U.S.
The Intercultural Nation
Second Edition

Alfred E. Prettyman

Rockland Community College
of the State University
of New York

**McGraw-Hill Primis
Custom Publishing**

New York St. Louis San Francisco Auckland Bogotá
Caracas Lisbon London Madrid Mexico Milan Montreal New
Delhi Paris San Juan Singapore Sydney Tokyo Toronto

McGraw-Hill Higher Education
A Division of The **McGraw-Hill** Companies

U.S. The Intercultural Nation

McGraw-Hill's Primis Custom Publishing Series consists of products that are produced from camera-ready copy. Peer review, class testing, and accuracy are primarily the responsibility of the author(s).

    6 7 8 9 0 QSR QSR 0 9 8 7 6 5 4 3 2 1

ISBN 0-07-229028-5

Editor: Constance Ditzel
Cover Design: William C. Whitman Jr.
Printer/Binder: Quebecor World

DEDICATIONS

For
*Meryl and Evan
and Julie*

❖   ❖   ❖

*Susan
and Martha*

❖   ❖   ❖

*Kathleen Conwell Prettyman
1942-1988
who shared the dream*

❖   ❖   ❖

*all of the cousins
Pat, Michelle, Great Tom, Michael, Shoni,
Mark, Maya and Alan*

❖   ❖   ❖

*and for
Albert E. Blumberg
fellow Baltimore emigre, colleague in philosophy,
perfect tennis partner,
Master of Coalitions*

Acknowledgments

For the First Edition

Dean of Arts and Sciences *Cora W. Wilder* of Rockland Community College / S.U.N.Y., co-author of a competing text, has been singularly supportive and of practical help toward the completion of this book. Past President *Neal A. Raisman* has been a strong supporter of my work, as has his Executive Assistant, *William E. Berry, Jr.*

Dean *Kathy Schatzberg,* of Rochester Community College, Minnesota, offered a challenge to my initial articulation of the theme of this book. It helped lead me to a greater precision which has found her favor. My colleagues *David Beisel, Bruce Delfini, Andrew Jacobs* and *Sylvia Miranda* offered valuable suggestions for the content of the book. I am especially grateful for permission from those among my colleagues whose work appears here.

McGraw-Hill's *Patricia A. Neidhart-Chiodi's* dedication to my project was the initial impetus for the ensuing enthusiastic support of *Constance Ditzel,* who is responsible for the superlative realization of this book on an impossible schedule. It has been a joy to work with so professional a publishing team.

It is a privilege to have so constant a coterie of critical thinkers and friends as the late *Albert E. Blumberg, Howard McGary, Wesley Brown, Thomas Slaughter, Dwight Murph, William Lawson, Frank Kirkland* and the new generation of members of the Association for the Study of Africana Philosophy. They, in ways they may scarcely realize, have helped make this book possible.

Susan Stedman often read my mind in locating material I needed. She certainly read every item I asked her to, and offered her insights and encouragement in many wonderful ways.

For the Second Edition

I am indebted to my colleagues of the McGregor School of Antioch University, the Intercultural Communication Institute and all of the members of Cohort 9 in Intercultural Relations.

Once again *Constance Ditzel* and *Jakarta M. Eckhart* have been ideal collaborators in the production of this book.

TABLE OF CONTENTS

Chapter Four—Politics and Social Practice

Chapter Five—Ourselves and Others

Chapter Six—Class and Power

PART III   THE UNITED STATES: DEMOCRACY'S GORGEOUS MOSAIC 303

Chapter Seven—Abilities

Chapter Eight—Values: Ethical and Religious

Chapter Nine—Consensus and Conflict in Contemporary Society

ALTERNATE TABLE OF CONTENTS FOR ENGLISH COMPOSITION

The readings are listed by their number in the Table of Contents. No attempt has been made to list each reading in every possible category of which it might be illustrative.

DESCRIPTION

NARRATION

CLASSIFICATION AND DIVISION

PROCESS

ANALYSIS

DEFINITION

COMPARISON AND CONTRAST

COMPARISON AND CONTRAST

ARGUMENT AND PERSUASION

RECOGNITIONS: HOW DO WE *SEE* EACH OTHER

Introduction (U.S.: The Intercultural Nation)

In a time when the variety of mediums for interpersonal and mass communication has never been more numerous, we truly *communicate* with one another less than in other times, we *understand* one another less than in other times —or so it seems.

What, then, fills these mediums of communication? Posturing, that excessive display of an attitude a speaker knows will appeal to his listeners whether he personally believes in it or not. Sound bites meant to catch the emotions with little thought required: "In your heart you know he's right," is a good example. Among the layered meanings of this catch- phrase from the Barry Goldwater presidential campaign of 1964 is the emotional appeal suggesting that whatever you believe, the candidate believes that too. Of course you are not expected to consider how one candidate could believe so many different things —given the wide variety of beliefs of the voting public in any election— and honestly stand for anything of principle.

Call-in bombast fills our air waves, whether on radio, television or a variety of internet "chat rooms." These are not forums for creating greater insight or mutual understanding, they are opportunities for letting off steam —steam too often carrying a foul odor. Equivocation frequently is another cheat of real communication, often found among candidates running for public office at any level. —lest the opinion polls shift. Consider a candidate who might say, "Every citizen has the right to choose the sanctity of life." Is this a pro- or anti-abortion position?

An increasingly serious impediment to communication in today's society is the alarming frequency with which anyone at odds with our individual views is demonized. The demonization of opposition political candidates through negative advertising, whatever their beliefs or party, has become a major, highly profitable business at every level of politics, local, state and national. Other forms of meanness or hatred have dominated our national discourse in other eras, but seldom in such deadening combination as they do today.

Why should what is printed and broadcast as news be determined predominantly by what is negative or titillating? When there is little demand for substantive news and an insatiable audience for gossipy or grim entertainment.

Why do conservative and liberal politicians present us with revitalized ideologies and programs that strike many of us as simply idiocies of different kind? When those driving political and social discourse believe that critical thinking is beyond the capacity of ordinary citizens; that economic, social and political issues are a simple matter of *we* who are up against *them*.

Why are bigotry, nativism and sexism fashionable, even excused, because of the vague claim that *everyone* at some time is guilty of such thoughts or behavior? By what civilizing principle can common guilt *sanction* these asocial behaviors that are such evils? When there is a deracinating conspiracy of silence, when few decry this theft of our common spirit.

In a time when, far too often, selfishness is exalted and mutual responsibility disclaimed, it is difficult to call on one another in continuing pursuit of our national *civicism*, that commitment to the principle that we share equally both the rights and duties of these United States of America. That this civic asks us, as collaborating citizens of this nation, for the *staying power* to expend our personal energies in learning to *recognize* others as we would have them *recognize* ourselves is a daunting expectation. But such a call, such an expectation are essential if we in this national society are to engage in *mutual* conversations. Without mutuality we shall learn little of each others differing lives and values. We do not have to agree with one another on everything, but we must work harder to *understand*, to *hear* unfiltered, to *recognize one another* with increasing frequency.

If we continue to make the effort over time, many more of us will be able to get on with our responsibilities in better humor, whether or not we agree. If we do not make this effort, we become complicit in the erosion of our national culture and its idea of a civic society.

What is our national culture? It is all of those shared beliefs, customs, skills, habits, traditions and knowledge common to us all and descriptive of our distinctive way of life. They are so familiar we take them for granted. E Pluribus Unum, the motto on our money, reminds us that we are a nation of "one out of many." We pledge allegiance to our flag and to the republic for which it stands. We celebrate national holidays. We are famous for our barbecue, whether it is a massive roast in some southern state or a backyard or rooftop cook-out in the neighborhood. We share a common language in a variety of dialects. We celebrate baseball as a unique national sport. What makes all of this possible is that we are a constitutional democracy the likes of which has never existed since life began on earth. The idea and existence of our civic society are founded on our traditions as a constitutional democracy, traditions intended to realize both the letter and the spirit of our Constitution.

Ours has always been a dynamic civic society, one of restless energy, growth and change. A society of contending forces and conflicting claims. An historic civic society committed to the commonweal, the good of all, as well as to individual freedom. What amazing conflicting commitments! Little wonder that government of a society with such conflicting ideological commitments has seen its share of years of forsaking the common good or ignoring individual freedom.

That we are a nation of diversity also is integral to our culture. What began as a nation of Anglo-Saxon immigrants, their subjugated Native American and enslaved African American cohabitants, grew to include other European immigrants —to meet labor demands of our industrial revolution, as well as Chinese and Mexican immigrants —to meet labor demands of our westward expansion. Now there is hardly an ethnic or national group in the world that is not represented in our national population. The demography of our democracy has continued to shift slowly, as do the tectonic plates undergirding the earth's continents. The prospect of a spectral shift in our demography within the next half century or so is viewed by many as a potential disaster, not unlike an earthquake that leaves the landscape forever changed. How we have, or have not, understood our diversity in the past, how we understand, or do not attempt to understand, our diversity at present, can shape what our diversity will become.

Perhaps it is best that we engage, if not dispel, structural myths about our diversity. That these United States of America constitute a "melting pot" of diverse ethnic, national peoples always has been largely a myth. Many who came here from other places with other cultures did assimilate, that is forsake their culture and assume our national culture. Some continue to do so. But in the past, the majority of immigrants adapted to our culture while maintaining their own. They acculturated. They did this, and continue to do this, by congregating in neighborhoods with others who share their ethnic or national heritage; while mingling at work, public events, on public transportation, sometimes in political, social or religious activities with members of other ethnic or national groups; by maintaining community or other social groups, formal or informal, that sustain their heritage; by organizing athletic organizations that compete with other groups. To describe these United States as a melting pot was always a metaphor for a desired situation, rather than a description of our reality as a national culture.

The "tossed salad" metaphor also does not work as descriptive of our society. Aside from the basically fricative process of making such a salad —a process we are not necessarily predisposed to— there is the contentious question of whose ethnic or national condiments will dress that tossed salad.

We could be described as, in ways, a kaleidoscope refracting different arrangements, combinations, collisions, possibilities. Or are we a mosaic, a composition created of different things —as are the colored ceramic, glass or marble compositions of an artist or group of artists?

As a mosaic we are bound to attend to whiteness as an element that is as marked as all others, rather than a singular composing hand by which the mosaic is valued. In other words, whiteness is simply not the norm which assigns everyone else value. That is a most difficult myth to dispel.

Nor is white a race. We must recall that at one time or another in our history as a nation Irish, Italians, Jews and Latinos have been described as "non-white." Whiteness is an insistence on privilege. A standpoint from which to look upon the world as a chosen people. It intrinsically defines itself against an "other." As Ruth Frankenberg puts it in her book *The Social Construction of Whiteness* (1995), "To speak of whiteness is, I think, to assign *everyone* a place in the relations of racism.... It is to emphasize that dealing with racism is not merely an option for white people —that, rather, racism shapes white people's lives and identities in a way that is inseparable from other facts of daily life." We should not flinch from so direct a gaze at our national socialization. We need to talk about it, often and at length. These are among the kinds of conversations that can shape what our diversity is to become.

Assuredly the institutions which form the basis of our civic society are a heritage of western civilization made new—from Egyptian and Mesopotamian bequeathals of legal and religious tradition to Israel and astronomical, magical and mathematical teachings to Greece, through Greek, Roman, British, French and German legal theories and political and social practices. The institutions we have devised from such an heritage and the national culture that has developed in the process provide all of us with a shared national identity.

It is the assumed denial of such a shared national identity that is alarming —understandably so— to those, such as the distinguished historian Arthur M. Schlessinger, Jr. (*The Disuniting of America,* 1992), who take a definition of our diversity as multicultural to be fundamentally divisive. This would be true only if multiculturalism were

assumed to mean an aggregate of encapsulated, *ethnocentric* groups. Members of such groups spend most of their time with one another, in the course of which they usually develop strong negative feelings towards people who are not like them. Sometimes members of these encapsulated groups come to feel threatened by people unlike themselves. That is not what is meant when describing our *multicultural* society as being comprised, for the most part, of acculturated ethnic and national immigrants as well as historically subjugated Native Americans and African Americans, people who maintain their own traditions, more or less, and are receptive to —if not really knowledgeable about— the distinctive traditions of others. We are, in fact, this latter type of multicultural society.

As such a society it is imperative that we be engaged in a continuing process of authentic mutual recognition. For as the eminent philosopher Charles Taylor has argued so cogently (*Multiculturalism* 1994), a crucial feature of human life is that it is fundamentally dialogical, through exchange with others —both "significant others", those dearest to us, and those with whom we socialize publicly in a variety of ways. So that if our identity is shaped through such interactions of recognition, so too can they be shaped, in part, by "the *mis*recognition of others, and so a person or group of people can suffer real damage, real distortion, if the people or society around them mirror back to them a confining or demeaning or contemptible picture of themselves." Both "nonrecognition and misrecognition can be a form of oppression, imprisoning someone in a false, distorted, and reduced mode of being." (25)

Historically subjugated African Americans and Native Americans consistently have had to cope with both nonrecognition and misrecognition. Many among the poor today suffer from nonrecognition and misrecognition. Women in patriarchal societies, such as ours is, must contend with misrecognition —some more often than others. Those who are disabled must contend with such misrecognition by many of us who are "temporarily able." Gays and lesbians must contend with such misrecognition by those who are homophobic or heterosexist. Chicanas, Chinese, Hmong, Koreans. Latinos, Japanese too must contend with various degrees of misrecognition, as must whites. Even some of the well-to-do, of whatever identity, at times must contend with misrecognition.

Equal recognition is not simply the appropriate mode for interacting in a democratic society, it is a necessary mode of interaction. This makes the politics of equal recognition both central to our social and institutional interactions, and stressful for such interactions. Contemporary feminism, race relations as well as discussions of multiculturalism "are undergirded by the premise that the withholding of recognition can be a form of oppression." (36)

It is certain that if our dialogical interactions are limited, for the most part, to a narrow range of associates and groups exhibiting little or no diversity, we are inadequately socialized, perhaps unsuited, to be effective and equable citizens in our diverse democratic society and its institutions. Certainly if we refuse to *mingle*—which, mythically, is quintessentially *American*—we will be increasingly unable to comprehend the political claims and social conflicts that compound the demands on our economy and strain the social fabric of this nation.

The expectations and demands of citizens of these United States have changed in significant ways since 1787, as well they should. Judith Shklar, the late John Cowles Professor of Government at Harvard and a MacArthur Fellow, reminds us that "every page of *The Federalist Papers* is a call to the people of America to take its fate into its own hands and to fashion its institutions in the light of the best political science of the present, rather than to look timidly to the past." I believe that in recognizing our individual identities and differences within the context of our shared national identity,

the good citizen of today must make the serious effort to fashion our institutions for the commonweal of today. For, as Shklar aptly notes, "from the nation's beginnings as an independent republic, Americans were torn by 'glaring inconsistencies between their professed principles of citizenship and their deep-seated desire to exclude certain groups permanently from the privileges of membership.' These tensions constitute the real history of its citizens. (*American Citizenship: The Quest for Inclusion*, 1991)

In this quest, each of us must be citizens who have "standing:" the same rights, the same recognition. For what has given "citizenship as standing its historical significance," Shklar points out, "is not that it was denied for so long to so many, but that this exclusion occurred in a republic that was overtly committed to political equality, and whose citizens believed theirs was a free and fair society." (17)

In this quest we also must seek coalitions not only of whose with whom we are comfortable and agree, but with those whom we know little or not at all and with whom we can make only occasional common cause.

Engaging in these dialogues surely will further our ability to disagree with civility, equably when we do not share a common cause. Contending effectively with such tensions and conflicting claims within our national society is, I believe, the complex responsibility each of us must *sustain* if we are actually to renew our pervasively troubled civil society so that it might reasonably endure for our children, certainly, and for their children with equal certainty.

Acknowledgments

(Sources listed in order of their appearance)

John Bierhorst, "Quetzalcoatl," an Aztec Hero Myth, from *Four Masterworks of American Indian Literature,* translated by John Bierhorst. Copyright © 1974 by John Bierhorst, University of Arizona Press, 1984. Reprinted with permission.

Gary B. Nash et al, "Three Worlds Meet," from *The American People, Creating a Nation and a Society,* Third Edition, Volume One: to 1877. Copyright © 1994 by HarperCollins Publishers, Inc. Reprinted with permission of Addison Wesley Educational Publications, Inc.

Ronald Takaki, "The "Tempest" in the Wilderness," from "The Racialization of Savagery," from *A Different Mirror, A History of Multicultural America.* Reprinted by permission of Little Brown and Company. Copyright © 1993 by Balkin Agency, Inc.

Suzanne Lebsock, "'No Obey': Women's Changing Status in the Seventeenth Century," from *A Share of Honour: Virginia Women.* Copyright © 1984 by the Virginia State Library and Archives. Reprinted by permission.

Jack Weatherford, "The Founding Indian Fathers," from *Indian Givers* by Jack Weatherford. Copyright © 1988 by Jack McIver Weatherford. Reprinted by permission of Crown Publishers, Inc.

John Higham, "The Immigrant in American History," from *Send These to Me, Immigrants in Urban America.* Copyright © 1984 by Johns Higham. Reprinted with permission.

John Hope Franklin, "Two Worlds of Race: A Historical View," from *Race and History: Selected Essays 1938-1988.* Copyright © 1989 by Louisiana State University Press.

Lewis Lipsitz and **David M. Speak,** "American Political Culture," from *American Democracy,* Third Edition. Copyright © 3/93 by St. Martin's Press. Reprinted by permission of St. Martin's Press.

Frances Moor Lappe and **Paul Martin DuBois,** "Mastering the Arts of Democracy: One-on-One Skills," from *The Quickening of America.* Copyright © 1994 by Jossey-Bass Inc. Reprinted with permission.

Edward C. Stewart and **Milton J. Bennett,** "American Pragmatism" and "Implications of American Ethnocentrism" from *American Cultural Patterns: A Cross-Cultural Perspective.* Copyright © 1991 by Intercultural Press. Reprinted with permission.

L. Luca Cavalli-Sforza, Paolo Menozzi and **Alberto Piazza,** "Scientific Failure of the Concept of Human Races," from *The History and Geography of Human Genes.* Copyright © 1994, Princeton University Press. Reprinted with permission.

Adalberto Aguirre, Jr. and **Jonathan H. Turner,** "Ethnicity and Ethnic Relations," from *American Ethnicity, The Dynamics and Consequences of Discrimination.* Copyright © 1995, McGraw-Hill, Inc. Reprinted with permission.

J. Milton Yinger, "Drawing the Boundaries of Ethnicity," from *Ethnicity, Source of Strength? Source of Conflict?* Copyright © 1994, State University of New York. Reprinted with permission.

Alfred Prettyman, "The Ring of the Bell Curve: Critical Reverberations and Resonance," delivered as one of the Inaugural Lectures upon the installation of Dr. Neal A. Raisman as President of Rockland Community College/State University of New York. Copyright © 1995 by A. E. Prettyman. All rights reserved.

Daniel Goleman, "When Smart is Dumb," from *Emotional Intelligence*. Copyright © 1995 by Daniel Goleman. Reprinted by permission of Bantam Books, a division of Bantam Doubleday Dell Publishing Group, Inc.

Catherine L. Albanese, "Civil Religion: Millennial Politics and History," from *America, Religious and Religion*. Copyright © 1995 by Wadsworth. Reprinted with permission.

Lawrence M. Hinman, "The Ethics of Diversity: Gender, Ethnicity, and Individuality," from *Ethics: A Pluralistic Approach to Moral Theory*. Copyright © 1994 by Harcourt Brace & Company. Reprinted with permission of the publisher.

Robert Coles, "The Disparity Between Intellect and Character," from *The Chronicle of Higher Education*, Sept. 22, 1995 issue. Copyright © 1995 by Robert Coles. Reprinted with permission.

Randall Kenan, "Things of This World" or "Angels Unawares," from *Let the Dead Bury Their Dead and Other Stories*. Copyright © 1992 by Randall Kenan. Reprinted by permission.

Bernard Gotfryd, "The Last Camp" from *Anton the Dove Fancier*. Reprinted with the permission of Pocket Books, a Division of Simon & Schuster. Copyright © 1990 by Bernard Gotfryd.

Jayne Cortez, "Madness Without Head," from *Mouth On Paper*. Copyright © 1995 by Jayne Cortez. Reprinted with permission.

Peter Edelman, "The Worst Thing Bill Clinton Has Done." Copyright © 1997 Peter Edelman, as first published in the *Atlantic Monthly*.

Wayne R. Ott and **John W. Roberts,** "Everyday Exposure to Toxic Pollutants" from *Scientific American*. Copyright 1998 by Scientific American.

Suzanne Oboler, "Hispanic Ethnicity, the Ethnic Revival, and Its Critique," from *Ethnic Labels, Latino Lives*. Copyright © 1992 Sage Publications. Reprinted with permission.

David Shipler, "Decoding Racism" from *A Country of Strangers*. Copyright © 1997 by David K. Shipler. Reprinted by permission of Alfred A. Knopf, Inc.

Genny Lim, "Children Are Color Blind," from *Forbidden Stitches: An Asian American Women's Anthology*. Copyright © 1989 Calyx Books. Reprinted with permission.

Fannie Lou Hamer, "It's in Your Hands" from *Black Women in White America*

Donald L. Fixico, "Termination and Relocation in Retrospect," from *Termination and Relocation*. Copyright © 1986 by the University of New Mexico Press. Reprinted with permission.

Part One

National Identity and the Democratic Process

National Identity

To say that these United States of America, this first *new* nation, has been an intercultural society from its beginnings would not meet with the approval of an early patriot such as John Jay (1745-1829). For him true Americans were "descended from the same ancestors, speaking the same language, professing the same religion... similar in their manners and customs." They were, in other words, Englishmen. Jay's description seems to slight his French protestant immigrant forebears, who arrived in New York in the late 1600s.

Jay's description contrasts with that of J. Hector St. John de Crevecoeur (1735-1813) in his imaginative recollections *Letters from an American Farmer* (1782). Before settling on a farm in Orange County, New York, sometime around 1769, de Crevecoeur had traveled through the Great Lakes and Ohio Valley regions and worked as a surveyor in Pennsylvania. Under the name Agricola, he also had written agricultural articles for American newspapers. In his *Letters* he wrote "What, then is the American, this new man? he is neither an European nor the descendant of a European, hence that strange mixture of blood, which you will find in no other country. I could point out to you a family whose godfather was an Englishman, whose wife was Dutch, whose son married a French woman, and whose present four sons now have four wives of different nations. He is an American, who, leaving behind him all his ancient prejudices and manners, receives new ones from the new mode of life he has embraced, the new government he obeys, and the new rank he holds.... Here individuals of all

nations are melted into a new race of men." This transformation is not simply the result of intermarriage, but, as Doreen Alvarez Saar (1993) has argued in analyzing the heritage of American ethnicity in *Letters* "the political and social environment shapes a new ethnic reality." But this assimilation is not offered to everyone, "both Native Americans and Africans brought to America as slaves remain outside the assimilation process." Saar finds it "disquieting to acknowledge that the patterns of ethnic relationships that dominate modern American culture were so strongly shaped by our colonial experience and so little altered."

While it is true that the English colonists "often went to great lengths to...protect their supposed racial purity, " as Colin G. Calloway has written in *New Worlds for All* (1997), "they could not prevent the mixing of peoples that occurred throughout North America as Indians, Europeans, and Africans met and intermarried." Mixing of many other cultures would occur on the pacific northwest coast in the eighteenth century, as trade in sea oters brought sailors and tradesmen—Asian, African, Russian, Spanish, Sandwich Islanders and even Yankees—who "met and often mated with, Chinooks, Nootkas, Bella Coolas, Aleuts, and others, leaving a mixed progeny."

Calloway would have us remember that the formation of early America cannot be encapsulated in picturesque moments such as the landings at Plymouth Rock, Massachusetts or Jamestown, Virginia. That formative growth went on for longer than the nearly two and a quarter centuries we have been a nation and "involved many different peoples adapting to many different situations. During those centuries, most of America was still Indian country, and even in areas of European settlement, Indians remained part of daily life. It was a world where Indian and European people lived, worked, worshiped, traveled and traded together, as well as a world where, often, they feared, avoided, despised, and killed each other."

The social environments that emerged, in time, from the interrelations of Indians, Europeans and Africans in colonial America were adaptive modes of interaction influenced by each of these cultures.

For the Europeans, political and economic life offered powerful incentives for assimilation. But there were degrees of social acculturation, exemplified by ethnic communities or the publication of foreign language newspapers for immigrant readers. However patriotic their content, these newspapers reinforced the British disposition to look upon non-English immigrants as not being *true* Americans. Who were the true Americans? The English, of course, were the true Americans, the *original* Americans. Other Europeans were immigrants. This marked the beginnings of nativism—the rejection of *alien* persons or cultures—in America.

THE DEMOCRATIC PROCESS

The new society grafted on this part of America which has become the United States(keeping in mind that Mexico and Canada are other parts of America) is not like the ancient civilizations Indians had known; nor those the Africans had been snatched or sold from; surely not like the ones Europeans had emigrated from for reasons of religious freedom, or to escape the sure prospect of limited social, political or economic lives institutionalized by traditions stemming from a history of feudal oppression. It is a society in which national identity is grounded in a *participatory constitutional democracy*. Citizenship is a birthright for the progeny of all those who built such a new nation as these United States — African, Asian, European and Indian. And citizenship is available, as well, to new immigrants who can become *naturalized citizens*. Many aspects of how this came to be are presented through the readings that follow. We should keep in mind, however, that for most of our history the imperatives assumed by our lawmakers and political leaders have resulted in enduring undemocratic conditions of citizenship based on ethnicity, gender, race or religion. The analysis of this history of the denial of individual liberties and opportunities for political participation is well-documented in Rogers M. Smith's CIVIC IDEALS (1997).

Recognitions: How Do We *See* Each Other? challenges the processes of interpersonal identification in U.S. society and political culture.

In Chapters 1 through 4, we review confluences of cultures in creating a new, complex society and the democratic processes, however imperfect, essential to that society's existence and mature growth.

Chapter 1, Grafting a New Society, begins with "The Creation of Life" from the Aztec Hero Myth *Quetzalcoatl*. In it Quetzalcoatl emerges from the underworld with the bones of earlier creations, which he brings to paradise, places in the womb of mother earth and, with his blood, inseminates them, creating a new human family. The underworld spirits were able to nibble the bones while Quetzalcoatl removed them, and this will forever deprive this new humanity of immortality. Similar interventions in the remainder of the selection underscore the uncertainty of life and the symbolic relation of birth to death, feast to famine. The relation of rain to rebirth is manifest in a concluding part of the myth not included here. Quetzalcoatl, as a bringer of culture, presents a challenging comparison to the bringers of culture in "Three Worlds Meet."

Ronald Takaki's "The Racialization of Savagery" explains the earliest demonizations of "the other" by those who would graft their culture on a "new world." Susanne Lebsock's "No Obey," provides a unique portrait of three worlds of seventeenth century women in Virginia. And in Hawthorne's short story "Alice Doane's Appeal," we are introduced to a "field where superstition won her darkest triumph, the high place where our fathers set up their shame, to the mournful gaze of generations far remote."

Although we often speak of our liberties and rights—less often our duties, as citizens of a constitutional democracy, too many citizens are vague about or unfamiliar with the founding documents of our government.

In **Chapter 2, Constitutional Government and the Commonweal,** students should find illuminating a reading of the *Declaration of Independence* and the *Constitution* along with Alexander Hamilton's "Conjectures About the New Constitution." Jack Weatherford's "The Founding Indian Fathers" offers a challenging counterpoint to our usual assumption that these documents grew out of exclusively western (non-American Indian) traditions and models of governance.

In **Chapter 3, Immigrant Lives,** the vignette from Willa Cather's *My Ántonia* is a quintessential immigrant tale for generations of immigrants, whatever their ethnicity. John Higham presents an excellent overview of the complex history of American immigration. John Hope Franklin's "Two Worlds of Race" traces how, from the beginning of our more than three and one-half centuries of colonial and national history, "law and custom" established a separate world for African Americans. "Equal rights for all" too often has meant "equal rights for some."

Two masters of American fiction, masters who also were contemporaries, begin **Chapter 4, Politics and Social Practice.** The episode from Henry James' *The Bostonians* provides a contrast in regional manners, class, and gender roles in the late nineteenth century U.S. Charles W. Chesnutt's "The Sheriff's Children," explores an altogether different dilemma of regional "manner" and "class" in that same period. How contradiction and conflict characterize U.S. society and political culture, historically and currently, is summarized in "American Political Culture: Liberty and Its Tensions" by Lipsitz and Speak.

Ten practical skills in "Master the Arts of Democracy" are present in Frances Moor Lappe and Paul Martin DuBois' article of that title. This is a real "how to" guide.

Chapter 5, Ourselves and Others, begins with Walt Whitman's poem in celebration of "Faces." Harry Irwin, in "Understanding Intercultural Communication," provides us with Asian cultural contexts for his exposition of how we might improve our intercultural communication performance. Why classification into races has proved to be a futile and unscientific enterprise is summarized in Cavalli-Sforza et al's "Scientific Failure of the Concept of Human Races." Aguirre and Turner review fundamental reasons for the tensions and conflicts among ethnic populations in the U.S. in "Ethnicity and Ethnic Relations." Milton Yinger provides a skillful analysis of the permeability of

ethnic boundaries in "The Boundaries of Ethnicity," and Eugene Eoyang offers an equally canny look at whiteness in "Coat of Many Colors: The Myth of a White America." Iris Creasy, "Who Am I? Idian, White, or Both" and Laura Bathurst, in "Potawatomi—To Be or Not To Be?, wrestle with issues of bicultural / multicultural personality identity— as do an increasing number of today's college students. "Communicating" by Primo Levi is a telling reminder of the horror of "incommunicability."

Suzanne Cleary's poetic celebration of stories in "Ivory Bracelets" enlivens and informs **Chapter 6, Class and Power.** Harold R. Kerbo answers the question of who gets what in the U.S. in "Dimensions of Inequality in the United States." Transformation in familiy structures and behaviors are presented clearly in Zinn and Eitzen's *Moving Away from the Nuclear Mold.* Diversity in families may readily lead to a "fuzzy logic" of interpersonal identification that we can appreciate in Maureen T. Reddy's personal narrative "Why Do White People Have Vaginas?"

The expansion of women's economic and sexual choices in U.S. society still does not deliver them from that ancient enemy, male violence—in all of its forms. Harassment, assault, abuse, and rape are discussed by John Scanzoni in "Aggression Against Women." John Allman's evocative "Sisters" is neither a comfortable nor simple tale of woman siblings.

With the largest segment, 23 percent of U.S. households headed by persons aged 35-44 and the second largest segment, 18 percent headed by person aged 45-54, we can see readily why aging has become a subject of concern even to young people. By the year 2010 the largest population segment in our society will be "baby boomers" aged 60-69 nearing retirement, if not already retired. John Scanzoni's "Aging, The Family Life Cycle, and its Life Courses" is a valuable reference. Death is integral to life, although many ignore its part; "Grandma's Wake" by Emilio Diaz Valcarel does not, nor does Dan Masterson's unforgettable "Calling Home." Julio Marzan's *Graduation Day* captures multiple rites of passage.

References:

Calloway, Colin G. (1997) *New Worlds For All*: Indians and the Remaking of Early America.

Deloria, Jr., Vine (1994) *God Is Red: A Native View of Religion*.

Saar, Doreen Alvarez (1993) The Heritage of American Ethnicity in Crevecoeur's *Letters from an American Farmer*. In Frank Shuffleton, (Ed.), *A Mixed Race: Ethnicity in Early America*.

Smith, Rogers M. (1997) *Civic Ideals: Conflicting Visions of Citizenship in U.S. History*.

Weatherford, Jack (1991) *Native Roots: How the Indians Enriched America*.

THE CREATION OF LIFE FROM

QUETZALCOATL

Translated from the Nahuatl by John Bierhorst
Fragment A / The Restoration of Life

And the gods assembled then, *and* they said, "Who shall live? The skies have dried, the Earth Lord has dried. *But* who, O gods, shall live?" They were therefore troubled:

Skirt-of-Stars Light-of-Day, Lord-*Drawn*-to-the-Water *Lord*-Issuing-Forth, Who-Firms-the-Earth Who-Tills-*the*-Earth, Quetzalcoatl Titlacahuan *were their names.*

But Quetzalcoatl went to the Dead Land then, *and* came to the Dead Land Lord, to the Dead Land Lady, saying, "These, the precious bones in your keeping, for these I have come, *and* these I would take." And he was answered at once: "To make what, Quetzalcoatl?" And therefore he spoke again: "The gods are troubled, *asking*, 'Who shall live on earth?'"

And so too the lord of the Dead Land spoke again: "Very well. Blow my trumpet shell and circle four times round my emerald realm." But his trumpet shell was not hollow.

Then *Quetzalcoatl* summoned worms, who hollowed it out, and at once bees and hornets went in. Then he blew. *And* the lord of the Dead Land heard.

And so too the lord of the Dead Land spoke once more: "Very well. Take them." But then to his subjects, the Micteca, the lord of the Dead Land said, "*My* holy ones, tell him he must but relinquish them!"

And at once Quetzalcoatl said, "But no! I have them already *and* forever." But his nahual said to him, "Merely answer: 'I do but relinquish them.'" *Quetzalcoatl* spoke at once, he cried out, "I do but relinquish them!" Yet in fact he ascended *with them.*

Then truly he took up the precious bones, the bones of man *where* they lay to one side, *and* so too the bones of woman *where* they lay to one side. Quetzalcoatl took them at once, then he wrapped them up, then he carried them off.

But the lord of the Dead Land now spoke again to his subjects: "Holy ones, Quetzalcoatl is truly removing the precious bones. Holy ones, make him a crypt!" Then they made it for him. He was startled by quail moreover, and so he fell into the crypt, he stumbled, he fell unconscious.

And the precious bones were therefore immediately scattered. Then the quail bit into them *and* nibbled them. And when Quetzalcoatl regained his senses, he wept. Then he said to his nahual, "My nahual! How will it be?" And at once he was answered, "How will it be? It *will* be undone. *But* let it be as it will."

And then he gathered *and* reassembled the bones and bundled them up. Then he brought them to Tamoanchan.

And when he arrived there, then she who is called Quilaztli, she, Cihuacoatl, reduced them to powder, which she even placed in a jadestone bowl. And thereupon Quetzalcoatl bled his member.

Then all the gods did penance, and they will be named herewith: Lord-Drawn-to-the-Water, Who-Tills-the-Earth, Lord-Issuing-Forth, Who-Firms-the-Earth, He-Who-Falls-Headlong– and the sixth who is Quetzalcoatl.

And then they spoke: "Born are the servants of the gods." For indeed they did penance for us.

Again they spoke: "But what will they eat, O gods? Let food be discovered." And then the ant brought maize kernels out of the heart of Food Mountain.

And at once Quetzalcoatl confronted the ant, asking, "Where did you find it? Tell me." But she would not tell him. Over and over he asked her and at last she said to him, "There!" Then she showed him the way and at once Quetzalcoatl changed himself into a black ant.

Then she showed him how to enter inside. Then together they dragged it out. The red ant, it seems, showed Quetzalcoatl the way. At the exit he laid down the kerneled maize. Then he took it to Tamoanchan. And the gods then chewed it. Then they laid it upon our lips so that we were made strong.

And they spoke then: "What shall we do with Food Mountain?" And at once Quetzalcoatl set out again, and he trussed it with cords and attempted to carry it with him. But he could not lift it.

And then Oxomoco divined with the kernels. And so too did Oxomoco's wife, Cipactonal, divine thereupon. Indeed the woman is Cipactonal.

And then Oxomoco and Cipactonal announced, "It is Nanahuatl who must break open Food Mountain. Indeed it has been determined."

But suddenly rain gods came forth: blue rain gods, white rain gods, yellow rain gods, red rain gods. Then Nanahuatl broke open the mountain, and then the rain gods stole the food: white, black, yellow, and red maize; beans, amaranth, sage, and argemone. All the foods were stolen.

THREE WORLDS MEET

by Gary Nash

In the late 1550s, a few years after Catholic King Philip II and Protestant Queen Elizabeth assumed the thrones in Spain and England, respectively, Opechancanough was born in Tsenacommacah. In the Algonquian language, the word *tsenacommacah* meant "densely inhabited land." Later, English colonizers would rename this place Virginia after their monarch, the virgin queen Elizabeth. Before he died in the 1640s, in the ninth decade of his life, Opechancanough had seen light-skinned, swarthy, and black-skinned newcomers from a half dozen European nations and African kingdoms swarm into his land. Like thousands of other Native Americans, he was witnessing the early moments of European expansion across the Atlantic Ocean.

Opechancanough was only an infant when Europeans first reached the Chesapeake Bay region. A small party of Spanish had explored the area in 1561, but they found neither gold nor silver nor anything else of value. Upon departing, they took with them the brother of one of the local chieftains, who was a member of Opechancanough's clan. They left behind something of unparalleled importance in the history of contact between the peoples of Europe and the Americas: a viral infection that spread like wildfire through a population that had no immunity against it. Many members of Opechancanough's tribe died, although their casualties were light compared with those of other tribes that caught the deadly European diseases.

In 1570, when Opechancanough was young, the Spanish returned and established a Jesuit mission near the York River. Violence occurred, and before the Spanish abandoned the Chesapeake in 1572, they put to death a number of captured Indians, including a chief who was Opechancanough's relative. The Native Americans learned that Europeans, even when they came bearing the crosses of their religion, were a volatile and dangerous people.

Opechancanough was in his forties when three ships of fair-skinned settlers disembarked in 1607 to begin the first permanent English settlement in the New World. For several months, he watched his half brother Powhatan, high chief of several dozen loosely confederated tribes in the region, parry and fence with the newcomers. Then Powhatan sent him to capture the English leader John Smith and escort him to the Indians' main village. Smith was put through a mock execution but then released. He later got the best of Opechancanough, threatening him with a pistol, humiliating him in front of his warriors, and assaulting one of his sons, whom Smith "spurned like a dog."

Opechancanough nursed his wounds for years while Powhatan grew old and the English settlements slowly spread in the Chesapeake region. Then, in 1617, he assumed leadership of the Powhatan Confederacy. Two years later, a Dutch trader sold 20 Africans to the settlers after docking at Jamestown. Three years after that, Opechancanough led a determined assault on the English plantations that lay along the rivers and streams emptying into the bay. The Indians killed nearly one-third of the intruders. But they paid dearly in the retaliatory raids that the colonists mounted in succeeding years.

As he watched the land-hungry settlers swarm in during the next two decades, Opechancanough's patience failed him. Finally, in 1644, now in his eighties, he galvanized a new generation of warriors and led a final desperate assault on the English. It was a suicidal attempt, but the "great general" of the Powhatan Confederacy, faithful to the tradition of his people, counseled death over enslavement and humiliation. Though the warriors inflicted heavy casualties, they could not overwhelm the colonizers, who vastly outnumbered them. For two years, Opechancanough was kept prisoner by the Virginians. Nearly blind and "so decrepit that he was not able to walk alone," he was fatally shot in the back by an English guard in 1646.

Over a long lifetime, Opechancanough painfully experienced the meeting of people from three continents. His land was one of many that would be penetrated by Europeans over the next three centuries, as Christian civilization girdled the globe. On the Chesapeake Bay, this clash of cultures formed the opening chapter of what we know as American history. That history, in turn, was one scene in a much broader drama of European colonization and exploitation of many indigenous cultures thousands of miles from the Old World. The nature of this violent intermingling of Europeans, Africans, and Native Americans is an essential part of early American history. But to understand how the destinies of red, white, and black people became intertwined in Opechancanough's land, we must look at the precontact history and cultural foundations of life in the homelands of each of them.

THE PEOPLE OF AMERICA BEFORE COLUMBUS

Thousands of years before the European voyages of discovery, the history of humankind in North America began. Nomadic bands from Siberia, hunting big game animals such as bison, caribou, and reindeer, began to migrate across a land bridge connecting northeastern Asia with Alaska. Geologists believe that this land bridge existed most recently between 25,000 and 14,000 years ago, when massive glaciers locked up much of the earth's moisture and left part of the Bering Sea floor exposed. Ice-free passage through Canada was possible only briefly at the beginning and end of this period, however. At other times melting glaciers flooded the land bridge and blocked foot traffic to Alaska. Paleoanthropologists remain dividend on the exact timing, but the main migration apparently occurred between 12,000 and 14,000 years ago, although possibly much earlier.

HUNTERS AND FARMERS

For thousands of years, these early hunters trekked southward and eastward, following vegetation and game. In time, they reached the tip of South America and the eastern edge of North America, thousands of miles from their Asian homeland. Thus did people from the "Old World" discover the "New World" thousands of years before Columbus.

Archaeologists have excavated ancient sites of early life in the Americas, unearthing tools, ornaments, and skeletal remains that can be scientifically dated. In this way they have tentatively reconstructed the dispersion of these first Americans over an immense landmass. Although much remains unknown, this archaeological evidence suggests that as centuries passed and population increased, the earliest inhabitants evolved into separate cultures, organizing life and adjusting to a variety of environments in distinct ways. Europeans who rediscovered the New World thousands of years later would indiscriminately lump together the myriad societies they found. But by the 1500s, the "Indians" of the Americas were enormously diverse in the size and complexity of their societies, the languages they spoke, and their forms of social organization.

Archaeologists and anthropologists have charted several phases of "Native American" history. A long Beringian epoch ended about 14,000 years ago. From that time a rich archaeological record indicates that the hunters had developed a new technology. Big game hunters now flaked hard stones into spear points and chose "kill sites" where they slew whole herds of Pleistocene mammals. This more reliable food source allowed population growth, and nomadism began to give way to settled habitations or local migration within limited territories.

In another phase of evolution, the Archaic era, from about 10,000 to 2,500 years ago, great geological changes brought further adaptations to the land. As the massive glaciers of the Ice Age slowly retreated, a warming trend deprived vast areas from Utah to the highlands of Central America of sufficient water and turned them from grasslands into desert. The Pleistocene mammals could not survive more arid conditions, but human populations ably adapted. They learned to exploit new sources of food, especially plant life. In time, a second technological breakthrough, the "agricultural revolution," occurred.

When Native Americans learned to domesticate plant life, they began the long process of transforming their relationship to the physical world. To learn how to harvest, plant, and nurture a seed

was to gain partial control over natural forces that before had been ungovernable. Anthropologists believe that this process began independently in widely separated parts of the world—Africa, Asia, Europe, and the Americas—about 7,000 to 9,000 years ago. Though agriculture developed very slowly, everywhere it eventually brought dramatic changes in human societies.

Over the millennia, humans progressed from doorside planting of a few wild seeds to systematic clearing and planting of bean and maize fields. As the production of domesticated plant food ended dependence on gathering wild plants and pursuing game, sedentary village life began to replace nomadic existence. The increase in food supply brought about by agriculture triggered other major changes. As populations grew, large groups split off to form separate societies. Greater social and political complexity developed because not everyone was needed as before to secure the society's food supply. Men cleared the land and hunted game, while women planted, cultivated, and harvested crops. Many societies empowered religious figures, who organized the common followers, directed their work, and exacted tribute as well as worship from them. In return they were trusted to protect the community from hostile forces.

Everywhere in the Americas, regional trading networks formed. Along trade routes carrying commodities such as salt, obsidian rock for projectile points, and copper for jewelry also traveled technology, religious ideas, and agricultural practices. By the end of the Archaic period, about 500 B.C. (to use the Christian European method of dating), hundreds of independent kin-based groups, like people in other parts of the world, had learned to exploit the resources of their particular area and to trade with other groups in their region.

NATIVE AMERICANS IN 1600

The last epoch of pre-Columbian development, the post-Archaic phase, occurred during the 2,000 years before contact with Europeans. It involved a complex process of growth and environmental adaptation among many distinct societies—and crisis in some of them. In the American Southwest, for example, the ancestors of the present-day Hopi and Zuni developed carefully planned villages composed of large terraced buildings, each with many rooms. By the time the Spanish arrived in the 1540s, the indigenous Pueblo people were using irrigation canals, dams, and hillside terracing to bring water to their arid maize fields. In their agricultural techniques, their skill in ceramics, their use of woven textiles for clothing, and their village life, Pueblo society resembled that of peasant communities in many parts of Europe and Asia.

Far to the east were the mound-building societies of the Mississippi and Ohio valleys. When European settlers first crossed the Appalachian Mountains a century and a half after arriving on the continent, they were amazed to find hundreds of ceremonial mounds, some of them 70 feet high, and gigantic sculptured earthworks in geometric designs or in the shapes of huge humans, birds, or writhing serpents. Believing all "Indians" to be forest primitives, they reasoned that these were the remains of an ancient civilization that had found its way to North America—perhaps Phoenicians, survivors of the sunken island of Atlantis, or the Lost Tribes of Israel spoken of in European mythology.

The mound-building societies of the Ohio valley declined many centuries before Europeans reached the continent, perhaps because of attacks from other tribes or severe climatic changes that undermined agriculture. But about A.D. 600 another mound-building culture, based on intensive cultivation of beans, maize, and squash, began to flourish in the Mississippi valley. Its center, a city of perhaps 40,000, stood near present-day St. Louis. Great ceremonial plazas, flanked by a temple that rose in four terraces to a height of 100 feet, marked this first metropolis in America. This was the urban center of a far-flung Mississippi culture that radiated out to encompass thousands of villages from Wisconsin to Louisiana and from Oklahoma to Tennessee.

Several centuries before Europeans arrived in North America, the mound-building cultures of the continental heartlands began to decline. But

their influence had already passed eastward to transform the woodlands societies along the Atlantic coastal plain. The numerous small tribes that settled from Nova Scotia to Florida never equaled the larger societies of the midcontinent in earthwork sculpture, architectural design, or development of large-scale agriculture. But they were far from the "savages" that the first European explorers described. They had added limited agriculture to their skill in exploiting natural plants for food, medicine, dyes, and flavoring and had developed food procurement strategies that used all the resources around them—cleared land, forests, streams, shore, and ocean.

Most of the eastern woodlands tribes lived in waterside villages. Locating their fields of maize near fishing grounds, they often migrated seasonally between inland and coastal village sites or situated themselves astride two ecological zones. In the Northeast, their birchbark canoes, light enough to be carried by a single man, gave them a means of trading and communicating over immense territories. In the Southeast, population was denser and social and political organization more elaborate.

As European exploration of the Americas drew near, the continent north of the Rio Grande contained perhaps 3-4 million people, of whom perhaps 500,000 lived along the eastern coastal plain and in the piedmont region accessible to the early European settlers. Though estimates vary widely, perhaps 40-60 million people lived in the entire hemisphere when Europeans first arrived. This contrasted with some 70-90 million in Europe about 1500 and about 40-70 million in Africa. The colonizers were not coming to a "virgin wilderness," as they often described it, but to a land inhabited for thousands of years by people whose village existence in many ways resembled that of the arriving Europeans.

CONTRASTING WORLD VIEWS

Colonizing Europeans called themselves "civilized" and typically described the people they met in the Americas as "savage," "heathen," or "barbarian." But the gulf separating people in Europe and North America was not defined so much by how the two cultures extracted a food supply from the land, housed themselves, or organized family life as by how they viewed their relationship to the environment and defined social relations in their communities. In these areas, a wide difference in values existed. This created the potential for a dangerous conflict once the Atlantic Ocean that had separated two ancient civilizations had been transformed from a barrier to a bridge by a technological and scientific leap forward by western Europeans in the fifteenth century.

In the view of Europeans, the natural world was a resource designed for man's use. "Subdue the earth," read the first book of the Old Testament, "and have dominion over every living thing that moves on the earth." God ruled the cosmos, bringing floods, droughts, and earthquakes, but humans could reshape their physical surroundings into a productive and secure world. Man's relationship to the natural environment was a secular matter, even if God, in the sacred sphere, sometimes intervened.

Native Americans, in contrast, were "a people that are contented with Nature as they find her," as one colonist phrased it. In their system of values, every part of the natural environment was sacred and interconnected. Rocks, trees, and animals all possessed spiritual power, and all were linked to form a sacred whole. To injure the environment, by overfishing or abusing it in any way, was to offend the spiritual power present throughout nature and hence to risk spiritual retaliation. In the villages of Europe, peasant people had similarly believed in spirits residing in trees and rocks, but such "superstition" was fading.

Regarding the soil as a resource to be exploited for man's benefit, Europeans believed that land should be privately possessed. Individual ownership of property became a fundamental concept, and an extensive institutional apparatus grew up to support it. Fences symbolized private property, inheritance became the mechanism for transmitting land from one generation to another within the same family, and courts gained the power to settle property disputes. Property was the basis not only of sustenance but also of independence, material wealth, political status, and personal

identity. The social structure directly mirrored patterns of land ownership, with a landwealthy elite at the apex of the social pyramid and a mass of propertyless individuals forming the broad base.

Native Americans also had concepts of property, and tribes recognized territorial boundaries. But they believed that land was invested with sacred qualities and should be held in common. As one German missionary to the Delaware Indians explained their view in the eighteenth century, the Creator "made the Earth and all that it contains for the common good of mankind. Whatever liveth on the land, whatsoever groweth out of the earth, and all that is in the rivers and waters…was given jointly to all and everyone is entitled to his share."

Communal ownership sharply limited social stratification in most tribal communities. Accustomed to wide disparities of wealth, Europeans often found this remarkable. Observing the Iroquois of the eastern woodlands in 1657, a French Jesuit noted with surprise that they had no almshouses because "their kindness, humanity and courtesy not only makes them liberal with what they have, but causes them to possess hardly anything except in common. A whole village must be without corn, before any individual can be obliged to endure privation." Not all Europeans were acquisitive, competitive individuals. The majority were peasants scratching a subsistence living from the soil, living in kin-centered villages with little contact with the outside world, and exchanging goods and labor through barter. But in Europe's urban centers a wealth-conscious, ambitious individual who valued and sought wider choices and greater opportunities to enhance personal status was coming to the fore. In contrast, Native American traditions stressed the group rather than the individual. Holding land and other resources in common, Indian societies were usually more egalitarian and their members more concerned with personal valor than personal wealth.

Exceptions to this cultural system occurred in the highly developed and populous Aztec and Inca empires and, in North America, among a few tribes such as the Natchez. But on the eastern and western coasts of the continent and in the Southwest—the regions of contact in the sixteenth and seventeenth centuries—the European newcomers encountered a people whose cultural values differed strikingly from theirs.

European colonizers in North America also found disturbing the matrilineal organization of many tribal societies. Contrary to European practice, family membership among the Iroquois, for example, was determined through the female line. A typical family consisted of an old woman, her daughters with their husbands and children, and her unmarried granddaughters and grandsons. When a son or grandson married, he moved from this female-headed household to one headed by the matriarch of his wife's family. Divorce was also the woman's prerogative. If she desired it, she merely set her husband's possessions outside their dwelling door. Clans were composed of several matrilineal kin groups related by a blood connection on the mother's side. To Europeans this was a peculiar and dangerous reversal of their sexual hierarchy in which men, from time immemorial, had been supreme.

In Native American societies, women also held subordinate positions, but not nearly to the extent found among European women. For example, European women, with rare exceptions, were entirely excluded from political affairs. By contrast, in Native American villages, again to take the Iroquois example, designated men sat in a circle to deliberate and make decisions, but the senior women of the village stood behind them, lobbying and instructing. The village chiefs were male, but they were named to their positions by the elder women of their clans. If they moved too far from the will of the women who appointed them, these chiefs were removed—or "dehorned." "Our ancestors," the Oneida chief Giod Peter explained, "considered it a great transgression to reject the counsel of their women, particularly the female governesses. Our ancestors considered them mistresses of the soil.... The women, they are the life of the nation."

The role of women in the tribal economy reinforced the sharing of power between male and female. Men were responsible for hunting, fishing,

and clearing land, but women controlled the cultivation, harvest, and distribution of food. They were responsible for probably three-quarters of their family's nutritional needs. When the men were away on hunting expeditions, women directed village life. Europeans, imbued with the idea of male superiority and female subordination, perceived such a degree of sexual equality as another mark of the uncivilized nature of tribal society.

In the religious beliefs of Native Americans, the English saw a final cultural defect. Europeans built their religious life around the belief in a single god, written scriptures, an organized clergy, and churches. Most Native American societies, sharing no literary tradition, expressed their religious beliefs in a less structured way. Animated by a belief in a spirit power dwelling throughout nature (polytheism), they seemed to Europeans to worship the Devil. European settlers, their fear and hatred of infidels intensified by the Protestant Reformation, saw a holy necessity to convert—or destroy—these enemies of their God.

AFRICA ON THE EVE OF CONTACT

Half a century before Columbus reached the Americas, a Portuguese sea captain, Antam Gonçalves, made the first European landing on the west coast of sub-Saharan Africa. If he had been able to travel the length and breadth of the immense continent, he would have encountered a rich variety of African peoples and cultures. The notion of African "backwardness" and cultural impoverishment was a myth perpetuated after the slave trade had begun transporting millions of Africans to the New World. During the period of early contact with Europeans, Africa, like pre-Columbian America, was recognized as a diverse continent with a long history of cultural evolution.

THE KINGDOMS OF AFRICA

The peoples of Africa, estimated at about 50 million in the fifteenth century, when Europeans began making extensive contact with them, lived in vast deserts, grasslands, and tropical forests. As in Europe and the Americas at that time, most people tilled the soil. Part of their skill in farming derived from the development of iron production which may have begun in West Africa while Europe was still in the Stone Age. More efficient iron implements increased agricultural productivity, which in turn spurred population growth. The pattern was repeated in other parts of the world—the Americas, Europe, the Far East, and the Middle East—when the agricultural revolution began.

By the time Europeans reached the west coast of Africa, a number of large empires had risen there. The first was the kingdom of Ghana. It embraced an immense territory between the Sahara and the Gulf of Guinea and stretched from the Atlantic Ocean to the Niger River.

The development of large towns, skillfully designed buildings, elaborate sculpture and metalwork depicting humans and animals, long-distance commerce, and a complex political structure marked the Ghanaian kingdom from the sixth to eleventh centuries. A thriving caravan trade with Arab peoples across the Sahara to Morocco and Algeria brought extensive Muslim influence by the end of this period. By the eleventh century the king of Ghana boasted an army of 200,000, maintained trading contacts as far east as Cairo and Baghdad, and was furnishing, through Muslim middlemen in North Africa, much of the gold supply for the Christian Mediterranean region.

An invasion of North African Muslim people beginning in the eleventh century introduced a period of religious strife that eventually destroyed the kingdom of Ghana. But in the same region arose the Islamic kingdom of Mali. Prospering through its control of the gold trade, Mali flourished until the fifteenth century. Its city of Timbuktu contained a distinguished faculty of scholars to whom North Africans and even southern Europeans came to study. Traveling there in the 1330s, the Arab geographer ibn-Battutu wrote admiringly of "the discipline of its officials and provincial governors, the excellent condition of public finance, and...the respect accorded to the decisions of justice and to the authority of the sovereign."

Lesser kingdoms such as Kongo, Songhay, and Benin had also been growing for centuries before Europeans reached Africa by water. In their towns, rivaling those of Europe in size, lived people skilled in metalworking, weaving, ceramics, architecture, and aesthetic expression. Codes of law, regional trade, and effective political organization all developed by the fifteenth century. Finding their way to Africa south of the Sahara, Europeans encountered not a backward area but a densely settled region with an ancient history of long-distance trade and cultural exchange with other peoples.

Population growth and cultural development in Africa, as elsewhere in the world, proceeded at different rates in different regions. Ecological conditions and geography had a great deal to do with this. Where soil was rich, rainfall was adequate, and minerals were abundant, as in western Sudan, for instance, population grew and cultures changed rapidly. Where inhospitable desert or impenetrable jungle ruled, societies remained small and changed at a very slow rate. Isolation from other cultures retarded development, while contact with other regions encouraged change. For example, cultural innovation accelerated in East African Swahili-speaking societies facing the Indian Ocean after trading contacts began with the Eastern world in the ninth century. Around the same time, traders from the Arab world began to spread Muslim influence in West Africa.

THE AFRICAN ETHOS

The many peoples of Africa, who were to supply more than half of all the immigrants who crossed the ocean to the Western Hemisphere in the three centuries after Europeans began colonizing there, came from a rich diversity of cultures. But most of them shared certain ways of life that differentiated them from Europeans.

As in Europe, the family was the basic unit of social organization. Unlike Europe, however, African societies were organized in a variety of kinship and political systems. In many African societies, as in many Native American ones, the family was matrilineal. Property rights and political inheritance descended through the mother rather than the father. It was not the son of a chief who inherited his father's position but the son of the chief's sister. When a man married, his wife did not leave her family and take his name; the bridegroom left his family to join that of his bride.

West Africans believed in a supreme creator of the cosmos and in an assortment of lesser deities associated with natural forces such as rain, fertility, and animal life. Since these deities could intervene in human affairs, they were elaborately honored. Like most North American Indian societies, the peoples of West Africa held that spirits dwelt in the trees, rocks, and rivers around them, and hence they exercised care in the treatment of these natural objects.

In Africa ancestors were also worshipped, for they mediated between the Creator and the living of the earth. Since the dead played such an important role for the living, relatives held elaborate funeral rites to ensure the proper entrance of a deceased relative into the spiritual world. The more ancient an ancestor, the greater was this person's power to affect the living; thus the "ancient ones" were devoutly worshipped. Deep family loyalty and regard for family lineage flowed naturally from this ancestor worship.

Social organization in much of West Africa by the time Europeans arrived was as elaborate as in fifteenth-century Europe. At the top of society stood the nobility and the priests, usually men of advanced age. Beneath them were the great masses of people. Most of them were farmers, but some worked as craftsmen, traders, teachers, and artists. At the bottom of society resided slaves. As in ancient Greece and Rome, they were "outsiders"—war captives, criminals, or sometimes people who sold themselves into servitude to satisfy a debt. The rights of slaves were restricted, and their opportunities for advancement were narrow. Nevertheless, as members of the community, they were entitled to protection under the law and allowed the privileges of education, marriage, and parenthood. Their servile condition was not permanent, nor was it automatically inherited by their children, as would be the fate of Africans enslaved in the Americas.

THE IBERIAN CONQUEST OF AMERICA

From 1492 to 1518, Spanish and Portuguese explorers opened up vast parts of Asia and the Americas to European knowledge. Yet during this age of exploration, only modest attempts at settlement were made, mostly by the Spanish on the Caribbean islands of Cuba, Puerto Rico, and Hispaniola. The three decades after 1518, however, became an age of conquest. In some of the bloodiest chapters in recorded history, the Spanish nearly exterminated the native peoples of the Caribbean islands, toppled and plundered the great inland empires of the Aztecs and Incas in Mexico and Peru, discovered fabulous silver mines, and built a westward oceanic trade of enormous importance to all of Europe. The consequences of this short era of conquest proved to be immense for the entire world.

Portugal, meanwhile, restricted by one of the most significant lines ever drawn on a map, concentrated mostly on building an eastward oceanic trade to southeastern Asia. In 1493, to settle a dispute, the pope had demarcated Spanish and Portuguese spheres of exploration in the Atlantic. Drawing a north-south line 100 leagues (about 300 miles) west of the Azores, the pope confined Portugal to the European side of the line. One year later, in the Treaty of Tordesillas, Portugal obtained Spanish agreement to move the line 270 leagues farther west. Nobody knew at the time that a large part of South America, as yet undiscovered by Europeans, bulged east of the new demarcation line and therefore fell within the Portuguese sphere. In time, Portugal would develop this region, called Brazil, into one of the most profitable areas of the New World.

THE SPANISH JUGGERNAUT

Within a single generation of Columbus' death in 1506, Spanish conquistadores explored, claimed, and conquered most of South America (except Brazil), Central America, and the southern parts of North America from Florida to California. Led by audacious explorers and military leaders, and usually accompanied by enslaved Africans, they established the authority of Spain and Catholicism over an area that dwarfed their homeland in size and population. They were motivated by religion, growing pride of nation, and dreams of personal enrichment. "We came here," explained one Spanish foot soldier in Cortés' legion, "to serve God and the king, and also to get rich."

In two bold and bloody strokes, the Spanish overwhelmed the ancient civilizations of the Aztecs and Incas. In 1519, Hernando Cortés set out with 600 soldiers from coastal Vera Cruz and marched over rugged mountains to attack Tenochtitlán (modern-day Mexico City), the capital of Montezuma's Aztec empire. At its height, centuries before, the ancient city in the Valley of Mexico had contained perhaps 200,000 people. But in 1521, following two years of tense relations between the Spanish and Aztecs, it fell before Cortés's assault. The Spanish use of horses and firearms provided an important advantage, but the alliance of dissident natives oppressed by Montezuma's tyranny was indispensable in overthrowing the Aztec ruler. From the Valley of Mexico, the Spanish extended their dominion over the Mayan people of the Yucatan and Guatemala in the next few decades.

In the second conquest, the intrepid Francisco Pizarro, marching from Panama through the jungles of Ecuador and into the towering mountains of Peru with a mere 168 men, most of them not even soldiers, toppled the Inca empire. Like the Aztecs, the populous Incas lived in a highly organized social system. But also like the Aztecs, violent internal divisions had weakened them. This ensured Pizarro's success in capturing their capital at Cuzco in 1533. From there, Spanish soldiers marched farther afield, plundering other gold- and silver-rich Inca cities. Further expeditions into Chile, New Granada (Colombia), Argentina, and Bolivia in the 1530s and 1540s brought under Spanish control an empire larger than any in the Western world since the fall of Rome.

By 1550, Spain had overwhelmed the major centers of native population throughout the Caribbean, Mexico, Central America, and the west coast of South America. Spanish ships carried gold, silver, dyewoods, and sugar east across the Atlantic and transported African slaves, coloniz-

ers, and finished goods west. In a brief half century, Spain had exploited the advances in geographical knowledge and marine technology made by their Portuguese rivals and brought into harsh but profitable contact with each other the people of three continents. The tri-racial character of the Americas was already firmly established by 1600.

For nearly a century after Columbus' voyages, Spain enjoyed almost unchallenged dominion over the fabulous hemisphere newly revealed to Europeans. Greedy buccaneers of various nations snapped at the heels of homeward-bound Spanish treasure fleets with cargoes of silver, but this was only a nuisance. France made gestures of contesting Spanish or Portuguese control by planting small settlements in Brazil and Florida in the mid-sixteenth century, but they were quickly wiped out. England remained island-bound until the 1580s. Until the seventeenth century, only Portugal, which staked out important claims in Brazil in the 1520s, challenged Spanish domination of the New World.

THE GREAT DYING

Spanish conquest of major areas of the Americas set in motion two of the most far-reaching processes in modern history. One involved microbes, the other precious metal. Spanish contacts with the natives of the Caribbean basin, central Mexico, and Peru in the early sixteenth century triggered the most dramatic and disastrous population decline ever recorded. The population of the Americas on the eve of European arrival had grown to an estimated 50 million or more. In some areas, such as central Mexico, the highlands of Peru, and certain Caribbean islands, population density exceeded that of most of Europe. But though they were less populous than the people of the Americas, the European colonizers had one extraordinary biological advantage over them. They were members of a population that for centuries had been exposed to nearly every lethal parasite that infects humans on an epidemic scale in the temperate zone. Over the centuries, Europeans had built up immunities to these diseases. Such biological defenses did not eliminate smallpox, measles, diphtheria, and other afflictions, but they limited their deadly power.

In contrast, the people of the Americas had been geographically isolated from these diseases. Arriving Europeans therefore unknowingly encountered a huge component of the human race that was utterly defenseless against the "domesticated" infections the explorers, traders, and settlers carried inside their bodies.

The results were catastrophic. On Hispaniola, a population of about one million that had existed when Columbus arrived had only a few thousand survivors by 1530. Of some 25 million inhabitants of the Aztec empire before Cortés' arrival, about 90 percent were felled by disease within a half century. Demographic disaster also struck the populous Inca peoples of the Peruvian Andes. Smallpox "spread over the people as great destruction," an old Indian told a Spanish priest in the 1520s. "There was great havoc. Very many died of it. They could not stir, they could not change position, nor lie on one side, nor face down, nor on their backs. And if they stirred, much did they cry out.... And very many starved; there was death from hunger, [for] none could take care of [the sick]." Such terrifying sickness led many natives to believe that their gods had failed them, and this belief left them ready to acknowledge the greater power of the Christian God that Spanish priests proclaimed.

In most areas where Europeans intruded in the hemisphere for the next three centuries, the catastrophe repeated itself. Whether Protestant or Catholic, whether French, English, Spanish, or Dutch, whether male or female, every newcomer from the Old World participated in the spread of disease that typically eliminated, within a few generations, at least two-thirds of the native population. Millions of Native Americans who never saw a European died of European diseases, which swept like wildfire through densely populated regions.

The enslavement and brutal treatment of the native people intensified the lethal effects of European diseases. After their spectacular conquests of the Incas and Aztecs, the Spanish enslaved thousands of native people and assigned them work regimens that severely weakened their resistance to disease. Some priests like Bartolome de Las Casas waged lifelong campaigns to reduce the exploitation of the Indians, but they had only limited power to control the actions of their colonizing compatriots.

SILVER, SUGAR, AND THEIR CONSEQUENCES

The small amount of gold that Columbus brought home from his explorations of the West Indies raised hopes that this metal, which along with silver formed the standard of wealth in Europe, might be found in the transatlantic paradise. Some gold was gleaned from the Caribbean islands and later from Colombia, Brazil, and Peru. But though men pursued it fanatically to the far corners of the hemisphere, more than three centuries would pass before they found gold in windfall quantities on the North American Pacific slope and in the Yukon. It was silver that proved most abundant— so plenteous, in fact, that when bonanza strikes were made in Bolivia in 1545 and then in northern Mexico in the next decade, much of Spain's New World enterprise focused on its extraction. The Spanish empire in America, for most of the sixteenth century, was a vast mining community.

Native people, along with some African slaves, provided the labor supply for the mines. The Spaniards permitted the highly organized Indian societies to maintain control of their own communities but exacted from them huge labor drafts for mining. By imposing themselves at the top of a highly stratified social order that had previously been organized around tributary labor, the Spanish enriched themselves beyond the dreams of even the most visionary explorers. At Potosí, in Bolivia, 58,000 workers labored at elevations of up to 13,000 feet to extract the precious metal from a fabulous sugarloaf "mountain of silver." The town's population reached 120,000 by 1570, making it larger than any in Spain at the time. Thousands of other workers toiled in the mines of Zacatecas, Taxco, and Guanajuato. By 1660, they had scooped up more than 7 million pounds of silver from the Americas, tripling the entire European supply.

The massive flow of bullion from the Americas to Europe triggered profound changes. It financed further conquests and settlement in Spain's American empire, spurred long-distance trading in luxury items such as silks and spices from the Far East, and capitalized agricultural development in the New World of sugar, coffee, cacao, and indigo. The bland diet of Europeans gradually changed as items such as sugar and spices, previously luxury articles for the wealthy, became accessible to ordinary people.

The enormous increase of silver in circulation in Europe after the mid-sixteenth century also caused a "price revolution." As the supply of silver increased faster than the volume of goods and services that Europeans could produce, the value of the metal declined. Put differently, prices rose. Between 1550 and 1600, they doubled in many parts of Europe and then rose another 50 percent in the next half century. Landowning farmers got more for their produce, and merchants thrived on the increased circulation of goods. But artisans, laborers, and landless agricultural workers (the vast majority of the population) suffered because their wages did not keep pace with rising prices. Skilled artisans, lamented one of the first English immigrants to America, "live in such a low condition as is little better than beggary."

Overall, the price revolution brought a major redistribution of wealth and increased the number of people in western Europe living at the margins of society. It thus built up the pressure to emigrate to the Americas, Europe's new frontier. At the same time, rising prices stimulated commercial development. Expansion overseas fed expansion at home and intensified changes toward capitalist modes of production already under way in the sixteenth century.

While the Spaniards organized their overseas empire around the extraction of silver from the highlands of Mexico, Bolivia, and Peru, the Portuguese staked their future on sugar production in the lowlands of Brazil. Spanish colonial agriculture supplied the huge mining centers, but the Portuguese, adapting techniques of cultivation worked out earlier on their Atlantic islands, produced sugar for the export market.

Whereas the Spanish mining operations rested primarily on the backs of the native labor force, the lowland Portuguese sugar planters scattered the indigenous people and replaced them with platoons of African slaves. By 1570, this regimented work force was producing nearly 6 million pounds of sugar annually; by the 1630s, output had risen to 32 million pounds per year. High in calories but low in protein, the sweet "drug food" revolutionized the tastes of millions of Europeans and caused the oceanic transport of millions of African slaves to the coast of Brazil and later to Colombia, Ecuador, and Peru.

From Brazil, sugar production jumped to the island-specked Caribbean. Here, in the early seventeenth century, England, Holland, and France challenged Spain and Portugal for the riches of the New World. Once they secured a foothold in the West Indies, Spain's enemies stood at the gates of the Hispanic New World empire. This ushered in a long period of conflict "beyond the line"—where European treaties had no force. Through contraband trading with Spanish settlements, piratical attacks on Spanish treasure fleets, and outright seizure of Spanish-controlled islands, the Dutch, French, and English in the seventeenth century gradually sapped the strength of the first European empire outside of Europe.

SPAIN'S NORTHERN FRONTIER

The crown jewels of Spain's New World empire were silver-rich Mexico and Peru, with the islands and coastal fringes of the Caribbean representing lesser, yet valuable, gemstones. Distinctly third in importance were the northern borderlands of New Spain—the present-day Sun Belt of the United States. The early Spanish influence in Florida, the Gulf region, Texas, New Mexico, Arizona, and California indelibly marked the history of the United States.

Spanish explorers began charting the southeastern region of North America in the early sixteenth century, beginning with Juan Ponce de León's expeditions to Florida in 1515 and 1521. For the next half century, Spaniards planted small settlements along the coast as far north as the Chesapeake Bay where their temporary settlement included many enslaved Africans. The Spanish traded some with the natives, but the North American coast, especially Florida, was chiefly important to the Franciscan priests who attempted to gather the local tribes into mission villages and convert them to Catholicism.

The Spanish made several attempts to bring the entire Gulf of Mexico region under their control. From 1539 to 1542, Hernando de Soto, a veteran of Pizarro's conquest of the Incas, led an expedition deep into the homelands of the Creeks and explored westward across the Mississippi to Arkansas. In 1559, Spaniards marched northward from Mexico in an attempt to establish their authority in the lower Gulf region. Everywhere they went, they enslaved Indians and used them as provision carriers. In 1565, they sought to secure Florida. Building a fort at St. Augustine, they evicted their French rivals. St. Augustine became the center of Spain's northeastern frontier, and Florida remained a Spanish possession for more than two centuries.

The Southwest became a more important region of Spanish activity in North America. Francisco Vásquez de Coronado explored the region from 1540 to 1542, leading an expedition of several hundred Spanish soldiers, a number of Africans, and a baggage train of 1,300 friendly Indians, servants, and slaves. Coronado never found the Seven Cities of Cibola, reported by earlier Spanish explorers to be fabulously decorated in turquoise and gold. But he opened much of Arizona, New Mexico, and Colorado to eventual Spanish control, happened upon the Grand Canyon, and probed as far north as the Great Plains. His interior explorations, together with the nearly simultaneous expedition of de Soto in the Southeast, established Spanish claims to the southern latitudes of North America and gave them contacts, often bloody, with the populous corn-growing Indian societies of the region.

The Southwest, like Florida, proved empty of the fabled golden cities. Hence, in the seventeenth century, the region chiefly interested cattle ranchers and Jesuit and Franciscan missionaries. The Spanish established presidios, or garrisons, such as those at Santa Fe (1609) and Albuquerque

(1706), to control these vast regions and serve as trade centers. But the Catholic mission became the primary institution of the Spanish borderlands. In the eighteenth century, the Catholic missions reached northward, bringing most of the Indians of the California coast, from San Diego to the San Francisco Bay, under the control of the Spanish padres.

The Spanish missionary frontier operated differently, depending on the Indian cultures encountered. In Florida and California, where the native people lived in small, often seminomadic tribes, the Spanish used persuasion mixed with force to gather them within the sound of the mission bell. Setting the Indians to agricultural labor, the Spanish attempted slowly to convert them to European ways of life.

In New Mexico, however, missionaries made no attempt to uproot Pueblo people and contain them within the mission walls. The natives they encountered had lived in settled villages and practiced agriculture for centuries, so here the Spanish aimed to graft Catholicism onto Pueblo culture by building churches on the edges of ancient native villages. When they attempted to do more than overlay Indian culture with a veneer of Catholicism, they encountered fierce resistance. Such was the case in Pope's revolt in 1680. For five years, the Spanish padres had tried to root out traditional Pueblo religious practices. In response, a Pueblo leader named Pope led an Indian uprising that destroyed most of the churches in New Mexico and for more than a decade drove the Spanish from the region. Spaniards and Indians declared a kind of cultural truce: the Spaniards agreed to allow certain Pueblo rituals in return for nominal acceptance of Christianity.

THE "TEMPEST" IN THE WILDERNESS FROM

THE RACIALIZATION OF SAVAGERY

by Ronald Takaki

The Wampanoags as well as the Pequots, Massachusets, Nausets, Nipmucks, and Narragansets cultivated corn. As the main source of life for these tribes, corn was the focus of many legends. A Narraganset belief told how a crow had brought this grain to New England: "These Birds, although they do the corn also some hurt, yet scarce one *Native* amongst a hundred will kill them, because they have a tradition, that the Crow brought them at first an *Indian* Grain of Corn in one Ear, and an *Indian* or French bean in another, from the Great God *Kautantouwits* field in the Southwest from whence...came all their Corn and Beans." A Penobscot account celebrated the gift of Corn Mother: During a time of famine, an Indian woman fell in love with a snake in the forest. Her secret was discovered one day by her husband, and she told him that she had been chosen to save the tribe. She instructed him to kill her with a stone ax and then drag her body through a clearing. "After seven days he went to the clearing and found the corn plant rising above the ground...When the corn had born fruit and the silk of the corn ear had turned yellow, recognized in it the resemblance of his dead wife. Thus originated the cultivation of corn."

These Indians had a highly developed agricultural system. Samuel de Champlain found that "all along the shore" there was "a great deal of land cleared up and planted with Indian corn." Describing their agricultural practices, he wrote: "They put in each hill three or four Brazilian beans [kidney beans]...When they grow up, they interlace with the corn...and they keep the ground very free from weeds. We saw there many squashes, and pumpkins, and tobacco, which they likewise cultivate." According to Thomas Morton, Indians "dung[ed] their ground" with fish to fertilize the

soil and increase the harvest. After visiting the Narragansets in Rhode Island, John Winthrop, Jr., noted that although the soil in that region was "sandy & rocky," the people were able to raise "good corn without fish" by rotating their crops. "They have every one 2 fields," he observed, "which after the first 2 years they let one field rest each year, & that keeps their ground continually [productive]." According to Roger Williams, when the Indians were ready to harvest the corn, "all the neighbours men and women, forty, fifty, a hundred," joined in the work and came "to help freely." During their green corn festival, the Narragansets erected a long house, "sometimes a hundred, sometimes two hundred feet long upon a plain near the Court...where many thousands, men and women," gathered. Inside, dancers gave money, coats, and knives to the poor. After the harvest, the Indians stored their corn for the winter. "In the sand on the slope of hills," according to Champlain, "they dig holes, some five or six feet, more or less, and place their corn and other grains in large grass sacks, which they throw into the said holes, and cover them with sand to a depth of three or four feet above the surface of the ground. They take away their grain according to their need, and it is preserved as well as it be in our granaries." Contrary to the stereotype of Indians as hunters and therefore savages, these Indians were farmers.

However, many colonists in New England disregarded this reality and invented their own representations of Indians. What emerged to justify dispossessing them was the racialization of Indian "savagery." Indian heathenism and alleged laziness came to be viewed as inborn group traits that rendered them naturally incapable of civilization. This process of Indian dehumanization developed a peculiarly New England dimension as the colonists associated Indians with the Devil. Indian identity became a matter of "descent": Their racial markers indicated inerasable qualities of savagery.

This social construction of race occurred within the economic context of competition over land. The colonists argued that entitlement to land required its utilization. Native men, they claimed, pursued "no kind of labour but hunting, fishing and fowling." Indians were not producers. "The *Indians* are not able to make use of the one fourth part of the Land," argued Reverend Francis Higginson in 1630, "neither have they any settled places, as Towns to dwell in, nor any ground as they challenge for their owne possession, but change their habitation from place to place." In the Puritan view, Indians were lazy. "Fettered in the chains of idleness," they would rather starve than work, William Wood of Boston complained in 1634. Indians were sinfully squandering America's resources. Under their irresponsible guardianship, the land had become "all spoils, rots," and was "marred for want of manuring, gathering, ordering, etc." Like the "foxes and wild beasts," Indians did nothing "but run over the grass."

The Puritan possession of Indian lands was facilitated by the invasion of unseen pathogens. When the colonists began arriving in New England they found that the Indian population was already being reduced by European diseases. Two significant events had occurred in the early seventeenth century. Infected rats swam to shore from Samuel de Champlain's ships, and some sick French sailors were shipwrecked on the beaches of New England. By 1616, epidemics were ravaging Indian villages. Victims of "virgin soil epidemics," the Indians lacked immunological defenses against the newly introduced diseases. Between 1610 and 1675, the Indian population declined sharply— from 12,000 to a mere 3,000 for the Abenakis and from 65,000 to 10,000 for the southern New England tribes.

Describing the sweep of deadly diseases among the Indians, William Bradford reported that the Indians living near the trading house outside of Plymouth "fell sick of the smallpox, and died most miserably." The condition of those still alive was "lamentable." Their bodies were covered with "the pox breaking and mattering and running one into another their skin cleaving" to the mats beneath them. When they turned their bodies, they found "whole sides" of their skin flaying off. In this terrible way, they died "like rotten sheep." After one epidemic, William Bradford recorded in his diary: "For it pleased God to visit these Indians with a great sickness and such a mortality that of a thousand, above nine and a half hundred of them

died, and many of them did rot above ground for want of burial."

The colonists interpreted these Indian deaths as divinely sanctioned opportunities to take the land. John Winthrop declared that the decimation of Indians by smallpox manifested a Puritan destiny: God was "making room" for the colonists and "hath hereby cleared our title to this place." After an epidemic had swept through Indian villages, John Cotton claimed that the destruction was a sign from God: When the Lord decided to transplant His people, He made the country vacant for them to settle. Edward Johnson pointed out that epidemics had desolated "those places, where the English afterward planted."

Indeed, many New England towns were founded on the very lands the Indians had been living on before the epidemics. The Plymouth colony itself was located on the site of the Wampanoag village of Pawtuxet. The Pilgrims had noticed the village was empty and the cornfields overgrown with weeds. "There is a great deal of Land cleared," one of them reported, "and hath beene planted with Corne three or foure yeares agoe." The original inhabitants had been decimated by the epidemic of 1616. "Thousands of men have lived there, which died in a great plague not long since," another Pilgrim wrote; "and pity it was and is to see so many goodly fields, and so well seated, without men to dress and manure the same." During their first spring, the Pilgrims went out into those fields to weed and manure them. Fortunately, they had some corn seed to plant. Earlier, when they landed on Cape Cod, they had come across some Indian graves and found caches of corn. They considered this find, wrote Bradford, as "a special providence of God, and a great mercy to this poor people, that here they got seed to plant them corn the next year, or else they might have starved." The survival of these pallid strangers was so precarious that they probably would have perished had it not been for the seeds they found stored in the Indian burial grounds. Ironically, Indian death came to mean life for the Pilgrims.

However, the Puritans did not see it as irony but as the destruction of devils. They had demonized the native peoples, condemning Indian religious beliefs as "diabolical, and so uncouth, as if...framed and devised by the devil himself." The Wampanoags of Martha's Vineyard, wrote Reverend Thomas Mayhew in 1652, were "mighty zealous and earnest in the Worship of False gods and Devils." They were under the influence of "a multitude of Heathen Traditions of their gods...and abounding with sins."

To the colonists, the Indians were not merely a wayward people: they personified something fearful within Puritan society itself. Like Caliban, a "born devil," Indians failed to control their appetites, to create boundaries separating mind from body. They represented what English men and women in America thought they were not—and, more important, what they must not become. As exiles living in the wilderness far from "civilization," the English used their negative images of Indians to delineate the moral requirements they had set up for themselves. As sociologist Kai Erikson explained, "deviant forms of behavior, by marking the outer edges of group life, give the inner structure its special character and thus supply the framework within which the people of the group develop an orderly sense of their own cultural identity...One of the surest ways to confirm an identity, for communities as well as for individuals, is to find some way of measuring what one is *not*." By depicting Indians as demonic and savage, the colonists, like Prospero, were able to define more precisely what they perceived as the danger of becoming Calibanized.

The Indians presented a frightening threat to the Puritan errand in America. "The wilderness through which we are passing to the Promised Land is all over fill'd with fiery flying serpents," warned Reverend Cotton Mather. "Our Indian wars are not over yet." The wars were now within Puritan society and the self: the dangers were internal. Self-vigilance against sin was required, or else the English would become like Indians. "We have too far degenerated into Indian vices. The vices of the Indians are these: They are very lying wretches, and they are very lazy wretches; and they are out of measure indulgent unto their children; there is no family government among them. We have [become] shamefully Indianized in all those abominable things."

To be "Indianized" meant to serve the Devil. Cotton Mather thought this was what had happened to Mercy Short, a young girl who had been a captive of the Indians and who was suffering from tormenting fits. According to Mather, Short had seen the Devil. "Hee was not of a Negro but of a Tawney, or an Indian colour," she said; "he wore an highcrowned Hat, with straight Hair, and had one Cloven-foot." During a witchcraft trial, Mather reported, George Burroughs had lifted an extremely heavy object with the help of the Devil, who resembled an Indian. Puritan authorities hanged an English woman for worshiping Indian "gods" and for taking the Indian devil-god Hobbamock for a husband. Significantly, the Devil was portrayed as dark complected and Indian.

For the Puritans, to become Indian was the ultimate horror, for they believed Indians were "in very great subjection" of the Devil, who "kept them in a continual slavish fear of him." Governor Bradford harshly condemned Thomas Morton and his fellow prodigals of the Merrymount settlement for their promiscuous partying with Indians: "They also set up a maypole, drinking and dancing about it many days together, inviting the Indian women for their consorts, dancing and frisking together like so many fairies." Interracial cavorting threatened to fracture a cultural and moral border—the frontier of Puritan identity. Congress of bodies, white and "tawney," signified defilement, a frightful boundlessness. If the Puritans were to become wayward like the Indians, it would mean that they had succumbed to savagery and failed to shrivel the sensuous parts of the self. To be "Indianized" meant to be decivilized, to become wild men.

But they could not allow this to happen, for they were embarking on an errand to transform the wilderness into civilization. "The whole earth is the Lord's garden and he hath given it to the sons of men [to] increase and multiply and replentish the earth and subdue it," asserted John Winthrop in 1629 as he prepared to sail for New England. "Why then should we stand starving here for the places of habitation...and in the meantime suffer a whole Continent as fruitful and convenient for the use of man to lie waste without any improvement."

Actually, Indians had been farming the land, and this reality led to conflicts over resources. Within ten years after the arrival of Winthrop's group, twenty thousand more colonists came to New England. This growing English population had to be squeezed into a limited area of arable land. Less than 20 percent of the region was useful for agriculture, and the Indians had already established themselves on the prime lands. Consequently, the colonists often settled on or directly next to Indian communities. In the Connecticut Valley, for example, they erected towns like Springfield (1636), Northampton (1654), Hadley (1661), Deerfield (1673), and Northfield (1673) adjacent to Indian agricultural clearings at Agawam, Norwottuck, Pocumtuck, and Squakheag.

Over the years, the expansion of English settlement sometimes led to wars that literally made the land "vacant." During the Pequot War of 1637, some seven hundred Pequots were killed by the colonists and their Indian allies. Describing the massacre at Fort Mystic, an English officer wrote: "Many were burnt in the fort, both men, women, and children...There were about four hundred souls in this fort, and not above five of them escaped out of our hands. Great and doleful was the bloody sight." Commander John Mason explained that God had pushed the Pequots into a "fiery oven," "filling the place with dead bodies." By explaining their atrocities as divinely driven, the English were sharply inscribing the Indians as a race of devils. This was what happened during King Philip's War of 1675-76. While one thousand English were killed during this conflict, over six thousand Indians died from combat and disease. Altogether, about half of the total Indian population was destroyed in southern New England, Again, the colonists quickly justified their violence by demonizing their enemies. The Indians, Increase Mather observed, were "so *Devil driven* as to begin an unjust and bloody war upon the English, which issued in their speedy and utter extirpation from the face of God's earth." Cotton Mather explained that the war was a conflict between the Devil and God: "The Devil decoyed those miserable savages [to New England] in hopes that the Gospel of the Lord Jesus Christ would never come here to destroy or disturb *His absolute empire* over them."

Indians, "such people" of this "brave new world," to use Shakespeare's words, personified the Devil and everything the Puritans feared—the body, sexuality, laziness, sin, and the loss of self-control. They had no place in a "new England." This was the view trumpeted by Edward Johnson in his *Wonder-working Providence*. Where there had originally been "hideous Thickets" for wolves and bears, he proudly exclaimed in 1654, there were now streets "full of Girls and Boys sporting up and down, with a continued concourse of people." Initially, the colonists themselves had lived in "wigwams" like Indians, but now they had "orderly, fair, and well-built houses...together with Orchards filled with goodly fruit trees, and gardens with variety of flowers." The settlers had fought against the Devil, who had inhabited the bodies of the Indians, Johnson observed, and made it impossible for the soldiers to pierce them with their swords. But the English had violently triumphed. They had also expanded the market, making New England a center of production and trade. The settlers had turned "this Wilderness" into "a mart." Merchants from Holland, France, Spain, and Portugal were coming here. "Thus," proclaimed Johnson, "hath the Lord been pleased to turn one of the most hideous, boundless, and unknown Wildernesses in the world in an instant...to a well-ordered Commonwealth."

But, in a sense, all of these developments had already been acted out in *The Tempest*. Like Prospero, the English colonists had sailed to a new land, and many of them also felt they were exiles. They viewed the native peoples as savages, as Calibans. The strangers occupied the land, believing they were entitled to be "the lord on't.

Still, in Shakespeare's fantasy, race as a social construction had not yet been firmly formed, and Caliban's qualities as "other" not yet definitely fixed by race. What happened in history, however, was a different story.

The English possessed tremendous power to define the places and peoples they were conquering. As they made their way westward, they developed an ideology of "savagery," which was given form and content by the political and economic circumstances of the specific sites of colonization. Initially, in Ireland, the English had viewed savagery as something cultural, or a matter of "consent": they assumed that the distance between themselves and the Irish, or between civilization and savagery, was quantitative rather than-qualitative. The Irish as "other" was educable: they were capable of acquiring the traits of civilization. But later, as colonization reached across the Atlantic and as the English encountered a new group of people, many of them believed that savagery for the Indians might be inherent. Perhaps the Indians might be different from the English in kind rather than degree; if so, then the native people of America would be incapable of improvement because of their race. To use Shakespeare's language, they might have a "nature" that "nurture" would never be able to "stick" to or change. Race or "descent" might be destiny.

What happened in America in the actual encounters between the Indians and the English strangers was not uniform. In Virginia, Indian savagery was viewed largely as cultural: Indians were ignorant heathens. In New England, on the other hand, Indian savagery was racialized: Indians had come to be condemned as a demonic race, their dark complexions signifying an indelible and inherent evil. Why was there such a difference between the two regions? Possibly the competition between the English and the Indians over resources was more intense in New England than in Virginia, where there was more arable land. More important, the colonists in New England had brought with them a greater sense of religious mission than the Virginia settlers. For the Puritans, theirs was an "errand into the wilderness"—a mission to create what John Winthrop had proclaimed as "a city upon a hill" with the eyes of the world upon them. Within this economic and cultural Indian "other" a "discovery" occurred: The Indian "other" became a manifest devil. Thus savagery was racialized as the Indians were demonized, doomed to what Increase Mather called "utter extirpation." Once the process of this cultural construction was under way, it set a course for the making of a national identity in America for centuries to come.

No Obey: Women's Changing Status in the Seventeenth Century

by Suzanne Lebsock

In the early seventeenth century, people from three parts of the world converged in the land the English named Virginia. In 1600 all Virginians were Indians. Before long their claim to the land was challenged by the colonizing English, who needed laborers to work the land they took from the Indians, and who were willing to fill the bill by buying slaves, people forcibly imported from Africa.

In all three groups, of course, there were women. Reconstructing their lives is a delicate and at times frustrating enterprise, for the evidence is thin, and we are dependent on whatever the English—and English men at that—saw fit to write down. But it appears that not one of the three groups had what we think of as "traditional" sex roles. In Indian Virginia, for example, and in much of West Africa, women were the farmers. Among the English, meanwhile, ideas about the proper roles of women were often undermined by the fluid conditions of life and death in the New World.

By 1700 the English had established dominion over Virginia, and English men were establishing increasingly effective dominion over women. But none of this was a foregone conclusion in 1607. In the beginning, almost anything seemed possible. From the writings of early English chroniclers, we learn of two powerful Indian women. One was Pocahontas, who, as legend had it, saved John Smith's head in 1607. The other was the queen of the Appamatuck, who had received an English exploring party a few months earlier. "She is a fatt lustie manly woman," wrote one of the admiring explorers. The queen wore a crown and jewelry of copper; she presented a "stayed Countenance"; "she would permit none to stand or sitt neere her." In other words, she reinforced her authority as rulers often did and in ways that Englishmen readily understood—by regal dress, by a dignified bearing, and by keeping her distance.

In the Indian's own language, this formidable woman was a *werowance*, the highest authority in her tribe. Among Virginia Indians, for women to hold such positions was not unusual and the English, fresh from the reign of Elizabeth I (1558-1603), knew a queen when they saw one. What was more difficult for them to grasp was the importance of Indian women in the texture of everyday life.

At that time, more than twenty thousand Indians lived in what came to be called Virginia. There were more than forty different tribes, and while each had its particular territory and tradition, the tribes were clustered in three language groups. South of the James River were the Iroquoian-speaking tribes, the Nottoway and Meherrin. In the Piedmont lived a number of Siouan speakers. About these groups, we unfortunately know little. Most numerous and by far the best known were the Algonquian-speaking tribes of the Tidewater region, among them the Appamatuck, Chickahominy, Mattaponi, Nansemond, Pamunkey, and Rappahannock. Long sharing a common language, many of these tribes had recently become political allies as well. Powhatan, the werowance of the Pamunkey, had inherited control of six tribes, and by the early seventeenth century he had wrestled two dozen other Algonquian tribes into a confederacy—some would say kingdom. The English, for their part, were impressed with the "terrible and tyrannous" Powhatan, just as he intended them to be.

So centralized a political structure could not have been built without a sound economy, and the economy was based on the work of women. Women were the farmers in a society in which farming was the central occupation. "Their victuall," as John Smith put it, "is their chiefest riches." Corn was the single most important product in the Virginia economy. During the growing season, the Indians drew together in towns of from ten to one hundred houses. Between the houses and sometimes on the town's edge were the fields, where women planted corn and

beans together in the same hills (this way the cornstalks doubled as beanpoles and the land stayed fertile longer). They also grew peas, sunflowers, and several kinds of squash.

The Virginia soil was generous with wild fruits, berries, acorns, hickory nuts, and walnuts, and the gathering of these foods fell to the women. So did all of the food processing and preparation. The making of clothing was women's work, too. This meant, among other things, dressing skins and making thread "very even and readily" by rolling bark, grass, or the sinews of animals between hand and thigh. The thread was good for fishing nets as well as for sewing. Pots were usually made by women. So were baskets, and the weaving of mats was a major industry, for these were used both as furniture and as siding for houses. The women also had to carry the wood, keep the fire alive, and "beare all kindes of burthens," including their babies, on their backs.

As for housework, there was little to do, for Indian houses were very simple—one room, furnished mainly with mats and skins. Made of bark or mats stretched over bent poles, the houses were snug and smokey, as fires burned along the center axis of the floor and the smoke was allowed to find its way out through a hole in the ceiling. It is not clear who built the houses in the summer villages. In winter, however, when the villagers separated into smaller groups and hiked to their hunting grounds, the women were once again in charge:

"In that time when they goe a Huntinge the weomen goes to a place apoynted before, to build houses for their husbands to lie in att night carienge matts with them to couer ther houses with all, and as the men goes further a huntinge the woemen goes before to make houses, always carrienge the mattes with them."

And what did the men do? One observer summed it up in a single sentence: "The men fish, hunt, fowle, goe to the warrs, make the weeres [fishtraps], botes, and such like manly exercises and all laboures abroad." The men, in short, hunted, fished, fought, and made the implements they needed for each activity. They also cleared the grounds for fields, though since they used the slash-and-burn method, this was not especially laborious; they cleared away small trees and underbrush by burning, while larger trees were stripped of their bark and allowed to die.

Since the English regarded hunting as sport and not as work, they quickly concluded that Indian men were lazy, that the women were drudges, and that the unequal division of labor between the sexes was proof of the general inferiority of Indian civilization. The English were wrong, for men did make substantial contributions to the Indian diet, even though the work of women was more essential to the material welfare of their people. English men and Indian men, meanwhile, had more in common than the English knew, both "scorning to be seene in any woman like exercise."

For all that, authority in Indian society did not belong to men alone. Succession among Virginia Indians was matrilineal: Political power was inherited through the mother rather than the father, and females were eligible to become rulers. John Smith explained how it worked with Powhatan: "His kingdome descendeth not to his sonnes nor children." Instead, Powhatan's position would pass first to his brothers, then to his sisters, "and after them to the heires male and female of the eldest sister; but never to the heires of the males."

Our knowledge of family life and family structure is otherwise confined to a few intriguing scraps of information; on the whole, the English chroniclers were much sharper observers of politics and the economy than they were of families. Sexual attitudes were somewhat different from those of the English, at least to the extent that women (whose individual status within the tribe is not clear) were sometimes offered as bedfellows for visiting male dignitaries. Some relatively wealthy men had more than one wife, and divorce was permissible. Parents were said to love their children "verie dearly." Mothers gave birth with no crying out, whereupon English men concluded that for Indian women, childbirth was not painful.

Would that we knew more. What we do know, however, adds up to an impressive record of female influence in Indian Virginia. And this is the significance of the Pocahontas story. Pocahontas was a girl with sparkle. Her name, according to

the English, translated as "Little Wanton"; we might say playful, mischievous, frisky. She was about twelve in 1607 when John Smith made his first appearance in the immediate domain of her father, Powhatan. Uncertain of Smith's intentions, Powhatan's warriors killed two of Smith's men and took Smith himself prisoner. After three weeks of captivity and feasting, Smith was led to a large stone and made to lay down his head. The warriors raised their clubs as though "to beate oute his braines." Suddenly, Pocahontas sprang forth, the clubs were stayed, and John Smith was spared.

Or so Smith told it. The authenticity of this story has been challenged many times, partly because in John Smith's earliest recountings of his exploits the Pocahontas episode does not appear at all, and partly because the dusky-princess-rescues-bold-adventurer theme was commonplace in European culture long before Smith set foot in Virginia. He could easily have borrowed it. On the other hand, it could have happened. In Indian warfare, women, children, and werowances were almost always spared. While male warriors were sometimes tortured and often killed, they, too, could be spared and adopted into the victorious tribe. Here the judges were women. Given women's importance as breadwinners and in the kinship structure, their deciding if and when a new person was needed made eminent sense. So Pocahontas could have saved John Smith after all. What Smith experienced, although he did not know it, may have been a ritual of mock execution and adoption.

As time went on, of course, Pocahontas was the one who was adopted by the English. After John Smith's release, Pocahontas continued to live up to her name; she was spotted turning cartwheels through Jamestown, for instance. Her story took a more serious turn in 1613, when she was taken hostage by Samuel Argall, who hoped to use Pocahontas to gain bargaining power with the Indians. While living under English authority, Pocahontas met John Rolfe, who would one day achieve fame as the primary promoter of tobacco culture. They were married in 1614 and had one son. In 1616 they sailed for England, where Pocahontas was received as both a curiosity and a celebrity; early in 1617 she was presented to James

I and Queen Anne. A few months later, just as she was preparing to return to Virginia, Pocahontas died. She was no more than twenty-two years old.

For a long time no one took much notice of her story. Then some 150 years after her death, Pocahontas took hold of the American imagination as no other woman has. She was brought to life on stage, in verse, and in the pages of novels and of countless children's books. Her name was given to people, places, and an astonishing variety of things, from tobacco and quack medicines to cotton mills and coal mines. As powerful legends usually do, the Pocahontas story had several symbolic meanings. But there is no doubt that the national romance with Pocahontas helped to soothe the troubled conscience of white America. Pocahontas had rescued one colonizer and had married another. She professed the Christian religion and was baptized "Rebecca." She learned to speak the English language, sat for her portrait in English costume, and met her death on English soil. Symbolically, Pocahontas put an Indian stamp of approval on white people, white culture, and white conquest.

We could opt for a different symbol. The queen of the Appamatuck—the "fatt lustie manly woman" the English encountered in 1607— thought it all very interesting when the first explorers appeared. She looked the visitors over, fed them, and asked them to shoot their guns, "whereat she shewed not neere the like feare as Arahatec [the werowance of the Arrohateck tribe] though he be a goodly man." The following year, when the English were desperate for food, she supplied them with corn. By 1611, however, she was alarmed. Launching an aggressive policy of expansion, the English began carving out plantations on her tribal territory. The queen of the Appamatuck decided to resist. She began by inviting fourteen colonists to a party. When the men arrived, they were ambushed and every one was killed. Reprisal was immediate. An English detachment attacked her town, burned it, and killed everyone they could find, including women and children. The queen herself was shot, probably fatally, as she tried to escape.

Or we could take for our symbol the queen of the Paspahegh tribe. In 1610, the English governor engaged Powhatan in negotiations over the return of some Englishmen who had run off to join the Indians. Frustrated by Powhatan's "disdaynefull Answers," the governor ordered punitive raids on nearby tribes. The English marched on the Paspahegh's chief town, killed several people, torched the houses, cut down the corn, and took the queen prisoner, along with her children. Returning to Jamestown by boat, some of the soldiers complained about the sparing of the children. This situation was resolved by throwing the children in the river and "shoteinge owtt their Braynes in the water." On hearing further complaints about the sparing of the mother, the commander decided against burning and instead had her led away and stabbed to death.

This was unspeakable brutality, even for a brutal age. After Pocahontas married John Rolfe, an uneasy peace was established for a few years, but the basic pattern was already in place. Regardless of the Indian's strategy—be it aloofness, cooperation, or armed resistance—the determination of the English to take Indian land for soil-depleting tobacco crops was paramount. The brutality escalated. Under the leadership of Opechancanough, the Powhatan Confederacy made a concerted effort to expel the English in 1622; this time women and children were not spared, and nearly 350 colonists were killed. The English reeled from the blow—and retaliated with extraordinary force. Somehow, after many years, Opechancanough's allies regrouped, and they struck again in 1644. By this time, the English were far stronger, and their counterattack demolished the Powhatan Confederacy. In a treaty of 1646 the surviving Indians were placed on reservations and promised protection in exchange for their help in fending off outlying tribes. Still, for the Indians there was no real safety. Whites were divided on Indian policy, and in 1676 the followers of renegade Nathaniel Bacon, Jr., made war on Indians of every description. A new treaty was signed in 1677, but in the meantime the Indians had suffered another bitter disaster. Killed in battle, wasted by disease, driven out and starved out, the Indian population of Virginia by 1700 was perhaps one-tenth of what it had been a century before. Among the survivors was Cockacoeske, the queen of the

Pamunkey. In the treaty of 1677, all the subscribing tribes pledged their allegiance to her as well as to the English king. And as a probable reward for her loyalty during Bacon's Rebellion, the government presented her with gifts including a dazzling silver badge. The English, it seems, were still willing to accept female political authority when they encountered it.

Virginia was named for a female ruler, of course, and the point was not lost on Virginia Ferrar. In 1650 Ferrar wrote to Lady Berkeley, the wife of Virginia's governor, offering encouraging words and a novel interpretation of history. Women, she claimed, deserved the credit for Europe's discovery of the New World. First there was Queen Isabella of Spain, "to the Eternall honour of her Sexe…(though laughed at by all the wise Conceited Courtiers)" sent Christopher Columbus on his famous voyage of 1492. Then Elizabeth I of England ordered the "planting" of a colony in North America, "giving it as she was a Virgin Queene the Happy and Glorious name of Virginia." Next, Ferrar suggested, the governor's lady herself might continue the "Heroyicke Interprize" by funding an expedition to find a route to the East Indies.

For Virginia Ferrar and many historians after her, heroism was found in exploration and conquest. For the women who helped colonize Virginia, there was heroism in survival. Wherever they came from—the British Isles, the West Indies, Africa—Virginia's new women faced a rugged existence. Thanks to Indian women, the colonists after a few years learned how to grow enough food to support themselves. Then in 1614 they began marketing the crop that would sustain their colony and run their lives. This was tobacco, of course, the seeds imported from the West Indies and the cultivation techniques once again borrowed from the Virginia Indians. Profits were high, at times spectacular, and so an entire society dedicated itself to putting more land in tobacco.

For the women, life was not easy. The death rate was appalling. Living conditions were crude, and all but the wealthiest could expect a lifetime of hard labor. Yet, if a woman lived long enough, she could sometimes experience a surprising degree of personal freedom. If she began as a slave, she might become free. If she started as a servant, she might become a planter. If she were a member of a wealthy family, she might become a politician. In the rough-and-ready world of the seventeenth century, almost anything might happen.

The gentlemen of the General Assembly had their moments of insight. "In a newe plantation," they declared in 1619, "it is not knowen whether man or woman be the most necessary." Believing that a permanent colony would not be established until the planters settled down and raised families, influential men had for some time tried to bring more women to Virginia. Decisions on who would come to America, however, were not made by legislators alone. Instead, they were made by hundreds of individuals, among them planters who decided that in the short run, on their particular plantations, men were the most necessary. The result was an extremely unbalanced sex ratio. Among blacks there were at least three men for every two women. Among whites, men outnumbered women by three or four to one.

The Virginia Company, chartered in 1606 to finance and oversee colonization, resolved to send shiploads of "Maydens," young English women who would dare an ocean voyage and marriage to a stranger on the other side. In her novel *To Have and to Hold,* Mary Johnston later imagined the commotion when the first group of maids arrived in Jamestown. "I saw young men, panting, seize hand or arm and strive to pull toward them some reluctant fair; others snatched kisses, or fell on their knees and began speeches out of Euphues; others commenced an inventory of their possession—acres, tobacco, servants, household plenishing. All was hubbub, protestation, frightened cries, and hysterical laughter." The narrator drew closer and heard some bargaining: "Says Phyllis, 'Any poultry?'"

Corydon: A matter of twelve hens and twa cocks.

Phyllis: A cow?

Phyllis: How much tobacco?

Corydon: Three acres, hinny, though I dinna drink the weed myself. I'm a Stewart, woman, an' the King's puir cousin.

Phyllis: What household plenishing?

Corydon: Ane large bed, ane flock bed, ane trundle bed, ane chest, ane trunk, ane leather cairpet, sax cawfskin chairs an' two-three rush, five pair o' sheets an' auchteen dowlas napkins, sax alchemy spunes—

Phyllis: I'll take you.

The legend of early Virginia was somehow brightened by the tales of this strange marriage market, although the Virginia Company in truth sent out only about 140 maids. Other English women made the crossing in ones and twos, sailing with their husbands or following husbands who had ventured over earlier. The vast majority of women colonists, however, were unfree laborers. Some, though their numbers were small in the first half of the seventeenth century, were slaves brought by force from different parts of Africa (and from Africa via the West Indies). About 80 percent of all English immigrants, meanwhile, were indentured servants. These people owed from four to seven years of faithful labor to whoever paid their passage from England. Until their time was up, they were not free to marry at all.

The new arrivals, single or married, bound of free, could expect rude beginnings. If, like the fictional Phyllis, her new household really contained five pairs of sheets, she would be doing very well indeed. The newcomer would need only a few seconds to size up her surroundings. From the outside the typical Virginia farmhouse looked (and was) small, and it probably needed patching. The inside could be inspected in three or four glances. This was a one-room house, measuring perhaps twenty-five by sixteen feet. It was a story and a half high and probably had a loft where children and servants slept. Otherwise, one space had to suffice for every indoor purpose.

Except for its enormous fireplace, it was something like an Indian house, and like an Indian house, it was sparsely furnished. Standard equipment for a house owned by a middling planter was one feather bed (not to say a bedstead), a chest for storage, a cooking pot, a mortar and pestle for pounding corn, an axe, some knives, a few wooden dishes, some odd spoons, and

containers for storing crops. Stools and benches were not standard, although some households had them, nor were tables, forks, sheets, skillets, lamps, or candles. Occasionally, some bright and beautiful object would light up a Virginia household, and some of the most prosperous planters lived in higher style. But the typical planter stuck to ruthless utility. If furnishings were spartan and houses leaked and leaned and all but tumbled down, no matter. The money was in tobacco, and the planter who wanted to succeed invested every spare shilling in laborers.

That, of course, is what brought most women to Virginia. Indentured servitude was the system that connected young English people in need of work to planters in need of workers. In the England of the middle seventeenth century, finding a place in life could be difficult. The population was exploding, wages were falling, and unemployment was acute. Looking for something better, the resourceful left villages for towns, towns for cities, and some of them took a chance on Virginia.

They were in for a few surprises. Servitude was no lark in England, but it was harsher still in Virginia. Masters were required by law to provide adequate food and clothing (including a send-off of three barrels of corn and a new suit of clothes when the servant's time was up), and they were instructed to keep punishments reasonable. The economic interest of masters, however, dictated squeezing their servants to the limit. By the same token, the interest of servants lay in resisting. This could be dangerous, though, because the master literally had the whip hand. Court records are rife with testimony concerning life-threatening punishments. One young woman was "sore beaten and her body full of sores and holes." Another was beaten "like a dogge." More than one was killed in the course of a whipping.

Sexual abuse was an added hazard. According to law, an indentured servant who became pregnant was obliged to serve her master an additional two years. Not until 1662 did the House of Burgesses respond to the logic of the situation: The old law encouraged masters to sexually exploit their own servants or to stand by while someone else did the exploiting. The new law of 1662 stipulated that the pregnant servant would still serve two more years, but she would serve them under a new master.

Another surprise was that some women servants were set to work in the fields. A popular ballad called "The Trappan'd Maiden: Or, the Distressed Damsel" made the point:

> I have play'd my part both at Plow and Cart, In the Land of Virginny, O;
>
> Billets from the Wood upon my back they load,
>
> *When that I am weary, weary, weary, weary, O*

Through ballads and by other means, the rumors about the nature of women's work in Virginia reached England. Because proper English women were not supposed to do heavy field work, this posed problem for Virginia's promoters. A pamphlet of 1656 offered a neat resolution to the problem: The only English women "put into the ground," it was explained, were those "wenches" who were "nasty, beastly, and…awkward."

It was not as though women needed work in the fields to keep them busy. Slaves, servants, mistresses, and daughters carried out all the day-to-day never-done tasks that made life possible. Every day they ground corn by hand and made it into soup or bread. If their children had milk, it was because the women tended cows. If there was butter or cheese, it was because the women made them from the milk. If there were eggs, it was because the women raised chickens. If there was meat, it was because the women had butchered it, preserved it, and boiled it. If there were vegetables, it was because the women gardened. If there was cider or beer, the women brewed it. While cloth was mainly imported, women did all the sewing, washing, and mending, major chores in a time when work meant sweat and when most people had few changes of clothing. If someone fell ill, women did the nursing; in large households someone was probably sick all of the time. And if the family prospered, chances were that the master would acquire a new male indentured servant. The women, as a result, acquired another bundle of laundry, another person to be nursed through inevitable illness, and another hearty appetite.

If the woman was married, she was likely to be pregnant, breastfeeding, or looking after a young child. This was a duty and a labor of love. It was also a major economic contribution as surely as growing tobacco or corn. The planters' primary economic problem in the seventeenth century was the shortage of labor. Anyone who brought children into the world, therefore, and nurtured them until they grew into productive adulthood, made direct and essential contributions to Virginia's economic development.

Rearing a child to adulthood, however, was often out of the parents' power. Death was simply everywhere. It came, as we have seen, from wars between colonists and Indians. It came much more often from disease, from what the colonists called "fluxes," "agues," and "fevers"; we would say typhoid, dysentery, smallpox, and malaria. A child born in Virginia had only a fifty-fifty chance of living to see adulthood. About a quarter of all babies died before they reached their first birthday.

Adults were vulnerable, too. Although experiences varied a great deal from one person to the next, we can reconstruct the life of a typical white woman. She was twenty when she arrived in Virginia as an indentured servant. If she lived through her term of service (her chances were not especially good), she would marry almost as soon as she was free. She was now about twenty-five, and she would begin bearing children, one every two years, as was commonly the case in societies without benefit of birth control. Two of her children would die in childhood. Whether she would live to see any of her children grown was doubtful. After seven years of marriage her husband (who was older) would die, and she would follow in a few years.

Some additional statistics (again, these are for whites) help us appreciate the disruption that death wrought in Virginia families. Only one marriage in three lasted as long as ten years. From the perspective of the children, losing a parent was the normal experience. By the time they reached the age of nine, half of the children had already lost one or both parents. Virginia was a land of widows, widowers, bachelors, and above all, orphans.

As a consequence, families hardly ever matched the English ideal. A family, in English theory, consisted of a father, a mother, their children, and servants. In Virginia practice, few children were raised exclusively by their own parents, and many people found themselves raising other people's children. Families were suddenly bereft, then just as suddenly recombined into new households as surviving parents remarried, each bringing with them the children, stepchildren, orphans, servants, and slaves from their previous households. The shape of the family, therefore, was complex, unpredictable, and always changing.

Virginia practice also challenged English views concerning the proper lines of authority within the family, and this was a major step forward for women. In theory, English families were "patriarchal." That is, the husband and father was responsible for the welfare and good behavior of the entire household; he ruled, and everyone else—wife, child, and servant—owed him unquestioning, uncomplaining obedience.

Virginians may have believed in patriarchal authority with all their hearts, but conditions in the New World at times made enforcement difficult. The patriarchs simply did not live long enough. In marrying, for example, young people often made their own decisions; they could hardly ask permission of fathers who were back in England or long since dead. Fathers often realized that their families might have to get along without protectors. Accordingly, the terms of men's wills tended to be generous, more so than in England. Virginia daughters stood a good chance of inheriting land, and Virginia wives were very often given larger legacies than the law required. What is more, the Virginia wife was usually named her husband's executrix—the pivotal person who controlled the property until it was finally handed over to the heirs.

Add in the sex ratio, and the result was a formula for considerable upward mobility among women. Because women were dramatically outnumbered, they could often "marry up." A former servant might marry a property owner, and if she outlived him, she might assume control of the property. She might marry still better a second or third time around.

If she was anything like Sarah Harrison of Surry County, she would have a strong sense of her own bargaining power. When Harrison was married to James Blair in 1687, the wedding ceremony began like any other. Presently, however, the minister intoned the standard question: Did Sarah promise to obey her husband? "No obey," said Sarah. The minister repeated the question. "No obey," said Sarah again. The minister tried yet again. "No obey," said Sarah, one more time. The minister was checked, and the ceremony went on, no obey.

Virginia had its share of Sarah Harrisons, women who were strong willed or rowdy or powerful, women who made their influence felt not only in families but in local communities and in the colony. Nothing in English law or thought encouraged their participation in public affairs. The prevailing idea, in fact, was that women were inferior to men in every way—in physical strength, in reasoning ability, in their capacity to withstand moral temptations—and thus was justified the exclusion of women from voting and holding public office. Yet officeholding was only one way to exert influence. In the seventeenth century, Virginia women explored some fascinating alternatives.

The obstacles to female participation in public affairs were formidable. Women were not allowed to vote, to serve on juries, or to hold office in either government or church. This in turn meant that women were seldom drawn out their immediate neighborhoods for court days and militia musters. Women ordinarily could not read, either. Church was as far as they could expect to go. Consequently, for most women the known world was isolated and small. It was perhaps five miles across and populated mainly by family and a few neighbors.

Within that small world, the challenge for women and men together was to forge some sense of community. In England and in Africa, most people lived in villages. In Virginia, Indians excepted, most people lived on scattered farms; thus for people to form bonds with their neighbors was especially important. Here the Sunday church service was central. So were weddings and funerals, and when a woman went into labor, she was attended by other women from the neighborhood. Women also served their communities by taking in orphans, paupers, and those who were physically and mentally disabled. In a time when there were no orphanages, almshouses, hospitals, or old people's homes, people in need were taken care of in households. Local authorities recognized this care as a community responsibility; the families who provided it were accordingly compensated by the taxpayers.

Since many of the surviving records for the seventeenth century are court records, we know more about the negative means of maintaining community. Enter the stocks, the whipping post, and the ducking stool—the instruments of public humiliation. Inflicting pain and shame was a practical means of controlling troublemakers in a society with no jails to speak of and with no police force. Transgressors were expected to confess and to beg forgiveness. In the process, they reaffirmed the neighborhood's notions about what was right and what was wrong.

Cases of fornication and adultery—the crimes that most frequently involved women—showed how the system worked. Virginians did not as a rule prosecute those who engaged in premarital sex; probably a third of Virginia brides were already pregnant at the wedding. Non-marital sex was another matter altogether, a violation of good order and, if a child was born to the offenders, a possible drain on the local welfare funds. Among the lawful penalties were whippings and fines. A third penalty required each offender to appear in church, draped in a white sheet and holding a white wand. Standing on a stool in front of the congregation, the offender was then expected to apologize.

Like other systems, this one did not work every time. Edith Tooker of Lower Norfolk was brought before her congregation in 1641 for the "foul crime of fornication." On being instructed to say she was sorry, she instead proceeded to "cut and mangle the sheet wherein she did penance." The court was not amused; "a most obstinate and graceless person," the clerk muttered. Tooker was resentenced to twenty lashes and, two Sundays hence, to another try at the sheet treatment.

Tooker was getting to be a regular. In an earlier case, the court had compelled her to apologize for slander, the other crime frequently perpetrated by women. In early Virginia, most information circulated by word of mouth, and personal reputation was extremely important. (Imagine your marriage prospects, your employment credentials, or your credit rating begin established by rumor.) Virginia was also a place in which bawdy joking was a way of life. It was therefore a thin line between conversation and slander, and legal actions were legion. In Northampton County, Goodwife Williams called John Dennis a "knave and base knave" and had the satisfaction of seeing him put into stock for calling her "a whore and a base whore" in return. Edward Drew sued Joane Butler for calling his wife a "common Cunted hoare." Ann Fowler of Lower Norfold was sentenced to twenty lashes and a public apology after she said, in reference to a high public official no less, "Let Capt. Thoroogood kiss my arse."

By 1662 the House of Burgesses was so vexed by the "brabling" women that a new law was passed; each country was required to build a ducking stool to quiet female scandalmongers. (Besides making the offender look ridiculous, the ducking stool held her under water until she spluttered out an apology.) This was testimony to the power of the spoken word. The power to wreck a reputation or to ignite conflict in a community—this was well within the reach of women, and some of them used it to even scores, to intimidate neighbors, or merely to show that they could not be pushed around. At the same time "gossip" could be a force for good. A man who beat his wife, a woman who whipped her servant, might both behave better when they found out their neighbors were talking about them.

Witchcraft demonstrated some of the same dynamics. A witch was someone who used supernatural powers to bring harm to someone else. Everyone believed that witchcraft was real, because it accounted for evil and suffering in a world where scientific explanations were not yet available. In 1671 in Northumberland, for example, Edward Cole's "people all fell sick and much of his cattle dyed." We would look for a germ or virus. Edward Cole suspected witchcraft.

That he accused a woman was no coincidence. In the witch traditions of Europe and Great Britain (Virginia's Indians and Africans probably had their own traditions, but we do not know the details), alleged witches were almost always female. Women, especially the old and poor, were easy scapegoats. For centuries, moreover, women had been stereotyped in the image of Eve—passionate, lusty, and easily seduced by the devil, the culprit who presumably gave witches their magical powers. Actually, a woman who was otherwise powerless might find her only leverage in behaving as though she might be a witch; that way neighbors who feared a bewitching would be likely to treat her with more care.

Or they might take her to court. Virginia seems to have had the dubious honor of hosting the first witch trial in British North America: Joan Wright of Surry was accused (and released) in 1626. No one was every executed for witchcraft in Virginia, however, and the most famous case on record suggests that the authorities tended to proceed with caution. In 1698 and at several times thereafter, Grace Sherwood was accused of bewitching various neighbors. In the investigations that followed, a gallows-happy set of justices could have found sufficient evidence to convict. A panel of matrons found "two things like titts" on her body, the extra nipples with which witches supposedly suckled the devil. Later, Sherwood was bound and thrown in the river to test whether she would sink or float; the spot in Virginia Beach is still called Witch Duck Point. She floated—more evidence of her guilt.

But Grace Sherwood was not condemned. Possibly, Virginia communities were too fragile to withstand the potentially explosive impact of witchcraft convictions. In the Sherwood case, the local population was apparently badly divided; when two subsequent panels of matrons were summoned to give evidence, they refused to appear. Were they deliberately protesting the proceedings?

They may have been, for seventeenth-century women did launch into political battles when the occasion arose, and highborn women were involved at the highest levels. Margaret Brent

arrived in Virginia around 1651. She lived out her days quietly on a Westmoreland plantation she named "Peace," a welcome change after a career in Maryland that had been anything but peaceful. Brent had served as the executrix of Maryland's governor, she had headed off a mutiny of hungry soldiers, and she had asked for the vote—the first woman in America to do so. In fact, she asked for two votes in the Maryland assembly, one as executrix and one in her own right. When she was denied, she lodged a protest against all the assembly's further actions.

Margaret Brent would probably have recognized kindred spirits in the women who were caught up in the turmoil of Bacon's Rebellion. Civil war broke out in Virginia in 1676. Indian policy precipitated the trouble; believing themselves too vulnerable to Indian attacks, planters on the frontier found a leader in Nathaniel Bacon and began making war on peaceful Indians. When Governor William Berkeley tried to stop them, Bacon's followers rebelled against their government, burning Jamestown and pillaging the plantations of Berkeley's supporters. Luckily for the forces of the governor, Bacon died in the fall of 1676 and the rebellion fizzled soon after. While Bacon's Rebellion was apparently set in motion by men, women were quickly embroiled, too. One of the most important histories of the rebellion was written on the scene by a woman. Anne Cotton apologized for writing 'too wordishly," but her *Account of Our Late Troubles in Virginia* was in fact an eloquent summary—and it earns her the distinction of having been Virginia's first woman historian. On the side of the rebels were several fiery women. One of them was Sarah Drummond, whose husband was executed for his role in the rebellion. Sarah herself was said to be "a notorious & wicked rebel, in inciting & incouraging the people to the late rebellion: persuading the soldiers to persist therein, telling them they need not fear the king, nor any force out of England, no more than a broken straw."

In this she was mistaken, for Lady Frances Berkeley soon returned from England with a thousand redcoats and orders to crush the rebels. Lady Berkeley was the wife of the governor and well connected at court. When the rebellion flared, the governor dispatched her to England to act as his representative. On returning to Virginia, she continued her vigorous defense of her husband's actions, and after he died in 1677, she harassed his successor unmercifully. She was joined by several influential men who met at her home, Green Spring, to plot strategy; they were collectively known as the Green Spring faction. Eventually Lady Berkeley married the governor of North Carolina (her third governor), but they lived at Green Spring and she remained a force in Virginia politics until her death in the 1690s.

From the widow who served as executrix of a small planter's will to the adventures of a Sarah Drummond or a Frances Berkeley, women in seventeenth-century Virginia frequently assumed positions of power, authority, or trust. There was a catch, however. No matter how well these women performed, their achievements did not undermine the prevailing belief in the natural inferiority or women Instead, these active women were thought of as exceptions, as honorary men; ideas about women as a group changed not at all.

As the century drew to a close, these ideas were expressed and given new strength by two developments. First was the founding of William and Mary in 1693. The college was for men only and would remain so for 226 years. Then in 1699 a new law spelled out who in Virginia could vote and who could not. While custom prevented women from voting everywhere, Virginia was the only colony to say explicitly that women could not vote. It was the beginning of a long tradition of legislative conservatism on issues affecting women.

As the seventeenth century gave way to the eighteenth, then, some doors began to close on women. For black women, unfortunately, this was nothing new. Their turning point seems to have come in the 1660s. Before then Africans in Virginia had at least a slim chance of becoming free people, and those who were slaves had work routines not very different from those of English indentured servants. But from 1662 on, Virginia lawmakers made a series or momentous decisions: One law after another made slavery more rigid, more degrading, and more difficult to escape.

So far as anyone knows, the first blacks arrived in Virginia in 1619. It is certain that they were brought by force. Less is known about their status over time—whether they remained slaves who were kept in bondage all their lives, or whether they became indentured servants who went free after a few years. Since there was no slavery in England, white Virginians had no fixed ideas about what they should do with their new laborers from Africa. We do know that among the relatively small numbers of Africans who came to Virginia in the early years, a few did achieve freedom.

An outstanding example was the family of Anthony and Mary Johnson of Northampton County. "'Antonio a Negro'" and "'Mary a Negro Woman'" arrived in separate ships in 1621 and 1622. They met when they were put to work on the same plantation; Mary was the only woman on the place. How they got free is not known, but at some point they married, and their family life proved to be a miracle of good health. They raised four children, and Mary and Anthony both lived to see grandchildren. Economically they did well. When the entire family moved to Maryland in the 1660s, Anthony sold a 250-acre plantation. Their grown son John owned a 450-acre plantation.

The Johnson family was surely not exempt from racial prejudice. Long before the English had laid eyes on actual Africans, they associated blackness with evil, and they made up their minds that darker-skinned peoples were inferior beings. English prejudice must have weighed on the Johnsons and all other black Virginians.

Still, there was a time in Virginia's early history when race relations were fluid, possibilities were open, and blacks and whites of the same class could expect roughly similar treatment. The best evidence of this comes from the courts' reactions to affairs of the heart. Black couples and interracial couples who were found guilty of adultery or fornication took the same punishments as white couples; in 1649 William Watts (white) and Mary (a "negro Woman" servant) found themselves "standing in a white sheete with a white Rodd in theire hands in the Chapell." Blacks and whites who actually married each other—and there were several documented cases of this—were left in peace.

But not for long. At midcentury the black population was still small—perhaps 500 people in a total population of about 14,000—and the great majority of bound laborers were still English servants. By century's end Virginia was fast making its fateful transition to slave labor. There were thousands of blacks in Virginia by 1700 (between 6,000 and 10,000, it is thought, in a total population of 63,000), and for every new indentured servant imported from England, four black slaves arrived from Africa or the Caribbean.

The legal system was ready for them. From 1662 to 1705 the assembly passed a series of laws that together defined the essential character of slavery and race relations in Virginia. It was a chilling list. Who was a slave? Any child born of a slave mother, the law answered (1662). Indians, too, could be made slaves (1682) . Could a slave ever become a free person? Hardly ever, the law answered. An owner who wanted to free a slave would have to pay to send the freed slave out of the colony (1691). In 1723 the law was revised; henceforth a slave could be freed only by special act of the assembly. Could a white person marry a black or an Indian? No, and any white who tried was to be banished from the colony (1691). Could

a slave own property? No, a slave was property, and any livestock belonging to slaves was to be confiscated and sold (1705). How could a slave be lawfully disciplined? If in the course of punishing a slave, the owner or overseer killed the slave, it was legal (1699). A runaway slave who resisted arrest was to be killed on the spot (1680). A slave who was merely unruly could legally have fingers or toes cut off (1705).

The law, fortunately, was not the only influence on the lives of slaves. As we shall see, slaves themselves continually invented ways of exerting influence on their owners, on the system, and on one another. Yet it is important to appreciate the law's full power. By 1700 the typical black Virginia woman was "chattel"—property—and as such she could be bought, sold, mortgaged, or swapped, or even gambled away in a card game. She would remain property all of her life, and so would her children, who could be taken away from her at any time. She could try to protest, but she did so knowing that her owner had life-and-death power over her. These were among the basic facts of life under slavery, and they would remain in force for more than a century and a half.

Alice Doane's Appeal

by Nathaniel Hawthorne

On a pleasant afternoon of June, it was my good fortune to be the companion of two young ladies in a walk. The direction of our course being left to me, I led them neither to Legge's Hill, nor to the Cold Spring, nor to the rude shores and old batteries of the Neck, nor yet to Paradise; though if the latter place were rightly named, my fair friends would have been at home there. We reached the outskirts of the town, and turning aside from a street of tanners and curriers, began to ascend a hill, which at a distance, by its dark slope and the even line of its summit, re-sembled a green rampart along the road. It was less steep than its aspect threatened. The eminence formed part of an extensive tract of pasture land, and was traversed by cow paths in various directions; but, strange to tell, though the whole slope and summit were of a peculiarly deep green, scarce a blade of grass was visible from the base upward. This deceitful verdure was occasioned by a plentiful crop of 'wood-wax,' which wears the same dark and glossy green throughout the summer, except at one short period, when it puts forth a profusion of yellow blossoms. At that season to a distant spectator, the hill appears absolutely overlaid with gold, or covered with a glory of sunshine, even beneath a clouded sky. But the curious wanderer on the hill will perceive that all the grass, and every thing that should nourish man or beast, has been destroyed by this vile and ineradicable weed its tufted roots make the soil their own, and permit nothing else to vegetate among them; so that a physical curse may be said to have blasted the spot, where guilt and phrenzy consummated the most execrable scene, that our history blushes to record. For this was the field where Superstition won her darkest triumph; the high place where our fathers set up their shame, to the mournful gaze of generations far remote. The dust of martyrs was beneath our feet. We stood on Gallows Hill.

For my own part, I have often courted the historic influence of the spot. But it is singular, how few come on pilgrimage to this famous hill; how many spend their lives almost at its base, and never once obey the summons of the shadowy past, as it beckons them to the summit. Till a year or two since, this portion of our history had been very imperfectly written, and, as we are not a people of legend or tradition, it was not every citizen of our ancient town that could tell, within half a century, so much as the date of the witchcraft delusion. Recently, indeed, an historian has treated the subject in a manner that will keep his name alive, in the only desirable connection with the errors of our ancestry, by converting the hill of their dis-grace into an honorable monument of his own antiquarian lore, and of that better wisdom, which draws the moral while it tells the tale. But we are a people of the present and have no heartfelt interest in the olden time. Every fifth of November, in commemoration of they know not what, or rather without an idea beyond the momentary blaze, the young men scare the town with bonfires on this haunted height, but never dream of paying funeral honors to those who died so wrongfully and, without a coffin or a prayer, were buried here.

Though with feminine susceptibility, my compan-ions caught all the melancholy associations of the scene, yet these could but imperfectly overcome the gayety of girlish spirits. Their emotions came and went with quick vicissitude, and sometimes combined to form a peculiar and delicious excite-ment, the mirth brightening the gloom into a sunny shower of feeling, and a rainbow in the mind. My own more sombre mood was tinged by theirs. With now a merry word and next a sad one, we trod among the tangled weeds, and almost hoped that our feet would sink into the hollow of a witch's grave. Such vestiges were to be found within the memory of man, but have vanished now, and with them, I believe, all traces of the precise spot of the executions. On the long and broad ridge of the eminence, there is no very decided elevation of any one point, nor other prominent marks, except the decayed stumps of two trees, standing near each other, and here and there the rocky substance of the hill, peeping just above the wood-wax.

There are few such prospects of town and village, woodland and cultivated field, steeples and country seats, as we beheld from this unhappy spot. No blight had fallen on old Essex; all was prosperity and riches, healthfully distributed. Before us lay our native town, extending from the foot of the hill to the harbor, level as a chess board, embraced by two arms of the sea, and filling the whole peninsula with a close assemblage of wooden roofs, overtopt by many a spire, and intermixed with frequent heaps of verdure, where trees threw up their shade from unseen trunks. Beyond, was the bay and its islands, almost the only objects, in a country unmarked by strong natural features, on which time and human toil had produced no change. Retaining these portions of the scene, and also the peaceful glory and tender gloom of the declining sun, we threw, in imagination, a veil of deep forest over the land, and pictured a few scattered villages, and this old town itself a village, as when the prince of hell bore sway there. The idea thus gained, of its former aspect, its quaint edifices standing far apart, with peaked roofs and projecting stories, and its single meeting house pointing up a tall spire in the midst; the vision, in short, of the town in 1692, served to introduce a wondrous tale of those old times.

I had brought the manuscript in my pocket. It was one of a series written years ago, when my pen, now sluggish and perhaps feeble, because I have not much to hope or fear, was driven by stronger external motives, and a more passionate impulse within, than I am fated to feel again. Three or four of these tales had appeared in the Token, after a long time and various adventures, but had incumbered me with no troublesome notoriety, even in my birth place. One great heap had met a brighter destiny: They had fed the flames; thoughts meant to delight the world and endure for ages, had perished in a moment, and stirred not a single heart but mine. The story now to be introduced, and another, chanced to be in kinder custody at the time, and thus by no conspicuous merits of their own, escaped destruction.

The ladies, in consideration that I had never before intruded my performances on them, by any but the legitimate medium, through the press, con-

sented to hear me read. I made them sit down on a moss-grown rock, close by the spot where we chose to believe that the death-tree had stood. After a little hesitation on my part, caused by a dread of renewing my acquaintance with fantasies that had lost their charm, in the ceaseless flux of mind, I began the tale, which opened darkly with the discovery of a murder.

A hundred years, and nearly half that time, have elapsed since the body of a murdered man was found, at about the distance of three miles, on the old road to Boston. He lay in a solitary spot, on the bank of a small lake, which the severe frost of December had covered with a sheet of ice. Beneath this, it seemed to have been the intention of the murderer to conceal his victim in a chill and watery grave, the ice being deeply hacked, perhaps with the weapon that had slain him, though its solidity was too stubborn for the patience of a man with blood upon his hand. The corpse therefore reclined on the earth, but was separated from the road by a thick growth of dwarf pines. There had been a slight fall of snow during the night, and as if Nature were shocked at the deed, and strove to hide it with her frozen tears, a little drifted heap had partly buried the body, and lay deepest over the pale dead face. An early traveller, whose dog had led him to the spot, ventured to uncover the features, but was affrighted by their expression. A look of evil and scornful triumph had hardened on them, and made death so life-like and so terrible, that the beholder at once took flight, as swiftly as if the stiffened corpse would rise up and follow.

I read on, and identified the body as that of a young man, a stranger in the country, but resident during several preceding months in the town which lay at our feet. The story described, at some length, the excitement caused by the murder, the unavailing quest after the perpetrator, the funeral ceremonies, and other common place matters, in the course of which, I brought forward the personages who were to move among the succeeding events. They were but three. A young man and his sister; the former characterized by a diseased imagination and morbid feelings; the latter, beautiful and virtuous, and instilling something of her own excellence into the wild heart of her brother, but not enough to cure the deep taint of his nature. The third person was a wizard; a small, gray, withered man, with fiendish ingenuity in devising evil, and superhuman power to execute it, but senseless as an idiot and feebler than a child, to all better purposes. The central scene of the story was an interview between this wretch and Leonard Doane, in the wizard's hut, situated beneath a range of rocks at some distance from the town. They sat beside a mouldering fire, while a tempest of wintry rain was beating on the roof. The young man spoke of the closeness of the tie which united him and Alice, the concentrated fervor of their affection from childhood upwards, their sense of lonely sufficiency to each other, because they only of their race had escaped death, in a night attack by the Indians. He related his discovery, or suspicion of a secret sympathy between his sister and Walter Brome, and told how a distempered jealousy had maddened him. In the following passage, I threw a glimmering light on the mystery of the tale.

'Searching,' continued Leonard, 'into the breast of Walter Brome, I at length found a cause why Alice must inevitably love him. For he was my very counterpart! I compared his mind by each individual portion, and as a whole, with mine. There was a resemblance from which I shrank with sickness, and loathing, and horror, as if my own features had come and stared upon me in a solitary place, or had met me in struggling through a crowd. Nay! The very same thoughts would often express themselves in the same words from our lips, proving a hateful sympathy in our secret souls. His education, indeed, in the cities of the old world, and mine in this rude wilderness, had wrought a superficial difference. The evil of his character, also, had been strengthened and rendered prominent by a reckless and ungoverned life, while mine had been softened and purified by the gentle and holy nature of Alice. But my soul had been conscious of the germ of all the fierce and deep passions, and of all the many varieties of wickedness, which accident had brought to their full maturity in him. Nor will I deny, that in the accursed one, I could see the withered blossom of every virtue, which by a happier culture, had been made to bring forth fruit in me. Now, here was a man, whom Alice might love with all the strength

of sisterly affection, added to that impure passion which alone engrosses all the heart. The stranger would have more than the love which had been gathered to me from the many graves of our household—and I be desolate!'

Leonard Doane went on to describe the insane hatred that had kindled his heart into a volume of hellish flame. It appeared, indeed, that his jealousy had grounds, so far as that Walter Brome had actually sought the love of Alice, who also had betrayed an undefinable, but powerful interest in the unknown youth. The latter, in spite of his passion for Alice, seemed to return the loathful antipathy of her brother; the similarity of their dispositions made them like joint possessors of an individual nature, which could not become wholly the property of one, unless by the extinction of the other. At last, with the same devil in each bosom, they chanced to meet, they two on a lonely road. While Leonard spoke, the wizard had sat listening to what he already knew, yet with tokens of pleasurable interest, manifested by flashes of expression across his vacant features, by grisly smiles and by a word here and there, mysteriously filling up some void in the narrative. But when the young man told, how Walter Brome had taunted him with indubitable proofs of the shame of Alice, and before the triumphant sneer could vanish from his face, had died by her brother's hand, the wizard laughed aloud. Leonard started, but just then a gust of wind came down the chimney, forming itself into a close resemblance of the slow, unvaried laughter, by which he had been interrupted. 'I was deceived,' thought he; and thus pursued his fearful story.

'I trod out his accursed soul, and knew that he was dead; for my spirit bounded as if a chain had fallen from it and left me free. But the burst of exulting certainty soon fled, and was succeeded by a torpor over my brain and a dimness before my eyes, with the sensation of one who struggles through a dream. So I bent down over the body of Walter Brome, gazing into his face, and striving to make my soul glad with the thought, that he, in very truth, lay dead before me. I know not what space of time I had thus stood, nor how the vision came. But it seemed to me that the irrevocable years, since childhood had rolled back, and a scene, that had long been confused and broken in my memory, arrayed itself with all its first distinctness. Methought I stood a weeping infant by my father's hearth; by the cold and blood-stained hearth where he lay dead. I heard the childish wail of Alice, and my own cry arose with hers, as we beheld the features of our parent fierce with the strife and distorted with the pain, in which his spirit had passed away. As I gazed, a cold wind whistled by, and waved my father's hair. Immediately, I stood again in the lonesome road, no more a sinless child, but a man of blood, whose tears were falling fast over the face of his dead enemy. But the delusion was not wholly gone; that face still wore a likeness of my father; and because my soul shrank from the fixed glare of the eyes, I bore the body to the lake, and would have buried it there. But before his icy sepulchre was hewn, I heard the voices of two travellers and fled.'

Such was the dreadful confession of Leonard Doane. And now tortured by the idea of his sister's guilt, yet sometimes yielding to a conviction of her purity; stung with remorse for the death of Walter Brome, and shuddering with a deeper sense of some unutterable crime, perpetrated, as he imagined, in madness or a dream; moved also by dark impulses, as if a fiend were whispering him to meditate violence against the life of Alice; he had sought this interview with the wizard, who, on certain conditions, had no power to withhold his aid in unravelling the mystery. The tale drew near its close.

The moon was bright on high; the blue firmament appeared to glow with an inherent brightness; the greater stars were burning in their spheres; the northern lights threw their mysterious glare far over the horizon; the few small clouds aloft were burthened with radiance; but the sky with all its variety of light, was scarcely so brilliant as the earth. The rain of the preceding night had frozen as it fell, and, by that simple magic, had wrought wonders. The trees were hung with diamonds and many-colored gems; the houses were overlaid with silver, and the streets paved with slippery brightness; a frigid glory was flung over all familiar things, from the cottage chimney to the steeple of the meeting house, that gleamed upward to the sky. This living world, where we sit by our firesides, or go forth to meet beings like ourselves, seemed rather the creation of wizard power, with so much of resemblance to known objects, that a man might shudder at the ghostly shape of his old beloved dwelling, and the shadow of a ghostly tree before his door. One looked to behold inhabitants suited to such a town, glittering in icy garments, with motionless features, cold, sparkling eyes, and just sensation enough in their frozen hearts to shiver at each other's presence.

By this fantastic piece of description, and more in the same style, I intended to throw a ghostly glimmer round the reader, so that his imagination might view the town through a medium that should take off its every day aspect, and make it a proper theater for so wild a scene as the final one. Amid this unearthly show, the wretched brother and sister were represented as setting forth, at midnight, through the gleaming streets, and directing their steps to a grave yard, where all the dead had been laid, from the first corpse in that ancient town, to the murdered man who was buried three days before. As they went, they seemed to see the wizard gliding by their sides, or walking dimly on the path before them. But here I paused, and gazed into the faces of my two fair auditors, to judge whether, even on the hill where so many had been brought to death by wilder tales than this, I might venture to proceed. Their bright eyes were fixed on me; their lips apart. I took courage, and led the fated pair to a new made grave, where for a few moments, in the bright and silent midnight, they stood alone. But suddenly, there was a multitude of people among the graves.

Each family tomb had given up its inhabitants, who, one by one, through distant years, had been borne to its dark chamber, but now came forth and stood in a pale group together. There was the gray ancestor, the aged mother, and all their descendants, some withered and full of years, like themselves, and others in their prime; there, too, were the children who went prattling to the tomb, and there the maiden who yielded her early beauty to death's embrace, before passion had polluted it. Husbands and wives arose, who had lain many years side by side, and young mothers who had forgotten to kiss their first babes, though pillowed so long on their bosoms. Many had been buried in the habiliments of life, and still wore their ancient garb; some were old defenders of the infant colony, and gleamed forth in their steel caps and bright breast-plates, as if starting up at an Indian war-cry; other venerable shapes had been pastors of the church, famous among the New England clergy, and now leaned with hands clasped over their grave stones, ready to call the congregation to prayer. There stood the early settlers, those old illustrious ones, the heroes of tradition and fireside legends, the men of history whose features had been so long beneath the sod, that few alive could have remembered them. There, too, were faces of former townspeople, dimly recollected from childhood, and others, whom Leonard and Alice had wept in later years, but who now were most terrible of all, by their ghastly smile of recognition. All, in short, were there; the dead of other generations, whose moss-grown names could scarce be read upon their tomb stones, and their successors, whose graves were not yet green; all whom black funerals had followed slowly thither, now re-appeared where the mourners left them. Yet none but souls accursed were there, and fiends counterfeiting the likeness of departed saints.

The countenances of those venerable men, whose very features had been hallowed by lives of piety, were contorted now by intolerable pain or hellish passion, and now by an unearthly and derisive merriment. Had the pastors prayed, all saintlike as they seemed, it had been blasphemy. The chaste matrons, too, and the maidens with untasted lips, who had slept in their virgin graves apart from all other dust, now wore a look from which the two trembling mortals shrank, as if the unimaginable sin of twenty worlds were collected there. The faces of fond lovers, even of such as had pined into the tomb, because there their treasure was, were bent on one another with glances of hatred and smiles of bitter scorn, passions that are to devils, what love is to the blest. At times, the features of those, who had passed from a holy life to heaven would vary to and fro, between their assumed aspect and the fiendish lineaments whence they had been transformed. The whole miserable multitude, both sinful souls and false spectres of good men, groaned horribly and

gnashed their teeth, as they looked upward to the calm loveliness of the midnight sky, and beheld those homes of bliss where they must never dwell. Such was the apparition, though too shadowy for language to portray; for here would be the moon-beams on the ice, glittering through a warrior's breast-plate, and there the letters of a tomb stone, on the form that stood before it; and whenever a breeze went by, it swept the old men's hoary heads, the women's fearful beauty, and all the unreal throng, into one indistinguishable cloud together.

I dare not give the remainder of the scene, except in a very brief epitome. This company of devils and condemned souls had come on a holiday, to revel in the discovery of a complicated crime; as foul a one as ever was imagined in their dreadful abode. In the course of the tale, the reader had been permitted to discover, that all the incidents were results of the machinations of the wizard, who had cunningly devised that Walter Brome should tempt his unknown sister to guilt and shame, and himself perish by the hand of his twin-brother. I described the glee of the fiends, at this hideous conception, and their eagerness to know if it were consummated. The story concluded with the Appeal of Alice to the spectre of Walter Brome; his reply, absolving her from every stain; and the trembling awe with which ghost and devil fled, as from the sinless presence of an angel.

The sun had gone down. While I held my page of wonders in the fading light, and read how Alice and her brother were left alone among the graves, my voice mingled with the sigh of a summer wind, which passed over the hill top with the broad and hollow sound, as of the flight of unseen spirits. Not a word was spoken, till I added, that the wizard's grave was close beside us, and that the wood-wax had sprouted originally from his unhallowed bones. The ladies started; perhaps their cheeks might have grown pale, had not the crimson west been blushing on them; but after a moment they began to laugh, while the breeze took a livelier motion, as if responsive to their mirth. I kept an awful solemnity of visage, being indeed a little piqued, that a narrative which had good authority in our ancient superstitions, and would have brought even a church deacon to Gallows Hill, in old witch times, should now be considered too grotesque and extravagant, for timid maids to tremble at. Though it was past supper time, I detained them a while longer on the hill, and made a trial whether truth were more powerful than fiction.

We looked again towards the town, no longer arrayed in that icy splendor of earth, tree and edifice, beneath the glow of a wintry midnight, which, shining afar through the gloom of a century, had made it appear the very home of visions in visionary streets. An indistinctness had begun to creep over the mass of buildings and blend them with the intermingled tree tops, except where the roof of a statelier mansion, and the steeples and brick towers of churches, caught the brightness of some cloud that yet floated in the sunshine. Twilight over the landscape was congenial to the obscurity of time. With such eloquence as my share of feeling and fancy could supply, I called back hoar antiquity, and bade my companions imagine an ancient multitude of people, congregated on the hill side, spreading far below, clustering on the steep old roofs, and climbing the adjacent heights, wherever a glimpse of this spot might be obtained. I strove to realize and faintly communicate, the deep, unutterable loathing and horror, the indignation, the affrighted wonder, that wrinkled on every brow, and filled the universal heart. See! The whole crowd turns pale and shrinks within itself, as the virtuous emerge from yonder street. Keeping pace with that devoted company, I described them one by one; here tottered a woman in her dotage, knowing neither the crime imputed her, nor its punishment; there another, distracted by the universal madness, till feverish dreams were remembered as realities, and she almost believed her guilt. One, a proud man once, was so broken down by the intolerable hatred heaped upon him, that he seemed to hasten his steps, eager to hide himself in the grave hastily dug, at the foot of the gallows. As they went slowly on, a mother looked behind, and beheld her peaceful dwelling; she cast her eyes elsewhere, and groaned inwardly, yet with bitterest anguish; for there was her little son among the accusers. I watched the face of an ordained pastor, who walked onward to the same death; his lips moved in prayer, no narrow petition for himself alone, but embracing all, his fellow sufferers and the frenzied multitude; he looked to heaven and trod lightly up the hill.

Behind their victims came the afflicted, a guilty and miserable band; villains who had thus avenged themselves on their enemies, and viler wretches, whose cowardice had destroyed their friends; lunatics, whose ravings had chimed in with the madness of the land; and children, who had played a game that the imps of darkness might have envied them, since it disgraced an age, and dipped a people's hands in blood. In the rear of the procession rode a figure on horseback, so darkly conspicuous, so sternly triumphant, that my hearers mistook him for the visible presence of the fiend himself; but it was only his good friend, Cotton Mather, proud of his well won dignity, as the representative of all the hateful features of his time; the one blood-thirsty man, in whom were concentrated those vices of spirit and errors of opinion, that sufficed to madden the whole surrounding multitude. And thus I marshalled them onward, the innocent who were to die, and the guilty who were to grow old in long remorse— tracing their every step, by rock, and shrub, and broken track, till their shadowy visages had circled round the hill-top, where we stood. I plunged into my imagination for a blacker horror, and a deeper woe, and pictured the scaffold—

But here my companions seized an arm on each side; their nerves were trembling; and sweeter victory still, I had reached the seldom trodden places of their hearts, and found the wellspring of their tears. And now the past had done all it could. We slowly descended, watching the lights as they twinkled gradually through the town, and listening to the distant mirth of boys at play, and to the voice of a young girl, warbling somewhere in the dusk, a pleasant sound to wanderers from old witch times. Yet ere we left the hill, we could not but regret, that there is nothing on its barren summit, no relic of old, nor lettered stone of later days, to assist the imagination in appealing to the heart. We build the memorial column on the height which our fathers made sacred with their blood poured out in a holy cause. And here in dark, funereal stone, should rise another monument, sadly commemorative of the errors of an earlier race, and not to be cast down, while the human heart has one infirmity that may result in crime.

The Declaration of Independence

In CONGRESS, July 4, 1776.

The unanimous Declaration of the thirteen united States of America, When in the Course of human events, it becomes necessary for one people to dissolve the political bands which have connected them with another, and to assume among the powers of the earth, the separate and equal station to which the Laws of Nature and of Nature's God entitle them, a decent respect to the opinions of mankind requires that they should declare the causes which impel them to the separation.—We hold these truths to be self-evident, that all men are created equal, that they are endowed by their Creator with certain unalienable Rights, that among these are Life, Liberty and the pursuit of Happiness.—That to secure these rights, Governments are instituted among Men, deriving their just powers from the consent of the governed,—That whenever any Form of government becomes destructive of these ends, it is the Right of the People to alter or to abolish it; and to institute new government, laying its foundation on such principles and organizing its powers in such form, as to them shall seem most likely to effect their Safety and Happiness. Prudence, indeed, will dictate that Governments long established should not be changed for light and transient causes; and accordingly all experience hath shown, that mankind are more disposed to suffer, while evils are sufferable, than to right themselves by abolishing the forms to which they are accustomed. But when a long train of abuses and usurpations, pursuing invariably the same Object evinces a design to reduce them under absolute Despotism, it is their right, it is their duty, to throw off such Government, and to provide new Guards for their future security.—Such has been the patient sufferance of these Colonies; and such is now the necessity which constrains them to alter their former Systems of Government. The history of the present King of Great Britain is a history of repeated injuries and usurpations, all having in direct object the establishment of an absolute Tyranny over these States. To prove this, let Facts be submitted to a candid world.—He has refused his Assent to Laws, the most wholesome and necessary for the public good.—He has forbidden his Governors to pass Laws of immediate and pressing importance, unless suspended in their operation till his Assent should be obtained; and when so suspended, he has utterly neglected to attend to them.—He has refused to pass other Laws for the accommodation of large districts of people, unless those people would relinquish the right of Representation in the Legislature, a right inestimable to them and formidable to tyrants only.—He has called together legislative bodies at places unusual, uncomfortable, and distant from the depository of their public Records, for the sole purpose of fatiguing them into compliance with his measures.—He has dissolved Representative Houses repeatedly, for opposing with manly firmness his invasions on the rights of the people.—He has refused for a long time, after such dissolutions, to cause others to be elected; whereby the Legislative powers, incapable of Annihilation, have returned to the People at large for their exercise; the State remaining in the mean time exposed to all the dangers of invasion from without, and convulsions within.—He has endeavoured to prevent the population of these States; for that purpose obstructing the Laws for Naturalization of Foreigners; refusing to pass others to encourage their migrations hither, and raising the conditions of new Appropriations of Lands.—He has obstructed the Administration of Justice, by refusing his Assent to Laws for establishing Judiciary powers —He has made Judges dependent on his Will alone, for the tenure of their offices, and the amount and payment of their salaries.—He has erected a multitude of New Offices, and sent hither swarms of Officers to harrass our people, and eat out their substance.— He has kept among us, in times of peace, Standing Armies without the Consent of our legislatures.— He has affected to render the Military independent of and superior to the Civil power.—He has combined with others to subject us to a jurisdiction foreign to our constitution, and unacknowledged by our laws; giving his Assent to their Acts of pretended Legislation:—For Quartering large bodies of armed troops among us:—For protecting them, by a mock Trial, from punishment for any Murders which they should commit on the Inhabitants of these States:—For calling off our Trade with all parts of the world:—For imposing Taxes on us without our Consent:—For depriving us in many cases, of the benefits of Trial by Jury:—For transporting us beyond Seas to be tried for pretended offences—For abolishing the free System of English Laws in a neighbouring Province, establishing therein an Arbitrary government, and enlarging its Boundaries so as to render it at once an example and fit instrument for introducing the same absolute rule into these Colonies:—For taking away our Charters, abolishing our most valuable Laws and altering fundamentally the Forms of our Governments:—For suspending our own Legislatures and declaring themselves invested with power to legislate for us in all cases whatsoever.—He has abdicated Government here, by declaring us out of his Protection and waging War against us.—He has plundered our seas, ravaged our Coasts burnt our towns, and destroyed the Lives of our people.—He is at this time transporting large Armies of foreign Mercenaries to compleat the works of death, desolation and tyranny, already begun with circumstances of Cruelty & perfidy scarcely paralleled in the most barbarous ages, and totally unworthy the Head of a civilized nation.—He has constrained our fellow Citizens taken Captive on the high Seas to bear Arms against their Country, to become the executioners of their friends and Brethren, or to fall themselves by their Hands.—He has excited domestic insurrections amongst us and has endeavoured to bring on the inhabitants of our frontiers, the merciless Indian Savages, whose known rule of warfare, is an undistinguished destruction of all ages, sexes and conditions. In every stage of these Oppressions we have Petitioned for Redress in the most humble terms: Our repeated Petitions have been answered only by repeated injury. A Prince, whose character is thus marked by every act which may define a Tyrant, is unfit to be the ruler of a free people. Nor have we been wanting in attentions to our British brethren. We have warned them from time to time of attempts by their legislature to extend an

unwarrantable jurisdiction over us. We have reminded them of the circumstances of our emigration and settlement here. We have appealed to their native justice and magnanimity, and we have conjured them by the ties of our common kindred to disavow these usurpations, which, would inevitably interrupt our connections and correspondence. They too have been deaf to the voice of justice and of consanguinity. We must, therefore, acquiesce in the necessity, which denounces our Separation, and hold them, as we hold the rest of mankind, Enemies in War, in Peace Friends.— We, therefore, the Representatives of the united States of America, in General Congress, Assembled, appealing to the Supreme Judge of the world for the rectitude of our intentions, do, in the Name, and by Authority of the good People of these Colonies, solemnly publish and declare, That these United Colonies are, and of Right ought to be Free and Independent States; that they are Absolved from all Allegiance to the British Crown, and that all political connection between them and the State of Great Britain, is and ought to be totally dissolved; and that as Free and Independent States, they have full Power to levy War, conclude Peace, contract Alliances, establish Commerce, and to do all other Acts and Things which Independent States may of right do.—And for the support of this Declaration, with a firm reliance on the protection of divine Providence, we mutually pledge to each other our Lives, our Fortunes and our sacred Honor.

John Hancock

Josiah Bartlett	Caesar Rodney
Wᵐ Whipple	Geo Read
Samˡ Adams	Tho M:Kean
John Adams	Samuel Chase
Robᵗ Treat Paine	Wᵐ. Paca
Elbridge Gerry	Thoˢ. Stone
Step. Hopkins	Charles Carroll of
William Ellery	Carrollton
Roger Sherman	George Wythe
Samˡ Huntington	Richard Henry Lee
Wᵐ Williams	Th Jefferson
Oliver Wolcott	Benj Harrison
Matthew Thornton	Thˢ Nelson Jr
Wᵐ Floyd	Francis Lightfoot Lee
	Carter Braxton

Phil. Livingston
Fran⁵. Lewis
Lewis Morris
Richᵈ Stockton
Jnᵒ Witherspoon
Fra⁵. Hopkinson
John Hart
Abra Clark
Robt Morris
Benjamin Rush
Benj. Franklin
John Morton
Geo Clymer
Jas. Smith
Geo. Taylor
James Wilson
Geo. Ross

Wᵐ Hooper
Joseph Hewes
John Penn
Edward Rutledge
Thoˢ Heyward Junʳ
Thomas Lynch Junr
Arthur Middleton
Button Gwilnnett
Lyman Hall
Geo Walton

LETTER FROM THE CONSTITUTIONAL CONVENTION TO THE PRESIDENT OF CONGRESS

In Convention, September 17, 1787.

SIR, WE have now the honor to submit to the consideration of the United States in Congress assembled, that Constitution which has appeared to us the most advisable.

The friends of our country have long seen and desired, that the power of making war, peace and treaties, that of levying money and judicial authorities should be fully and effectually vested in the general government of the Union: But the impropriety of delegating such extensive trust to one body of men is evident—Hence results the necessity of a different organization.

It is obviously impracticable in the federal government of these States; to secure all rights of independent sovereignty to each, and yet provide for the interest and safety of all—Individuals entering into society, must give up a share of liberty to preserve the rest. The magnitude of the sacrifice must depend as well on situation and circumstance, as on the object to be obtained. It is at all times difficult to draw with precision the line between those rights which must be surrendered, and those which may be reserved; and on the

present occasion this difficulty was encreased by a difference among the several States as to their situation, extent, habits, and particular interests.

In all our deliberations on this subject we kept steadily in our view, that which appears to us the greatest interest of every true American, the consolidation of our Union, in which is involved our prosperity, felicity, safety, perhaps our national existence, This important consideration, seriously and deeply impressed on our minds, led each State in the Convention to be less rigid on points of inferior magnitude, than might have been otherwise expected; and thus the Constitution, which we now present, is the result of a spirit of amity, and of that mutual deference and concession which the peculiarity of our political situation rendered indispensable.

That it will meet the full and entire approbation of every State is not perhaps to be expected; but each will doubtless consider, that had her interests been alone consulted, the consequences might have been particularly disagreeable or injurious to others; that it is liable to as few exceptions as could reasonably have been expected, we hope and believe; that it may promote the lasting welfare of that country so dear to us all, and secure her freedom and happiness, is our most ardent wish.

With great respect, WE have the honor to be SIR, Your Excellency's most Obedient and humble servants.

George Washington, President.
By unanimous Order of the
Convention

RESOLUTIONS OF THE CONVENTION CONCERNING THE RATIFICATION AND IMPLEMENTATION OF THE CONSTITUTION

In Convention Monday September 17th. 1787.

Present The States of New Hampshire, Massachusetts, Connecticut, Mr. Hamilton from New York, New Jersey, Pennsylvania, Delaware, Maryland, Virginia, North Carolina, South Carolina and Georgia.

RESOLVED, That the preceeding Constitution be laid before the United States in Congress assembled, and that it is the Opinion of this Convention, that it should afterwards be submitted to a Convention of Delegates, chosen in each State by the People thereof, under the Recommendation of its Legislature, for their Assent and Ratification; and that each Convention assenting to, and ratifying the Same, should give Notice thereof to the United States in Congress assembled.

Resolved, That it is the Opinion of this Convention, that as soon as the Conventions of nine States shall have ratified this Constitution, the United States in Congress assembled should fix a Day on which Electors should be appointed by the States which shall have ratified the same, and a Day on which the Electors should assemble to vote for the President, and the Time and Place for commencing Proceedings under this Constitution. That after such Publication the Electors should be appointed, and the Senators and Representatives elected: That the Electors should meet on the Day fixed for the Election of the President, and should transmit their Votes certified, signed, sealed and directed, as the Constitution requires, to the Secretary of the United States in Congress assembled, that the Senators and Representatives should convene at the Time and Place assigned; that the Senators should appoint a President of the Senate, for the sole Purpose of receiving, opening and counting the Votes for President; and, that after he shall be chosen, the Congress, together with the President, should, without Delay, proceed to execute this Constitution.

By the Unanimous Order of the Convention
W. Jackson Secretary.   Geo: Washington Presidt.

THE CONSTITUTION

[The footnotes in this appendix, keyed to the line number on the page, indicate portions of the Constitution that have been altered by subsequent amendment.]

We the People of the United States, in Order to form a more perfect Union, establish Justice, insure domestic Tranquility, provide for the common defence, promote the general Welfare, and secure the Blessings of Liberty to ourselves and our Posterity, do ordain and establish this Constitution for the United States of America.

Article I.

Section. 1. All legislative Powers herein granted shall be vested in a Congress of the United States, which shall consist of a Senate and House of Representatives.

Section. 2. The House of Representatives shall be composed of Members chosen every second Year by the People of the several States, and the Electors in each State shall have the Qualifications requisite for Electors of the most numerous Branch of the State Legislature.

No Person shall be a Representative who shall not have attained to the Age of twenty five Years, and been seven Years a Citizen of the United States, and who shall not, when elected, be an Inhabitant of that State in which he shall be chosen.

Representatives and direct Taxes shall be apportioned among the several States which may be included within this Union, according to their respective Numbers, which shall be determined by adding to the whole Number of free Persons, including those bound to Service for a Term of Years, and excluding Indians not taxed, three fifths of all other Persons. The actual Enumeration shall be made within three Years after the first Meeting of the Congress of the United States, and within every subsequent Term of ten Years, in such Manner as they shall by Law direct. The Number of Representatives shall not exceed one for every thirty Thousand, but each State shall have at Least one Representative; and until such enumeration shall be made, the State of New Hampshire shall be entitled to chuse three, Massachusetts eight, Rhode-Island and Providence Plantations one, Connecticut five, New-York six, New Jersey four, Pennsylvania eight, Delaware one, Maryland six, Virginia ten, North Carolina five, South Carolina five, and Georgia three.

When vacancies happen in the Representation from any State, the Executive Authority thereof shall issue Writs of Election to fill such Vacancies.

The House of Representatives shall chuse their Speaker and other Officers; and shall have the sole Power of Impeachment.

Section. 3. The Senate of the United States shall be composed of two Senators from each State, chosen by the Legislature thereof, for six Years; and each Senator shall have one Vote.

Immediately after they shall be assembled in Consequence of the first Election, they shall be divided as equally as may be into three Classes. The Seats of the Senators of the first Class shall be vacated at the Expiration of the second Year, of the second Class at the Expiration of the fourth Year, and of the third Class at the Expiration of the sixth Year, so that one third may be chosen every second Year; and if Vacancies happen by Resignation, or otherwise, during the Recess of the Legislature of any State, the Executive thereof may make temporary Appointments until the next Meeting of the Legislature, which shall then fill such Vacancies.

No Person shall be a Senator who shall not have attained to the Age of thirty Years, and been nine Years a Citizen of the United States, and who shall not, when elected, be an Inhabitant of that State for which he shall be chosen.

The Vice President of the United States shall be President of the Senate, but shall have no Vote, unless they be equally divided.

The Senate shall chuse their Officers, and also a President pro tempore, in the Absence of the Vice President, or when he shall exercise the Office of President of the United States.

The Senate shall have the sole Power to try all Impeachments. When sitting for that Purpose, they

shall be on Oath or Affirmation. When the President of the United States is tried, the Chief Justice shall preside: And no Person shall be convicted without the Concurrence of two thirds of the Members present.

Judgement in Cases of Impeachment shall not extend further than to removal from Office, and disqualification to hold and enjoy an Office of honor, Trust or Profit under the United States. But the Party convicted shall nevertheless be liable and subject to Indictment, Trial, Judgement and Punishment, according to Law.

Section 4. The Times, Places and Manner of holding Elections for Senators and Representatives, shall be prescribed in each State by the Legislature thereof; but the Congress may at any time by Law make or alter such Regulations, except as to the Places of chusing Senators.

The Congress shall assemble at least once in every Year, and such Meeting shall be on the first Monday in December, unless they shall by Law appoint a different Day.

Section 5. Each House shall be the Judge of the Fictions, Returns and Qualifications of its own Members, and a Majority of each shall constitute a Quorum to do Business; but a smaller Number may adjourn from day to day, and may be authorized to compel the Attendance of absent Members, in such Manner, and under such Penalties as each House may provide.

Each House may determine the Rules of its Proceedings, punish its members for disorderly Behaviour, and, with the Concurrence of two thirds, expel a Member. Each House shall keep a Journal of its Proceedings, and from time to time publish the same, excepting such Parts as may in their Judgement require Secrecy; and the Yeas and Nays of the Members of either House on any question shall, at the Desire of one fifth of those Present, be entered on the Journal.

Neither House, during the Session of Congress, shall, without the Consent of the other, adjourn for more than three days, nor to any other Place than that in which the two Houses shall be sitting.

Session 6. The Senators and Representatives shall receive a Compensation for their Services, to be ascertained by Law, and paid out of the Treasury of the United States. They shall in all Cases, except Treason, Felony and Breach of the Peace, be privileged from Arrest during their Attendance at the Session of their respective Houses, and in going to and returning from the same; and for any Speech or Debate in either House, they shall not be questioned in any other Place.

No Senator or Representative shall, during the Time for which he was elected, be appointed to any civil Office under the Authority of the United States which shall, during the Time for which he was elected, be appointed to any civil Office under the Authority of the United States which shall have been created, or the Emoluments whereof shall have been encreased during such time; and no Person holding any Office under the Untied States, shall be a Member of either House during his Continuance in Office.

Section 7. All Bills for raising Revenue shall originate in the House of Representatives; but the Senate may propose or concur with Amendments as on other Bills.

Every Bill which shall have passed the House of Representatives and the Senate shall, before it becomes a Law, be presented to the President of the United States; If he approve he shall sign it, but if not he shall return it, with his Objections to that House in which it shall have originated, who shall enter the Objections at large on their Journal, and proceed to reconsider it. If after such Reconsideration two thirds of that House shall agree to pass the Bill, it shall be sent, together with the Objections, to the other House, by which it shall likewise be reconsidered, and if approved by two thirds of that House, it shall become a Law. But in all such Cases the Votes of both Houses shall be determined by yeas and Nays, and the Names of the Persons voting for and against the Bill shall be entered on the Journal of each House respectively. If any Bill shall not be returned by the President within ten Days (Sundays excepted) after it shall have been presented to him, the Same shall be a Law, in like Manner as if he had signed it, unless the Congress by their Adjournment prevent its Return, in which Case it shall not be a Law.

Every Order, Resolution, or Vote to which the Concurrence of the Senate and House of Representatives may be necessary (except on a question of Adjournment) shall be presented to the President of the United States; and before the Same shall take Effect, shall be approved by him, or being disapproved by him, shall be repassed by two thirds of the Senate and House of Representatives, according to the Rules and Limitations prescribed in the Case of a Bill.

Section. 8. The Congress shall have Power To lay and collect Taxes, Duties, Imposts and Excises, to pay the Debts and provide for the common Defence and general Welfare of the United States; but all Duties, Imposts and Excises shall be uniform throughout the United States;

To borrow Money on the credit of the United States;

To regulate Commerce with foreign Nations, and among the several States, and with the Indian Tribes;

To establish an uniform Rule of Naturalization, and uniform Laws on the subject of Bankruptcies throughout the United States;

To coin Money, regulate the Value thereof, and of foreign Coin, and fix the Standard of Weights and Measures;

To provide for the Punishment of counterfeiting the Securities and current Coin of the United States;

To establish Post Offices and post Roads;

To promote the Progress of Science and useful Arts, by securing for limited Times to Authors and Inventors the exclusive Right to their respective Writings and Discoveries;

To constitute Tribunals inferior to the supreme Court;

To define and punish Piracies and Felonies committed on the high Seas, and Offences against the Law of Nations;

To declare War, grant Letters of Marque and Reprisal, and make Rules concerning Captures on Land and Water;

46

To raise and support Armies, but no Appropriation of Money to that Use shall be for a longer Term than two Years;

To provide and maintain a Navy;

To make Rules for the Government and Regulation of the land and naval Forces;

To provide for calling forth the Militia to execute the Laws of the Union, suppress Insurrections and repel Invasions;

To provide for organizing, arming, and disciplining, the Militia, and for governing such Part of them as may be employed in the Service of the United States, reserving to the States respectively, the Appointment of the Officers, and the Authority of training the Militia according to the discipline prescribed by Congress;

To exercise exclusive Legislation in all Cases whatsoever, over such District (not exceeding ten Miles square) as may, by Cession of particular States, and the Acceptance of Congress, become the Seat of the Government of the United States, and to exercise like Authority over all Places purchased by the Consent of the Legislature of the State in which the same shall be, for the Erection of Forts, Magazines, Arsenals, dock-Yards, and other needful Buildings; —And

To make all Laws which shall be necessary and proper for carrying into Execution the foregoing Powers, and all other Powers vested by this Constitution in the Government of the United States, or in any Department or Officer thereof.

Section. 9. The Migration or Importation of such Persons as any of the States now existing shall think proper to admit, shall not be prohibited by the Congress prior to the Year one thousand eight hundred and eight, but a Tax or duty may be imposed on such Importation, not exceeding ten dollars for each Person.

The Privilege of the Writ of Habeas Corpus shall not be suspended, unless when in Cases of Rebellion or Invasion the public Safety may require it.

No Bill of Attainder or ex post facto Law shall be passed.

No Capitation, or other direct, Tax shall be laid, unless in

Proportion to the Census or Enumeration herein before directed to be taken.

No Tax or Duty shall be laid on Articles exported from any State.

No Preference shall be given by any Regulation of Commerce or Revenue to the Ports of one State over those of another: nor shall Vessels bound to, or from, one State, be obliged to enter, clear, or pay Duties in another.

No Money shall be drawn from the Treasury, but in Consequence of Appropriations made by Law; and a regular Statement and Account of the Receipts and Expenditures of all public Money shall be published from time to time.

No Title of Nobility shall be granted by the United States: And no Person holding any Office of Profit or Trust under them, shall, without the Consent of the Congress, accept of any present, Emolument, Office, or Title, of any kind whatever, from any King, Prince, or foreign State.

Section. 10. No State shall enter into any Treaty, Alliance, or Confederation; grant Letters of Marque and Reprisal; coin Money; emit Bills of Credit; make any Thing but gold and silver Coin a Tender in Payment of Debts; pass any Bill of Attainder, ex post facto Law, or Law impairing the Obligation of Contracts, or grant any Title of Nobility.

No State shall, without the Consent of the Congress, lay any Imposts or Duties on Imports or Exports, except what may be absolutely necessary for executing its inspection Laws: and the net Produce of all Duties and Imposts, laid by any State on Imports or Exports, shall be for the Use of the Treasury of the United States; and all such Laws shall be subject to the Revision and Controul of the Congress.

No State shall, without the Consent of Congress, lay any Duty of Tonnage, keep Troops, or Ships of War in time of Peace, enter into any Agreement or Compact with another State, or with a foreign Power, or engage in War, unless actually invaded, or in such imminent Danger as will not admit of delay.

Article II.

Section. 1. The executive Power shall be vested in a President of the United States of America. He shall hold his Office during the Term of four Years, and, together with the Vice President, chosen for the same Term, be elected, as follows

Each State shall appoint, in such Manner as the Legislature thereof may direct, a Number of Electors, equal to the whole Number of Senators and Representatives to which the State may be entitled in the Congress: but no Senator or Representative, or Person holding an Office of Trust or Profit under the United States, shall be appointed an Elector.

The Electors shall meet in their respective States and vote by Ballot for two Persons, of whom one at least shall not be an Inhabitant of the same State with themselves. And they shall make a List of all the Persons voted for, and of the Number of Votes for each; which List they shall sign and certify, and transmit sealed to the Seat of the Government of the United States, directed to the President of the Senate. The President of the Senate shall, in the Presence of the Senate and House of Representatives, open all the Certificates, and the Votes shall then be counted. The Person having the greatest Number of Votes shall be the President, if such Number be a Majority of the whole Number of Electors appointed; and if there be more than one who have such Majority, and have an equal Number of Votes, then the House of Representatives shall immediately chuse by Ballot one of them for President; and if no Person have a Majority, then from the five highest on the List the said House shall in like Manner chuse the President. But in chusing the President, the Votes shall be taken by States, the Representation from each State having one Vote; A quorum for this Purpose shall consist of a Member or Members from two thirds of the States, and a Majority of all the States shall be necessary to a Choice. In every Case, after the Choice of the President, the Person having the greatest Number of Votes of the Electors shall be the Vice President. But if there should remain two

or more who have equal Votes, the Senate shall chuse from them by Ballot the Vice President.

The Congress may determine the Time of chusing the Electors, and the Day on which they shall give their Votes; which Day shall be the same throughout the United States.

No Persons except a natural born Citizen, or a Citizen of the United States, at the time of the Adoption of this Constitution, shall be eligible to the Office of President; neither shall any Person be eligible to that Office who shall not have attained to the Age of thirty five Years, and been fourteen Years a Resident within the United States.

In Case of the Removal of the President from Office, or of his Death, Resignation, or Inability to discharge the Powers and Duties of the said Office, the Same shall devolve on the Vice President, and the Congress may by Law provide for the Case of Removal, Death, Resignation or Inability, both of the President and Vice President, declaring what Officer shall then act as President, and such Officer shall act accordingly, until the Disability be removed, or a President shall be elected.

The President shall, at stated Times, receive for his Services, a Compensation, which shall neither be increased nor diminished during the Period for which he shall have been elected, and he shall not receive within that Period any other Emolument from the United States, or any of them.

Before he enter on the Execution of his Office, he shall take the following Oath or Affirmation:—"I do solemnly swear (or affirm) that I will faithfully execute the Office of President of the United States, and will to the best of my Ability, preserve, protect and defend the Constitution of the United States."

Section. 2. The President shall be Commander in Chief of the Army and Navy of the United States, and of the Militia of the several States, when called into the actual Service of the United States; he may require the Opinion, in writing, of the principal Officer in each of the executive Departments, upon any Subject relating to the Duties of their respective Offices, and he shall have Power to grant

Reprieves and Pardons for Offences against the United States, except in Cases of Impeachment.

He shall have Power, by and with the Advice and Consent of the Senate, to make Treaties, provided two thirds of the Senators present concur; and he shall nominate, and by and with the Advice and Consent of the Senate, shall appoint Ambassadors, other public Ministers and Consuls, Judges of the supreme Court, and all other Officers of the United States, whose Appointments are not herein otherwise provided for, and which shall be established by Law: but the Congress may by Law vest the Appointment of such inferior Officers, as they think proper, in the President alone, in the Courts of Law, or in the Heads of Departments.

The President shall have Power to fill up all Vacancies that may happen during the Recess of the Senate, by granting Commissions which shall expire at the End of their next Session.

Section. 3. He shall from time to time give to the Congress Information of the State of the Union, and recommend to their Consideration such Measures as he shall judge necessary and expedient; he may, on extraordinary Occasions, convene both Houses, or either of them, and in Case of Disagreement between them, with Respect to the Time of Adjournment, he may adjourn them to such Time as he shall think proper; he shall receive Ambassadors and other public Ministers; he shall take Care that the Laws be faithfully executed, and shall Commission all the Officers of the United States.

Section. 4. The President, Vice President and all civil Officers of the United States, shall be removed from Office on Impeachment for, and Conviction of Treason, Bribery, or other high Crimes and Misdemeanors.

Article III.

Section. 1. The judicial Power of the United States, shall be vested in one supreme Court, and in such inferior Courts as the Congress may from time to time ordain and establish. The Judges, both of the supreme and inferior Courts, shall hold their Offices during good Behaviour, and shall, at stated Times, receive for their Services, a Compensation, which shall not be diminished during their Continuance in Office.

Section. 2. The judicial Power shall extend to all Cases, in Law and Equity, arising under this Constitution, the Laws of the United States, and Treaties made, or which shall be made, under their Authority;—to all Cases affecting Ambassadors, other public Ministers and Consuls;—to all Cases of admiralty and maritime Jurisdiction;—to Controversies to which the United States shall be a Party;—to Controversies between two or more States—between a State and Citizens of another State;—between Citizens of different States,—between Citizens of the same State claiming Lands under Grants of different States, and between a State, or the Citizens thereof, and of foreign States, Citizens or Subjects.

In all Cases affecting Ambassadors, other public Ministers and Consuls, and those in which a State shall be Party, the supreme Court shall have original Jurisdiction. In all the other Cases before mentioned, the supreme Court shall have appellate Jurisdiction, both as to Law and Fact, with such Exceptions, and under such Regulations as the Congress shall make.

The Trial of all Crimes, except in Cases of Impeachment, shall be by Jury; and such Trial shall be held in the State where the said Crimes shall have been committed; but when not committed within any State, the Trial shall be at such Place or Places as the Congress may by Law have directed.

Section. 3. Treason against the United States, shall consist only in levying War against them, or in adhering to their Enemies, giving them Aid and Comfort. No Person shall be convicted of Treason unless on the Testimony of two Witnesses to the same overt Act, or on Confession in open Court.

The Congress shall have Power to declare the Punishment of Treason, but no Attainder of Treason shall work Corruption of Blood, or Forfeiture except during the Life of the Person attainted.

Article IV.

Section. I. Full Faith and Credit shall be given in each State to the public Acts, Records, and judicial

Proceedings of every other State. And the Congress may by general Laws prescribe the Manner in which such Acts, Records and Proceedings shall be proved, and the Effect thereof.

Section. 2. The Citizens of each State shall be entitled to all privileges and Immunities of Citizens in the several States.

A Person charged in any State with Treason, Felony, or other Crime, who shall flee from Justice, and be found in another State, shall on Demand of the executive Authority of the State from which he fled, be delivered up, to be removed to the State having Jurisdiction of the Crime.

No Person held to Service or Labour in one State, under l the Laws thereof, escaping into another, shall, in Consequence of any Law or Regulation therein, be discharged from such Service or Labour, but shall be delivered up on Claim of the Party to whom such Service or Labour may be due.

Section. 3. New States may be admitted by the Congress into this Union; but no new State shall be formed or erected within the Jurisdiction of any other State; nor any State be formed by the Junction of two or more States, or Parts of States, without the Consent of the Legislatures of the States concerned as well as of the Congress.

The Congress shall have Power to dispose of and make all needful Rules and Regulations respecting the Territory or other Property belonging to the United States; and nothing in this Constitution shall be so construed as to Prejudice any Claims of the United States, or of any particular State.

Section 4. The United States shall guarantee to every State in this Union a Republican Form of Government, and shall protect each of them against Invasion; and on Application of the Legislature, or of the Executive (when the Legislature cannot be convened) against domestic Violence.

Article V.

The Congress, whenever two thirds of both Houses shall deem it necessary, shall propose Amendments to this Constitution, or, on the Application of the Legislatures of two thirds of the several States, shall call a Convention for proposing Amendments, which, in either Case, shall be valid to all Intents and Purposes, as Part of this Constitution, when ratified by the Legislatures of three fourths of the several States, or by Conventions in three fourths thereof, as the one or the other Mode of Ratification may be proposed by the Congress; Provided that no Amendment which may be made prior to the Year One thousand eight hundred and eight shall in any Manner affect the first and fourth Clauses in the Ninth Section of the first Article; and that no State, without its Consent, shall be deprived of its equal Suffrage in the Senate.

Article VI.

All Debts contracted and Engagements entered into, before the Adoption of this Constitution, shall be as valid against the United States under this Constitution, as under the Confederation.

This Constitution, and the Laws of the United States which shall be made in Pursuance thereof; and all Treaties made, or which shall be made, under the Authority of the United States, shall be the supreme Law of the Land; and the Judges in every State shall be bound thereby, any Thing in the Constitution or Laws of any State to the Contrary notwithstanding.

The Senators and Representatives before mentioned, and the Members of the several State Legislatures, and all executive and judicial Officers; both of the United States and of the several States, shall be bound by Oath or Affirmation, to support this Constitution; but no religious Test shall ever be required as a Qualification to any Office or public Trust under the United States.

Article VII.

The Ratification of the Convention of nine States, shall be sufficient for the Establishment of this Constitution between the States so ratifying the Same.

DONE in Convention by the Unanimous Consent of the States present the Seventeenth Day of September in the Year of our Lord one thousand seven hundred and Eighty seven and of the

Independance of the United States of America the Twelfth In Witness whereof We have hereunto subscribed our Names,

Attest William Jackson Secretary   Go: Washington—Presidt.
                                     and deputy from Virginia

Delaware:	Geo: Read	**New Hamp-shire:**	John Langdon
	Gunning Bedford junr		Nicholas Gilman
	John Dickinson		
	Richard Bassett	**Massa-chusetts:**	Nathaniel Gorham
	Jaco: Broom		Rufus King
Maryland:	James McHenry	**Connec-ticut:**	Wm: Saml. Johnson
	Dan of St Thos. Jenifer		Roger Sherman
	Danl Carroll	**New York:**	Alexander Hamilton
Virginia:	John Blair—		
	James Madison Jr.	**New Jersey:**	Wil: Livingston
North Carolina:	Wm. Blount		David Brearly
	Richd. Dobbs Spaight.		Wm. Paterson.
	Hu Williamson		Jona: Dayton
South Carolina:	J. Rurledge	**Pennsyl-vania:**	B. Franklin
	Charles Cotesworth Pinckney		Thomas Mifflin
	Charles Pinckney		Robt Morris
	Pierce Butler		Geo. Cylmer
Georgia:	William Few		Thos. FitzSimons
	Abr Baldwin		Jared Ingersoll
			James Wilson
			Gouv. Morris

ARTICLES in Addition to, and Amendment of, the Constitution of the United States of America, proposed by Congress, and ratified by the Legislatures of the several States, pursuant to the fifth Article of the original Constitution.

Article I.

Congress shall make no law respecting an establishment of religion, or prohibiting the free exercise thereof; or abridging the freedom of speech, or of the press; or the right of the people peaceably to assemble, and to petition the Government for a redress of grievances.

Article II.

A well regulated Militia, being necessary to the security of a free State, the right of the people to keep and bear Arms, shall not be infringed.

Article III.

No Soldier shall, in time of peace be quartered in any house, without the consent of the Owner, nor in time of war, but in a manner to be prescribed by law.

Article IV.

The right of the people to be secure in their persons, houses, papers, and effects, against unreasonable searches and seizures, shall not be violated, and no Warrants shall issue, but upon probable cause, supported by Oath or affirmation, and particularly describing the place to be searched, and the persons or things to be seized.

Article V.

No person shall be held to answer for a capital, or otherwise infamous crime, unless on a presentment or indictment of a Grand Jury, except in cases arising in the land or naval forces, or in the Militia, when in actual service in time of War or public danger; nor shall any person be subject for the same offence to be twice put in jeopardy of life or limb; nor shall be compelled in any criminal case to be a witness against himself, nor be deprived of life, liberty, or property, without due process of law; nor shall private property be taken for public use, without just compensation.

Article VI.

In all criminal prosecutions, the accused shall enjoy the right to a speedy and public trial, by an impartial jury of the State and district wherein the crime shall have been committed, which district shall have been previously ascertained by law, and to be informed of the nature and cause of the accusation; to be confronted with the witnesses against him; to have compulsory process for obtaining witnesses in his favor, and to have the Assistance of Counsel for his defence.

Article VII.

In Suits at common law, where the value in controversy shall exceed twenty dollars, the right of trial by jury shall be preserved, and no fact tried by a jury, shall be otherwise reexamined in any Court of the United States, than according to the rules of the common law.

Article VIII.

Excessive bail shall not be required, nor excessive fines imposed, nor cruel and unusual punishments inflicted.

Article IX.

The enumeration in the Constitution, of certain rights, shall not be construed to deny or disparage others retained by the people.

Article X.

The powers not delegated to the United States by the Constitution, nor prohibited by it to the States, are reserved to the States respectively, or to the people.

Articles I.–X. proposed to the states by Congress, September 25, 1789
Ratification completed, December 15, 1791
Ratification declared, March 1, 1792

Article XI.

The Judicial power of the United States shall not be construed to extend to any suit in law or equity, commenced or prosecuted against one of the United States by Citizens of another State, or by Citizens or Subjects of any Foreign State.

Proposed to the states by Congress, March 4, 1794
Ratification completed, February 7, 1795
Ratification declared, January 8, 1798

Article XII.

The Electors shall meet in their respective states, and vote by ballot for President and Vice-President, one of whom, at least, shall not be an inhabitant of the same state with themselves; they shall name in their ballots the person voted for as President, and in distinct ballots the person voted for as Vice-President, and they shall make distinct lists of all persons voted for as President, and of all persons voted for as Vice-President, and of the number of votes for each, which lists they shall sign and certify, and transmit sealed to the seat of the government of the United States, directed to the President of the Senate;—The President of the Senate shall, in the presence of the Senate and House of Representatives, open all the certificates and the votes shall then be counted;—The person having the greatest number of votes for President, shall be the President, if such number be a major-ity of the whole number of Electors appointed; and if no person have such majority, then from the persons having the highest numbers not exceeding three on the list of those voted for as President, the House of Representatives shall choose immediately, by ballot, the President. But in choosing the President, the votes shall be taken by states, the representation from each state having one vote; a quorum for this purpose shall consist of a member or members from two-thirds of the states, and a majority of all the states shall be necessary to a choice. And if the House of Representatives shall not choose a President whenever the right of choice shall devolve upon them, before the fourth day of March next following, then the Vice-President shall act as President, as in the case of the death or other constitutional disability of the President.—The person having the greatest number of votes as Vice-President, shall be the Vice-President, if such number be a majority of the whole number of Electors appointed, and if no person have a majority, then from the two highest numbers on the list, the Senate shall choose the Vice-President; a quorum for the purpose shall consist of two-thirds of the whole number of Senators, and a majority of the whole number shall be necessary to a choice. But no person constitutionally ineligible to the office of President shall be eligible to that of Vice-President of the United States.

Proposed to the states by Congress, December 9, 1803
Ratification completed, June 15, 1804
Ratification declared, September 25, 1804

Article XIII.

Section 1. Neither slavery nor involuntary servitude, except as a punishment for crime whereof the party shall have been duly convicted, shall exist within the United States, or any place subject to their jurisdiction.

Section 2. Congress shall have power to enforce this article by appropriate legislation.

Proposed to the states by Congress, January 31, 1865
Ratification completed, December 6, 1865
Ratification declared, December 18, 1865

Article XIV.

Section 1. All persons born or naturalized in the United States, and subject to the jurisdiction thereof, are citizens of the United States and of the State wherein they reside. No State shall make or enforce any law which shall abridge the privileges or immunities of citizens of the United States; nor shall any State deprive any person of life, liberty, or property, without due process of law; nor deny to any person within its jurisdiction the equal protection of the laws.

Section 2. Representatives shall be apportioned among the several States according to their respective numbers, counting the whole number of persons in each State, excluding Indians not taxed. But when the right to vote at any election for the choice of electors for President and Vice President of the United States, Representatives in Congress, the Executive and Judicial officers of a State, or the members of the Legislature thereof, is denied to any of the male inhabitants of such State, being twenty-one years of age, and citizens of the United States, or in any way abridged, except for participation in rebellion, or other crime, the basis of representation therein shall be reduced in the proportion which the number of such male citizens shall bear to the whole number of male citizens twenty-one years of age in such State.

Section 3. No person shall be a Senator or Representative in Congress, or elector of President and Vice President, or hold any office, civil or military, under the United States, or under any State, who, having previously taken an oath, as a member of Congress, or as an officer of the United States, or as a member of any State legislature, or as an executive or judicial officer of any State, to support the Constitution of the United States, shall have engaged in insurrection or rebellion against the same, or given aid or comfort to the enemies thereof. But Congress may by a vote of two-thirds of each House, remove such disability.

Section 4. The validity of the public debt of the United States, authorized by law, including debts incurred for payment of pensions and bounties for services in suppressing insurrection or rebellion, shall not be questioned. But neither the United States nor any State shall assume or pay any debt or obligation incurred in aid of insurrection or rebellion against the United States, or any claim for the loss or emancipation of any slave; but all such debts, obligations and claims shall be held illegal and void.

Section 5. The Congress shall have power to enforce, by appropriate legislation, the provisions of this article.

Proposed to the states by Congress, June 13, 1866
Ratification completed, July 9, 1868
Ratification declared, July 28, 1868

Article XV.

Section 1. The right of citizens of the United States to vote shall not be denied or abridged by the United States or by any State on account of race, color, or previous condition of servitude.

Section 2. The Congress shall have power to enforce this article by appropriate legislation.

Proposed to the states by Congress, February 26, 1869
Ratification completed, February 3, 1870
Ratification declared, March 30, 1870

Article XVI.

The Congress shall have power to lay and collect taxes on incomes, from whatever source derived, without apportionment among the several States, and without regard to any census or enumeration.

Proposed to the states by Congress, July 12, 1909
Ratification completed, February 3, 1913
Ratification declared, February 25, 1913

Article XVII.

The Senate of the United States shall be composed of two Senators from each State, elected by the people thereof, for six years; and each Senator shall have one vote. The electors in each State shall have the qualifications requisite for electors of the most numerous branch of the State legislatures.

When vacancies happen in the representation of any State in the Senate, the executive authority of such State shall issue writs of election to fill such vacancies: Provided, that the legislature of any State may empower the executive thereof to make temporary appointments until the people fill the vacancies by election as the legislature may direct.

This amendment shall not be so construed as to affect the election or term of any Senator chosen before it becomes valid as part of the Constitution.

Proposed to the states by Congress, May 13,1912
Ratification completed, April 8, 1913
Ratification ration declared, May 31, 1913

Article XVIII.

Section 1. After one year from the ratification of this article the manufacture, sale, or transportation of intoxicating liquors within, the importation thereof into, or the exportation thereof from the United States and all territory subject to the jurisdiction thereof for beverage purposes is hereby prohibited.

Section 2. The Congress and the several States shall have concurrent power to enforce this article by appropriate legislation.

Section 3. This article shall be inoperative unless it shall have been ratified as an amendment to the Constitution by the legislatures of the several States, as provided in the Constitution, within seven years from the date of the submission hereof to the States by the Congress.

Proposed to the states by Congress, December 18, 1917
Ratification completed, January 16,1919
Ratification declared, January 29, 1919

Article XIX.

The right of citizens of the United States to vote shall not be denied or abridged by the United States or by any State on account of sex.

Congress shall have power to enforce this article by appropriate legislation.

Proposed to the states by Congress, June 4, 1919
Ratification completed, August 18, 1920
Ratification declared, August 26, 1920

Article XX.

Section 1. The terms of the President and Vice President shall end at noon on the 20th day of January, and the terms of Senators and Representatives at noon on the 3d day of January, of the years in which such terms would have ended if this article had not been ratified; and the terms of their successors shall then begin.

Section 2. The Congress shall assemble at least once in every year, and such meeting shall begin at noon on the 3d day of January, unless they shall by law appoint a different day.

Section 3. If, at the time fixed for the beginning of the term of the President, the President elect shall have died, the Vice President elect shall become President. If a President shall not have been chosen before the time fixed for the beginning of his term, or if the President elect shall have failed to qualify, then the Vice President elect shall act as President until a President shall have qualified; and the Congress may by law provide for the case wherein neither a President elect nor a Vice President elect shall have qualified, declaring who shall then act as President, or the manner in which one who is to act shall be selected, and such person shall act accordingly until a President or Vice President shall have qualified.

Section 4. The Congress may by law provide for the case of the death of any of the persons from whom the House of Representatives may choose a President whenever the right of choice shall have devolved upon them, and for the case of the death of any of the persons from whom the Senate may choose a Vice President whenever the right of choice shall have devolved upon them.

Section 5. Sections I and 2 shall take effect on the 15th day of October following the ratification of this article.

Section 6. This article shall be inoperative unless it shall have been ratified as an amendment to the Constitution by the legislatures of three-fourths of the several States within seven years from the date of its submission.

Proposed to the states by Congress, March 2,1932
Ratification completed, January 23, 1933
Ratification declared, February 6,1933

Article XXI.

Section 1. The eighteenth article of amendment to the Constitution of the United States is hereby repealed.

Section 2. The transportation or importation into any State, Territory, or possession of the United States for delivery or use therein of intoxicating liquors, in violation of the laws thereof, is hereby prohibited.

Section 3. This article shall be inoperative unless it shall have been ratified as an amendment to the Constitution by conventions in the several States, as provided in the Constitution, within seven years from the date of the submission hereof to the States by the Congress.

Proposed to the states by Congress, February 20, 1933
Ratification completed, December 5, 1933
Ratification declared, December 5, 1933

Article XXII.

Section 1. No person shall be elected to the office of the President more than twice, and no person who has held the office of President, or acted as President, for more than two years of a term to which some other person was elected President shall be elected to the office of the President more than once. But this Article shall not apply to any person holding the office of President when this Article was proposed by the Congress, and shall not prevent any person who may be holding the office of President, or acting as President, during the term within which this Article becomes operative from holding the office of President or acting as President during the remainder of such term.

Section 2. This article shall be inoperative unless it shall have been ratified as an amendment to the Constitution by the legislatures of three-fourths of the several States within seven years from the date of its submission to the States by the Congress.

Proposed to the states by Congress, March 21, 1947
Ratification completed, February 27, 1951
Ratification declared, March 1, 1951

Article XXIII.

Section 1. The District constituting the seat of Government of the United States shall appoint in such manner as the Congress may direct:

A number of electors of President and Vice President equal to the whole number of Senators and Representatives in Congress to which the District would be entitled if it were a State, but in no event more than the least populous State; they shall be in addition to those appointed by the States, but they shall be considered, for the purposes of the election of President and Vice President, to be electors appointed by a State; and they shall meet in the District and perform such duties as provided by the twelfth article of amendment.

Section 2. The Congress shall have power to enforce this article by appropriate legislation.

Proposed to the states by Congress, June 17, 1960
Ratification completed, March 29, 1961
Ratification declared, April 3, 1961

Article XXIV.

Section 1. The right of citizens of the United States to vote in any primary or other election for President or Vice President, for electors for President or Vice President, or for Senator or Representative in Congress, shall not be denied or abridged by the United States or any State by reason of failure to pay any poll tax or other tax.

Section 2. The Congress shall have power to enforce this article by appropriate legislation.

Proposed to the states by Congress, August 27, 1962
Ratification completed, January 23, 1964
Ratification declared, February 4, 1964

Article XXV

Section 1. In case of the removal of the President from office or of his death or resignation, the Vice President shall become President.

Section 2. Whenever there is a vacancy in the office of the Vice President, the President shall nominate a Vice President who shall take office upon confirmation by a majority vote of both Houses of Congress.

Section 3. Whenever the President transmits to the President pro tempore of the Senate and the Speaker of the House of Representatives his written declaration that he is unable to discharge the powers and duties of his office, and until he transmits to them a written declaration to the contrary, such powers and duties shall be discharged by the Vice President as Acting President.

Section 4. Whenever the Vice President and a majority of either the principal officers of the executive departments or of such other body as Congress may by law provide, transmit to the

President pro tempore of the Senate and the Speaker of the House of Representatives their written declaration that the President is unable to discharge the powers and duties of his office, the Vice President shall immediately assume the powers and duties of the office as Acting President.

Thereafter, when the President transmits to the President pro tempore of the Senate and the Speaker of the House of Representatives his written declaration that no inability exists, he shall resume the powers and duties of his office unless the Vice President and a majority of either the principal officers of the executive department or of such other body as Congress may by law provide, transmit within four days to the President pro tempore of the Senate and the Speaker of the House of Representatives their written declaration that the President is unable to discharge the powers and duties of his office. Thereupon Congress shall decide the issue, assembling within forty-eight hours for that purpose if not in session. If the Congress, within twenty-one days after receipt of the latter written declaration, or, if Congress is not in session, within twenty-one days after Congress is required to assemble, determines by two-thirds vote of both Houses that the President is unable to discharge the powers and duties

of his office, the Vice President shall continue to discharge the same as Acting President; otherwise, the President shall resume the powers and duties of his office.

Proposed to the states by Congress, July 6, 1965
Ratification completed, February 10, 1967
Ratification declared, February 23, 1967

Article XXVI.

Section 1. The right of citizens of the United States, who are eighteen years of age or older, to vote shall not be denied or abridged by the United States or by any State on account of age.

Section 2. The Congress shall have power to enforce this article by appropriate legislation.

Proposed to the states by Congress, March 23, 1971
Ratification completed, July 1, 1971
Ratification declared, July 5, 1971

Article XXVII.

No law, varying the compensation for the services of the Senators and Representatives, shall take effect, until an election of Representatives shall have intervened.

Proposed to the states by Congress, September 25, 1789
Ratification completed, May 7, 1992
Ratification declared, May 18, 1992

ALEXANDER HAMILTON'S CONJECTURES ABOUT THE NEW CONSTITUTION

September 1787

The new constitution has in favour of its success these circumstances—a very great weight of influence of the persons who framed it, particularly in the universal popularity of General Washington,—the good will of the commercial interest throughout the states which will give all its efforts to the establishment of a government capable of regulating protecting and extending the commerce of the Union—the good will of most men of property in the several states who wish a government of the union able to protect them against domestic violence and the depredations which the democratic spirit is apt to make on property; and who are besides anxious for the respectability of the nation—the hopes of the Creditors of the United States that a general government possessing the means of doing it will pay the debt of the Union. A strong belief in the people at large of the insufficiency of the present confederation to preserve the existence of the Union and of the necessity of the union to their safety and prosperity; of course a strong desire of a change and a predisposition to receive well the propositions of the Convention.

Against its success is to be put, the dissent of two or three important men in the Convention; who will think their characters pledge to defeat the plan—the influence of many *inconsiderable* men in possession of considerable offices under the state governments who will fear a diminution of their consequence power and emolument by the establishment of the general government and who can hope for nothing there— the influence of some *considerable* men in office possessed of talents and popularity who partly from the same motives and partly from a desire of *playing* a part in a convulsion for their own aggrandisement will oppose the quiet adoption of the new government—(some considerable men out of office, from motives of ambition may be disposed to act the same part)—add to these causes the disinclination of the people to taxes and of course to a strong government—the opposition of all men much in debt who will not wish to see a government established one object of which is to restrain this means of cheating Creditors—the democratical jealousy of the people which may be alarmed at the appearance of institutions that may seem calculated to place the power of the community in few hands and to raise a few individuals to stations of great preeminence—and the influence of some foreign powers who from different motives will not wish to see an energetic government established throughout the states.

In this view of the subject it is difficult to form any judgment whether the plan will be adopted or rejected. It must be essentially matter of conjecture. The present appearances and all other circumstances considered the probability seems to be on the side of its adoption.

But the causes operating against its adoption are powerful and there will be nothing astonishing in the Contrary—

If it do not finally obtain, it is probable the discussion of the question will beget such struggles, animosities and heats in the community that this circumstance conspiring with the *real necessity* of an essential change in our present situation will produce civil war. Should this happen, whatever parties prevail it is probable governments very different from the present in their principles will be established—A dismemberment of the Union and monarchies in different portions of it may be expected. It may however happen that no civil war will take place; but several republican confederacies be established between different combinations of particular states.

A reunion with Great Britain, from universal disgust at a state of commotion, is not impossible, though not much to be feared. The most plausible shape of such a business would be the establishment of a son of the present monarch in the supreme government of this country with a family compact.

If the government is adopted, it is probable general Washington will be the President of the United States—This will ensure a wise choice of men to administer the government and a good administration. A good administration will conciliate the confidence and affection of the people and perhaps enable the government to acquire more consistency than the proposed constitution seems to promise for so great a Country—It may then triumph altogether over the state governments and reduce them to an entire subordination, dividing the large states into smaller districts. The *organs* of the general government may also acquire additional strength.

If this should not be the case, in the course of a few years, it is probable that the contests about the boundaries of power between the particular governments and the general government and the *momentum* of the larger states in such contests will produce a dissolution of the Union. This after all seems to be the most likely result.

But it is almost arrogance in so complicated a subject, depending so entirely on the incalculable fluctuations of the human passions, to attempt even a conjecture about the event.

It will be Eight or Nine months before any certain judgment can be formed respecting the adoption of the Plan.

The Founding Indian Fathers

by Jack Weatherford

Every day of the school year, troops of children march across the lawn of the United States Capitol perched atop the District of Columbia's highest elevation. The building dominates the Washington skyline, a model of classical symmetry and precision. Two giant wings of precisely equal proportion reach out from a Roman dome that surveys the city of Washington. If reduced to a ruin, the forest of Greek columns decorating the building would appear to be as much at home in Rome or Naples as in Athens or Corinth. The building revels in its Old World heritage.

Indian schoolchildren walking through the halls of Congress would rarely see a hint that the building sits in America overlooking the Potomac River and not along the shores of the Mediterranean Sea. The building copies European, primarily classical, styles, and its halls proudly display pictures, friezes, and busts of famous political thinkers from Hammurabi and Solomon to Rousseau and Voltaire. In the hallways stand statues of American politicians posing in Greek tunics and Roman togas as though they were Roman senators or Athenian orators. Greek busts of the vice-presidents of the United States line the halls of the Senate, lending them the aura of a classical cemetery.

The children pass under doorways that bear weighty engravings and quotations from European documents such as the Magna Carta interspersed with quotes from the United States Declaration of Independence or Constitution. The building and its appointments proudly proclaim their part in the great march of European progress and civilization. They portray the blessed dove of democracy hatching in Athens and then taking wing for a torturous flight of two millennia, pausing only momentarily over Republican Rome, the field of Runnymede, and the desk of Voltaire before finally alighting to rest permanently and securely in the virgin land of America.

A child standing squarely in the middle of the Capitol beneath the great dome sees a painted band circling the upper wall representing the history of America. In that work, the Indians appear as just one more dangerous obstacle, like the wild animals, the Appalachian Mountains, the Mississippi River, and the western deserts, that blocked the progress of European civilization and technology in the white man's march across America. The most peaceful picture with an Indian theme in the rotunda shows the baptism of Pocahontas, daughter of the Indian leader Powhatan. Surrounded by Europeans and dressed in English clothes, she symbolically renounces the savage life of the Indians for the civilization of the British.

The lesson in this august setting presents itself forcefully on every visitor. The United States government derives from European precedents, and the Americans gave civilization to the Indians. Nothing in the Capitol hints that contemporary Americans owe the slightest debt to the Indians for teaching us about democratic institutions.

Despite these civic myths surrounding the creation of American government, America's settlers from Europe knew little of democracy. The English came from a nation ruled by monarchs who claimed that God conferred their right to rule and even allowed them to wage wars of extinction against the Irish. Colonists also fled to America from France, which was wandering aimlessly through history under the extravagances of a succession of kings named Louis, most of whom pursued debauched and extravagant reigns that oppressed, exploited, and at times even starved their subjects.

Despite the ideal government sketched by Plato in The Republic, and the different constitutions analyzed by Aristotle in his Politics, the Old World offered America few democratic models for government. Democratic government had no fortress in the Old World. Despite the democratic rhetoric that came into fashion in

eighteenth-century Europe, no such systems existed there at that time. The monarchy and the aristocracy of England were engaged in a protracted struggle that would eventually lead to the supremacy of Parliament (and a closely limited electoral franchise until the reforms of the nineteenth century). France had not yet begun its experiments with participatory democracy. The Founding Fathers of the United States judiciously assembled bits and pieces of many different systems to invent a completely new one. In fashioning the new system, they even borrowed some distinctive elements from the American Indians.

The Founding Fathers faced a major problem when it came time to invent the United States. They represented, under the Articles of Confederation, thirteen separate and sovereign states. How could one country be made from all thirteen without each one yielding its own power?

Reportedly, the first person to propose a union of all the colonies and to propose a federal model for it was the Iroquois chief Canassatego, speaking at an Indian-British assembly in Pennsylvania in July 1744. He complained that the Indians found it difficult to deal with so many different colonial administrations, each with its own policy. It would make life easier for everyone involved if the colonists could have a union which allowed them to speak with one voice. Me not only proposed that the colonies unify themselves, but told them how they might do it. He suggested that they do as his people had done and form a union like the League of the Iroquois [Johansen, pp. 12, 61].

Hiawatha and Deganwidah founded the League of the Iroquois sometime between A.D. 1000 and 1450 under a constitution they called the *Kaianerekowa* or Great Law of Peace. When the Europeans arrived in America, the league constituted the most extensive and important political unit north of the Aztec civilization. From earliest contact the Iroquois intrigued the Europeans, and they were the subject of many amazed reports. Benjamin Franklin, however, seems to have been the first to take their system as a potentially important model by which the settlers might be able to fashion a new government.

Benjamin Franklin first acquainted with the operation of Indian political organization in his capacity as official printer for the colony of Pennsylvania. His job included publication of the records and speeches of the various Indian assemblies and treaty negotiations, but following his instinctive curiosity, he broadened this into a study of Indian culture and institutions. Because of his expertise and interest in Indian matters, the colonial government of Pennsylvania offered him his first diplomatic assignment as their Indian commissioner. He held this post during the 1750s and became intimately familiar with the intricacies of Indian political culture and in particular with the League of the Iroquois. After this taste of Indian diplomacy, Franklin became a lifelong champion of the Indian political structure and advocated its use by the Americans. During this time he also refined his political techniques of persuasion, compromise, and slow consensus building that proved so important to his later negotiations as the ambassador to France and as a delegate to the Constitutional Convention.

Echoing the original proposal of Canassatego, Franklin advocated that the new American government incorporate many of the same features as the government of the Iroquois [Wilson, p. 46]. Speaking to the Albany Congress in 1754, Franklin called on the delegates of the various English colonies to unite and emulate the Iroquois League, a call that was not heeded until the Constitution was written three decades later [Hecht, p. 71]. Even though the Founding Fathers finally adopted some of the essential features of the Iroquois League, they never followed it in quite the detail advocated by Franklin.

The Iroquois League united five principal Indian nations—the Mohawk, Onondaga, Seneca, Oneida, and Cayuga. Each of these nations had a council composed of delegates called sachems who were elected by the tribes of that nation. The Seneca Nation elected eight sachems to its council, the Mohawk and Oneida nations each had councils of nine sachems, the Cayuga Nation had a council of ten, and the Onondaga Nation had a council of fourteen. Each of these nations governed its own territory, and its own council met to decide the issues of public policy for each one. But these councils exercised jurisdiction over the internal concerns of that one nation only; in this regard they exercised powers somewhat like the individual governments of the colonies.

In addition to the individual councils of each separate nation, the sachems formed a grand Council of the League in which all fifty sachems of the six nations sat together to discuss issues of common concern. The sachems represented their individual nations, but at the same time they represented the whole League of the Iroquois, thereby making the decisions of the council the law for all five nations. In this council each sachem had equal authority and privileges, with his power dependent on his oratorical power to persuade. The council met in the autumn of at least one year in five in a longhouse in the Onondaga Nation; if needed they could be called into session at other times as well. Their power extended to all matters of common concern among the member nations. In the words of Lewis Henry Morgan, America's first modern anthropologist, the council "declared war and made peace, sent and received embassies, entered into treaties of alliance, regulated the affairs of subjugated nations, received new members into the League, extended its protection over feeble tribes, in a word, took all needful measures to promote their prosperity, and enlarge their dominion" [Morgan, pp. 66-67].

Through this government the nations of the Iroquois controlled territory from New England to the Mississippi River, and they built a league that endured for centuries. Unlike European governments, the league blended the sovereignty of several nations into one government. This model of several sovereign units united into one government presented precisely the solution to the problem confronting the writers of the United States Constitution. Today we call this a "federal" system in which each state retains power over internal affairs and the national government regulates affairs common to all. Henry Steele Commager later wrote of this crucial time that even "if Americans did not actually invent federalism, they were able to take out an historical patent on it" [Commager, p. 207]. The Indians invented it even though the United States patented it.

Another student of the Iroquois political organization was Charles Thomson, the perpetual secretary of the Continental Congress. He spent so much energy studying the Indians and their way of life that the Delaware Nation adopted him as a full member. Following Thomas Jefferson's request, Thomson wrote at length on Indian social and political institutions for inclusion in an appendix to Jefferson's *Notes on the State of Virginia*. According to his description of Indian political tradition, each Indian town built a council house for making local decisions and for electing delegates to the tribal council. The tribal council in turn elected delegates to the national council [Thomson, p. 203]. Even though Thomson wrote this several years before the Constitutional Convention, this description reads like a blueprint for the United States Constitution, especially when we remember that the Constitution allowed the state legislatures (rather than the general populace) to elect senators. Thomson stresses that the sachems or political leaders do not acquire their positions by heredity but by election, and he adds that because outsiders can be naturalized into the Indian nation, even they can be elected to such offices.

The Americans followed the model of the Iroquois League not only in broad outline but also in many of the specific provisions of their *Kalanerekowa*. According to the *Kaianerekowa*, the sachems were not chiefs, a position frequently associated with leadership in war. As a lawmaker, the sachem could never go to war in his official capacity as a sachem. "If disposed to take the warpath, he laid aside his civil office, for the time being, and became a common warrior" [Morgan, p. 72]. This followed the tradition in many Indian tribes that relied upon separate leaders for peace and for war. The colonists followed this model too in eventually separating civilian authorities from military ones. Members of Congress, judges, and other officials could not also act as military leaders without giving up their elected office; similarly, military leaders could not be elected to political office without first resigning their military position. This contrasted with British traditions; church and military leaders frequently served as members of the House of Lords and frequently played major political roles in the House of

Commons as well. Similarly, this inability to separate the civil government and the military has doomed many of the imitators of American democracy, particularly in Africa and Latin America.

If the conduct of any sachem appeared improper to the populace or if he lost the confidence of his electorate, the women of his clan impeached him and expelled him by official action, where upon the women then choose a new sachem [Goldenweiser, p. 570]. This concept of impeachment ran counter to European tradition, in which the monarch ruled until death, even if he became insane or incapacitated, as in the case of George III. The Americans followed the Iroquois precedent of always providing for ways to remove leaders when necessary, but the Founding Fathers saw no reason to follow the example of the Iroquois in granting women the right to vote or any other major role in the political structure.

One of the most important characteristics of the Iroquois League permitted it to expand as needed; the council could vote to admit new members. This proved to be an important feature of the system after the Tuscarora Indians of North Carolina faced attack in 1712 by the army of Colonel John Barnwell and again in 1713 by the army of Colonel James Moore. Having thoroughly defeated the Tuscaroras, the Carolina colonists demanded reparations from the Indians to pay the colonists' expenses incurred in the war. Because the Indians had no money to pay, the colonists seized four hundred of them and sold them into slavery at the rate of ten pounds sterling apiece. The surviving Tuscaroras fled North Carolina to seek refuge among the Iroquois. In 1714 the Tuscaroras applied for formal membership in the league, and the Iroquois admitted them in 1722 as the Sixth Nation [Waldman, p. 104]. Similarly the league later incorporated other decimated groups such as the Erie, but the league did not allow for an entity such as a colony, which had played such an important part in European governments since the times of the ancient Greeks.

In a radical break with Old World tradition, the emerging government of the United States emulated this Iroquois tradition of admitting new states as members rather than keeping them as colonies. The west became a series of territories and then states, but the United States treated each new territory as a future partner rather than as a colony. The new government codified this Indian practice into American law through the Congressional Resolution of 1780, the Land Ordinances of 1784 and 1785, and the Northwest Ordinance, together with similar provisions written directly into the Constitution. No direct proof links these laws with the Iroquois, but it seems likely to be more than mere coincidence that both the Iroquois and the United States governments enacted such similar procedures.

Although the Iroquois recognized no supreme leader in their system analogous to the president of the United States, the framers of the Constitution deliberately or inadvertently imitated the Great Council in establishing the electoral college system to select a president. Each state legislature a group of electors equal in number to that state's combined total of senators and representatives. Like the sachems, each elector then had one vote in the electoral college.

In the two centuries since the Constitution went into effect, some aspects of the system have changed. The voters rather than the state legislatures now elect both the electoral college and the senators through popular vote, but the system preserves the general features of the League of the Iroquois.

Upon election to the council, the new sachem "lost" his name and thenceforth other sachems called him by the title of his office. In much the same way, proceedings of the United States Senate do not permit the use of names such as "Senator Kennedy" or "Rudy Boschwitz." Instead the senators must be addressed by their office title as "the Senior Senator from Massachusetts" or "the Junior Senator from Minnesota." Other titles such as "Majority Leader," "Mr. Chairman," or "Mr. President" may be used, but all personal names remain strictly taboo.

Another imitation of the Iroquois came in the simple practice of allowing only one person to speak at a time in political meetings. This contrasts with the British tradition of noisy interruptions of

one another as the members of Parliament shout out agreement or disagreement with the speaker. Europeans were accustomed to shouting down any speaker who displeased them; in some cases, they might even stone him or inflict worse damage.

The Iroquois permitted no interruptions or shouting. They even imposed a short period of silence at the end of each oration in case the speaker had forgotten some point or wished to elaborate or change something he had said (Johansen, p. 87]. Even though the American Congress and legislatures did not adopt the practice of silence at the end, they did allow speakers "to revise and extend" the written record after speaking.

The purpose of debate in Indian councils was to persuade and educate, not to confront. Unlike European parliaments, where opposing factions battle out an issue in the public arena, the council of the Indians sought to reach an agreement through compromise. This important difference in nuance led Bruce Burton to observe in his study of American law that "American democracy owes its distinctive character of debate and compromise to the principles and structures of American Indian civil government" [Burton, p. 5]. Still today, this difference separates the operation of the United States Congress and the state legislatures from their European counterparts. American legislative bodies are composed primarily of individuals forming shifting factions from one issue to another, whereas the legislative bodies of Europe operate through opposing political parties that control the votes of individual representatives.

In keeping with Iroquois tradition, Franklin proposed that since the sachems did not own land or receive any financial compensation for their work, the officials of the United States should not be paid. They should perform their work as a sacred trust freely given to the communal welfare. Even though the Founding Fathers did not incorporate this, they did work to prevent property qualifications for holding office and for exercising the right to vote. They also tended to limit salaries paid to officeholders to a minimum to cover basic expenses of life rather than making public office a sinecure or a route to wealth.

In his democratic zeal to imitate the system of the Indians, Franklin even proposed that military officers should be elected by the men whom they ordered into battle. The Indians routinely fought this way, and Franklin organized such a militia himself in 1747 to protect Philadelphia from harassment by French and Dutch pirates. Even though the American army did not adopt the practice of electing officers, it gradually abandoned the European practice of allowing the purchase of commissions by the wealthy. The American system did allow for mobility within the ranks and prevented the officer corps of the army from resembling too closely an aristocratic class as in Europe or an oligarchy as in many Latin American nations.

The League of the Iroquois operated with only a single chamber in its council. Franklin became an ardent supporter of this unicameral organization, and he even wanted to use the English translation of the Iroquois term meaning "grand council" rather than the Latinism "congress." The United States government relied on only a single chamber during the years of the Continental Congress, and some states, such as Pennsylvania and Vermont, reduced their state legislatures to unicameral bodies for a while. The unicameral congress and legislature, however, did not endure, and today only Nebraska has a unicameral legislature, instituted to save money and not to emulate the Iroquois.

In addition to Benjamin Franklin, Thomas Paine, and Charles Thomson, many of the Founding Fathers of American federalism had worked closely with the Indian political institutions. George Washington had extensive contacts with the Indians in his surveying expeditions into the western part of Virginia and fought with Indians and against Indians in the French and Indian War. Washington showed a greater interest in land speculation and making money than in observing the political life of the Indians. Thomas Jefferson, author of the Declaration of Independence, also lived close to the frontier, and he himself was the son of a pioneer. He studied and wrote numerous articles and essays on the Indians, leading a later historian to call Jefferson "the most enlightened of amateur ethnologists" [Commager, p. 179]. In his

recommendations for the University of Virginia, he became the first person to propose a systematic ethnological study of the Indians in order "to collect their traditions, laws, customs, languages and other circumstances" [Jefferson, p. 151].

Because of men such as Thomas Paine, Benjamin Franklin, Charles Thomson, and Thomas Jefferson, we today know a great deal about the League of the Iroquois and some of the other Indian groups of the eastern United States. Subsequent years of ethnological research into the political organizations of the New World have shown that the League of the Iroquois seems representative of political institutions throughout all of America north of Mexico and much of Central and South America as well. Councils chosen by the clans, tribes, or villages governed most Indian nations.

From Hollywood films and adventure novels Americans often conclude that strong chiefs usually commanded the Indian tribes. More often, however, as in the case of the Iroquois, a council ruled, and any person called the "head" of the tribe usually occupied a largely honorary position of respect rather than power. Chiefs mostly played ceremonial and religious roles rather than political or economic ones. Unlike the words "caucus" and "powwow," which are Indian-derived and indicative of Indian political traditions, the word "chief" is an English word of French origin that British officials tried to force onto Indian tribes in order that they might have someone with whom to trade and sign treaties.

In Massachusetts the British tried to make one leader into King Philip. The British imputed monarchy to the Indian system when no such institution existed. Thus while the English settlers learned from the Indians how to speak and act in group councils, they simultaneously pushed the Indians toward a monarchical and thus less democratic system.

We see the same collective system in the early 1500s in the pueblos of the southwest when one of Francisco Coronado's soldiers wrote that the Zuni had no chiefs "but are ruled by a council of the oldest men" whom they called papas. The Zuni word papa means "elder brother," and each clan probably elected its papa the way the Iroquois clans elected their sachems.

Even the Aztecs' government conformed to this pattern. They divided themselves into twenty *calpulli* or corporate clans, each of which owned property in common. Each *calpulli* elected a number of administrative officers to oversee the administration of property and law within its clan, and they elected a *tlatoani*, literally a "speaker," who functioned as the representative of the *calpulli* to the outside world. All the *tlatoani* met together to form the supreme council of the nation, and they elected the supreme speaker, or *huey-tlatoani*, an office with life tenure. By the time the Spanish arrived, this highest office of the nation had been reserved for a single family, but the council decided who within that family would have the office. The Spanish assumed that the Aztec system was like their own system or like that of their neighbors the Moors; they translated *huey-tlatoani* as "emperor" and called the *tlatoani* the "nobles" of the empire. Moctezuma, the Aztec leader captured by Hernando Cortes, held office as the supreme speaker of the Aztec nation, not as its emperor.

This Aztec system was no more of a democracy or a federal union because of these councils than was the Holy Roman Empire, which also had a council to elect its emperor from one family. Still, in the Aztec system we can see the outlines of a political format common throughout the Americas and in many ways closer to our democratic system in the United States today than to the systems of Europe of that time. The difference in the Aztec system and a European monarchy appeared most clearly when the Aztec people removed Moctezuma from office after the Spaniards captured him. The people even stoned him when he tried to persuade them to acquiesce to the Spanish. The Spaniards had expected the people to revere and obey their "emperor" no matter what, but they assumed erroneously that Moctezuma held the same power over the Aztec people that the Spanish king held over themselves.

The depth of democratic roots among North American Indian groups shows clearly in the detailed study of the Yaqui by historian Evelyn

Hu-DeHart. Living in the present-day states of Sonora and Sinaloa of northwestern Mexico lust south of the Apaches of Arizona, the Yaquis coaxed a livelihood from this desert setting through hunting and simple agriculture. In July 1739 the Yaquis sent two emissaries named Muni and Bernabe to Mexico City for a rare audience with the Spanish viceroy to plead for free elections of their own government administrators in place of the Jesuits appointed over them. After 1740 the government allowed the Yaquis to elect their own captain general as head of their tribe, but the government still sought to exercise control over the Yaquis through clerical and civilian administrators [Hu-DeHart, p. 17]. Thus in the wilds of Mexico a full generation before the Revolution in the English colonies of North America, we see evidence of the Indians demanding the franchise and free elections in order to maintain their traditional political values.

In almost every North American tribe, clan, or nation for which we have detailed political information, the supreme authority rested in a group rather than in an individual. It took many generations of close interaction between colonists and Indians before the principles of group decision-making replaced the European traditions of relying on a single supreme authority. The importance of these Indian councils and groups shows clearly in the English lack of words to explain such a process.

One of the most important political institutions borrowed from the Indians was the caucus. Even though the word appears to be proper Latin and some law students with a semester of Latin occasionally decline the plural as *cauci*, the word comes from the Algonquian languages. The caucus permits informal discussion of an issue without necessitating a yea or nay vote on any particular question. This agreed with the traditional Indian way of talking through an issue or of making a powwow; it made political decisions less divisive and combative. The caucus became a mainstay of American democracy both in the Congress and in political and community groups all over the country. The caucus evolved into such an important aspect of American politics that the political parties adopted it to nominate their presidential candidates. In time this evolved into the political convention. which still functions as an important part of contemporary American politics but is largely absent from European politics.

Not all the Founding Fathers showed interest in Indian political traditions. They turned Instead toward models such as the British Parliament and some of the Greek and Italian city-states. Many of them had been deeply trained in classic literature, in ways that Franklin and Paine had not been trained, and they sought to incorporate the classic notions of democracy and republicanism into the new nation.

Often this proved to be a tricky undertaking, for the ancient Greeks observed democracy far more in the breach than in its enactment. The Greeks who rhapsodized about democracy in their rhetoric rarely created democratic institutions. A few cities such as Athens occasionally attempted a system vaguely akin to democracy for a few years. These cities functioned as slave societies and were certainly not egalitarian or democratic in the Indian sense. Most of the respected political thinkers of Greece despised democracy both theoretically and in practice. The people of Athens executed Socrates during one of their democratic eras because he had conspired with the oligarchs to destroy democracy. On the other hand, Plato favored rule by a philosopher-king and even went to Syracuse to help the tyrant Dionysius rule.

In the United States, the southerners identified much more closely with the ideals of Greek democracy based on massive slavery than with lroquois democracy, which did not permit slavery. As historian Vernon Parrington wrote, the "dream of a Greek civilization based on black slavery was discovered in the bottom of the cup of southern romanticism" [Parrington, p. 130].

Carolinians, Georgians, and Virginians identified so closely with the so-called democracies of Greece that they considered the south to be a virtual reincarnation or at least renaissance of Greek life. By the beginning of the nineteenth century, southerners had created a virtual Greek cult as an intellectual bulwark to protect their way of life. European romantics such as Lord Byron and John Keats flirted with Greek aesthetics, but the Euro-

peans quickly dropped them in favor of a more personal form of romanticism.

The American south, however, embraced everything Greek. The southern gentleman with his leisurely life of relaxation in the study, friendly conversation in the parlor, fine meals in the dining room, courting in the ballroom, and hunting in the forest identified closely with the good life of Greek literature. At least a passing acquaintance with the Greek and Latin languages became the true mark of a gentleman in the south, and the Greek ideal of a sound mind in a sound body became the creed of the southern leisure class. Southerners wrote poems in mock-Greek style and wrote letters in a classical form. In their excess they even gave their house slaves, horses, and hunting dogs names such as Cicero, Athena, Cato, Pericles, Homer, Apollo, and Nero.

They adorned their plantations with Greek names, and even built their homes in the style of Greek temples. Greek architecture prevailed so widely in the South that today the stereotyped image of a plantation house includes Corinthian columns in Greek Revival style. In their gardens they built gazebos that were styled after Greek shrines, and they set Greek statues out among the magnolia trees and the palms. Even the churches of the south added porticos and rows of columns to their fronts, topped off by very un-Greek steeples.

In making itself over in the Greek image, America neglected a major part of its democratic roots in the long house of the Iroquois and the humble caucus of the Algonquians in favor of the ostentatious props and models looted from the classical Mediterranean world. For almost the whole first century of American independence this Greek architecture and Greek oratory helped to disguise the fact that the nation was based on slavery, an institution that could never be compatible with democracy no matter how much that architectural and verbal edifice tried to cover it.

Prior to this Greek cult, most government buildings in America had been built in a very simple style, as in the state capitol of Massachusetts, Independence Hall in Philadelphia, or the government buildings of colonial Williamsburg. But with the rise of the Greek cult in the south, government architects moved away from the simple Federal style to make public buildings appear Greek. At the height of this classical obsession the United States government began work on a new Capitol. The Senate chamber took the form of a small Greek amphitheater covered in excessive classical ornaments, while the House of Representatives crowned itself with a large clock encased in a sculpture of Clio, the muse of history, riding in her winged chariot and recording the historic events below her.

Although the Greek cult spread out of the south, New Englanders never embraced it very fondly. For them mystic philosophies such as Transcendentalism, often accompanied by ideas of liberty and abolition of slavery, seemed far more alluring. For them the existence of slavery at the foundations of democracy bastardized the whole system.

Even in the south the Greek cult did not reign as the only intellectual and social fashion. In stark contrast to this indulgence of the rich, the black population and the poor whites embraced a strict form of Old Testament fundamentalism closely associated with Moses, the liberator of the slaves, and of New Testament salvation focused on a very personal savior and protector.

Meanwhile in the west the process of learning democracy through experience of the frontier and Indians continued without regard to the supposed classical models. Even after the founding of the United States, the Indians continued to play a significant role in the evolution of democracy because of their sustained interactions with Americans on the frontier. The frontiersmen constantly reinvented democracy and channeled it into the eastern establishment of the United States.

Time and again the people of the frontier rebelled against the entrenched and conservative values of an ever more staid coastal elite. As the frontier gradually moved westward, the settlements on the edge sent such rebels as Henry Clay, Andrew Jackson, David Crockett, and Abraham Lincoln back to reinvest the spirit of democracy into the political institutions of the east. Some of these men, such as Sam Houston, lived for long periods with Indians. Houston spent so much time with

the Cherokee that they adopted him into their nation about 1829. The influence of the Cherokees stayed with him throughout his tenure as president of Texas from 1836 to 1838 and again from 1841 to 1844. Throughout his life he maintained close working relations with a variety of Indian nations and a strong commitment to liberty.

Even Alexis de Tocqueville, who denigrated the achievements of the Indians, noticed that the settlers "mix the ideas and customs of savage life with the civilization of their fathers." In general he found this reprehensible, for it made their "passions more intense" and "their religious morality less authoritative" [Tocqueville, Vol. 1, p. 334], but these traits certainly may be interpreted by others as among the virtues of a democratic people.

Most democratic and egalitarian reforms of the past two hundred years in America originated on the frontier and not in the settled cities of the east. The frontier states dropped property and religious requirements for voters. They extended the franchise to women, and in 1916 Montana elected Jeannette Rankin as the first woman in Congress four years before the Nineteenth Amendment to the Constitution gave women the right to vote. The western states started the public election of senators in place of selection by the legislature. They also pioneered the use of primary elections and electoral recalls of unpopular officers. Even today they have more elective offices, such as judges; such offices in the east are usually filled by appointment by the governor or the legislature. This strong bias toward the electoral process and equal votes for all has been reinforced repeatedly by the people who have had the closed and the longest connections with the Indians on the frontier.

The final extension of the federal principles used in the Iroquois Nation and later in the formation of the United States came in 1918 with establishment of the League of Nations. The framers of this new league also chose the Iroquois federal system of allowing each member an equal voice no matter how small or large a country he represented. The same principle underlay creation of the General Assembly of the United Nations a generation later. By ironic coincidence, the founders of this international body located it in New York in the very territory that once belonged to the League of the Iroquois. In one respect the United Nations was an international version of that Indian league.

Washington, D.C., has never recognized the role of the Indians in the writing of the United States Constitution or in the creation of political institutions that seem so uniquely American. But an inadvertent memorial does exist. An older woman from Israel pointed this out to me one spring day as I cut across the lawn of the United States Capitol, where I then worked for Senator John Glenn. She stopped me, and in a husky voice asked me who was the Indian woman atop the Capitol dome. Suddenly looking at it through her eyes, I too saw the figure as an Indian even though I knew that it was not.

When the United States government embarked on an expansion of the Capitol in the middle of the nineteenth century, the architects proposed to cap the dome with a symbol of freedom. They chose for this a nineteen-foot bronze statue of a Roman woman who would stand on the pinnacle of the Capitol. Sculptor Thomas Crawford crowned the woman with a Phrygian cap, which in Roman history had been the sign of the freed slave. At that time Jefferson Davis, the future president of the Confederate States of America, still served as the secretary of war for the United States, and he objected strongly to what he interpreted as an antisouthern and antislavery symbol. He compelled Crawford to cap her with something less antagonistic to southern politicians. Crawford designed a helmet covered with a crown of feathers, but in putting this headdress on the figure, her whole appearance changed. Now instead of looking like a classical Greek or Roman, she looked like an Indian.

She still stands today on the pseudoclassical Capitol overlooking the city of Washington. The Washington Monument rises to the same height, but no other building has been allowed to rise higher than she. Even though no one intended her to be an Indian, she now reigns as the nearest thing to a monument that Washington ever built to honor the Indians who contributed to the building of a federal union based on democracy.

Introduction

Last summer, in a season of intense heat, Jim Burden and I happened to be crossing Iowa on the same train. He and I are old friends, we grew up together in the same Nebraska town, and we had a great deal to say to each other. While the train flashed through never-ending miles of ripe wheat, by country towns and bright-flowered pastures and oak groves wilting in the sun, we sat in the observation car, where the woodwork was hot to the touch and red dust lay deep over everything. The dust and heat, the burning wind, reminded us of many things. We were talking about what it is like to spend one's childhood in little towns like these, buried in wheat and corn, under stimulating extremes of climate: Burning summers when the world lies green and billowy beneath a brilliant sky, when one is fairly stifled in vegetation, in the colour and smell of strong weeds and heavy harvests; blustery winters with little snow, when the whole country is stripped bare and gray as sheet-iron. We agreed that no one who had not grown up in a little prairie town could know anything about it. It was a kind of freemasonry, we said.

Although Jim Burden and I both live in New York, I do not see much of him there. He is legal counsel for one of the great Western railways and is often away from his office for weeks together. That is one reason why we seldom meet. Another is that I do not like his wife. She is handsome, energetic, executive, but to me she seems unimpressionable and temperamentally incapable of enthusiasm. Her husband's quiet tastes irritate her, I think, and she finds it worth while to play the patroness to a group of young poets and painters of advanced ideas and mediocre ability. She has her own fortune and lives her own life. For some reason, she wishes to remain Mrs. James Burden.

As for Jim, disappointments have not changed him. The romantic disposition which often made him seem very funny as a boy, has been one of the strongest elements in his success. He loves with a personal passion the great country through which his railway runs and branches. His faith in it and his knowledge of it have played an important part in its development.

During that burning day when we were crossing Iowa, our talk kept returning to a central figure, a Bohemian girl whom we had both known long ago. More than any other person we remembered, this girl seemed to mean to us the country, the conditions, the whole adventure of our childhood. I had lost sight of her altogether, but Jim had found her again after long years, and had renewed a friendship that meant a great deal to him. His mind was full of her that day. He made me see her again, feel her presence, revived all my old affection for her.

'From time to time I've been writing down what I remember about Ántonia,' he told me. 'On my long trips across the country, I amuse myself like that, in my stateroom.'

When I told him that I would like to read his account of her, he said I should certainly see it—if it were ever finished.

Months afterward, Jim called at my apartment one stormy winter afternoon, carrying a legal portfolio. He brought it into the sitting-room with him, and said, as he stood warming his hands,

'Here is the thing about Ántonia. Do you still want to read it? I finished it last night. I didn't take time to arrange it; I simply wrote down pretty much all that her name recalls to me. I suppose it hasn't any form. It hasn't any title, either.' He went into the next room, sat down at my desk and wrote across the face of the portfolio the word 'Ántonia.' He frowned at this a moment, then prefixed another word, making it 'My Ántonia.' That seemed to satisfy him.

THE SHIMERDAS

by Willa Cather

I first heard of Ántonia on what seemed to me an interminable journey across the great midland plain of North America. I was ten years old then; I had lost both my father and mother within a year, and my Virginia relatives were sending me out to my grandparents, who lived in Nebraska. I travelled in the care of a mountain boy, Jake Marpole, one of the 'hands' on my father's old farm under the Blue Ridge, who was now going West to work for my grandfather. Jake's experience of the world was not much wider than mine. He had never been in a railway train until the morning when we set out together to try our fortunes in a new world.

We went all the way in day-coaches, becoming more sticky and grimy with each stage of the journey. Jake bought everything the newsboys offered him: candy, oranges, brass collar buttons, a watch-charm, and for me a 'Life of Jesse James,' which I remember as one of the most satisfactory books I have ever read. Beyond Chicago we were under the protection of a friendly passenger conductor, who knew all about the country to which we were going and gave us a great deal of advice in exchange for our confidence. He seemed to us an experienced and worldly man who had been almost everywhere; in his conversation he threw out lightly the names of distant states and cities. He wore the rings and pins and badges of different fraternal orders to which he belonged. Even his cuff-buttons were engraved with hieroglyphics, and he was more inscribed than an Egyptian obelisk.

Once when he sat down to chat, he told us that in the immigrant car ahead there was a family from 'across the water' whose destination was the same as ours.

'They can't any of them speak English, except one little girl, and all she can say is "We go Black Hawk, Nebraska." She's not much older than you, twelve or thirteen, maybe, and she's as bright as a new dollar. Don't you want to go ahead and see her, Jimmy? She's got the pretty brown eyes, too!'

This last remark made me bashful, and I shook my head and settled down to 'Jesse James.' Jake nodded at me approvingly and said you were likely to get diseases from foreigners.

I do not remember crossing the Missouri River, or anything about the long day's journey through Nebraska. Probably by that time I had crossed so many rivers that I was dull to them. The only thing very noticeable about Nebraska was that it was still, all day long, Nebraska.

I had been sleeping, curled up in a red plush seat, for a long while when we reached Black Hawk. Jake roused me and took me by the hand. We stumbled down from the train to a wooden siding, where men were running about with lanterns. I couldn't see any town, or even distant lights; we were surrounded by utter darkness. The engine was panting heavily after its long run. In the red glow from the fire-box, a group of people stood huddled together on the platform, encumbered by bundles and boxes. I knew this must be the immigrant family the conductor had told us about. The woman wore a fringed shawl tied over her head, and she carried a little tin trunk in her arms, hugging it as if it were a baby. There was an old man, tall and stooped. Two half-grown boys and a girl stood holding oilcloth bundles, and a little girl clung to her mother's skirts. Presently a man with a lantern approached them and began to talk, shouting and exclaiming. I pricked up my ears, for it was positively the first time I had ever heard a foreign tongue.

Another lantern came along. A bantering voice called out: 'Hello, are you Mr. Burden's folks? If you are, it's me you're looking for. I'm Otto Fuchs. I'm Mr. Burden's hired man, and I'm to drive you out. Hello, Jimmy, ain't you scared to come so far west?'

I looked up with interest at the new face in the lantern-light. He might have stepped out of the pages of 'Jesse James.' He wore a sombrero hat, with a wide leather band and a bright buckle, and the ends of his moustache were twisted up stiffly, like little horns. He looked lively and ferocious, I thought, and as if he had a history. A long scar ran across one cheek and drew the corner of his mouth up in a sinister curl. The top of his left ear was gone, and his skin was brown as an Indian's. Surely this was the face of a desperado. As he walked about the platform in his high-heeled boots, looking for our trunks, I saw that he was a rather slight man, quick and wiry, and light on his feet. He told us we had a long night drive ahead of us, and had better be on the hike. He led us to a hitching-bar where two farm-wagons were tied, and I saw the foreign family crowding into one of them. The other was for us. Jake got on the front seat with Otto Fuchs, and I rode on the straw in the bottom of the wagon-box, covered up with a buffalo hide. The immigrants rumbled off into the empty darkness, and we followed them.

I tried to go to sleep, but the jolting made me bite my tongue, and I soon began to ache all over. When the straw settled down, I had a hard bed. Cautiously I slipped from under the buffalo hide, got up on my knees and peered over the side of the wagon. There seemed to be nothing to see; no fences, no creeks or trees, no hills or fields. If there was a road, I could not make it out in the faint starlight. There was nothing but land: not a country at all, but the material out of which countries are made. No, there was nothing but land—slightly undulating, I knew, because often our wheels ground against the brake as we went down into a hollow and lurched up again on the other side. I had the feeling that the world was left behind, that we had got over the edge of it, and were outside man's jurisdiction. I had never before looked up at the sky when there was not a familiar mountain ridge against it. But this was the complete dome of heaven, all there was of it. I did not believe that my dead father and mother were watching me from up there; they would still be looking for me at the sheep-fold down by the creek, or along the white road that led to the mountain pastures. I had left even their spirits behind me. The wagon jolted on, carrying me I knew not whither. I don't think I was homesick. If we never arrived anywhere, it did not matter. Between that earth and that sky I felt erased, blotted out. I did not say my prayers that night: here, I felt, what would be would be.

I do not remember our arrival at my grandfather's farm sometime before daybreak, after a drive of nearly twenty miles with heavy work-horses. When I awoke, it was afternoon. I was lying in a little room, scarcely larger than the bed that held me, and the window-shade at my head was flapping softly in a warm wind. A tall woman, with wrinkled brown skin and black hair, stood looking down at me; I knew that she must be my grandmother. She had been crying, I could see, but when I opened my eyes she smiled, peered at me anxiously, and sat down on the foot of my bed.

'Had a good sleep, Jimmy?' she asked briskly. Then in a very different tone she said, as if to herself, 'My, how you do look like your father!' I remembered that my father had been her little boy; she must often have come to wake him like this when he overslept. 'Here are your clean clothes,' she went on, stroking my coverlid with her brown hand as she talked. 'But first you come down to the kitchen with me, and have a nice warm bath behind the stove. Bring your things; there's nobody about.'

'Down to the kitchen' struck me as curious; it was always 'out in the kitchen' at home. I picked up my shoes and stockings and followed her through the living-room and down a flight of stairs into a basement. This basement was divided into a dining-room at the right of the stairs and a kitchen at the left. Both rooms were plastered and white-washed—the plaster laid directly upon the earth walls, as it used to be in dugouts. The floor was of hard cement. Up under the wooden ceiling there were little half-windows with white curtains, and pots of geraniums and wandering Jew in the deep sills. As I entered the kitchen, I sniffed a pleasant smell of gingerbread baking. The stove was very large, with bright nickel trimmings, and behind it there was a long wooden bench against the wall, and a tin washtub, into which grandmother poured hot and cold water. When she brought the soap and towels, I told her that I was used to taking my bath without help.

'Can you do your ears, Jimmy? Are you sure? Well, now, I call you a right smart little boy.'

It was pleasant there in the kitchen. The sun shone into my bath-water through the west half-window, and a big Maltese cat came up and rubbed himself against the tub, watching me curiously. While I scrubbed, my grandmother busied herself in the dining-room until I called anxiously, 'Grandmother, I'm afraid the cakes are burning!' Then she came laughing, waving her apron before her as if she were shooing chickens.

She was a spare, tall woman, a little stooped, and she was apt to carry her head thrust forward in an attitude of attention, as if she were looking at something, or listening to something, far away. As I grew older, I came to believe that it was only because she was so often thinking of things that were far away. She was quick-footed and energetic in all her movements. Her voice was high and rather shrill, and she often spoke with an anxious inflection, for she was exceedingly desirous that everything should go with due order and deco-rum. Her laugh, too, was high, and perhaps a little strident, but there was a lively intelligence in it. She was then fifty-five years old, a strong woman, of unusual endurance.

After I was dressed, I explored the long cellar next the kitchen. It was dug out under the wing of the house, was plastered and cemented, with a stairway and an outside door by which the men came and went. Under one of the windows there was a place for them to wash when they came in from work.

While my grandmother was busy about supper, I settled myself on the wooden bench behind the stove and got acquainted with the cat—he caught not only rats and mice, but gophers, I was told. The patch of yellow sunlight on the floor travelled back toward the stairway, and grandmother and I talked about my journey, and about the arrival of the new Bohemian family; she said they were to be our nearest neighbours. We did not talk about the farm in Virginia, which had been her home for so many years. But after the men came in from the fields, and we were all seated at the supper table, then she asked Jake about the old place and about our friends and neighbours there.

My grandfather said little. When he first came in he kissed me and spoke kindly to me, but he was not demonstrative. I felt at once his deliberateness and personal dignity, and was a little in awe of him. The thing one immediately noticed about him was his beautiful, crinkly, snow-white beard. I once heard a missionary say it was like the beard of an Arabian sheik. His bald crown only made it more impressive.

Grandfather's eyes were not at all like those of an old man; they were bright blue, and had a fresh, frosty sparkle. His teeth were white and regular—so sound that he had never been to a dentist in his life. He had a delicate skin, easily roughened by sun and wind. When he was a young man his hair and beard were red; his eyebrows were still coppery.

As we sat at the table, Otto Fuchs and I kept stealing covert glances at each other. Grandmother had told me while she was getting supper that he

was an Austrian who came to this country a young boy and had led an adventurous life in the Far West among mining-camps and cow outfits. His iron constitution was somewhat broken by moun-tain pneumonia, and he had drifted back to live in a milder country for a while. He had relatives in Bismarck, a German settlement to the north of us, but for a year now he had been working for grandfather.

The minute supper was over, Otto took me into the kitchen to whisper to me about a pony down in the barn that had been bought for me at a sale; he had been riding him to find out whether he had any bad tricks, but he was a 'perfect gentleman,' and his name was Dude. Fuchs told me everything I wanted to know: how he had lost his ear in a Wyoming blizzard when he was a stage-driver, and how to throw a lasso. He promised to rope a steer for me before sundown next day. He got out his 'chaps' and silver spurs to show them to Jake and me, and his best cowboy boots, with tops stitched in bold design—roses, and true-lover's knots, and undraped female figures. These, he solemnly explained, were angels.

Before we went to bed, Jake and Otto were called up to the living-room for prayers. Grandfather put on silver-rimmed spectacles and read several Psalms. His voice was so sympathetic and he read so interestingly that I wished he had chosen one of my favourite chapters in the Book of Kings. I was awed by his intonation of the word 'Selah.' 'He shall choose our inheritance for us, the excellency of Jacob whom He loved. Selah.' I had no idea what the word meant; perhaps he had not. But, as he uttered it, it became oracular, the most sacred of words.

Early the next morning I ran out-of-doors to look about me. I had been told that ours was the only wooden house west of Black Hawk—until you came to the Norwegian settlement, where there were several. Our neighbours lived in sod houses and dugouts—comfortable, but not very roomy. Our white frame house, with a storey and half-storey above the basement, stood at the east end of what I might call the farmyard, with the windmill close by the kitchen door. From the windmill the ground sloped westward, down to the barns and granaries and pig-yards. This slope was trampled hard and bare, and washed out in winding gullies by the rain. Beyond the corncribs, at the bottom of the shallow draw, was a muddy little pond, with rusty willow bushes growing about it. The road from the post-office came directly by our door, crossed the farmyard, and curved round this little pond, beyond which it began to climb the gentle swell of unbroken prairie to the west. There, along the western sky-line it skirted a great cornfield, much larger than any field I had ever seen. This cornfield, and the sorghum patch behind the barn, were the only broken land in sight. Everywhere, as far as the eye could reach, there was nothing but rough, shaggy, red grass, most of it as tall as I.

North of the house, inside the ploughed fire-breaks, grew a thick-set strip of box-elder trees, low and bushy, their leaves already turning yellow. This hedge was nearly a quarter of a mile long, but I had to look very hard to see it at all. The little trees were insignificant against the grass. It seemed as if the grass were about to run over them, and over the plum-patch behind the sod chicken-house.

As I looked about me I felt that the grass was the country, as the water is the sea. The red of the grass made all the great prairie the colour of wine-stains, or of certain seaweeds when they are first washed up. And there was so much motion in it; the whole country seemed, somehow, to be running.

I had almost forgotten that I had a grandmother, when she came out, her sunbonnet on her head, a grain-sack in her hand, and asked me if I did not want to go to the garden with her to dig potatoes for dinner.

The garden, curiously enough, was a quarter of a mile from the house, and the way to it led up a shallow draw past the cattle corral. Grandmother called my attention to a stout hickory cane, tipped with copper, which hung by a leather thong from her belt. This, she said, was her rattlesnake cane. I must never go to the garden without a heavy stick or a corn-knife; she had killed a good many rattlers on her way back and forth.

A little girl who lived on the Black Hawk road was bitten on the ankle and had been sick all summer.

I can remember exactly how the country looked to me as I walked beside my grandmother along the faint wagon-tracks on that early September morning. Perhaps the glide of long railway travel was still with me, for more than anything else I felt motion in the landscape; in the fresh, easy-blowing morning wind, and in the earth itself, as if the shaggy grass were a sort of loose hide, and underneath it herds of wild buffalo were galloping, galloping…

Alone, I should never have found the garden—except, perhaps, for the big yellow pumpkins that lay about unprotected by their withering vines—and I felt very little interest in it when I got there. I wanted to walk straight on through the red grass and over the edge of the world, which could not be very far away. The light air about me told me that the world ended here: only the ground and sun and sky were left, and if one went a little farther there would be only sun and sky, and one would float off into them, like the tawny hawks which sailed over our heads making slow shadows on the grass. While grandmother took the pitchfork we found standing in one of the rows and dug potatoes, while I picked them up out of the soft brown earth and put them into the bag, I kept looking up at the hawks that were doing what I might so easily do.

When grandmother was ready to go, I said I would like to stay up there in the garden awhile.

She peered down at me from under her sunbonnet. 'Aren't you afraid of snakes?'

'A little,' I admitted, 'but I'd like to stay, anyhow.'

'Well, if you see one, don't have anything to do with him. The big yellow and brown ones won't hurt you; they're bull-snakes and help to keep the gophers down. Don't be scared if you see anything look out of that hole in the bank over there. That's a badger hole. He's about as big as a big 'possum, and his face is striped, black and white. He takes a chicken once in a while, but I won't let the men harm him. In a new country a body feels friendly to the animals. I like to have him come out and watch me when I'm at work.'

Grandmother swung the bag of potatoes over her shoulder and went down the path, leaning forward a little. The road followed the windings of the draw; when she came to the first bend, she waved at me and disappeared. I was left alone with this new feeling of lightness and content.

I sat down in the middle of the garden, where snakes could scarcely approach unseen, and leaned my back against a warm yellow pumpkin. There were some ground-cherry bushes growing along the furrows, full of fruit. I turned back the papery triangular sheaths that protected the berries and ate a few. All about me giant grasshoppers, twice as big as any I had ever seen, were doing acrobatic feats among the dried vines. The gophers scurried up and down the ploughed ground. There in the sheltered draw-bottom the wind did not blow very hard, but I could hear it singing its humming tune up on the level, and I could see the tall grasses wave. The earth was warm under me, and warm as I crumbled it through my fingers. Queer little red bugs came out and moved in slow squadrons around me. Their backs were polished vermilion, with black spots. I kept as still as I could. Nothing happened. I did not expect anything to happen. I was something that lay under the sun and felt it, like the pumpkins, and I did not want to be anything more. I was entirely happy. Perhaps we feel like that when we die and become a part of something entire, whether it is sun and air, or goodness and knowledge. At any rate, that is happiness; to be dissolved into something complete and great. When it comes to one, it comes as naturally as sleep.

On Sunday morning Otto Fuchs was to drive us over to make the acquaintance of our new Bohemian neighbours. We were taking them some provisions, as they had come to live on a wild place where there was no garden or chicken-house, and very little broken land. Fuchs brought up a sack of potatoes and a piece of cured pork from the cellar, and grandmother packed some loaves of Saturday's bread, a jar of butter, and several pumpkin pies in the straw of the wagon-box. We clambered up to the front seat and jolted off past the little pond and along the road that climbed to the big cornfield.

I could hardly wait to see what lay beyond that cornfield; but there was only red grass like ours, and nothing else, though from the high wagon-seat one could look off a long way. The road ran about like a wild thing, avoiding the deep draws, crossing them where they were wide and shallow. And all along it, wherever it looped or ran, the sunflowers grew; some of them were as big as little trees, with great rough leaves and many branches which bore dozens of blossoms. They made a gold ribbon across the prairie. Occasionally one of the horses would tear off with his teeth a plant full of blossoms, and walk along munching it, the flowers nodding in time to his bites as he ate down toward them.

The Bohemian family, grandmother told me as we drove along, had bought the homestead of a fellow countryman, Peter Krajiek, and had paid him more than it was worth. Their agreement with him was made before they left the old country, through a cousin of his, who was also a relative of Mrs. Shimerda. The Shimerdas were the first Bohemian family to come to this part of the county. Krajiek was their only interpreter, and could tell them anything he chose. They could not speak enough English to ask for advice, or even to make their most pressing wants known. One son, Fuchs said, was well-grown, and strong enough to work the land; but the father was old and frail and knew nothing about farming. He was a weaver by trade; had been a skilled workman on tapestries and upholstery materials. He had brought his fiddle with him, which wouldn't be of much use here, though he used to pick up money by it at home.

'If they're nice people, I hate to think of them spending the winter in that cave of Krajiek's,' said grandmother. 'It's no better than a badger hole; no proper dugout at all. And I hear he's made them pay twenty dollars for his old cookstove that ain't worth ten.'

'Yes'm,' said Otto; 'and he's sold 'em his oxen and his two bony old horses for the price of good workteams. I'd have interfered about the horses—the old man can understand some German—if I'd 'a' thought it would do any good. But Bohemians has a natural distrust of Austrians.'

Grandmother looked interested. 'Now, why is that, Otto?'

Fuchs wrinkled his brow and nose. 'Well, ma'm, it's politics. It would take me a long while to explain.'

The land was growing rougher; I was told that we were approaching Squaw Creek, which cut up the west half of the Shimerdas' place and made the land of little value for farming. Soon we could see the broken, grassy clay cliffs which indicated the windings of the stream, and the glittering tops of the cottonwoods and ash trees that grew down in the ravine. Some of the cottonwoods had already turned, and the yellow leaves and shining white bark made them look like the gold and silver trees in fairy tales.

As we approached the Shimerdas' dwelling, I could still see nothing but rough red hillocks, and draws with shelving banks and long roots hanging out where the earth had crumbled away. Presently, against one of those banks, I saw a sort of shed, thatched with the same wine-coloured grass that grew everywhere. Near it tilted a shattered windmill frame, that had no wheel. We drove up to this skeleton to tie our horses, and then I saw a door and window sunk deep in the drawbank. The door stood open, and a woman and a girl of fourteen ran out and looked up at us hopefully. A little girl trailed along behind them. The woman had on her head the same embroidered shawl with silk fringes that she wore when she had alighted from the train at Black Hawk. She was not old, but she was certainly not young. Her face was alert and lively, with a sharp chin and shrewd little eyes. She shook grandmother's hand energetically.

'Very glad, very glad!' she ejaculated. Immediately she pointed to the bank out of which she had emerged and said, 'House no good, house no good!'

Grandmother nodded consolingly. 'You'll get fixed up comfortable after while, Mrs. Shimerda; make good house.'

My grandmother always spoke in a very loud tone to foreigners, as if they were deaf. She made Mrs. Shimerda understand the friendly intention of our visit, and the Bohemian woman handled the loaves of bread and even smelled them, and examined the pies with lively curiosity, exclaiming, 'Much good, much thank!'—and again she wrung grandmother's hand.

The oldest son, Ambroz—they called it Ambrosch —came out of the cave and stood beside his mother. He was nineteen years old, short and broad-backed, with a close-cropped, flat head, and a wide, flat face. His hazel eyes were little and shrewd, like his mother's, but more sly and suspicious; they fairly snapped at the food. The family had been living on corncakes and sorghum molasses for three days.

The little girl was pretty, but Án-tonia—they accented the name thus, strongly, when they spoke to her—was still prettier. I remembered what the conductor had said about her eyes. They were big and warm and full of light, like the sun shining on brown pools in the wood. Her skin was brown, too, and in her cheeks she had a glow of rich, dark colour. Her brown hair was curly and wild-looking. The little sister, whom they called Yulka (Julka), was fair, and seemed mild and obedient. While I stood awkwardly confronting the two girls, Krajiek came up from the barn to see what was going on. With him was another Shimerda son. Even from a distance one could see that there was something strange about this boy. As he approached us, he began to make uncouth noises, and held up his hands to show us his fingers, which were webbed to the first knuckle, like a duck's foot. When he saw me draw back, he began to crow delightedly, 'Hoo, hoo-hoo, hoo-hoo!' like a rooster. His mother scowled and said sternly, 'Marek!' then spoke rapidly to Krajiek in Bohemian.

'She wants me to tell you he won't hurt nobody, Mrs. Burden. He was born like that. The others are smart. Ambrosch, he make good farmer.' He struck Ambrosch on the back, and the boy smiled knowingly.

At that moment the father came out of the hole in the bank. He wore no hat, and his thick, iron-grey hair was brushed straight back from his forehead. It was so long that it bushed out behind his ears, and made him look like the old portraits I remembered in Virginia. He was tall and slender, and his thin shoulders stooped. He looked at us understandingly, then took grandmother's hand and bent over it. I noticed how white and well-shaped his own hands were. They looked calm, somehow, and skilled. His eyes were melancholy, and were set back deep under his brow. His face was ruggedly formed, but it looked like ashes —like something from which all the warmth and light had died out. Everything about this old man was in keeping with his dignified manner. He was neatly dressed. Under his coat he wore a knitted grey vest, and, instead of a collar, a silk scarf of a dark bronzegreen, carefully crossed and held together by a red coral pin. While Krajiek was translating for Mr. Shimerda, Ántonia came up to me and held out her hand coaxingly. In a moment we were running up the steep drawside together, Yulka trotting after us.

When we reached the level and could see the gold tree-tops, I pointed toward them, and Ántonia laughed and squeezed my hand as if to tell me how glad she was I had come. We raced off toward Squaw Creek and did not stop until the ground itself stopped—fell away before us so abruptly that the next step would have been out into the tree-tops. We stood panting on the edge of the ravine, looking down at the trees and bushes that grew below us. The wind was so strong that I had to hold my hat on, and the girls' skirts were blown out before them. Ántonia seemed to like it; she held her little sister by the hand and chattered away in that language which seemed to me spoken so much more rapidly than mine. She looked at me, her eyes fairly blazing with things she could not say.

'Name? What name?' she asked, touching me on the shoulder. I told her my name, and she repeated it after me and made Yulka say it. She pointed into the gold cottonwood tree behind whose top we stood and said again, 'What name?'

We sat down and made a nest in the long red grass. Yulka curled up like a baby rabbit and played with a grasshopper. Ántonia pointed up to the sky and questioned me with her glance. I gave her the word, but she was not satisfied and pointed to my eyes. I told her, and she repeated the word, making it sound like 'ice.' She pointed up to the sky, then to my eyes, then back to the sky, with movements so quick and impulsive that she distracted me, and I had no idea what she wanted. She got up on her knees and wrung her hands. She pointed to her own eyes and shook her head, then to mine and to the sky, nodding violently.

'Oh,' I exclaimed, 'blue; blue sky.'

She clapped her hands and murmured, 'Blue sky, blue eyes,' as if it amused her. While we snuggled down there out of the wind, she learned a score of words. She was quick, and very eager. We were so deep in the grass that we could see nothing but the blue sky over us and the gold tree in front of us. It was wonderfully pleasant. After Ántonia had said the new words over and over, she wanted to give me a little chased silver ring she wore on her middle finger. When she coaxed and insisted, I repulsed her quite sternly. I didn't want her ring, and I felt there was something reckless and extravagant about her wishing to give it away to a boy she had never seen before. No wonder Krajiek got the better of these people, if this was how they behaved.

While we were disputing about the ring, I heard a mournful voice calling, 'Án-tonia, Án-tonia!' She sprang up like a hare. *'Tatinek! Tatinek!'* she shouted, and we ran to meet the old man who was coming toward us. Ántonia reached him first, took his hand and kissed it. When I came up, he touched my shoulder and looked searchingly down into my face for several seconds. I became somewhat embarrassed, for I was used to being taken for granted by my elders.

We went with Mr. Shimerda back to the dugout, where grandmother was waiting for me. Before I got into the wagon, he took a book out of his pocket, opened it, and showed me a page with two alphabets, one English and the other Bohemian. He placed this book in my grandmother's hands, looked at her entreatingly, and said, with an earnestness which I shall never forget, 'Te-e-ach, te-e-ach my Án-tonia!'

The Immigrant in American History

by John Higham

In the late 1770's a well-to-do French farmer who had settled in the Hudson River Valley posed a question that has fascinated subsequent generations and reverberated through American history. "What then is the American, this new man?" asked St. John de Crèvecoeur in writing an affectionate sketch of his adopted country. Crèvecoeur's answer elaborated a claim already advanced by another recent arrival from Europe, Tom Paine. Paine's famous revolutionary pamphlet, *Common Sense* (1776), was the first stentorian call for independence from Britain. It declared, and Crèvecoeur heartily agreed, that the Americans were not transplanted Englishmen. They were a mixture of many European peoples, a nation of immigrants.

The idea that all Americans, except possibly the Indians, once were immigrants has never had unqualified acceptance. It was undoubtedly a minority view in Crèvecoeur's time. John Jay, writing the second of the *Federalist* papers, probably commanded wider assent. Jay defined Americans as "one united people—a people descended from the same ancestors, speaking the same language, professing the same religion, attached to the same principles of government, very similar in their manners and customs." Many writers still describe America not as an eclectic and cosmopolitan society, but as the creation of one dominating group. Today a unitary conception of America, emphasizing stability and power rather than migration and freedom, crops up on the left as well as on the right.

Both interpretations tell us something about the American conundrum; but neither Crèvecoeur nor Jay comprehended its complexity. Diversity and homogeneity intertwine so densely in American experience that neither theme alone can do it justice. This complicates enormously the problem of understanding immigration. The historian must thread his way between rival legends, each an amalgam of partial truths and potent myths. One legend puts the immigrant, and all he represents, at the center of American experience. Another relegates him to the periphery.

In recent years the legend of the American as immigrant has been widely stressed. One finds a classic statement in a posthumous little book written for and attributed to President John F. Kennedy, entitled *A Nation of Immigrants* (1964). The ideas summarized there influence serious scholarship as well. A British historian, making an excellent survey of American immigration, turns aside in his preface from a straightforward narrative to pay deference to the legend. Immigration, Maldwyn Jones tells us, is "America's historic *raison d'être*...the most persistent and the most pervasive influence in her development." Still more sweepingly, an eminent historian declared a few years ago that the immigrants *were* American history. An adequate description of the course and effects of immigration would require him to write the whole history of the country.

In some senses, of course, immigration does ramify into every aspect of American life. Conceived as the quintessential act of mobility, or as the starting point of the great American success story, immigration exemplifies conditions general to the whole society. Since the common experience of all Americans is the memory of displacement from somewhere else, migration may be seen as the key to the American character. In the absence of a truly rooted national tradition, Americans have been united—it might be argued—by their commitment to the future. And the future-looking orientation of the American people has shaped the most notable American traits: idealism; flexibility and adaptability to change; a dependence on the self and the immediate family more than the wider community; a high respect for personal achievement; a tendency to conform to the values of peers and neighbors instead of holding stubbornly to ancestral ways.

These are plausible attributes of migration as a social process; but they do enlarge the immigrant, as a specific type, to the dimensions of myth. In view of such large conceptions of the matter, it is little wonder that scholars have been hard put to specify what particular features of American life derive in some distinctive way from immigration. Insofar as we conceive it as a kind of rite of passage to an American identity, it eludes us as a historical variable. By visualizing the immigrant as the representative American, we may see him building America; we cannot see him changing it. Whatever significance immigration may have in some inclusive or representative way, it has also been a major differentiating force. It has separated those who bear the marks of foreign origin or inheritance from others who do not. The importance of immigration in this more limited sense—as a source of distinctions, divisions, and changes within the United States— remains as yet only dimly grasped. We shall have to disentangle the special effects of immigration from the encompassing legend; and that will require all the light comparative history can shed.

Let us begin with the word. In 1809 a traveler noted, "Immigrant is perhaps the only new word of which the circumstances of the United States has in any degree demanded the addition to the English language." The word materialized simultaneously with the creation of a national government. In 1789 Jedidiah Morse's famous patriotic textbook, American Geography, mentioned the "many immigrants from Scotland, Ireland, Germany, and some from France" who were living in New York. Paine, Crèvecoeur, and earlier writers had referred only to "emigrants." But by 1789 our language was beginning to identify newcomers with the country they entered rather than the one they had left. Thus the term immigrant presupposed the existence of a receiving society to which the alien could attach himself. The immigrant is not, then, a colonist or settler who *creates a new soci*ety and lays down the terms of admission for others. He is rather the bearer of a foreign culture.

Morse explicitly differentiated the "immigrants" from "the original inhabitants," the Dutch and English "settlers." The Dutch had planted in 1624 the settlement on the Hudson River that became the province of New York forty years later when it fell into the hands of the English. At the time of the American Revolution, Dutch was still spoken fairly extensively in churches and homes in New York and New Jersey. By that time people of English origin composed the preponderant element, as indeed they did in all thirteen states. The best estimate identifies as English about 60 per cent of the white population of 1790. Like the Dutch in New York, the English in all of the colonies before the Revolution conceived of themselves as founders, settlers, or planters—the formative population of those colonial societies— not as immigrants. Theirs was the polity, the language, the pattern of work and settlement, and many of the mental habits to which the immigrants would have to adjust. To distinguish immigration from other aspects of American history, we shall have to exclude the founders of a society from the category of immigrant.

The English seizure of the Dutch settlements illustrates another mode of ethnic aggregation that does not belong within the scope of immigration. It should not include peoples who are forcibly incorporated into the host society. Those groups join the society on terms that shape their subsequent experience in special ways. Americans tend to forget how many alien groups joined them involuntarily. The great American success story features the saga of the immigrant, for the immigrant chose America, however circumscribed was his choice and however involuntary his dislodgement from home. In the process of immigration the alien seeks a new country; and it encourages his aspiration. Most of the captured groups, on the other hand, do not fit the success story because their entry into the Anglo-American community did not depend on the real freedom and mobility that propelled the immigrant.

Two types of coercion have contributed to the peopling of the United States. The most obvious was slavery. The English founders imported African slaves who accounted in 1790 for about 19 per cent of the population of the new nation. Virtually from the beginning, blacks constituted an inferior caste in the American social order. Immigrants were expected sooner or later to blend with the rest of the society or go back where they came from. Blacks were permitted only a limited degree of assimilation, and they were unable to leave.

Meanwhile, expansion and conquest engulfed many Indian tribes and other groups already established in the New World. Unlike the Negroes and the immigrants, these groups belonged to a particular place, to which they tried to cling in their encounter with the dominant American society. The Indians, after proving resistive both to assimilation and to enslavement, were steadily driven westward. Treated as foreign nations until 1871 and expected to die out, most of them became part of the United States only when they could not otherwise survive at all. With far less cruelty and destruction, the Anglo-Americans also overran various French and Spanish settlements. In 1755, they uprooted several thousand French Acadians from villages on the Bay of Fundy and dispersed them to other English colonies. Subsequent annexations took in, and left relatively undisturbed, the languid French settlements in the Illinois country, at St. Louis and, most important, New Orleans. As a result of the War with Mexico (1846-1848) the Anglo-Americans took possession of a considerable Spanish population in the Southwest. The widely scattered "Californios" lost their patrimony and disappeared. In the Rio Grande Valley of New Mexico, on the other hand, tightly knit village settlements enabled the "Hispanos" to preserve their culture and their identity as ancient inhabitants of the place, proudly distinct from the "Anglos" around them and from the Mexican immigrants in adjacent states.

Altogether, the United States has participated in almost all of the processes by which a nation or empire can incorporate a variety of ethnic groups. It has acquired a diverse people by invasion and conquest, by enslavement, and by immigration. The one incorporative process America has not attempted on a significant scale is a federation between contiguous but unlike peoples. This is a dangerous form of nation-building. It leaves entirely distinct ethnic groups in control of different parts of the country and so leads often to disruption and secessionist movements. In Canada, Nigeria, and the old Austro-Hungarian Empire, federation gave territorially based ethnic majorities a threatening veto power against one another. When the individual American states

federated into a single national community in 1789, however, the event had no direct ethnic import. In every state of the American Union the dominant group sprang from approximately the same British ancestry. And by the time federation extended to Hawaii and Alaska, society there had been Americanized. Thus the American experience with federation has increased the variety of minorities without altering the distribution of ethnic power.

What then can be said about ethnic groups formed by the voluntary process of immigration? After taking account of the descendants of English colonizers, African slaves, and the more or less indigenous groups adopted in the course of expansion, what remains? Actually, a great deal. The 40 per cent of the white population of 1790 who were not English, plus the 46,000,000 immigrants who have entered the United States since that time, have produced a very considerable part of the American people. For example, in 1920, the best authorities estimated, nearly 15 per cent of the population of the continental United States might be ascribed to German immigration and another 10 per cent attributed to southern—i.e., Catholic—Ireland (Table 1).

Suggestive though such figures are, they leave us uncertain about the extent to which most people actually identify with the origins imputed to them. The effort in the 1920's to assign all Americans to specific national origins arose at a time of unusual anxiety over the menace of immigration to the whole social order. It assumed that nearly everyone had a clear ethnic identity: an uncomplicated attachment to a specific line of descent originating outside the United States. The assumption that we are all ethnics—an assumption shared by some who would disdain to think of themselves as immigrants—has never been testable because the boundaries of most American ethnic groups are so vague. A second attempt to determine the ethnic composition of the American people was made in 1972 by census-takers who asked a broad national sample, "What is your origin or descent?" If the respOndents said they were "American," the interviewers probed for a more specific and earlier origin. A large proportion of the white respondents, however—about four out of every ten—would not claim descent from any of the eight nationalities which the census-takers offered as possible choices. Some of this unclassified population can be assigned to small national strains, such as the Swedish and the Dutch; some were simply uncooperative. But a great many derived from an ancestry that was either too mixed or too remote from European antecedents to sustain any consciousness of an Old World heritage.

The size of the unclassified group in the 1972 ethnic survey is one indication of a gradual erosion that besets American immigrant groups after the supply of fresh immigration has dwindled. At some point the initial effort to constitute an organized group life is succeeded by a struggle to survive. A strong religious heritage, compact settlement, or pronounced phenotypical characteristics will check the decline. Intergroup conflict may reverse it. In the typical process of

development, however, a substantial proportion of every generation after the first marries outside the group and becomes more interested in other associations. Those who lose close contact with their immigrant origins are assimilated into a partially de-ethnicized host society.

On the other hand, the triumph of assimilation is not nearly as complete or as rapid as the official ideal of the melting pot has sometimes persuaded us to think. For many, ethnic identity remains a viable option. Almost every ethnic group that has survived its formative encounter with American culture retains a loyal core, which keeps it alive and encourages a periodic rekindling of group consciousness. In recent years a renewed appreciation of the ethnic bond as a source of political power and personal integration has inspired scholars to look more closely than ever before at its persistence in American politics. Much research has shown that people usually inherit their politi-

TABLE 1. National and Racial Origins, Population of the United States: 1920 and 1972 (in thousands)

	1920 NATIONAL ORIGINS ASCRIBED		PER CENT	1972 NATIONAL ORIGINS DECLARED	PER CENT
British (inc. Anglo-Canadian)		42,066	39.5	29,548	14.4
German		15,489	14.6	25,543	12.5
Irish		10,653	10.0	16,408	8.0
Polish		3,893	3.7	5,105	2.5
Italian		3,462	3.3	8,764	4.3
French (inc. Fr.-Canadian)		3,029	2.8	5,420	2.6
Russian		1,661	1.6	2,188	1.1
Spanish (inc. Sp.-American)		1,313	1.2	9,178	4.5
Other white		13,140	12.3	77,031	37. 6
Swedish	1,977		1.9		
Dutch	1,881		1.8		
Norwegian	1,419		1.3		
Negro		10,463	9.8	22,737	11.1
Indian		244	0.2	819	0.4
Asian		182	0.2	2,099	1.0

Sources: Adapted from Warren S. Thompson and P. K. Whelpton, *Population Trends in the United States* (New York, 1933), 90-91; Leon S. Truesdell, *The Canadian Born in the United States* (New Haven, 1943), 60; U.S. Bureau of the Census, *Statistical Abstract of the United States: 1973* (Washington, D.C., 1973), 30, 34; U.S. Bureau of the Census, "Characteristics of the Population by Ethnic Origin: March 1972 and 1971," *Current Population Reports*, P-20, No. 249 (Washington, D.C., 1973), 19. Data on racial groups are not included in the 1972 study of ethnic origins, although it encompasses a cross section of the entire population. I have therefore used the 1970 Census to fractionalize the 50.1 per cent who are grouped as "Other" and "No Report" in the 1972 study.

cal predispositions. They grow up with, and commonly pass on to their children, a set of values that defines their friends, their enemies, and ultimately themselves. To take an extreme example, the Irish were already enthusiastic Jeffersonians in 1800—"the most God-provoking Democrats this side of Hell," Uriah Tracy called them. One hundred and seventy-two years later their stronghold—Massachusetts—was the only state the Democratic party carried.

The wider significance of these new studies is still obscure. One scholar, examining the history of New Haven, Connecticut, has hypothesized that ethnic voting becomes most salient in the second or third generation, when the emergent ethnic group has produced a middle class capable of providing skilled and visible leadership. Yet we also know that the attainment of middle-class status tends to weaken ethnic identity by tempting the recipients of that status into new residential and friendship patterns; occupation replaces ancestry as the foundation of social life. There may be an irony here: ethnic voting intensifies as ethnic identity becomes problematical.

Between evidence of some striking continuities in ethnic life and contrary evidence of great flux and change, reconciliation seems impossible without appreciating the characteristic indistinctness of national and class boundaries in American society. "The distinctions among groups, whether identified as occupational class or ascribed status groupings, tend to merge, almost imperceptibly, into one another," a leading sociologist has concluded. "Thus the 'model' of urban pluralism that we see developing for the American case must necessarily take into account the relatively high permeability of the boundaries between groups and the corresponding tendencies toward fusion." Due to this permeability, it has been possible to shed the outward marks of foreign origin without undergoing total assimilation. Some differences of attitude and world-view linger after the group itself has ceased to figure largely in a person's consciousness. In other countries minorities usually stand out more sharply. Either a more complete absorption is demanded, as in the case of Brazil, or a fuller separateness is tolerated, as in Canada. In the United States, Joshua Fishman has

said, ethnicity has learned a great secret: "To exist and yet not to exist, to be needed and yet to be unimportant, to be different and yet to be the same, to be integrated and yet to be separate."

Thus, leaving aside the special situation of the indigenous groups and the blacks, American society may be visualized as a cluster of immigrant-ethnic communities lapped by an expanding core population of mixed origins and indeterminate size. An inflow from the ethnic communities slowly enlarges the fuzzy perimeter of the core population. Cross-cut with memories of ancestral diversities, the host society becomes less and less capable of defining itself in an exclusive way. The Pilgrim and the Puritan have faded as American symbols. Craggy-featured Uncle Sam has gone too, and the Statue of Liberty has largely replaced Plymouth Rock. The newly minted term WASP became in the 1960's the only ethnic slur that could safely be used in polite company; for it was part of a largely successful assault on certain remaining bastions of ethnic exclusiveness.

Although the immigrant sector has at times been large in America, it has never been overwhelming. Some other new countries present more striking statistics. For example, Canada's people in 1911 were 22 per cent foreign-born. In Argentina nearly one-third of the population in 1914 was foreign-born. Foreigners outnumbered natives in some provinces of Canada and Argentina by two to one. In Buenos Aires, they comprised three-fourths of all adults. Immigration never reached anything like those heights in the United States. At most, the proportion of the foreign-born was half as great as it was in Argentina. Immigrants rarely exceeded a third of the population in a state, and then only in an occasional frontier state during its early years. Wisconsin was 36 per cent foreign-born in 1850, Nevada 44 per cent in 1870, North Dakota 43 per cent in 1890. But these levels fell off sharply in later decades. First- and second-generation immigrants combined never exceeded 35 per cent of the total American population (Table 2).

In some states and localities at certain periods the impact of immigration has indeed been massive. At the time of the American Revolution, German stock alone comprised about a third of the population of Pennsylvania, to say nothing of the many Ulstermen from Northern Ireland. At the time of the Civil War, more than half the residents of Chicago, Milwaukee, and St. Louis were foreign-born. In Milwaukee in the late nineteenth century, 20 per cent of the adult population could not speak English. At the beginning of the twentieth century 75 per cent of Minnesota, 71 per cent of Wisconsin, 64 per cent of Rhode Island, 62 per cent of Massachusetts, and 61 per cent of Utah were people with at least one parent born outside the United States. The great immigration of the early twentieth century concentrated heavily on the cities, so that three-quarters of the population of New York, Chicago, Cleveland, Detroit, and Boston consisted of first- and second-generation immigrants in 1910. But the immigrants never swamped the older Americans in any major city because the latter participated in the urban movement just as vigorously as did the immigrants. The proportion of foreign-born in the twenty-five principal cities actually declined steadily every decade after 1860.

More important, the sheer size of the immigrant population is less striking than its truly extraordinary diversity. Other immigrant-receiving countries have tended to draw disproportionately from a few favored ethnic backgrounds. In a century of immigration to Argentina, for instance, 40 per cent of the newcomers came from Italy, another 27 per cent from Spain. The same nationalities, together with a large Portuguese contingent, made up 76 per cent of Brazil's immigration. Canada, between 1851 and 1950, got almost half its immigrants from the British Isles and a quarter of the remainder from the United States. Australia, too, recruited overwhelmingly from the British Isles. As recently as 1947, only 11 per cent of the Australian white population was traceable to other origins. In contrast, the United States during the period 1820-1945 recruited 12 per cent of its total immigration from Italy, 13 per cent from Austria-Hungary and its successor states, 16 per cent from Germany, 10 per cent from Russia and Poland, 6 per cent from Scandinavia, and a third from the British Isles. New England sustained a major invasion of French Canadians. Hundreds of thousands of Mexicans poured into the Southwest. About half a

million Greeks reached the United States before the Second World War. Substantial concentrations of Japanese materialized in the San Francisco Bay area, of Finns in the lumber and copper towns of the Northwest, of Armenians in the orchards around Fresno, of Netherlanders in South Dakota and Michigan, of Portuguese in New Bedford, of Arabs in New York City. In some mining and mill towns one might find a dozen ethnic groups intermixed in more or less the same neighborhood. No other country has gathered its people from so many different sources.

TABLE 2. Foreign-Born and Their Children in the United States, 1790—1980

	FOREIGN-BORN		NATIVES OF FOREIGN OR MIXED PARENTAGE
	Number	*Per Cent of Total Pop.*	*Per Cent of Total Pop.*
1790	500,000[a]	12.8	
1800	600,000[a]	11.3	
1810	800,000[a]	11.1	
1820	1,000,000[a]	10.4	
1830	1,200,000[a]	9.3	
1840	1,400,000[a]	8.2	
1850	2,244,602	9.7	
1860	4,138,697	13.2	
1870	5,567,229	14.0	13.8
1880	6,679,943	13.3	16.5
1890	9,249,560	14.7	18.3
1900	10,444,717	13.6	20.6
1910	13,630,073	14.7	20.5
1920	14,020,203	13.7	21.5
1930	14,283,255	14.8	21.0
1940	11,656,641	8.8	17.5
1950	10,431,093	6.9	15.6
1960	9,738,143	5.4	13.6
1970	9,619,302	4.7	11.8
1980	14,079,906	6.2	

Sources: Niles Carpenter, *Immigrants and Their Children, 1920* (U.S. Bureau of the Census, Census Monographs, VII, Washington, D.C., 1927), 6, 308; *U.S. Census, 1970: Populations,* I, part 1, p. 361; Ernest Rubin, "Immigration and the Economic Growth of the U.S.: 1790-1914, *R.E.M.P. Bulletin* (Research Group for European Migration Problems), VII (Oct.-Dec. 1959), 87-95; U.S. Bureau of the Census, *U.S. Census, 1980: Summary Tape File, 3c.*

[a] Provisional estimate by Ernest Rubin.

The very diversity of the immigration makes its impact difficult to measure. In some ways diversity limited that impact. Where one immigrant culture predominates, it can impart its own distinctive flavor to an area and perhaps affect decisively the allocation of power. Thus Chinese immigration created a deep and lasting social cleavage in Malaya and Thailand, as East Indians did in Guyana. In Argentina, Latin immigration overwhelmed the Indian, mestizo, and Negro elements. A nation that had an Indian and mestizo majority in the mid-nineteenth century has become overwhelmingly white. Only tiny pockets of Indians survive, and the rural people who are identifiably mestizo have dwindled to perhaps 10 per cent of the total population. In Canada, immigration has strengthened the English culture to the disadvantage of the French, since the immigrants send their children to English-speaking schools and press for privileges that threaten the special status of French. But an influx as miscellaneous as that which the United States has received cannot easily alter preexisting relationships. Competing against one another, immigrants have ordinarily found themselves on all sides of the choices America has thrust upon them. Except in relatively isolated, rural areas, no immigrant enclave—no close-knit neighborhood or favored occupation—has been safe from invasion by some newer, less advantaged group. Employers learned to set one group against another and thus manage their labor force more easily, a policy they called "balancing nationalities." Politicians learned to rally miscellaneous support, while exploiting ethnic division, by a strategy known as "balancing the ticket." Accordingly, the immigrants have never been arrayed solidly against the native population on economic issues, and no political party has ever captured the whole "foreign vote."

All of this is not to say that immigrants have exercised only fleeting and localized influence before melting away into America's great majority. Neither the commanding position of the majority group nor the fragmentation of the immigrants into many disunited minorities deprives them of a major role in American history. To delimit the scope of their role is rather to make possible a judgment of its distinctive import. Even so, the crux of the matter still eludes us unless—concentrating on the process of immigration—we can somehow separate what it may have made possible from what it merely reinforced. No one has yet wrestled hard with that question. But we can make a tentative start by noting that immigration occurred in two large and quite distinct phases.

Beginning in the 1680's, the English colonies in America attracted a sizable, voluntary inpouring of other ethnic groups, which continued without slackening until the American Revolution. Then it resumed in 1783 and continued strong until 1803. This First Immigration, as I shall call it, followed a sharp decline in English fears of overpopulation at home and a consequent falling off of English emigration. The proprietors of the newer colonies, notably Pennsylvania and Carolina, turned to foreign sources for the people essential to their promotional designs. Prior to 1680 the occasional Scot, Irishman, or Jew had left no special imprint on the long Atlantic seaboard except in the motley Dutch town of New Amsterdam. Now advertising, the promise of religious liberty, and other inducements attracted French Huguenots, Irish Quakers, German pietists. Their coming started a wider movement—particularly from Ireland, Scotland, Switzerland, and the Rhineland—which soon acquired its own momentum. Altogether, about 450,000 immigrants arrived in the course of the eighteenth century, over half of them Irish, predominantly Presbyterian, who suffered terribly from English landlords and English mercantilist policies. The colonies, dependent on local initiative and competing with one another for people, became so avid for immigration that their Declaration of Independence in 1776 charged the king with obstructing it.

Actually, Britain permitted a latitude in the admission of foreigners to rights in her colonies that was inconceivable in the mother country or elsewhere in the world. Although the English maintained at home restrictions designed to prevent foreign immigration, their own society was too pluralistic to make a monolithic policy seem essential overseas. The crown therefore delegated the responsibility for colonization to private promoters. Within certain limits they could bring in "any other strangers that will become our loving subjects." An Act of Parliament in 1740, which applied only to America, laid down a uniform procedure for naturalizing foreign Protestants and Jews. Catholics, though denied civil rights, could not be altogether excluded from so decentralized a society. The other great colonizing powers, Spain and France, kept authority centralized and policies uniform. They admitted only native-born Catholics to their overseas domains, so immigration to those parts did not begin until after the end of the colonial era.

The United States not only had a colonial immigration, but by the time of the American Revolution a significant portion of the immigrants of the preceding century had been fully accepted in the new society. The first major ethnic crisis in American history boiled up in Pennsylvania in the 1740's, when the mushrooming German settlements temporarily seemed an unassimilable alien mass. The threat soon passed, however. The Germans proved to be disunited; and the society in which they lived was itself too differentiated to exclude them systematically. A Schwenkfelder leader wrote wonderingly in 1768, "You can hardly imagine how many denominations you will find here.... We are all going to and fro like fish in water but always at peace with each other. . . . Dear Friend, think of the unlimited freedom…and you will understand in what dangers we are concerning our children." The seduction of the children was in effect an enlargement of the core population. Consequently the founders of the new nation did not consist exclusively or perhaps even primarily of rebellious Englishmen, Germans, and the like. America's "charter group" (to use a helpful phrase Canadian sociologists have coined) was already becoming a blend—a blend not of races but of closely related ethnic strains.

This widening of the Anglo-American community took on a special ideological significance when Americans needed, in 1776 and after, to differentiate themselves from Englishmen. The immigration of the eighteenth century enabled Paine and other formulators of the national legend to claim that Americans, unlike Englishmen, are a truly cosmopolitan people, the heirs of all mankind. Thus a universalistic and eclectic sense of national identity was created. In the long run this has probably

been the most important single effect of the First Immigration. The English have tended to assume that all groups should retain their own cultural distinctiveness and remain at a comfortable distance from one another. That assumption has survived and flourished in Canada, where the English permitted the French settlers (they were not immigrants) to keep their own special privileges. Accordingly, immigrant groups also received special concessions; Canadians came to describe their society as a "mosaic." Neither Canada nor other countries that came out of the expansion of Europe have felt the deep commitment the First Immigration implanted in American culture: the commitment to breed a "new man."

The Second Immigration, like the First, lasted for a century. It ran from the 1820's to the stiff immigration restriction law of 1924. This human flood vastly extended the diversity its predecessor had created. During the first two decades of the nineteenth century war and other restraints on emigration had kept the transatlantic movement at a low level. The proportion of the foreign-born in the American population fell by the 1830's to about 8 per cent. Then a transportation revolution made America accessible from more and more remote points, while a population crisis in rural Europe and the breakdown of the traditional agricultural system put millions of people to flight. The tide surged to a high point in the 1850's, to a higher one in the early 1880's, and to a crest in the opening decade of the twentieth century. Whereas the First Immigration had been entirely white and predominantly English-speaking, the Second brought a Babel of tongues and an array of complexions ranging from the blond Scandinavian through the swarthy south Italian to the West Indian Negro. And whereas the First Immigration had been very largely Protestant, the second was heavily Catholic from the outset; and by the end of the century it was increasingly Jewish and Eastern Orthodox.

Primarily because of immigration, the Roman Catholic Church as early as 1850 became the largest single religious body in America; and so it has remained. Immigration transformed the church into an ethnic fortress, in which immigrant peoples through their own ethnic parishes, their own parochial schools, hospitals, and orphanages resisted the onslaught of the surrounding Protestant culture on their faith and traditions. As long as the Second Immigration lasted, Catholicism in America was mostly defensive and conservative: an anomaly, in spite of brave assertions to the contrary, in a Protestant country. Ultimately, however, Catholicism identified itself so closely with Americanism that Americanism ceased to be Protestant. By the 1950's, informed observers of all faiths recognized that America was no longer distinctively or predominantly a Protestant country. This in itself was a major consequence of the Second Immigration. Elsewhere in the western hemisphere, immigration has tended to reinforce, rather than alter, the preexisting religious pattern.

In the secular sphere, the Second Immigration was perhaps most important in shaping an urban, industrial way of life. On this subject, it is not possible to distinguish the influence of immigration sharply from that of other forces. Many influences intermingled in transforming the United States from a decentralized, rural republic to a consolidated, industrial nation. But a comparative approach underlines the special ways in which immigration met the demands of an urban, industrial order in the United States. To a degree unequaled elsewhere, the immigrants supplied an industrial labor force and an urban state of mind.

Initially, the promise of land and the wealth it contained lured many of the 50,000,000 people who poured out of Europe in the nineteenth and early twentieth centuries. Like the eastward migration across the Russian steppes, the overseas movement to North and South America, to Australasia, and to parts of Africa was in good part an insatiable land rush. Immigrants broke the soil and harvested the wheat of the Argentine pampas and the Canadian prairies; they cleared forests in southern Brazil; they dug gold in California and Australia; they spread rich farms over large parts of the American Middle West. Where they could acquire land, they took root. Increasingly, however, the newcomers in the immigrant-receiving countries gravitated toward the cities. This was especially so in the United States. In 1890, 62 per cent of America's foreign-

born lived in urban places, as against only 26 per cent of the native whites born of native parents.

The urban immigrants played a unique role in the United States. Industrialization in the other immigrant-receiving countries before the First World War was quite limited. They needed immigrants not only for the hard labor that built the cities and the transportation network but even more to provide a wide range of commercial, technical, clerical, and professional skills. In Canada, for example, British immigration supplied a large proportion of skilled and clerical workers in the early twentieth century. In Argentina, European immigrants virtually created an energetic middle class in a nation that had been sharply divided between a creole aristocracy and apathetic mestizo masses. Seeking immigrants as the representatives of a higher civilization, the ruling elite intended them to "Europeanize" the native population, to produce, in Sarmiento's phrase, "a regeneration of the races." The United States, on the other hand, already had its own vigorous middle class. What its more highly developed economy lacked was an industrial working class. The Second Immigration coincided with the industrialization of the United States and furnished the bulk of the manpower for it. Irish and French Canadians gave a tremendous impetus to the textile industry of New England. Germans, Jews, and Italians transformed the clothing industry of New York. A dozen nationalities collaborated in the blast furnaces and rolling mills of Pennsylvania and the meat-packing houses of the Middle West.

To make adequate use of the enormous supply of illiterate European peasants who became available around the end of the nineteenth century, it was necessary to simplify and routinize factory work. Accordingly, a dependence on unskilled immigrant labor encouraged the introduction of automatic machines and processes. In bituminous coal mining, machines which largely replaced the pick miner increased the proportion of unskilled labor. In cotton factories, automatic looms that an inexperienced immigrant could operate did the work formerly requiring skilled weavers. Only in America did the immigrants constitute a mass proletariat engaged in manufacturing; and because they did, America was able to develop to the fullest a system of mass production.

Adjustment to the standardized, mechanized life of the industrial city was a stressful, often lacerating experience, whatever resources a person brought to it. Particularly for those who started at the bottom of the ladder in an incomprehensible, alien society, the ordeal could be harrowing. In some respects, however, the immigrants were relatively well prepared to meet the challenge. The older Americans cherished ideals of individualism that were ill suited to the interdependent character of the new urban world. They were slow to respond to collective needs, slow to reach out for mutual support beyond the immediate family. The foreigners, remembering the intimate villages they had left, probably liked the big impersonal cities of America no better than most native Americans did. But the immigrant cultures were far less individualistic. In seeking means of self-protection—in striving to make their homes and jobs decent and secure—the immigrants had no inhibitions about resorting to collective action.

One means at hand was the trade union. First- and second-generation immigrants in the late nineteenth and early twentieth centuries dominated the labor movement, the most prominent leaders of which were Irish, German, and Jewish. When fully mobilized, the immigrants could throw themselves into a strike with the selfless passion of a communal uprising. But most of the unions belonged to skilled workers from northern Europe, who held aloof from the southern and eastern European masses and took pride in the exclusiveness of their craft. Throughout industrial America intricate ethnic divisions dissipated class consciousness. The immigrants tended to identify not with a downtrodden class but with exemplars of success among their own people. For most immigrants, therefore, the trade union offered a less accessible or responsive channel for collective action than the political party.

In the cities, immigrant politics was machine politics: a politics of loyalty, authority, reciprocal obligation, and personal service. Although the machine served self-interest, it worked through disciplined group effort and unquestioning obedience. Its style of operation, therefore, was antithetical to American individualism. Without the Second Immigration, the machine could hardly have become so distinctive and notable an American institution. And when its traditional ministrations could no longer cope with the immense needs of the urban masses—when the psychological "recognition" it gave and the favors and jobs it dispensed no longer appeased them—the political machines gradually adapted to the immigrants' requirements. Detroit's independent reform mayor, Hazen Pingree, showed in the 1890's how an aroused immigrant working class could be rallied to support a program of cheap transit fares and equalized taxes even against the opposition of the old-style bosses. After 1910, the Democratic machines in major cities came increasingly under the control of politicians like Alfred E. Smith of New York, who recognized the value of welfare legislation to their organizations as well as their constituents. Through a new politics of welfare, the Democratic party won the allegiance of more and more of the urban ethnic groups. In the process, it broke the Republicans' grip on the industrial states and became, after 1930, America's majority party.

While coming to terms with the city in these ways, the immigrants were also forging an urban mass culture to replace the traditions they could not transplant intact. It is hardly surprising that heterogeneous people, cut adrift from their past and caught up in the machine process, should have found the substance of a common life in the stimuli of the mass media. Beginning as early as 1835, when the Scottish-born journalist James Gordon Bennett started the raucous New York Herald, immigrants have pioneered in the production of mass culture. Hungarian-born Joseph Pulitzer modernized the sensationalism that Bennett began. Pulitzer's New York World, with its special appeal to immigrant readers, showed how a newspaper could speak for, as well as to, the urban masses. Meanwhile, a transplanted Irishman, Robert Bonner, developed the promotional techniques that created in the late 1850's the first mass-circulation weekly, the New York Ledger. Of the four outstanding editors *at t*he turn of the century who expanded the magazine audience still further, two were foreign-born— S. S. McClure and Edward Bok. The prominence of immigrant editors in *the* creation of mass-circulation newspapers and magazines suggests that the need to adjust to a cosmopolitan society and an unfamiliar culture nurtured a burning passion to communicate and an instinctive feeling for what is immediately transmissible to an amorphous public. Americans became a *nation* of newspaper readers because what they shared was not a common past but rather the immediate events of the present: the "news."

Other immigrants and their children have thronged the popular stage, the music shops of Tin Pan Alley, the film studios of Hollywood. Spyros Skouras created a theatrical empire. Edward L. Bernays professionalized the field of public relations. The early history of radio broadcasting is in large measure a story of struggle between David Sarnoff's R.C.A. and William Paley's C.B.S.—one of them a first-generation Jewish immigrant, the other a second. A remarkable number of Hollywood moguls and popular comedians in the period between the two world wars were sons and daughters of Jewish immigrants. Through their experience of displacement and assimilation, many second-generation immigrants gained a special capability for the arts of the theatre: for playing a role, for transforming the self, for projecting an instant identity, and for achieving these effects in a milieu of illusion and surprise.

There is, for example, a world of significance in the fact that few entertainers in the early twentieth century rivaled the dazzling fame of an immigrant specializing in the art of escape. Harry Houdini, America's foremost magician, billed himself "The World-Famous Self-Liberator." What captivated audiences was Houdini's symbolic re-enactment of hIs (and their) crucial experience—a very urban, very American liberation from old traditions and confining circumstances. Escape was the recurrent pattern of Houdini's formative years. His father fled Hungary to escape arrest. At twelve, the son ran away from home to escape the crushing poverty of a family dependent on an unsuccessful

rabbi who never learned to speak English. At eighteen, he eloped with a Catholic girl whose parents would not accept him. As a young magician, he began to specialize in escapes because of the enthusiasm of audiences for a stunt he called "Metamorphosis," in which two people exchange positions across a seemingly impenetrable barrier. Thereafter he acted out, more and more strenuously, the promethean fantasy of individual triumph over every external constraint. He escaped from all handcuffs and straight jackets; from iron collars, padlocked water tanks, safes, and Chinese torture devices; from jail cells, the bottom of rivers, and buried coffins. Houdini's career, like the careers of many makers of modern American mass culture, suggests how immigrants driven by the tremendous pressures for assimilation in the late nineteenth and early twentieth centuries added a searing intensity to the old American myth of freedom and mobility.

So we come finally to a paradox in assessing the impact of immigration. Clearly, it has enhanced the variety of American culture. Its diversifying influence is imprinted in the American ideal of nationality, in the American religious pattern, and in the sheer presence of so many different human types. On the other hand, the diversities have given way time and again to pressures for uniformity, which have come not just from older Americans but which immigrants and their children have also shaped and inspired. Through the systems of mass production and mass communications, America and its immigrants assimilated one another within an urban, technological culture that overrode distinctions of place, class, and ethnic type.

Yet the distinctions were never obliterated, the assimilation never wholly satisfying or complete. Today many Americans are rebuilding ethnic identities, and are discovering that America no longer looks as monolithic as it did a few years ago. Other societies have had a simpler experience with immigrant groups, either absorbing them or acquiescing in their separateness. In American life these contrary impulses mingle, their tensions unresolved, their implications still unfolding.

THE TWO WORLDS OF RACE: A HISTORICAL VIEW

by John Hope Franklin

Measured by universal standards the history of the United States is indeed brief. But during the brief span of three and one-half centuries of colonial and national history Americans developed traditions and prejudices which created the two worlds of race in modern America. From the time that Africans were brought as indentured servants to the mainland of English America in 1619, the enormous task of rationalizing and justifying the forced labor of peoples on the basis of racial differences was begun; and even after legal slavery was ended, the notion of racial differences persisted as a basis for maintaining segregation and discrimination. At the same time, the effort to establish a more healthy basis for the new world social order was begun, thus launching the continuing battle between the two worlds of race, on the one hand, and the world of equality and complete human fellowship, on the other.

For a century before the American Revolution the status of Negroes in the English colonies had become fixed at a low point that distinguished them from all other persons who had been held in temporary bondage. By the middle of the eighteenth century, laws governing Negroes denied to them certain basic rights that were conceded to others. They were permitted no independence of thought, no opportunity to improve their minds or their talents or to worship freely, no right to marry and enjoy the conventional family relationships, no right to own or dispose of property, and no protection against miscarriages of justice or cruel and unreasonable punishments. They were outside the pale of the laws that protected ordinary humans. In most places they were to be governed, as the South Carolina code of 1712 expressed it by special laws "as may restrain the disorders, rapines, and inhumanity to which they are naturally prone and inclined." A separate world for

them had been established by law and custom. Its dimensions and the conduct of its inhabitants were determined by those living in a quite different world.

By the time that the colonists took up arms against their mother country in order to secure their independence, the world of Negro slavery had become deeply entrenched and the idea of Negro inferiority well established. But the dilemmas inherent in such a situation were a source of constant embarrassment. "It always appeared a most iniquitous scheme to me," Mrs. John Adams wrote her husband in 1774, "to fight ourselves for what we are daily robbing and plundering from those who have as good a right to freedom as we have." There were others who shared her views, but they were unable to wield much influence. When the fighting began General George Washington issued an order to recruiting officers that they were not to enlist "any deserter from the ministerial army, nor any stroller, negro, or vagabond, or person suspected of being an enemy to the liberty of America nor any under eighteen years of age." In classifying Negroes with the dregs of society, traitors, and children, Washington made it clear that Negroes, slave or free, were not to enjoy the high privilege of fighting for political independence. He would change that order later, but only after it became clear that Negroes were enlisting with the "ministerial army" in droves in order to secure their own freedom. In changing his policy if not his views, Washington availed himself of the services of more than five thousand Negroes who took up arms against England.[1]

Many Americans besides Mrs. Adams were struck by the inconsistency of their stand during the War for Independence, and they were not averse to making moves to emancipate the slaves. Quakers and other religious groups organized antislavery societies, while numerous individuals manumitted their slaves. In the years following the close of the war most of the states of the East made provisions for the gradual emancipation of slaves. In the South, meanwhile, the antislavery societies were unable to effect programs of statewide emancipation. When the southerners came to the Constitutional Convention in 1787 they succeeded in winning some representation on the basis of slavery, in securing federal support for the capture and rendition of fugitive slaves, and in preventing the closing of the slave trade before 1808.

Even where the sentiment favoring emancipation was pronounced, it was seldom accompanied by a view that Negroes were the equals of whites and should become a Dart of one family of Americans. Jefferson, for example, was opposed to slavery; and if he could have had his way, he would have condemned it in the Declaration of Independence. It did not follow, however, that he believed Negroes to be the equals of whites. He did not want to "degrade a whole race of men from the work in the scale of beings which their Creator may *perhaps* have given them.... I advance it therefore, as a suspicion only, that the blacks, whether originally a distinct race, or made distinct by time and circumstance, are inferior to the whites in the endowment both of body and mind." It is entirely possible that Jefferson's later association with the extraordinarily able Negro astronomer and mathematician, Benjamin Banneker, resulted in some modification of his views. After reading a copy of Banneker's almanac, Jefferson told him that it was "a document to which your whole race had a right for its justifications against the doubts which have been entertained of them."[2]

In communities such as Philadelphia and New York, where the climate was more favorably disposed to the idea of Negro equality than in Jefferson's Virginia, few concessions were made, except by a limited number of Quakers and their associates. Indeed, the white citizens in the "City of Brotherly Love" contributed substantially to the perpetuation of two distinct worlds of race. In the 1780s, the white Methodists permitted Negroes to worship with them, provided the Negroes sat in a designated place in the balcony. On one occasion, when the Negro worshippers occupied the front rows of the balcony, from which they had been excluded, the officials pulled them from their knees during prayer and evicted them from the church. Thus, in the early days of the republic and in the place where the republic was founded, Negroes had a definite "place" in which they were expected at all times to remain. The white Methodists of New York had much the same attitude

toward their Negro fellows. Soon, there were separate Negro churches in these and other communities. Baptists were very much the same. In 1809 thirteen Negro members of a white Baptist church in Philadelphia were dismissed, and they formed a church of their own. Thus the earliest Negro religious institutions emerged as the result of the rejection by white communicants of their darker fellow worshippers. Soon there would be other institutions—schools, newspapers, benevolent societies—to serve those who lived in a world apart.

Those Americans who conceded the importance of education for Negroes tended to favor some particular type of education that would be in keeping with their lowly station in life. In 1794, for example, the American Convention of Abolition Societies recommended that Negroes be instructed in "those mechanic arts which will keep them most constantly employed and, of course, which will less subject them to idleness and debauchery, and thus prepare them for becoming good citizens of the United States." When Anthony Benezet, a dedicated Pennsylvania abolitionist, died in 1784 his will provided that on the death of his wife the proceeds of his estate should be used to assist in the establishment of a school for Negroes. In 1787 the school of which Benezet had dreamed was opened in Philadelphia, where the pupils studied reading, writing, arithmetic, plain accounts, and sewing.

Americans who were at all interested in the education of Negroes regarded it as both natural and normal that Negroes should receive their training in separate schools. As early as 1773 Newport, Rhode Island, had a colored school, maintained by a society of benevolent clergymen of the Anglican Church. In 1798 a separate private school for Negro children was established in Boston, and two decades later the city opened its first public primary school for the education of Negro children. Meanwhile, New York had established separate schools, the first one opening its doors in 1790. By 1814 there were several such institutions that were generally designated as the New York African Free Schools.[3]

Thus, in the most liberal section of the country, the general view was that Negroes should be kept out of the mainstream of American life. They were forced to establish and maintain their own religious institutions, which were frequently followed by the establishment of separate benevolent societies. Likewise, if Negroes were to receive any education, it should be special education provided in separate educational institutions. This principle prevailed in most places in the North throughout the period before the Civil War. In some Massachusetts towns, however, Negroes gained admission to schools that had been maintained for whites. But the school committee of Boston refused to admit Negroes, arguing that the natural distinction of the races, which "no legislature, no social customs, can efface renders a promiscuous intermingling in the public schools disadvantageous both to them and to the whites." Separate schools remained in Boston until the Massachusetts legislature in 1855 enacted a law providing that in determining the qualifications of students to be admitted to any public school no distinction should be made on account of the race, color, or religious opinion of the applicant.

Meanwhile, in the southern states, where the vast majority of the Negroes lived, there were no concessions suggesting equal treatment, even among the most liberal elements. One group that would doubtless have regarded itself as liberal on the race question advocated the deportation of Negroes to Africa, especially those who had become free. Since free Negroes "neither enjoyed the immunities of freemen, nor were they subject to the incapacities of slaves," their condition and "unconquerable prejudices" prevented amalgamation with whites, one colonization leader argued. There was, therefore, a "peculiar moral fitness" in restoring them to "the land of their fathers." Men like Henry Clay, Judge Bushrod Washington, and President James Monroe thought that separation—expatriation—was the best thing for Negroes who were or who would become free.[4]

While the colonization scheme was primarily for Negroes who were already free, it won, for a time, a considerable number of sincere enemies of slavery. From the beginning Negroes were bitterly opposed to it, and only infrequently did certain Negro leaders, such as Dr. Martin Delany and the Reverend Henry M. Turner, support the idea.

Colonization however, retained considerable support in the most responsible quarters. As late as the Civil War, President Lincoln urged Congress to adopt a plan to colonize Negroes, as the only workable solution to the race problem in the United States. Whether the advocates of colonization wanted merely to prevent the contamination of slavery by free Negroes or whether they actually regarded it as the just and honorable thing to do, they represented an important element in the population that rejected the idea of the Negro's assimilation into the mainstream of American life.

Thus, within fifty years after the Declaration of Independence was written, the institution of slavery, which received only a temporary reversal during the Revolutionary era, contributed greatly to the emergence of the two worlds of race in the United States. The natural rights philosophy appeared to have little effect on those who became committed, more and more, to seeking a rationalization for slavery The search was apparently so successful that even in areas where was declining, the support for maintaining two worlds of race strong. Since the Negro church and school emerged in northern communities where slavery was dying, it may be said that the free society believed almost as strongly in racial separation as it did in racial freedom.

The generation preceding the outbreak of the Civil War witnessed development of a set of defenses of slavery that became the basis much of the racist doctrine to which some Americans have subscribed from then to the present time. The idea of the inferiority of the Negro enjoyed wide acceptance among southerners of all classes and among many northerners. It was an important ingredient in the theory of society promulgated by southern thinkers and leaders. It was organized into a body of systematic thought by the scientists and social scientists of the South, out of which emerged a doctrine of racial superiority that justified any kind of control over the slave. In 1826 Dr. Thomas Cooper said that he had not the slightest doubt that Negroes were an "inferior variety of the human species; and not capable of the same improvement as the whites." Dr. S. C. Cartwright of the University of Louisiana insisted that the capacities of the Negro adult for learning were equal to those of a white infant; and the Negro could properly perform certain physiological functions only when under the control of white men. Because of the Negro's inferiority, liberty and republican institutions were not only unsuited to his temperament, but actually inimical to his well-being and happiness.

Like racists in other parts of the world, southerners sought support for their ideology by developing a common bond with the less privileged. The obvious basis was race; and outside the white race there was to be found no favor from God, no honor or respect from man. By the time that Europeans were reading Gobineau's *Inequality of Races,* southerners were reading Cartwright's *Slavery in the Light of Ethnology.* In admitting all whites into the pseudo-nobility of race, Cartwright won their enthusiastic support in the struggle to preserve the integrity and honor of *the* race. Professor Thomas R. Dew of the College of William and Mary comforted the lower-class whites by indicating that they could identify with the most privileged and affluent of the Community. In the South, he said, "no white man feels such inferiority of rank as to be unworthy of association with those around him. Color one is here the badge of distinction, the true mark of aristocracy, and all who are white are equal in spite of the variety of occupation."[5]

Many northerners were not without their own racist views and policies in the turbulent decades before the Civil War. Some, as Professor Louis Filler has observed, displayed a hatred of Negroes that gave them a sense of superiority and an outlet for their frustrations. Others cared nothing one way or the other about Negroes and demanded only that they be kept separate.[6] Even some of the abolitionists themselves were ambivalent on the question of Negro equality. More than one anti slavery society was agitated by the suggestion that Negroes be invited to join. Some members thought it reasonable for them to attend, but not to be put on an "equality with ourselves." The New York abolitionist Lewis Tappan admitted "that when the subject of acting out our profound principles in treating men irrespective of color is discussed heat is always produced."[7]

In the final years before the beginning of the Civil War, the view that the Negro was different, even inferior, was widely held in the United States. Leaders in both major parties subscribed to the view, while the more extreme racists deplored any suggestion that the Negro could ever prosper as a free man. At Peoria, Illinois, in October, 1854, Abraham Lincoln asked what stand the opponents of slavery should take regarding Negroes. "Free them, and make them politically and socially, our equals? My own feelings will not admit of this; and if mine would, we well know that those of the great mass of white people will not. Whether this feeling accords with justice and sound judgment, is not the sole question, if indeed, it is any part of it. A universal feeling, whether well or ill founded, cannot be safely disregarded. We cannot, then, make them equals."

The Lincoln statement was forthright, and it doubtless represented the views of most Americans in the 1850s. Most of those who heard him or read his speech were of the same opinion as he. In later years, the Peoria pronouncement would be used by those who sought to detract from Lincoln's reputation as a champion of the rights of the Negro. In 1964, the White Citizens Councils reprinted portions of the speech in large advertisements in the daily press and insisted that Lincoln shared their views on the desirability of maintaining two distinct worlds of race.

Lincoln could not have overcome the nation's strong predisposition toward racial separation if he had tried. And he did not try very hard. When he called for the enlistment of Negro troops, after issuing the Emancipation Proclamation, he was content not only to set Negroes apart in a unit called "U. S. Colored Troops," but also to have Negro privates receive $10 per month including clothing, while whites of the same rank received $13 per month plus clothing. Only the stubborn refusal of many Negro troops to accept discriminatory pay finally forced Congress to equalize compensation for white and Negro soldiers.[8] The fight for union that became also a fight for freedom never became a fight for equality or for the creation of one racial world.

The Lincoln and Johnson plans for settling the problems of peace and freedom never seriously touched on the concomitant problem of equality. To be sure, in 1864 President Lincoln privately raised with the governor of Louisiana the question of the franchise for a limited number of Negroes, but when the governor ignored the question the president let the matter drop. Johnson raised a similar question in 1866, but he admitted that it was merely to frustrate the design of radical reformers who sought a wider franchise for Negroes. During the two years following Appomattox southern leaders gave not the slightest consideration to permitting any Negroes, regardless of their service the Union or their education or their property, to share in the political life of their communities. Not only did every southern state refuse to permit Negroes to vote, but they also refused to provide Negroes with any of the educational opportunities that they were providing for the whites.

The early practice of political disfranchisement and of exclusion from public educational facilities helped to determine subsequent policies that the South adopted regarding Negroes. While a few leaders raised their voices against these policies and practices, it was Negroes themselves who made the most eloquent attacks on such discriminations. As early as May, 1865, a group of North Carolina Negroes told resident Johnson that some of them had been soldiers and were doing everything possible to learn how to discharge the higher duties of citizenship. "It seems to us that men who are willing on the field of battle to carry the muskets of the Republic, in the days of peace ought to be permitted to carry the ballots; and certainly we cannot understand the justice of denying the elective franchise to men who have been fighting *for* the country, while it is freely given to men who have just returned from *four* years fighting against it." Such pleas fell on deaf ears, however; and it was not until 1867, when Congress was sufficiently outraged by the inhuman black codes, widespread discriminations in the South, and unspeakable forms of violence against Negroes, that new federal legislation sought to correct the evils of the first period of Reconstruction.

The period that we know as Radical Reconstruction had no significant or permanent effect on the status of the Negro in American life. For a period of time, varying from one year to fifteen or twenty years, some Negroes enjoyed the privileges of voting. They gained political ascendancy in a very few communities only temporarily, and they never even began to achieve the status of a ruling class. They made no meaningful steps toward economic independence or even stability; in no time at all, because of the pressures of the local community and the neglect of the federal government, they were brought under the complete economic subservience of the old ruling class. Organizations such as the Ku Klux Klan were committed to violent action to keep Negroes "in their place" and, having gained respectability through sponsorship by Confederate generals and the like, they proceeded to wreak havoc in the name of white supremacy and protection of white womanhood.[9]

Meanwhile, various forms of segregation and discrimination, developed during the years before the Civil War in order to degrade the half-million free Negroes in the United States, were now applied to the four million Negroes who had become free in 1865. Already the churches rid and the military were completely segregated. For the most part the schools, even in the North, were separate. In the South segregated schools persisted, even in the places where the radicals made a halfhearted attempt to desegregate them. In 1875 Congress enacted a Civil Rights Act to guarantee the enjoyment of equal rights in carriers and all places of public accommodation and amusement. Even before it became law northern philanthropists succeeded in forcing the deletion of the provision calling for desegregated schools. Soon, because of the massive resistance in the North as well as in the South and the indifferent manner in which the federal government enforced the law, it soon became a dead letter everywhere. When it was declared unconstitutional by the Supreme Court in 1883, there was universal rejoicing, except among the Negroes, one of whom declared that they had been "baptized in ice water."

Neither the Civil War nor the era of Reconstruction made any significant step toward the permanent elimination of racial barriers. The radicals of the post-Civil War years came no closer to the creation of one racial world than the patriots of the Revolutionary years. When Negroes were, for the first time, enrolled in the standing army of the United States, they were placed in separate Negro units. Most of the liberals of the Reconstruction era called for and worked for separate schools for Negroes. Nowhere was there any extensive effort to involve Negroes in the churches and other social institutions of the dominant group. Whatever remained of the old abolitionist fervor, which can hardly be described as unequivocal on the question of true racial equality, was rapidly disappearing. In its place were the sentiments of the businessmen who wanted peace at any price. Those having common railroad interests or crop-marketing interests or investment interests could and did extend their hands across sectional lines and joined in the task of working together for the common good. In such an atmosphere the practice was to accept the realities of two separate worlds of race. Some even subscribed to the view that there were significant economic advantages in maintaining the two worlds of race.

The post-Reconstruction years witnessed a steady deterioration in the status of Negro Americans. These were the years that Professor Rayford Logan has called the "nadir" of the Negro in American life and thought. They were the years when Americans, weary of the crusade that had, for the most part, ended with the outbreak of the Civil War, displayed almost no interest in helping the Negro to achieve equality. The social Darwinists decried the very notion of equality for Negroes, arguing that the lowly place they occupied was natural and normal. The leading literary journals vied with each other in describing Negroes as lazy, idle, improvident, immoral, and criminal.[10] Thomas Dixon's novels *The Clansman* and *The Leopard's Spots* and D. W. Griffith's motion picture *The Birth of a Nation* helped to give Americans a view of the Negro's role in American history that "proved" he was unfit for citizenship, to say nothing of equality. The dictum of William Graham Sumner and his followers that "stateways cannot change folkways" convinced many Americans that legislating equality and creating one

great society where race was irrelevant was out of the question.

But many Americans believed that they *could* legislate inequality; and they proceeded to do precisely that. Beginning in 1890, one southern state after another revised the suffrage provisions of its constitution in a manner that made it virtually impossible for Negroes to qualify to vote. The new literacy and "understanding" provisions permitted local registrars to disqualify Negroes while permitting white citizens to qualify. Several states, including Louisiana, North Carolina, Oklahoma, inserted "grandfather clauses" in their constitutions in order to permit persons, who could not otherwise qualify, to vote if their fathers or grandfathers could vote in 1866. (This was such a flagrant discrimination against Negroes, whose ancestors could not vote in 1866, that the United States Supreme Court in 1915 declared the "grandfather clause" unconstitutional.) Then came the Democratic white primary in 1900 that made it impossible for Negroes to participate in local elections in the South, where, by this time, only the Democratic party had any appreciable strength. (After more than a generation of assaults on it, the white primary was finally declared unconstitutional in 1944.)

Inequality was legislated in still another way. Beginning in the 1880s, many states, especially but not exclusively in the South, enacted statutes designed to separate the races. After the Civil Rights Act was declared unconstitutional in 1883, state legislatures were emboldened to enact numerous segregation statutes. When the United States Supreme Court, in the case of *Plessy v. Ferguson,* set forth the "separate but equal" doctrine in 1896, the decision provided a new stimulus for laws to separate the races and, of course, to discriminate against Negroes. In time, Negroes and whites were separated in the use of schools, churches, cemeteries, drinking fountains, restaurants, and all places of public accommodation and amusement. One state enacted a law providing for the separate warehousing of books used by white and Negro children. Another required the telephone company to provide separate telephone booths for white and Negro customers. In most communities housing was racially separated by law or practice.[11]

Where there was no legislation requiring segregation, local practices filled the void. Contradictions and inconsistencies seemed not to disturb those who sought to maintain racial distinctions at all costs. It mattered not that one drive-in snack bar served Negroes only on the inside, while its competitor across the street served Negroes only or the outside. Both were committed to making racial distinctions; and communities where practices and mores had the force of law, the distinction was everything. Such practices were greatly strengthened when, in 1913, the federal government adopted policies that segregated the races in its offices as well as in its eating and restroom facilities.

By the time of World War I, Negroes and whites in the South and in parts of the North lived in separate worlds, and the apparatus for keeping the worlds separate was elaborate and complex. Negroes were regaled by law in the public schools of the southern states, while those in the northern ghettos were sent to predominantly Negro schools, except where their numbers were insufficient. Scores of Negro newspapers sprang up to provide news of Negroes that the white press consistently ignored. Negroes were as unwanted in the white churches as they had been in the late eighteenth century; and Negro churches of virtually every denomination were the answer for a people who had accepted the white man's religion even as the white man rejected his religious fellowship.

Taking note of the fact that they had been omitted from any serious consideration by the white historians, Negroes began in earnest write the history of their own experiences as Americans. There had been Negro historians before the Civil War, but none of them had challenged the white historians' efforts to relegate Negroes to a separate, degraded world. In 1882, however, George Washington Williams published his *History of the Negro Race in America* in order to "give the world more correct ideas about the colored people." He wrote, he said, not "as a partisan apologist, but from a love for the truth of history."[12] Soon there were other historical works by Negroes describing

their progress and their contributions and arguing that they deserved to be received into the full fellowship of American citizens.

It was in these post-Reconstruction years that some of the most vigorous efforts were made to destroy the two worlds of race. The desperate pleas of Negro historians were merely the more articulate attempts of Negroes to gain complete acceptance in American life. Scores of Negro organizations joined in the struggle to gain protection and recognition of their rights and to eliminate the more sordid practices that characterized the treatment of the Negro world by the white world. Unhappily, the small number of whites who were committed to racial equality dwindled in the post-Reconstruction years, while government at every level showed no interest in eliminating racial separatism. It seemed that Negro voices were indeed crying in the wilderness, but they carried on their attempts to be heard. In 1890 Negroes from twenty-one states and the District of Columbia met in Chicago and organized the Afro-American League of the United States. They called for more equitable distribution of school funds, fair and impartial trial for accused Negroes, resistance "by all legal and reasonable means" to mob and lynch law, and enjoyment of the franchise by all qualified voters. When a group of young Negro intellectuals, led by "W.E. B. Du Bois, met at Niagara Falls, Ontario, in 1905, they made a similar call as they launched their Niagara Movement.

However eloquent their pleas, Negroes alone could make no successful assault on the two worlds of race. They needed help—a great al of help. It was the bloody race riots in the early years of the twentieth century that shocked civic-mined and socially conscious whites into answering the Negro's pleas for support. Some whites began to take the view that the existence of two societies whose distinction was based solely on race was inimical to the best interests of entire nation. Soon, they were taking the initiative and in 1909 organized the National Association for the Advancement of Colored People. They assisted the following year in establishing the National Urban League. White attorneys began to stand with Negroes before the United States Supreme Court to challenge the "grandfather clause," local segregation ordinances, and flagrant miscarriages of justice in which Negroes were the victims. The patterns of attack developed during these years were to become invaluable later. Legal action was soon supplemented by picketing, demonstrating, and boycotting, with telling effect particularly in selected northern communities.[13]

The two world wars had a profound effect on the status of Negroes in the United States and did much to mount the attack on the two worlds of race. The decade of World War I witnessed a very significant migration of Negroes. They went in large numbers—perhaps a half-million—from the rural areas of the South to the towns and cities of the South and North. They were especially attracted to the industrial centers of the North. By the thousands they poured into Pittsburgh, Cleveland, and Chicago. Although many were unable to secure employment, others were successful and achieved a standard of living they could not have imagined only a few years earlier. Northern communities were not altogether friendly and hospitable to the newcomers, but the opportunities for education and the enjoyment of political self-respect respect were greater than they had ever been for these Negroes. Many of them felt that they were entirely justified in their renewed hope that the war would bring about a complete merger of the two worlds of race.

Those who held such high hopes, however, were naive in the extreme. Already the Ku Klux Klan was being revived—this time in the North as well as in the South. Its leaders were determined to develop a broad program to unite "native-born white Christians for concerted action in the preservation of American institutions and the supremacy of the white race." By the time that the war was over, the Klan was in a position to make capital of the racial animosities that had developed during the conflict itself. Racial conflicts had broken out in many places during the war; and before the conference at Versailles was over race riots in the United States had brought about what can accurately be described as the "long, hot summer" of 1919.

If anything, the military operations which aimed to save the world for democracy merely fixed more permanently the racial separation in the United States. Negro soldiers not only constituted entirely separate fighting units in the United States Army, but, once overseas, were assigned to fighting units with the French Army. Negroes who sought service with the United States Marines or the Air Force were rejected, while the Navy relegated them to menial duties. The reaction of many Negroes was bitter, but most of the leaders, including Du Bois, counseled patience and loyalty. They continued to hope that their show of patriotism would win for them a secure place of acceptance as Americans.

Few Negro Americans could have anticipated the wholesale rejection they experienced at the conclusion of World War I. Returning Negro soldiers were lynched by hanging and burning, even while still in their military uniforms. The Klan warned Negroes that they must respect the rights of the white race "in whose country they are permitted to reside." Racial conflicts swept the country, and neither federal nor state governments seemed interested in effective intervention. The worlds of race were growing farther apart in the postwar decade. Nothing indicated this more clearly than the growth of the Universal Negro Improvement Association, led by Marcus Garvey. From a mere handful of members at the end of the war, the Garvey movement rapidly became the largest secular Negro group ever organized in the United States. Although few Negroes were interested in settling in Africa—the expressed aim of Garvey— they joined the movement by the hundreds of thousands to indicate their resentment of the racial duality that seemed to them to be the central feature of the American social order.[14]

More realistic and hardheaded were the Negroes who were more determined than ever to engage in the most desperate fight of their lives to destroy racism in the United States. As the editor of the *Crisis* said in 1919, "We return from fighting. We return fighting. Make way for Democracy! We saved it in France, and by the Great Jehovah, we will save it in the U.S.A., or know the reason why." This was the spirit of what Alain Locke called "The New Negro." He fought the Democratic white primary, made war on the whites who consigned him to the ghetto, attacked racial discrimination in employment, and pressed legislation to protect his rights. If he was seldom successful during the postwar decade and the depression, he made it quite clear that he unalterably opposed to the un-American character of the two worlds of race.

Hope for a new assault on racism was kindled by some of the New Deal policies of Franklin D. Roosevelt. As members of the economically disadvantaged group, Negroes benefited from relief and recovery legislation. Most of it, however, recognized the existence of the two worlds of race and accommodated itself to it. Frequently bread lines and soup kitchens were separated on the basis of race. There was segregation in the employment services, while many new agencies recognized and bowed to Jim Crow. Whenever agencies, such as the Farm Security Administration (FSA), fought segregation and sought to deal with people on the basis of their needs rather than race, they came under the withering fire of the racist critics and seldom escaped alive. Winds of change, however slight, were discernible, and nowhere was this in greater evidence than in the new labor unions. Groups like the Congress of industrial trial Organizations, encouraged by the support of the Wagner Labor Relations Act, began to look at manpower resources as a whole and to attack the old racial policies that viewed labor in terms of race.

As World War II approached, Negroes schooled in the experiences of the 1920s and 1930s were unwilling to see the fight against Nazism carried on in the context of an American racist ideology. Some white Americans were likewise uncomfortable in the role of freeing Europe of a racism that still permeated the United States; but it was the Negroes who dramatized American inconsistency by demanding an end to discrimination in employment in defense industries. By threatening to march on Washington in 1941 they forced the president to issue an order forbidding such discrimination. The opposition was loud and strong. Some state governors denounced the order, and some manufacturers skillfully evaded it. But it

was a significant step toward the elimination of the two worlds.

During World War II the assault on racism continued. Negroes, more than a million of whom were enlisted in the armed services, bitterly fought discrimination and segregation. The armed services were, for the most part, two quite distinct racial worlds. Some Negro units had white of officers, and much of the officer training was desegregated. But was not until the final months of the war that a deliberate experiment was undertaken to involve Negro and white enlisted men in the same fighting unit. With the success of the experiment and with the glow of victory over Nazism as a backdrop, there was greater inclination to recognize the absurdity of maintaining a racially separate military force to protect the freedoms of the country.[15]

During the war there began the greatest migration in the history Negro Americans. Hundreds of thousands left the South for the industrial trial centers of the North and West. In those places they met hostility, but they also secured employment in aviation plants, automobile factories, steel mills, and numerous other industries. Their difficulties persisted as they faced problems of housing and adjustment. But they continued to move out of the South in such large numbers that by 1965 one-third of the twenty million Negroes in the United States lived in twelve metropolitan centers of the North and West. The ramifications of such large-scale migration were numerous. The concentration of Negroes in communities where they suffered no political disabilities placed in their hands an enormous amount of political power. Consequently, some of them went to the legislatures, to Congress, and to positions on the judiciary. In turn, this won for them political respect is well as legislation that greatly strengthened their position as citizens.

Following World War II there was a marked acceleration in the war against the two worlds of race in the United States. In 1944 the Supreme Court ruled against segregation in interstate transportation, and three years later it wrote the final chapter in the war against the Democratic white primary. In 1947 the President's Committee on Civil Rights called for the "elimination of segregation, based on race, color, creed, or national origin, from American life."[16] In the following year President Truman asked Congress to establish a permanent Fair Employment Practices Commission. At the same time he took steps to eliminate segregation in the armed services. These moves on the part the judicial and executive branches of the federal government by no means destroyed the two worlds of race, but they created a more wealthy climate in which the government and others could launch an attack on racial separatism.

The attack was greatly strengthened by the new position of world leadership that the United States assumed at the close of the war. Critics of the United States were quick to point to the inconsistencies an American position that spoke against racism abroad and countenanced it at home. New nations, brown and black, seemed reluctant to plow the lead of a country that adhered to its policy of maintaining two worlds of race—the one identified with the old colonial ruling powers and the other with the colonies now emerging as independent nations. Responsible leaders in the United States saw the weakness of their position, and some of them made new moves to repair it.

Civic and religious groups, some labor organizations, and many individuals from the white community began to join in the effort to destroy segregation and discrimination in American life. There was no danger, after World War II, that Negroes would ever again stand alone in their fight. The older interracial organizations continued, but they were joined by new ones. In addition to the numerous groups that included racial equality in their over-all programs, there were others that made the creation of one racial world their principal objective. Among them were the Congress of Racial Equality, the Southern Christian Leadership Conference, and the Student Non-Violent Coordinating Committee. Those in existence in the 1950s supported the court action that brought about the decision against segregated schools. The more recent ones have taken the lead in pressing for new legislation and in developing new techniques to be used in the war on segregation.

The most powerful direct force in the maintenance of the two worlds of race has been the state and its political subdivisions. In states and communities where racial separation and discrimination are basic to the way of life, the elected officials invariably pledge themselves to the perpetuation of the duality. Indeed, candidates frequently vie with one another in their effort to occupy the most extreme segregationist position possible on the race question. Appointed officials, including the constabulary and, not infrequently, the teachers and school administrators, become auxiliary guardians of the system of racial separation. In such communities Negroes occupy no policy-making positions, exercise no influence over the determination of policy, and are seldom even on the police force. State and local resources, including tax funds, are at the disposal of those who guard the system of segregation and discrimination; and such funds are used to enforce customs as well as laws and to disseminate information in support of the system.

The white community itself acts as a guardian of the segregated system. Schooled in the specious arguments that asserts the supremacy of the white race and fearful that a destruction of the system would be harmful to their own position, they not only "go along" with it but, in many cases, enthusiastically support it. Community sanctions are so powerful, moreover, that the independent citizen who would defy the established order would find himself not only ostracized but, worse, the target of economic and political reprisals.

Within the community many self-appointed guardians of white supremacy have emerged at various times. After the Civil War and after World War I it was the Ku Klux Klan, which has shown surprising strength in recent years. After the desegregation decision of the Supreme Court in 1954 it was the White Citizens Council, which one southern editor has called the "uptown Ku Klux Klan." From time to time since 1865, it has been the political demagogue, who has not only made capital by urging his election as a sure way to maintain the system but has also encouraged the less responsible elements of the community to take the law into their own hands.

Violence, so much a part of American history and particularly of southern history, has been an important factor in maintaining the two worlds of race. Intimidation, terror, lynchings, and riots have, in succession, been the handmaidens of political entities whose officials have been unwilling or unable to put an end to such tactics. Violence drove Negroes from the polls in the 1870s and has kept them away in roves since that time. Lynchings, the spectacular rope and faggot kind or the quiet kind of merely "doing away" with some insubordinate Negro, have served their special purpose by terrorizing whole communities of Negroes. Riots, confined to no section of the country, have demonstrated how explosive the racial situation can be in urban communities burdened with the strain of racial strife.

The heavy hand of history has been a powerful force in the maintenance of a segregated society and, conversely, in the resistance to change. Americans, especially southerners whose devotion to the past is unmatched by that of any others, have summoned history to support their arguments that age-old practices and institutions cannot be changed overnight, that social practices cannot be changed by legislation. Southerners have argued that desegregation would break down long-established customs and bring instability to a social order that, if alone, would have no serious racial or social disorders. After all, them whites "know" Negroes; and their knowledge has come from many generations of intimate association and observation, they insist.

White southerners have also summoned history to support them in their resistance to federal legislation designed to secure the civil rights of Negroes. At every level—in local groups, state governments, and in Congress—white southerners have asserted that federal civil rights elation is an attempt to turn back the clock to the Reconstruction era, when federal intervention, they claim, imposed a harsh and unjust peace.[17] To make effective their argument, they use such emotion-laden phrases as "military occupation," "Negro rule," and "black-out of honest government." Americans other than southerners have been frightened by the southerners' claim that civil

rights for Negroes would cause a return to the "evils" of Reconstruction. Insecure in their own knowledge of history, they have accepted the erroneous assertions about the "disaster" of radical rule after the Civil War and the vengeful punishment meted out to the South by the Negro and his white allies. Regardless of the merits of these arguments that seem specious on the face of them—to say nothing of their historical inaccuracy—they have served as effective brakes on the drive to destroy the two worlds of race.

One suspects, however, that racial bigotry has become more expensive in recent years. It is not so easy now as it once was to make. political capital out of the race problem, even in the deep South. Local citizens—farmers, laborers, manufacturers—have become a bit weary of the promises of the demagogue that he will preserve the integrity of the races if he is, at the same time, unable to persuade investors to build factories and bring capital to their communities. Some southerners, dependent on tourists, are not certain that their vaunted racial pride is so dear, if it keeps visitors away and brings depression to theirs economy. The cities that see themselves bypassed by a prospective manufacturer because of their reputation in the field of race relations might have some sober second thoughts about the importance of maintaining their two worlds. In a word, the economics of segregation and discrimination is forcing, in some quarters, a reconsideration of the problem.

It must be added that the existence of the two worlds of race has created forces that cause some Negroes to seek its perpetuation. Some Negro institutions, the product of a dual society, have vested interests in the perpetuation of that society. And Negroes who fear the destruction of their own institutions by desegregation are encouraged white racists to fight for their maintenance. Even where Negroes have a desire to maintain their institutions because of their honest commitment to the merits of cultural pluralism, the desire becomes a strident struggle for survival in the context of racist forces that seek with vengeance to destroy such institutions. The firing of a few hundred Negro schoolteachers by a zealous, racially oriented school board forces some second thoughts on the part of the Negroes regarding merits of desegregation.

The drive to destroy the two worlds of race has reached a new, dramatic, and somewhat explosive stage in recent years. The forces arrayed in behalf of maintaining these two worlds have been subjected to ceaseless and powerful attacks by the increasing numbers committed to the elimination of racism in American life. Through techniques of demonstrating, picketing, sitting-in, and boycotting they have not only harassed their foes but marshaled their forces. Realizing that another ingredient was needed, they have pressed for new and better laws and the active support of government. At the local and state levels they began to secure legislation in the 1940s to guarantee the civil rights of all, eliminate discrimination in employment, and achieve decent public and private housing for all.

While it is not possible to measure the influence of public opinion in the drive for equality, it can hardly be denied that over the past five or six years public opinion has shown a marked shift toward vigorous support of the civil rights movement. This can be seen in the manner in which the mass-circulation magazines as well as influential newspapers, even in the South, have stepped up their support of specific measure that have as their objective the elimination of at least the worst features of racism. The discussion of the problem of race over radio and television and the use of these media in reporting newsworthy and dramatic events in the world of race undoubtedly have had some impact. If such activities have not brought about the enactment of civil rights legislation, they have doubtless stimulated the public discussion that culminated in such legislation.

The models of city ordinances and state laws and the increased political influence of civil rights advocates stimulated new action on federal level. Civil rights acts were passed in 1957,1960,1964, and 1965 after almost complete federal inactivity in this sphere for more three-quarters of a century. Strong leadership on the part of the executive and favorable judicial interpretations of old as well as new laws have made it clear that the war against

the two worlds of race now enjoys the sanction of the law and its interpreters. In many respects constitutes the most significant development in the struggle against racism in the present century.

The reading of American history over the past two centuries impresses one with the fact that ambivalence on the crucial question of quality has persisted almost from the beginning. If the term "equal rights for all" has not always meant what it appeared to mean, the inconsistencies and the paradoxes have become increasingly apparent. This is not to say that the view that "equal rights for some" has disappeared or has even ceased to be a threat to the concept of real equality.

It is to say, however, that the voices supporting inequality, while no less strident, have been significantly weakened by the very force of the numbers and elements now seeking to eliminate the two worlds of race.

Footnotes:

1. Benjamin Quarles, *The Negro in the American Revolution* (Chapel Hill, 1961), 15-18.

2. John Hope Franklin, *From Slavery to Freedom: A History of American Negroes* (New York, 1956), 156-57.

3. Carter G. Woodson, *The Education of the Negro Prior to 1861* "Washington, D.C., 1919), 93-97.

4. P. J. Staudenraus, *The African Colonization Movement, 1816-1865* (New York, 1961), 22-32.

5. John Hope Franklin, *The Militant South, 1800-1861* (Cambridge, Mass., 1956), 83-86.

6. Louis Filler, *The Crusade Against Slavery, 1830-1860* (New York, 1960), 142-45

7. Leon F. Litwack, *North of Slavery: The Negro in the Free States, 1790-1860* (Chicago, 1961), 216-17.

8. Benjamin Quarles, *The Negro in the Civil War* {Boston, 1953), 200.

9. John Hope Franklin, *Reconstruction After the Civil War* (Chicago, 1961), 154-58.

10. Rayford W. Logan, *The Negro in American Life and Thought: The Nadir, 1877-1901* (New York, 1954), 239-74.

11. John Hope Franklin, "History of Racial Segregation in the United States," *Annals of the Academy of Political and Social Science*, CCCIV [March, 1956], 1-9.

12. George W. Williams, *History of the Negro Race in America from 1619 to 1880* (New York, 1882), x.

13. Franklin, *From Slavery to Freedom,* 437-43.

14. Edmund David Cronon, Black Moses: The Story of Marcus Garvey and the Universal Negro Improvement Association Madison, Wisc., 1951, 202-206.

15. Lee Nichols, Breakthrough on the Color Front (New York, 1954), 221-26.

16. To Secure These Rights: The Report of the President's Committee on Civil Rights (New York, 1947), 166.

17. John Hope Franklin, "As for Our History," herein, pp. 59-70.

THE BOSTONIANS

by Henry James

Olive will come down in about ten minutes; she told me to tell you that. About ten; that is exactly like Olive. Neither five nor fifteen, and yet not ten exactly, but either nine or eleven. She didn't tell me to say she was glad to see you, because she doesn't know whether she is or not, and she wouldn't for the world expose herself to telling a fib. She is very honest, is Olive Chancellor; she is full of rectitude. Nobody tells fibs in Boston; I don't know what to make of them all. Well, I am very glad to see you, at any rate.

These words were spoken with much volubility by a fair, plump, smiling woman who entered a narrow drawing-room in which a visitor, kept waiting for a few moments, was already absorbed in a book. The gentleman had not even needed to sit down to become interested: Apparently he had taken up the volume from a table as soon as he came in, and, standing there, after a single glance round the apartment, had lost himself in its pages. He threw it down at the approach of Mrs. Luna, laughed, shook hands with her, and said in answer to her last remark, 'You imply that you do tell fibs. Perhaps that is one.'

'Oh no; there is nothing wonderful in my being glad to see you, Mrs. Luna rejoined, when I tell you that I have been three long weeks in this unprevaricating city.'

'That has an unflattering sound for me,' said the young man. 'I pretend not to prevaricate.'

'Dear me, what's the good of being a Southerner?' the lady asked. 'Olive told me to tell you she hoped you will stay to dinner. And if she said it, she does really hope it. She is willing to risk that.'

'Just as I am?' the visitor inquired, presenting himself with rather a work-a-day aspect.

Mrs. Luna glanced at him from head to foot, and gave a little smiling sigh, as if he had been a long sum in addition. And, indeed, he was very long,

Basil Ransom, and he even looked a little hard and discouraging, like a column of figures, in spite of the friendly face which he bent upon his hostess's deputy, and which, in its thinness, had a deep dry line, a sort of premature wrinkle, on either side of the mouth. He was tall and lean, and dressed throughout in black; his shirt-collar was low and wide, and the triangle of linen a little crumpled, exhibited by the opening of his waistcoat, was adorned by a pin containing a small red stone. In spite of this decoration the young man looked poor—as poor as a young man could look who had such a fine head and such magnificent eyes. Those of Basil Ransom were dark, deep, and glowing; his head had a character of elevation which fairly added to his stature; it was a head to be seen above the level of a crowd, on some judicial bench or political platform, or even on a bronze medal. His forehead was high and broad, and his thick black hair, perfectly straight and glossy, and without any division, rolled back from it in a leonine manner. These things, the eyes especially, with their smouldering fire, might have indicated that he was to be a great American statesman; or, on the other hand, they might simply have proved that he came from Carolina or Alabama. He came, in fact, from Mississippi, and he spoke very perceptibly with the accent of that country. It is not in my power to reproduce by any combination of characters this charming dialect; but the initiated reader will have no difficulty in evoking the sound, which is to be associated in the present instance with nothing vulgar or vain. This lean, pale, sallow, shabby, striking young man, with his superior head, his sedentary shoulders, his expression of bright grimness and hard enthusiasm, his provincial, distinguished appearance, is, as a representative of his sex, the most important personage in my narrative; played a very active part in the events I have undertaken in some degree to set forth. And yet the reader who likes a complete image, who desires to read with the senses as well as with the reason, is entreated not to forget that he prolonged his consonants and swallowed his vowels, that he was guilty of elisions and interpolations which were equally unexpected, and that his discourse was pervaded by something sultry and vast, something almost African in its rich, basking tone, something that suggested the teeming expanse of the cotton-field. Mrs. Luna looked up at all this, but saw only a part of it; otherwise she would not have replied in a bantering manner, in answer to his inquiry: 'Are you ever different from this?' Mrs. Luna was familiar—intolerably familiar.

Basil Ransom coloured a little. Then he said: 'Oh yes: when I dine out I usually carry a six-shooter and a bowie knife.' And he took up his hat vaguely—a soft black hat with a low crown and an immense straight brim. Mrs. Luna wanted to know what he was doing. She made him sit down; she assured him that her sister quite expected him, would feel as sorry as she could ever feel for anything —for she was a kind of fatalist, any-how—if he didn't stay to dinner. It was an immense pity—she herself was going out; in Boston you must jump at invitations. Olive, too, was going somewhere after dinner, but he mustn't mind that; perhaps he would like to go with her. It wasn't a party—Olive didn't go to parties; it was one of those weird meetings she was so fond of.

'What kind of meetings do you refer to? You speak as if it were a rendezvous of witches on the Brocken.'

'Well, so it is; they are all witches and wizards, mediums, and spirit-rappers, and roaring radicals.'

Basil Ransom stared; the yellow light in his brown eyes deepened. 'Do you mean to say your sister's a roaring radical?'

'A radical? She's a female Jacobin—she's a nihilist. Whatever is, is wrong, and all that sort of thing. If you are going to dine with her, you had better know it.'

'Oh, murder!' murmured the young man vaguely, sinking back in his chair with his arms folded. He looked at Mrs. Luna with intelligent incredulity. She was sufficiently pretty; her hair was in clusters of curls, like bunches of grapes; her tight bodice seemed to crack with her vivacity; and from beneath the stiff plaits of her petticoat a small fat foot protruded, resting upon a stilted heel. She was attractive and impertinent, especially the latter. He seemed to think it was a great pity, what

she had told him; but he lost himself in this consideration, or, at any rate, said nothing for some time, while his eyes wandered over Mrs. Luna, and he probably wondered what body of doctrine *she* represented, little as she might partake of the nature of her sister. Many things were strange to Basil Ransom; Boston especially was strewn with surprises, and he was a man who liked to understand. Mrs. Luna was drawing on her gloves; Ransom had never seen any that were so long; they reminded him of stockings, and he wondered how she managed without garters above the elbow. 'Well, I suppose I might have known that,' he continued, at last.

'You might have known what?'

'Well, that Miss Chancellor would be all that you say. She was brought up in the city of reform.'

'Oh, it isn't the city; it's just Olive Chancellor. She would reform the solar system if she could get hold of it. She'll reform you, if you don't look out. That's the way I found her when I returned from Europe.'

'Have you been in Europe?' Ransom asked.

'Mercy, yes! Haven't you?'

'No, I haven't been anywhere. Has your sister?'

'Yes; but she stayed only an hour or two. She hates it; she would like to abolish it. Didn't you know I had been to Europe?' Mrs. Luna went on, in the slightly aggrieved tone of a woman who discovers the limits of her reputation.

Ransom reflected he might answer her that until five minutes ago he didn't know she existed; but he remembered that this was not the way in which a Southern gentleman spoke to ladies, and he contented himself with saying that he must condone his Boeotian ignorance (he was fond of an elegant phrase); that he lived in a part of the country where they didn't think much about Europe, and that he had always supposed she was domiciled in New York. This last remark he made at a venture, for he had, naturally, not devoted any supposition whatever to Mrs. Luna. His dishonesty however, only exposed him the more.

'If you thought I lived in New York, why in the world didn't you come and see me?' the lady inquired.

'Well, you see, I don't go out much, except to the courts.'

'Do you mean the law-courts? Every one has got some profession over here! Are you very ambitious? You look as if you were.'

'Yes, very,' Basil Ransom replied, with a smile, and the curious feminine softness with which Southern gentlemen enunciate that adverb.

Mrs. Luna explained that she had been living in Europe for several years—ever since her husband died—but had come home a month before, come home with her little boy, the only thing she had in the world, and was paying a visit to her sister, who, of course, was the nearest thing after the child. 'But it isn't the same,' she said. 'Olive and I disagree so much.'

'While you and your little boy don't,' the young man remarked.

'Oh no, I never differ from Newton!' And Mrs. Luna added that now she was back she didn't know what she should do. That was the worst of coming back; it was like being born again, at one's age—one had to begin life afresh. One didn't even know what one had come back for. There were people who wanted one to spend the winter in Boston; but she couldn't stand that—she knew, at least, what she had not come back for. Perhaps she should take a house in Washington; did he ever hear of that little place? They had invented it while she was away. Besides, Olive didn't want her in Boston, and didn't go through the form of saying so. That was one comfort with Olive; she never went through any forms.

Basil Ransom had got up just as Mrs. Luna made this last declaration; for a young lady had glided into the room, who stopped short as it fell upon her ears. She stood there looking, consciously and rather seriously, at Mr. Ransom; a smile of exceeding faintness played about her lips—it was just perceptible enough to light up the native gravity of her face. It might have been likened to a thin ray of moonlight resting upon the wall of a prison.

'If that were true,' she said, 'I shouldn't tell you that I am very sorry to have kept you waiting.'

Her voice was low and agreeable—a cultivated voice—and she extended a slender white hand to her visitor, who remarked with some solemnity (he felt a certain guilt of participation in Mrs. Luna's indiscretion) that he was intensely happy to make her acquaintance. He observed that Miss Chancellor's hand was at once cold and limp; she merely placed it in his, without exerting the smallest pressure. Mrs. Luna explained to her sister that her freedom of speech was caused by his being a relation—though, indeed, he didn't seem to know much about them. She didn't believe he had ever heard of her, Mrs. Luna, though he pretended, with his Southern chivalry, that he had. She must be off to her dinner now, she saw the carriage was there, and in her absence Olive might give any version of her she chose.

'I have told him you are a radical, and you may tell him, if you like, that I am a painted Jezebel. Try to reform him; a person from Mississippi is sure to be all wrong. I shall be back very late; we are going to a theatre-party; that's why we dine so early. Good-bye, Mr. Ransom,' Mrs. Luna continued, gathering up the feathery white shawl which added to the volume of her fairness. 'I hope you are going to stay a little, so that you may judge us for yourself. I should like you to see Newton, too; he is a noble little nature, and I want some advice about him. You only stay to-morrow? Why, what's the use of that? Well, mind you come and see me in New York; I shall be sure to be part of the winter there. I shall send you a card; I won't let you off. Don't come out; my sister has the first claim. Olive, why don't you take him to your female convention?' Mrs. Luna's familiarity extended even to her sister; she remarked to Miss Chancellor that she looked as if she were got up for a sea-voyage. 'I am glad I haven't opinions that prevent my dressing in the evening!' she declared from the doorway. 'The amount of thought they give to their clothing, the people who are afraid of looking frivolous!'

Whether much or little consideration had been directed to the result, Miss Chancellor certainly would not have incurred this reproach. She was

habited in a plain dark dress, without any ornaments, and her smooth, colourless hair was
confined as carefully as that of her sister was
encouraged to stray. She had instantly seated
herself, and while Mrs. Luna talked she kept her
eyes on the ground, glancing even less toward
Basil Ransom than toward that woman of many
words. The young man was therefore free to look
at her; a contemplation which showed him that
she was agitated and trying to conceal it. He
wondered why she was agitated, not foreseeing
that he was destined to discover, later, that her
nature was like a skiff in a stormy sea. Even after
her sister had passed out of the room she sat there
with her eyes turned away, as if there had been a
spell upon her which forbade her to raise them.
Miss Olive Chancellor, it may be confided to the
reader, to whom in the course of our history I shall
be under the necessity of imparting much occult
information, was subject to fits of tragic shyness,
during which she was unable to meet even her
own eyes in the mirror. One of these fits had
suddenly seized her now, without any obvious
cause, though, indeed, Mrs. Luna had made it
worse by becoming instantly so personal. There
was nothing in the world so personal as Mrs.
Luna; her sister could have hated her for it if she
had not forbidden herself this emotion as directed
to individuals. Basil Ransom was a young man of
first-rate intelligence, but conscious of the narrow
range, as yet, of his experience. He was on his
guard against generalisations which might be
hasty; but he had arrived at two or three that were
of value to a gentleman lately admitted to the New
York bar and looking out for clients. One of them
was to the effect that the simplest division it is
possible to make of the human race is into the
people who take things hard and the people who
take them easy. He perceived very quickly that
Miss Chancellor belonged to the former class. This
was written so intensely in her delicate face that he
felt an unformulated pity for her before they had
exchanged twenty words. He himself, by nature,
took things easy; if he had put on the screw of late,
it was after reflection, and because circumstances
pressed him close. But this pale girl, with her light-
green eyes, her pointed features and nervous
manner, was visibly morbid; it was as plain as day
that she was morbid. Poor Ransom announced this

fact to himself as if he had made a great discovery,
but in reality he had never been so 'Boeotian' as at
that moment. It proved nothing of any importance, with regard to Miss Chancellor, to say that
she was morbid; any sufficient account of her
would lie very much to the rear of that. Why was
she morbid, and why was her morbidness typical?
Ransom might have exulted if he had gone back
far enough to explain that mystery. The women he
had hitherto known had been mainly of his own
soft clime, and it was not often they exhibited the
tendency he detected (and cursorily deplored) in
Mrs. Luna's sister. That was the way he liked
them—not to think too much, not to feel any
responsibility for the government of the world,
such as he was sure Miss Chancellor felt. If they
would only be private and passive, and have no
feeling but for that, and leave publicity to the sex
of tougher hide! Ransom was pleased with the
vision of that remedy; it must be repeated that he
was very provincial.

These considerations were not present to him as
definitely as I have written them here; they were
summed up in the vague compassion which his
cousin's figure excited in his mind, and which was
yet accompanied with a sensible reluctance to
know her better, obvious as it was that with such a
face as that she must be remarkable. He was sorry
for her, but he saw in a flash that no one could
help her: that was what made her tragic. He had
not, seeking his fortune, come away from the
blighted South, which weighed upon his heart, to
look out for tragedies; at least he didn't want them
outside of his office in Pine Street. He broke the
silence ensuing upon Mrs. Luna's departure by
one of the courteous speeches to which blighted
regions may still encourage a tendency, and
presently found himself talking comfortably
enough with his hostess. Though he had said to
himself that no one could help her, the effect of his
tone was to dispel her shyness; it was her great
advantage (for the career she had proposed to
herself) that in certain conditions she was liable
suddenly to become bold. She was reassured at
finding that her visitor was peculiar; the way he
spoke told her that it was no wonder he had
fought on the Southern side. She had never yet
encountered a personage so exotic, and she always

felt more at her ease in the presence of anything strange. It was the usual things of life that filled her with silent rage; which was natural enough, inasmuch as, to her vision, almost everything that was usual was iniquitous. She had no difficulty in asking him now whether he would not stay to dinner—she hoped Adeline had given him her message. It had been when she was upstairs with Adeline, as his card was brought up, a sudden and very abnormal inspiration to offer him this (for her) really ultimate favour; nothing could be further from her common habit than to entertain alone, at any repast, a gentleman she had never seen.

It was the same sort of impulse that had moved her to write to Basil Ransom, in the spring, after hearing accidentally that he had come to the North and intended, in New York, to practise his profession. It was her nature to look out for duties, to appeal to her conscience for tasks. This attentive organ, earnestly consulted, had represented to her that he was an offshoot of the old slave-holding oligarchy which, within her own vivid remembrance, had plunged the country into blood and tears, and that, as associated with such abominations, he was not a worthy object of patronage for a person whose two brothers—her only ones—had given up life for the Northern cause. It reminded her, however, on the other hand, that he too had been much bereaved, and, moreover, that he had fought and offered his own life, even if it had not been taken. She could not defend herself against a rich admiration—a kind of tenderness of envy—of any one who had been so happy as to have that opportunity. The most secret, the most sacred hope of her nature was that she might some day have such a chance, that she might be a martyr and die for something. Basil Ransom had lived, but she knew he had lived to see bitter hours. His family was ruined; they had lost their slaves, their property, their friends and relations, their home; had tasted of all the cruelty of defeat. He had tried for a while to carry on the plantation himself, but he had a millstone of debt round his neck, and he longed for some work which would transport him to the haunts of men. The State of Mississippi seemed to him the state of despair; so he surrendered the remnants of his patrimony to his mother

and sisters, and, at nearly thirty years of age, alighted for the first time in New York, in the costume of his province, with fifty dollars in his pocket and a gnawing hunger in his heart.

That this incident had revealed to the young man his ignorance of many things—only, however, to make him say to himself, after the first angry blush, that here he would enter the game and here he would win it—so much Olive Chancellor could not know; what was sufficient for her was that he had rallied, as the French say, had accepted the accomplished fact, had admitted that North and South were a single, indivisible political organism. Their cousinship—that of Chancellors and Ransoms—was not very close; it was the kind of thing that one might take up or leave alone, as one pleased. It was 'in the female line,' as Basil Ransom had written, in answering her letter with a good deal of form and flourish; he spoke as if they had been royal houses. Her mother had wished to take it up; it was only the fear of seeming patronising to people in misfortune that had prevented her from writing to Mississippi. If it had been possible to send Mrs. Ransom money, or even clothes, she would have liked that; but she had no means of ascertaining how such an offering would be taken. By the time Basil came to the North—making advances, as it were—Mrs. Chancellor had passed away; so it was for Olive, left alone in the little house in Charles Street (Adeline being in Europe), to decide.

She knew what her mother would have done, and that helped her decision; for her mother always chose the positive course. Olive had a fear of everything, but her greatest fear was of being afraid. She wished immensely to be generous, and how could one be generous unless one ran a risk? She had erected it into a sort of rule of conduct that whenever she saw a risk she was to take it; and she had frequent humiliations at finding herself safe after all. She was perfectly safe after writing to Basil Ransom, and, indeed, it was difficult to see what he could have done to her except thank her (he was only exceptionally superlative) for her letter, and assure her that he would come and see her the first time his business (he was beginning to get a little) should take him to Boston. He had now come, in redemption of his grateful vow, and even this did not make Miss Chancellor feel that she had courted danger. She saw (when once she had looked at him) that he would not put those worldly interpretations on things which, with her, it was both an impulse and a principle to defy. He was too simple—too Mississippian—for that; she was almost disappointed. She certainly had not hoped that she might have struck him as making unwomanly overtures (Miss Chancellor hated this epithet almost as much as she hated its opposite); but she had a presentiment that he would be too good-natured, primitive to that degree. Of all things in the world contention was most sweet to her (though why it is hard to imagine, for it always cost her tears, headaches, a day or two in bed, acute emotion), and it was very possible Basil Ransom would not care to contend. Nothing could be more displeasing than this indifference when people didn't agree with you. That he should agree she did not in the least expect of him; how could a Mississippian agree? If she had supposed he would agree, she would not have written to him.

The Sheriff's Children

by Charles W. Chestnutt

(The first pages of this story describe the village of Troy, county seat of Branson County, North Carolina.)

A murder was a rare event in Branson County. Every well-informed citizen could tell the number of homicides committed in the county for fifty years back, and whether the slayer in any given instance had escaped, either by flight or acquittal, or had suffered the penalty of the law. So when it became known in Troy early one Friday morning in summer, about ten years after the war, that old Captain Walker, who had served in Mexico under Scott and had left an arm on the field of Gettysburg, had been foully murdered during the night, there was intense excitement in the village. Business was practically suspended, and the citizens gathered in little groups to discuss the murder and speculate upon the identity of the murderer. It transpired from testimony at the coroner's inquest held during the morning, that a strange mulatto had been met going away from Troy early Friday morning by a farmer on his way to town. Other circumstances seemed to connect the stranger with the crime. The sheriff organized a posse to search for him, and early in the evening, when most of the citizens of Troy were at supper, the suspected man was brought in and lodged in the county jail.

By the following morning the news of the capture had spread to the farthest limits of the county. A much larger number of people than usual came to town that Saturday—bearded men in straw hats and blue homespun shirts, and butternut trousers of great amplitude of material and vagueness of outline; women in homespun frocks and slat-bonnets, with faces as expressionless as the dreary sandhills which gave them a meager sustenance.

The murder was almost the sole topic of conversation. A steady stream of curious observers visited the house of mourning and gazed upon the rugged face of the old veteran, now stiff and cold in death;

and more than one eye dropped a tear at the remembrance of the cheery smile, and the joke—sometimes superannuated, generally feeble, but always good-natured—with which the captain had been wont to greet his acquaintances. There was a growing sentiment of anger among these stern men toward the murderer who had thus cut down their friend, and a strong feeling that ordinary justice was too slight a punishment for such a crime.

Toward noon there was an informal gathering of citizens in Dan Ayson's store.

"I hear it 'lowed that Square Kyahtah's too sick ter hol' co'te this evenin'," said one, "an' that the purlim'nary hearin' 'll haf ter go over 'tel nex' week." A look of disappointment went round the crowd.

"Hit's the durndes', meanes' murder ever committed in this caounty," said another, with moody emphasis.

"I s'pose the nigger 'lowed the Cap'n had some greenbacks," observed a third speaker.

"The Cap'n," said another, with an air of superior information, "has left two bairls of Confedrit money, which he 'spected'd be good some day er nuther."

This statement gave rise to a discussion of the speculative value of Confederate money; but in a little while the conversation returned to the murder.

"Hangin' air too good fer the murderer," said one; "he oughter be burnt, stider bein' hung."

There was an impressive pause at this point, during which a jug of moonlight whiskey went the round of the crowd.

"Well," said a round-shouldered farmer who, in spite of his peaceable expression and faded gray eye, was known to have been one of the most daring followers of a rebel guerrilla chieftain, "what air ye gwine ter do about it? Ef you fellers air gwine ter set down an' let a wuthless nigger kill the bes' white man in Branson, an' not say nuthin' ner do nuthin', *I'll* move outen the caounty."

This speech gave tone and direction to the rest of the conversation. Whether the fear of losing the round-shouldered farmer operated to bring about the result or not is immaterial to this narrative; but at all events the crowd decided to lynch the Negro. They agreed that this was the least that could be done to avenge the death of their murdered friend, and that it was a becoming way in which to honor his memory. They had some vague notions of the majesty of the law and the rights of the citizen, but in the passion of the moment these sunk into oblivion; a white man had been killed by a Negro.

"The Cap'n was an ole sodger," said one of his friends solemnly. "He'll sleep better when he knows that a co'te-martial has be'n hilt an' jestice done."

By agreement the lynchers were to meet at Tyson's store at five o'clock in the afternoon and proceed thence to the jail, which was situated down the Lumberton Dirt Road (as the old turnpike antedating the plank-road was called) about half a mile south of the court house. When the preliminaries of the lynching had been arranged and a committee appointed to manage the affair, the crowd dispersed, some to go to their dinners and some to secure recruits for the lynching party.

It was twenty minutes to five o'clock when an excited Negro, panting and perspiring, rushed up to the back door of Sheriff Campbell's dwelling, which stood at a little distance from the jail and somewhat farther than the latter building from the courthouse. A turbaned colored woman came to the door in response to the Negro's knock.

"Hoddy, Sis' Nance."

"Hoddy, Brer Sam."

"Is de shurff in?" inquired the Negro.

"Yas, Brer Sam, he's eatin' his dinner," was the answer.

"Will yer ax 'im ter step ter de do' a minute, Sis' Nance?"

The woman went into the dining room, and a moment later the sheriff came to the door. He was a tall, muscular man, of a ruddier complexion than is usual among Southerners. A pair of keen, deep-set gray eyes looked out from under bushy eyebrows, and about his mouth was a masterful expression, which a full beard, once sandy in color but now profusely sprinkled with gray, could not entirely conceal. The day was hot; the sheriff had discarded his coat and vest, and had his white shirt open at the throat.

"What do you want, Sam?" he inquired of the Negro, who stood hat in hand, wiping the moisture from his face with a ragged shirt-sleeve.

"Shurff, dey gwine ter hang de pris'ner w'at lock' up in de jail. Dey're comin' dis a-way now. I wuz layin' down on a sack er corn down at de sto', behine a pile er flour-bairls, w'en I hearn Doc' Cain en Kunnel Wright talkin' erbout it. I slip' outen de back do', en run here as fas' as I could. I hearn you say down ter de sto' once't dat you wouldn't let nobody take a pris'ner 'way fum you widout walkin' over yo' dead body, en I thought I'd let you know 'fo' dey come, so yer could pertec' de pris'ner."

The sheriff listened calmly, but his face grew firmer, and a determined gleam lit up his gray eyes. His frame grew more erect, and he unconsciously assumed the attitude of a soldier who momentarily expects to meet the enemy face to face.

"Much obliged, Sam," he answered. "I'll protect the prisoner. Who's coming?"

"I dunno who-all *is* comin'," replied the Negro. "Dere's Mistah McSwayne, en Doc' Cain, en Maje' McDonal', and Kunnel Wright en a heap er yuthers. I wuz so skeered I done furgot mo' d'n half un em. I spec' dey mus' be mos' here by dis time, so I'll git outen de way, fer I don't want nobody fer ter think I wuz mix' up in dis business." The Negro glanced nervously down the road toward the town, and made a movement as if to go away.

"Won't you have some dinner first?" asked the sheriff.

The Negro looked longingly in at the open door, and sniffed the appetizing odor of boiled pork and collards.

"I ain't got no time fer ter tarry, Shurff," he said, "but Sis' Nance mought gin me sump'n I could kyar in my han' en eat on de way."

A moment later Nancy brought him a huge sandwich of split cornpone, with a thick slice of fat bacon inserted between the halves, and a couple of baked yams. The Negro hastily replaced his ragged hat on his head, dropped the yams in the pocket of his capacious trousers and, taking the sandwich in his hand, hurried across the road and disappeared in the woods beyond.

The sheriff reentered the house, and put on his coat and hat. He then took down a double-barreled shotgun and loaded it with buckshot. Filling the chambers of a revolver with fresh cartridges, he slipped it into the pocket of the sackcoat which he wore.

A comely young woman in a calico dress watched these proceedings with anxious surprise.

"Where are you going, Father?" she asked. She had not heard the conversation with the Negro.

"I am goin' over to the jail," responded the sheriff. "There's a mob comin' this way to lynch the nigger we've got locked up. But they won't do it," he added, with emphasis.

"Oh, Father, don't go!" pleaded the girl, clinging to his arm. "They'll shoot you if you don't give him up."

"You never mind me, Polly," said her father reassuringly, as he gently unclasped her hands from his arm. "I'll take care of myself and the prisoner, too. There ain't a man in Branson County that would shoot me. Besides, I have faced fire too often to be scared away from my duty. You keep close in the house," he continued, "and if anyone disturbs you just use the old horse-pistol in the top bureau drawer. It's a little old-fashioned, but it did good work a few years ago."

The young girl shuddered at this sanguinary allusion, but made no further objection to her father's departure.

The sheriff of Branson was a man far above the average of the community in wealth, education, and social position. His had been one of the few families in the county that before the war had owned large estates and numerous slaves. He had graduated at the State University at Chapel Hill, and had kept up some acquaintance with current literature and advanced thought. He had traveled some in his youth, and was looked up to in the county as an authority on all subjects connected with the outer world. At first an ardent supporter of the Union, he had opposed the secession movement in his native state as long as opposition availed to stem the tide of public opinion. Yielding at last to the force of circumstances, he had entered the Confederate service rather late in the war and served with distinction through several campaigns, rising in time to the rank of colonel. After the war he had taken the oath of allegiance, and had been chosen by the people as the most available candidate for the office of sheriff, to which he had been elected without opposition. He had filled the office for several terms and was universally popular with his constituents.

Colonel or Sheriff Campbell, as he was indifferently called, as the military or civil title happened to be most important in the opinion of the person addressing him, had a high sense of the responsibility attached to his office. He had sworn to do his duty faithfully, and he knew what his duty was as sheriff perhaps more clearly than he had apprehended it in other passages of his life. It was therefore with no uncertainty in regard to his course that he prepared his weapons and went over to the jail. He had no fears for Polly's safety.

The sheriff had just locked the heavy front door of the jail behind him when a half dozen horsemen, followed by a crowd of men on foot, came round a bend in the road and drew near the jail. They halted in front of the picket fence that surrounded the building, while several of the committee of arrangements rode on a few rods farther to the sheriff's house. One of them dismounted and rapped on the door with his riding whip.

"Is the sheriff at home?" he inquired.

"No, he has just gone out," replied Polly, who had come to the door.

"We want the jail keys," he continued.

"They are not here," said Polly. "The sheriff has them himself." Then she added, with assumed indifference, "He is at the jail now."

The man turned away, and Polly went into the front room, from which she peered anxiously between the slats of the green blinds of a window that looked toward the jail. Meanwhile the messenger returned to his companions and announced his discovery. It looked as though the sheriff had learned of their design and was preparing to resist it.

One of them stepped forward and rapped on the jail door.

"Well, what is it?" said the sheriff, from within.

"We want to talk to you, Sheriff," replied the spokesman.

There was a little wicket in the door; this the sheriff opened, and answered through it.

"All right, boys, talk away. You are all strangers to me, and I don't know what business you can have." The sheriff did not think it necessary to recognize anybody in particular on such an occasion; the question of identity sometimes comes up in the investigation of these extrajudicial executions.

"We're a committee of citizens and we want to get into the jail."

"What for? It ain't much trouble to get into jail. Most people want to keep out."

The mob was in no humor to appreciate a joke, and the sheriff's witticism fell dead upon an unresponsive audience.

"We want to have a talk with the nigger that killed Cap'n Walker."

"You can talk to that nigger in the courthouse, when he's brought out for trial. Court will be in session here next week. I know what you fellows want, but you can't get my prisoner today. Do you want to take the bread out of a poor man's mouth? I get seventy-five cents a day for keeping this prisoner, and he's the only one in jail. I can't have my family suffer just to please you fellows."

One or two young men in the crowd laughed at the idea of Sheriff Campbell's suffering for want of seventy-five cents a day; but they were frowned into silence by those who stood near them.

"Ef yer don't let us in," cried a voice, "we'll bus' the do' open."

"Bust away," answered the sheriff, raising his voice so that all could hear. "But I give you fair warning. The first man that tries it will be filled with buckshot. I'm sheriff of this county; I know my duty, and I mean to do it."

"What's the use of kicking, Sheriff?" argued one of the leaders of the mob. "The nigger is sure to hang anyhow; he richly deserves it; and we've got to do something to teach the niggers their places or white people won't be able to live in the county."

"There's no use talking, boys," responded the sheriff. "I'm a white man outside, but in this jail I'm sheriff; and if this nigger's to be hung in this county, I propose to do the hanging. So you fellows might as well right-about-face, and march back to Troy. You've had a pleasant trip, and the exercise will be good for you. You know me. I've got powder and ball, and I've faced fire before now, with nothing between me and the enemy, and I don't mean to surrender this jail while I'm able to shoot." Having thus announced his determination, the sheriff closed and fastened the wicket and looked around for the best position from which to defend the building.

The crowd drew off a little, and the leaders conversed together in low tones.

The Branson County jail was a small, two-story brick building, strongly constructed, with no attempt at architectural ornamentation. Each story was divided into two large cells by a passage running from front to rear. A grated iron door gave entrance from the passage to each of the four cells. The jail seldom had many prisoners in it, and the lower windows had been boarded up. When the sheriff had closed the wicket, he ascended the steep wooden stairs to the upper floor. There was no window at the front of the upper passage, and the most available position from which to watch the movements of the crowd below was the front window of the cell occupied by the solitary prisoner.

The sheriff unlocked the door and entered the cell. The prisoner was crouched in a corner, his yellow face, blanched with terror, looking ghastly in the semidarkness of the room. A cold perspiration had gathered on his forehead, and his teeth were chattering with affright.

"For God's sake, Sheriff," he murmured hoarsely, "don't let 'em lynch me; I didn't kill the old man."

The sheriff glanced at the cowering wretch with a look of mingled contempt and loathing.

"Get up," he said sharply. "You will probably be hung sooner or later, but it shall not be today if I can help it. I'll unlock your fetters, and if I can't hold the jail you'll have to make the best fight you can. If I'm shot, I'll consider my responsibility at an end."

There were iron fetters on the prisoner's ankles, and handcuffs on his wrists. These the sheriff unlocked, and they fell clanking to the floor.

"Keep back from the window," said the sheriff. "They might shoot if they saw you."

The sheriff drew toward the window a pine bench which formed a part of the scanty furniture of the cell, and laid his revolver upon it. Then he took his gun in hand, and took his stand at the side of the window where he could with least exposure of himself watch the movements of the crowd below.

The lynchers had not anticipated any determined resistance. Of course they had looked for a formal protest, and perhaps a sufficient show of opposition to excuse the sheriff in the eye of any stickler for legal formalities. They had not however come prepared to fight a battle, and no one of them seemed willing to lead an attack upon the jail. The leaders of the party conferred together with a good deal of animated gesticulation, which was visible to the sheriff from his outlook, though the distance was too great for him to hear what was said. At length one of them broke away from the group and rode back to the main body of the lynchers, who were restlessly awaiting orders.

"Well, boys," said the messenger, "we'll have to let it go for the present. The sheriff says he'll shoot, and he's got the drop on us this time. There ain't any of us that want to follow Cap'n Walker jest yet. Besides, the sheriff is a good fellow and we don't want to hurt 'im. But," he added, as if to reassure the crowd, which began to show signs of disappointment, "the nigger might as well say his prayers, for he ain't got long to live."

There was a murmur of dissent from the mob, and several voices insisted that an attack be made on the jail. But pacific counsels finally prevailed, and the mob sullenly withdrew.

The sheriff stood at the window until they had disappeared around the bend in the road. He did not relax his watchfulness when the last one was out of sight. Their withdrawal might be a mere feint, to be followed by a further attempt. So closely indeed was his attention drawn to the outside, that he neither saw nor heard the prisoner creep stealthily across the floor, reach out his hand and secure the revolver which lay on the bench behind the sheriff, and creep as noiselessly back to his place in the corner of the room.

A moment after the last of the lynching party had disappeared there was a shot fired from the woods across the road; a bullet whistled by the window and buried itself in the wooden casing a few inches from where the sheriff was standing. Quick as thought, with the instinct born of a semi-guerrilla army experience, he raised his gun and fired twice at the point from which a faint puff of smoke showed the hostile to have been sent. He stood a moment watching, and then rested his gun against the window and reached behind him mechanically for the other weapon. It was not on the bench. As the sheriff realized this fact, he turned his head and looked into the muzzle of the revolver.

"Stay where you are, Sheriff," said the prisoner, his eyes glistening, his face almost ruddy with excitement.

The sheriff mentally cursed his own carelessness for allowing him to be caught in such a predicament. He had not expected anything of the kind. He had relied on the Negro's cowardice and

subordination in the presence of an armed white man as a matter of course. The sheriff was a brave man, but realized that the prisoner had him at an immense disadvantage. The two men stood thus for a moment, fighting a harmless duel with their eyes.

"Well, what do you mean to do?" asked the sheriff with apparent calmness.

"To get away, of course," said the prisoner in a tone which caused the sheriff to look at him more closely, and with an involuntary feeling of apprehension; if the man was not mad, he was in a state of mind akin to madness, and quite as dangerous. The sheriff felt that he must speak to the prisoner fair and watch for a chance to turn the tables on him. The keen-eyed, desperate man before him was a different being altogether from the groveling wretch who had begged so piteously for life a few minutes before.

At length the sheriff spoke:—

"Is this your gratitude to me for saving your life at the risk of my own? If I had not done so, you would now be swinging from the limb of some neighboring tree."

"True," said the prisoner, "you saved my life, but for how long? When you came in, you said court would sit next week. When the crowd went away they said I had not long to live. It is merely a choice of two ropes."

"While there's life there's hope," replied the sheriff. He uttered this commonplace mechanically, while his brain was busy in trying to think out some way of escape. "If you are innocent you can prove it."

The mulatto kept his eye upon the sheriff. "I didn't kill the old man," he replied; "but I shall never be able to clear myself. I was at his house at nine o'clock. I stole from it the coat that was on my back when I was taken. I would be convicted even with a fair trial unless the real murderer were discovered beforehand."

The sheriff knew this only too well. While he was thinking what argument next to use, the prisoner continued:—"Throw me the keys—no, unlock the door."

The sheriff stood a moment irresolute. The mulatto's eye glittered ominously. The sheriff crossed the room and unlocked the door leading into the passage.

"Now go down and unlock the outside door."

The heart of the sheriff leaped within him. Perhaps he might make a dash for liberty and gain the outside. He descended the narrow stairs, the prisoner keeping close behind him.

The sheriff inserted the huge iron key into the lock. The rusty bolt yielded slowly. It still remained for him to pull the door open.

"Stop!" thundered the mulatto, who seemed to divine the sheriff's purpose. "Move a muscle, and I'll blow your brain out."

The sheriff obeyed; he realized that his chance had not yet come.

"Now keep on that side of the passage and go back upstairs."

Keeping the sheriff under cover of the revolver, the mulatto followed him up the stairs. The sheriff expected the prisoner to lock him into the cell and make his own escape. He had about come to the conclusion that the best thing he could do under the circumstances was to submit quietly and take his chances of recapturing the prisoner after the alarm had been given. The sheriff had faced death more than once upon the battlefield. A few minutes before, well armed, and with a brick wall between him and them, he had dared a hundred men to fight; but he felt instinctively that the desperate man confronting him was not to be trifled with, and he was too prudent a man to risk his life against such heavy odds. He had Polly to look after and there was a limit beyond which devotion to duty would be quixotic and even foolish.

"I want to get away," said the prisoner, "and I don't want to be captured; for if I am I know I will be hung on the spot. I am afraid," he added somewhat reflectively, "that in order to save myself I shall have to kill you."

"Good God!" exclaimed the sheriff in involuntary terror; "you would not kill the man to whom you owe your own life."

"You speak more truly than you know," replied the mulatto. "I indeed owe my life to you."

The sheriff started. He was capable of surprise, even in that moment of extreme peril. "Who are you?" he asked in amazement.

"Tom, Cicely's son," returned the other. He had closed the door and stood talking to the sheriff through the gated opening. "Don't you remember Cicely—Cicely whom you sold with her child to the speculator on his way to Alabama?"

The sheriff did remember. He had been sorry for it many a time since. It had been the old story of debts, mortgages, and bad crops. He had quarreled with the mother The price offered for her and her child had been unusually large, and he had yielded to the combination of anger and pecuniary stress.

"Good God!" he gasped; "you would not murder your own father?"

"My father?" replied the mulatto. "It were well enough for me to claim the relationship, but it comes with poor grace from you to ask anything by reason of it. What father's duty have you ever performed for me? Did you give me your name, or even your protection? Other white men gave their colored sons freedom and money, and sent them to the free states. You sold me to the rice swamps."

"I at least gave you the life you cling to," murmured the sheriff.

"Life?" said the prisoner, with a sarcastic laugh. "What kind of a life? You gave me your own blood, your own feathers—no man need look at us together twice to see that—and you gave me a black mother. Poor wretch! She died under the lash, because she had enough spirit, and you made me a slave, and crushed it out."

"But you are free now," said the sheriff. He had not doubted, could not doubt, the mulatto's word. He knew whose passions coursed beneath that swarthy skin and burned in the black eyes opposite his own. He saw in this mulatto what he himself might have become had not the safeguards of parental restraint and public opinion been thrown around him.

"Free to do what?" replied the mulatto. "Free in name, but despised and scorned and set aside by the people to whose race I belong far more than to my mother's."

"There are schools," said the sheriff. "You have been to school." He had noticed that the mulatto spoke more eloquently and used better language than most Branson County people.

"I have been to school, and dreamed when I went that it would work some marvelous change in my condition. But what did I learn? I learned to feel that no degree of learning or wisdom will change the color of my skin and that I shall always wear what in my own country is a badge of degradation. When I think about it seriously I do not care particularly for such a life. It is the animal in me, not the man, that flees the gallows. I owe you nothing," he went on, "and expect nothing of you; and it would be no more than justice if I should avenge upon you my mother's wrongs and my own. But still I have to shoot you; I have never yet taken human life—for I did *not* kill the old captain. Will you promise to give no alarm and make no attempt to capture me until morning, if I do not shoot?"

So absorbed were the two men in their colloquy and their own tumultuous thoughts that neither of them had heard the door below move upon its hinges. Neither of them had heard a light step come stealthily up the stairs, nor seen a slender form creep along the darkening passage toward the mulatto.

The sheriff hesitated. The struggle between his love of life and his sense of duty was a terrific one. It may seem strange that a man who could sell his own child into slavery should hesitate at such a moment, when his life was trembling in the balance. But the baleful influence of human slavery poisoned the very fountains of life, and created new standards of right. The sheriff was conscientious; his conscience had merely been warped by his environment. Let no one ask what

his answer would have been; he was spared the necessity of a decision.

"Stop," said the mulatto, "you need not promise. I could not trust you if you did. It is your life for mine; there is but one safe way for me; you must die."

He raised his arm to fire, when there was a flash—a report from the passage behind him. His arm fell heavily at his side, and the pistol dropped at his feet.

The sheriff recovered first from his surprise, and throwing open the door secured the fallen weapon. Then seizing the prisoner he thrust him into the cell and locked the door upon him; after which he turned to Polly, who leaned half-fainting against the wall, her hands clasped over her heart.

"Oh, Father, I was just in time!" she cried hysterically and, wildly sobbing, threw herself into her father's arms.

"I watched until they all went away," she said. "I heard the shot from the woods and I saw you shoot. Then when you did not come out I feared something had happened, that perhaps you had been wounded. I got out the other pistol and ran over here. When I found the door open I knew something was wrong, and when I heard voices I crept upstairs, and reached the top just in time to hear him say he would kill you. Oh, it was a narrow escape!"

When she had grown somewhat calmer, the sheriff left her standing there and went back into the cell. The prisoner's arm was bleeding from a flesh wound. His bravado had given place to a stony apathy. There was no sign in his face of fear or disappointment or feeling of any kind. The sheriff sent Polly to the house for cloth, and bound up the prisoner's wound with a rude skill acquired during his army life.

"I'll have a doctor come and dress the wound in the morning," he said to the prisoner. "It will do very well until then if you will keep quiet. If the doctor asks you how the wound was caused, you can say that you were struck by the bullet fired from the woods. It would do you no good to have it known that you were shot while attempting to escape."

The prisoner uttered no word of thanks or apology, but sat in sullen silence. When the wounded arm had been bandaged, Polly and her father returned to the house.

The sheriff was in an unusually thoughtful mood that evening. He put salt in his coffee at supper, and poured vinegar over his pancakes. To many of Polly's questions he returned random answers. When he had gone to bed, he lay awake for several hours.

In the silent watches of the night, when he was alone with God, there came into his mind a flood of unaccustomed thoughts. An hour or two before, standing face to face with death, he had experienced a sensation similar to that which drowning men are said to feel—a kind of clarifying of the moral faculty, in which the veil of the flesh, with its obscuring passions and prejudices, is pushed aside for a moment, and all the acts of one's life stand out, in the clear light of truth, in their correct proportions and relations—a state of mind in which one sees himself as God may be supposed to see him. In the reaction following his rescue, this feeling had given place for a time to far different emotions. But now, in the silence of midnight, something of this clearness of spirit returned to the sheriff. He saw that he had owed some duty to this son of his—that neither law nor custom could destroy a responsibility inherent in the nature of mankind. He could not thus, in the eyes of God at least, shake off the consequences of his sin. Had he never sinned, this wayward spirit would never have come back from the vanished past to haunt him. As these thoughts came, his anger against the mulatto died away, and in its place there sprang up a great pity. The hand of parental authority might have restrained the passions he had seen burning in the prisoner's eyes when the desperate man spoke the words which had seemed to doom his father to death. The sheriff felt that he might have saved this fiery spirit from the sloth of slavery; that he might have sent him to the free North and given him there, or in some other land, an opportunity to turn to usefulness and honorable pursuits the talents that

had run to crime, perhaps to madness; he might, still less, have given this son of his the poor simulacrum of liberty which men of his caste could possess in a slave-holding community; or least of all, but still something, he might have kept the boy on the plantation, where the burdens of slavery would have fallen lightly upon him.

The sheriff recalled his own youth. He had inherited an honored name to keep untarnished; he had had a future to make; the picture of a fair young bride had beckoned him on to happiness. The poor wretch now stretched upon a pallet of straw between the brick walls of the jail had had none of these things, no name, no father, no mother—in the true meaning of motherhood—and until the past few years no possible future, and that one vague and shadowy in its outline, and dependent for form and substance upon the slow solution of a problem in which there were many unknown quantities.

From what he might have done to what he might yet do was an easy transition for the awakened conscience of the sheriff. It occurred to him, purely as a hypothesis, that he might permit his prisoner to escape; but his oath of office, his duty as sheriff, stood in the way of such a course, and the sheriff dismissed the idea from his mind. He could, however, investigate the circumstances of the murder and move Heaven and earth to discover the real criminal, for he no longer doubted the prisoner's innocence; he could employ counsel for the accused, and perhaps influence public opinion in his favor. Acquittal once secured, some plan could be devised by which the sheriff might in some degree atone for his crime against this son of his—against society—against God.

When the sheriff had reached this conclusion he fell into an unquiet slumber, from which he awoke late the next morning.

He went over to the jail before breakfast and found the prisoner lying on his pallet, his face turned to the wall; he did not move when the sheriff rattled the door.

"Good morning," said the latter, in a tone intended to waken the prisoner.

There was no response. The sheriff looked more keenly at the recumbent figure; there was an unnatural rigidity about its attitude.

He hastily unlocked the door and, entering the cell, bent over the prostrate form. There was no sound of breathing; he turned the body over—it was cold and stiff. The prisoner had torn the bandage from his wound and bled to death during the night. He had evidently been dead several hours.

American Political Culture

**by Lewis Lipsitz
and David M. Speak**

Liberty and Its Tensions

The American political experience seems at first glance simple and straightforward enough. In the traditional view of grammar school textbooks, the United States was created as a full-fledged democracy, born in a revolution that rallied around the call for liberty and equality. Since that time, according to this version of history, the nation has gone on to greater and greater heights as a democratic society and as a defender of democracy elsewhere in the world. A closer look at our political history, however, reveals a far more ambiguous and troubling picture. The American experiment with government by the people was certainly innovative and has had worldwide significance. But there have been many rough moments in the evolution of U.S. democracy, from its beginnings to the present day. The very meaning of democracy has sometimes been called into question, and many battles have been waged over the concept of making democracy more meaningful.

One key factor in determining how democracy evolves is the character of a society's political culture. Let us now turn to that issue in connection with democracy in America.

What Is Political Culture?

In this text the phrase *political culture* is given a very broad meaning, befitting the roots of its component words. The ancient Greek *polis* is the basis for our world *political*. The polis was a city-state, like Athens in the Golden Age—a country the size of a city in which life was not so easily divided into such categories as politics, economics, religion, and social life. The polis was the center of an interwoven fabric of relationships that included all of these. In the United States, *political* has come to have a very narrow, decidedly negative meaning. It is often used to refer to the manipulative, underhanded behavior of candidates and elected officials. In this text we use the word much more broadly and positively to refer to everything that binds us together as a people.

Culture grew from its Latin root, *cultura*, which referred to cultivating the soil. *Culture* came to mean cultivating the mind and then to mean the products of such cultivation—the whole way of life (material, intellectual, and spiritual) of a given society.

Political culture, then, means the collection of beliefs, institutions, and artifacts that have to do with our shared life as Americans. What should we as a society and as citizens strive for? What is the proper role of government? What institutions allow for the expression of political opinions? What obligations and rights belong to citizens? In the following sections we will examine the interplay between political culture and democratic values and the role of consensus in political culture.

POLITICAL CULTURE AND DEMOCRACY

Is it possible to characterize the kind of culture that is compatible with democracy? It is easy, after all, to cite attitudes hostile to democratic government. If, for example, citizens feel that they play no legitimate role in their nation's politics, if a nation's leaders distrust its citizens, and one another, if force is accepted as a necessary means of political action, if dissent and opposition are considered unacceptable—such feelings are unlikely to spawn a democratic form of government. But even though it may be easy to point out undemocratic aspects of political culture, it is not so simple to describe the sort of political milieu likely to support democracy. We can, however, specify certain elements that any democratic society would have to include in its cultural repertoire: for example, belief in citizen participation, in the legitimacy of dissent and opposition, and in the meaningfulness of public debate and elections; reasonable respect for law and demo-

cratic principles; and tolerance toward other social groups.

In describing the kind of society likely to develop and maintain a democratic political culture, some political scientists have cited high levels of education, affluence, and a large middle class as crucial elements. Yet it is difficult to argue that any or all of these factors actually promote democracy. Democracies have developed under many conditions, and the vagaries of history sometimes help to shape political life in ways that could never be anticipated. At the end of World War II, for example, democracy was actually imposed on West Germany and Japan, two rabidly antidemocratic, fascist societies. Many authorities argued, not surprisingly, that the cultures of these nations were inherently inhospitable to democratic practices. Yet democracy has not only survived but actually thrived in both nations.

COHESIVENESS IN POLITICAL CULTURE

Consensus, more than any other element, distinguishes stable political cultures. Where political culture lacks consensus, political life is likely to be conflict-ridden, marked by disagreement over fundamentals. In U.S. society, certain basic elements of the political culture, such as the near-sacred status of the Constitution, are virtually unchallengeable. Other facets of U.S. political culture, such as the interplay between religion and politics, have long sparked intense controversy. Our political culture, like most others, encompasses contradictory values, as well as conflicts between the values people proclaim and the values reflected in how they actually behave.

But if conflicts and contradictions characterize much of the style and dynamics of U.S. politics, some key areas of basic agreement, or consensus, mark U.S. political culture as well. Many observers of U.S. history have remarked on the strong consensus on political attitudes achieved in a society made up of so many disparate ethnic and racial groups. Ethnic diversity alone, obviously, does not rule out the development of a cohesive political culture. British colonists, who comprised 60 percent of the original colonial population, established the political processes, dominant language, and social and economic norms of interaction to which subsequent immigrant groups adjusted.

On one occasion in U.S. history the political consensus broke down and the issue had to be settled by war. This was, of course, the Civil War, which erupted out of the clash of differing concepts of citizenship and basic rights, as well as disagreements over how political power should be exercised. The legacy of that conflict still shapes over political life today.

Overall, U.S. political culture has remained sufficiently cohesive to permit orderly government to carry on in spite of the many conflicts and contradictions in our society and our political life. In fact, looking back over the years since the Kennedy administration, it may seem remarkable that our political processes have been able to survive, relatively unchanged, in the face of assassinations, domestic violence, a bitterly opposed and costly war in Asia, and the resignation of a president. Whether this is a testimony to the resilience of our political culture or to its irrelevance is a question we will consider at the conclusion of this text.

We will now look at the pattern of our political culture, exploring the many ways it has supported and strengthened our democratic behavior. We will examine the fundamental values that have shaped U.S. political life, beginning with the liberal democratic tradition that informs much of our political culture. Then we will turn to the limitations of that same political culture, to analyze some cultural and political patterns that have thwarted the evolution of democracy in the United States.

THE LIBERAL TRADITION

The United States was conceived in the tradition of eighteenth-century **liberalism,** a social and political set of values that decisively shaped our democratic politics. The cornerstones of this political value system were a belief in government based on the consent of the governed and a belief that certain rights are guaranteed to all persons simply because they are human beings. These

rights, as enunciated so eloquently by Thomas Jefferson in the Declaration of Independence, included "life, liberty and the pursuit of happiness." Government, according to eighteenth-century liberals, gains legitimacy by protecting these rights. And when a government violates the rights of its citizens, those citizens have a right to rebel—which is exactly what some of the colonists did.

Liberals placed great emphasis on the liberty of the individual. The concept of the free individual actually evolved over the course of several centuries. In the Renaissance era (roughly 1350-1600), as the tenets of classical humanism were revived and reinterpreted, intellectuals and artists celebrated what they saw as the uniqueness of human potential and the virtually unlimited possibilities of human creativity. To the Renaissance celebration of humanism was added, beginning in the early 1500s, the Protestant Reformation's emphasis on the primacy of the individual conscience and the solitary relation of the individual to God. Paralleling those developments, an economic movement called capitalism—based on private property and individual initiative—advocated freedom for every individual to buy and sell, to invest and gamble, to work and to relocate, as that person saw fit. Finally, seventeenth-century political philosophers such as John Locke applied the concept of the free individual to the political realm, arguing that government existed only to safeguard the **natural rights** of individuals. These rights are considered essential human guarantees (such as freedom) that a government cannot curtail or eliminate arbitrarily and remain just.

The ideal society of free individual envisioned by the liberal thinkers of the seventeenth and eighteenth centuries was a society based entirely on merit and open to all, in which each person was free to pursue any course of action, so long as it did not impinge on the freedom or rights of others. In such an open society, you had only yourself to blame if you failed to take advantage of life's opportunities. In the fledgling United States, a nation consisting primarily of small, individually owned farms and located on the edge of a vast, unexplored continent, these liberal ideas set down particularly tenacious roots.

ECONOMIC, SOCIAL, AND POLITICAL VALUES

Given the tenets of the liberal creed, it is easy to see why the United States acted as a magnet for immigrants. Although some immigrants were refugees from political or religious persecution, most came to the United States to find a better life, lured by the liberal promise that even the lowest born person could, through hard work, climb the ladder of success. The United States, with no hereditary nobility and seemingly no social or political restrictions on individual initiative, drew great waves of immigrants looking for a chance to better themselves.

Along with Americans' faith in individual responsibility went a belief in the small business or individually owned farm as the appropriate vehicle for economic success. Throughout the nation's history, Americans have generally believed that although bigger may be better in some matters, too much bigness was a dangerous thing. Recurrently in U.S. political history, populist, or grass-roots, movements have arisen to defend the interests of the common citizen against institutions or power elites perceived as too big and oppressive. In the 1890s the Populist party attacked the big corporations and the railroads. More recently, populist movements have focused their attacks on so-called big government.

Populist agitation, however, has rarely been directed against the capitalist system itself—only against perceived abuses of it. True to their liberal democratic heritage, most Americans continue to believe that capitalism is the best economic system. Private ownership has remained popular, although most people now accept the idea that sometimes big business must be regulated for the public good.

Together with these economic values, eighteenth-century liberalism encompassed political and social values predicated on a considerable degree of equality among citizens. Because all individuals are born with certain rights, all are entitled to have those rights protected by society and government. Each person should be equal before the law—a person cannot claim superiority before a judge, for example, simply by virtue of belonging to a richer or more privileged class. In addition, each person is entitled to basic political rights, starting with the right to participate meaningfully in political life.

Eighteenth-century liberals were also suspicious of the power of governments in general. Government power, they felt, could be abused all too easily, subverting the rights of the individual—through excessive taxation, for example. As a safeguard, liberals argued for a contractual arrangement between government and the governed. Government, they said, should be limited to specific functions, and the governed should be guaranteed certain rights; if any of those rights are violated, moreover, individuals have cause for disobedience or even rebellion.

Let us summarize the values that eighteenth-century liberalism contributed to the U.S. democratic tradition:

Individualism: A belief in the central value of the individual, whose rights government is created to defend. Each individual is responsible for his or her own fate.

Liberty: Each person should have the maximum freedom possible, compatible with equal freedom for others.

Equality: All are entitled to equal legal and political rights.

An open society: Each person should be judged on individual merits and be free to enter various occupations and pursuits.

Rule of law: Government must be nonarbitrary, exercising power through equitable laws that are fairly administered.

Limits on government: Since power can easily corrupt, governments must be watched closely and hedged with restrictions lest they infringe on citizens' rights. A written constitution helps to set such limits.

As noble as these tenets of eighteenth-century liberalism sounded in theory, however, applying them to concrete situations proved extremely difficult. For example, early liberals had grave doubts about whether everyone ought to have the right to vote. In both England and America many liberals were wary of the potential power of "the many" that political equality might create. They feared what was sometimes called the tyranny of the majority, or, less politely, mob rule. The U.S. Constitution, significantly, left the issue of voting rights up to the individual states, many of which stipulated that only male citizens who owned a certain amount property could vote. Still, for white males the right to vote was achieved earlier in the United States (by 1830) than it was anywhere else in the world.

Interestingly, the liberal values on which the United States was founded actually made it a purer liberal society than the European societies that gave birth to liberalism. In Europe, liberals were forced to do combat with the defenders of monarchy, of which there were few in the new United States. Of course, there was (and remains) tremendous disagreement over what "democratic liberalism" actually means, but the United States was from the start more egalitarian, despite the vast differences in wealth that have always existed here.

Of course, many Americans throughout history have neither supported nor acted on these core liberal values, preferring beliefs and practices often at great variance with the liberal tradition. Nevertheless, liberalism is the American creed. We many not honor it, but it haunts our conscience. It represents our collective ideal, even if it is not always reflected in our collective practice.

THE LEGACY OF LIBERALISM

The strength of the liberal tradition in the United States has helped democratic government to survive here for more than two centuries. In our political history, apart from the Civil War, there has been no serious challenge to the legitimacy of democratic government and constitutional authority. As the nation's conscience, the liberal tradition has kept alive the hope of equal treatment and basic civil rights for all. Despite long periods of religious, racial, and political intolerance, respect for civil liberties has gradually increased throughout our history. Legal equality for American blacks, long believed to be a virtual impossibility, was achieved after a long struggle. The fundamen-

tal liberal commitment to political equality served as a goad in that struggle.

Liberalism has also sustained a considerable distrust of government, which continues to show itself in grass-roots resistance to government intrusions, in tax revolts, and in attacks on the growth of government budgets at all levels. The liberal belief in equality before the law also served as the basis of the Watergate investigations of the early 1970s, leading to the first resignation of a president in U.S. history.

Finally, Americans embrace liberalism's deep commitment to the individual. The capitalist economic system, the central premise of which is private ownership of the means of production, mirrors this emphasis on individual accomplishment. Despite many modifications in this economic system and much greater government involvement in economic life, most Americans still consider capitalism essential to the American way of life.

TWO TYPES OF LIBERALISM

U.S. political debate today revolves around two seemingly opposing viewpoints, usually labeled "liberalism" and "conservatism." But ironically, eighteenth-century liberal ideas and assumptions stand at the core of both views. Regardless of the labels, U.S. political life basically operates within the framework and norms established at the founding of the nation. We will now examine how the beliefs of today's conservatives and liberals both derive from the same liberal tradition and how that tradition has hampered the growth of radical groups in the U.S. political arena.

CONSERVATISM: TRADITIONAL LIBERALISM

By and large, most U.S. conservatives are traditional liberals who have kept faith with liberalism as it was propounded more than two hundred years ago. Conservative politicians such as former President Ronald Reagan and Senator Jesse Helms of North Carolina reflect the individualist, anti-government tenets of the liberal tradition. They believe in the strength of U.S. capitalism, as represented by free enterprise—allowing supply and demand to regulate the marketplace with minimal government interference. Out of a belief in individual responsibility, they generally disapprove of government programs to aid the disadvantaged. Because of their commitment to capitalism, they prefer to leave dollars in private hands, rather than redistributing wealth through social programs. They want less economic regulation by government and see virtue in what Reagan called the "magic of the marketplace"—the creation of wealth through individual initiative and free enterprise in business and finance, unfettered by government restrictions.

Occasionally, powerful forces on the political right (the Ku Klux Klan, for instance) have championed ideals contrary to the liberal creed, but such fringe elements have never entered the mainstream of conservatism. Today's conservatives usually think of themselves as upholding the truest traditions of the nation, and they are fond of citing the words of the Founders on such issues as the danger of too much government power and the importance of the individual. Unlike most conservatives in Europe, U.S. conservatives are not usually comfortable with paternalistic government—with using the power of the state to protect or assist individuals.

NEW DEAL LIBERALISM

The Great Depression of the 1930s prompted a major shift in U.S. politics. At that time, millions of Americans were out of work, banks were failing, many stocks were practically worthless, and much of the population was afraid and in want. President Franklin D. Roosevelt said he saw "one third of the nation ill-housed, ill-clothed and ill-fed." The U.S. economic system had failed, and there was widespread agreement on the need for a restructuring of the economy, in which government would gain far more power over economic affairs and make a firm commitment to the well-being of the common citizen. President Roosevelt's solution was a wide range of social and economic initiatives called the **New Deal**, which involved government regulations and subsidies in the economic sphere and welfare programs in the social sector.

FDR's New Deal was the crystallization of the "new" liberalism, an activist creed committed to the improvement of the average person's conditions of life and particularly to elimination of the worst forms of poverty and deprivation. Politicians committed to the new liberalism, such as Senators Edward Kennedy of Massachusetts and Tom Harkin of Iowa, are not satisfied with letting the economy run according to its own laws, preferring to direct economic activity toward larger social interests. In general, this means initiating social programs aimed at aiding the unemployed, improving health care and housing for low-income people, raising educational opportunities for all, and so on.

The new liberals, like the conservatives, are not entirely consistent in their views and policies. Despite their commitment to social change, liberals often favor balanced budgets and reduced government spending. Conservatives, for their part, frequently defend government subsidies to groups such as farmers while maintaining a general opposition to government spending. Conservatives also are the chief champions of government involvement in matters of personal morality such as abortion, pornography, and sexuality.

When it comes to an activist government, then, conservatives usually prefer action in the realm of personal life while opposing regulation of business. Liberals tend to take the opposite view—that morals are a matter of personal choice, whereas economic matters have general social significance and therefore legitimately fall within the areas that government may regulate.

THE FAILURE OF RADICALISM

One consequence of the strength of the U.S. liberal tradition has been the relative failure of radical movements to gain national power. The Untied States is, in fact, the only industrial democracy without a significant **socialist** political party. The socialist ideology usually favors collective and government ownership over individual or private ownership. In comparison with the United States, socialists have played a key part in the national politics of European democracies since the nineteenth century, and in recent years democratic socialist parties have held power in France, Spain, Great Britain, Germany, Sweden, Denmark, Norway, Finland, Austria, Greece, the Netherlands, and Portugal. Even in Canada, where the political left has not been a major force nationally until recently, the socialist New Democratic party has elected provincial governments in British Columbia, Saskatchewan, and Manitoba. In the 1990 provincial elections, the New Democratic party won an absolute majority (74 seats of 130) in Ontario, the most populous Canadian province. A socialist state government in the United States is just about unimaginable, as is any significant socialist presence in the federal government.

Many arguments have been advanced to explain the weakness of the American left. Some observers argue that the United States is simply too rich a country: General affluence has made socialism less appealing to the masses. Others contend that the country's many ethnic, racial, religious, and regional divisions have made organizing a party based on social class very difficult. Most observers believe, however, that one of the central factors has been the strength of the liberal tradition. The American emphasis on individualism, with its ideology of opportunity and success, together with this nation's relative equality and lack of feudal heritage, has prevented radical ideas from catching on. European socialists, by contrast, have benefited from the greater class consciousness and solidarity of the working class, as well as a more closed social system than in the United States. It has even proved more difficult to organize trade unions here, and union membership today is much lower in the United States than in most other democratic nations.

This is not to say, however, that socialists have seen no success at all in the United States. Many socialists mayors and legislators were elected around World War I, for example, and California came close to electing a socialist governor during the Depression. We saw something of a left-wing revival in the 1960s. It is also important to note that many programs advocated by socialists have, in fact, become accepted U.S. policies, from social security and unemployment insurance to the many efforts to protect consumers or the very idea of government responsibility for the performance of the economy. Nonetheless, socialist Bernie Sander's election to Congress from Vermont in 1990 was a political novelty (he chose to caucus with the Democrats so as not to be entirely isolated). The failure of a socialist party to play a significant role in America has had many important political consequences, among them the relative weakness of the American welfare state.

Looking to the other side of the American political spectrum, we see that the far right, including such antidemocratic groups as the Ku Klux Klan, has also failed to gain national power. Outright racist groups have had much greater success at the state and local levels. The Klan, for example, exerted some influence in several states during the 1920s but never succeeded on a national level at anything more than a march in the nation's capital. The Klan had a minor effect on national politics in 1992 when its former Grand Dragon, David Duke, mounted a bid for the Republican presidential nomination. Despite early media attention, Duke encountered difficulty getting on state primary ballots and failed to win much support in states where his name did appear. He suspended his campaign well before the Republican convention.

Clearly on the margin of American politics but harder to characterize in left-right terms is **libertarianism**, an extreme form of the least-government position. While opposing government regulation of the economy (a right-wing position), libertarians also oppose government intervention in personal, moral matters and do not favor a large military establishment (positions from the left). Like most parties out of the center, the Libertarian party in the United States has never fared well in elections.

Both the far left and the far right, then, have played a less significant role in our history than they have in many other democratic nations. Shaped by our own brand of liberalism, the American political spectrum has remained narrower than that of most other democratic nations.

LIMITS OF LIBERALISM

As we have seen, our nation's liberal heritage has in many ways supported democratic values and practices. Yet we have often failed to live up to the standards of this heritage. Americans are proud to recite the tenets of the liberal faith, but we sometimes find it difficult to put our beliefs into practice. Too often the doors of the "open society" have been shut to some citizens. Respect for law has not prevented bouts of violence. Our attempts to spread democracy to the world have become ensnared in national self-interest. Religious beliefs, supposedly matters of individual concern, have occasionally been thrust into the political arena.

This is not to imply that liberal values are not upheld much of the time. The United States justly deserves its reputation as the "land of opportunity," and many Americans are respectful of the rights of others and generous in sharing their resources. This section focuses on our lapses—areas where contradictions and problems persist in our culture.

INTOLERANCE AND DISCRIMINATION

"Fellow immigrants," President Franklin Roosevelt once began an address to the Daughters of the American Revolution, a group sometimes noted for its snobbish celebration of special hereditary connections. Roosevelt's irony was well placed. Except for the American Indians, whose journey here came centuries earlier, we are all immigrants. Social and economic distinctions often boil down to who got here first and made the most of it.

Despite assimilation by the various immigrants who settled here, however, enough lumps have remained in the so-called melting pot that politicians frequently find it advantageous to pitch their campaigns to specific ethnic groups. Particular ethnic groups have even taken firm hold on local politics in certain areas. Still, only in the later half of the twentieth century have the members of some ethnic groups been able to attain high elective office. The first Catholic president, John F. Kennedy, was elected in 1960, and it will probably be quite some time before an African-American or a Hispanic-American is elected president.

MASTERING THE ARTS OF DEMOCRACY: ONE-ON-ONE SKILLS

by Frances Moor Lappe and Paul Martin DuBois

You've met many people in these pages. Their lives are becoming more satisfying, because they are learning how to move from hopelessness to effective problem solving. For them, a new way of thinking is becoming a new way of being.

But to translate understanding into action requires that we hone new skills. We call the skills that make possible effective public life *the arts of democracy*. Here we'll highlight just ten of the democratic arts we've seen people practicing to achieve breakthroughs in public life.

We've chosen the term *art* quite deliberately. Art to us sounds pretty important. It's something people take seriously, and that's exactly the point. We want to elevate the notion of democratic practice to something that is highly valued, prized— something that is actively sought by all of us.

Yes, but we know some people are put off by the notion of art, as in, "I could never be an artist; I don't have what it takes." So we need to explain further.

Art doesn't *have* to suggest something exclusive, something at which only the talented few can succeed. Developing an art is possible for each of us, but—and we want to underline this—it can't be learned by rote or formula. In any art, individuals add their own twists. Plus, we like the idea of an art because its practice calls on not just one but many of our faculties.

Most important, an art can be learned. Being born with certain talents—manual dexterity, great vocal cords, or perfect pitch, for example—is not enough. Artistry develops over time. And in art

there is no end point to the learning. The same is true of a Living Democracy. It has no end. It is always in flux, fluid, in development.

WE LEARN BY DOING

Like sports or the art of dance, we learn the arts of Living Democracy by *doing* them and by reflecting on our doing. Practicing the democratic arts means participating in democratic decision making and action.

After all, human beings are innately social creatures meaning that we're obviously dependent on each other. But we're not born *effective* social creatures. While virtually all of us have the potential to listen, to communicate well, to envision a better society, to imagine ourselves in the shoes of others, to resolve conflict, and so forth, we do not all realize that potential. Realizing that potential requires deliberate learning.

TEN ARTS OF DEMOCRACY

Art One: Active listening—encouraging the speaker and searching for meaning

Art Two: Creative conflict—confronting others in ways that produce growth

Art Three: Mediation—facilitating interaction to help people in conflict hear each other

Art Four: Negotiation—problem solving that meets some key interests of all involved

Art Five: Political imagination—reimaging our futures according to our values

Art Six: Public dialogue—public talk on matters that concern us all

Art Seven: Public judgment—public decision making that allows citizens to make choices they are willing to help implement

Art Eight: Celebration and appreciation— expressing joy and appreciation for what we learn as well as what we achieve

Art Nine: Evaluation and reflection—assessing and incorporating the lessons we learn through action

Art Ten: Mentoring—supportively guiding others in learning these arts of public life

---

DEMOCRATIC ART ONE: ACTIVE LISTENING

Hallmarks

✓ Stays engaged
✓ Is supported of the speakers' efforts whether or not there's agreement
✓ Searches for underlying meaning
✓ Is nonjudgmental

Benefits	**Some 'How-To's'**
✓ Uncovers deeper interests	✓ Reach out for the ideas of others
✓ Permits the discovery of mutual interests	✓ Sometimes, just be quiet
✓ Spurs creativity	✓ Be encouraging and feed back what you hear
✓ Changes the speaker as well as the listener	✓ Ask probing questions
✓ Creates positive bonds	✓ Take in more than the words
	✓ Make the speaker comfortable

How often have you been asked—by a colleague at work, your spouse, or even a canvasser at your doorstep—to sign on to somebody else's agenda before first being asked about your own concerns?

If you disagreed with their position, did you feel free to offer another view? How did their approach make you feel?

But how? In this chapter we highlight just a few of the many capacities— the democratic arts—that we see regular people in all walks of life actively cultivating in order to make a difference. We can't give you, in this one book, a detailed, step-by-step training manual. But we *can* help you understand the importance of each art in your life. And we can help you choose the next steps you can take to achieve ends you care about deeply.

In this chapter, we begin with four arts that we often—though not exclusively—practice one-on-one.

The first step in old-style politics or old-style management is drawing up one's manifesto, plan, or agenda and then selling it to others.

In contrast, the first art of Living Democracy is *simply listening.*

But is it really so simple? Listening and really hearing is an art that most of us must actively learn. It is the basis of any successful organization, whether it be a business, a community group, or even our family.

Active Listening Uncovers Mutual Interests. At its most complete, active listening suggests putting oneself in another's shoes, seeing the world—even if for just a fleeting moment—from their vantage point. This carries several benefits. First, we can then perceive another's interests fully. That's critical in finding the links to our own interests. And if both parties are to agree on action, common ground is key.

Earlier we recounted how COPS (Communities Organized for Public Service), a citizen organization in San Antonio, reacted to its frustration at high unemployment rates among Hispanics. COPS members were upset because the city's biggest employers were bringing in outsiders to fill local jobs. COPS might have simply staged an angry protest. Instead, they invited corporate leaders to the table. COPS members *listened.* They listened to the concerns of those they might have seen only as adversaries. They listened to the companies' CEOs tell them of their own frustrations in not being able to find qualified employees locally. COPS members discovered a common interest with the business leaders; improving the city's job training efforts. From there, as Tom Holler described, COPS went on to develop an innovative redesign of the city's job training programs, which the city council passed unanimously.

Active Listening Spurs Creativity. Active listening spurs creativity because it opens us to new ways of seeing. That's why English professor Peter Elbow at the University of Massachusetts uses active listening as a teaching tool. He calls it "The Believing Game." Peter believes that our culture overemphasizes the importance of critical thinking, looking for flaws in any argument. The problem with using only this approach is that it can make even the best idea look bad. A creative idea with far-reaching advantages may be ignored because it contradicts conventional wisdom, or is poorly stated. To see its virtues, Peter argues, we must make a conscious, disciplined effort to *pretend* it is the best proposal, and then see what we notice.

THE BELIEVING GAME

Play it when a proposal or idea gets roundly rejected before anyone has taken the time to explore it fully.

Rules:

1. Everyone tries as hard as possible to believe in the proposal, even briefly. As they listen nonjudgmentally, they look for possible strengths only.

2. Participants offer only positive elaborations—ways to bolster the idea. No criticism!

3. Don't try to evaluate an idea until people have been able to bolster it with the believing game.

Sometimes you have to play the believing game with yourself on your own ideas.

Source: Adapted from Peter Elbow, "Methodical Belief," in *Embracing Contraries* (New York: Oxford University Press, 1985) and "Believing Game," appendix essay in *Writing Without Teachers* (New York: Oxford University Press, 19073). Used with permission.

What's required is a special kind of active listening—the temporary suspension of disbelief. We drop our tendency to first identify all the problems, freeing our creative input.

Peter uses this approach to enhance his teaching. But he encourages any group to try something similar.

Active Listening Changes the Speaker. In private life, when we go to a friend for advice and that friend simply listens, we're often amazed *to* discover *it* is we ourselves who have the answers. We've had them all along. But formulating our ideas in order to make ourselves clear to someone else enables us to "see" those answers for the first time.

The same possibility exists in public life. In North Carolina, for example, the Listening Project bases its community improvement work on hundreds of in-depth, one-on-one interviews with people in their homes. Instead of quick, check-off surveys, organizers ask open-ended questions about people's values and concerns. In one home, a middle-aged white man complained that the biggest problem he saw was the noisy black teenagers who hung out on the streets and caused trouble.

On a simple survey, that one comment might have gotten him labeled a racist. But the organizers just listened. They didn't argue. As the man talked, he began to reflect as well. By the end of the interview, he himself had restated—and re-understood—the problem in his neighborhood as the lack of decent recreational and job opportunities for young people.

So while we think of listening as passive, at best having some impact on the listener, this story suggests much more. The very act of being truly listened to can change the speaker's own understanding.

Active Listening Creates Positive Bonds. Because being listened to is such a powerful experience—in all the ways we just mentioned and more—it creates strong bonds among people. In Chapter Four we described a growing appreciation of the power of such bonds—relationships of trust—in public life. These relationships help sustain our commitment to tasks over time, and help us survive the disappointments that all rewarding effort entails.

ACTIVE LISTENING HOW-TO'S

Here are some steps you can take to ensure that your listening becomes more active.

Reach Out for the Ideas of Others. Americans often think that social change occurs when someone "who cares" comes up with a plan and then mobilizes others to make the change. But over and over again in our research we found that this is not what happens in the most effective organizations.

In Nashville, Tennessee, to give one example, a congregation-based effort, associated with the IAF, began with almost two years of listening. By this we mean the pastors and others (who were committed to working throughout the city to unite citizens across race and class lines) didn't begin by mapping out the issues *they* cared about most. They began by simply listening to the concerns of their colleagues, parishioners, and neighbors, listening to understand why *others* might want to be part of such an effort. They expanded that listening process to include dozens of "house meetings" to listen to the concerns of diverse congregations and housing project residents, among others. Out of this lengthy listening process TNT (Tying Nashvillians Together) was born.

Sometimes, Just Be Quiet. The most simple, and maybe most difficult, how-to of active listening is how to keep quiet. Most of us want to be heard more than we want to listen. It feels like this is the only way to protect our interests. Actually, talking can undermine our interests, since our interests are often tied to the other person's feeling positive and heard.

So one skill in active listening is the habit of pausing after the other person speaks. Get comfortable with a little space there. The pause will allow you to be sure that the other person has finished. It will allow you to compose a more thoughtful question or a more balanced and calm response.

Be Encouraging and Feed Back What You Hear. Most of us have a hard time talking without an audience. If you as a listener want someone to talk, demonstrate that you are taking it all in. Make eye contact. Lean toward the speaker, never away. Nod your encouragement. Add "uh-huh" or other encouraging expressions as often as is comfortable. And take the time to summarize what you're hearing. Only then do your listeners know they're being heard. Check in to see whether the speaker thinks you "got it."

Ask Probing Questions. Juanita Mitchell of The Metropolitan Organization (TMO) in Houston stresses another aspect of active listening. Involves asking questions that encourage the speaker to reflect on his and her own words. "We help people go deeper," Juanita told us. "We ask, what do you mean? What do you really mean? We get people to think about the words they use."

Take in More Than the Words. Disciplining oneself to talk less and to pause more allows you to become a better observer. Communication is about a lot more than the words spoken, as we all know. The speaker's facial expression, tone of voice, and body language (positioning and movement) all communicate feelings that we can take it in. We're not suggesting that it is always possible to read these expressions accurately, but we can register them and weigh them in light of everything else we know about the speaker.

DEMOCRATIC ART TWO: CREATIVE CONFLICT

Hallmark

✓ Constructive, honest confrontation.

Benefits

✓ Demonstrates that diverse stakeholders are involved.
✓ Uncovers interests.
✓ Can deepen understanding.
✓ Generates more options.
✓ Can build group confidence.

Some 'How-To's'

✓ Value and incorporate diversity.
✓ Create an environment "safe" for difference.
✓ Leave labels at the door.
✓ Agree to disagree when there's no common ground.
✓ Focus on the present and on solutions.
✓ Allow some "venting" but limit reactions.
✓ Use self-discipline in expressions of anger.
✓ Be well prepared.
✓ Make no permanent enemies.
✓ Model the "surfacing" of conflict.

Make Sure the Speaker Is Comfortable. Joe Szakos is a low-key, highly effective citizen organizer with Kentuckians for the Commonwealth (KFTC). He told us: "If you want people to talk, you can't just invite them to a meeting to discuss an issue you think is important." Then he emphasized to us: "You have to go sit on their porch. You have to sit with them and drink coffee, not worrying about what the agenda is. What they care most about may not even come up on the first sit." In other words, it's important to go to a place where people feel most at ease and aware of their feelings.

At home or on the job, effective listeners go to where people feel most comfortable, and they take in more than the words. Effective listeners reach out to the ideas of others; they ask probing questions and feed back what they hear. And sometimes they're just quiet.

"To live is to have conflict," a leader in Allied Communities of Tarrant (ACT) told us when we visited him in Fort Worth. "If you don't have problems, you're not doing anything. This is what we're teaching our children. Friction means fire—and fire is power."

Is his view typical? Hardly. Most Americans abhor conflict. Whether in politics or at work, school, or home, most of us learn to see conflict as negative—as something to avoid. Typically, an employer promotes a subordinate for being "a good team player" who "doesn't make waves." A principal believes his good teachers are those who maintain orderly classrooms without noise and—above all—without conflict. A parent praises his teenager for being "a good kid" who "never gives me problems." Entire minority communities are cursed or praised according to whether they "cause trouble," or are seen as "peaceful, good folk."

When we ask Americans what comes to mind when they hear the word conflict, we receive answers like "tension," "power grabs," "nastiness," "fights," "win-lose," "war," and "anger." This limited perspective understandably leads to a version of the "flight or fight" response; either avoid conflict or be prepared to "duke it out."

There is hope, however, in this limited picture. Millions of Americans, including many of those introduced in this book, are acknowledging that neither fight nor flight is a very successful strategy.

Instead, many people are experimenting with techniques for negotiating conflict constructively, as books like Getting to Yes soar to the top of the bestseller list. But before we Americans make the effort to learn new skills, we have to uproot our own prejudices, fully grasping the positive functions of conflict.

Conflict Demonstrates that Diverse Stakeholders Are Involved. If there's no conflict, it might just mean that important perspectives have been excluded from the decision-making table.

Conflict Can Uncover Interests. Conflict can shake us out of our narrowly defined interest, as we see the consequences of our views through the eyes of those who disagree.

Conflict Can Deepen Our Understanding of a Problem. Considering several definitions of a problem—and the consequences of different solutions—helps sharpen our understanding of even the most complex issues.

Conflict Can Provide More Options for Action. Conflict avoids one of the most common mistakes in problem solving—leaping to a premature commitment to one solution. Conflict gives us more choices.

Conflict Can Be About Learning Instead of "Winning or Losing." Every difference, discomfort, or disagreement can be used to better know ourselves and others. Conflict provides clues to prejudices, needs, values, and goals—all information we need to successfully interact with others.

Conflict Can Build Group Confidence. Groups that successfully use conflict for learning come to believe in themselves more strongly. With confidence in their ability to use conflict well, they can take more risks. Healthy conflict can get us more engaged in the problem-solving process— deepening our sense of ownership, both of the process and, eventually, the solution. As Belle Zars, a member of a social justice group in West Virginia, told us: "It's good just to know that any time you get change you get conflict." Further, adds Belle, "I've learned that any time we have a good rip-roaring fight, the quality of our decisions is much better. Heat isn't necessarily bad."

Conflict will not go away. Yet, think how much energy and time we waste trying to avoid it or engaging in destructive battles. Simply perceiving conflict as both inevitable and useful—even essential—to healthy public discussion is the first step in turning it from a curse to a creative tool.

How do we create positive conflict, conflict with all its potential benefits?

CREATIVE CONFLICT HOW-TO'S

Here are some pointers to help you accept and embrace conflict as a healthy part of public inter-action. First, positive conflict requires that we welcome diversity, in all its forms.

Value and Incorporate Diversity. By the 1990s, nothing could be more PC—politically correct—than to swear allegiance to the principle of diversity. It's one of the biggest "shoulds" of our time. Living Democracy, however, approaches diversity from another angle: diversity can pro-duce better results. If it helps spur creative conflict, diversity contributes all of the benefits we just listed. From more perspectives come more understanding, more creativity, and more commit-ment to implementation.

So appreciating diversity is not a moralistic "should. " It creates better solutions. That's Ken Galdston's experience. As you may recall from Chapter Five, Ken works with the Merrimack Valley Project in Massachusetts, which includes both unions and churches, each with very different styles of action.

> I see the way the church people challenge the union people and vice versa. That's good. An example is when two companies announced they were closing. Hundreds of jobs were at stake. This brought church, union, and chamber of commerce people together.

> Once it was clear that the plant closures couldn't be reversed, we decided to ask for job-retraining money from the companies. The union people were ready to write it off. They didn't trust the compa-

nies. They wanted to jump on the companies for bad faith. But the church people were inclined to give the companies a timetable and to just see how it went. They said, 'We can be more principled.' If we'd just taken this go-slow approach or just had the jump-the-gun approach, it wouldn't have worked. In the end, the combination worked. We got $55,000 from the company for retraining 140 workers, and that leveraged other funds.

Jean True of Kentuckians for the Commonwealth put this lesson quite simply: "The best decisions are those made with the most input by the most people."

Create an Environment "Safe" for Difference. Making conflict constructive begins by creating environments in which people feel free to dissent, to offer opposing views. Conflict by which we grow is "open, public, and often very noisy," writes educational philosopher Parker Palmer. What blocks such creative conflict is fear, he says. "It is fear of exposure, of appearing ignorant, of being ridiculed." People feel safe to expose their ignorance only when we work to communicate that "every attempt at truth, no matter how off the mark," contributes to the search.

Recently we heard about a marvelously successful high school history teacher, very popular with his students. "That's a brilliant wrong answer!" he's been known to say to a student who ventured beyond his or her own sure knowledge. This teacher was creating a public environment free from fear of embarrassment. He was preparing young people who will be able to deal with differences without fear that being wrong will bring humiliation.

Even about what appears to be a no-compromise issue—abortion— some advocates on both sides have tired of battling. They've worked hard to create an environment safe for differences.

Beginning in 1991, abortion rights advocates and those opposed in Milwaukee came together in what turned into half- or even full-day meetings every four to six weeks. Initially, what made the meetings possible were commitments to keep the encounters safe. Everyone agreed; no media coverage, and "the only agenda would be to have a dialogue," Maggi Cage, one of the conveners, told us.

Agree to Leave Labels at the Door. Participants in the abortion discussion arrived at certain rules to foster active listening. For one, they agreed to ban the use of clichés, labels, and rhetoric. Without the distraction of defending themselves against each other's labels, they could see beneath differences to discover that they all, as Maggi explained, do have a shared interest. It's a "common desire to prevent unwanted pregnancies." Stereotypes broke down; trust grew. Out of this dialogue came ideas for "sexuality education" for youth, which the group later presented to legislators.

Agree to Disagree, Then Explore Common Ground. In St. Louis, representatives from the two abortion camps took a very different approach. While the Milwaukee participants believed it was important to really listen to each others' views on abortion before finding common ground, in St. Louis they "decided to table the abortion issue and talk about everything else in between," said Jean Cavender of Reproductive Health Services. Since most of the participants were providers of services to women and children, they found that "everything else in between" covered quite a lot of ground—including common ground.

So even in the most divisive battles, participants can deliberately create conditions allowing all sides to discover their shared interests. The idea is catching on in the abortion debate; such groups are now forming in several other cities.

Keep the Focus on the Present—and on Solutions. In Berkeley, California, a zoning plan had been stalled for years. Labor union members and other workers wanted zoning in order to keep high-paying manufacturing jobs. But environmentalists and some residents applauded the exit of polluting industries. How could such opposing interests ever converge?

Planning Commission member Babette Jee agreed to chair a subcommittee on the West Berkeley Plan, but only with the understanding that she would bring every interested party to the table. And she did, in a series of face-to-face meetings that continued over many months.

"At first the meetings were a little tense," she told us, "because people were complaining about the past.... So we made people talk about the present and a little about the future. We would focus not just on the rhetorical or political point of view, but a real situation: 'practically speaking, how do we deal with this problem?'"

Discipline Expressions of Anger. Meeting facilitators encouraged participants in the West Berkeley Plan to get their competing feelings out on the table but to resist reacting to inflammatory statements or "under-your-breath" jabs. They encouraged people not to interrupt each other and to reflect back on a speaker's interests before stating competing interests. After a while, participants realized that they didn't need to be abrasive to be heard.

The process generated a plan that none had started with but that held to the highest environmental standards while still protecting good jobs. By the end, "Almost anyone in the group could articulate the other's side," Babette Jee marveled. When it came time for the city council to vote on the plan, thirty or forty citizens testified—all in favor. "Speaker after speaker got up, basically supporting the proposition, not because it was exactly what they wanted, but because it supports the entire group of people," said one of the participants.

The outcome of this creative conflict surprised even the participants. They learned that creative conflict requires disciplining anger if we hope to be effective.

Undisciplined anger can cause others to shut down: their fear response renders them unable to perceive the reasons for the anger. So its intent backfires. Rather than the hoped-for change, undisciplined anger provokes greater resistance to change.

After much work before the 1991 election, Shelby County Interfaith in Memphis had finally gotten a meeting with the mayor. Hear Gerald Taylor tell it: "In the middle of the mayor's remarks, some of our members snickered. This offense gave the mayor an excuse to try to end the meeting. A small-scale confrontation blew up into a large one.

And it took us some time to get back on track toward our goals.

"In the evaluation we did after the meeting, everyone in the group agreed the snickering gave the mayor an opening to deflect the meeting from our agenda. We still ended the meeting better positioned than when we began, but we all learned from that."

Here, the group's internal evaluation session encouraged SCI members to reinforce their commitment to disciplining their expression of anger.

And there's another drawback in undisciplined anger: It often strikes the wrong target.

Take, for instance, the temptation to rail against a government or corporate official about something his or her bureaucracy is doing. If you make the person feel personally blamed, you may have alienated a potential ally. Citizens in Seattle, upset about a development proposed for a wooded ravine in their neighborhood, invited a city planner to a block meeting. These neighbors decided not to attack the planner for the city's role, but to listen instead. They read between the lines of her remarks and discovered that she was actually sympathetic to their cause. They built on that relationship and ultimately triumphed. Disciplining anger is critical to constructive confrontation.

Be Well Prepared. Jean True of Kentuckians for the Commonwealth described why discipline is so important in, say, testifying before the legislature or state agencies: "They'll bait you. They'll try to get you mad. Then they'll turn around and make you look like a fool. They'll say, 'oh, she's not rational. She's too emotional. We can't invite her to meetings.' They also tend to pick on certain people they know are more vulnerable."

That's why, Jean told us, the training KFTC provides is so important. It prepares people to keep calm, to not react to baiting, to prepare themselves mentally beforehand.

Make No Permanent Enemies. Many of the most effective citizens we've met have learned that in public life it doesn't pay to create permanent foes, whether in the workplace, school, or citizens'

organization. Someone who opposes you on one issue might become your greatest asset on the next.

Model the "Surfacing" of Conflict. No group can deal creatively with conflict if its participants refuse to acknowledge it. So Rick Surpin, co-founder of the Bronx worker-owned home care service you read about in Chapter Five, works to model the "surfacing of conflict, so that the group can deal with it." And Rick describes the payoff: "If body language shows something different than what people are saying, I used to have to make sure that the real feeling came out. Now, others are starting to do it. People will put out more of what they're thinking. Some number of people will—even if only a few. This creates space for a broader middle to speak. It starts the ball rolling. It was like pulling teeth in the beginning. Now that isn't necessary." Rick was pleased at that. "A belief that conflict should be out on the table is part of our culture now," Rick told us.

Too often in public life, as well as in private, people in conflict feel reluctant to confront each other directly. They may fear embarrassment. They may fear the other person's anger. They may fear they won't be heard, or treated fairly. So they tell everyone *else* about their conflict. Or those in conflict simply lock horns. They attack. And their anger and fear of not being heard makes them unable to listen. In either mode, there's little hope for positively resolving conflict. Mediation may be needed.

Meditation is a fancy word for a simple process—a neutral listener plays a facilitating role. Its power lies in people feeling they've had a chance to express themselves fully in a safe context. Feeling heard, in and of itself, often reduces the intensity of people's anger. It taps many of the benefits of active listening, including hearing oneself perhaps for the first time. New options can emerge.

DEMOCRATIC ART THREE: MEDIATION

Hallmark

✓ A skilled, neutral listener helps those in conflict "hear" each other.

Benefits

✓ Avoids destructive conflict.
✓ Makes problem solving more possible.
✓ Reduces the likelihood of unproductive conflict in the future.
✓ Enhances personal dignity and mutual respect.

Some 'How-To's'

✓ Someone who's neutral—the mediator—invites those in conflict to state their views.
✓ The mediator listens in order to bring differences to the surface.
✓ The mediator doesn't judge, but asks questions to uncover common interests.
✓ The mediator stresses points in common that the disputants may not see.
✓ Disputants search for a solution that meets some interests of both parties.

MEDIATION HOW-TO'S

For this art of democracy we've woven the how-to's into two stories about Americans learning mediation skills. Do these stories suggest ways mediation could improve problem solving in your workplace, organization, school, or family?

San Francisco's Community Boards Resolve Conflicts. In 1976, in a racially mixed, working-class neighborhood in San Francisco, several residents decided that many problems creating stress and bad blood couldn't be addressed simply by calling in the police. In fact, bringing in the police was deepening the antagonism.

These citizens looked for a better way to resolve conflict, be it barking dogs, vandalism, petty theft, fender-benders, lousy service, whatever. Volunteers set out to train residents to mediate conflicts among neighbors. And the Community Board Program was born with this motto: "Neighbors helping neighbors resolve conflicts that keep us apart."

Today, the Community Boards' full-time staff trains and oversees the work of three hundred volunteer conciliators, ranging in age from fourteen to seventy. Over a third are people of color. Its volunteer mediators handle and settle more cases in San Francisco than the municipal court.

"I think it's not so much that these programs do problem resolution, but they allow for problem *reformations*" explained Terry Amsler, who heads the Community Boards. "They help people get off their stuckness, off the conflict, into 'what are the bigger positives we can shoot for by doing it together?' . . . It's not how we resolve the problem, it's how do we talk enough to establish a relationship."

Terry explained the four steps in mediation that allow this problem-reformation:

> **Disputants introduce themselves and tell their stories to the mediation panel.** The sense of being heard "brings out the best in people," reports staff person Rita Adrian. "It's the fact that people who, not getting paid, give so much sympathetic attention to them. . . and take everything they say so seriously. That's incredibly disarming," she says.

> **The mediation panel responds.** The panel then praises the disputants for being willing to conciliate. It summarizes the nature of the dispute and stresses the common points of agreement, which often the disputants have not noticed.

> **Disputants turn their chairs and talk directly to each other, while the mediation panel listens attentively.** Sometimes the mediators might intervene to say: "Please repeat back what you heard the other person say." But the main goal is to give people the time just to talk to each other, Terry

told us, so they begin to break down "the evil, mean monster" picture they've created of each other.

The disputants and the mediation panel then talk together to come up with "win-win" solutions. The point, says Terry, is to "satisfy to some degree the self-interest—if not all the issues—of the parties."

The resolution arrived at then gets committed to paper and all parties sign what is a moral, though not legally binding, agreement. In a few weeks, Community Boards follow up to see how things are going and to offer any additional assistance if necessary.

Eighty percent of the time, neighborhood mediations resolve problems to the satisfaction of all parties. Considering that a third of the cases involve violence or threats of violence, Terry says he's pleased.

The impact of Community Boards goes far beyond the prevention of violence and neighborhood tension. The volunteer mediators—one-third of whom first became involved as disputants themselves—learn skills that enrich the community. "Volunteers from Community Boards marshal parade routes and facilitate community meetings," Terry observes. "[They are] a resource to the community in many ways."

ANALYZING DISPUTES AND YOUR ROLE IN THEM

Think of the three disputes you listed earlier that you have observed in the recent past. Could a mediator have helped?

In each cause, who might have served as a mediator? Where would the best mediation have occurred? When? How?

Answers to these questions—who, where, when, and how—add up to your analysis of what mediation might offer in each of these conflicts.

Now what about your role in mediation? What could you have done to facilitate the reach of a constructive agreement?

Students Learn Mediation Skills and Reduce Violence. In the early 1980s, San Francisco's Community Boards became one of the trailblazers in the movement to teach dispute resolution and to train children to mediate conflict among their peers. Since then, a half-dozen other centers around the country have also developed training programs in positive conflict resolution for school children. Most require that the young, would-be mediators receive ten to fifteen hours of training in how to resolve the disputes they see developing among other kids.

Now, from Sacramento to Iowa and New York, some two thousand schools are involved. In the Community Boards' approach, the young disputants must agree to four key rules: (1) agree to solve the problem; (2) tell the truth; (3) don't interrupt; and (4) no name-calling.

New York's Board of Education, jointly with the organization Educators for Social Responsibility, launched the Resolving Conflict Creatively program in 1985. It now involves forty thousand students in over one hundred schools. At P.S. 321, for example, fourth and fifth graders elect students who receive special training to negotiate their classmates' disputes. Sporting special T-shirts and working in pairs, the youngsters patrol the playground and lunchroom. If they see fighting or arguing, they ask, "Can we help?" If the disputants agree to mediation, they follow steps similar to the four that San Francisco's Community Board Program uses.

The results are striking: Young mediators have dramatically decreased the discipline problems in their schools. At a middle school in Tucson, Arizona, for example, peer mediation cut the number of physical fights by half in just three months.

These two developments—one community based, one school based— provide guidelines for successful mediation. They suggest that mediation could become part of our public culture, and aid our private lives as well.

DEMOCRATIC ART FOUR: NEGOTIATION

Hallmark

✓ Problem solving that meets some key needs of each party.

Benefits

✓ Makes resolution more possible.
✓ Maintains the dignity of all parties.
✓ Makes it more likely that agreements will be upheld.
✓ Prepares the ground for future problem solving.

Some 'How-To's'

✓ Know your interests so well, you know what you can compromise.
✓ Focus on crucial interests; don't get bogged in debate over means.
✓ Search for common interests; work to narrow differences.
✓ Maintain respectful communication—it's in your interest.
✓ Take the pressure off and keep talking.

Every day, we're involved in negotiation, whether it's with our spouse about who will do the grocery shopping, with a colleague about how to share tasks, as part of a parents' group dealing with a rigid school principal, or as part of a citizens' organization getting banks to invest in our neighborhood. If we negotiate well, we ensure that agreements will be honored and that they meet some needs of everybody involved. Plus, we can feel confident we're preparing the ground for resolving any future problems.

NEGOTIATION HOW-TO'S

To achieve these benefits, what does effective negotiation require? It requires all the other arts we've mentioned, such as active listening and constructive conflict, and more.

Know Your Interests Well. One obstacle to effective negotiation is a fear of compromise (fear of being "had"). To overcome it, we must reflect ahead of time. If we're clear on our real interests, we know what we can compromise without sacrificing that interest.

Consider a citizens' organization asking for the school board's commitment to an annual community-wide survey evaluating the school's performance—a "community report card." Before meeting with the board, members decide they

would be willing to compromise on *when* the survey would first be introduced and whether the school would allocate funds for mailing it. But, members agree, the community-wide school evaluation itself is not negotiable.

Focus on Interests, Not the Means to Achieve Them. A related danger is getting sidetracked in disputes about the *ways* to achieve a goal, instead of remaining focused on the goal itself. In this case, the citizens know that their goal is a genuine evaluation process in which all citizens could participate. They remain open to suggestions about *how* that evaluation might best be done.

Search for Common Interests; Work to Narrow Differences. In the school-evaluation example, the citizens' group can ask itself, what might be the *school board's* interest in annual school evaluations by the community? The citizens would look for ways to demonstrate the value to the board—such as a higher profile for the school, identification of problems before they become intractable, a greater sense of ownership by the community.

Maintain Respectful Communication—It's in Your Interest. Sometimes you can't achieve what you *most* want. But if you've maintained respectful give-and-take, you leave the door open for identifying a different, more feasible objective. When the Merrimack Valley Project in Massachusetts realized it couldn't save the jobs it wanted, for example, members and staff were able to negotiate funds for retraining because they had maintained good communication with the company throughout the negotiation.

Take the Pressure off and Keep Talking. A dramatic labor dispute offers another lesson about effective negotiation. In April 1989, seventeen hundred members of the United Mine Workers of America struck the Pittston Coal Group. The ensuing struggle was bitter: It lasted nine months and involved sympathy strikes reaching ten other states and affecting forty-six thousand additional workers.

Finally, the secretary of labor appointed long-time mediator Bill Usery. Bill pledged to bring Pittston's CEO and the union president face to face. But his approach was not typical of adversarial, labor-management wrangles. When asked how he managed to arrive at a "win-win" contract, he explained that it was by breaking out of the formal negotiation process: "For seven days and into the nights, I kept them [labor and management] talking to each other, not even asking them to make a proposal. We talked about concepts. How would they see the best relationship working? How could they best achieve the productivity they wanted? . . . For seven days— for ten to fifteen hours at a time—we just kept them talking to each other, and relaxing, and hearing one another and understanding one another. Then we broke for two days, and we came back.... We tried to back away, to look at it anew with a better understanding of one another."

This process of just talking, without pressure to take positions, broke through feelings that Bill described as "total mistrust" and "animosity" between the two sides. Bill kept both sides talking, but in such a way that they didn't fear that a mistaken remark could kill them. The process led to a settlement both sides could accept.

So the next time you lock horns with someone, take a tip from the mine workers: Call a moratorium for a few days. Just be together without trying to find out the answer. See whether a resolution comes more easily when you resume.

Before going on, you might wish to pause here and review the four democratic arts introduced in this chapter.

MASTERING THE ARTS OF DEMOCRACY: GROUP SKILLS

Next we turn to those arts of democracy that we practice more frequently in group settings. But for many of us, the very thought of group settings is off-putting. We have sat—bored and frustrated—through too many bad meetings. If Living Democracy means more meetings, you may be thinking, then it's not for me!

But perhaps the problem is not with bad meetings but with meeting badly. In our research for this book, we have observed meetings that left participants feeling energized, not depleted. People walked out with a sense of solid accomplishment. They'd even had fun. Such meetings almost never happen spontaneously. But learning how to create them isn't difficult, even though as youngsters few of us ever had the chance to learn.

Now to the six arts of democracy that can vastly enrich our satisfaction in any group endeavor.

When today's world can look so grim, when all the evils of our time—poverty, violence, and environmental decay—are worsening, how is it possible to envision positive alternatives?

Yet, without an image of where we want to go, we're not likely to get there. Thus *political imagination* is a primary art of Living Democracy. It's the ability to suspend the givens of today's social and political order in order to envision new possibilities. It's the capacity to reimage the world. Political imagination is what philosopher Peter Kropotkin was getting at in his advice to students in the last century: "Think about the kind of world you want to live and work in. What do you need to build that world? Demand that your teachers teach you that."

DEMOCRATIC ART FIVE: POLITICAL IMAGINATION

Hallmark

✓ Reimaging current reality to more nearly match our values and needs.

Benefits

✓ Spurs creativity.
✓ Motivates action.
✓ Releases and focuses positive energy.
✓ Enables goal setting.

Some 'How-To's'

✓ Contrast the world as it is with the world as you wish it to be. Be concrete.
✓ Learn to hold both images in your consciousness at once—to avoid either cynicism or naiveté.
✓ Try cultural expressions such as art.

POLITICAL IMAGINATION HOW-TO'S

Here are some guidelines to assist you in imagining the world you can help to build.

Contrast the World as It Is with the World as You Wish It to Be. From business groups to community-based organizations, people are experimenting with exercises in political imagination. Training and workshop facilitators ask participants to describe the world—or community, or workplace—in which they wish to live. Such exercises can be much more than wishful thinking when they remind participants that the world is not static; it is remade daily by our choices.

Learn to Hold Both Images in Your Consciousness at Once. The exercise opens a discussion of the contrast between the world as it is and the world as we wish it to be. Living in the tension between the two—avoiding both cynicism and naiveté—is what makes people effective in public life. In the citizen training offered by the Industrial Areas Foundation, learning to hold both realities in us at once is an important theme.

Try Cultural Expressions Such as Art. Art is a powerful vehicle for sparking political imagination. In the northern California community of Ukiah, residents temporarily transformed their city hall into a gallery. People of all ages were asked to offer their visual images of what they want their community to look like a decade hence. The result: A map of the future with a sense of differences and shared values. A similar process has been repeated in hundreds of towns and cities across America.

Once we understand where we wish to go, Living Democracy involves us with others whose visions are not the same as ours. Dialogue is then required.

What we call public dialogue our friend and political philosopher, Benjamin Barber, calls "public talk." "It is not about the world; it is talk that makes and remakes the world," he writes. Public dialogue is how citizens learn to incorporate varied interests and come to public judgment. At its fullest, it means creating an ongoing conversation about public matters in which differences are valued because they help us explore underlying assumptions and new sources of information.

In stark contrast, today's public talk is dominated by media broadcasts in which even the sound bites are shrinking. Political campaigns have become more fund-raising machines than forums for face-to-face discussion. And Annie's small-town café—serving up community gab along with hot coffee—has been replaced by Dunkin Donuts and suburban sprawl.

Where and how do we engage in public dialogue? Some Americans are coming up with innovative answers, from issue-focused talk shows to community problem-solving meetings.

135

DEMOCRATIC ART SIX: PUBLIC DIALOGUE

Hallmarks

✓ Public talk on matters that affect all of us.
✓ Talk in which differences are valued.

Benefits

✓ Reveals interests.
✓ Expands and deepens knowledge.
✓ Generates more creative alternatives.

Some 'How-To's'

✓ Use face-to-face discussion.
✓ Use a neutral facilitator; where feasible.
✓ Use resource materials with diverse perspectives.
✓ Probe beneath positions to explore values.
✓ Sometimes start small; let trust build gradually.

IGNITING AN ENVISIONING PROCESS

To think about the value of an envisioning process for your community, workplace, or school, make believe you are preparing a fifteen-minute talk on the importance of political imagination to help create positive change. What will you tell your audience?

Now imagine a process to help your fellow citizens create a community that more nearly matches their values. Who should be involved? How might they become involved? What would be necessary to make people feel their views will be heard? What role might community and religious leaders and organizations play? And what result would you find most satisfying?

In our chapter on making the media our voice, we cited El Paso's televised issue discussions. Ismael Legarreta, an engineer for a steel company, was one of many who discovered that these discussions met a real need for people who rarely had opportunities to talk about important concerns.

PUBLIC DIALOGUE HOW-TO'S

Here are ways some everyday citizens have initiated public dialogue.

Use Face-to-Face Discussion. "When we looked around, we saw there were plenty of places to go to fight with each other. What we wanted to do was just talk to each other," said Glenn Gross of the Connecticut Environment Round Table. So Glenn and his colleagues created a "study circle" on environmental issues. "Our real goal is not just to talk to each other, but to get other people out in the world talking to each other."

Study circles that Glenn mentioned are hardly new. The term is borrowed from Sweden, where study circles are a way of life: Today over three hundred thousand study circles meet in that small country. Today, Americans, too—in workplaces, union halls, schools, communities, and places of worship—are experimenting with these loosely structured discussion groups.

Use a Neutral Facilitator and Use Resource Materials with Diverse Perspectives. In one type of study group, diverse participants read a common set of background materials, offering a variety of perspectives on one issue. Then they come together with a neutral facilitator to share their reactions and "to work through" their differences. They often gain a deeper understanding and, in some cases, a course of action.

In Maine, Sarah Campbell is communications director of that state's Council of Churches. During the Gulf War, the council agonized over an appropriate response. Since its member organizations held "varying points of view," wrote Sarah, "a public position on the war was out of the question." Instead, we defined our role as facilitator and educator, she explained. The council used the Study Circle Resource Center's booklet *Crisis in the Gulf* to initiate discussion groups.

Probe Beneath Positions to Explore Values. In El Paso, Ismael Legarreta explained to us how being involved in discussion groups changed his way of relating to people: "You start looking at what people *are*. People say things, and even though they might not make sense, you start learning why they're saying them, where they came from, what their environment was, how they grew up. And you're not judging. What you're trying to do is find out what makes them say the things they say."

Sometimes Start Small, Let Trust Build Gradually. Dan Kemmis is the mayor of Missoula, Montana. He had long been frustrated by the divisiveness of Missoula's political culture. In the 1980s, Dan and the head of the chamber of commerce took a bold step: Each agreed to invite two other people to talk about how to do things differently.

START A STUDY CIRCLE

Is there an issue in your workplace, school, or community that study circles could address? Perhaps it's school reform, health care, or drug abuse.

Two national organizations, the Study Circles Resource Center and the Kettering Foundation's National Issues Forums, could offer you help. They develop materials on critical national issues—from AIDS to homelessness to the Arab-Israeli conflict—for use by study circles and discussion groups. Their booklets and study guides contrast different perspectives and encourage participants to engage their differences. They also offer guidance on how to generate study groups.

Eventually their group grew to twenty-four, with members hand-picked to represent both sides of the ideological fence. It called itself the Missoula Roundtable. To join the group, each person had to agree to honor one basic covenant: "Although they would disagree about much, the goal was a better way of doing public business, a better way of listening to each other, and to say things so they could be heard," Dan told us. "It was hard. It took time."

Confidence grew slowly. But eventually, group members moved past their differences and took on a major issue together. The issue, a proposal to build a ski resort, "had all the elements that normally would have guaranteed years of divisiveness," said Dan. Instead, the Roundtable asked citizens to come and talk to them from both sides of the issue. They asked that everyone approach the issue in a way that "does the least harm to the community."

The two sides agreed that there must at least be a way to collect the data in a less adversarial way. So instead of having two sides amassing contradictory data, they made one effort. In the end, the data itself settled the issue.

The Roundtable languished when Dan ran for mayor against the chamber of commerce director. But when Dan became mayor he reconvened it as the Mayor's Roundtable. He's tried to balance the group by gender and income, as well as by ideology. "It's invaluable," he says enthusiastically. "I can bring big and divisive issues to the Roundtable and people must think about what's good for Missoula, as well as their own positions."

Public talk of the type just described makes possible what many call *public judgment.*

Public judgment is not public opinion. What gets polled in surveys as public opinion usually registers our knee-jerk reactions—our undigested private thoughts about issues and controversies. Public judgment is something quite different. It emerges only in hearing other points of view, thinking through the clash of values. It is the difficult, rewarding process people in Connecticut and Montana went through in our examples earlier.

DEMOCRATIC ART SEVEN: PUBLIC JUDGMENT

Hallmark

✓ Discriminating reason, arrived at through talk and reflection.

Benefits

✓ Better solutions.
✓ Greater willingness to accept tough trade-offs.
✓ Releases and focuses positive energy.

Some 'How-To's'

✓ Learn to accept the consequences of one's choices.
✓ Explore the values that underlie alternative choices.
✓ Try deliberation by randomly selected groups of citizens.

Public judgment involves dialogue, of course. But it is distinguished by a willingness to *make choices*—even tough choices.

PUBLIC JUDGMENT HOW-TO'S

Here are several lessons from Americans who are learning how to come to public judgment.

Learn to Accept the Consequences of Our Choices. In his book, *Coming to Public Judgment*, Daniel Yankelovitch argues that a key measure of high-quality public opinion is not how much information we citizens have under our belts. Rather, "the quality of public opinion [should] be considered good," he writes, "when the public accepts responsibility for the consequences of its views, and poor when the public, for whatever reason, is unprepared to do so." Citizens' demanding more public services but refusing to pay the taxes to cover them is a prime example of his point.

In 1988, the Maverick Institute, along with the University of Arizona's 4-H, involved 360 young people, aged twelve to eighteen, in small group talk about pressing social issues. The process clearly affected the teenagers: In one county, after thoroughly discussing alternative perspectives, the young people's willingness to increase taxes to pay for public improvements changed from a slight majority in favor to a seven-to-one majority in favor.

How do people come to accept tough trade-offs? Only as we ourselves weigh alternatives, so that the choices are *ours*, not trade-offs forced upon us by others.

Explore the Values That Underlie Alternative Choices. The Oregon Health Decisions movement we described in Chapter Eight offers a powerful example of how ordinary citizens began by exploring underlying values, which then guided their discussion about health care. After agreeing on one core, shared value—that access to basic health care is a commitment that citizens make to one another through democratic government—these Oregon citizens were then able to make difficult choices about how to allocate public funds.

Try Deliberation by Randomly Selected Groups of Citizens. Some Americans who refuse to accept the shrinking of political debate into ten-second sound bites are responding with citizen juries. In citizen juries, randomly chosen citizens join together to study an issue and make public their findings.

An example from the 1992 elections gives a taste of their potential. That year, the League of Women Voters sponsored citizen juries in both Philadelphia and Pittsburgh. Two groups of eighteen average citizens were selected by random telephone survey. The juries studied the two senate candidates' records, held two days of hearings with knowledgeable witnesses, and on the third day questioned the candidates. They released their findings, along with their reasoning, believing their deliberations offered other citizens a real service.

Citizen juries are no substitute for the ongoing practice of developing public judgment we've seen in citizen organizations featured throughout this book. But they do, along with many other models, offer an enrichment of public deliberation. They can demonstrate the distinct contribution that citizens can make to evaluating public issues.

Too many organizations and businesses feel that they can't take time to celebrate and express appreciation. There's just too much to *do*. They see celebration and appreciation as "extras" that can happen *after* all the work gets done. But in the most effective organizations, celebration and appreciation are integral to their very purpose.

CELEBRATION AND APPRECIATION HOW-TO'S

Here are just a few suggestions from citizens who are learning the importance of celebration and appreciation.

Celebrate the Learning, Not Just the Winning. We don't always get what we want. But out of every effort comes learning to be appreciated. After one citizen group's legislative campaign failed, we noticed that their newsletter celebrated how much their members had learned about both the issue and the citizen lobbying process. So by "celebration" we don't necessarily mean throwing a party. We also mean acknowledging and express-ing satisfaction in what has been accomplished, even when an intended target is not met.

Create a Celebratory Spirit. Colored balloons. Noisemakers. Streamers. Amusing props. Live music. All these features create a mood of celebra-tion, even in a public gathering dealing with deadly serious problems. Each time we've at-tended public meetings held by the Sonoma County Faith-Based Organizing Project, for example, our moods are lifted as soon as we enter the auditorium. These techniques infuse their meetings with a spirit of celebration, despite the fact that this group faces such difficult issues as affordable housing and school reform.

What are they celebrating? Not just a victorious moment. One feels that we—all of us in these meetings—are celebrating the power of citizens to come together with a common vision. (And that power is not lost on the public officials present.) We're celebrating the hard work required to pull off the event. We're celebrating the power of hope over fear.

And it works. After two hours, members walk out feeling new energy, not drained from another boring meeting.

Show Appreciation of Your Adversaries as Well as Your Allies. Many of the groups you've read about in this book thrive because of the unpaid efforts of volunteers. Feeling appreciated can substitute for a lot of nonexistent paychecks. The most successful groups that we know acknowl-edge their volunteers at events in which the particular contribution of each individual is described. As members hear what others do, appreciation becomes a means of building a sense of interdependence within the group.

DEMOCRATIC ART EIGHT: CELEBRATION AND APPRECIATION

Hallmark

✓ Celebration and appreciation integrated into the daily practices of public life.

Benefits

✓ Sustains and recharges.
✓ Builds loyalty and strengthens relationships.
✓ Releases and focuses positive energy.

Some 'How-To's'

✓ Celebrate the learning as much as the winning.
✓ Create a celebratory spirit.
✓ Show appreciation of your adversaries as well as your allies.

But the tough part is showing appreciation of our adversaries. Recall the earlier advice to make no permanent enemies. It was one how-to of creative conflict. Sometime in the future, you may need your present adversary's good will. Members of Kentuckians for the Commonwealth, at the close of one legislative session, passed out buttons to legislators whom they had been battling all year. The buttons read "I survived the 1990 legislative session!" In this gesture, KFTC members expressed their good will and appreciation for their adversaries' hard work. At another point, KFTC set up a lemonade and cookies stand for legislators near the state rotunda. The message of appreciation was mixed but good-spirited: "The lobbyists take you out for expensive meals. Come have some lemonade with us!"

Gestures like these, along with letters and calls of thanks (even when you disagree with the person), do not signal weakness. You'll establish your credibility as a person or group with strength, who knows you'll be around for the long haul.

Unfortunately, human beings have short memories. We tend to focus on the challenges of today, often failing to see or appreciate the distance we've traveled. This human tendency underscores the importance of the art of reflection and evaluation.

The most effective organizations and workplaces use every meeting, every discussion, every significant public event as an opportunity for learning—in part by immediately evaluating what went on. How, for example, did the event help them move toward their goals? An in-depth evaluation reviews the overall strategy and the effectiveness of the individual participants. It also examines any changes in the development and distribution of power.

EVALUATION AND REFLECTION HOW-TO'S

Here are several suggestions for how to make evaluation and reflection part of the culture of your organization or business.

Make an Evaluation of Each Meeting or Public Action a Habit. A good evaluation is far from a rote exercise. It deeply probes not only what we learned but *how we might change* based on what we've learned.

In the Youth Action Program (YAP) in New York City, both the staff and the trainees get together every Friday for an evaluation. Christopher Hatcher, who joined YAP to learn the building trades and escape inner-city poverty, told us that he appreciates the evaluation because "everybody has time to talk. Everybody listens." There's praise and there's criticism. The leadership is knowingly

---

DEMOCRATIC ART NINE: PUBLIC DIALOGUE

Hallmark

✓ Public and private assessments of lessons learned through action.

Benefits

✓ Helps participants to improve their practice of all the other arts of democracy.
✓ Develops group and individual memory.

Some 'How-To's'

✓ Create a new habit: immediately after each public action, discuss what worked, what didn't, and what lessons were learned.
✓ Encourage self-evaluation.
✓ Record lessons, so that history becomes a basis for ongoing learning.
✓ Reflect by digging deeper; it complements public evaluation.

creating camaraderie in the group. At YAP, terms like *good* or *bad* are avoided in evaluations. The staff is acutely aware of the low self-esteem these young inner-city residents carry into the program. Staff person Richard Green explained that these kids are too often called *bad*. "We don't want to continue that," he says. "So we simply talk about specific behaviors and note whether they are occurring 'more frequently' or 'less frequently.'"

Group Evaluation

The structure of a good evaluation can be elegantly simple. A few basic questions can become powerful tools of change. For example:

How do you feel about what happened? (Answers can be in one-word descriptions of emotions: upset, happy, relieved, angry, energized. No intellectualizing allowed.)

What worked?
What didn't work?
What could we do better?

Encourage Self-Evaluation. In the most effective evaluations, citizen groups that are concerned about building the leadership strengths of their members are careful not to let criticism demoralize people. At Brockton Interfaith Community in Massachusetts, organizer Scott Spencer explained to us that after any "action" they always begin by encouraging participants first to evaluate their *own* performance before anyone else makes a critical comment. Acknowledging one's own mistakes is easier for most of us than hearing others' criticisms. The approach also fosters self-awareness.

Record Lessons So That History Becomes a Basis for Ongoing Learning. In most organizations and institutions, participants know little about the experiences of those who've gone before them. To create *group memory*, participants create records from which others can draw over time. Without them, members can't learn from group experience or feel rooted in the efforts of others. Kentuckians for the Commonwealth, for example, celebrated its tenth anniversary by publishing its own history as a handsome hardback book. And Cooperative Home Care Associates (CHCA) has recorded its group memory for others who are starting worker-

owned and -managed enterprises. There's no blueprint to follow, CHCA stresses, but it wants to provide a "sense of history."

Reflect by Digging Deeper; It Complements Public Evaluation. By *reflection* we mean deeper thought—sitting back and asking, What did I learn from all this? Why am I doing it? What do I need to learn to become more effective in the future? While we can be aided by the penetrating questions of others, our most important insights come when we take the time to be alone, in order to listen to ourselves and record how we perceive our own growth.

Ken Galdston at the Merrimack Valley Project describes how his group encourages reflection: "We do one-on-one meetings with people about where they are going with their lives. At the Leadership Retreat, we reflect on their self-interest. What's the fit between their stated self-interest— things like personal growth and family—and how they are spending their time? We try to help people bring them into alignment."

In conversations with hundreds of people who are learning the arts and skills of Living Democracy, the concept of mentoring came up often. We learned to think of a mentor as an on-the-scene guide or coach. This is a person who asks the leading questions, offers suggestions and feedback, and also demonstrates the skills being learned.

MENTORING HOW-TO'S

The following examples suggest guidelines for using mentoring to help individuals and groups develop new skills in the practice of Living Democracy.

Model the Arts. Jeanne Gauna of the Southwest Organizing Project (SWOP) is convinced that people learn the art of positive conflict by seeing it in action: "We teach it by doing, by modeling. We encourage people to see the value of different points of view. A lot of it has to do with facilitation of our meetings. We show facilitators how to point out the value of differing views—to say 'that's a good point. He's right. That's another good point,' even when the points seem radically opposed."

141

DEMOCRATIC ART TEN: MENTORING

Hallmark

✓ Encouragement and guidance to motivate learning.

Benefits

✓ Makes learning possible, regardless of the starting point.
✓ Motivates.
✓ Builds self-esteem and feelings of accomplishment for all.

Some 'How-To's'

✓ Model the arts.
✓ Supportively "push."
✓ Break learning down into small steps.
✓ Team up newcomers with old-timers.

Supportively "Push." Preschool teacher Dulcie Giadone described how mentoring—with some friendly pushing—allowed her to become president of HART, an influential citizens' organization in Hartford, Connecticut. "The organizers keep pestering you," she told us. "'The meeting two weeks from now—would you chair it?' Jim [a staff person] would come early to the meeting and go over everything with you. He would always support you. It took me one year to handle the meeting completely on my own."

Elena Hanggi, who moved from homemaker to head one of the nation's largest citizen organizations, ACORN, used her own story to explain the importance of being pushed: "The first time, I literally had to be shoved to the podium to speak to the city council. The staff organizer knew that I could do it. I even knew that I could do it, but I *still* was afraid. If all that stands in the way is fear, sometimes you need others to help you get past that fear."

Break Learning Down into Small Steps. Mentors guide people, training them step-by-step in the new skills they need. "We teach people facilitation [of meetings] by having people do it," says Jeanne Gauna of SWOP. "People learn by watching others. So we start in pairs at first. One person handles names and calls on people. The other handles the summing up process and keeps the meeting moving." Soon the person in the less challenging role of just calling on speakers can take on the more difficult tasks.

Team up Newcomers with Old-Timers. Businesses, too, are learning that peer coaching works. Rather than use a training manual or have a boss serve as instructor, a company will have an experienced peer build a mentoring relationship with a new employee. W.L. Gore, maker of Goretex, is a good example. Gore calls his approach a "sponsor system." For each new hire, an experienced employee volunteers to be his or her starting sponsor. The sponsor, not the person in authority over you, teaches you the ropes. And it's the sponsor who decides after three months whether your contribution to the company warrants a permanent position. A second type of sponsor is the advocate sponsor, whose job it is to know your accomplishments and to speak on your behalf.

Teaming up with more experienced participants in public life whether from community organizations, churches, schools, or workplaces—helps us manage our fears, learn new skills, and grasp the context within which we are working.

We've briefly discussed ten arts of effective public life that Americans are learning in diverse settings, from the workplace to the community group. And we've woven into the entire book the suggestions of many people as to where you can practice these arts.

As we deliberately develop the arts of democratic public life, we help to reshape the institutions of everyday living from workplaces to schools—so that their rules and practices support, instead of thwart, growth in these skills. And in the process we begin to shape the very qualities of character so needed for a living, working democracy.

EMBRACING THE DEMOCRATIC SELF

The arts of democracy we touched on in this book suggest more than a distinct set of skills. They add up to a certain *quality of character*. Someone who, for example, listens actively, uses anger effectively, develops judgment through dialogue, and regularly practices reflection and evaluation is more than just highly skilled. Such a person has honed attitudes, values, habits of mind, and a temperament that support those skills. We call the sum of these qualities of character the democratic self.

The emergence of the democratic self in a Living Democracy poses a radical challenge to long-held assumptions about the human personality.

The classical eighteenth-century liberal view of the self as a social "atom," isolated from others and driven by narrow self-interest, has been largely discredited by modern social science even though it continues to shape our "you've got to look out for Number One" culture. That human beings are profoundly social creatures is increasingly appreciated: We become who we are through interaction with others. Abraham Maslow, one of this century's most celebrated psychologists, urged individuals to develop a wider circle of identifications...what he called the 'more inclusive Self.'

One problem blocking the emergence of Living Democracy, however, is that most popular psychology still defines quite narrowly this social aspect of the human personality. Even though it has left behind its simplistic self-fulfillment theme of the seventies and eighties, the prevailing message in popular psychology remains: We grow, we change ourselves, we find happiness by pursuing our *private* relationships. Best-selling self-help books coach us in finding ourselves through introspection—through personal journals, dream analysis, body work—and by working through issues of love and control in our intimate relationships. While many of these techniques can enhance our lives, they are simply not sufficient either to produce the individual happiness we want or the society we want.

Living Democracy—what we've found *working* in the lives of people who shaped this book—suggests that a myopic focus on self, and on intimate private relationships, ignores a huge part of the human personality. Human beings also grow, find ourselves, and find meaning as we act with others on concerns beyond ourselves. As we discover what we uniquely bring to the community in which we live. As we reshape who we are by interacting with others who are different from us.

Because the prevailing culture has so long devalued the contribution of regular citizens, too many of us have acquiesced to the notion that private life is all there is. Public life comes to be viewed as only what celebrities and activists have. But the effective people whom you have met in this book are teaching us something else: Without rich public lives our growth remains stunted, our private lives impoverished.

Perhaps as you have read this book you have tried to imagine what some of the people are like who are doing the things we describe. Just who *are* they? Are they people like me? you might wonder.

We believe that people who are bringing democracy to life are developing distinct qualities. A number of these qualities cluster around a common theme; the democratic self keeps the big picture in mind. Because it would take another book to explore the qualities of the democratic self in the depth they deserve, we've chosen to focus here on this cluster.

FOUR QUALITIES OF THE DEMOCRATIC SELF

The democratic self:

- Has patience even with oneself
- Values learning as much as winning
- Takes some discomfort in stride
- Is creative in the face of ambiguity

PATIENCE, EVEN WITH ONESELF

Patience as a democratic art goes much deeper than being able to wait for the bus without getting upset. It is a frame of mind—a large frame of mind.

Anyone consciously setting out to improve a human-made institution— a workplace, an organization, a bureaucratic agency, a school, any structure at all—is likely to encounter frustration, disappointment, sometimes even betrayal. Things are always more complicated than we imagine they will be. Every change creates unanticipated outcomes. Sometimes people act against even their own best interests.

When philosophers ponder this fact of inevitable disappointment, they simply call it the human condition. From Shakespeare's graceful pen, it was what occurs too often "twixt the cup and the lip." The less poetic among us simply groan, "life's tough," while the more coarse reduce it to that unlovely bumper sticker, "s—t happens."

As we develop a public life in which we work for ends we care about deeply, these painful truths— that life and social change can be deeply frustrating—require something even deeper than ordinary patience. We need an appreciation of the unevenness of human growth.

Gerald Taylor, for example, the citizen organizer with the Industrial Areas Foundation, pondered aloud how he manages to derive enormous satisfaction from his work, despite inevitable setbacks. "Philosophically I do not believe in the inevitability of progress," he said. "I only believe in change. The beauty of this work is that you are participating fully in the human condition. That means it's not linear—not a straight line going up. So I don't get upset when things don't go as planned.

"This work has taught me the meaning of real patience. Every success has seeds of new problems. I try to prepare leaders for this, so they don't get the idea that they can find *the* solution . . . To be effective, you have to be at ease with the human condition—its irrationality, its pathos."

And Carol Ford at Save Our Cumberland Mountains voiced a very similar idea "With SOCM, I learned that you may not move a mountain in a day, you chip away at it. With that kind of thinking, things don't have to overwhelm you."

Gerald's and Carol's views were echoed by Adam Urbanski, head of Rochester's teachers' union. "Democracy means not dramatic changes but pragmatic improvements," he says. The greatest danger facing Rochester's school reform, he feels, is not from its opponents but from those supporters who expect results too soon.

The importance of cultivating the quality of patience also arose when we talked with business analysts about democratizing the workplace. Henry Sims warned, "You cannot expect people to take over new responsibilities too fast." Learning takes time. He stressed that sometimes introducing self-managed teamwork produces a "temporary fall in productivity that is difficult to accept." And he went on to emphasize that "Managers have to accept this. Persistence is needed here."

AN EMPHASIS ON LEARNING

Gerald's, Carol's, and Henry's comments suggest a new way of thinking about growth itself. As some wiser than we have said, it's not about solving all our problems. Growth is about moving from one set of problems to a better set of problems. In other words, as long as we can take satisfaction in our own learning, we never feel defeated. Even if we have not reached a goal, we can appreciate the capacities we've gained in the process of trying, capacities that make it possible for us to tackle new challenges.

SOME DISCOMFORT GOES WITH THE TERRITORY

Developing the democratic self may not always be comfortable. In fact, things can feel worse before they feel better. Learning any new skill feels awkward at first, whether it's playing tennis, mastering the piano, or learning how to make a democratic classroom work.

Remember teacher Kim Wile in Ohio, whose students became a key source of information for voters of their county? She acknowledges that "democracy can be an untidy and challenging business." Recall that she acknowledged feeling "quite comfortable in the traditional role of the directive teacher. It is far more nerve-racking to take the back seat and let the students take the reins of control." But, she adds, "watching the students' pride, excitement, and growth" made this major change worth the effort.

Similarly, corporate CEO Ralph Stayer decided to abandon authoritarian management, but that turned out to be more difficult than he'd imagined. "Initially, I had hoped the journey would be as neat and orderly as it now appears on paper. Fortunately—since original mistakes are an important part of learning—it wasn't. There were lots of obstacles and challenges, much backsliding, and myriad false starts and wrong decisions."

BEING CREATIVE DESPITE AMBIGUITY

Like Gerald Taylor, Larry McNeil is an organizer with the Industrial Areas Foundation. Larry works in southern California, and he talked with us about a related quality that he feels is essential to democratic public life. "In IAF, we teach that there's tension between the world as it is and the world as you wish it to be. Sure, there's part of the world as it is that you don't want to mimic, but it's not simple. You can't live in the world as you *wish* it to be. So public life has an edge. You have to live with the tension.... You have to learn how to act when things aren't simple, clear-cut. You have to learn that it's possible to have core values but be flexible about how you get there. The successful people live with the tension."

The statements we've heard from Gerald, Carol, and Larry capture key qualities that can be cultivated in public life. But their words also suggest an additional dimension of the democratic personality: Not simply living with ambiguity, but *being creative* in the face of ambiguity.

"I used to say apologetically that democracy is messy," Jerry Jenkins told us. She was Citizen Participation Coordinator in St. Paul for many years. "Now I've decided that I don't need to apologize for democracy. You just have to wade in. You learn the value of creative conflict. You learn how deeply interdependent we all are."

And as you've noticed throughout this book, Jerry and hundreds of other citizens have found ways to turn this "messiness" into creative solutions to the problems that disturb them. Refusing to wallow in despair, they are developing themselves and working with others to devise pragmatic approaches that build realistic hope.

The democratic self doesn't express itself in only one arena of our lives. As we learn the arts of effective problem solving in, say, a democratic work-place, that learning spills over into other areas.

Recall the experiences of those in Chapter Two who described the effect of a changed workplace, or participation in a democratic community organization, on their lives outside of work. One worker in a team-run plant noted a similar spillover: "I'm in a Cub Scout organization," he said. "The meetings there used to be atrocious. [Then] I instituted an agenda system like we have at team meetings here at the plant." And a co-worker described his success in "getting more participation" in meetings of his volunteer fire department. "It *has* worked," he says.

And young people we've spoken with have seen how the experience of discovering public life beyond school has altered their experience *in* school. Sixteen-year-old Kathy Rivera of Brooklyn is one. At thirteen she joined the Toxic Avengers, a group of teenagers started just months earlier from a project in a high school science class for youngsters who had dropped out of regular school. The Avengers' first big victory was forcing a glue factory in the neighborhood to stop dumping toxic wastes into the sewer. "Before I joined I was a more timid person. I kept to myself. I let people suppress my ideas," Kathy told us. "But I've learned to let people know what I believe in." She explained that now she's more motivated in school "because in the future I want to make a difference."

Formal democracy requires little of us. In formal democracy, it's the laws and institutions that count—and they're *already* established, many of them two hundred years ago. All that's really asked of us is that we pay the bill each April 15th and show up at the polls every few years.

In contrast, Living Democracy requires a great deal—not *from* us, but *of* us. Rather than being an added burden we have to bear, Living Democracy means attending energetically to the development of our democratic selves.

EMBRACING THE EFFORT THAT CHANGE REQUIRES

Some popular psychology that focuses on individual fulfillment suggests that healthy gratification is effortless: "What's right is what feels good. Anything else means self-sacrifice, and that's unhealthy."

The understanding of human beings that makes Living Democracy possible is based on a much older tradition. This tradition assumes that most of us naturally desire what is best for our community, even when we find it difficult to achieve. We *want* to contribute. Even when such work is challenging. Even when it doesn't offer immediate gratification. Even when it entails suffering through self-doubt and fear.

The people you've met in this book confirm this view of human nature. Making a positive difference in their communities or workplaces or schools is what they genuinely want to do. Yet it obviously entails effort. They, and, we believe, most Americans, are willing—given encouragement, examples, and training—to go to a great deal of effort in order to develop the capacities they need to become effective contributors to our larger society.

Developing the democratic self takes effort, of course. But why might we bother? As we address that question, teacher Nancy Corbett comes to mind. For nineteen years she taught as a traditional stand-in-front-of-the-classroom teacher. It was comfortable. She was in control. Then she began to challenge her democratic self, and as a consequence, she writes, "I need not fear drying up (like a crinkled apple doll . . .) behind my desk, just because I have taught for so long. While projects like these [involving students in the community] will mean extra work and extra time, my own staying alive in the classroom is more than sufficient reason to adventure democratically with learners."

The people we've met in writing this book are convincing; they *are* becoming more alive. They are taking charge of their lives and solving their problems. They live in hope, not despair. We hope this book can serve as *their* invitation to millions of Americans.

Part Two

Contending Claims and Intercultural Communication

Chapter 5, Ourselves and Others, begins with Walt Whitman's poem in celebration of "Faces." Why classification into races has proved to be a futile and unscientific enterprise is summarized in Cavalli-Sforza et al's "Scientific Failure of the Concept of Human Races." Aguirre and Turner review fundamental reasons for the tensions and conflicts among ethnic populations in the U.S. in "Ethnicity and Ethnic Relations." Milton Yinger provides a skillful analysis of the permeability of ethnic boundaries in "The Boundaries of Ethnicity," and Eugene Eoyang offers an equally canny look at whiteness in "Coat of Many Colors: The Myth of a White American." Sam Roberts' "Our National Obsession" enumerates some of the costs of color consciousness in contemporary national life. "Intercultural Communication: Theory" by Newmark and Asante outlines the skills needed to enhance intercultural awareness and sensitivity. "Communicating" by Primo Levi is a telling reminder of the horror of "incommunicability."

Suzanne Cleary's poetic celebration of stories in "Ivory Bracelets" enlivens and informs **Chapter 6, Class and Power.** Harold R. Kerbo answers the question of who gets what in the U.S. in "Dimensions of Inequality in the United States." Transformations in family structures and behaviors are presented clearly in Zinn and Eitzen's *"Moving Away from the Nuclear Modl."* The Structural transformation of U.S. families and the economy is assayed substantially in Zinn and Eitzen's "The Reshaping of Society and Families." Diversity in families may readily lead to a "fuzzy logic" of interpersonal identification that we can

appreciate in Maureen T. Reddy's personal narrative "Why Do White People Have Vaginas?"

The expansion of women's economic and sexual choices in U.S. society still does not deliver them from that ancient enemy, male violence—in all of its forms. Harassment, assault, abuse, and rape are discussed by John Scanzoni in "Aggression Against Women." John Allman's evocative "Sisters" is neither a comfortable nor simple tale of woman siblings. And Christina Hoff Sommers' "The Backlash Myth" takes Susan Faludi and other feminist critics to task for betraying women they claim to champion. Julio Marzan's *Graduation Day"* captures multiple rites of passage.

With the largest segment, 23 percent of U.S. households headed by persons aged 35-44 and the second largest segment, 18 percent headed by person aged 45-54, we can see readily why aging has become a subject of concern even to young people. By the year 2010 the largest population segment in our society will be "baby boomers" aged 60-69 nearing retirement, if not already retired. John Scanzoni's "Aging, The Family Life Cycle, and its Life Courses" is a valuable reference. Death is integral to life, although many ignore its part; "Grandma's Wake" by Emilio Diaz Valcarel does not, nor does Dan Masterson's unforgettable "Calling Home."

Within the recent past we have come to appreciate how insufficient a short, one-size-fits-all set of communication skills is for effective understanding of a different culture or for the understanding of different groups within the same general culture. This has been a lesson of our broadening international relations, whether through the experiences of Peace Corps members or U.S. international economics experts. It also is among the clear lessons of our thwarted domestic dialogues on such issues as immigration, health care, education or ethnic relations. Mastering the arts of democracy one-on-one, as Lappe and DuBois tell us, cannot be done by rote. It requires creative responses to emerging interpersonal interactions.

There are numerous particular things we cannot generalize about different cultures — as well as about different individual people.

Consider, for example, the challenge an actress or actor accepts in playing a role. Simply reading the words will not bring a character to life. The words are a threshold into the character: who is this person? what have they been doing in their life until this moment? what is the history of this situation I (as the character) am now in? who are these other people with me in this dramatic environment? what is my interrelationship with them? how do I really feel about them? how do they feel about me? what are we doing here together?

And then the characters begin to rehearse their interactions on the stage, their movements, their inflections, their thoughts. They must then create the physical and psychological nuances that really bring the play alive.

Too often when meeting someone whose culture is different from ours, whether regionally —the culture of Appalachia is not like that of Dayton, Ohio, Portland, Oregon or southern California— ethnically or nationally, we begin that interaction as the main character of a play. But do we ask the same questions in trying to get to know these new people before us as does an effective actress who not only must understand her role but that of others? Usually not. We come with preconceptions (stereotypes) we expect these different people to confirm. Sometimes those preconceptions are so strong (prejudices) that we don't pay real attention to the gestures and inflections of words, or the body movements, the eye movements of that person. Whatever they do confirms what we expect because our eyes really have gone opaque; our minds have closed.

But our challenge in those situations is even more difficult than that of the actor. Why? *There is no script!* That is, there is no script unless we bring one in our heads: based on stereotypes, biases, prejudices, hostility.

What we really need on such occasions is curiosity, openness, perhaps even wonder. I am continually amazed, at times, by how different I am from someone I have known a long time or have met recently: how lively and interesting they are in

ways I could not possibly be. Or those who are pessimistic about others, and guarded in their personal interactions in ways that I could not possibly be.

If culture is communication, if our every mode of self-identification reflects elements of our culture, then our task is even more complex when we engage or meet someone from a different ethnic or national culture because each of us comes to such an interaction speaking —to a lesser or greater degree— *a different language.* For example, if we are from the south of the U.S., we have to slow down, so to speak, and listen more acutely before we begin to get the hang of a Boston accent. True, it is the same language, but it is a different dialect. I recall the first meeting of a woman from Nachadoches, Texas and another from Brooklyn, New York. They spontaneously laughed at the difference in one another's American English dialect; and one of them even said, devilishly,, "What in the world is she saying?" That was a natural and effective way to break the ice.

Think of how much more difficult our job is if the person we are meeting speaks a different language altogether. We then are limited to beginning our communication with gestures and vocal inflections.

To the degree that we become more effective in meeting these challenges of intracultural (within our own culture) and intercultural (between our culture and different cultures) communication, we will become increasingly effective in understanding, if not completely resolving, the competing claims of different economic, ethnic, national, political, and social groups in our nation.

References

Brislin, Richard (1993) *Understanding Culture's Influence on Behavior.*

Stuart, Edward C. and Bennet, Milton J. (1991) *American Cultural Patters: A Cross-Cultural Perspective.*

Faces from Leaves of Grass

by Walt Whitman

Sauntering the pavement or riding the country
byroad here then are faces,
Faces of friendship, precision, caution,
suavity, ideality,
The spiritual prescient face, the always welcome
common benevolent face,
The face of the singing of music, the grand faces of
natural lawyers and judges broad at the
backtop,
The faces of hunters and fishers, bulged at the
brows .... the shaved blanched faces of orthodox citizens,
The pure extravagant yearning questioning artist's
face,
The welcome ugly face of some beautiful soul ....
the handsome detested or despised face,
The sacred faces of infants .... the illuminated face
of the mother of many children,
The face of an amour .... the face of veneration,
The face as of a dream .... the face of an immobile
rock,
The face withdrawn of its good and bad...a
castrated face,
A wild hawk... his wings clipped by the clipper,
A stallion that yielded at last to the thongs and
knife of the gelder.

Sauntering the pavement or crossing the ceaseless
ferry, here then are faces;
I see them and complain not and am content with
all.

Do you suppose I could be content with all if I
thought them their own finale?

This now is too lamentable a face for a man;
Some abject louse asking leave to be . . cringing for
it,
Some milknosed maggot blessing what lets it wrig
to its hole.

This face is a dog's snout sniffing for garbage;
Snakes nest in that mouth . . I hear the sibilant
threat.

This face is a haze more chill than the arctic sea,
Its sleepy and wobbling icebergs crunch as they
go.

This is a face of bitter herbs .... this an emetic ....
they need no label,
And more of the drugshelf . .laudanum, caoutch-
ouc, or hog's lard.

This face is an epilepsy advertising and doing
business .... its wordless tongue gives out the
unearthly cry,
Its veins down the neck distend .... its eyes roll till
they show nothing but their whites,
Its teeth grit...the palms of the hands are cut by
the turned-in nails,
The man falls struggling and foaming to the
ground while he speculates well.

This face is bitten by vermin and worms,
And this is some murderer's knife with a
halfpulled scabbard.

This face owes to the sexton his dismalest fee,
An unceasing deathbell tolls there.

Those are really men! .... the bosses and tufts of the
great round globe.

Features of my equals, would you trick me with
your creased and cadaverous march?
Well then you cannot trick me.

I see your rounded never-erased flow,
I see neath the rims of your haggard and mean
disguises.

Splay and twist as you like .... poke with the
tangling fores of fishes or rats,
You'll be unmuzzled .... you certainly will.
I saw the face of the most smeared and slobbering
idiot they had at the asylum,
And I knew for my consolation what they knew
not;

I knew of the agents that emptied and broke my
brother,
The same wait to clear the rubbish from the fallen
tenement;
And I shall look again in a score or two of ages,
And I shall meet the real landlord perfect and
unharmed, every inch as good as myself.

The Lord advances and yet advances:
Always the shadow in front .... always the reached
    hand bringing up the laggards.

Out of this face emerge banners and horses .... O
    superb! .... I see what is coming,
I see the high pioneercaps .... I see the staves of
    runners clearing the way,
I hear victorious drums.

This face is a lifeboat;
This is the face commanding and bearded .... it
    asks no odds of the rest;
This face is flavored fruit ready for eating;
This face of a healthy honest boy is the programme
    of all good.

These faces bear testimony slumbering or awake,
They show their descent from the Master himself.

Off the word I have spoken I except not one . . . .
    red white or black, all are deific,
In each house is the ovum .... it comes forth after a
    thousand years.

Spots or cracks at the windows do not disturb me,
Tall and sufficient stand behind and make signs to
    me;
I read the promise and patiently wait.

This is a fullgrown lily's face,
She speaks to the limber-hip'd man near the
    garden pickets,
Come here, she blushingly cries .... Come nigh to
    me limber-hip'd man and give me your finger
    and thumb,

Stand at my side till I lean as high as I can upon
    you,
Fill me with albescent honey .... bend down to me,
Rub to me with your chafing beard . . rub to my
    breast and shoulders.

The old face of the mother of many children:
Whist! I am fully content.

Lulled and late is the smoke of the Sabbath morn-
    ing,
It hangs low over the rows of trees by the fences,
It hangs thin by the sassafras, the wildcherry and
    the catbrier under them.

I saw the rich ladies in full dress at the soiree,
I heard what the run of poets were saying so long,
Heard who sprang in crimson youth from the
    white froth and the water-blue.

Behold a woman!
She looks out from her quaker cap .... her face is
    clearer and more beautiful than the sky.

She sits in an armchair under the shaded porch of
    the farmhouse,
The sun just shines on her old white head.

Her ample gown is of creamhued linen,
Her grandsons raised the flax, and her grand-
    daughters spun it with the distaff and the
    wheel.

The melodious character of the earth!
The finish beyond which philosophy cannot go
    and does not wish to go!
The justified mother of men!

AMERICAN PRAGMATISM AND IMPLICATIONS OF AMERICAN ETHNOCENTRISM

by Edward C. Stewart *and*
Milton J. Bennett

AMERICAN PRAGMATISM

American thinking distinguishes between the internal world of thought and the external world of action but emphasizes operations such as decision making that straddle the two. American mental formations favor what is called *procedural knowledge,* which focuses on how to get things done. In contrast, Germans favor *declarative knowledge,* which consists of descriptions of the world (Ryle 1949). The American approach is functional and emphasizes solving problems and accomplishing tasks. The measure of success lies in the consequences of concept-driven action. This distinctive functional style is embodied in American pragmatism. Pragmatism lacks the theoretical commitment that Edmund Glenn identifies with the Russians (1981, 80) and the perceptual commitment of the Japanese, lying somewhere in between. The American drive to attain impact has led to the cultivation of a variety of approaches to problem solving, decision making, and conflict resolution intended to avoid the deficiencies of intuition and common sense. Pragmatism employs psychology, game theory, and mathematics to channel human thinking and judgment into applications. This technical approach to human behavior, sometimes called *technicism* (Stanley 1978, 200), is deeply embedded in the consciousness of most Americans, many of whom mistakenly consider it universal. It clearly is not, as indicated by the fact that the Japanese and other cultures lack this prototype of conceptual decision making. The concepts of *alternatives, probability* and *criterion,* to mention three that we

shall discuss, mean something very different to the Japanese than they do to Americans.

When selecting a course of action, the Japanese seldom consider alternatives systematically. Instead, they are more likely to arrive intuitively at one course of action. The difference between the Japanese and American approaches is illustrated in the following episode which illustrates the different attitudes of the American and the Japanese toward planning in general.

> A Japanese and an American administrator were planning a program for a group of visitors who were arriving in Tokyo from overseas. The American collected cost information on four different places where the visitors could be lodged during their one-week visit. These were a business hotel, a guesthouse, a dormitory (or similar lodgings), and an apartment complex. He weighed the advantages of each according to convenience, accessibility of transportation, food, etc. against the different prices involved. He then showed the results to his Japanese colleague. The Japanese looked at the figures and asked how they were going to stay at four different places at the same time. The American answered that of course they were not going to stay at four different places. The figures were simply a feasibility study. His colleague replied, "We also do feasibility studies, but most often we just pick the best one, and we do that very well."

The use of probability has seeped through American culture to a degree unknown to the Japanese and others. When Westerners cooperate with Japanese in technical areas, a number of conceptual gaps can arise to produce misunderstandings and tensions. Two examples given below illustrate some of these difficulties. Both episodes occurred in Japan in the course of conducting research with Japanese and Western technical companies.

> An American manager, situated in Tokyo, received an order for his company's products produced at a plant three hours away by train. He knew that the plant was running near full capacity, but he decided to call his plant manager, an excellent Japanese engineer trained in a leading Japanese university, and ask him for his estimate of how long it would take to fill the order. The Japanese declined to give an answer. The American pressed for an estimate but failed to persuade the Japanese to respond. The

151

stand-off led to tension between the two men, which came out weeks later when they accidentally met face-to-face in a training session and discussed the situation with assistance from the trainer.

The Japanese explained his response or lack of response by saying that, for him, numbers represented countdowns, commitments to deliver. The American understood his position but said that he had only been asking for a "guesstimate," not a commitment. The American was comfortable using data to estimate probable but indeterminate outcomes. The Japanese was not.

This episode conveys a fundamental difference in how Americans and Japanese work with measurements, probability, and plans. It is particularly important because it demonstrates again how these kinds of differences are often interpreted as interpersonal conflict. American technicism includes a readiness to speculate freely with numbers. American production figures, for example, are often reported as a percentage of the full capacity of the plant, and they invariably include small errors. Japanese production figures are strictly counts of actual units produced. The same difference holds in the area of quality control. In the American system, product samples are inspected and the results used to generalize about the quality of the total production. This is also an example of technicism—the use of statistics and probability to increase efficiency. The Japanese adopt the attitude of craftsmen and insist on quality inspection for each item produced, making an inspection of samples irrelevant. Responsibility for Japanese quality control naturally falls to the production line and to each individual worker.

The Japanese manager in the above episode acted in the best Japanese style. First, he did not share with the American uncertainties of planning for the order; Japanese typically do not discuss their plans until after the countdown. Second, he would not commit himself to deliveries based on probability rather than countdowns. Therefore, he was caught in a difficult cultural predicament.

A second episode presents a technical view of speculation, probability, and risk analysis. The incident was reported by a Scandinavian assigned to survey and approve the construction of a ship contracted to a Japanese ship-building company.

The surveyor, who was working with the Japanese, identified a structural problem in the design of the ship. He insisted that a horizontal component of the structure be changed from a rectangular to a triangular shape to improve the distribution of forces on the vertical components of the structure. The Japanese responded by accumulating an enormous amount of data supporting their design, which they brought to the surveyor a few days later. Overwhelmed by the data, he approved the design presented by the Japanese. Nevertheless, the surveyor remained uneasy, believing that the metal in the ship's structure would develop fissures after some years of service because of metal fatigue. Later, the surveyor recognized that the Japanese calculations had taken into account normal functioning but had not included risk analysis and had specifically omitted speculations about long-term metal fatigue. The Japanese considered it superfluous to conduct experiments to test the design. If the design was as good as its representation in the drawings, they expected the ship to be good. Their approach to safety consisted of a refined and detailed examination, but their testing ordinarily omitted speculations about improbable conditions that would test the limits of the technology. The Scandinavian surveyor, with experiences in the tempestuous North Sea, was more willing to speculate about unusually severe conditions.

This Scandinavian surveyor's experience would probably be very similar to that of an American technician placed in the same position. On the surface there appears to be miscommunication or perhaps an effort to cut corners, but the deep message is another story. The American (and in this case Scandinavian) approach to probability and the analyses of risk differ from that of the Japanese. If we consider the differences in the context of patterns of thinking, we can see that the Japanese attitude is compatible with perceptual thinking, while the Western attitude is functional and based more on abstract considerations. The use of speculations and probability in risk analysis requires a strong commitment to find out what will happen if certain conditions are fulfilled, which by assumption are possible but improbable. This attitude is unduly abstract for a mental disposition inclined toward rigid and measurable perceptions.

We have introduced these lengthy episodes and their analyses as evidence that the American pattern of thinking directs American actions along very different channels from those of the Japanese (and others), even when it involves technical personnel working with abstractions such as probability. The Japanese, relying on perceptual thinking, choose to work with the certainty of precedents and rules—even those of bureaucracies—rather than with probability.

The operational cast of American (and European) thought apparent in the preceding discussion places it closer to the symbolic end of the perception/symbolism continuum. For instance, Americans are oriented toward the future, an abstract state of mind lying outside perception. Reliance on a vision of the future may raise doubts about the practicality of American thinking. These doubts, though, can be laid to rest by noting that the temporal aim is toward the near future, making the orientation more functional than that in other societies where people orient themselves to a future measured by decades and generations. Second, the future appears in American thinking in the form of anticipated consequences of actions. The projection into the future is conveyed by human intentions and actions rather than by abstract time. Anticipated consequences of actions is a functional concept used in models of decision making and provides a link between thinking and action. We shall return to this subject when we discuss the value of activity. Here it is sufficient to note that the American time orientation represents a midpoint on the continuum—a position that combines some aspects of concrete action with the symbolism of abstract probability.

The primary content of perceptual thinking has been described here as images that are classified according to such perceptual dimensions as color, shape, size, and position. In American thinking, perceptual dominance yields to functional attributes of what a person can do with things in the form of concepts instead of images (a computer is not just a high tech instrument used for games; it is a high-speed tool used for calculating data). Further along the continuum, operations for classifying objects increase in abstraction and scope until classifications can be based on a single common feature, a *criterial attribute* (Cole and

Scribner 1974, 101-02). Any one system of thought has access to each level of abstraction, but Japanese thinking tends to dwell on complex perceptual attributes and avoids all-encompassing general principles while American thinking reaches for that single dimension, the criterial attribute.

IMPLICATIONS OF AMERICAN ETHNOCENTRISM

Many of the difficulties with intercultural communication can be traced to the obstacles created by *ethnocentrism*, which means, literally, "centrality of culture." When one's own culture is considered central to all reality, the values, assumptions, and behavioral norms of that culture may be elevated to the position of absolute truth. There are several implications of this definition. First, ethnocentric beliefs about one's own culture shape a social sense of identity which is narrow and defensive. Second, ethnocentrism normally involves the perception of members of other cultures in terms of stereotypes. Third, the dynamic of ethnocentrism is such that comparative judgments are made between one's own culture and other cultures under the assumption that one's own is normal and natural. As a consequence, ethnocentric judgments usually involve invidious comparisons that ennoble one's own culture while degrading those of others. With these costs, ethnocentrism establishes identity and belonging in the context of culture.

Ethnocentrism produces significant effects on cross-cultural interaction and international affairs. The patterns of other cultures may be ignored in deference to the naturalness of the reference culture. Or the other cultures may simply be treated as deviations from reality or normality rather than as variations. In either case, the effects of ethnocentrism can be seen in the way Americans perceive themselves and in their perception of others. First, we shall look at the inward face of ethnocentrism and briefly suggest some of the factors in American ethnocentrism that affect cross-cultural interactions.

The image of the ugly American prevalent in the 1960s has become increasingly rare. Although an occasional traveler still behaves as if the world owes him or her tribute as an American, overt displays have yielded to more subtle expressions of ethnocentrism. Statements such as "Deep down, everyone in the world is really just the same" and the advice to fellow Americans, "Just be yourself," betray the peculiarly American mix of individualism and egalitarianism that pervades American cultural self-perception. While these values and their attendant behavior may function well within American culture, their application, as we have seen, is not universal. Yet Americans are inclined to act on the false assumption that all people consider themselves autonomous individuals, that all people desire maximum material gain, or that all people value social mobility.

Americans commonly assume that circumstances such as oppressive governments or restrictive social norms have frustrated people's "natural" desire to value those things that Americans also value. When this assumption is used in intercultural communication, the result is likely to be misunderstanding. For example, a recent United States president on a trip to Central America called for governments in the area to "get off people's backs" so they could do what they really wanted to do—engage in individual entrepreneurship. Since many Central Americans do not share the American value of individual entrepreneurship, the statement was interpreted as another attempt by North Americans to impose their way of life on others. In another case, an American businessman responsible for hosting some Japanese visitors to his U.S. company was asked about what problems he thought might occur during the visit. "Nothing," he was reported as saying, "except that they won't want to go home after they have a taste of the social freedom we have in this country." The American's lack of acknowledgment that the Japanese visitors may find their own ways preferable will almost certainly be interpreted by the Japanese as disrespect, and communication will suffer in subtle but definite ways.

Ethnocentric self-perception tends to vary from culture to culture. The Japanese, for instance, generally assume that they are different from people of all other cultures. Superficially, this stance may seem to be less ethnocentric than the American view, but it is not. The Japanese commonly assume that because they are so different, foreigners can never really understand them, nor can foreigners really be understood. European ethnocentric self-perceptions are more likely to be based on yet another premise: cultures are "evolving" toward more civilized states, and the pinnacle of civilization is assumed (mostly by Europeans) to be in Europe.

An American form of the premise of cultural evolution can be found in the notion of "developing nations," where the goal of development is American technicism. As we have seen in previous examples, advisors may be drawn by this idea to help people (whom they frequently misunderstand) develop towards a goal that is also misunderstood and perhaps, if understood fully, would be spurned. Cultural, political, economic, and religious "missionaries" are particularly inclined to accept cultural evolution. Even if adept at intercultural communication, they may nevertheless use those skills to further their own ethnocentrism by helping other cultures to be like them. The point is not that there is anything wrong with cultural, social, and economic change but that the assumptions about how these changes should take shape are too easily derived from the values of foreigners.

The outward-looking face of ethnocentrism directs the perception of others and the interpretation of events in simple terms, conforming to familiar cultural experience. Judgments are parochial and lack a base for making objective interpretations. Insofar as people are restricted to the categories of only their reference culture, they may fail to perceive the meaning of specific events in other cultures. Indeed, they may fail to perceive the events at all. For example, American tourists sometimes return from Tokyo or other large foreign cities and report that "It's just like New York" (or some other large American city). These Americans have perceived as figure only the large buildings, heaving traffic, and fast-food outlets that do, indeed, exist in most large cities of the world. The unique conditions that make these cities different from one another remain hidden from the travelers' views by the constraints of their own culture-bound perceptions. It is not just Americans who suffer from parochial perception. Japanese tourists in the U.S. are more attuned to recognizing differences than similarities, but their perception still tends to depend on already existing categories of meaning. Thus, it is common for the Japanese to report extensively on the wide-open spaces of America—which are made important in Japan by their absence—and which don't exist in most of the large American cities they visit any more than they do in Tokyo.

An ethnocentric perception of others has no single name but is based on "units" which are called *stereotypes*. This form of social perception is not an aberration of cross-cultural contact; it is the individual's natural defense in confronting cultural difference (M. Bennett 1986). An ethnocentric vision composed of stereotypes simplifies the social perception of others by means of a rigid belief that all members of a culture or group share the same characteristics, and thus, challenges to ethnocentric assumptions are avoided. It is not surprising that simple contact between ethnocentric members of two cultures is likely to exacerbate existing stereotypes and perhaps generate new ones. Unless intercultural communicators are aware of these processes, face-to-face interaction is not likely to improve awareness of and tolerance for cultural differences. Stereotypes can be attached to any assumed indicator of group membership, such as race, religion, ethnicity, age, or gender as well as national culture.

Stereotypes fail to distinguish among members of broad categories. For instance, many Americans do not differentiate among Gulf State Arabs (in particular, Saudi Arabians), other Middle Eastern Arabic speakers (e.g., Syrians), and Iranians. To lump these different cultures into a single broad category of "Arabs" is both inaccurate and a source of great frustration to people of those cultures. Similarly, the category "Asian" or "Oriental" clouds important cultural differences among Japanese, Koreans, and Chinese. Although Americans now commonly differentiate Southeast Asians from Asians in general, even this category ignores crucial differences among Vietnamese, Cambodians, and Laotians. This kind of restricted or

parochial perception can have dramatic practical consequences. One case occurred in the Portland, Oregon Rose Parade, where a float was entered honoring Sapporo, Japan, Portland's sister city. Dignitaries flown from Japan were quite upset when they observed that some of the young women waving from the float were Chinese, not Japanese. The parade director, when questioned on the point, responded with a statement of stereotypic perception: "Japanese...Chinese—close enough." More troubling, many Saudi Arabian students were subjected to verbal (and sometimes physical) abuse during the Iranian hostage crisis. Aside from the questionable justification for abusing anyone because of nationality or culture, this confusion of Arabs and Iranians, who have quite different histories and cultures, again indicates the practical consequences of inadequately developed categories for cross-cultural perception.

We should not leave the topic of parochial perception without mentioning one of the chief sources of irritation to foreigners in communicating with Americans. Foreign visitors to the U.S. universally report that Americans ask them stupid questions. Typical of these questions is (to Africans) "Do you have lions around your house?" Europeans are surprised when Americans ask them if they have ice cream or cars in their countries, and nearly everyone is irritated by geographical questions that place their countries on the wrong continent. While these questions may occasionally be expressions of negative stereotypes, more often they are well-motivated attempts by Americans to express interest or friendliness toward the foreigner. Of course the questions betray ignorance about other countries, but beyond that, they display parochial perception. Operating with broad categories that fail to differentiate critical differences among peoples and societies, Americans may have to select from a small array of elements to formulate their questions. For instance, the mental category for Africa may include only the elements "blacks live there" and "lions live there." Thus, the only question or comment that can occur is one that links an African black person with lions.

The realities of ethnocentrism and of limited information obstruct the development of objective assessment of cultural differences. Our examples thus far have been drawn from the area of stereotypes which typically involve beliefs, concepts, and images. Many of these stereotypes derive their content from simplistic word-of-mouth sources and from woefully incomplete information on television and in cartoons and comic books. While these cultural distortions are troublesome for communication, the content of the stereotypes is based on deep culture and is thereby accessible to description and analysis and is responsive to education.

Furthermore, deep-culture ethnocentrism among Americans is not so different from that in other cultures. The true challenge for intercultural communication appears when we consider procedural culture. In the next section, we examine some of the issues involving ethnocentrism in the American style of communication. The novelty of this section is that we associate obstacles to understanding with procedural rather than with deep culture.

PROCEDURAL ETHNOCENTRISM IN COMMUNICATION

The ethnocentric impression that one's communication style is natural and normal predisposes Americans to evaluate other styles negatively. Such evaluation is likely to elicit a defensive reaction, forming a mutual negative *evaluation* that stems from blindness toward differences between procedural cultures. For instance, Americans may evaluate Japanese indirect communication style as "ambiguous," while American directness may be received by Japanese as "immature." When communicators engage in mutual negative evaluation, the recriminatory interaction may be enough to block communication. If the communicators then attempt to overcome the difficulty through ethnocentric procedures, the communication event may deteriorate even further. The American, sensing Japanese reluctance to confront a problem, becomes even more personal and aggressive. The Japanese, reacting to an embarrassing social indiscretion, becomes even more formal and indirect. With each turn of this regressive *spiral,* negative evaluations are intensified; "ambiguity"

may spiral to "evasion," "deviousness," "deception," and finally to "dishonesty." On the other side of the culture curtain, "immature" may spiral to "impolite," "brash," "impertinent," and finally to "offensive." In this pattern of mutual compensation, the actions of each person intensify the reactions of the other (Wilmot 1987). Recognizing regressive spirals and predicting their effects are major concerns in the procedural domain of intercultural communication.

Negative evaluations and spirals are not limited merely to American-Japanese interactions. The following situations illustrate regressive spirals common to Americans communicating with people of a variety of other cultures.

> An American student listens with growing impatience to a Nigerian student, who is responding to a simple question about his religion with several long stories about his childhood. Finally, the American breaks in and makes her own point clearly and logically. The American evaluates the Nigerian negatively as being stupid or devious (for talking "in circles"). The Nigerian evaluates the American as being childish or unsophisticated (for being unable to understand subtlety). The American urges the Nigerian to state his point more clearly, and in response the Nigerian intensifies his efforts to provide more context.

> The American states that there is a problem that needs solving (by direct action of a participant). An Arab counterpart denies there is any problem at all, stating that the situation is ill-fated. The American evaluates the Arab as lazy and unreceptive while the Arab sees the American as unreceptive (of the larger context) and egotistic (in thinking he can change things). The American seeks to convince the Arab of the severity of the problem, prompting the Arab to emphasize even more the inevitability of the situation.

> To avoid appearing "status conscious," the American manager requests that a Thai employee address him by his first name. The employee agrees but continues to use the manager's formal title in conversations. The American evaluates this action as unduly subservient and unfriendly. The Thai evaluates the American as naive and disrespectful (of the special place held by the employee in the organization's hierarchy). The American insists on pursuing casual friendliness, engendering even more formality in the employee's behavior.

An American trainer presents a proposal to her British counterpart. The Briton states that it is the most ridiculous hogwash she has ever seen. The American responds by saying that her feelings are hurt (by the attacking tone of her counterpart). The British woman enlarges on her original statement by pointing out the specific shortcomings of the proposal. The American says she must have been mistaken about considering the woman her friend, and the Briton becomes silent.

The main factor in these and endless other examples of intercultural communication spirals is a lack of awareness of specific cultural differences in communication style. In the first case of the Nigerian, both people are unaware of the American preference for a direct and explicit style in contrast to the more contextual African style. Both these communicators are likely to leave the situation less inclined to ask or answer questions of each other again. The Arab example illustrates a typical tendency for people to "educate" each other. Unfortunately, the education is not about cultural difference but is instead an unconscious attempt to convert the other to the "best" way of interpreting a situation. As in the Nigerian example, all participants are likely to leave with their negative stereotypes of the others as "obtuse" confirmed. In the Thai case, there might be an ironic conclusion: the Thai may eventually acquiesce in calling the supervisor by his first name, but rather than the action being one of American egalitarianism, it will be a confirmation of the higher-status person's right to demand compliance. The misunderstanding will go underground.

The British situation illustrates a particularly troublesome clash of American personal and European intellectual styles, and it deserves closer attention. Europeans tend to use a low-context approach to intellectual confrontation—they state their points explicitly and without the ambivalence considered polite by Americans in intellectual matters. In personal matters of feeling and relationship, however, Europeans use a more high-context style, relying on suggestion and nonverbal nuance. One is far more likely to hear a European say "I think..." than "I feel...". Americans, on the other hand, treat a relationship in a low-context manner. They verbalize emotions far more often, including direct expressions of how

they feel about the person with whom they are communicating. But Americans are more likely to handle intellectual confrontation in a high-context manner. They tend to indicate disagreement non-verbal with tone of voice or facial expression, for example, "well (pause), that idea certainly has **some** merit." Americans commonly stereotype Europeans as being adamant in intellectual matters, while Europeans stereotype Americans as lacking strong convictions (or as being ignorant). On the other side of the coin, Americans often think Europeans are unnecessarily coy about interpersonal relationships, while Europeans see Americans as lacking subtlety in personal affairs.

Certainly not all negative evaluation is inappropriate. People in most cultures are critical of aspects of their own society. While it is possible that a long-term visitor will achieve enough understanding of the host culture to be knowledgeably critical, such ability is long in coming, rarely insightful, and nearly always unappreciated by host-country nationals. To avoid complicating the already difficult task of intercultural communication, participants in a cross-cultural situation need to consider first the possibility that a negative evaluation might be based on an unrecognized cultural difference rather than the result of astute cross-cultural analysis. Each person needs to be aware that he or she is evaluating the other, often on similarly ethnocentric grounds, and seek to suspend these kinds of evaluations until the potential spiraling effects of the action have been considered. Suspension of judgment is particularly difficult for professionals, since much of their credibility and self-esteem may lie in being able to exercise quick, accurate evaluation. Professionals operating cross-culturally might usefully define their primary goal as communication rather than evaluation. It would then become apparent that swift evaluation is likely to be ethnocentric and detrimental to effective intercultural communication.

Americans can overcome the tendency to stereotype and generate negative evaluations by approaching every cross-cultural situation as a kind of experiment. They should assume that some kind of cultural difference exists but that the nature of the difference is unclear. Using available generalizations about the other culture, they can formulate a hypothesis and then test it for accuracy. Lacking a generalization about the other culture, the hypothesis can be based on possible contrasts to a typical American pattern in the situation. The hypothesis should be tested by acting tentatively as if it were accurate and by watching carefully to see what happens, as illustrated in the following example:

> An American student in a homestay in Germany is sitting down to her first dinner with her host family. (The family speaks English.) She avoids the initial pitfall in a cross-cultural encounter—intolerable ambiguity—by treating the occasion as a chance to learn and not as a "command performance" at which she might fail. Nor does she fall back on her American behavior patterns, which might involve somewhat nervous chatter about what happened during the day and how she felt about it (importance of personal experience). By allowing the family to initiate the conversation, the student may be able to ascertain the pattern of topics that are appropriate for dinner conversation. But what if they wait for her? One hypothesis she might consider is that Germans typically do not engage in conversation during a meal. Thinking over what she knows about Europeans in general, she decides that this is not likely (although it is typical in some other cultures). Because she has not received a very complete predeparture orientation, the student is unaware of the generalization that Germans prefer to discuss intellectual or political issues over meals (and at other times as well). But the student does remember her mother telling her never to discuss politics and religion at the dinner table. Perhaps the German pattern is a contrast to this American social norm? She tentatively broaches the topic of the political problems of American forces stationed on German soil, ready to back off from the topic if it seems uncomfortable. However, the family engages this subject heartily, the student is relieved, and the homestay is off to a good start.[1]

Generating and using cultural generalizations effectively while avoiding stereotyping is one of the most demanding skills of intercultural communication. Cultural self-awareness is necessary, as is some knowledge of predominant patterns in the target culture and their variations (e.g., generational, gender, ethnic group). Although this knowledge is usually limited, it can still be used to hypothesize likely areas of contrast and possible communication problems. As more knowledge of relevant cultural differences is acquired, generalizations can become more specific, hypotheses more particular, and communication difficulties more predictable. However, if Americans (and others) seek sure answers that will eliminate all ambiguity from communication, the result is likely to be stereotyping.

Footnote

1. This example represents dozens of reports by exchange students interviewed by the authors. Unfortunately, most students did not discover the procedure described until well after the first dinner.

Scientific Failure of the Concept of Human Races

by L. Luca Cavalli-Sforza, Paolo Menozzi *and* Alberto Piazza

The classification into races has proved to be a futile exercise for reasons that were already clear to Darwin. Human races are still extremely unstable entities in the hands of modern taxonomists, who define from 3 to 60 or more races (Garn 1971). To some extent, this latitude depends on the personal preference of taxonomists, who may choose to be "lumpers" or "splitters." Although there is no doubt that there is only one human species, there are clearly no objective reasons for stopping at any particular level of taxonomic splitting. In fact, the analysis we carry out for purposes of evolutionary study shows that the level at which we stop our classification is completely arbitrary. Explanations are statistical, geographic, and historical. Statistically, genetic variation within clusters is large compared with that between clusters (Lewontin 1972; Nei and Roychoudhury 1974). All populations or population clusters overlap when single genes are considered, and in almost all populations, all alleles are present but in different frequencies. No single gene is therefore sufficient for classifying human populations into systematic categories.

As one goes down the scale of the taxonomic hierarchy toward the lower and lower partitions, the boundaries between clusters become even less clear. The evolutionary explanation is simple. There is great genetic variation in all populations, even in small ones. This individual variation has accumulated over very long periods, because most polymorphisms observed in humans antedate the separation into continents, and perhaps even the origin of the species, less than half a million years ago. The same polymorphisms are found in most populations, but at different frequencies in each, because the geographic differentiation of humans is recent, having taken perhaps one-third or less of the time the species has been in existence. There

has therefore been too little time for the accumulation of a substantial divergence. The difference between groups is therefore small when compared with that within the major groups, or even within a single population. In addition, our species and its immediate predecessor, *Homo erectus,* showed considerable migratory activity in all directions, some of which are likely to have resulted in admixtures between branches that had separated a long time before. Whatever genetic boundaries may have developed, given the strong mobility of human individuals and populations, there probably never were any sharp ones, or if there were, they were blurred by later movements. There may still exist weak genetic boundaries in some regions, but they only mean that there has been less local admixture across certain barriers. For instance, Barbujani and Sokal (1990; Sokal et al. 1988) have found a number of weak genetic boundaries in Europe linked with geographic, ecological, and linguistic differences.

From a scientific point of view, the concept of race has failed to obtain any consensus; none is likely, given the gradual variation in existence. It may be objected that the racial stereotypes have a consistency that allows even the layman to classify individuals. However, the major stereotypes, all based on skin color, hair color and form, and facial traits, reflect superficial differences that are not confirmed by deeper analysis with more reliable genetic traits and whose origin dates from recent evolution mostly under the effect of climate and perhaps sexual selection. By means of painstaking multivariate analysis, we can identify "clusters" of populations and order them in a hierarchy that we believe represents the history of fissions in the expansion to the whole world of anatomically modern humans. At no level can clusters be identified with races, since every level of clustering would determine a different partition and there is no biological reason to prefer a particular one. The successive levels of clustering follow each other in a regular sequence, and there is no discontinuity that might tempt us to consider a certain level as a reasonable, though arbitrary, threshold for race distinction. Minor changes in the genes or methods used shift some populations from one cluster to the other. Only "core" populations, selected because they presumably underwent less admixture, confer greater compactness to the clusters and stability to the classification tree. Although the hope of producing a good taxonomy is a lost cause—a minor scientific loss—that of reconstructing evolutionary history retains full strength and has the advantage that hypotheses can be tested on the basis of other, independent sources of data. Greater confidence in the conclusions must come from agreement with external sources of relevant evidence rather than from internal analysis.

The word "race" is coupled in many parts of the world and strata of society with considerable prejudice, misunderstanding, and social problems. Xenophobia, political convenience, and a variety of motives totally unconnected with science are the basis of racism, the belief that some races are biologically superior to the others and that they have therefore an inherent right to dominate. Racism has existed from time immemorial but only in the nineteenth century were there attempts to justify it on the basis of scientific arguments. Among these, social Darwinism, mostly the brainchild of Herbert Spencer (1820-1903), was an unsuccessful attempt to justify unchecked social competition, class stratification, and even Anglo-Saxon imperialism. Not surprisingly, racism is often coupled with caste prejudice and has been invoked as motivation for condoning slavery, or even genocide. There is no scientific basis to the belief of genetically determined "superiority" of one population over another. None of the genes that we consider has any accepted connection with behavioral traits, the genetic determination of which is extremely difficult to study and presently based on soft evidence. The claims of a genetic basis for a general superiority of one population over another are not supported by any of our findings. Superiority is a political and socioeconomic concept, tied to events of recent political, military, and economic history and to cultural traditions of countries or groups. This superiority is rapidly transient, as history shows, whereas the average genotype does not change rapidly. But racial prejudice has an old tradition of its own and is not easy to eradicate.

ETHNICITY AND ETHNIC RELATIONS

by Adalberto Aguirre, Jr. and Jonathan H. Turner

Why did early white settlers in America kill millions of Native Americans? Why did slavery exist, and why are its vestiges still evident today? Why are so many Americans fearful of immigrants? Why are Poles, Italians, the Irish, and other groups still the subjects of ethnic jokes? And on the world scene, why do Protestants and Catholics in northern Ireland try to kill each other? Why have the new freedoms in the former Soviet Union unleashed a torrent of hostility between ethnic groups? Why has the former Yugoslavia degenerated into a war of ethnic hatred? Why is there a "new Nazi" underground in Germany fifty years after the death camps closed? Why are neo-Nazi, skinhead, and Klan hate groups a part of the American scene at the close of the twentieth century? Why is it so difficult to dismantle apartheid in South Africa?

Such questions could go on and on, but the point is clear: people who define each other as "different" often have trouble developing harmonious relations. Our goal in this book is to understand why this is so, and in the chapters to follow, we explore the fundamental reasons for the tensions and conflicts among prominent ethnic populations in the United States. Unfortunately, ethnic strife exists worldwide; ever since early subpopulations of human beings first came into contact, strife has been an aspect of that contact. Ethnic tensions are thus not only very volatile and widespread, but also very old. How, then, are we to understand and deal with this ubiquitous and long-standing feature of human organization? Let us begin with some definitions; in the next chapter we can explore the ideas surrounding them.

RACE AND ETHNICITY

The term "race" connotes biological differences among peoples—skin color, facial features, stature, and the like—which are transmitted from generation to generation. As such, these biological differences are seen as permanent characteristics of people. The notion of race does not make much sense as a biological concept, however, because the physical characteristics that make people distinctive are trivial. A few alleles on genes are what account for these differences, and, most importantly, these alleles are on genes that are not determinative of basic biological functions. These biological differences are, in essence, superficial. Moreover, they do not mark clear boundaries: Where does "black" end and "white" begin? Is the child of an Asian mother and a European father more Asian or more European?

Even though biological differences are superficial and difficult to use as markers of boundaries between peoples, they are important sociologically. For if people believe that others are biologically distinctive, they tend to respond to them as being different. And, when people associate superficial biological differences with variations in people's psychological, intellectual, and behavioral makeup, they may feel justified in treating members of a distinctive group in discriminatory ways. For example, if someone considers black skin an important distinction, and this distinction becomes associated in that person's mind with differences in behavior and psychological functioning, then that superficial biological difference influences how that person relates to people with black skin.

How, then, should we conceptualize the notion of "race" if it does not make much biological sense? Our answer is to subordinate and incorporate the idea of race into a broad definition of *ethnicity*. When a subpopulation of individuals reveals, or is perceived to reveal, shared historical experiences as well as unique organizational, behavioral, and cultural characteristics, it exhibits its ethnicity. For instance, when country of origin, religion, family practices, interpersonal style, language, beliefs, values, and other characteristics are used to demark a population of individuals from others, then ethnicity is operating. The more visible the characteristics marking ethnicity, the more likely those in an ethnic category are to be treated differently.

Here is where race or presumptions of biological differences become a part of ethnicity. Physical features like skin color and facial features can be used as highly visible markers of organizational, behavioral, and cultural differences among individuals. When someone is labeled "black," more than skin color is involved; there is also a whole cluster of assumptions about historical experiences, behavior, organization, and culture associated with this label. The same is true for labels such as "white," "Asian," "Mexican," "Jew," "Indian," and so on.

In fact, as we will come to see, labels often are self-fulfilling in creating and sustaining ethnicity. If people are given a label because of their skin color, and then discriminated against as if they are different, they will react to such treatment by behaving and organizing in ways that are indeed distinctive. Once behavioral and organizational differences exist and are elaborated culturally into norms, beliefs, and other systems of symbols, they become an additional marker of differences, both justifying the earlier label and the distinctive treatment of these others as somehow "different." So, if biology or race can become a part of the label for denoting populations, it can also be considered an aspect of the dynamics producing and sustaining ethnicity. Indeed, racial labels are like turbochargers in ethnic relations: They escalate the heat and power of emotions and tensions.

ETHNIC GROUPS

What is a group? Sociologists generally define a group as a gathering of individuals in face-to-face interaction. According to this definition, an ethnic "group" would be a number of interacting individuals distinguished by their ethnicity. Not every one of these individuals interacts face to face, but they may interact in various social settings. Obviously, when we use the term "ethnic group," we have something much bigger, broader, more inclusive in mind. *Subpopulations* of individuals in a society can be distinguished by their history as well as their distinctive behavior, organization, culture, and, perhaps, biology. An ethnic group is a subpopulation of individuals who are labeled and categorized by the general population and, often, by the members of a group itself as being of a particular type of ethnicity: They reveal a unique history as well as distinctive behavioral, organizational, and cultural characteristics, and, as a result, often are treated differently by others. In addition to the term "ethnic group," in this text we use the terms "ethnic subpopulation" and "ethnic population," which more accurately describe the groups we are discussing.

Minority Groups

What is a *minority group?* Louis Wirth (1945:347) long ago offered the basic definition, the general thrust of which is still used today: "A group of people who, because of their physical or cultural characteristics, are singled out from others in the society in which they live for differential and unequal treatment and who therefore regard themselves as objects of collective discrimination." There are many problems with this definition, however. First, it is not a group but members of a larger subpopulation rather that is singled out for unequal treatment. Second, the label "minority" is not always accurate; sometimes it is a majority, as is the case in South Africa, that is discriminated against. Thus, we should begin to revise this traditional definition of "minority group" by acknowledging what it really means: an ethnic subpopulation in a society subject to discrimination by members of more powerful ethnic subpopulations. Usually the victimized subpopulation is a numerical minority, and the more powerful discriminators are in the majority. Since this is not always true, the important issue is this: Which ethnic subpopulation has the power to discriminate? The more powerful subpopulation is the dominant or superordinate ethnic group, and the less powerful ethnic subpopulation is the subordinate group. This latter terminology, which revolves around dominance and subordination, more accurately frames the issues that were once classified as "minority group relations."

Ethnic Discrimination

Phrases like "unequal treatment" and "distinctive treatment" have been used rather loosely thus far. These and related terms can be consolidated by one key term: discrimination. In general, *discrimination*

is the process by which an individual, group, or subpopulation of individuals acts in ways that deny another individual, group, or subpopulation access to valued resources. So, in the context of ethnic relations, *ethnic discrimination* is the process by which the members of a more powerful and dominant ethnic subpopulation deny the members of another, less powerful and subordinate ethnic subpopulation full access to valued resources—jobs, income, education, health, prestige, power, or anything that the members of a society value.

Today, the term *reverse discrimination* is often used to emphasize that programs designed to overcome the effects of past discrimination against members of a subordinate subpopulation often deny some members of the dominant subpopulation equal access to valued resources. What makes these programs so controversial is that those denied access to resources—say, particular classes of jobs—are usually not the ones who engaged in discrimination in the past. Thus, they feel cheated and angry—emotions that the victims of discrimination almost always feel. The phrase "reverse discrimination" is pejorative in that it emphasizes the net loss of resources for those who may no longer discriminate but whose forefathers did; and so, they ask: Is this fair? On the other side, those who must live with the legacy of past discrimination ask: How are the effects of past discrimination to be overcome? There is no easy answer to either of these questions, but one thing is clear: The definition of the term "discrimination" often becomes the centerpiece of ideological and political debate over ethnic tensions (Kinder and Sanders, 1990; Thomas, 1990; Feagins, 1990; and Ross, 1990).

The process of discrimination is the most important force sustaining ethnicity in a society. Discrimination denies some people access to what is valued, making it a highly volatile process. Because discrimination varies in nature, degree, and form, we need to identify some of its dimensions.

Types of Discrimination

The type of discrimination against an ethnic population varies considerably. The most intense form is *genocide,* where members of an ethnic subpopulation are killed or, potentially, an entire ethnic group is exterminated. The Nazi death camps with their gas chambers constituted an effort at genocide; the exposure of Native Americans to diseases and then the carnage of the Indian wars resulted in the virtual genocide of the original population in America. More recently, the "ethnic cleansing" policies of the Serbians in the former Yugoslavia is another example of genocidal behavior.

Expulsion is a somewhat less intense form of discrimination because those who are exiled from a society retain access to at least one highly valued resource: life. Expulsion is a common form of discrimination. For example, during the time of slavery in the United States, several American Presidents, including Abraham Lincoln, considered the creation of a black state in Africa to which "free" black people would be sent. Expulsion is usually forced, but it is often the case that one group makes life miserable for another and "forces" the latter to leave "voluntarily." Thus, the concept of expulsion has ambiguity: if we confine its use only to cases where people are thrown out of a country by direct coercion, the importance of more indirect expulsion, where people's lives are made so miserable that they pack up and leave, is underemphasized.

Segregation is a process of spatially isolating an ethnic subpopulation in areas where they cannot have the same access to valued resources as those who are not isolated. For instance, as we will see in Chapter 4, most African Americans were confined to the decaying cores of large cities during the post-World War II era by governmental and private housing policies and, as a result, they were denied access to the jobs, schools, and housing enjoyed by white Americans who moved to suburbia. The black townships and various rules of residence in South Africa mark another segregation pattern that denies access to resources. The Indian reservations that dot the American landscape are yet another form of segregation.

Exclusion is a pattern of discrimination that denies members of an ethnic group certain positions, independent of the effects of segregation. Slaves were denied basic citizenship rights. Up to just a few decades ago, African Americans were excluded

from most craft unions; even in industrial unions, they were allowed to rise only to certain grade levels and not beyond. For many decades, African Americans and Hispanics were excluded from the political arena through poll taxes, literacy tests, gerrymandering of districts, and other exclusionary tactics. Exclusion in the job sphere is especially harmful because it denies members of an ethnic group the money they could use to buy other valued resources—health care, housing, education, and political power. Exclusion from the political arena denies an ethnic group the power to move out of its subordinate position.

Selective inclusion is the process of allowing members of ethnic subpopulations into certain positions, while at the same time excluding them from other positions. For instance, Jewish people in Europe historically were excluded from most economic, social, and political positions but were included in the world of finance. In the United States, early Asian immigrants were allowed access to some positions—the Chinese were laborers on the railroads and later in small service businesses. According to Takaki (1993), the Japanese were denied access to the industrial labor market in the 1920s California; as a result, many moved into the agricultural labor market where they used their entrepreneurial skills to become successful farmers and land owners. Today many Asian immigrants are given easy access to ownership of small retail businesses but are excluded, to some degree, from white- and blue-collar positions in large companies. Historically, Mexican American laborers were included in the low-wage farm labor work force and, later, in other low-paying jobs in light industry, but they were excluded from better-paying economic positions as well as positions in the political and educational arena. Thus exclusion and selective inclusion tend to operate simultaneously, in a pincerlike movement that denies access to some positions and opens access only to those areas that are often (though not always) financially unrewarding or lacking in power and prestige.

BOX 1.1
The Gender Dimension of Discrimination

Discrimination denies people access to valued resources, such as jobs and income. Most of the analyses of ethnic groups in this text emphasize the ethnic subpopulation as a whole, but it is also necessary to emphasize that ethnic discrimination reveals a gender dimension: Men and women of any ethnic population have different degrees of access to many important resources, indicating that women and men are treated differently in American society. For example, examine the figures in the table below. Across the board, women received less income than their male counterparts. These differences reflect not only the income discrepancies between men and women in the same occupation, but also the disproportionate numbers of women in lower-paying occupations.

Ethnic Population	Male	Female	Proportion of Median Female Earnings to Male Earnings, %
White American	$28,540	$18,920	0.66
African American	20,430	17,390	0.85
Hispanic	14,047	9,861	0.70
Asian	22,168	14,122	0.63

The next table compares the occupational distribution of men and women in 1990. In the top-paying category—managerial and professional—the proportion of women equals or tops that of men, except within the Asian American population. But in the lower-paying technical, sales, and administrative support jobs (mostly secretarial), the proportion of women nearly doubles that of men. Coupled with the virtual exclusion of minority women from higher-skill, better-paying blue-collar positions such as precision production workers, craft laborers, repair people, operators, fabricators, and laborers (who are often unionized), the reason for the lower incomes of most minority women becomes clear: These women are excluded from most higher-paying occupations.

Selected Occupations by Sex, Race, and Ethnicity: 1990

Occupation	White Americans, % Male	White Americans, % Female	African Americans, % Male	African Americans, % Female	Hispanics, % Male	Hispanics, % Female	Asian Americans, % Male	Asian Americans, % Female	Native Americans, % Male	Native Americans, % Female
Managerial and professional specialty	27.3	27.4	13.4	18.8	10.7	16.0	35.9	27.9	13.5	20.9
Technical, sales, and administrative support	20.8	45.7	16.6	39.7	14.7	38.4	24.3	43.3	13.9	39.1
Service	8.7	16.1	17.5	27.0	16.2	25.1	14.6	15.7	10.0	23.8
Precision production, craft, and repair	19.9	2.1	16.3	2.3	20.6	2.7	12.4	3.0	22.1	3.2
Operations, fabrication, and labor	19.2	7.6	33.4	12.0	29.8	16.7	11.6	10.0	35.1	11.8
Farming, forestry, and fishing	4.1	1.1	2.8	0.2	8.0	1.1	1.2	0.1	5.4	1.2
	100.0	100.0	100.0	100.0	100.0	100.0	100.0	100.0	100.0	100.0

Source: 1990 Census Detailed Occupations EEO File for the United States.

The intensity of discrimination varies according to its type: from genocide and expulsion to physical segregation to exclusion and selective inclusion. None is pleasant, if you are on the receiving end. Historically, these patterns of discrimination have been implemented in various ways. Despite the variations, however, the underlying mechanisms of each type of discrimination are similar and are based on both informal and institutional practices. Let us now examine these mechanisms to see how ethnic discrimination is institutionalized and maintained over long stretches of time.

THE INSTITUTIONALIZATION OF DISCRIMINATION

Acts by individuals who seek to deny others access to valued resources are the most salient form of discrimination. When a white person refuses to sell a house to an Asian person, when a police officer physically abuses a member of a minority group, or when a supervisor refuses to promote an ethnic worker and these actions are taken simply because a person is a member of an ethnic group, discrimination is at work. These examples are isolated acts of discrimination if (1) they are not sanctioned by cultural values, beliefs, and norms; (2) they are not performed as a matter of policy within an organized structure such as a corporation, police department, board of realtors, school, or factory and (3) they are not frequent and pervasive in the informal contact among people within an organization. In contrast, *institutionalized discrimination* exists when these individual acts are sanctioned by cultural values, beliefs, laws, and norms; when they are part of the way a social structure normally operates; and when they are a pervasive and persistent feature of the contact among people.

The distinction between isolated acts of discrimination and institutionalized discrimination is easier to make in a definition than in practice. For example, when discrimination is institutionalized in one sphere—say, housing practices—it becomes easier to commit acts of discrimination in other arenas, such as schooling, politics, or jobs. If enough people practice such isolated acts of informal discrimination, these acts become institutionalized. In the United States, civil rights laws and cultural beliefs do not condone discrimination as they once did; indeed, they demand that all individuals be given equal access to schools, jobs, housing, and other important areas. They even mandate punishments for those who discriminate, and they have led to the creation of watchdog and enforcement agencies. Yet, individual acts of informal discrimination are so widespread in many communities that discrimination is informally institutionalized even in the face of formal prohibitions.

Thus, the process of institutionalized discrimination is subtle and complex. It can operate at formal and informal levels, and these two levels can even be in contradiction. Isolated acts of discrimination can increase in frequency when they constitute a normatively sanctioned and, hence, institutionalized form of discrimination.

The subtlety and complexity of institutionalized discrimination is demonstrated in past patterns of discrimination which are now formally banned and no longer practiced. Yet, the legacy and cumulative effects of past discrimination can be so great that they prevent ethnic subpopulations from gaining equal access to resources. For example, many African Americans today live in urban slums away from decent schools, housing, and jobs because of past patterns of discrimination. In this environment, many African Americans do not acquire the education, job skills, or motivation that would enable them to leave the slums and take advantage of new opportunities that were not available even thirty years ago. Thus, sometimes the legacy of the past operates as a barrier in the present and constitutes a pervasive pattern of discrimination. For example, many blacks (Native Americans, Hispanics, and others) are systematically denied by their present circumstances the same access to valued resources as whites. Even if we could assume that no employer, realtor, teacher, or police officer currently acts in a discriminatory way, many African Americans would not have the same degree of access to resources as white Americans because of their present location, segregated in slums with a long history of exclusion from most spheres of mainstream life in America. The same is true of other ethnic groups, and so we must appreciate that institutionalized discrimination has a lag effect beyond the period in the past when individuals and organizations practiced discrimination routinely.

Another facet of institutionalized discrimination is that it is often unintentional. This is certainly the case with the holdover effects of past discrimination discussed above, but more is involved. To take the most obvious example in the United States today—schools—it is now clear that the school curriculum, testing procedures, and classroom activities place some ethnic students at a disadvantage in comparison with others. Such is not intentionally the case, at least in most instances; and it could be argued (albeit problematically) that schools facilitate the acquisition of the critical skills necessary for success and for overcoming the effects of past discrimination. Yet, if the schools are organized in ways that are, for example, alien to students, that are not responsive to the problems of poor children or immigrant children, and that are insensitive to the distinctive culture of a minority population, then the schools can become a source of discrimination. Students will have difficulty adjusting and will become discouraged—dropping out and finding themselves with few prospects for jobs and income. The school may not have intended this to occur—indeed just the opposite—but the very nature of its structure and operation have worked to discourage students and, in so doing, have subtly and inadvertently discriminated against students whose access to resources is dramatically lowered when they drop out (Hilliard, 1988; Medina, 1988; Trueba, 1986; McCarth, 1990). In a society that uses educational credentials as a quick and easy way to sort people out in a labor market, the consequences for members of ethnic subpopulations who find the school experience unrewarding extend to all spheres of their life—their job, home, income, and health.

Thus, the institutionalization of discrimination is an important force in ethnic relations. The pattern of institutionalization affects the type of segregation, exclusion, and selective inclusion that a subordinate ethnic subpopulation experiences, if it is not killed off or sent away. As the pattern of institutionalized discrimination changes, so does the pattern of segregation, exclusion, and selective inclusion.

ETHNIC STRATIFICATION

Discrimination, as it operates to segregate, exclude, and selectively include members of a subordinate ethnic subpopulation within a society, produces a system of ethnic stratification. Because discrimination determines how many and which types of valued resources the members of an ethnic subpopulation are likely to have, it establishes the location of an ethnic subpopulation within the stratification system of a society. Moreover, discrimination also determines the patterns of mobility, if any, across social class lines.

For our purposes, *ethnic stratification* refers to several interrelated processes:

1. The amount, level, and type of resources—such as jobs, education, health, money, power, and prestige—an ethnic subpopulation typically receives

2. The degree to which these shares of resources locate most members of an ethnic subpopulation in various social hierarchies

3. The extent to which these resource shares contribute to those distinctive behaviors, organizations, and cultural systems that provide justification to the dominant group for making them targets of discrimination

We can take almost any ethnic group—Hispanics, for example—and determine their average income, their level of political representation, and their average years of education. In performing this exercise, we soon find that, on the whole, most Hispanics in America have relatively low incomes, are underrepresented in the halls of political power, and attain less education than Anglo Americans. The statistics can be determined by simple counts of average income, years of education, and number of political offices held. The numbers show the amount of resources Hispanics possess in American society. One often finds, in addition, differences in the shares of resources within an ethnic subpopulation. There are affluent Hispanics; their average level of affluence, power, and prestige tends to vary in terms of which type of Hispanic—Mexican American, Cuban, Puerto Rican, South or Central American—is being addressed. Yet, when ethnic stratification is in evidence, a majority of a subpopulation does reveal a particular level and configuration of resource shares. On various social hierarchies—power, income and wealth, prestige, and education—this profile of resource shares locates a majority of the ethnic group. There are always deviations, of course, but when stratification is in force, these deviations apply to a minority of cases. Some Hispanics, such as Mexican Americans, are located near the bottom of the power, income and wealth, prestige, and education hierarchies, thereby placing them in the lower and working classes. There are middle- and upper-class Mexican Americans, to be sure, but they are a tiny minority. This profile of resource shares and the resulting location on various social hierarchies contribute to the distinctiveness of Mexican Americans and, as a consequence, justify new and continuing occurrences of prejudice and discrimination against them, thereby perpetuating the ethnic dimensions of social stratification.

In general, discrimination causes members of an ethnic subpopulation to be (1) overrepresented in lower and working classes, or (2) overrepresented in a narrow range of middle-class positions, usually in small businesses of various kinds. As discrimination lessens, mobility to other classes and positions within classes occur, but a holdover effect persists that limits such mobility for many.

Specifically, institutionalized discrimination, as it segregates, excludes, and selectively includes, determines the kinds and shares of resources received by members of an ethnic subpopulation; these shares locate them on society's hierarchies. By virtue of its pattern of resource shares and location on various social hierarchies, an ethnic subpopulation's distinctiveness is created and sustained. Thus, the principal consequence of ethnic discrimination is to give the broader stratification system in a society an ethnic dimension, one which is often more tension-producing and volatile than the normal antagonisms between members of different social classes.

ETHNIC PREJUDICE

The terms "prejudice" and "discrimination" are often uttered together, for it is presumed that prejudiced people discriminate, and vice versa. *Prejudice* is a set of beliefs and stereotypes about a category of people; hence, *ethnic prejudices* are beliefs and stereotypes about designated subpopulations who share certain identifying characteristics—biological, behavioral, organizational, or cultural—or at least are perceived to share these identifying characteristics. Those prejudices that lead to, and are used to justify, discrimination are negative, emphasizing the undesirable features of a subpopulation.

Does prejudice invariably lead to discrimination? In a classic study in the early 1930s, Richard La Piere (1934) observed in his travels with a Chinese couple that, despite a climate of hostility toward Asians in the United States at that time, the couple was served and treated courteously at hotels, motels, and restaurants. He was puzzled by this observation, because all the attitude surveys at that time revealed extreme prejudice by white Americans toward the Chinese. La Piere sent a questionnaire to the owners of the establishments where he and his companions had experienced courteous service to Asians asking if they would "accept members of the Chinese race as guests in your establishment." More than 90 percent said no, thus demonstrating that prejudice and discrimination do not always go together.

Robert Merton (1949) defined four categories of people in his analysis of the relationship between prejudice and discrimination:

1. All-weather liberals who are not prejudiced and do not discriminate

2. Reluctant liberals who are unprejudiced but will discriminate when it is in their interest to do so

3. Timid bigots who are prejudiced but afraid to show it

4. Active bigots who are prejudiced and quite willing to discriminate

In La Piere's study of motel owners, then, he encountered timid bigots who, in face-to-face contact with an ethnic group, did not implement their prejudices.

Even though prejudice does not always translate into discrimination, it is an important force in ethnic relations, for several reasons. First, prejudicial beliefs and stereotypes highlight, usually unfairly and inaccurately, certain characteristics of an ethnic subpopulation. By spotlighting these characteristics, they make ethnic group members become more identifiable, alerting others to their existence, separating them from the majority, and potentially, making them easier targets for discrimination. Second, prejudices present negative images of an ethnic group, legitimizing discrimination against such "undesirable" persons. Third, prejudices arouse fears about, and anger toward, an ethnic group, placing members of the ethnic group in constant tension with those who are prejudiced and, often, making them vulnerable to unprovoked acts of discrimination. Fourth, prejudice creates a general climate of intolerance for differences not only in a selected ethnic group, but in other categories of individuals as well (such as the disabled or the elderly).

Prejudice may generate potential or actual discrimination, but the reverse is also true: Acts of discrimination can generate prejudice or, as is often the case, reinforce existing prejudices. Most people feel they must justify their acts of discrimination; in a society like the United States, where cultural values emphasize equality and freedom, discrimination, which violates these values, has to be rationalized and made to seem appropriate. Prejudice is one mechanism for doing this because it makes the denial of freedom and equality seem acceptable "in this one case," since "after all, these people are so . . . (fill in the prejudice)." Those who are victims of discrimination react in different ways: sometimes passively and other times aggressively. The results vary: Prejudicial stereotypes are sometimes reinforced, other times changed or eliminated.

Thus, prejudicial beliefs based on negative and stereotypical portrayals of an ethnic subpopulation stimulate and sustain ethnic tensions. Such beliefs do not always translate into direct discriminatory action, but they target, highlight the negative, arouse fears and anger, and create a culture of intolerance that can erupt into discriminatory acts, or legitimate those that have been practiced in the past. Prejudice provides the rationale for discrimination, either before or after the fact, and is thus central to understanding discrimination and patterns of ethnic stratification.

ADAPTATIONS TO PREJUDICE AND DISCRIMINATION

When confronted with discrimination, members of a subordinate subpopulation respond. Usually, they seek to make the best of a difficult situation. Depending upon the nature and magnitude of discrimination, as well as upon other social conditions, several responses are possible: (1) passive acceptance, (2) marginal participation, (3) assimilation, (4) withdrawal, (5) rebellion, and (6) organized protest. Different segments of a minority population may resort to several of these adaptations at the same time, or a population may pass through different patterns of adaptation.

PASSIVE ACCEPTANCE

If the power of an ethnic group is small and the magnitude of the discrimination great, members of the group may have no choice but to accept the discrimination. For example, during the slavery era in the United States it was virtually impossible for African Americans to do anything but accept subjugation. Under severely oppressive conditions, populations acquire interpersonal techniques for dealing with their oppressors while maintaining their sense of identity and dignity. The stereotypic slave, as portrayed in Harriet Beecher Stowe's *Uncle Tom's Cabin*, offers a vivid example of such techniques. Uncle Tom's bowing and scraping and repeated use of the phrase, "Yes sir, yes sir," allowed him to gain favor with white people and to enjoy some degree of privilege. Passive acceptance, then, often is not passive, but active manipulation of a situation. Some slaves were able to develop their own culture and to enjoy some of the basic pleasures of life through the appearance of "passive acceptance." Of course, such a pattern of adjustment tends to perpetuate itself; the subordinate population does not initiate change, and the majority is not pressured to cease its discriminatory practices.

MARGINAL PARTICIPATION

At times, subordinate ethnic subpopulations can find a niche where they can use their creative resources and prosper. For example, Jews have often been able to find business opportunities and to prosper in societies that actively discriminated against them. At the turn of the century and up to the present, many Chinese Americans were able to prosper in small businesses providing services to the white American majority. Such marginal niches are created when the majority is not inclined to enter a specialized field. Marginal adaptation tends to be most successful when the minority population is small and does not enter areas dominated by the majority. It is probably for this reason that African Americans and Chicanos have been unable to find specialized niches; their numbers are simply too great.

ASSIMILATION

Assimilation is the process by which the members of an ethnic group become part of the broader culture and society, losing their distinctive character. Minorities that are less identifiable biologically and culturally are more readily assimilated. Ethnic populations that can be easily identified, however, have greater difficulty assimilating. It is for this reason that white ethnic groups in America, such as the Protestant Irish and Germans, have become largely assimilated, although enclaves are thriving in some large Eastern cities. Other Caucasian migrants, such as Poles, Italians, and Catholic Irish, have also tended to assimilate, although the east and midwest have cohesive ethnic cultures of these populations. African Americans, on the other hand, have had a more difficult time assimilating because of their visibility and the resulting ease with which the majority can locate them as targets of discrimination.

WITHDRAWAL AND SELF-SEGREGATION

Another adaptation to discrimination is withdrawal and the creation of a self-sustaining "society" within the broader society. Such subsocieties create and support their own communities, businesses, schools, leadership, churches, and other social forms. For example, the early black Muslim movement in America advocated a separate African American community, self-supporting and isolated from "white" institutions. Urban communities as well as rural communes were established and still prosper, although there has been a clear trend away from withdrawal and isolation among the black Muslims.

Self-segregation is a difficult adaptation to maintain. Opportunities are necessarily limited compared to those in the broader society. As a result, some seek these outside opportunities. Moreover, economic, political, and social isolation is often difficult to sustain in urban, media-dominated societies.

REVOLT AND REBELLION

Subordinate ethnic subpopulations do not always accept, assimilate, withdraw, or marginally participate. Frequently they rebel. Such rebellion can take a number of forms, one being general hostility and aggressive behavior toward the majority. For example, few white Americans would feel comfortable walking through a black ghetto or a Chicano barrio, because they fear that there is some likelihood of intimidation and assault. The urban riots of the 1960s and the turmoil in Los Angeles in the early 1990s are other examples of minorities "striking back" and venting their frustrations.

BOX 1.2
BOX 1.2
Where Minorities Are a Majority

When minorities—African Americans, Hispanics, and Asians—are all counted together, the 1990 census shows that in the 200 cities with at least 100,000 population, minorities constitute a majority in 51 of them. Most of the increase in such cities comes from Hispanic and Asian immigration over the last decade. Since 1980, 22 cities have seen minorities become the majority (these are starred). These shifts in the relative numbers of ethnic groups foretell of changes in power and patterns of discrimination.

City	*Percent Minority*		City	*Percent Minority*	
	1990	1980		1990	1980
Atlanta	69.7	67.9	Los Angeles	62.4	51.0
Baltimore	61.3	56.3	Macon*	53.1	45.3
Birmingham	64.2	56.3	Memphis*	56.3	48.5
Bridgeport*	54.0	39.6	Miami, Fla.	87.7	80.1
Chicago	61.9	56.0	New Haven*	50.8	40.6
Chula Vista*	50.0	31.3	New Orleans	66.8	59.5
Cleveland*	52.1	47.3	New York*	56.5	47.2
Corpus Christi	56.0	52.3	Newark	83.1	76.7
Dallas*	52.2	42.7	Oakland	71.5	64.0
Detroit	79.2	65.9	Ontario*	52.7	32.4
East Los Angeles	97.0	95.7	Oxnard	67.5	56.5
El Monte	84.6	65.1	Pasadena*	53.1	43.9
El Paso	73.5	66.5	Paterson	75.1	62.7
Elizabeth*	60.0	45.6	Pomona	71.6	52.5
Flint*	51.6	44.5	Richmond	57.0	52.3
Fresno*	50.3	36.2	Salinas*	61.0	47.0
Gary, Ind.	85.8	77.8	San Antonio	63.6	61.6
Hartford	69.1	54.5	San Bernadino*	54.2	42.1
Hialeah	89.0	75.8	San Francisco*	53.2	46.2
Honolulu	74.3	69.7	San Jose*	50.2	35.1
Houston*	59.2	47.1	Santa Ana	76.7	53.8
Inglewood	91.1	77.6	Savannah	53.8	50.6
Jackson*	56.6	47.7	Stockton*	56.2	41.2
Jersey City	63.1	50.1	Vallejo	53.7	38.7
Laredo	94.3	93.2	Washington	72.5	73.6
Long Beach	50.2	30.9			

Source: The Associated Press.

ORGANIZED PROTEST

Rebellious outbursts are often part of a larger social movement. Subordinate ethnic groups frequently become organized and begin to make broad-based and concerted efforts to change patterns of discrimination. The civil rights movement represented one such effort. Beginning with sit-ins and freedom rides, progressing to large-scale demonstrations, teeming over into riots, and culminating in several national organizations that effectively changed many legal and social patterns, African Americans successfully challenged pervasive discriminatory practices. The movement has been far from successful, however, since substantial integration of African Americans into the American mainstream has not occurred. But when an ethnic population is large and organized, it can generate political power and initiate some degree of social change. When minorities become majorities in cities and regions, as has often been the case in late twentieth century in the United States, they can wield additional power and can force changes in old patterns of discrimination.

SUMMARY

Ethnic antagonism is one of the oldest and most pervasive phenomenon affecting patterns of human social organization. To study this phenomenon, it is necessary to define commonly used terms and discuss key concepts in order to understand the dynamics of ethnicity. The term "race" is of little importance biologically, but it is relevant sociologically. For if people perceive and believe others to be biologically distinctive and different, superficial biological traits become an important consideration in the formation of ethnicity. For our purposes, ethnicity refers to the history as well as the behavioral, organization, and cultural features of people that make them distinctive and distinguishable from others. People can be distinguished on the basis of superficial biological traits, but these traits are associated with presumed behavioral, organizational, and cultural features—that is, with ethnicity.

The term "ethnic group" is commonly used, but we prefer the term "ethnic subpopulation." The latter term emphasizes the fact that people who are distinguished on the basis of an interrelated cluster of characteristics—biological, cultural, behavioral, and organizational—constitute a population more than a closed group. They are not all necessarily engaged in face-to-face contact, as the notion of "group" implies. To be sure, people's involvement in local groups and other structures sustain their distinctive patterns of organization, but these do not embrace the population as a whole. Ethnic subpopulations exist, instead, within a larger, more inclusive population. This point is not merely semantic; it is fundamental to an understanding of the dynamics of ethnicity.

The term "minority group" is also limited. Not all ethnic subpopulations subject to discrimination are minorities. They can constitute the majority in a community or in a nation as a whole. The underlying issue is power. Which groups have the power to limit the activities of other groups? More accurate terms are "superordinate ethnic subpopulations" and "subordinate ethnic subpopulations."

Discrimination is the process of denying others access to valued resources. Ethnic discrimination occurs when members of a superordinate ethnic subpopulation are able to limit or deny members of a subordinate ethnic population access to valued resources—jobs, income, education, power, health care, and anything that is valued and prized in a society. Ethnic discrimination surfaces in several different forms: genocide, or the systematic killing of members in a subordinate ethnic population; expulsion, or the exiling of all or selected members of an ethnic population; segregation, or the spatial confinement or isolation of members of an ethnic group so that they have difficulty gaining access to resources; exclusion, or the denial of rights to positions in a society that provide access to valued resources; and selective inclusion, or the confinement of members of an ethnic subpopulation to a narrow range of positions in the society. These types of discrimination gain effectiveness as discrimination becomes institutionalized. We define institutionalized discrimination as individual acts of discrimination that are: (1) pervasive; (2) culturally supported in norms, beliefs, and values; and (3) lodged in social structures as matters of policy and practice. The more institutionalized the discrimination is, the more a subordinate ethnic subpopulation is segregated, excluded, and selectively included, while being vulnerable to genocide and expulsion. Discrimination is thus the central process underlying ethnic problems in society.

Institutionalized discrimination produces ethnic stratification. When members of a subordinate ethnic subpopulation receive only certain types and levels of valued resources, it becomes possible to establish their location on the social hierarchies of society. On the basis of this location, the distinctiveness of an ethnic group is retained, thereby making it a target of further prejudice and discrimination.

Prejudice refers to negative and stigmatizing beliefs, concepts, and stereotypes about people; ethnic prejudice is based on negative beliefs, conceptions, and stereotypes about members of a subpopulation distinguishable in terms of their history and biological, behavioral, cultural, and organizational features. Prejudice and discrimination are not perfectly correlated, but discrimination cannot be easily institutionalized without widespread prejudice among dominant ethnic subpopulations.

Prejudice and discrimination force their targets to respond and adapt. Assimilation, or the elimination of ethnically distinct characteristics and adoption of those of the superordinate ethnic population, is one method of adaptation. At the other extreme are rebellion and revolt against superordinate ethnic groups, the goal being redistribution of power and, hence, the patterns of discrimination. Another response to discrimination is organized protest, often arising out of or even prompting acts of rebellion, in which ethnic groups and their allies organize to change patterns of discrimination. Yet another response is withdrawal and self-segregation of the subordinate ethnic group in order to isolate itself from the discriminatory acts of others. Members of an ethnic group may choose to accept their position passively, or they may participate marginally, finding narrow niches where they can secure resources. This chapter has presented many useful terms and distinctions which will deepen our understanding of and provide a perspective on ethnic relations in America. These distinctions do not explain ethnic relations; they only describe

them. We also need to know why people make ethnic distinctions, why they discriminate, *why* they hold prejudices, and *why* superordinate populations force subordinate groups to adapt in certain ways. Explaining these "why" issues is the job of theory. Within this framework of definitions and distinctions we can explore the theories that have been used to explain ethnicity, prejudice, discrimination, and other aspects of ethnic relations.

POINTS OF DEBATE

In any society where distinct ethnic subpopulations exist, the issue of ethnicity is a subject of debate and controversy. No society revealing ethnic differences has ever been able to organize itself in ways that avoid the tension and conflict accompanying ethnic identity. The United States is no exception; indeed, American society is one of the few in history that has sought to integrate so many large and diverse ethnic subpopulations into its cultural core. The problems of ethnicity in the United States have stimulated and continue to create many points of debate. When reading the coming chapters, keep in mind the following controversial issues.

1. The "first American dilemma": How can a society that values equality and freedom engage in systematic discrimination against minority subpopulations? This question is rhetorical, because the evidence is irrefutable that discrimination has occurred, and continues to occur, on a massive and long-term scale. Can the accumulated effects of such discrimination be undone?

2. The "second American dilemma": Can the values of freedom and equality be used to justify efforts to compensate the descendants of past discrimination? An affirmative answer to this question has many implications, all of which are debatable: (a) Are Americans willing to spend billions of tax dollars to create jobs, housing, and educational programs to overcome the effects of past discrimination? (b) Is private enterprise willing or able to participate on a massive scale in creating jobs for members of particular ethnic groups who have been the victims of this legacy of discrimination? (c) Are

white Americans willing to give up some of their access to valued resources so that disadvantaged minority groups can increase their access, or is such action simply going to encourage accusations of "reverse discrimination?"

3. If Americans are unwilling to meet the challenges posed by the second American dilemma, what is the alternative? Conflict and violence among ethnic groups is escalating, poverty among ethnic groups is on the rise; out-of-wedlock childbearing is reaching epidemic proportions (now 63 percent) among African Americans; substance abuse and other social problems among minority groups are growing; crimes committed by minority group members are increasing; and innumerable problems are arising from the accumulated effects of past discrimination. This reality confronts Americans in their daily lives. What is to be done? Nothing? Build more prisons? Hire more police? Actively try to address the problems at enormous cost? What are the viable options? Such questions are ultimately part of any discussion of ethnicity in America.

DRAWING THE BOUNDARIES OF ETHNICITY

by Milton Yinger

This was to have been a fairly straightforward essay on ethnicity, built upon a long-standing interest. Then somebody started a revolution, tore down a wall, declared independence. People of many different inclinations leaped into the openings thus created. This is a fluid moment in human history, which, "taken at the flood" can "lead on to fortune." But it can be a time during which, opportunities neglected, we drift "in shallows and in miseries."

Humane goals, wise policies, and personal courage in the midst of ethnic conflicts mingle with revenge, personal ambition, and the fanaticism that grows out of the release of suppressed needs and desires. The conflicts command most of our attention. One is tempted to declare with Horatio, in the last scene of *Hamlet:*

> And let me speak to the yet unknowing world
> How these things came about. So shall you hear
> Of carnal, bloody, and unnatural acts,
> Of accidental judgments, casual slaughters,
> Of deaths put on by cunning and forced cause,
> And, in the upshot, purposes mistook
> Fall'n on the inventors' heads.

Those lines, written nearly four hundred years ago, could have been written in recent months about Bosnia, Los Angeles, Nagorno-Karabakh, Iraq, Somalia, Afghanistan, Kenya, Mozambique, Zaire, India, or Peru. This list could be greatly extended.

Other lines are being written, however, telling stories that are not so shattering. A score of African states, after reveling in their independence, have begun to discover that their homegrown tyrants have proved no better—and with the added ethnic violence, probably worse—than their foreign oppressors. Little is to be gained by backing away from the jaws of a crocodile, they are discovering, only to be torn by the claws of a tiger. The Republic of South Africa has also taken the precious early steps on a long journey toward democracy. And western European states, a generation late, are beginning to face the complex multi-ethnic situation they are carrying into their Community.

Particularly in the early chapters, I pull away from such critical and immediate events in an effort to build a solid foundation for the analytic study of ethnicity. Throughout the essay, however, the stubborn facts—often tragic, sometimes heartening—command attention.

THE DEFINITION AND MEASUREMENT OF ETHNICITY

The boundaries of things of interest to social scientists are often drawn in different ways by different observers. Theoretical perspectives, ideologies, and the data being examined all affect the process of definition. Thus "ethnic groups" range, in various usages, from small, relatively isolated, nearly primordial kin-and-culture groups within which much of life proceeds, all the way to large categories (not groups) of people defined as alike on the basis of one or two shared characteristics (e.g., Latino Americans, Asian Americans, Blacks in South Africa, the Maghrebi Muslims in France).

If groups with vastly different size, historical depth, links to other groups, and self-perceptions are all going to be called "ethnic," we must be acutely aware of the scope of the definition. Ethnic groups are a "family," a "class," or perhaps even a "phylum"—not a "species," to use the terminology of biological classification. It is of value to know that the whale, the bat, and the lion are mammals, all members of the same class to which *Homo sapiens* belongs. They share important traits; however they are also enormously different. Much would be lost if only their similarities or only their differences were studied.

And so it is with ethnic groups. It seems unlikely that the term will be pared down to some small part of the present usages. We have not yet developed a clear typology marking different points— in terms of salience, strength of individual identities, importance to societies, and the like—within the range. We can perhaps suggest the outer limits by

noting that current ethnic movements in developed societies are different in many ways from what can be called primary ethnic groups in developing societies.

Ethnicity as a social phenomenon converges, by imperceptible steps, with related yet distinctive phenomena. Where shall we draw the line, stating that "here is ethnicity," in efforts to suggest a definition that will maximize our understanding? Both broad and narrow definitions have scientific advantages and disadvantages. One helps us to see similarities amidst differences (similarities in world views among Native Americans—three hundred or more quite diverse tribes). The other helps us to see differences amidst similarities (e.g., Oneidas and Seminoles and Sioux). In our examination of the seamless web of life, both perspectives are needed.

In a general definition, an ethnic group is a segment of a larger society whose members are thought, by themselves or others, to have a common origin and to share important segments of a common culture and who, in addition, participate in shared activities in which the common origin and culture are significant ingredients. We need to distinguish a sociologically and psychologically important ethnicity from one that is only administrative or classificatory. We might call these "hard" and "soft" ethnicities. The former connects directly with many aspects of life; the latter is marginal. A hard ethnic order is thoroughly institutionalized, with clear separating boundaries and a strong ideology. A soft ethnic order has blurred, permeable lines, incomplete institutionalization, and an ambivalent ideology. To draw this distinction we need to expand our behavioral measures of ethnic identity; we cannot be content with naming and counting.

The definition of an ethnic group I have suggested has three ingredients: 11) The group is perceived by others in the society to be different in some combination of the following traits: language, religion, race, and ancestral homeland with its related culture; (2) the members also perceive themselves as different; and (3) they participate in shared activities built around their (real or mythical) common origin and culture. Each of these is a variable, of course; hence we need to devise a scale of ethnicity. Measured by these three criteria, one can be fully ethnic or barely ethnic. Moreover, these factors vary independently of one another to some degree. If one transposes each of the three criteria into a question and answers it, for simplicity, either yes or no, there are eight possible combinations. Different forms of ethnicity have different causes and consequences. Putting them into a table, one gets a formal, and at this stage rather arid, typology of ethnic groups (see table 1.1) In particular times and places, several of the categories may be unimportant. Showing the full possible range, however, may help us to see ethnicity as a variable.

Authors concentrate on different combinations of the three variables that together mark the parameters of ethnicity. This helps to account for some of the disagreements in the literature. In my judgment, if even one of the three questions is answered yes, there is an ethnic factor operating that deserves attention, in terms of its causes and consequences. Type 4, for example, which I have called "Hidden Ethnicity," is not perceived as such

either by the participants or by others. But if in fact there are activities built around a common origin and ancestral culture, perhaps hidden by a national ideology that obscures the presence of ethnic lines, the consequences may be quite significant. This is most likely to be true among members of dominant groups. One need scarcely say that type 6, Stereotyped Ethnicity, can have important consequences, even in the absence of shared activities or perception by the individuals involved that they are ethnically distinct. Imagined Ethnicity, type 7, exists only in the beliefs of the members, but it doubtless affects their behavior and is potentially more important if the situation within which they live changes.

If the three criteria were seen as variables, rather than attributes, more subtle and refined distinctions among types and intensities of ethnicity could be drawn. We are a long way, however, from being able to measure and compare an 8-8-2 profile, let us say, with a 2-2-8 or a 5-5-5.

TABLE 1.1 VARIETIES OF ETHNIC IDENTITY

		I. Are They Perceived by Others as Ethnically Distinct?			
		Yes		No	
	II.	Do Individuals Perceive Themselves as Ethnically Distinct?		Do Individuals Perceive Themselves Ethnically Distinct?	
III. Do they participate in shared activities?		Yes	No	Yes	No
Yes		1. Full	2. Unrecognized	3. Private	4. Hidden
No		5. Symbolic	6. Stereotyped	7. Imagined	8. Nonethnic

Examination of the relationships of ethnic groups to the societies of which they are a part reveals a different way of looking at ethnic variations. At least four major types can be found among multi-ethnic societies in the contemporary world:

A. A society can be built out of formally equal ethnic groups.

B. A society can be characterized by a major national cultural group, separated from one or more ethnic groups by a highly permeable boundary.

C. One or more ethnic groups can be strongly oriented toward an outside mother society.

D. One or more ethnic groups can be "imprisoned" as disprivileged minorities within the larger society.

These four types of societal patterns might be sketched as shown in figure 1.1.

These types are not mutually exclusive. One might think of a society built up of two or more layers each of which exhibits, to a greater or lesser degree, the characteristics of one of the societal types. It can well be argued that the United States has elements of all four types, each limiting the full applicability of the others but not excluding them entirely.

Failure to distinguish among such different societal patterns as these would deprive us of many crucial observations regarding ethnicity. It is also important to recognize that these patterns are not fixed. Societies move from one to another—or more accurately, the mix of the four types changes: boundaries become more or less permeable; equality among ethnic groups increases or decreases; orientation to outside societies grows stronger or weaker.

In defining ethnicity, some contemporary writers state that everyone belongs to an ethnic group. In those rare instances where there is minimal ethnic variation, societies are described simply as ethnically homogeneous. The association of a theory of ethnicity with the study of social conflict and discrimination—which for long has been a major emphasis—is reduced or eliminated. In that case,

societal type B (Fig. 1.1) could not exist, since the inner core would itself be an ethnic group.

A. Society composed of several ethnic groups

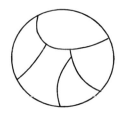

B. Society with a core cultural group surrounded by ethnic groups

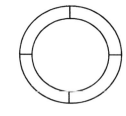

C. Society containing an ethnic group with outside orientation

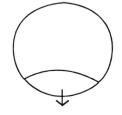

D. Society with one or more disadvantaged ethnic minorities

FIGURE 1.1

VARIETIES OF MULTI-ETHNIC SOCIETIES

If such shifts of definition as this can bring new insights they can also blur important distinctions. They may come about not because of major developments in theory or a flood of new data, but out of political or ideological interests. Arguing that a large and dominant population in a society is or is not an ethnic group is a political-moral position as well as an intellectual one. The choice depends on values and needs. Obviously, one does not argue against action in service of those values and needs; but it is appropriate to distinguish such action from scientific efforts to understand the sources and consequences of emphasis on ethnicity. Does one better understand England, for example, by dividing the population into an English core-group surrounded by others of Welsh, Irish, Scottish, Pakistani, Indian, Nigerian, Jamaican, and other descents, or by saying that the British population is made up of a multiplicity of ethnic groups, the largest of which is of Anglo-Saxon descent? To answer this question, I would need information on how the several groups perceive the situation and on the patterns of intragroup and intergroup behavior—that is, on the criteria of my definition of ethnicity.

In a similar way we can ask: is there an American core group joined by a series of ethnic Americans—Mexican Americans, African Americans, Jewish Americans, Asian Americans, Native Americans, and the like? Or are we all ethnics? We all have ancestors who came from other shores—some only a few years ago, others perhaps fifteen thousand years ago.

Franklin D. Roosevelt once startled members of the Daughters of the American Revolution by opening an address to them with the greeting, "fellow immigrants." (He was never invited back.) Margaret Mead, with calculated exaggeration, said that we are all "third generation." Most Americans share the sentiments implicit in such statements. It seems much more democratic to affirm that nobody—or everybody—is a hyphenated American. It seems wise, however, not to affirm that everybody is equal if thereby we obscure the fact that some are more equal than others or make it more difficult to recognize the conflict and dissension intrinsic to many multi-ethnic systems. The idea that many large and heterogeneous societies have a core group, however diverse its origins, adds a valuable perspective to the study of social process. This is not to affirm that the core culture is intrinsically better or worse than the ethnic cultures that surround it. It is an estimation that many people, in the United States and elsewhere, place little value on identity with their ancestral groups. They primarily are identified by others simply as Americans; they participate in few if any activities in which shared ancestry is important as symbol or substance. In addition, extensive ethnic mixture in their backgrounds makes shifts in orientation toward greater ethnic identification, unlikely.

In their recent study, Lieberson and Waters note that "there are a substantial number of people who recognize that they are white, but lack any clear-cut identification with, and/or knowledge of, a specific European origin." Despite heightened awareness of ethnicity in recent years, many Americans are unaware of their ethnic origins, choose to identify with none of the ethnic groups, see themselves simply as Americans, or do not answer an ancestry question on recent polls and census surveys.

A similar situation is found in France, where 80 percent or more of the population think of themselves and are thought of simply as French, despite two millennia of mixtures among a diverse group of migrants. The same can be said of China and even more strongly of Japan, where the mixed origins of the large majorities have been almost obliterated by the passage of centuries.

Invention of an ethnic label for the core group may seem to make it an ethnic group—and indeed words do both reflect and affect reality. But words can also deflect us from reality. Being a WASPish fellow, I find no difficulty in being categorized as a WASP. It is purely a category, however; it has little or no social reality for me. Like tens of millions of Americans, my ancestry is so mixed that the Anglo-Saxon part of WASP has somehow to absorb a bit of Scottish, Irish, Dutch, German, and Swedish. I belong to no organizations in which WASPishness is, even informally, a criterion for membership. If everyone is ethnic, then I am a WASP, but surely a weak one, a stingless one.

In renewing our attention to the important ethnic factor, we must not lose sight of earlier understandings. I would emphasize the point, made particularly by Linton, that many modern nations have as their core culture a great melange on which most members draw and to which they have contributed. Indeed, the hybrid vigor from such mixtures has been crucial to their development.

Many will remember how Linton put it:

> [I]nsidious foreign ideas have…wormed their way into [the American's] civilization without his realizing what was going on. Thus dawn finds the unsuspecting patriot garbed in pajamas, a garment of East Indian origin, and lying in a bed built on a pattern which originated in either Persia or Asia Minor. He is muffled to the ears in un-American materials: cotton, first domesticated in India; linen, domesticated in the Near East; wool from an animal native to Asia Minor; or silk whose uses were first discovered by the Chinese…
>
> On awakening he glances at the clock, a medieval European invention, uses one potent Latin word in abbreviated form, rises in haste, and goes to the

bathroom. Here, if he stops to think about it, he must feel himself in the presence of a great American institution…and will know that in no other country does the average man perform his ablutions in the midst of such splendor. But the insidious foreign influence pursues him even here. Even his bathtub and toilet are but slightly modified copies of Roman originals…

Breakfast over, as he scans the latest editorial pointing out the dire results to our institutions of accepting foreign ideas, he will not fail to thank a Hebrew God in an Indo-European language that he is a one hundred percent {decimal system invented by the Greeks) American (from Americus Vespucci, Italian geographer.

Perhaps today we should change the well-known saying to "That's as American as apple pie, pizza, dim sum, burritos, and nouvelle cuisine." The cultural landscape would be seen as even more diverse had Linton added attention to the influence of America's indigenous population and of the many streams of immigrants and refugees. I do not need to detail here the degree to which residents of the United States are all culturally Native American, African American, Irish, Jewish, Italian, German, and so forth. It is difficult to be much of a WASP in such a setting; and it is difficult for members of some other groups, after two or three generations of ancestors in the United States, to be closely bound into a particular ethnic group, from the cultural point of view.

Ethnicity is a topic filled with so many assumptions, guided by such poorly defined terms, and evocative of such strong emotions that we often fail to see the culture-building process going on before our eyes. This is clearly not a one-way process; nor is there the least danger of producing dead-level homogeneity. A special issue of the *American Ethnologist* on "Intra-cultural Variation" demonstrates that the fear of narrow uniformity in the absence of ethnic differences is not well founded, even in small and superficially uniform societies. With reference to the United States, the evidence does not support Novak's assertion that "the melting pot is a kind of homogenized soup." Most people are aware of the great variety of persons within their own groups. Failure to see it in others is a mark of our strong inclinations toward stereotype. When thinking of persons of Irish Catholic background, should one think of Joseph McCarthy or Eugene McCarthy? Is Harry Truman or Richard Nixon the typical WASP? Is Louis Farrakhan or Martin Luther King, Jr. the standard for African Americans?

Ethnic differentiation can add strength to a society, but not because it protects us from bland homogeneity. The development of a complex core culture, drawn from many sources, may make it possible, in Cooley's words, to move from differentiation based on isolation to differentiation based on choice.

COAT OF MANY COLORS: THE MYTH OF A WHITE AMERICA

by Eugene Eoyang

But the things you will learn from the Yellow
an' Brown, They'll 'elp you a lot with the White!

RUDYARD KIPLING, *The Ladies*

In the traditional translations of the story of
Joseph in the Book of Genesis, the coat of
many colors figures prominently. This gift,
which Jacob confers on Joseph, his favorite son, is
emblematic of Joseph's privileged state; it is the
symbol against which the envy of his brothers is
directed. To make matters worse, Joseph tells his
brothers about a dream—and, given Joseph's
particular gift for interpreting dreams, this cannot
be a frivolous dream—in which his sheaf of grain
rose up and stood upright while theirs formed a
ring around his and bowed down to it (Gen. 37:7).
His brothers are resentful: "And they hated him all
the more for his talk about his dreams" (Gen.
37:8). A second dream makes the symbolism of
hegemony and power even more explicit: the sun
and eleven stars bowed down to him (Gen. 37:9).
Now, Jacob is incensed: " 'What is the meaning,'
he asked him, 'of this dream of yours? Shall I and
your mother and your brothers come bowing to
you to the ground?' "Later in the story, the coat of
many colors also figures prominently as "evidence": The brothers daub it with blood and
present it as "proof" that Joseph has been de-
voured by wild beasts.

This biblical tale may be a parable of arrogance on
the part of Joseph and jealousy on the part of his
brothers. But the Bible makes it clear that Joseph is
Yahweh's (God's) favorite as well for, when he is
sent to Egypt, he prospers, and, when he is thrown
into jail because Potiphar's wife falsely accuses
him of rape, Yahweh blesses him: "And whatever

he undertook, Yahweh made prosper" (Gen.
39:23).

The latter part of the story depicts Joseph's
spectacular rise to power in Egypt, his prophetic
gifts being translated into economic power,
wielded with an authority second only to
Pharaoh's. Eventually, Joseph is able, even during
the seven years of famine that he had predicted, to
bring to Egypt Jacob and all his surviving offspring—including the brothers who, at the outset
of the story, had victimized Joseph and to whom,
ironically, Joseph owes his subsequent good
fortune.

The story of Joseph and his brothers is well worth
pondering in the context of race relations in the
United States. "Whites" in America are, in a
positive sense, reminiscent of Joseph: they have
been favored by history; they enjoy the highest
standard of living; they have "foretold" the future
more accurately than their brethren; and they have
the gift of oneiric creativity of making their
dreams come true. Their shrewdness in economic
affairs reminds one of Joseph's spectacular land
acquisitions in Egypt, augmenting Pharaoh's
holdings by exploiting those who had been reduced to poverty and starvation by the famine,
offering part of the ample provisions stored up
during the seven years of plenty to buy land.

The coat of many colors turns out to be a doubly
ambivalent gift: A token of Jacob's love, it brings
down on Joseph the envy and hostility of his
brothers, which in turn motivates their dire plot
against him; but it also leads to his exile in Egypt
as well as the ultimate deliverance of Jacob's
family during the years of famine. The image of
"white" has had the same import in the United
States. Emblem of privilege and favoritism,
symbol of suspected arrogance, the insignia of
political domination and ambition, "whites" in
America for most of our history are very reminiscent of Joseph in a negative sense as well:
Opportunistic in their ambitions, ruthless in
capitalizing on their economic opportunities,
manipulative in the marketplace of ideas and of
human resources. Their success has also made
whites the target of a great deal of animosity, from
the "have-nots" both in the United States and in

the world. "White America"—like Joseph—is the envy of the world, for both positive and negative reasons, to both favorable and unfavorable effect.

To meditate on the story of Joseph might be a more fruitful approach to an appreciation of white American culture than wading through the polemics of race relations or sifting through volumes of less than dispassionate rhetoric, for there is much to admire as well as to deplore about white America. But the sad truth is that most analyses polarize themselves unduly by depicting the white American either as the devil incarnate (Ahab's version of Moby Dick) or as an angel of purity personified (Snow White and her seven—ethnic?—dwarfs). There is another connection between Joseph's coat of many colors and the color white: While common custom "sees" white as a color among other colors, the science of optics tells us that white is a figment of our visual imaginations. There is no color white, per se; what we see as the color white is a composite of many colors. White can be thought of as a coat of many colors.

It is the composite nature of white, and the ambivalent character of Joseph in the biblical tale, that we must understand if any light is to be shed on the conundrum of race relations in America. Much of what is regarded as mainstream "white" culture in the United States comes from ethnic origins that are decidedly un-English and un-European. A proper definition of *white culture* in America must take into account the nonwhite elements as well.

Those who are wary of the recognition of America's multicultural past, who insist on seeing such discriminations as discriminatory, often appeal to the importance of a common belief system to the very survival of America as a nation. The concepts of unity in diversity and *e pluribus unum* (one out of many) are often compromised when the country as a whole is under attack. Opposition parties historically rally around the president during times of military crisis, and differences of opinion are not as easily tolerated when the polity as a whole is threatened. The debate in Congress over whether the United States should enter the Persian Gulf War was an inspir-

ing moment in American democracy, for, whatever side of the issue one stood on, few challenged the loyalty of those who disagreed with what turned out to be the majority view (which constituted a healthy change from the prevailing wind during the Vietnam War). Justifications of unconstitutional actions in terms of "national security" did not die out with the perfidies of Richard Nixon: Others have invoked the concept since. It is a disturbing kind of patriotism that believes it necessary to lie to the American people in order to protect their freedoms.

Is it un-American to recognize one's roots? Is it un-American to identify the foreign sources of one's talent and vision? Has there ever been an America that wasn't anything but the sum total of immigrant dreams? Why is it necessary to "white out" one's immigrant origins in order to become American? Imperceptibly, a myth has grown up in this country that a native-born American is more American than someone who is not native born. Some of us have forgotten that one of the complaints lodged against King George III in the Declaration of Independence was that he obstructed "laws for naturalization of foreigners."

Naturalization strikes me as a uniquely American concept. Counterparts in other countries include *sinicization* for Chinese, *anglicization* for English culture *gallicization* for French. But there is something distinct about *naturalization* in America: the word means: "to invest (an alien) with the rights and privileges of a citizen." Whereas the other terms identify the process by which the foreigner acquires the native culture in each respective country, the word *naturalization* merely points to the process by which the rights and privileges of a citizen are conferred on a foreigner. Nowhere is it said, neither in the Declaration of Independence nor in the Constitution, that one has to give up one's native (foreign) culture in order to become or be American The act of naturalization is not cultural but institutional: The recognition of, and allegiance to, the basic principles of American government is all that is required of an American citizen or of an alien who wants to be "naturalized." In other words, anyone who is willing to subscribe to the ideals of the American form of society, whatever his/her ethnic origins or social status, can become an American. The most natural American is also a "naturalized" American: the problem is that some native-born Americans are not as familiar with the institutional history of America as some immigrants, who have to learn the Declaration of Independence and the Constitution practically by heart in order to qualify for "naturalization." Being born American is not the only way to become American: As a nation that prides itself on our colonial history and that believes in the importance that Jefferson attached to the laws of "naturalization of foreigners," we can ill afford to forget that.

I have lived in a small Midwestern community for more than twenty-five years. Once I had some business to conduct with a local merchant. Our discussions reached an amicable conclusion. Unbeknownst to me, a colleague happened to visit the same merchant shortly after my visit to inquire about the same project. The merchant repeated what he had told me, and then, scarcely able to contain his curiosity, he asked my colleague about me: "Your friend, he's…he's not from around here, is he?" In hearing my friend's report, I was touched that the local merchant was too shy to admit that I looked a little different from his usual customers. Perhaps he was curious about *which* country I came from. In retrospect, I appreciated his discretion about asking me: Obviously, he was made somewhat uncertain because my English sounded thoroughly native.

Which raises the interesting question, What does *from around here* mean? I later found out that this merchant had moved into the community fifteen years after I had arrived. Yet, I could not deny that, notwithstanding our actual tenure in town, I would always be perceived as being "not from around here" whereas he could always appear to belong, no matter how recent a newcomer he was. The contrast is that he would look at home virtually anywhere in the United States, no matter how recently he took up residence, whereas I would always look as if I were "not from around here," no matter how long I had lived in one place.

There is a Custer's Last Stand mentality among certain defenders of WASP culture: they are beleaguered by foreign competition in the market-

place, beset by waves of immigrants from all countries, and besieged by assaults on their values and precepts by radical activists. The pressures against the white majority in the United States have escalated to such an extent that even moderate white Americans are feeling threatened by the onslaught of ethnic and racial rhetoric. They are circling the wagons against the intellectual and political tyrannies of "political correctness." Typically, profoundly complex issues are being co-opted by oversimplifications to produce a great deal of friction and heat, yielding very little understanding or light. We are being asked to choose up sides, as in a pickup stickball game, but the false dichotomies are mischievous, if not malicious. Unless we sort out the issues and see them clearly, the disputes will fester and conflicts multiply without any real progress toward solutions. The sad thing is that it is all so unnecessary.

If the hypocrisies and deceits of WASP culture have been amply documented, perhaps it is time to focus on the unique WASP contribution to human civilization. Whatever other cultures, each with its own virtues, have to claim, in no other than white Anglo-Saxon Protestant culture has the tradition of democracy and freedom been so passionately articulated. From the Magna Carta to Jimmy Carter (a peanut farmer who became president), the commitment to egalitarian forms of government is that culture's most glorious contribution to civilization. The great civilizations and cultures of the world each have their particular achievements, but in none has the idea of egalitarian rule been pursued with as much dedication, imagination, and sacrifice as in white Anglo-Saxon Protestant culture. These principles are the higher cause that must unite the various cultural and political constituencies in these United States.

These are the principles that have allowed the various mixes of people to unite in a common cause, however disparate their customs and backgrounds, however at odds their belief systems and religions, however contradictory and contrary their political views. But, if this is the achievement of WASP culture, then, ironically, it cannot be undermined by an interpretation of equal opportunity that is restricted only to WASP culture. These principles become a travesty when "we, the people" must be interpreted as "we, the white people," or "we, the rich people," or "we, the male people." And, so long as the reality in America fails to redeem the promises made in the Declaration of Independence and the Constitution, the very achievement of WASP culture is undermined. There is a quantum leap in this magnanimity of vision, greater than that of the Greeks, whose definition of freedom was not extended to their slaves; greater than that of the Romans, whose notion of power did not include women; greater than that of the Chinese, whose notion of culture did not recognize the contribution of the foreigner—for the crowning achievement of the WASP vision of the world is that it confers on all peoples, not just WASPs, "the right to life, liberty, and the pursuit of happiness." The multicultural vision, therefore, does nothing to diminish the achievement of WASP culture or the triumph of Western civilization; on the contrary, it demonstrates irrefutably the genius of this uniquely compelling vision of humanity.

It is as wrong to presume that all nonwhites are actually or incipiently "antiwhite" as it is foolish, categorically wrong, to dismiss all whites as racists and cultural bigots. Those who have attributed the term political correctness to those in favor of the multicultural movement wish to discredit that movement, and those in the movement who believe in political correctness do not truly understand multiculturalism. The issue is not to replace a white orthodoxy with a nonwhite orthodoxy. The issue of multiculturalism should be about culture rather than politics; it should be concerned with sensitivities rather than categorical correctness. Being politically correct is no guarantee that ethnic sensitivities will not be offended: as a minority, I am more impressed by the human concern of someone who might be politically incorrect than by the doctrinaire liberal formulas of the politically correct. Minorities are not interested in correct behavior; what they want is responsive behavior. The notion of political correctness is at bottom intensely insulting to minorities because it suggests that ethnic individuals be treated "by the book" and that there is a right and a wrong way to deal with other human beings. Nothing could be more obnoxious than a handbook of political correctness; it reflects the

same thinking as a manual on the care and feeding of animals. As a minority, I may wish to be treated kindly, or candidly, or circumspectly, or courteously, or sympathetically, or considerately, or honestly; but God spare me from anyone bent on treating me "correctly."

If multiculturalism means anything, it also includes WASP culture as a primary component of the American experience. To insist that the whole story of American history be told is not the same thing as erasing the contribution of white Americans to that history. Indeed, just as one argues that the black contributions to white culture deserve to be recognized, the genetic contributions of whites to black culture must also be acknowledged. If there is nothing pure about white culture, there is also nothing pure about black culture. Although no official statistics are available, a considerable number of blacks in the United States have at least one white among their ancestors. The fact that many blacks were the offspring of rape and miscegenation was perhaps the reason to be discreet about the "white" genes interspersed among the "black." There is ample inferential proof of the infusion of white blood in the black population, often from the very people who wish to downgrade blacks as inferior.

In Louisiana, state law defines anyone with one part black blood out of sixty-four as being black. If we assume as many as sixty-four great-great-great-great-grandparents, that means that anyone with as few as one black ancestor out of these sixty-four is considered, according to Louisiana law, black. In other words, the sixty-three other great-great-great-great-grandparents could be white, but they wouldn't count. One would still be black in the eyes of Louisiana law. Leaving aside the ethical and eugenic dimensions of this law, its existence, and the severely prejudicial ratio that it enshrines, would suggest a high incidence of blacks with one or more white progenitors. Such a law would not have been enacted were the number of blacks with white blood negligible. The implicit cut-off imposed by this law is that, if one had a great-great-great-great-great-grandparent who was black (in other words, if a black could prove that 127 out of 128 progenitors of that generation were white), one would be considered, in the eyes of

Louisiana law, white. However, if one could do no better than sixty-three out of sixty-four progenitors in the subsequent generation, then one had to be considered legally black. Somehow it seems so pointless a distinction: one is considered black if one of the sixty-four ancestors six generations ago was black, but one isn't considered black if 127 of the 128 ancestors seven generations ago were white!

Nothing betrays the myth of white purity more than these ridiculously persnickety distinctions. One can fairly ask about the validity of a distinction that rests on such flimsy genealogical grounds, especially when most Americans can hardly identify their ancestors past a few generations, much less six or seven.

Multiculturalism must also recognize the proportion of white progenitors in the black population. White is a culture too. It is as foolish to be for or against whites as it is to be for or against blacks. The dynamics of prejudice apply in any direction. The black who stereotypes whites is just as racist as the white who stereotypes blacks. It is racism that all races should be against, and there is no way to eradicate another person's racism by opposing it with your own.

What we should all be against is the "whitewash" mentality. Whitewash is my term for leaving out salient parts of the truth and then glossing over those omissions; the appropriation of a valid cause for an invalid purpose. Whitewash is the dedicated insistence on ideals with no regard to how those ideals are controverted and undermined in reality. Whitewash is the false attribution of treason to those who will not accept the predominant ideology. Whites are not the only ones capable of whitewash. There are the "Oreos" and the "bananas" and the "coconuts"—the blacks who are black on the outside and white on the inside; the Asians who are yellow on the outside and white on the inside; and the Latinos/Latinas or East Indians who are brown on the outside but white on the inside. These intercultural symbols indicate a white heart in a skin of color, and they are instances of what might be called internal whitewash—where the psyche has been brainwashed into thinking that one is white when one isn't.

There is also the phenomenon of the external whitewash— where one "puts on a white face," as it were. There are ethnics who have mastered the art of "whiteface"—playing the white man's game to get ahead in white society. The interesting thing is that whites scarcely notice these racial caricatures, and they are not as offended by blacks playing in "whiteface" as blacks are by whites playing in blackface. Richard Pryor, for example, gets as many laughs from whites as blacks imitating a "honky." Could it be that blackface unfairly caricatures an oppressed people whereas whiteface merely acknowledges the dominant culture? (There is an entire psychology of humor to be explored that would explain why ethnics insulting themselves can be funny but nonethnics insulting ethnics is not funny—except to bigots.)

But there are more subtle forms of ethnic whitewash, in which individuals take umbrage behind their ethnic masks rather than assume responsibility for their own limitations and failures. We have all met such moral hypocrites: those who cry "racism" at the drop of a hat, despite the fact that others of the same race have succeeded in the same job or in the same situation; those who cry anti-Semitism, even when Jews have preceded them in the same profession; and those who cry sexism to avoid admitting their own shortcomings. The irony is that those most often offended by these "cry-wolfers" are those minority individuals who are successful and who achieved their success, sometimes against racism, through extra hard work and dedication. The ambivalence of these minority individuals is profound: they hate the racism that has made their road to success difficult, but they feel indebted to those very difficulties for making them better and tougher than their white counterparts. Shelby Steele touches on some of these perspectives in The Content of Our Character (1990).

I am reminded of an incident years ago in New York City, when my wife and I lived in a small one-and-half-room apartment on Riverside Drive. Late one Saturday night, actually, it was early Sunday morning, around three o'clock, I woke up to the thumping and shaking of loud music and dancing next door. Bleary eyed, I got up and knocked on my neighbor's door. An African opened up, amid gales of merriment. When I said that the party was perhaps a bit too boisterous, my African neighbor accused me of racism. I suspected that this response was his knee-jerk response in all such situations, and he was not even disconcerted to notice that, with my Chinese face, I did not at all resemble the white racists he was in the habit of impugning.

It is eyewash to teach the Fourteenth Amendment and not point out its violation throughout American history since it was passed in 1866. One can never be reminded too often of the text of the Fourteenth Amendment: "All persons born or naturalized in the United States, and subject to the jurisdiction thereof, are citizens of the United States and of the State wherein they reside. No State shall make or enforce any law which shall abridge the privileges or immunities of the citizens of the United States; nor shall any State deprive any persons of life, liberty, or property, without due process of law; nor deny to any person within its jurisdiction the equal protection of the law" (section I). The teaching of history that underscores the magnanimity and the nobility of the Fourteenth Amendment, yet neglects the internment of sixty thousand American citizens of Japanese descent in 1942, is whitewashing reality and making a travesty of history. And to read "No State shall…deny to any person within its jurisdiction the equal protection of the law" without any concern for the differential proportions by which blacks are sentenced to the death penalty, especially when whites are the victims, without recognizing the repeated abrogation of the rights of Native Americans in broken treaty after broken treaty, without acknowledging the injustices perpetrated on Latino/ Latina immigrants, especially those characterized cynically by fruit growers as "wetbacks," is whitewashing the truth. We cannot celebrate lofty sentiments and at the same time ignore instances in which those sentiments are conveniently disregarded.

There is also a blitheness among some whites about the ethnic experience, a blindness that indicates that they have no sense of what it is to live day after day in one's own country and yet be made to feel a stranger in it. Only minorities have experienced the special hurt of living in a country

and being told by someone much younger that they don't belong here. Whites who know nothing of this experience might be instructed by a German-American friend who traveled in Japan and was stunned to find herself, for the first time in her life, in the minority. Whites who have not been alienated in their own country blithely suggest that ethnics are wrong to point to their own traditions; they insist that it is divisive and separatist to use such hyphenated designations as African-American, Chinese-American, Italian-American, etc. Two examples from popular journalism, from respected and intelligent commentators on the American scene, will suffice to illustrate this blindness.

The first comes from Marilyn Vos Savant: "I believe one of the greatest threats to the stability of the United States may well be the declining number of people who call themselves Americans. I wonder how long the hyphenation of nationalities can continue without bringing the hyphenations of loyalties. Whenever people ask me whether I'm a French-American, for example, because of my name, it irritates me, and I tell them, 'No. I was born in this country, I'm a citizen, and I'm an American!'" (Parade Magazine, 26 May 1991). Ms. Vos Savant is totally oblivious to the experience of non-European immigrants or the descendants of non-European immigrants: they aren't even asked the hyphenized version of their nationality. If they look "Oriental," they are asked, "Are you Chinese or Japanese?" (Of course, the more circumspect and thoughtful ask where your ancestors come from.) We are not asked, "Are you Chinese-American or Japanese-American?" Indeed, in the eyes of some, we are seen as not being American.

And then there are times when Americans of Chinese descent are misidentified at the peril of their lives. In 1989, James Liu in Raleigh, North Carolina, a Chinese-American, was taken to be Vietnamese, so two pool-hall bullies bashed his head in, as an act of vengeance for the trauma that they, and America, had suffered as a result of the Vietnam War. In 1981, Vincent Chin was erroneously taken for Japanese, and two autoworkers, disgruntled at being put out of work (by the

Japanese, they thought, not by mismanaged American corporations), beat his brains in. Vincent Chin and Jim Liu would have been proud to be called, simply, American, but their assailants were, evidently, unwilling to recognize their citizenship.

In fact, it may come as a surprise to Marilyn Vos Savant that many ethnic Americans do not like the hyphen because it makes them feel like second-class citizens; the hyphen represents Americans whose citizenship is somehow compromised. Most ethnics would be delighted to eliminate the hyphen as well as the ethnic marker and call themselves simply Americans. What is to Ms. Vos Savant a choice—to be called a hyphenated American or to be called, simply, American—is, unfortunately, not an option for those who are physiognomically at variance with what, mythically, an American is "supposed" to look like. Vos Savant has the situation on backward: The divisive forces—racism—impose the need for hyphenated Americans; the labels are not assumed voluntarily. But, since the hyphenation has become inevitable, some of the militant ethnics (much like the blacks of the 1960s) have insisted on the label as a reminder of white racism. Vos Savant wants to remove the symptom without attending to the disease.

A similar form of *whitewash*—here its cognate is *Americanization*—may be found in the writing of Peggy Noonan, speechwriter for Presidents Reagan and Bush. Too savvy politically to offend any constituency, Noonan is, on the whole, positive about the recent influx of immigrants—"the biggest...since the great wave that ended in the 1920's." Noonan puts forth a concept of *Americanism* that she characterizes as "the Sunday stew—rich, various and roiling, and all of it held together by a good strong broth" (1991, 39). After celebrating the successes of several recent immigrants, Noonan goes on to say, "Nationwide, the small shops the immigrants run create thousands of jobs and contribute billions to the economy. In return, the newcomers get the possibility of dreams. But these dreams aren't free. There's a price to pay: Once you're here, you have to become Americanized." Just what does *becoming Americanized* mean? If it means to become acculturated to WASP culture (as it does in the minds of many, and not only in the minds of whites), then Americanization is merely another form of cultural hegemony. Noonan avoids this ethnocentric interpretation: She talks about the "moral and philosophical underpinnings of what they've joined, the things that keep us together. These include the reasons we fought the Revolutionary War and the Civil War, the meaning of the civil-rights movement and the reasons we have sent armies across oceans to liberate other nations. To know what we were is to know who we are."

These are fine sentiments, and few would take issue with them. It's only when one looks at the substance and the concrete examples of what Noonan talks about that this rhetoric begins to sound hollow. She says, "This is why we must not permit school texts to imply, as some do, that 'America was founded by white male Euros who broke from Britain over taxes but retained slaves, and two centuries later the liberation is not complete because racism is still rampant'" The "we" in "we must not permit" betrays Noonan's provinciality, for this "we" is evidently addressed to orthodox white Americans, not to blacks, whose role in the Revolutionary War has been obscured by the previous textbooks, and not to Japanese-Americans, who fought in the all-Nisei 44^{2d} Regimental Combat team in World War II (one of the most decorated in the war), and not to the Japanese-Americans whose lands were confiscated and whose civil rights were violated. And Noonan says nothing to contradict the version of American history she sneers at. America as the history books present *it was* founded by white male Euros, wasn't it? And where is the egalitarian spirit in Noonan's exclusive and imperious "we"? Some of the "we's" are committed to rewriting American history by telling the truth, and we seek no one's permission to do so. As Noonan says, "To know what we were is to know who we are." But that's exactly what "revisionist" history is after: To truly know what we truly were. How can she be against a more accurate depiction of America's history, and why does she characterize this search for more accurate history as "sour revisionism"? Are we talking about ideologies, party lines, or the facts of history? Why is a revision of knowledge revisionism? The whole notion of revisionism smacks of totalitarian excuses to discipline the wayward. And why should the restoration of truth ever be considered sour? Is it divisive, sour, and spoilsport to insist that the errors of previous scientific textbooks be corrected? If so, Copernicus, Galileo, Newton, Darwin, and Einstein were "sour revisionists."

When we read Noonan complaining that this view of American history "omits a salient truth: those seeking justice over the years were lucky enough to be operating in a country that had not only a Constitution, but a conscience, to which an appeal could be made. This is a triumph of idealism that is forever a tribute to the human spirit." Again, in the abstract, this sounds fine. But there are some who would not have thought themselves so lucky—not the Scottsboro boy who was lynched; not the Native Americans who were run off their land; not the innumerable nameless victims of racial prejudice whose sufferings find no voice in American history. To espouse these "ideals" without recognizing the disparity between the rhetoric of these claims and the reality of history is to indulge in the most callous form of whitewash.

"Whites," "blacks," "reds," "yellows," and "browns" should all be against the hypocrisy of whitewash. Our national solidarity will be the stronger if it comprises masses of wildly diverse individuals: The solidarity consisting of masses of individuals exactly like each other, cookie-cutter clones of a conformist model, is itself an abnegation of individuality, an invitation to tyrants and demagogues who look for goose-stepping precision in national parades.

I began this chapter with the biblical story of Joseph, and I considered the parallels to the myth of white America. In a sense, Joseph represents the fortunate sibling, the one who is blessed with natural ability, given precious opportunity, and empowered with status and authority. In that sense, every one of the brothers would like to be Joseph, the favorite not only of his father but of the Supreme Father as well. Which minority would not like to attain the status of the white majority in America? If white is the symbol of empowerment, who would not like to be white? But if white is to

be properly understood, it cannot be the white of white lies or the white of whitewash; it must be the white that physics identifies for us, the white of many colors. If we understand white in this way, then a coat of white is exactly what this country needs.

I am using the Joseph story as a parable, not as a symbol. It is merely an analogy enabling us to think through some of the situational dilemmas that we face and to understand some of the complex psychologies involved. I am by no means suggesting that the United States is favored of the Almighty or that Americans are the chosen people. Joseph, after all, is a patriarch of the Jews, who may have regarded themselves as the chosen people, but whose lot in history, especially in the twentieth century, has been anything but lucky. Each language, each culture, has a tendency to see itself as the center of the universe, whether it's the Greeks, who regarded all non-Greeks as barbarians, or the Chinese, who saw their country as the "central kingdom." When such a highly civilized culture as Germany in the early twentieth century can spawn National Socialism, we can no longer take it for granted that civilization and barbarism are mutually exclusive. We now realize that there are not only "barbarians within"; there are also "nobles without."

As an analogy, comparing the United States to Joseph does make a certain amount of sense. The United States is literally the most attractive country on earth: we attract more immigrants than any other country. (Japan, by contrast, attracts few immigrants—despite its economic power.) We are the most blessed country in the world—blessed with natural resources, blessed with its favorable place in history, blessed with the richness of its human resources, drawn from every corner of the world. America is Joseph, and it has been favored, more than any other country, with a coat of many colors. This white America must never forget its colorful history.

The United States is a crazy quilt of cultures; its energy, its verve, its good nature, its imagination, its daring, have attracted people from all over the world. Every American is either an immigrant or descended from immigrants: Even the Native American probably migrated to the Western hemisphere from Asia. The essence of being American is neither racial nor cultural nor political: Those who seek a common thread overlook the most obvious—cultural exiles unified by the belief in the ultimate worth of each individual and the conviction that our strength as a country lies precisely in the diversity of its citizens. The United States—note the plural singular—is a collective unity. A pluralistic one. *E pluribus unum* (out of many, one); *e pluribus pigmentis album* (out of many colors, white). In more than one sense, America is a family *album* of many colors, creeds, and faiths.

"WHY DO WHITE PEOPLE HAVE VAGINAS?"

by Maureen T. Reddy

When Sean was born in November of 1983, Doug and I had been married for four years and living in Minneapolis for almost all of that time, half a continent away from our families. My younger brother, Tom, had recently moved out to live with us, but everyone else awaited from a distance the birth of this first member of the next generation of our families.

The couples in our childbirth class and the women who were in my prenatal exercise class all had their babies before us, and every one had a boy. Both Doug and I assumed we would have a girl, based on some vague, mathematically insupportable idea about odds and just a feeling we both had. We were proved wrong when Sean appeared. When we made our calls an hour or so after Sean was born, everyone was effusively delighted, demanded photos by overnight mail, and announced various plans to fly out to us. The only odd comment came from my mother-in-law, who said, "A boy! That's *wonderful*—Daddy will be so happy! I'm relieved!" Relieved? "Oh, I probably shouldn't tell you this, but it's okay now that Sean's here and he's a boy," Marguerite said, "but Daddy said that if it wasn't a boy, he didn't care what it was." I spluttered a bit, and my mother-in-law said, "Don't take it personally, Maureen; that's what Daddy said to me, too, every time I was pregnant."

Well, *of course*, I took it personally: I am a woman, and a feminist, and objected to this valuing of boys over girls. I also was troubled by this vivid, early reminder that Doug and I would have to struggle with inequitable gender roles for our child, and to help him to resist a racist, sexist system that, on one of its axes, favored him because of his maleness. Or, more accurately, *seemed* to favor him: Although maleness carries certain privileges, most of those privileges are in fact reserved for white males. Stereotypes of black masculinity—rapacious sexuality, violence, danger, threat—shorten black men's lives and mock the very notion of male privilege.

I also knew that simply resisting stifling race/gender definitions would not be enough: We would have to provide alternatives to fill the space resistance creates. In a world that offers few positive public images of black maleness, we would have to seek them out while also countering the vast number of soul-destroying stereotypes. As Ishmael Reed has remarked, the most familiar image of black men in the popular media is naked from the waist up, handcuffed, and thrown across a police car. We did not want Sean to see black men in general or himself in particular through that racist lens, but I was not at all certain how Doug and I could help him to see himself through his own eyes, unclouded by racism or sexism. In addition to the obvious counter to racism unconditional love and real self-esteem provide, we both wanted to foster in Sean a sense of wide possibility through carefully choosing books and toys for him, and through encouraging lots of fantasy play.

One of the simpler pleasures of parenting, we thought, would be giving Sean toys and playing with him—wrong, wrong, wrong, as we learned on our first excursion to a toy store when Sean was just a few weeks old. Because Doug and I were among the first of our friends to have children, we had not been toy shopping since we were little more than children ourselves, and we therefore had no clear idea about what toys were available. Before our baby's birth, we had decided to buy toys on a gender-neutral basis—blocks, trucks, stuffed animals, and dolls, regardless of our child's sex—and to ban war toys and Barbie, for obvious reasons. We had guessed that black dolls would be hard to find, but otherwise we had given little thought to race as a factor in toy shopping. After all, what could race have to do with blocks? Plenty, we discovered. That first trip to a big toy store was enlightening: We found aisle upon aisle of toys of all varieties in packages that depicted only white children playing with them. At most, one-fifth of the toys we saw incorporated no exclusionary race or gender codes on their packages. Even fancy yuppie toys, carefully aimed

at both sexes—European crib mobiles and the like—came in packages adorned with pictures of white babies. In the doll aisle, blond, blue-eyed dolls outnumbered black dolls fifty to one, and the only black male dolls were Cabbage Patch Kids, which were new to the market the year Sean was born and almost impossible to get. In an effort to support progressive manufacturers, we tried to buy toys that showed some sensitivity to racial diversity in their packaging, but we also ended up buying a lot of things that had to be removed from their boxes before we gave them to Sean. Obviously, though, we could not control everything in Sean's life as easily as we discarded troubling toy wrappings, and we knew that he would be bombarded by images and messages quite contrary to the vision of self we hoped to foster. What effect would these images have on him? And how powerful would our parental influence be? We waited, and hoped.

At about two and a half or three, Sean began to say things that suggested he understood both race and sex as categories—as interrelated categories, in fact—and that he was trying to figure out the principles that govern those categories. Like most preschoolers, Sean had a passion for categorization and a sometimes overwhelming desire to organize the elements of his world into a system that made sense to him. He was single-mindedly dedicated to grasping the abstract principles to be extrapolated from specific observations. Sean was a tiny scientist, Doug and I were his reference library, and the world was his laboratory.

One evening, Sean asked me if he would get a vagina when he grew up. After explaining that he would always have a penis but no vagina, I remarked that I had been born with a vagina and still have one, and that his father was born with a penis and still has that. "Your sex doesn't change when you grow up," I concluded. A series of questions from Sean followed, focusing on people we know and whether they have vaginas or penises. That was the end of that, I thought. Months later, Sean once again brought up the penis/vagina issue, but phrased it this way: "Why do white people have vaginas, Mom?" He evidently thought genitalia determined race, not sex: Generalizing from me and his father, Sean assumed all black people have penises, and all white people have vaginas. I had to return to our list of friends, reiterate who had penises and who vaginas, and remind him of each person's race before Sean would believe that a penis meant you were male, whether black or white, and a vagina meant you were female, independent of race.

Racial differences were apparently more noticeable to Sean than were sex differences, and I suppose this could have been predicted. After all, we were making major efforts to raise Sean in a gender-free way, emphasizing that the only real differences between boys and girls were biological. We were supported by friends and by the enlightened day-care center Sean attended, where both staff and parents identified themselves as feminists. Perhaps most important, when he was a toddler Sean never saw commercial television. At three, he did not choose playmates or toys on a gender-appropriate basis, nor did he seem to think much about differences between boys and girls, especially in comparison to several other children we knew, who made a big deal about gender roles from an early age. Sean could see skin-color differences between Doug and me, and knew that I have a vagina and Doug has a penis. He never saw other people naked, so he had no opportunity to notice black females with vaginas and white males with penises. It makes perfect sense, then, that he would jumble everything up and figure that skin color and genitalia were linked.

After figuring out the vagina/penis issue, Sean decided that other physical characteristics were sex-linked as well, once telling us that girls have blue eyes and boys have brown eyes. This statement emerged at a very unlikely time—quite late at night when he had awakened to go to the bathroom—which made me realize just how deeply such issues concerned him. I explained that girls can have brown eyes and boys blue, and that many other possibilities exist, which Sean seemed to accept after recalling his brown-eyed aunt and blue-eyed uncle. He moved on to a different topic ("Why do I have to wash my hands if I don't touch the toilet?") and that seemed to be the end of it. As I tucked him back into bed, he said sleepily, "But boys have curly hair and girls don't," stuck his

thumb in his mouth, and closed his eyes to signal the end of our discussion.

Sean's comments about race and his confusion about racial and sexual characteristics mirror social confusion. Race, unlike sex, has little to do with biology, popular mythology notwithstanding. As Henry Louis Gates trenchantly remarks, "Race is the ultimate trope of difference because it is so very arbitrary in its application. The biological criteria used to determine 'difference' in sex simply do not hold when applied to 'race.' Yet we carelessly use language in such a way as to *will* this sense of *natural* difference into our formulations." Sex—but not gender—is an objective term of classification and therefore is comparatively easy to explain to a small child. Race and gender are subjective categories, social constructions, whose parameters constantly shift, change shape, mutate. Further, although both race and gender are socially constructed categories of analysis, they are *differently* constructed; consequently, understanding these constructions and resisting them requires quite different strategies.

From about age three, Sean began to realize that racial differences were meaningful in some way beyond mere skin color, but he wasn't clear on what these meanings might be. For instance, he announced to me that people get darker as they get older and that dark people are older than light people. This makes sense as a general statement about the origins of humankind, but that wasn't his point. "No," I explained, "skin color isn't age-related. People come in all different colors and pretty much stay that way. Daddy was dark brown when he was little, and he's still dark brown. I was sort of pink when I was a baby and I'm still pink. You were light brown as a baby and you're still light brown." This seemed to make sense to Sean, and he moved on to another question ("Why is Big Bird yellow?").

A few weeks later, though, Sean once again said darker people are older than lighter people. I offered some examples of younger dark people (his friend Maggie, age two) and older light people (his grandfather, mid-sixties), and we laid that issue to rest, after agreeing that it's nice to have so many different shades of skin and hair and eyes in the world. Months passed with no further age/race commentary, but then one night while Doug was giving Sean a bath, Sean made a remark about "when you get old." It was the end of a long and exhausting day, and Doug jokingly replied, "I already *am* old!" Sean responded angrily, touching Doug's arm, *"That's* not old, Daddy! *That* [pointing to my skin} is old!" If dark skin doesn't signify age, then it must signify youth; Sean still wasn't willing to accept that skin color is independent of age and sex, all evidence of that independence carrying no weight with him.

As I look back now, Sean's early determination to figure out race's meaning strikes me as a nascent rage for order that rebelled against the intimations of chaos coming to him from the outside world. He was beginning to sense the social significance attached to race, and went looking for clues to explain that significance. The arbitrariness not only of racial distinctions themselves but also of race's social significance—when we think about it, using race as *the* crucial category depends on arbitrary historical choices that could just as easily have fastened on height or hair color or anything else for that matter—must have been apparent to him, and therefore Sean went looking for reassurances that the world was indeed an orderly place, with rules he could grasp. I think Sean felt that race *meant* something, and believed that meaning must attach to real, measurable, understandable differences, else the world might be terrifyingly unfathomable.

Sometimes Sean's mistakes about race and/or gender amused us, as when he first saw a program on commercial television and I had to explain advertisements to him. The short version of this long explanation was that you can't believe everything you see in ads, because the advertisers are trying hard to sell their products, not to let you know all sides of any issue. Sean snorted knowingly and said, "I *know*, Mom. Commercials are stupid. Like that ad for washing soap. Everyone knows that Moms don't do the laundry!"

Occasionally, Sean's mistakes alerted Doug and me to real problems. For instance, from his early

infancy, we sought out books for Sean that showed both girls and boys engaged in various activities, rejecting books that encoded gender stereotypes. We also found books for him that featured black children in a variety of roles, not just as the background figures they too often are in children's literature. When we couldn't find books that incorporated racial diversity, we purchased stories about humanoid animals, figuring these were better than all-white texts. Then, at three, Sean started critiquing the pictures in his books. *"That's* not the mom," he'd say, pointing to the black mother in *Jamaica's Find*, or "Where's the dad?" as we looked at a page in a book about a white boy who was shown sitting on his father's lap. We realized that there was not a single children's book available that reflected Sean's family situation. Although many books showed black and white children playing together, no book that we found showed black and white people as members of the same family: in the world of children's literature we were invisible, nonexistent.

Actually, that's not quite true: searching through bibliographies of children's literature, I did find books about interracial families, but none I wanted to share with Sean. Rather like the literary and sociological treatments of interracial couples as pathological I mentioned in the first chapter, most children's books about interracial families fall into the problem/solution genre, treating interracial families as posing special problems. Most of these books are about adoption, such as Catherine and Sherry Bunin's is That Your Sister?, and therefore did not reflect Sean's life. Others, such as Adrienne Jones's so, Nothing is Forever, treat the initial rejection of the interracial family by white relatives—the problem—and the eventual growth of love between white grandparents and black children—the solution. Although well-meant and perhaps valuable, such books were of no use to us. At that stage in his life, Sean's interracial family was simply a fact, not a problem, and we wanted to find materials that acknowledged or reflected that fact. Most children's books depicting relationships between blacks and whites—even nonfamilial ones—posit such relationships as problem-ridden. Generally, the white characters are at the center of the story, which focuses on their learning about blacks and simultaneously discovering the evils of racism.

In this highly theoretical age, talking about the impact of popular culture or the uses of literature in simple terms is faintly embarrassing. However, whenever I ask students in my introduction to theory course why they are English majors, they inevitably respond with some version of "I like to read. Literature teaches me about myself and about other people." Although these students realize that literature does a lot of other things as well, this sort of comment is always their first response to the question. Numerous autobiographies by black writers remark on the poisonous lesson they learned as children from books that completely ignored their existence. Indeed, a recognition of literature's reflective or reinforcing function underlay early efforts to integrate African-American and women's literature into the curricula of colleges and universities. Sean's remarks to us indicated that he was certainly looking for images of himself and his world when he looked at books. At that young age, however, he doubted the books and thought they were wrong, as opposed to seeing our family as unusual, unlike others, "wrong."

Looking now for Ailis, who is fascinated by books, as well as for Sean, we have found exactly one "nonproblem" book about interracial families— Sarah Garland's Billy and Belle, which a black librarian at our local library put aside for me because she thought Belle resembled Ailis—and few about blacks and whites together in any kind of relationship that do not centralize the white child's consciousness. This may be one reason that Sean now most often reads fantasy books featuring characters that are other than human, such as Brian Jacques's Redwall series and J.R.R. Tolkein's Hobbit books. Toni Morrison has described her writing of The Bluest Eye as partly motivated by her need to write the book she wanted to read; I am convinced that this same desire, this hunger, for self-affirming, truth-telling tales fuels the current boom in black women's literature. Adult children of interracial couples will have to write their own books, as their experience is not only

marginalized but totally erased in currently available children's literature.

My unsuccessful quest for children's literature that reflected Sean's daily environment paralleled my own search for child-care books that seriously addressed issues of race and gender, and that did more than merely acknowledge the existence of interracial families—sadly, few books did even that much. The books that addressed race progressively (such as James P. Comer and Alvin F. Poussaint's Black Baby and Child Care) said little about gender, while the books that addressed parents like us who wanted to avoid reinscribing traditional gender definitions (such as Letty Cottin Pogrebin's Growing up Free) said little about race. At the same time, I continued to hunt for fiction for myself that depicted interracial relationships, and found very little other than tragic tales of sorrow, loss, and death. Even fewer of the few exceptions I found included children, and I was hungry for information about this crucial part of my life. I needed something to rub up against, to give me some sense of history, of shared experience. Jane Lazarre's The Mother Knot was the only book I found that gave me what I needed, and the sheer relief, the amazing exhilaration I felt while reading Lazarre's book taught me how deep my need was. In looking for literature that reflected my family's circumstances, I was looking for visibility, for verification of our existence, in some sense. Of course, that was exactly what Sean wanted, too, and our absence from literature—and from movies, television programs, catalogues, and even toy boxes—obviously worried him.

Who Am I?
American Indian, White, or Both?

by Iris Creasy

"Who am I?" is a question I have asked myself every day of my life for 48 years. Who I am is a "card carrying" (an enrolled member of a American Indian tribe) Native American. Who I am not is a half-breed nor a full-blood American Indian. My father was a full-blood and my mother was one-fourth, both of Cherokee descent. Thus, I am five-eighths Cherokee which does not qualify me as a half-breed, and less than four-fourths which does not qualify me as a full- blood. Who am I, an American Indian or white? The problem of who I am appears to rest with who I believe I am.

When I am among the Western Band of Cherokees of the Cherokee Nation in Oklahoma or the Eastern Band of Cherokees in Cherokee, North Carolina, the problem of who I am occurs when someone sees me for the first time because I am very light-skinned. There are two logical reasons why: (1) my mother tended to be very light-skinned and, (2) some full- blood Cherokees have a tendency to be. Unfortunately, when I attend pow wows of my people, as well as other tribes, I am regarded as an outsider and am never given the chance to prove that I am a "card carrying" member of the Cherokee Indian tribe. If I could wear my "card" like a name badge, other Indians would recognize me as Indian because they understand the importance of the card. They know what difficulties are encountered in obtaining the card that proves the degree of Indian blood. They are also aware of the importance of the procedure because of the number of people who claim to have Indian heritage without documentation. I am fortunate that my father and my mother, although uneducated and unable to read or write beyond an elementary school level, realized the importance of the Roll Numbers that placed them on the Dawes Roll that evolved from the Dawes Bill of 1901. Even without prestigious births, my parents were concerned with providing documentation of who I am.

While growing up and attending elementary school in a small town, other Cherokees and myself were the target of racism and prejudice. In one instance, I recall being told by a second grade teacher that I was stupid, filthy and dirty, and would never amount to anything. I also vividly recall the humiliation of being automatically treated for head lice because I was a "dirty" Indian. In third grade, I was slapped across the face for telling a classmate that I thought we were related. The teacher told me I deserved to be slapped for the embarrassment I had caused the white student. Who I was appeared to be less than desirable at this point in my life and I believed that white was good.

At 12 years of age I was taught a different kind of prejudice when I was sent to an Indian boarding school in Lawrence, Kansas. I remember my father telling me when I was very young that I was the lucky one because I was light-skinned and could pass for white. At that time, I did not know what he meant. Once at the boarding school, I began to understand what he had been trying to tell me. This is where I learned that if my parents had chosen to live on a reservation as I was growing up, life would have been degrading and humiliating for me because I would have been considered an outcast. Therefore, at 17 years of age I made a conscious choice to live my life as a white person. I consciously chose to let people assume that I was white. But, at 18, my first child was born. Since I had married a nearly full- blood Ponca/Omaha Indian, our child was very dark- skinned. My husband became an alcoholic; and I was forced to rear our child alone. When people would see me with my child they would act prejudicial and suspicious. This was not a popular time to claim to be Indian or any part thereof. As time passed, who I was became less important as I watched my child suffer from the same racism and prejudice I had experienced in my life.

After more than one failed marriage, 34 years had passed, and I married a white man who encouraged me to return to school. With this passage of time, it had become socially acceptable and popular to be a minority, so l applied for a minority scholarship through the Cherokee Nation in Oklahoma. When I made the first step into the world of academics I did not realize that all of the prejudices from my childhood would rise up to haunt me. Little did I realize that in my pursuit of a college degree, the question of *who I am* would arise again and again.

After passing the GED exam in the State of Delaware, my first attempt at college was in Dover, Delaware, at a vocational and technical community college. I worked full time and went to college part time. I worked hard for good grades but did not graduate because my husband was transferred to Scott Air Force Base in Illinois. Upon arriving at Scott AFB I did not return to school for five years. In 1989 my husband suffered a heart attack, and it became the catalyst I needed to complete my education. I enrolled at the local community college in Centralia, Illinois, and was awarded a tennis scholarship to complete my associate's degree. I graduated in 1990 and promptly enrolled at Southern Illinois University at Edwardsville (SIUE) from which I graduated in 1992 with a bachelor of science in psychology. I entered graduate school at Southern Illinois University at Edwardsville and graduated in 1995 with a master's in psychology. While attending graduate school, I had begun teaching part-time for Kaskaskia Community College. SIUE notified me of a minority fellowship program known as PROMPT (Proactive Recruitment of Multicultural Professionals of Tomorrow) being offered at SlUC. The program offered minority teachers an opportunity to obtain a Ph.D. in selected fields of study and was being offered to five candidates throughout the midwest United States. I was encouraged to apply.

I applied even though I felt it was an effort in futility in July, I was notified that I had been selected to receive one of the five fellowships. During the application process, I was required to list my academic accomplishments on paper. As I read through the list, it looked as though the degrees came easily. This was definitely an illusion. Although I have just completed the first

semester at SIUC in the Ph.D. program with good grades, it has not been easy. All of my degrees have been obtained because I swallowed my pride and sought out the campus counseling center while an undergraduate at SIUE. Although I studied longer and harder than other students, I continued to receive low grades. I knew I had a problem but wrestled with it much longer than was necessary to prove to myself that I was unable to solve it alone. This was the ultimate degradation for an Indian: asking for help from white people (the counseling center was staffed by white personnel). This proved to be a mental setback in finding out who I was!

I realized that somewhere during my life I had accepted the ideas planted in my mind by that second grade teacher. I further realized that I had to overcome the idea that I was stupid, filthy and dirty and begin to believe that I could succeed in my pursuit of becoming a good and whole person. The realization that learning problems would continue to plague me as long as the root cause went unidentified, became stronger and stronger as time passed. Recognition of the fact I did not know how to solve the problem made me feel ashamed, so I swallowed my pride and went to the counseling center. There I received help and learned that the potential for change and growth through education was present inside of me; it was hidden and in need of nurturing. Thus, my quest for who I am continued through self-evaluation.

As a result of the quest, I have begun to change the way I study and view the subjects that I must take to obtain my Ph.D. A part of my problem was that a part of me resented having to take subjects dictated to me by the white culture which had no bearing on subjects in the Indian culture. The other necessary change in myself was to stop fighting with myself and believing that I was meant to fail because I was stupid. Occasionally I still struggle when I am faced with a particularly difficult class.

During my search, I set two major goals for myself. I began the long process of teaching myself that I can fit into both worlds and be successful in either one. Teaching myself that I am both Native American and white without a need to be either one or the other, and a huge success no matter which one my mood dictates that I be, was the foundation I laid to be built upon. My second goal was to complete my Doctor of Philosophy degree in Education with a counselor education specialty no matter how difficult it may become at times. When these two goals are completed, I hope to move to Cherokee, North Carolina, and teach at one of the major universities near the Cherokee Indian reservation and do part-time counseling for the reservation since my area of specialty within counselor education is substance abuse. In this way, I feel that I can partially repay a debt that I feel I owe. I view all the minority scholarships and awards that I have received as constituting a debt owed to my people that needs repayment. The recognition of my accomplishments as debts that require repayment is a part of who I am.

The main reason for writing this autobiography is to reach other American Indians who are part Indian and assure them that they are not alone in trying to decide who they are. I would like to offer reassurance that whether they are four-fourths or one-eighth degree, American Indians can obtain a balance in their lives and need not let go of one culture to embrace another. American Indians can have the best of both worlds, if they are willing to let go of a lot of anger and stereotypical beliefs. We need to realize that there is no shame or loss of face in admitting a need for help in dealing with the problems that we have carried for a lifetime. Lastly, and perhaps most important, is that we cease to judge one another based on the color of our skins. We live in an ordered society and to maintain this society, we must accept assimilation to obtain peace and harmony in our lives. This concept applies to all people, regardless of color or culture. However, this does not mean that we relinquish our culture, but simply that we put it in a proper frame of reference that will allow for growth and development and allow us to decide who we are.

Potawatomi—To Be or Not to Be—Reflections on Ethnicity

By Aura Bathurst

I grew up in predominantly white rural Kansas aware that I was a member of what was then called the Citizen Band Potawatomi Tribe of Oklahoma, but clueless as to what that meant. My relatives in Oklahoma were family, not "Indians." They didn't wear loincloths, beat tomtoms, or raise their right hands and say, "How" whenever I went to visit—all things the mass media would have had me believe "real" Indians did. It was, and continues to be, hard for me to sort through images of Indianness to form a coherent picture of what it is to be Potawatomi.

By common perception, there are two avenues through which I could claim to be Potawatomi—cultural and biological. By cultural definition, I could claim to be Potawatomi through outsiders—if non-group members identify me as such; through self-identification—if I identify myself as such, or through the group's definition; if the group (in this case, the Citizen Potawatomi Nation) identifies me as a member based upon their criteria. Criteria for Potawatomi identity could include shared cultural traits such as distinct language, worldview, way of life, dress and shared history.

Based on a biologically defined Potawatomi identity, I would still have to rely on a culturally constructed definition of "how Potawatomi" I am. To be "biologically" Potawatomi is to conform to a culturally determined notion of what percentage of Potawatomi ancestry constitutes "Potawatomi." By this method, called "blood quantum," I could claim to be a certain percentage Potawatomi. The actual blood quantum would have to be legally "provable" through official documents which show direct descendency from Potawatomi ancestors. In the United States today, a blood quantum of 1/16 is usually acceptable as sufficiently "Indian" to be labeled a "minority." Depending on which figures are to be believed, I am either 1/16, 1/32, 1/64, or 1/128 "Indian." Several of my ancestors found it advisable to lie and say they were less "Indian" than they actually were, given the political · situation at the time, so l am "officially" 1/128 Potawatomi.

Under many laws, only if I am 1/16 "Indian" could I call myself such, and I cannot "prove" that I am 1/16. However, I am a member of the Citizen Potawatomi Nation, so I am Indian by law—sometimes. Which definition should define my ethnic identity? Should it be the fiction of a 'biologically" determined identity which draws an arbitrary, culturally defined line and uses this line to tell me my ethnicity, ignoring the three culture-based identifiers I mentioned earlier? Or should a group have the right to identify its own members?

If the "biological" definition were to take precedence, it would continue the injustice of one culture dominating another, which many anthropologists are striving to correct. To decide that the "biological" definition of Potawatomi identity—which is actually a thinly disguised cultural definition—should be the prevailing definition is to disempower, once again, a people who have repeatedly been disempowered since Europeans first arrived in the Americas. The only fair and culturally sensitive way to determine ethnicity is for groups to have power to set their own criteria for membership.

Based upon the four ways through which I could come to call myself Potawatomi outlined above, I currently fill three of the four. I don't officially fulfill the 1/16 blood quantum requirement, but I am identified by the United States government as Potawatomi because of my tribal membership, self-identified as a Potawatomi Indian, and accepted by the Citizen Potawatomi nation, which has granted me membership. Since I fulfill these three criteria, why do I still feel apologetic when I claim to be Native American? Is it not enough that I fulfill established criteria set forth by my tribe and the U.S. government? I still do not feel like I have the right to call myself a "real Indian."

My ambivalence toward my Native American identity reflects my consciousness of the motivations behind my desire to embrace it. When I am asked my ethnicity on official forms, I have the legal right to fill in the bubble marked Native American, but why should I identify more with my Native heritage than my European ancestry? What purpose does it serve? I can say that I am "Indian," but does that mean I should? Or is my Native identity solely a construct (although a legal one) to allow me special treatment as a "minority?" Why do I say I'm Potawatomi?

In considering the motivations behind Native rights movements, neither the subjugated nor the oppressor should be demonized or romanticized. My desire to identify myself as a Potawatomi Indian reflects complex political circumstances as well as the emotional benefits gained from identification with and membership in a group. If there were no ramifications, personal as well as tribal, negative as well as positive, by my checking the box marked "American Indian," I doubt that I would think the issue important enough to warrant a paper. If there were no benefits, I doubt that I would check the box and therefore have any need to write this essay.

I am not the only one struggling with these identity issues. Looking deeper into Potawatomi history sheds light upon the role that the larger political situation plays in a group's self-defined ethnicity. Expanding the criteria for group membership can be an adaptive mechanism, benefiting both those previously excluded and the original members. However, such an expression also weakens the cohesive bonds of the group, pushing the limits of what ^ethnicity" means. My tribe, the Citizen Potawatomi, is an excellent example of both the benefits and detriments of "diluting" the group.

From their first contact with Europeans to their acceptance or rejection of land allotments, my ancestors have both embraced and resisted the dominant culture, adapting to changing circumstances and losing most of the pre-contact cultural practices. I am part of a large movement by many Potawatomi today who are attempting to go "back to the blanket," reconstructing a unique

Potawatomi identity. Many of us are looking to early records of Potawatomi contact with Europeans in order to find out what "true" Potawatomi were like. However, when we look to past records in our search for ourselves, we not only have to be aware of European ideology that infiltrates such records, but we also have to accept findings that sometimes invalidate our identity.

Like many Native American tribes, the Potawatomi considered themselves superior to other groups. The Neshnabek, the True People, as we called ourselves, explained our origins with the Earth Diver myth[1]:

"In the beginning, the Old People taught, there was no land, only water. Floating on this Great Sea was a birchbark canoe. In it, weeping, sat a man, Our Grandfather. He wept because he had no idea of his fate."

In the story, Muskrat, Beaver, Snapping Turtle, and Otter dove to the bottom of the sea to bring dirt which the man, the Master of All Life, Wiske, formed into an island.

As a result of diverse coping mechanisms used when Europeans and then the United States pressured the Potawatomi for precious resources, Wiske's people are now separated into several "islands" after 350 years of both accommodation and resistance.

Today, groups of Potawatomi have their respective centers in Oklahoma, Southern Michigan, Northern Michigan, Kansas, Wisconsin, Indiana, and Canada. These diverse groups of Potawatomi Indians have chosen varied strategies to hold onto their "islands." Some are now working toward reuniting into one cohesive group again, but others believe that our respective differences are better reflected and our interests are better served as separate entities.

Archeological and linguistic evidence suggests that the Potawatomi were once part of a Central Algonquian-speaking population which included the Chippewa, or Ojibwa, and the Ottawa.[2] Just as changing circumstances have resulted in the separation of contemporary Potawatomi into smaller groups, so, too, did the evolving situation of my ancestors result in an earlier split of these traditionally joined Algonquian-speakers.

The Potawatomi ranged throughout the Great Lakes region during the 1600s and 1700s, as tensions with enemy tribes and competition over scarce resources demanded. These included pressures put on them by the Iroquois, who had entered the fur trade and acquired guns, playing their part in the Beaver Wars.[3] The Potawatomi spread into what is now Michigan, Wisconsin, Indiana, and Illinois. In 1642, they were near the east end of Lake Superior; in 1654, they were recorded living in Wisconsin; in 1670 they populated the island around Green Bay.[3] As they spread throughout the Great Lakes region, they formed geographically scattered groups which would later be permanently separated, both culturally and politically.

A close look at kinship system of my ancestors as it was recorded when they lived in the Great Lakes region could weaken my claim to be Potawatomi if a fluid concept of ethnicity is not accepted. The Potawatomi were strongly patrilineal, with membership in a clan traced through a line of men to a mythical ancestor in the distant past.[1] If this system were still accepted as the defining mechanism for Potawatomi ethnicity, than I could not claim to be Potawatomi because my father is not Potawatomi. I derive my Potawatomi ethnicity from my mother and my mother's mother. However, the Potawatomi have redefined, several times, what constitutes a Potawatomi Indian.

A casual observer might be tempted to argue that the "original" definition of Potawatomi ethnicity should be upheld, and that we should not be able to change our self-definition as a group. Such a person would reject attempts of groups to restructure membership requirements—restructuring that is currently taking place in Indian Country when groups like the Apache decide to adopt criteria for membership similar to that of today's Citizen Potawatomi, where the only requirement is to be a descendent of a tribal member. However, an argument for maintaining the "original" requirements fails to recognize that cultures are in constant flux. Cultures are adaptive mechanisms that change as circumstances demand. To choose one moment in history and claim that the state of a culture at that moment is the "original state" is to believe in a fallacy. Thus, we must accept the right of groups to constantly adjust to new circumstances, redefining their collective identities as they see fit. The Citizen Potawatomi—and groups like the Apache—have seized upon their right to do just that, to reconstruct membership requirements and better adapt to complex political situations.

One benefit of easing membership restrictions is to increase group size, a characteristic that could be deemed more important than upholding a "traditional," uniform sense of group identity.

This is the path my people, the people of the Citizen Potawatomi Nation, have chosen. By this choice, we have created a large population base which reaches into "mainstream" United States culture, increasing the chances of ensuring a continuing Potawatomi ethnicity by appealing to people like me. However, by choosing this path, we also change what it means to be Potawatomi.

I do not speak Potawatomi, nor did I grow up in Indian Country; however, I vote in our tribal elections and participate in our tribal councils, thus altering the future of our tribe to reflect values I gained outside of Indian Country. This is the route my people have chosen, but it has ramifications that may or may not have been foreseen. It is ironic that the very step that increases the political power of the Citizen Potawatomi—by increasing its numbers and its members in power positions in the dominant society— also decreases the dire need for such political power. (When people are not marginalized, degraded, and set apart as "Indian," as most of the Citizen Band are not, the imperative need for special status as "Indians"—to right ongoing wrongs—also declines.)

By opening up tribal membership to those already assimilated into mainstream United States culture, the Citizen Potawatomi Nation weakens any claim to special status founded on continuing marginalization. We are more able, however, to regain control of our resources and aggressively pursue tribal goals. We are more able to reconstruct a Potawatomi identity. We can look into the

past for culture heroes of our heritage—heroes like Wiske, waking him from his long slumber to once again send the earth divers to the bottom of the sea, creating a new island for us, the Neshnabek, the "true people." This time, however, Wiske can create an island for us within land, not water, and this time we can understand that we are one of many "true peoples." Our way is not the only way, but it is our way, and we are choosing it. In the end, this is all any group has the right to ask: that they be allowed to govern themselves, and define themselves, as they see fit—as we see fit.

So it is with my people, and so it will be with other groups, because as groups search for effective ways to seize control of their own lives and gain political clout, strategies similar to those adopted by the Citizen Potawatomi Nation will undoubtedly be utilized by other groups. Just as the Apache have recently decided to restructure their membership criteria, accepting descendency as the only requirement for membership and opening themselves up for even faster culture change, so too, will other groups. This restructuring will stretch the boundaries of the "Indian problem" making it even more difficult to sort through its complexities.

When does the situation of the Citizen Potawatomi nation change from an issue of the Fourth World to a purely political issue of fully assimilated people claiming dual citizenship for purely economic reasons? Some people will argue that tribes that choose the route of the Citizen Potawatomi should lose their entitlement to "special" treatment under the law when the majority of their members are successfully integrated into the mainstream society; however, such a stand would impose a naive idea of what it is to be "Native" upon people who are refusing to carry this projection of "savagery" for the larger population. To move to take away the hard won rights and privileges of Native Americans just because we refuse to act out the "noble savage" or "wild Indian" roles romanticized by the media and many members of the dominant culture would be unjust.

Each group deserves the right to choose for itself its membership criteria. Each group must weigh, for itself, the potential results, both positive and negative, of strategies like that of the Citizen

Potawatomi Nation. Does the group want the benefits of larger numbers when it may be "watered down" and lose its "traditional" sense of ethnicity? Is the group willing to embrace new members and renegotiate what it means to be a member of that group? Or is the group willing to chance a continuing decline in numbers which may result in complete extinction? Each group must be allowed to decide for itself. The dominant culture should not push alien ideas of how "the Natives" should appear or act upon such groups. My people have chosen their path. Now I, and all other new members' must learn/create what it means to be Potawatomi.

So I've come full circle—from feeling like I had an illegitimate claim to my American Indian identity to believing that the feeling of illegitimacy is exactly what I share with "my people," the Citizen Potawatomi. We do share a common identity, a common ethnicity. We are all Citizen Potawatomi struggling to reconcile images of "Indianness" shoved upon us by outsiders with what we see in the mirror each day. We, and our ancestors, are the recipients of that dynamic birthright called culture, and ours is chipping away at stereotypes of what a "culture" truly is. We are proof that a culture is truly an adaptive mechanism that, if successful, allows people to overcome obstacles and adjust to rapid changes.

Laura Bathurst is a member of the Citizen Potawatomi Nation and has a B.A. in anthropology and Spanish from Kansas State University She is now a graduate student in anthropology at the University of California, Berkeley.

Footnotes:

1. Clifton, James. *The Potawatomi.* New York: Chelsea House Publishers, 1987: p. 15, p. 13, p. 30

2. Sulcer, Patricia. "Final Winter for Potawatomis in Valley of the St. Joseph. *"South Bend Tribune."* 8 Jan. 1984: p. 3.

3. Landes, Ruth. *The Prairie Potawatomi: Tradition and Ritual in the Twentieth Century.* Madison, Wis.:University of Wisconsin Press 1970: p. 15.

COMMUNICATING

by Primo Levi

I never liked the term *incommunicability, so* fashionable in the 1970s, first of all because it is a linguistic horror, and secondly for more personal reasons.

In today's normal world, which by convention and contrast we call from time to time "civilized" or "free," one almost never encounters a total linguistic barrier, that is, finds oneself facing a human being with whom one must absolutely establish communication or die, and then is unable to do so.

A famous but incomplete example of this is in Antonioni's film *Red Desert,* when one night the protagonist meets a Turkish sailor who knows not a word of any language but his own and tries in vain to make himself understood. Incomplete because on both sides, the sailor's as well, the will to communicate exists, or, at least, the will to reject contact is lacking.

According to a theory fashionable during those years, which to me seems frivolous and irritating, "incommunicability" supposedly was an inevitable ingredient, a life sentence inherent to the human condition, particularly the life style of industrial society: We are monads, incapable of reciprocal messages, or capable only of truncated messages, false at their departure, misunderstood on their arrival. Discourse is fictitious, pure noise, a painted veil that conceals existential silence; we are alone, even (or especially) if we live in pairs. It seems to me that this lament originates in and points to mental laziness; certainly it encourages it, in a dangerous vicious circle. Except for cases of pathological incapacity, one can and must communicate, and thereby contribute in a useful and easy way to the peace of others and oneself, because silence, the absence of signals, is itself a signal, but an ambiguous one, and ambiguity generates anxiety and suspicion. To say that it is impossible to communicate is false; one always can. To refuse to communicate is a failing; we are biologically and socially predisposed to communication, and in particular to its highly evolved and noble form, which is language. All members of the human species speak, no nonhuman species knows how to speak.

From the standpoint of communication—indeed, of failed communication—we survivors have known a peculiar experience. It is an irksome habit of ours to intervene when someone (our children!) speaks about cold, hunger, or fatigue. What do you know about it? You should have gone through what we did. In general, for reasons of good taste and good neighborliness, we try to resist the temptation of such *miles glorious* interventions; nevertheless I find it imperative to intervene precisely when I hear people talking about failed or impossible communication. "You should have experienced ours." There can be no comparison to the tourist in Finland or Japan who finds interlocutors who do not speak his language but are professionally (or even spontaneously) polite or well intentioned and make an effort to understand and help him. Besides, who, in what corner of the world, cannot string together a few words of English? In any event the questions of tourists are few, always the same, hence uncertainties are rare, and almost understanding each other can be as amusing as a game.

IVORY BRACELETS

by Suzanne Cleary

I am fascinated by ivory bracelets, thick and
     heavy
and carved like cathedral doors, the pictures
wrought from them

in layers, like successive rooms, this carving
reinforcing my belief that each surface hides a
     story

in bas-relief, an Atlantis where there is a table set
     for dinner
and a bracelet worn, at the moment her world
     ends,

by a girl holding a cup with two hands.

I stare into store windows at these bracelets on
     blue velvet
but see only a braille in the polished, buttery ivory

which is the color of my grandfather's fingernails
thickened and hardened by 43 years in the shoe
     factory.

The carvings could be the long room I saw once
when I was five years old, the workbenches high
     as my forehead.

It was piecework. I didn't know what I saw
but I saw the leather tongues strung together in
stacks,

each stack with a paper tag to be saved, counted at
     the end of the week,

dangling, waving in the breeze from the fans.

I saw the brooms, the canvas bins for scraps,

beneath the benches, pots: you wouldn't leave
     your work to pee.

Someone opened the window, which looked like a
     barn door
and slid sideways, and this I remember best: how
     blue the sky looked

over the factories' tar roofs.

On certain days the sky is the color of ivory
but ivory is a more substantive beauty, throughout
time

associated with power and death.
When it circles the wrist

it is often worn in pairs that clack dully together
or worn singly, as those things we prize most.

When I look at an ivory bracelet I want to imagine
that it is carved with figures of both animals and
     humans

and the men carry bowls to the horses,
who lower their heads and drink

and the women, tall, are naked and shaded by fir
     trees,
beyond the trees a stream.

I know this is too much for one bracelet
but that is how it is true to life. The pieces

of this story cannot be woven together.
I want to imagine the stories on the bracelet

cover time, and cross it, in harmony
and some of the braille is in fact for the blind

and some of the shadow opaque,
the ivory dark-veined, flawed.

I am fascinated by what has been left out
to create the beautiful shapes, and deepen them.

I want to imagine that nothing died for this.

DIMENSIONS OF INEQUALITY IN THE UNITED STATES

by Harold R. Kerbo

A few years ago I met an American friend of mine at a train station in California. He had been living in Japan for ten years, and except for a couple of short visits to Hawaii had not been in the United States during those ten years. He arrived in San Francisco, spent a few days across the Bay in Oakland, traveled by train to Los Angeles, and then completely across the country to spend a few weeks gathering information in Washington, D.C. Upon arriving in California, and then more so as he traveled across the United States, he was shocked at the poverty and signs of inequality he saw everywhere. "This is not the country I remember," he told me. "It almost seems like a third world country today." A couple of years later, while I was living in Germany, American relatives who came for a visit asked, "So where do the poor people live?" They were unaware that, such as there are, I had already shown them.

These are not uncommon reactions. Indeed, in the United States we find a mix of third world and first world characteristics more than in other industrial nations. Traveling around this country, you find the third world and first world in separate regions, with people of first world America trying to isolate themselves from what they find in the other. The third world parts, it must be stressed, are not mostly due to recent immigration: The vast majority of poor people in the United States were born of parents whose ancestors had been Americans for many generations.

As noted toward the end of the previous chapter, the United States is in the process of change. Poverty and inequality *have again been* growing. But this is not the only reason why my friend, returning to his homeland for the first time in ten years, was shocked: He also had been living in a country with one of the lowest levels of inequality among industrial nations. There are some homeless, mostly mentally ill, people, sleeping in subway stations in Tokyo. There is one particular section of Tokyo with many poor workers, and certainly another in Osaka. But there is today in Japan nothing like the poverty and homelessness we find in many cities of the United States. With much exaggeration, I like to make the point by referring to the city of Hiroshima, where I recently lived for a year: "There *are* homeless people in Hiroshima—I saw both of them sleeping in the park on Peace Boulevard across from my apartment one morning."

It is time to turn to some details of the inequality in the United States compared with earlier history and compared with other countries. But it must be stressed that our intent in this chapter is primarily *descriptive* rather than analytical. We will begin by describing the distribution of income and wealth, then proceed to standards of living and health. In the final section we will describe inequalities in government services and the tax policies that lead to inequalities in who pays for these services. These types of inequalities are among the most important, although by no means the only ones of importance. There are, for example, other nonmaterial inequalities, and inequalities based upon caste like divisions of race and sex. These will be examined in other chapters. But the patterns of inequality examined here will provide us with a base image of inequality in a Western industrial society that will make further study of social stratification more meaningful.

INCOME AND WEALTH INEQUALITY

Two of the most important types of inequality are inequalities of income and wealth. These are of major importance because it is income and wealth that bring other valued goods and services, not to mention the basic necessities of life. The relationship between income and necessities like food, shelter, and health care will be described after our discussion of income and wealth. Income and wealth, however, are also generalized commodities that, depending upon the quantity and how they are used, bring power and influence. The relationship income and wealth have to power and influence will be the subject of later chapters.

By *income* we mean money, wages, and payments that periodically are received as returns from an occupation or investments. Income is the means by which most Americans obtain the necessities and simple luxuries of life; a wage or salary (rather than investments) sustains the vast majority of people in this country. *Wealth is* accumulated assets in the form of various types of valued goods, such as real estate, stocks, bonds, or money held in reserve. Wealth is anything of economic value that is bought, sold, stocked for future disposition, or invested to bring an economic return. As might be expected, most Americans have little or no wealth; whatever they have attained in the form of wages and salaries cannot be accumulated because it must be used for immediate necessities. Income is certainly distributed in an unequal manner in this country, but wealth is distributed even more unequally.

INCOME INEQUALITY

A simple method of considering income inequality is by looking at a population distribution within specified income categories. Table 2-1 presents such a distribution for all families (as well as for whites, blacks, and Hispanics) in the United States

as of 1992. Of more than 96 million households, for example, 4.6 percent had annual incomes of less than $5000; 10 percent had incomes between $5000 and $9999; and, at the other end of the spectrum, 4.9 percent had incomes of $100,000 or more.

As we will see in later chapters, an important issue in the study of social stratification and inequality, especially in the United States, is inequality by race and ethnic origin. We will see that race, ethnicity, and class are related to each other in complex ways, with racial divisions often having, to some degree, class divisions at their base. But for now we first need to consider the level of income inequality by race and Hispanic origin. In Table 2-1 we find that both blacks and Hispanics had a much higher percentage of people with incomes of $5000 or less in 1992, and a much lower percentage with incomes of $100,000 or more compared with whites.

In contrast to considering the distribution of people or families within income categories (as in Table 2-1), we can consider the distribution of total income among select population categories. A standard method of doing so is to divide the population into income fifths (20 percent population segments) and compare population shares

TABLE 2-1
PERCENTAGE DISTRIBUTION OF FAMILIES (WHITE AND NONWHITE) BY INCOME LEVEL, 1992

Annual income (dollars)	Percentage of all families	Percentage of white families	Percentage of black families	Percentage of families of Spanish origin
Under 5,000	4.6	3.6	11.8	6.6
5,000-9,999	10.0	8.9	18.7	13.8
10,000-14,999	9.5	9.1	12.2	12.6
15,000-24,999	16.8	16.7	18.3	20.8
25,000-34,999	14.8	15.1	13.2	16.3
35,000-49,999	17.1	17.7	12.8	14.5
50,000-74,999	16.1	17.0	8.8	10.5
75,000-99,999	6.1	6.6	2.7	3.2
100,000 & over	4.9	5.3	1.5	1.8

Source: U.S. Bureau of the Census, 1993, *Current Population Reports,* "Money Income and Poverty Status of Families and Persons in the United States: 1992," Table B-2.

with income shares. Table 2-2 presents this information for 1992. In this year the lowest fifth of households in the United States received 3.8 percent of the income, the next- lowest fifth received 9.4 percent, and the highest fifth received 46.9 percent of all income. In other words, the lowest 20 percent of households received only 3.8 percent of the total income, while the highest 20 percent of households received 46.9 percent of the total. Table 2-2 also shows that the highest 5 percent of households alone received 18.6 percent of aggregate income.

It is useful to note at this point that the mean household income in 1992 was $39,020, while the mean income of the lowest 20 percent of households was only $7328, that of the upper 20 percent of households was $91,494, and that of the upper 5 percent was $145,244. The mean income for the second lowest fifth was $18,281 while it was $30,794 for the third fifth, and $47,235 for the fourth fifth.

TABLE 2-2
PERCENTAGE OF AGGREGATE HOUSEHOLD INCOME RECEIVED BY EACH FIFTH AND HIGHEST 5 PERCENT, 1992

All households	Percentage of aggregate income
Lowest fifth	3.8
Second fifth	9.4
Middle fifth	15.8
Fourth fifth	24.2
Highest fifth	46.9
Highest 5 percent	18.6

Source: U.S. Bureau of the Census, 1993, *Current Population Reports,* "Money Income and Poverty Status of Families and Persons in the United States: 1992." Table B-3

The vast majority of people in this country must depend upon some type of employment (as opposed to wealth) for their income, and the occupational structure is of primary importance in creating an unequal distribution of income. Table 2-3 presents the median incomes within general occupational categories for 1992. For males, the highest occupational category (executive, adminis-

trative, and managerial occupations) shows a median income of $40,081, while the lowest (farmworkers) shows a median income of only $7858. It is also interesting to note that for females the highest figure is substantially lower than that for men ($25,239). Roughly the same income discrepancy is found between males and females with respect to education level in Table 2-3. As we will see in later chapters, part of the male-female inequality is due to sex discrimination, but this discrimination operates within the occupational structure in a number of important ways.

The extent of income inequality by occupation is severely underestimated in Table 2-3 because we are considering only very general occupational categories. Within each occupational category many people are making much less and others much more than is indicated by the median. This underestimation is especially evident at the top, where many managers of major corporations have exceptionally high salaries. For example, a 1991 survey of top executive incomes in the biggest 838 corporations in the United States found an average of $1.2 million (*Wall Street Journal Europe,* October 9, 1992; *Los Angeles Times,* March 3, 1993).

Having considered some aspects of current income inequality, we will go on to three further questions. What was the previous pattern of income inequality in the United States? How does the United States compare with other industrialized nations in this respect? And has the distribution of income in this country become more or less unequal, or has it remained the same over the years? This last question has become one of the most important at the end of the twentieth century and pertains to a troubling trend in the nature of inequality in the United States.

Trends in U.S. Income Inequality We have data showing that income inequality was reduced somewhat during the 1930s and early 1940s due to depression reforms and full employment during World War II. The most significant change occurred within the top 20 percent and the top 5 percent of families, who had their share of income reduced from 54.4 percent and 30 percent, respectively, in 1929 to 44 percent and 17.2 percent by 1945 (Turner and Starnes 1976:51).

TABLE 2-3
MEDIAN INCOME BY OCCUPATIONAL CATEGORY AND EDUCATION MALE AND FEMALE, 1992

| | Median income | |
Occupation	Male	Female
Executive, administrative, and managerial	$40,081	25,239
Professional	40,059	25,759
Technical, sales, and administrative support	23,823	14,023
Sales	23,485	8,565
Administrative support and clerical	20,708	15,746
Precision production and craft	23,219	14,794
Operators and laborers	16,879	11,045
Service	10,739	6,506
Farming, forestry, fishing	7,858	3,686

Educational level		
Less than 9 years	17,445	13,000
9 to 12 years	21,411	14,613
High school graduate	27,357	19,462
Some college	32,187	23,223
Associate degree	33,477	25 643
Bachelor's degree	41,406	30 394
Master's degree	50,001	36,062
Professional degree	76,321	46,422
Doctorate degree	58,035	45,776

Source: U.S. Bureau of the Census, 1993, *Current Population Reports,* "Money Income of Households, Families, and Persons in the United States: 1992," consumer Income series P-60, no. 184, pp. 152-155, 94-95

As shown in Table 2-4, however, there is again change in the income distribution among families.[1] There was a slight decrease in income inequality between 1947 and 1975. The percentage of income going to the bottom 20 percent of the people increased somewhat, and the percentage of income going to the top 20 percent and top 5 percent of the people decreased. *However,* as noted in the beginning of this chapter, there has been significant change since 1980. There has been a rather rapid and significant increase in income inequality between 1980 and 1992 because, as they say, the income rich have been getting richer while the income poor have been getting poorer. As we see in Table 2-4, the bottom income group now has

only 4.4 percent of the income, compared with 5.1 percent in 1980, and the top 20 percent income group now has 44.6 percent of all income, compared with only 41.6 percent in 1980. (Note that Table 2-2 is based upon household income compared with actual multiperson (family) income in Table 2-4.) And it should be noted that this income inequality is even higher if we use Federal Reserve data, which include more complete income sources than the standard Census Bureau study (Thurow 1987). Using these Federal Reserve data, for example, we find that the top 2 percent of people received about 14 percent of all income during the early 1980s.

TABLE 2-4

PERCENTAGE OF AGGREGATE FAMILY INCOME BY INCOME FIFTHS AND TOP 5 PERCENT, 1947-1992

Year	Percentage of aggregate family income					
	Lowest fifth	Second fifth	Third fifth	Fourth fifth	Highest fifth	Top 5 percent
1992	4.4	10.5	16.5	24.0	44.6	17.6
1990	4.6	10.8	16.6	23.8	44.3	17.4
1985	4.7	10.9	16.8	24.1	43.6	16.7
1980	5.1	11.6	17.5	24.3	41.6	15.3
1975	5.4	11.8	17.6	24.1	41.1	15.5
1970	5.4	12.2	17.6	23.8	40.9	15.6
1965	5.2	12.2	17.8	23.9	40.9	15.5
1960	4.8	12.2	17.8	24.0	41.3	15.9
1955	4.8	12.3	17.8	23.7	41.3	16.4
1950	4.5	12.0	17.4	23.4	42.7	17.3
1947	5.0	11.9	17.0	23.1	43.0	17.5

Source: U.S. Bureau of the Census, 1981, *Current Population Reports, 1980*:63, Table 13; U.S. Bureau of the Census, 1980, *Current Population Reports,* "Money Income of Families and Persons in the United States: 1978," series P-60, no. 123, Table L; U.S. Bureau of the Census, 1993, *Current Population Reports* "Money Income and Poverty Status of Families and Persons in the United States: 1992," series P-M, no. 166, Table B-7.

Figure 2-l indicates this growing inequality by using these data to construct what is known as a **Gini index** to measure income inequality. With Figure 2-l we can see that, since World War II, income inequality in the United States hit its lowest level between 1965 and 1970 but then rose dramatically in the 1980s to its highest point in 1992. In addition to this trend of increasing income inequality in the 1980s, there has been a decline in real income for most Americans since the 1970s.

Another way to consider this growing income inequality is by looking at the percentage change in the number of households at certain income levels as presented for 1992 in Table 2-1 (using consistent 1992 dollars). This is done in Table 2-5 for income data from 1967 to 1992. When we look down the columns for all families under $5,000 to $14,999 annual income, we find slight increases or no significant change in the percentage of households in these columns. But, most interesting, we find a *big decrease* from 1967 to 1992 in the

middle-income columns of $15,000 to $49,999. That is clearly shrinkage of the middle class in the United States. Then, at the upper income levels $50,000 to over $100,00 we find rather large increases in the number of people at the same time the middle is shrinking. The percentage of households in the $100,000 and over column increased from 2.5 percent in 1970 to 6.2 percent in 1992. The middle is falling away, while the affluent and the poor steadily grow more numerous.

For the 1980s, Figure 2-2 shows most clearly what was happening, and continues to happen, as we have seen. From 1980 to 1989 the bottom 20 percent of the U.S. population lost 4.6 percent in real income, the next 20 percent of people lost 4.1 percent, while the middle 20 percent lost a bit less than 1 percent (0.8). After that real income goes up—way up. The upper 10 percent of people gained 9.1 percent in their income, while the top 1 percent of people gained 62.9 percent.

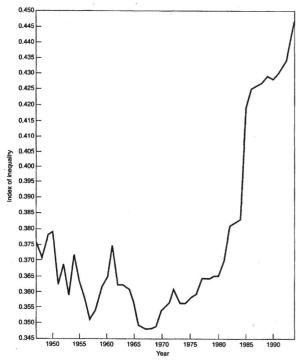

FIGURE 2-1
Family income inequality (Gini index), 1947-1992. *Source:* U.S. Bureau of the Census, 1993.

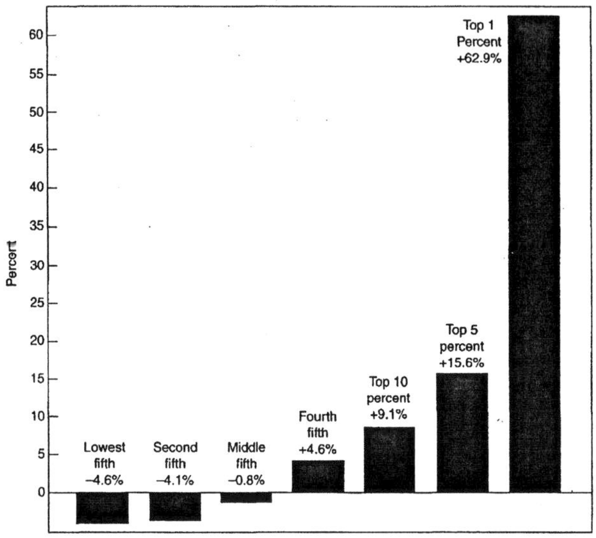

FIGURE 2-2
Income gains and losses, 1980-1989. *Source:* Mishel and Bernstein (1993:48).

The picture for minorities is more extreme when we consider data like that presented for all races in Table 2-5. For whites we find that the percentage of people with incomes under $5000 increased somewhat between 1967 and 1992. However, for blacks and Hispanics, and especially blacks, there is considerable increase in the lowest-income column during this period. The shrinkage of the middle-income class for both of these minorities is considerably greater than for whites, while the increase in the affluence of some minorities is much less than for whites. In the case of blacks and Hispanics between 1967 and 1992, compared with whites, the poor were getting even poorer, while the rich were increasing only slightly.

This is not the place to get into a full explanation of why income inequality has grown significantly in the 1980s, but we can briefly cover some of the most important reasons. These reasons fall into two main categories: (1) political policies since the late 1970s and (2) changes in the U.S. economy.

Among the political policies that increased income inequality were changes in tax policies (reducing taxes for the wealthy, while taxes for lower-income groups increased) and cuts in transfer payments such as the means-tested welfare programs for the poor (Harrison and Bluestone 1988). Among the most important changes in the economy, as noted earlier, has been the reduction in middle-paying jobs in the l980s and 1990s, while jobs in both the highest-paid and lowest-paid areas of the economy increased (Thurow 1987). This change can be seen in Figure 2-3 for the periods 1963-1973, 1973-1979, and 1979-1986. Further, of all the new jobs created in the economy from 1979 to 1986, over 55 percent have wages at the poverty level or below (Bluestone 1988). During the early 1990s there has been some alteration in this pattern: A slight majority of new jobs have been in the higher income levels, with a continuing increase in low-paying jobs and a continuing decrease in middle-paying jobs (U.S. Census, *New York Times,* October 17, 1994).

TABLE 2-5

DISTRIBUTION OF FAMILES BY INCOME LEVELS, 1970-1992*

All Races	Number (thous.)	Total	Under $5,000	$5,000 to $9,999	$10,000 to $14,999	$15,000 to $24,999	$25,000 to $34,999	$35,000 to $49,999	$50,000 to $74,999	$75,000 to $99,999	$100,000 and over	Median income Value (dollars)	Median income Standard error (dollars)	Mean income Value (dollars)	Mean income Standard error (dollars)
							Percent distribution								
1992	68,144	100.0	3.7	5.8	7.3	15.5	15.0	19.2	19.6	7.7	6.2	36,812	186	44,483	205
1991	67,173	100.0	3.5	5.9	7.0	15.6	15.2	19.6	19.2	7.8	6.2	37,021	184	44,539	202
1990	66,322	100.0	3.2	5.4	6.7	15.4	15.2	20.0	19.4	8.2	6.6	37,950	181	45,785	211
1989	66,090	100.0	3.0	5.3	7.1	14.8	14.6	19.7	20.1	8.4	7.0	38,710	221	46,962	225
1988	65,837	100.0	3.2	5.5	6.8	15.4	14.7	19.9	20.0	8.1	6.5	38,177	199	45,788	224
1987[1]	65,204	100.0	3.1	5.7	6.7	15.3	14.8	20.0	20.3	8.0	6.3	38,249	177	45,553	204
1986	64,491	100.0	3.2	5.7	6.8	15.5	15.3	20.1	19.9	7.6	6.0	37,709	202	44,707	196
1985	63,558	100.0	3.2	6.1	7.2	16.1	15.7	20.1	19.3	7.1	5.1	36,164	196	42,956	186
1984	62,706	100.0	3.4	6.0	7.7	16.1	15.8	20.3	19.2	6.8	4.8	35,693	158	41,931	166
1983[2]	62,015	100.0	3.6	6.3	7.7	16.6	16.3	20.6	18.4	6.2	4.4	34,757	(NA)	40,597	(NA)
1962	61,393	100.0	3.4	6.2	7.9	16.9	16.6	21.0	18.0	6.0	4.1	34,390	170	40,198	160
1981	61,019	100.0	2.9	5.9	7.6	17.4	16.5	21.4	18.4	6.4	3.5	34,862	149	40,234	154
1980	60,309	100.0	2.6	5.7	7.4	16.5	16.8	21.8	19.2	6.3	3.7	35,839	153	40,869	159
1979[3]	59,550	100.0	2.4	5.3	6.9	16.4	15.8	22.5	19.9	6.6	4.2	37,136	173	42,310	169
1978	57,804	100.0	2.4	5.3	7.4	16.3	16.0	22.6	19.9	6.1	4.0	36,665	168	41,760	166
1977	57,215	100.0	2.4	5.5	7.9	16.6	16.9	22.5	19.0	5.7	3.5	35,539	127	40,545	129
1976	56,710	100.0	2.2	5.7	8.0	16.8	17.0	23.5	18.5	5.2	3.2	35,330	128	39,846	128
1975	56,245	100.0	2.3	5.9	8.3	17.4	17.8	23.1	17.5	4.7	2.9	34,249	130	38,810	125
1974[4]	55,698	100.0	2.3	5.3	7.8	16.7	18.4	22.8	18.4	5.3	3.1	34,878	(NA)	39,768	(NA)
1973	55,053	100.0	2.1	5.5	7.5	16.3	17.5	23.5	18.8	5.5	3.4	35,821	(NA)	40,491	(NA)
1972	54,373	100.0	2.3	5.8	7.3	16.6	18.6	23.0	17.9	5.3	3.2	35,126	(NA)	39,894	(NA)
1971	53,296	100.0	2.6	6.2	7.5	17.8	19.7	23.2	16.0	4.5	2.4	33,480	(NA)	37,705	(NA)
1970	52,227	100.0	2.7	5.9	7.5	17.4	20.2	23.1	16.3	4.3	2.5	33,519	(NA)	37,728	(NA)
1969	51,586	100.0	2.6	6.0	7.5	17.0	20.0	24.4	16.1	4.0	2.4	33,590	(NA)	37,664	(NA)
1968	50,823	100.0	2.9	5.9	8.1	18.2	21.3	23.6	14.6	3.4	2.0	32,124	(NA)	35,987	(NA)
1967	50,111	100.0	3.1	7.2	7.9	19.4	22.6	21.8	12.8	3.3	2.0	30,661	(NA)	34,016	(NA)

* In constant 1992 dollars.
Source: U.S. Bureau of the Census, 1993, *Current Population Reports,* "Money Incom of Hourseholds, Families, and Persons in the United States; 1992," Table B-6.

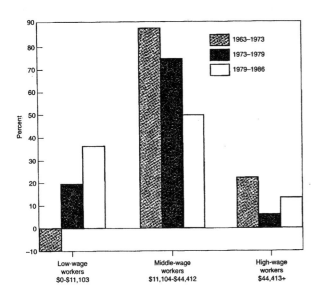

FIGURE 2-3
Net change in employment by wage categories, 1963-1986.
Source: U.S. Bureau of the Census, *Current Population Reports, 1964-1987;* Harrison and Bluestone (1988:122).

Comparative Income Inequality Our next question pertains to what the U.S. income inequality looks like compared with that of other industrial nations. In the beginning, it is useful to point out that during the 1960s the United States was generally ranked about midway in terms of income inequality when compared with other industrial nations (Jain 1975). France had the highest amount of income inequality at the time, with West Germany, England, and Australia showing the lowest levels in the 1960s.

The most recent comparative income inequality figures that can be obtained are generally for the 1980s because these data are not collected every year in other countries, in contrast to the United States. These data show some very important changes compared with the 1960s. As we might expect from the preceding discussion of growing income inequality in the United States, Figure 2-4 now shows that the overall highest level of income inequality is found in the United States, with the lowest level found in Japan (see also Menard 1986; Verba et al. 1987). The gap between the average income of the top 20 percent group and the bottom 20 percent income group in the United States is twelve to one (meaning the top average is twelve times that of the bottom), while this same gap is only four to one in Japan (World Bank 1986:227). Although Japan and the United States had had similar levels of income inequality, since the 1960s Japan has had a substantial reduction in income inequality, while the United States has experienced increased income inequality. We will examine why this was so for Japan, as well as why both Japan and Germany today have much less inequality, in our last two chapters.

We have more recent income figures for different occupational groups in major industrial nations, which show the same basic pattern. Table 2-6 indicates the average annual incomes for 1992 in the seven leading industrial nations of the world. Looking down the column for manufacturing employees, we find American workers are paid on average only above British workers. But at the other end of the table, we find that American chief executive officers of corporations have average incomes ($717,237) far above those of other industrial nations. Japan and Germany, on the other hand, show generally the opposite pattern: Their workers are among the highest-paid in the world, while their top executives are the lowest-paid of the seven leading industrial nations. Thus, the gap between incomes is lowest in Japan and Germany, while the gap is highest in the United States.

WEALTH INEQUALITY

Despite the importance of income inequality in the United States, in some ways wealth inequality is more significant. Most people use income for day-to-day necessities. Substantial wealth, however, often brings income, power, and independence. On the one hand, wealth in significant quantities relieves individuals from dependence upon others for an income. As we will see, the authority structure associated with occupational differentiation is one of the most important aspects of the stratification system in the United States, and the impact of this authority

structure is reduced when people have substantial wealth. On the other hand, if wealth is used to purchase significant ownership of the means of production in the society (most importantly, stock ownership in major corporations), it can bring authority to the holder of such wealth (depending on the amount of ownership). Substantial wealth is also important because it can be transferred from generation to generation more easily than income, producing greater inheritance of position and opportunity within the stratification system. This has been especially true since 1982, when one of President Reagan's tax bills substantially reduced inheritance taxes in this country.

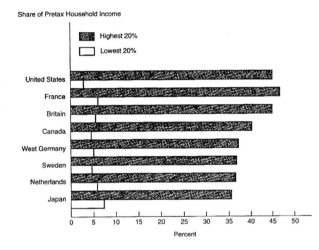

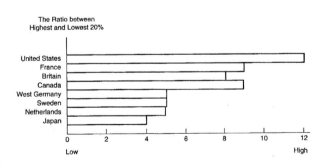

FIGURE 2-4

Comparative income inequality, leading capitalist nations, 1980s. *Source:* World Bank (1986).

TABLE 2-6
COMPARATIVE EMPLOYEE AND EXECUTIVE INCOMES, 1992

Manufacturing employee	White-collar employee	Managers	CEOs
Germany **$36,857**	Britain **$74,761**	Italy **$219,573**	**United States** **$717,237**
Canada $34,935	France $62,279	France $190,354	France $479,772
Japan $34,263	Germany $59,916	Japan $185,437	Italy $439,441
Italy $31,537	Italy $58,263	Britain $162,190	Britain $439,441
France $30,019	**United States** **$57,675**	**United States** **$159,575**	Canada $416,066
United States **$27,606**	Canada $47,231	Germany $145,627	Germany $390,933
Britain $26,084	Japan $40,990	Canada $132,877	Japan $390,723

Source: Towers Perrin, *Wall Street Journal Europe,* October 9, 1992; Mishel and Bernstein: (1993:204).

Estimates of wealth holdings and wealth are difficult to come by in any society, including the United States. This is so not only because much wealth can be and is always hidden for those trying to make an estimate but also because most countries, including the United States, seldom try to collect the figures annually, as is more often done with income figures. Table 2-7 reports wealth inequality data that exists for 1983 and 1989. Wealth holdings are estimated by fifths of the population, as were shown for income inequality, and are presented with figures on income inequality for the same year for comparison purposes. With the 1989 data, wealth and income shares are listed for the top 1 percent of people and the top 10 percent. Although income is highly unequal in the United States, these data show wealth to be even more unequally distributed. For example, in 1983, while the top fifth of the population received 42.7 percent of the *income,* the top fifth held over 78.7 percent of family *wealth.* Moreover, the top 0.5 percent of the population controlled 27 percent of all wealth, and the top 10 percent of the population controlled about 68 percent of all wealth, according to a study by James Smith (Institute for

Social Research 1986/1987).[2] In contrast, while the bottom fifth received 4.7 percent of the income, the bottom fifth held even less of the wealth (-0.4 percent). Considered another way, we find that the top 40 percent of the population held 93.2 percent of the wealth, leaving only 6.8 percent of the wealth for the remaining 60 percent of the population. The 1989 data show roughly the same type of distribution: The top 1 percent of people held 38.3 percent of the wealth, while the top 10 percent of people held 71.2 percent of the wealth.

As we did with income, we need to consider race and ethnic inequality with respect to wealth. When we do so, we find even greater inequality in wealth compared with income. Table 2-8 presents the 1991 median net worth by race and Hispanic origin.[3] As can be seen, wealth inequalities by race and Hispanic origin are even greater than income inequalities. While the median net worth for white households was $44,408 (down from $50,204 in 1988, we might add), the median worth for black households was $4,604 (down from $4836 in 1988) and $5345 for households of Hispanic origin (down from $6408 in 1988).

TABLE 2-7

DISTRIBUTION OF WEALTH AND INCOME BY FAMILY
FIFTHS, 1983 AND 1989

Family fifths	Percentage of total wealth	Percentage of total income
Highest fifth	78.7	42.7
Fourth fifth	14.5	24.4
Middle fifth	6.2	17.1
Second fifth	1.1	11.1
Lowest fifth	-0.4	4.7
	100.0%	100.0%

Percentage of population (1989)	Percentage of all wealth	Percentage of income
Top 1 percent	38.3%	14.7%
Top 10 percent	71.2	38.9

Source: U.S. Bureau of the Census, 1 1989, *Current Population Reports,* series P-60, no. 146; Mishel and Bernstein (1993:254). Note: Also see note 1.

TABLE 2-8

DISTRIBUTION OF HOUSEHOLD NET WORTH BY
RACE AND SPANISH ORIGIN, 1991

	1991 Median net worth
White households	$44,408
Black households	$4,604
Hispanic origin households	$5,345

Source: U.S. Bureau of the Census, 1994, *Current Population Reports,* Household Economic Studies, "Household Wealth and Asset Ownership: 1991," series P-70, no, 34, p. xiii.

Another way to look at wealth inequality, of course, is by examining the superrich. *Forbes* magazine (October 24, 1988) estimated that there were fifty-one billionaires in 1988, making the 1980s obviously a fine climate for the rich to get richer because the number of billionaires *doubled* between 1986 and 1988. By 1992 the *Forbes* (October 1992) list of U.S. billionaires had grown to seventy-one. And of the most wealthy 101 people in the world, the United States counted 26, with Japan a distant second with 13, and Germany third with 9 (*Fortune,* June 28, 1993). Heading the list of billionaire families in the United States for 1993 were the Waltons of the Wal-Mart discount store empire, with $23.5 billion controlled by five family members. Next came the Mars family wealth (as in candy bars) at $14.0 billion. As for the individual controlling the most wealth in the United States, that position was held by William Gates of Microsoft.

As noted earlier, wealth inequality data for the overall population are not gathered as often as for income inequality in the United States, and, before the 1980s, the last time a complete study such as this was made was in 1962 (U.S. Office of Management and Budget 1973: 164). But in contrast to

income inequality, the data indicate somewhat less change in wealth inequality between 1962 and 1983. However, it is most likely that wealth inequality shows only some change when comparing 1962 and 1986, but that there has been more change between these two points in time. As indicated by Table 2- 9, the percentage of wealth held by the top was going down at least until 1972, and would have had to come back up since 1972 to make the 1962 and 1983 distributions similar. Thus, we probably have been experiencing an upward trend in wealth inequality in recent years, and especially so since 1983 (again, see note 2). Differing data sets always make comparisons difficult with respect to wealth, but data for the top 1 percent of the population in 1989 certainly show a big increase in wealth concentration in the mid-1980s, from 24.1 percent held by this top 1 percent in 1972 to 38.3 percent in 1989. Much the same is suggested by new Internal Revenue Service data showing that the number of millionaires had almost doubled (from 475,000 to 941,000) between 1982 and 1986 (see the Los *Angeles Times,* August 23, 1990).

Another important question pertains to the source of wealth for the top wealth holders in the United

States. As indicated in Table 2-10, in 1989 the top 1 percent and the top 0.5 percent of the population (in terms of wealth) held 46.7 percent and 37.4 percent, respectively, of all personally owned corporate stock in the United States. As noted earlier, and as will be discussed more fully in later chapters, ownership of corporate stock is most important because such ownership can bring significant economic power. The ownership of real estate, for example, brings certain rights pertaining to how the real estate is used, but significant ownership of corporate stock can influence the overall economy through influence in major corporations in this country. (We emphasize *can* because there are many questions about such influence that must be considered further.)

TABLE 2-9
PERCENT OF TOTAL WEALTH HELD BY TOP 1 PERCENT AND TOP 0.5 PERCENT.

Year	Percentage of wealth held by	
	Top 1%	Top 0.5%
1958	25.5	20.4%
1962	26.2	20.7
1969	24.4	19.3
1972	24.1	18.9
1989	38.3	-

Source: U.S. Bureau of the Census, 1980, *Statistical Abstracts of the United States,* Table 786, p. 471; Mishel and Bernstein (1993:254).

TABLE 2-10
TOP WEALTH MOLDERS BY TYPE OF WEALTH, 1989

Richest	% of all stock	% of all bonds	% of all trusts
0.5 percent	37.4	64.0	33.3
1 percent	46.7	72.9	52.6
10 percent	83.8	94.0	90.1

Source: Mishel and Bernstein (1993:256).

In another study looking at some other sources of wealth in 1983, the Federal Reserve Board found that the most wealthy 10 percent of the U.S. population held 41 percent of all money in checking accounts, 72 percent of all the corporate stock, 50 percent of all physical property, and 78 percent of all business property (Harrison and Bluestone 1988: 136).

Historical Trends in Wealth Inequality As with income inequality, a major question pertains to the historical trends in wealth inequality in the United States. We saw in Table 2-9 that wealth inequality went down somewhat between 1958 and 1972 before going up dramatically again in the 1980s (with the holdings of the top 1 percent and 0.5 percent of the population). Table 2- 11 shows that the proportion of wealth held by the top 1 percent of the population had mostly been going down

slowly between World War II (1945) and 1972, only to jump again dramatically in the 1980s. We do find a significant increase and then a drop in the wealth holdings of the top 1 percent between 1922 and 1945, which (along with the change in income distribution) is no doubt related to the major changes in this country brought about by the great depression of the 1930s and World War II. But despite these changes since 1922, we have other evidence that the amount of wealth held by the most wealthy 1 percent did not change much between 1810 and 1945 (see Gallman 1969:6). Since the 1980s, it is important to note, the level of wealth inequality has returned to where it was before the great depression in 1929.

As noted previously, while both wealth and income are distributed very unequally in the United States, wealth is distributed even more unequally. A comparison of wealth and income inequality can be made most strikingly with what is known as a **Lorenz curve,** which is constructed by indicating how much wealth or income is held by various percentages of the total population. As shown in Figure 2-5, a condition of equality would show a straight diagonal line across the graph. In other words, 20 percent of the population would receive 20 percent of the wealth or income, 40 percent of the population would receive 40 percent of the wealth or income, and so on. On the other hand, the farther the curve is from the diagonal, the greater the inequality. Using 1983 data, Figure 2-5 graphically shows the magnitude of both income and wealth inequality in the United States.

TABLE 2-11
PERCENTAGE OF TOTAL WEALTH HELD BY TOP 1 PERCENT, 1922- 1989

Year	Percentage of wealth held by top 1 percent*
1922	31.6
1929	36.3
1933	28.3
1939	30.6
1945	23.3
1949	20.8
1953	24.3
1954	24.0
1956	26.0
1958	23.8
1962	22.0
1965	23.4
1969	20.1
1972	20.7
1989	38.3

* Figures vary slightly in some years compared with Table 2-9 due to sample differences. *Source:* U.S. Bureau of the Census, 1980, *Statistical Abstracts of the United States,* Table 785, p. 471; Mishel and Bernstein (1993:254).

INEQUALITY IN BASIC NECESSITIES

With the extent of income and wealth inequality reviewed here, it would seem quite obvious that other material goods are distributed unequally in the United States. However, there are other issues that must be noted with respect to the distribution of basic necessities. An unequal distribution of income is not always an accurate indication of

how basic necessities such as food, housing, and medical care are distributed. There are two reasons for this: First, we must consider the possibility of state subsidies of necessities; second, we must consider the relative cost of basic necessities.

In considering state subsidies for basic necessities, we need only mention at this point that, contrary to political rhetoric, the United States spends at best an *average* amount for welfare-type programs when compared with other industrialized nations (Mishel and Bernstein 1993; Shapiro 1992). The United States is the only industrialized nation that does not have a basic guaranteed income program for all families below the poverty level or a comprehensive national health program meeting the medical needs of all families (Mishel and Bernstein 1993; Moynihan 1973:95; Kahn and Kamerman 1977; Ozawa 1978:39; Harrington 1984). And when families do receive welfare support for basic necessities, the money they receive places them well below the income needed for those necessities. For example, with a median family income of $36,812 for 1992, the median family income for those existing on income from welfare payments was only $7853 (U.S. Bureau of the Census, *Current Population Reports* 1992:88). What is more, this 1992 level of welfare support for individuals declined more than 40 percent between 1970 and 1992. Despite what one would think given the political debate in the mid-1990s, only about *1 percent* of the federal budget goes to the main poverty program (AFDC) every year. We will have much more to say on this subject when we consider poverty in the United States.

Even with a highly unequal distribution of income, the distribution of basic necessities may be less unequal if the cost of such basic items is relatively low. If this is the case, luxuries and savings, not basic necessities, become most unequal. But to the extent tent that this has ever been the case in the United States, it is rapidly becoming less so. Inflation has been rather low in the late 1980s to the mid-1990s, but the decade of the 1970s was one of rapid inflation; between 1967 and 1978 the consumer price index almost doubled. More importantly, the cost of basic necessities rose 44 percent *faster* than the cost of non-necessities between 1970 and 1976 (Blumberg 1980:182), which means that those toward the bottom of the income scale find it even harder to maintain an adequate standard of living. We do not have studies such as these since the 1970s, but all of the poverty, income, and cost-of-living statistics indicate the standard of living has gone down for low-income people.

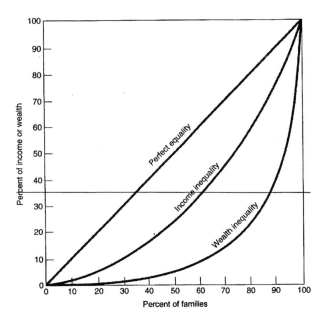

FIGURE 2-5
Lorenz curves on wealth and income inequality. These curves are estimates from data presented in Table, 2-7.

Food, of course, is one of the basic necessities; Duncan (1976) shows that the lowest 10 percent of the population (in terms of income) had to spend over 40 percent of its income for food in the early 1970s. And just between 1972 and 1974, the proportion of this group's income going for food increased from 40.1 percent to 46.6 percent. At the same time, however, the proportion of income going for food among those in the highest income decile increased only from 10.8 percent to 11.4 percent.

A broader picture of the cost of basic necessities in 1974 was given by Nulty (1977) who included the cost of energy, shelter, and medical care, as well as food. The picture presented in this study was even more striking because it is based on net family income (after taxes, and so on). Although income at the bottom was probably underestimated by this study (see Blumberg 1980:183), it is clear that people toward the bottom of the income scale would need to go into *debt* if they were to buy all necessities in the United States. In contrast to the bottom 20 percent in income who would have had to go into debt to buy necessities, the top 10 percent in income spent only 38.4 percent of their net income for these necessities.

As noted, inflation has not been a major problem in the second half of the 1980s and up to the mid-1990s, but neither was there a change in this ratio of the cost of necessities versus non-necessities, meaning the cost of obtaining basic necessities remains beyond the reach of the poor and lower classes in this society. What has changed most dramatically in the 1980s and 1990s is the number of people who are poor or near-poor and cannot afford these basic necessities.

HEALTH INEQUALITIES

Good health is an obviously important human condition; but unfortunately for those toward the bottom of the stratification system, good health is to some degree unequally distributed through the stratification system. There are two basic reasons for this: First, adequate health care is unequally distributed; and second, conditions promoting better health are unequally distributed.

Much like income and wealth, health care is in constant demand. People seldom have enough health care; there are often new aches, new procedures, brighter and straighter teeth to attain, and preventive medicine. Thus, because health care is a scarce quantity, as with any scarce quantity, there must be a method of distribution. With health care there are two opposing methods of distribution. On the one hand, health care can be distributed through a pricing mechanism. Those who can afford to pay for it get it; those who cannot afford to pay do without. On the other hand, health care distribution can be based on some principle of need. Those in greatest need get it first; those with less need must wait. Between these opposing methods of distribution, the distribution of health care in the United States is based more on the ability to pay, whereas in virtually all other industrialized nations distribution is based more on need (although no society today is at either extreme).

Since 1915 there have been attempts in the United States to enact legislation establishing a national health care system that would help distribute health care on the basis of need (Morris 1979:77). It was not until 1965 that a small achievement in this direction was gained with the Medicare and Medicaid programs. But the way these programs were designed, especially with Medicaid for the poor, it was only a small achievement. In all states in this country Medicaid does not pay for all kinds of medical needs, and what is paid for is done at a reduced level. Hospitals and doctors accepting Medicaid patients must accept a lower fee (usually 80 percent of standard fees). Studies have shown that with this program the poor now get more medical care than in the past, but it is care of lower quality than that received by the more affluent (Dutton 1978). Health care quality continues to be unequally distributed in the United States through the ability to pay.

The preceding points were made most clearly by two studies that were widely reported in newspapers for the first time during the summer of 1989, with much similar information distributed during President Clinton's failed attempt to pass new health care programs during 1993. At least 20 percent of all Americans lack any major coverage for medical care, either through a private insurance company or a government health program such as Medicare for the elderly (receiving Social Security) or Medicaid for the very poor. Another federal government study released in 1989 found that almost half of all the people unemployed up to nine months had no health care coverage (U.S. Bureau of the Census, *Current Population Reports,* Household Economic Studies 1989:8). This condition has developed because of the growing expense of private medical insurance and the increasing number of people in low-paying jobs who cannot pay for private health coverage but at the same time do not qualify for

government-funded Medicaid. This second condition was caused by the Reagan cuts in the Medicaid program (Piven and Cloward 1982). As with the other welfare programs, such as Aid to Families with Dependent Children (AFDC), many of the Reagan reductions in Medicaid were made by cutting off the working poor. The Medicaid program (before Reagan's presidency) had coverage for what was called the "medically indigent," which meant that a family that was not "poor enough" to receive assistance from other major poverty programs could count its medical bills against its income so that, for eligibility purposes, it would be considered poor enough to receive Medicaid.

If you do not have either government or private medical coverage, however, you wild usually receive some medical treatment for serious injury or disease in the United States through "charity hospitals" or county- (or state-) funded hospitals. The problem, as noted earlier, is this is where the poor, with or without Medicaid, must go, and these hospitals are usually overcrowded, understaffed, and unable to provide adequate health care. This was the theme of the second news story cited previously. A study of the many hospitals in the Los Angeles area, for example, found huge differences in death rates for people admitted to the hospitals for the same illness or injury *(Los Angeles Times,* July 7, 1989). And it was the hospitals where the poor must receive treatment that had the highest death rates.

As of 1995, of course, the United States continues to be the *only* major industrial nation without some type of comprehensive government-sponsored health care system for all citizens. President Clinton's attempt to change this situation was blocked by many interest groups working through Congress: With both houses of Congress as of 1995 controlled for the first time since the 1950s by Republicans who were key opponents of health care legislation, it is doubtful that the United States will stop being the exception among industrial nations any time soon.

A second reason good health is unequally distributed in the United States is that a low income often means poor nutrition, less sanitary living conditions, and (less important) less knowledge about how to maintain better health. But also, as we are increasingly finding, a lower position in the stratification system means a more unhealthy work environment. With more and more dangerous machines and industrial chemicals, the working class must put its lives and health on the line for corporate profits.

The outcome of these two sources for an unequal distribution of good health can be found in a number of statistics. For example, infant mortality is an often-used indicator because it is a condition that can be reduced with better medical care. Consistently, data indicate that the lower the income, the higher the infant mortality rate in the United States. Furthermore, it is important to note that with the best medical technology and knowledge in the world, the United States has a relatively high infant mortality rate among industrialized nations (see Table 2-12). A prime reason for this poor standing by the United States may be that its distribution of medical care is based more on the ability to pay than on need. Studies have shown that it *is* the lack of adequate medical care that explains much of the higher infant mortality rate among the poor in this country (Gortmaker 1979).

All of the preceding help us understand why in the United States death rates are strongly related to class and income. In a unique study conducted by officials of the National Center for Health Statistics, the death rates for people making less than $9000 *were found to be three times higher* than for people with incomes of $25,000 or more. What is more, this inequality in death rates had more than doubled between just 1960 and 1986 (*New York Times*, July 8, 1993). And as might be expected from what we already know about inequalities between race and ethnic groups in the United States, the death rates for blacks are higher even within the same income categories. As can be seen in Table 2-13, for example, the death rate for white men (25 to 64 years old) with $9000 income or less was 16.0 per 1000, while it was 19.5 for black men in the same income category. At the other end of the table, the death rate for men making $25,000 or more was only 2.4 for whites and 3.6 for blacks.

UNEQUAL POLITICAL OUTPUTS

By unequal political outputs, or simply political inequalities, we refer to outcomes of the political process that favor some class interests more than others. In this section our focus is not on inequalities of political power per se but rather on the outcomes of differing amounts of political power—or the benefits flowing from the attainment of political power. This subject, as one may suspect, is rather broad when we consider the extent of government outputs today. But our goal at this point is simply to indicate a pattern using a few basic examples.

TABLE 2-12
COMPARATIVE INFANT MORTALITY RATES, 1987

Country	Infant mortality rate (rate per 1000 live births)
Japan	5.0
Sweden	5.7
Finland	5.8
Switzerland	6.8
Canada	7.3
Ireland	7.4
Netherlands	7.6
France	7.6
Denmark	8.3
West Germany	8.3
Norway	8.4
East Germany	8.5
Australia	8.8
United Kingdom	9.1
Belgium	9.7
Italy	9.8
Austria	9.9
New Zealand	10.0
United States	10.1
Israel	11.4
Greece	12.6

*Rate is for 1986. *Source:* United Nations, *Population and Vital Statistics Report,* April 1989.

When examining political inequalities, we find that the pattern that emerges is one in which those toward the top of the stratification system receive more of the services or general outputs provided by government agencies. Despite the common misconception of a welfare state, the poor do not receive most government benefits, and the benefits going to those toward the bottom of the stratification system are the ones most likely to be cut back in times of government retrenchment.

At this point, and for our purpose (which is to describe inequality), the state can be considered as a *redistributive institution*. That is, one function of the state is to take from some and redistribute to others. In this regard, of course, the state is an important mechanism in a system of social stratification. It is based in class conflict to the extent that one class wants to be sure that it gets from the state what has been taken from other classes, while at the same time having to give up as little as possible. There are other functions of the state that are related to social stratification, one of the most important being the maintenance of the class system. Again, however, our focus at present is on the inequality in government outputs.

TABLE 2-13
CLASS, RACE, AND DEATH

	Death rates per 1000 people, 25 to 64 years old		
Income		Whites	Blacks
Less than $9,000	males	16.0	19.5
	females	6.5	7.6
$9,000-$14,999	males	10.2	10.8
	females	3.4	4.5
15,000-18,999	males	5.7	9.8
	females	3.3	3.7
$19,000-24,999	males	4.6	4.7
	females	3.0	2.8
$25,000 Or more	males	2.4	3.6
	females	1.6	2.3

Source: National Center for Health Statistics, 1993; New *York Times,* July 8,1993, p. c-18.

TABLE 2-14
INTERNAL REVENUE COLLECTIONS BY SELECTED SOURCES, 1960-1993

	Percentage of total			
Source of revenue	1960	1970	1980	1993
Individual income taxes	49.0	53.0	47.2	45.0
Employment taxes such as old-age and disability insurance, unemployment insurance	12.2	19.1	30.5	37.3
Corporation income taxes	24.2	17.9	12.5	9.3
Estate and gift taxes	1.8	1.9	1.1	1.2
Excise taxes	12.9	8.1	4.7	4.2

Source: U.S. Bureau of the Census, 1980, *Statistical Abstracts of the United States,* Table 446, p. 268; U.S. Bureau of the Census, 1993, *Statistical Abstracts of the United States,* Table 510.

TAXES

One very important type of political inequality pertains to government tax policies. Government services and functions must be paid for by someone. The question becomes, who pays? Because most states in industrialized nations emerged when the old aristocratic privileges of the Middle Ages were under attack, new ideas of democracy

and equality (or equality of opportunity) were built into these new states. With respect to government tax policies, this often meant that those most able to pay would pay more in taxes—that there would be **progressive taxation.** In reality, however, this philosophy is often subverted.

We can begin by noting the sources of total federal tax revenue in the United States. As shown in

Table 2-14, money from individuals and families accounts for over 80 percent of tax revenues in the form of individual income taxes and Social Security deductions (called employment taxes). These sources of tax revenue have been increasing most since 1960, while corporate income taxes have been decreasing.

If we look back farther than 1960, this pattern becomes even clearer. In 1916, individual and employment taxes made up only 9.4 percent of tax revenues; in 1930, 31.6 percent; and in 1950, 43.6 percent. In contrast, corporate income taxes accounted for 34.8 percent of federal tax revenues in 1930, 27.6 percent in 1950, 12.5 percent in 1980, and, as shown in Table 2-14, only 9.3 percent in 1993 (U.S. Department of Commerce, *Statistical Abstracts of the United States,* 1993:510; U.S. Department of Commerce, *Historical Statistics of the United States,* 1960:713).

TABLE 2-15
THE EFFECTS OF TAXES AND WELFARE PAYMENTS ON THE DISTRIBUTION OF INCOME BY INCOME QUINTILES, 1992

Definition of income	Lowest quintile	Second quintile	Third quintile	Fourth quintile	Highest quintile
Income before taxes:					
1. Money income excluding capital gains (current measure)	3.8	9.4	15.9	24.1	46.8
2. Definition 1 less government money transfers	1.0	7.8	15.6	25.3	50.4
3. Definition 2 plus capital gains	0.9	7.6	15.4	24.8	51.3
4. Definition 3 plus health insurance supplements to wage or salary income	0.9	7.4	15.4	25.3	51.0
Income after taxes:					
5. Definition 4 less Social Security payroll taxes	0.9	7.4	15.4	25.0	51.3
6. Definition 5 less federal income taxes	1.1	8.1	16.0	25.6	49.1
7. Definition 6 less state income taxes (and plus earned tax credit)	1.1	8.4	16.3	25.5	48.6

Source: U.S. Bureau of the Census, *Current Population Reports, 1993,* Consumer Income, "Measuring the Effect of Benefits and Taxes on Income and Poverty, 1992," series P-60, no. 186-RD, p. xii.

When we turn more directly to individual and family income taxes, a major question, of course, is who pays? And one way we can approach this question is by looking at how the distribution of income is affected by the tax system. If we have a truly progressive income tax, one in which the rich are taxed at a higher rate than the poor and the not so rich, then the after-tax income distribution should be less unequal than the before-tax income distribution. This question is addressed by Table 2-15.

This table shows five income distributions by 20 percent population segments, from the poorest 20 percent of the population to the richest 20 percent of the population. The first line in Table 2-15 shows the distribution of income before taxes, but after government transfers (such as welfare and Social Security payments) are added to income. Thus, the first line shows that the poorest 20 percent of the population receives 3.8 percent of the income, while the richest 20 percent of the population receives 46.8 percent of the income.

The next line shows what the distribution of income would look like without the government transfer payments. As would be expected, in this case the income share of the poorest 20 percent is reduced sharply to 1.0 percent, which then leaves more of the total income to go to other groups, with the upper 20 percent group gaining most. The third line adds the value of capital gains to what is counted as income, which of course adds to the income of the rich. The fourth line adds in the value of health insurance supplements by employers, which has only a small effect on the income distribution. Finally, lines 5 through 7 include the effects of Social Security payroll taxes and federal income taxes and then state income taxes to the distribution of income. We find only a slight effect on the distribution of income because of income taxes. And we find that it is welfare benefits that have the most effect on the distribution of income by improving the income of the poorest 20 percent.

We must look further into the effects of taxes on the distribution of income, however, because Table 2-15 includes only income taxes in the analysis. Another form of taxation is a sales tax, which is regressive rather than being even close to progressive, as with income taxes in the United States. Sales taxes are called regressive because the less affluent pay more as a percentage of their income than do the more affluent. (For example, if a person with an income of $10,000 and a person with $100,000 both pay a total of $300 in sales taxes in a year, this represents a much greater share of the first person's income.) A study of the effects of all forms of taxes on the distribution of income has found that all forms of taxation taken together actually increase the level of income inequality in the United States (Devine 1983).

Much was said about the tax law changes during the Reagan administration because these changes purposely reduced the tax rates for the wealthy early in the 1980s. Reagan's tax bill certainly did that, but what also happened due to increases in other more regressive income taxes, such as the Social Security payroll tax, is that the overall tax rates for the less affluent and poor actually went up in the 1980s (Harrison and Bluestone 1988).

It was said at the time that this change in the tax rates would finally benefit the poor and the less affluent because the benefits given the rich would "trickle down" to those below in the form of more jobs and income when the rich invested this money. As we have already seen with the increasing income inequality and drop in real wages during the 1980s, it did not happen this way. The extra money in the pockets of the rich was not always invested in the economy to produce more jobs and income for those below. A study conducted soon after the tax law changes in the early 1980s found that, in fact, the "trickle-down" effect from increases in the income of the rich has almost never worked to improve the incomes and jobs of the poor (Treas 1983). The only group somewhat improved by this trickle-down effect since World War II has been white males. And not only are women and minorities less helped by investments by the rich in good economic times, they are more harmed in times of economic stagnation (Parcel and Mueller 1989).

Finally, it should be noted that the tax laws were again changed shortly before Reagan left office in 1988, but the effect on income distribution by this last change is expected to be very small. Reagan's first tax law change brought the "possible" tax rate on the highest income group down to somewhat above 50 percent from the earlier rate in the 60 percent range. But we must say "possible" tax rate because, by taking advantage of what are called *tax loopholes* the wealthy seldom pay this amount, and the real tax rate (effective tax rate) for the highest income group most often ended up being in the 30 percent range (Stern 1973). What Reagan's last tax change did, in effect, was to bring down the top tax rates to this 30 to 35 percent range and do away with some of the tax loopholes. Thus, how taxes were figured changed. Some among the rich gained, while others in different circumstances, because of previous favoritism of tax loopholes that were lost, were hurt. The result was that the overall income distribution effect of these tax changes at the end of the 1980s was almost none. And by 1992, the IRS estimated that more than half of those making $200,000 or more paid less than 25 percent in taxes (*Los Angeles Times*, June 30, 1993). There was, however, a much bigger effect on money saved by the *richest 1 percent;* without Reagan's tax changes the richest 1 percent would have paid $70 billion more in taxes by 1993 *(Los Angeles Times,* March 7, 1993). That much money could have easily covered the $15 billion paid to all the U.S. poor for AFDC in 1992, plus the $27 billion paid for food stamps and the $9 billion in housing assistance for the poor, with $19 billion still left for something like improvements in education.

GOVERNMENT SERVICES

In this final section on inequalities we approach a vast subject that can be treated at this point with only a brief description and a few examples. When the subject of government services is raised, welfare for the poor most often comes to mind. But such an image of government services is highly misleading. There is another side of government services often called wealthfare. Most of what government does, it does *not* for the poor, but for the nonpoor. And among the nonpoor, it is often the wealthy and corporations that benefit most. This is yet another aspect of how the stratification system and unequal power affect the state as a redistributive mechanism.

In addition to providing welfare for the poor, consider what else the federal government does. The federal government provides subsidies to many industries like agriculture, research and development that directly benefit major corporations, tariff protection for many industries, regulatory agencies that protect major industries, and other direct services that industries would otherwise have to pay for out of their own profits (such as the Federal Aviation Administration's maintenance of air guidance systems, airport landing systems, and research and development for new airline technology).

Let us look at a few examples. About one-half of all 1994 federal spending went for various programs that provide money or services (such as health care) for individuals. On the one hand, most of these programs and money transfers do not go to poor people; on the other hand, most of these transfers are paid for through specific or additional regressive withholding taxes that

operate much like pension programs or insurance programs.

The largest example of federal money going to the nonpoor as well as the poor is Social Security. The Social Security program operates much like a pension or insurance program (that is, workers pay for the system by contributing to a special fund), and it accounted for almost $320 billion, or about 28 percent, of the federal budget in 1994. Another $46 billion went to federal employees' retirement and insurance benefits. In contrast to this total of $386 billion, the federal government spent only about $55 billion on direct-transfer payments to the poor, aged, or disabled under public assistance programs like Supplemental Security Income (SSI) and AFDC (U.S. Bureau of the Census *Statistical Abstracts of the United States,* 1994:334). As for other 1994 federal expenditures, about $279 billion went for the military, $37.5 billion for transportation programs, $16.8 billion for agriculture, $17.2 billion for scientific and technology research and $4.9 billion for energy programs, to name only a few.

The main point in presenting these examples of federal spending is to demonstrate the expanse of government programs and services going to the nonpoor. But the actual benefit these services provided to the wealthy cannot be judged solely in government outlays. A relatively inexpensive government program for price supports, business regulation, or protection from foreign and domestic business competition can result in billions of dollars in greater profits or in transfers from consumers to business.

It can be argued that many of these government services that directly help the wealthy and corporations also help the general public, and hence the working class and poor. The question becomes one of who is helped most, and by how much. If we find that the wealthy and corporate classes have more resources that are used to influence government policies and programs, we must recognize that it is their interests that are probably most directly served. Information supporting such a conclusion is central to the study of social stratification and will be considered in coming chapters. We can conclude this discussion by simply noting again that the wealthfare system is equally, if not more importantly, an aspect of the state as is welfare for the poor. Along with the many other inequalities described in this chapter, inequalities in government services must be added.

DIMENSIONS OF INEQUALITY: A CONCLUSION

The design of this chapter has been to present descriptive information on the extent of inequality in the contemporary United States. Toward this end, inequalities in income and wealth, standards of living and health, and taxation and government services were examined. These primarily material inequalities are among the most important, but they are by no means the only important ones.

We have said nothing about educational opportunities and inequalities in the actual attainment of education. Educational attainment, as might be expected, is in many ways linked to divisions in the stratification system—as both an outcome of this system and a means of its maintenance. This subject receives considerable attention later.

Neither have we said anything substantial about inequalities in power and authority. Authority divisions (or institutionalized power) are obvious outcomes of social organization in complex societies with an expanded division of labor. We need not describe the fact that some people give many orders, while others only take orders. And power inequalities per se, or the ability to influence others whether such power is institutionalized or not, are difficult to measure in the absence of a specific context. We have no simple scales with which to rank people in terms of power as people can be ranked in terms of income or wealth. We will consider the importance of inequalities in both power and authority in later chapters.

In addition to the inequalities already outlined, it should now be evident that any material good, condition, or service that people come to value, for whatever reason, may be unequally distributed by or through a stratification system. One such valued condition, of course, is life itself. Those lower in the stratification system, however, are more likely to be victims of violent crime and find they must fight and die for their country, as shown in studies of the Korean War (Mayer and Hoult 1955) and the Vietnam War (Zeitlin, Lutterman, and Russel 1973). But there are other inequalities that require brief mention.

Along with various material goods and services, the stratification system also provides an unequal distribution of status or honor, self-esteem or self-evaluations, and social deference. As briefly noted in the previous chapter, because human beings tend to evaluate things, conditions, behavior, and people differently, a status hierarchy will emerge that tends to correspond with hierarchical divisions within a stratification system. Thus, people and groups are ranked by others in terms of status, prestige, or honor. They usually receive social deference from those of lower status rank in ritual interactions, and they tend to rank or evaluate themselves unequally in terms of their positions in a system of social stratification.

Many sociologists, in fact, have argued that this status dimension of social stratification is of primary importance. Among functional theorists (such as Parsons 1951, 1970) there is the view that status inequality produces an unequal distribution of material goods and services as rewards for attaining high status. There is, as we will see, extensive research on the distribution of status within the occupational structure.

For several reasons outlined in subsequent chapters, however, more sociologists now reject the causal logic of this functional argument. Especially in complex societies, status is considered more a product than a cause of unequal power and wealth. In other words, power and material wealth usually bring status or prestige, not the other way around (see Lenski 1966). But none of this rejection of the functional view of status inequality is to deny its existence or its secondary importance for understanding social stratification.

Status divisions are of considerable importance in understanding the *maintenance* of social stratification. For example, individuals of a particular class often establish status boundaries (based upon lifestyle) to protect their privilege by excluding people from lower class divisions. Also, there is everyday social interaction that requires prescribed deference rituals among members of unequal status. These deference rituals give everyday meaning and reinforcement to the stratification system (Collins 1975:161-215). Finally, such status divisions can lead to differing amounts of self-esteem and differing self-evaluations that lead people to accept their place in the stratification system and to accept the system's legitimacy (Della Fave 1980). These nonmaterial inequalities will be discussed more fully when we have occasion to explain their use in maintaining a system of social stratification.

The point that inequalities of many, many kinds are shaped and produced by a system of social stratification has been made. It is time to consider why and how such inequality is produced. We will first explore how stratification systems have evolved throughout the history of human societies. That is the task of our next chapter.

SUMMARY

The main objective of this chapter has been to describe the exact details of inequality in the contemporary United States. We found that income inequality is growing in the United States and is now the highest among the major industrial nations, with Japan and Germany having among the lowest levels of income inequality. Wealth inequality is more difficult to measure than is income inequality, but data indicate that wealth is much more unequally distributed compared with income, with wealth inequality also growing. We then examined a number of other types of inequality that are also very important but often more difficult to measure such as health inequalities, government services, and tax rates.

NOTES

1. It must be noted here that going back before 1967 we must use income figures for families rather than households. The definition of family is more limited and thus does not include as many people who are poor and on their own, thus indicating less inequality than that for household income presented in Table 2-2. If we look at household income, we find that the bottom 20 percent received 4.3 percent in 1975 compared with 3.8 percent in 1992, while the top 20 percent received 43.6 percent in 1975 compared with 46.9 percent in 1972.

2. Until the early 1980s there had not been a comprehensive study of wealth inequality in the United States since the early 1960s. In the most discussed study of wealth inequality in the early 1980s, James D. Smith was able to work with the Internal Revenue Service to collect a random sample of 3824 individuals, plus 438 individuals among the top wealth holders in the United States (see Smith 1986; Institute for Social Research 1986/1987:3). When this study was released in 1986, most newspapers in the country ran front-page stories about the reported "extensive increase" in wealth inequality between 1963 and 1983 (for the *Washington Post* story, see Berry 1986).

CONTEMPORARY LIFESTYLE VARIATIONS

by Maxine Baca-Zinn *and* D. Stanley Eitzen

Since the 1960s, new social practices regarding marriage, divorce, childbearing, child-rearing, and women's participation in the labor force have fundamentally altered the ways in which most Americans structure their lives. Fewer than one in ten American families currently fits the breadwinner/ homemaker model. Today, families and households take a multitude of forms.

Although the traditional definition excludes most American households, it remains the idealized model in our society. Although at any given point in time, the majority of adults are not living in traditional families, over the course of a lifetime most will do so (Macklin, 1987:317). But it is important to keep in mind that the idealized traditional nuclear family has never been the typical family. Factors such as economics, ethnicity, and demography have always produced diversity in family patterns. We must also realize that although traditional and nontraditional tend to be categorized as polar opposites, variations on the traditional family actually make up a broad continuum, with many different social and personal factors involved.

Family changes and variations are greater, more widespread, and likely to affect more individuals than at any previous time in history. Many people now choose from a wide range of family and lifestyle options. For others, alternative lifestyles evolve as adaptations to changes and constraints in the surrounding society. Yet alternatives have not replaced conventional monogamous marriage as the ideal form. Rather than posing a threat, the new lifestyles have taken their place alongside conventional families. They have become permanent and legitimate social forms.

The past two decades have brought momentous changes. What is happening to the family is a continuation of what has been happening for several centuries (Bumpass, 1990:483). The proliferation of family forms has deep historical roots. It is less a "revolution" in lifestyles than an outgrowth of several social and economic trends. The current diversification of family forms muse be placed in the context of larger societal changes set in motion when industrialization separated family and work (see Chapter 3). Familism declined, and individualism took hold as people gained more power to determine the course of their own lives. Advances in technology made it possible to separate sexuality from procreation, reduced the risk involved in nonmarital emotional and physical interchange, facilitated family planning, and prolonged the period after child-rearing. Energy once expended on meeting physical and security needs could now be devoted to personal development and the pursuit of pleasure. By the end of the 1960s, the scene had been set; premarital sexuality had become a generally accepted reality; contraception and sterilization were increasingly available; women and men discovered new role options and became increasingly disillusioned with the traditional avenues to happiness; age at first marriage continued to rise; and divorce had become a viable alternative (Macklin, 1980:906).

The rise of lifestyle variations is associated with (1) new patterns of divorce and remarriage; (2) a massive reordering of work, class, and gender relations; (3) new expectations about individual needs, human fulfillment, and personal life; and (4) greater societal tolerance of alternative lifestyles. These are closely related. Changes in the economy requiring large numbers of female workers have made women less economically dependent on marriage. As the success of economic enterprises has become less crucial to husbands and wives, their personal satisfaction with their marriage has become more important. According to Andrew Cherlin, "husbands and wives are more likely today than in the recent past to evaluate their marriage primarily according to how it satisfies their individual emotional needs. If their evaluation on these terms is unsuccessful, they are likely to turn to divorce and then, perhaps, to another marriage" (Cherlin, 1981:75). Marriage and divorce trends go hand in hand with individualism and the search for fulfillment.

Contemporary society has created new conditions for experimenting with lifestyles. This invites the questioning of all traditional institutions. The rise of alternatives reflects, in pare, the search to satisfy new needs. R. N. Whitehurst has explained how alternative forms develop out of social structure and new expectations.

> In a society changing as rapidly as ours, it is impossible to maintain stable marriage forms not aligned with people's real needs. If we free women to go into the marketplace, give people leisure, money, and opportunity to meet others, and take them away from home for long periods, solidarity in the old-fashioned sense cannot be the result. The need for intimacy is probably a constant in humans, but our sense of legitimizing multiple ways of searching for it is subject to radical changes over time. We have expected more intimacy from relationships today, and we have provided more means of searching for it than in former times. It is doubtful that people have ever been able to find much intimacy, but the fact that we expect it today and have expanded means of seeking it makes the search for alternatives an understandable imperative (Whitehurst, 1978:373).

These changes in how individuals organize their living patterns are driven by changing preferences and behaviors of individuals that demonstrate a reduced commitment to the nuclear family and to married life as the preferred status (Wetzel, 1990:5). Many people now choose from a wide range of family and lifestyle options. For others, alternative lifestyles evolve as they adapt to changes and constraints in the surrounding society. Yet alternatives have not replaced conventional monogamous marriage as the ideal form. Rather than posing a threat, the new lifestyles have taken their place alongside conventional families. They have become permanent and legitimate social forms. The question "What is the family?" grows increasingly contested.

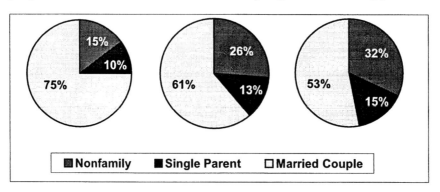

Figure 12.1 Changing Composition of U.S. Households: 1960 to 2000. *(Source: America in the 21st Century: A Demographic Overview,* [Washington, DC: Population Reference Bureau, May 1989] p.7)

One of the most striking changes is the decline of persons maintaining families of their own. More young adults are delaying marriage, living at home with their parents, are living alone or sharing their home with a roommate or other nonrelative, and fewer are maintaining families of their own. (See Figure 12.1). According to Frances Goldscheider and Linda Waite (1991), this aspect of family decline is one of the two most important trends in American living. They call this trend "No Families." It refers to the tendency of more and more adults to avoid marriage and parenthood and to live independently. The other trend, which they call "New Families," describes more equalitarian relationships and divisions of labor within families, especially between women and men. Both "new families" and "no families," are on the rise.

This suggests a system of pluralism in which various structures coexist at one point in time for different individuals (Gerstel, 1977:357). As individuals move through various phases of life, their family and household arrangements will take different forms. As children, they may live with both parents, alone with their mothers after a divorce, and then with their mothers and stepfathers. As adults they may live alone for a time, live at home, live with someone of the opposite sex without marrying, marry, divorce, live alone again, remarry, and live alone after the death of a spouse (Cherlin and Furstenberg, 1983). Although not everyone will have a family history as complex as this, the lives of many individuals are increasingly marked by family pluralism.

As family changes have affected more and more people, a national debate has arisen about their significance. Are families disintegrating, or are they changing? Are the changes good or bad? Such questions are impossible to answer because they are value judgments (Bumpass, 1990:492). Furthermore, transformations affect people differently (Gerson, 1991). Family changes today are uneven, with different costs for adults and children, women and men. Increased independence for adults often means that children pay a great price.

Despite the unequal costs of social change, family transformations reflect ongoing adaptation. In the words of Kathleen Gerson, this "stability-within-change" perspective provides an important rebuttal to the gloomy and accusatory picture presented by the "family breakdown" thesis. This perspective emphasizes the resilience of families, which are adapting rather than disintegrating in the face of social change, and the resourcefulness of individuals who are able to build meaningful interpersonal bonds amid the uncertainty and fragility of modern relationships (Gerson, 1991:35).

Some variations on the traditional nuclear family form, such as dual-earner marriages, single-parent families, voluntarily child-free marriages, and extended and augmented families were discussed earlier in this book. This chapter focuses on four others: singlehood as either a temporary or permanent lifestyle, heterosexual cohabitation, homosexual cohabitation, and marriage in which couples commute between households.

Nontraditional alternatives may be called lifestyles. The term lifestyle refers to the "relational patterns around which individuals organize their living arrangements" (Stayton, 1985:17). Understanding the relationship between nontraditional forms and the larger society is clarified by an understanding of the concepts of life chances

and lifestyle. Lifestyles are simply the way people live their lives, for example, as a partner in an unmarried couple, as a single parent, or as part of the gay scene. These ways of life are often based on the resources available to individuals at given points in their lives. Many single mothers must support families on meager job earnings or welfare payments. Their lifestyles are constrained by the amount of money available to them. In contrast, a well-educated single professional living in an urban area has a very real choice about living arrangements, spending, leisure activities, and interaction with others. The better a person's life chances, the more choice one has of a satisfying lifestyle (Stein, 1981:3). Furthermore, the more resources a person has, the more likely it is that a particular lifestyle he or she chooses will be accepted as legitimate by the surrounding society.

Throughout this book, we have argued that social and economic forces in society produce and require diversity in family life. Therefore, family pluralism is not new. What is new is a greater recognition and tolerance of persons who choose some nontraditional lifestyles. Alternative lifestyles do not carry the same kind of social and cultural legitimacy that the traditional family does. Furthermore, lifestyle variations also differ in the degree to which the larger society accepts them. For example, lifestyles created by same-sex preference are stigmatized, whereas lifestyles created by career choices are more likely to be viewed as legitimate. When alternatives are associated with subordinate class and racial categories, they are judged against a standard model and found to be deviant. Yet many alternative lifestyles that appear new to middle-class Americans are actually variant family patterns that have been traditional within Black and other ethnic communities for many generations. Presented as the "new lifestyles of the young mainstream elite, "they are in fact the same lifestyles that have in the past been defined as pathological, deviant, or unacceptable when observed in Black families" (Peters and McAdoo, 1983:288). Many of the family patterns among racial ethnics have been adopted as available and logical life choices in a society that has denied them a full range of resources. Lifestyle variations should include the adaptations imposed by restricted life chances as well as those involving choices made by the more privileged who seek meaning and self -actualization.

The contemporary lifestyle variations discussed here represent additional adaptations to those already discussed in previous chapters. Like the variations in family living produced by class, race, and gender inequality, these lifestyle variations have always existed.

Singlehood, heterosexual cohabitation, lesbian and gay alternatives, and commuter marriage represent an array of alternatives that cannot be neatly tied to a single cause. They are part of a larger web of economic, demographic, and social trends. Women's economic independence, later age at marriage, and the high divorce rate are some of the trends associated with these nontraditional alternatives, but no one explanation covers all of them. Although though these forms appear to be a heterogeneous mixture of lifestyles, in fact they all embody new definitions of women's and men's public and private roles. Singlehood, heterosexual and homosexual cohabitation, and commuter marriage expand the traditional boundaries and behaviors associated with gender. Each form, in its unique way, modifies the relational patterns around which women and men organize their living arrangements. In this way, these alternatives challenge the fundamental assumptions on which the traditional nuclear family is based.

The question "what is a family?" will grow more contested as more arrangements fall outside the nuclear mold. The Census Bureau's definition of "two or more persons related by birth, marriage or adoption who live in the same household" fails to include many arrangements in which people live and relate as families. Yet practical and legal considerations require that we pin down what the family is all about.

SINGLE LIFE

"Single" used to mean what people were *before* they settled down to marriage and family. Over the past two decades, a growing proportion of adults are spending a larger proportion of their lives in a single status and in one-person house-

holds. For young women and men today, it is plausible to assume that approximately 10 percent will never marry in their lifetime. For those who do marry, approximately 50 percent will divorce, and the surviving marriages will eventually end in widowhood.

Adults in all age groups are more likely to be single today than they were in 1970. The singles population aged 18 and older rose from 38 million in 1970 (28 percent of all adults) to 66 million in 1988 (37 percent of all adults). (Saluter, 1989a:1).

THE SINGLES POPULATION

Although most persons marry at some point in their lives, a larger number of adults are single at any given time. Popular fascination with the singles world is growing. Singles are apt to be portrayed as a trendy group in the forefront of social change and new lifestyles. "Do You Wish You Were Single?" is the title of an article in the magazine *Family Weekly*:

> One out of every three married persons reading this article will be single within the next five years. One out of every two will be single in the next decade. They will join the ranks of the 67 million adults in America, a group comprised of divorced and widowed individuals as well as those who have chosen to postpone marriage or never marry at all (Simenauer and Carroll, 1984:214).

There are several reasons many people today are opting for a single lifestyle. First, historical changes accompanying urbanization and industrialization have made marriage less attractive (Thornton and Freedman, 1982). In colonial times, almost all unmarried persons lived in a family environment, either with parents or in the homes of their employers. Only with marriage did they become fully independent members of society. This pattern began to change in the nineteenth century, when increasing numbers of single people worked for wages outside the family and lived in boarding houses. The dramatic strife, however, occurred in recent years. Most singles now work at jobs outside the family and live away from home. Most significant has been the employment of women outside of family enterprises with careers that often provide both satisfaction and economic independence. It is far easier today for singles to enjoy an active social and sexual life.

The changing roles of women have had a significant impact on the rise of singlehood as a viable option. New social and work roles for women have provided opportunities rare in earlier times. Since women now have a much greater chance for financial independence, they no longer require a husband for material success and social status. Many women with strong career aspirations have opted for singlehood because marriage, the demands of domesticity, children, and the remnants of patriarchy that persist in so many relationships greatly lessen their chances for career success.

SINGLE LIFE AND GENDER

Singlehood is not always a matter of choice, however. Demography and culture combine to create a condition known as the "marriage squeeze," which operates to increase the number of single women. Until 1940, the adult male population exceeded the number of adult women, but now the situation is reversed. This imbalance is exacerbated by the cultural push for women to marry somewhat older men. This shortage of eligible male partners results in many women remaining single.

Although women are more likely to remain single, research suggests that long-term singlehood has traditionally been a more positive state for women than for men, and that women who remain single are superior to single men in terms of education, occupation, and mental health (summarized in Macklin, 1987:320). Apparently, singlehood has quite the opposite effect on women than does marriage.

Single women, however, have special problems. The older they become, the greater the gender imbalance. The result of the marriage squeeze is that, as women advance in age, there are fewer eligible men. The ratio of unmarried men to unmarried women by age suggests that the marriage prospects are better for younger women than for older women. Overall, in 1988, there were about four unmarried men for every five unmarried women. However, the ratio was much lower

for persons 40 years of age and older than it was for persons under 40 years of age. In fact, the largest ratio of unmarried men to unmarried women was for the age groups 25 to 29 and 30 to 34 years (127 and 121 unmarried men for every unmarried women, respectively) (Saluter, 1989b:5). The situation is worse for successful professional women. The men they want are the least available. Successful women and men are on the opposite marriage gradient:

> Educated, professional men marry earlier and stay married longer than other men, while their female peers marry later and have a higher probability of divorce than other women. These contradictory patterns create a crunch which has been exacerbated by the rapid emergence of the new class of single professional women. There's been a sudden growth on the demand side of the market and very little movement in the supply lines. The female elite have become demographic losers; they've priced themselves out of the market. The problem that used to concern only heiresses—where to find a suitable mate among the sparsely stocked and heavily fished pool of men at the top—now afflicts an entire class (Doudna and McBride, 1981:22).

The reasons for the increasing ranks of single women are demographic, social, and psychological and include the following (from Gross, 1987: 12):

- These women were born in the baby-boom years, and as they seek to marry men older then themselves, as is common, they find fewer around. This problem gets worse as women get older because of longer life expectancy.

- Although women tend to marry "up" both in age and status, men tend to marry "down, " leaving a surplus of successful women, particularly in the older age groups.

- Men classified as unmarried by the U.S. Bureau of the Census include homosexuals, who (various studies show) outnumber lesbians by at least three to one.

- Many women, thanks to the feminist movement, no longer derive their economic and social status from their husbands and therefore do not rush into early marriages as often as did their predecessors.

• Many single women in their thirties and forties have histories of relationships with unavailable men. frequently married ones.

As women acquire higher levels of education and income, the female singles category grows ever larger. The irony of this development is that men who are statistically available are the least educated. So we have a puzzle with completely mismatched pieces. As Jessie Bernard has put it, in the pool of eligibles, the men are at the "bottom of the barrel" and the women are the "cream of the crop" (quoted in Doudna and McBride, 1981:23).

The disadvantageous sex ratio for women, together with changing norms about women's sexuality, are contributing to new patterns of intimacy between single women and men. The demographic imbalance creates a phenomenon that sociologist Laurel Richardson calls "the new other woman," a category of single women who are involved in affairs with married men. Her analysis, based on interviews with 55 highly educated women, reveals that "other women" share a great deal in common, based on an intimate connection with a married man that must be hidden from friends, family, and the larger society [Richardson, 1985]. Despite the disadvantageous sex ratio, single professional women are adapting. With support from others, they have found themselves part of a new lifestyle that does not center on men and challenges the notion that to be single is to miss out on life. *Ms.* magazine published a survey of the 14 best cities for single women, based not on where the single men are but on where women have (1) good opportunities and acceptance in leadership positions, (2) health and safety facilities, and (3) access to transportation and legal rights (Abott and Starker, 1984: 129-132).

RACE AND SINGLES

The proportion of those who have never married is higher for Blacks than for Whites and Latinos. Black women outnumber men in the ages when most people marry and scare families, ages 20 to 49. Following this reasoning, fewer Black women marry because there are not enough eligible Black men available (O'Hare et al., 1991:19). In 1988, three-fourths (75 percent) of Black women in their early twenties had not married, compared with 59 percent of White women. Among Black women in their late twenties, one-half (50 percent) had not married, compared with 26 percent of White women. The same is true for men, although the differences between the proportions of never-married Black men and White men are not as large as between Black and White women. Persons of Hispanic origin had large proportions of never-married individuals. The proportions for Hispanics were more similar to chose of Whites than those of Blacks (Saluter, 1989a:2).

Many Blacks will continue to remain unmarried because of demographic factors. There remains in the Black community an imbalanced sex ratio resulting from the institutional discrimination against Black men who cannot get jobs. The Black single world is characterized by a large proportion of uneducated men with low incomes and an equally disproportionate number of women with college degrees and high incomes.

LIFESTYLES OF SINGLES

Singlehood's new respectability has not dispelled myths and stereotypes about single people. Old beliefs about unmarried people being somehow flawed have given way to newer stereotypes. Two of the more prominent stereotypes are that singles must be terribly lonely and that they are "swingers" (i.e., sexually nonexclusive). A study conducted by Leonard Cargan examined these two stereotypes by comparing the responses of single people with those of married people to determine whether singles felt undesirable, lonely, and incomplete. The singles included never-married and divorced women and men. The stereotype of loneliness was shown to be true, in that singles had no one with whom to share happy or sad moments or with whom to discuss problems. But these findings were qualified by the relatively large numbers of the married who also felt these facets of loneliness. The other stereotype of sexual "swinging" was upheld in the sense that singles have more sexual partners. However, it was the divorced singles, not single people in general, who tended to be sexually nonexclusive. Furthermore,

228

"swingers" appeared in all of the categories examined (Cargan, 1984:546-557).

Like other nontraditional alternatives, singlehood can be an ambivalent experience: autonomous and euphoric at some times, lonely and unconnected at other times. Even amidst the joys of self-discovery, people require companionship. Methods of meeting among singles have moved from the private sector (introductions made through family, friends, school, church, neighbors, and so on) to the public sector (for example, meeting at bars, singles groups, dances, health spas, dating services, and pickups) (Simenauer and Carroll, 1984:216). A diverse network of enterprises has sprung up—dating agencies, magazines, singles bars, travel bureaus, and a host of others. Singles look for "someone special" through video recordings, personal advertisements, or singles condominium complexes. Advertisers are targeting singles as a burgeoning new market with substantial discretionary income. A New York advertising agency concludes that singles, especially those between the ages of 18 and 34, are above-average consumers of such commodities as liquor, stereo equipment, books, foreign cars, and most sporting goods (Sanoff, 1983:54).

The desire to connect with other people remains strong for most singles. Life outside of a traditional family structure does not always preclude family like relationships that are supportive and nourishing. Throughout history, people have been able to bond with one another, sometimes creating familial relationships with people who are not blood kin. For example, Blacks in slavery adopted kin into the conventional family as aunts, uncles, and other relatives People have also formed strong familial friendships at the workplace—in offices and factories—and in suburban neighborhoods. Many singles have made alternative families out of friends. New kinds of families formed out of friendship provide support in times of emergencies and a history of involvement in the lives of others (Lindsey, 1981). The support networks that people create for themselves are called "network families." They provide resources and enrichment for many of those who are without traditional families (Rossman, 1985:19).

HETEROSEXUAL COHABITATION

The term *heterosexual cohabitation* refers to the practice of a male and female who are not married sharing a household. Cohabitation is an emotional and physical relationship without the benefit of legal or religious sanctions (Newcomb, 1984:484). Once considered "living in sin," this arrangement is experienced by many at some point during their lifetime and is increasingly common. The number of American couples living in such an arrangement grew 80 percent during the 1980s; from 1.6 million in 1980 to 2.9 million in 1990 (U. S. Bureau of the Census; Marital Status and Living Arrangement, 1991:14). Four percent of the U. S. population age 19 and older are now cohabiting, and 25 percent of adult Americans have cohabited at some point during their adult lives.

These official data from the census are based on households of unmarried couples, that is, households containing only two adults with or without children under 15 years present, in which the adults are of opposite sex and are not related to each other.

THE RISE OF COHABITATION

Noted demographer Larry Bumpass asks "how has it happened that what was once morally reprehensible has become the majority experience in just two decades?" (Bumpass, 1990:486). A number of possible factors help explain this phenomenon. First, young people are postponing marriage. Second, divorced persons are increasingly not remarrying but are choosing instead to cohabit (Goldscheider and Waite, 1991:15). Underlying these changes is the erosion of normative objections to living together. Bumpass explains that, "shacking up was offensive after all, not because couples were sharing cooking and the laundry, but because they were sharing a bed. The revolution in the sexual experience of unmarried persons over the same period has seriously weakened the basis for disapproving of cohabitation. Only a fifth of young adults now disapprove of cohabitation under any circumstances (Bumpass, 1990:486). Not only have normative objections faded, but other conditions have promoted the increase in cohabitation. The trends associated with singlehood and living away from parents in dormitories and apartments opens up new possibilities for women and men. Women have attained financial personal options beyond marriage, while men no longer face the same pressures from employers to be married (Goldsheider and Waite, 1991:61).

Something else has changed to make living together a common experience. People are much less confident about marital stability. Many choose cohabitation because they worry about marriage, given the high divorce rate. Bumpass reports that in a series of questions about reasons for cohabitation, couples reported wanting to make sure that they are compatible before getting married. This reason was indicated far more than any other options offered. (Bumpass, 1990:407).

Still another reason for cohabitation is an economic one. It is a means by which two persons can pool their resources to share the costs of rent, food, and utilities. But of all the possible reasons, surely the most likely explanation of this increase is that young Americans are becoming increasingly attracted to this lifestyle, and their parents are becoming less critical of this behavior as long as it does not result in childbearing and as long as those involved directly are economically independent (Glick and Spanier, 1980:21).

WHO ARE COHABITORS?

Cohabitation is not a new phenomenon. Throughout American history, some couples have lived together without formal marriage. In the past, the practice was concentrated among the poor. The characteristics of cohabitors have changed over time. Surra (1991:56) summarizes the personal characteristics of cohabitors in the late eighties:

- They were mostly young adults (in 1988, 68 percent were under the age of 35) and never-marrieds (53 percent).

- A sizable proportion (34 percent) had divorced.

- Cohabitation rates were higher for women than for men, and for Whites than Blacks once other variables such as age were taken into account.

- Contrary to the stereotype of cohabitation as a college student phenomenon, cohabitation and education were inversely related.

- Cohabitors were likely to be homogamous in race, age, and education.

- Compared with noncohabitors, cohabitors had more liberal attitudes toward family life and were more unconventional.

COHABITATION AND TRADITIONAL COURTSHIP

Changes in the practice of cohabitation have led many to conclude that cohabitation is simply a new stage in the American courtship process. Still, many cohabiting couples anticipate parental disapproval. They may try to conceal their relationships. They may do this with "his" and "her" phones and mailboxes. Or they may even maintain separate residences while living together in one. There are other complicated schemes of deception as this one:

> A student at the University of Texas at Austin, for example, offers her services as a "roommate"—a front for women who don't want their parents to know whom they are really living with. For $25 a month, she supplies an address, forwards letters, and answers phone calls from parents (explaining each time that the daughter is out and will "return the call"). For an additional fee, the young entrepreneur allows her clients to move in with her when their parents visit (Middleton and Roark, 1981b:3).

The other prominent difference between cohabitation and courtship is that in cohabitation the partners have more or less continuous intimacy. This requires a number of personal adjustments to meet the requirements of living together, adjustments not found in steady dating relationships or even among engaged couples. The partners muse determine the division of labor and the division of economic responsibilities, as well as adjusting to each other's habits, personalities, needs for space, intimacy, and the like. As such, this time of trial intimacy, although not considered part of traditional courtship, actually serves as a very useful last stage of courtship.

COHABITATION COMPARED WITH MARRIAGE

Cohabitation differs from marriage in several fundamental respects. A major difference is in the presumption of the length of the relationship and its arrangement. Cohabitation does not assume permanence. In fact, the average length of cohabitation is short—only 1.5 years (Bumpass, 1990:487). The second difference centers on the public versus the private nature of the two arrangements. Marriage symbolically sets people apart by bestowing a new status signified by public rituals and rules. Cohabitation has no symbolic equivalents. It remains covert and private, without celebrations, announcements, or terms that designate the relationship and affirm the status of cohabitors. Cohabitation, unlike marriage, is not institutionalized, nor is it surrounded by standard expectations (Henslin, 1980:108). The lack of institutionalization poses far-reaching problems:

> Cohabitors may be dismayed by this because they feel their love is enough and that all it takes to create a way of life is two people who see eye to eye. But they do not take into account the importance of society's reactions and how poorly society is equipped to accommodate them. For example, parents may not want to acknowledge a cohabitor's partner as a family member. Even if they want to be welcoming, they may be unsure of what to expect of such a person; they may not know how to act toward him or her. One symptom of this confused state of affairs is that cohabitation has been widely discussed and openly practiced for the past fifteen years, yet we still do not have a term the two people can use for one another. Couples who want to create an institution should be aware of what an awesome task they have taken on (Blumstein and Schwartz, 1983:321).

Cohabitants feel these difficulties intensely, but they perceive that the rewards of the relationship, especially companionship, sexual gratification, and economic gain, outweigh the costs. Newcomb's summary of these studies (1984:486) reports little difference between cohabitants and marrieds in stability, emotional closeness, role expectations, and role performances.

GENDER

Gender is an important variable in cohabiting relationships. The research shows that the male, at least at the beginning of the relationship, tends to view it in pragmatic terms, with less emotional involvement and less personal commitment than the female, who tends to define the arrangement as a step toward a stable, long-term relationship (Jackson, 1983; Macklin, 1983). Women cohabitors are more likely than men to desire marriage (Lyness, Lipetz, and Davis, 1972:308; Blumstein and Schwartz, 1983). This tendency may be greater among previously unmarried women. Philip Blumstein and Pepper Schwartz found cohabiting women who had been married before less eager to marry than women who had never been married, but previous marriage had no negative impact on the men. These findings suggest the different consequences of marriage for women and men. Perhaps the gendered marital experience defines the desire to marry again.

In addition to the gender differences in commitment and desire to marry, there are differences in the division of labor. The strong tendency appears to be for household duties to be split along traditional gender role lines, with the women doing most of the domestic chores. Gender role inequality is also indicated by the high probability that the bills, lease, and phone are put in the man's name. In short, "one cannot make the assumption that because people violate conventional norms and engage in cohabitation that they are therefore 'liberated' and striving for sex-role equality" (Jackson, 1983:44). In Blumstein and Schwartz's study, women cohabitors did more housework, even when they worked full time and earned as much as their partners.

> This inclination on the part of cohabiting men to sidestep housework causes arguments between partners. The more he pitches in, the more peaceful the relationship. The more he leaves for her to do, the less satisfied she becomes with the whole situation (Blumstein and Schwartz, 1983: 148).

COHABITATION AND THE FUTURE OF MARRIAGE

Comparisons between cohabiting and noncohabiting couples imply that all cohabiting relationships are alike, which is not true. Macklin (1983:268-269) has identified five types along a continuum from least to most commitment.

1. Temporary casual convenience in which two persons share the same living quarters because it is expedient to do so.

2. The affectionate dating/going-together type of relationship, in which the couple stays together because they enjoy being with one another and will continue to stay together as long as both prefer to do so.

3. The trial-marriage type, which includes the "engaged to be engaged" and partners who are consciously testing the relationship before making a permanent commitment.

4. The temporary alternative to marriage, in which the individuals are committed to staying to-gether but are waiting until it is more convenient to marry.

5. The permanent alternative to marriage, in which couples live together in a long-term, committed relationship similar to marriage, but without the traditional religious or legal sanctions.

Considering the differences among these types, we muse not treat unmarried cohabitants as one homogeneous group. They may also be divided into two broad categories: those couples who enter into cohabiting relationships with no intention of permanence and those who expect their intimate relationship to endure. Given the increasing numbers of cohabiting couples, and the fact that many do not intend to marry their partner eventu-ally, does this mean that the institution of marriage is in jeopardy? Bumpass, after reviewing the evidence, does not think so. However, he notes several implications of cohabitation for marriage (from Bumpass, 1990:481:

1. Cohabitation changes the meaning of "single." Singlehood (and the rapid decline of marriage) no longer means unattached living.

2. Marriage is now a less specific marker of other transitions such as sex, living arrangements, and parenting.

3. Cohabitation requires a new way of marking those unions that eventually become marriages. For some couples, "marriage" began when they started living together, whereas others avoid an unstable marriage by splitting up before they reach the altar.

4. "Premarital divorces" help keep the divorce rate from going even higher, since many couples are using cohabitation to test their relationship.

5. Not all cohabitations are part of the marriage process. Some are better characterized as relationships of convenience in which marriage is not an issue.

Does cohabitation enhance marital stability and lessen the likelihood of divorce? Although the association between cohabitation and marital outcome is not well understood, the current answer to this question is a qualified *no*. Research conducted on large samples demonstrates that cohabitation is negatively related to marital stability, measured as dissolution as well as the propensity to divorce. Why? Perhaps cohabitors enter marriage in the same way that they enter cohabitation, with the notion that a relationship should be ended if either partner is dissatisfied.

If cohabitation is an alternative to legal marriage it is one that is temporary alternative in the life course of young adults. It does not threaten marriage but rather serves as an option that is practiced before, between, or even after marriage in contemporary society.

LESBIAN AND GAY ALTERNATIVES

Heterosexuality is a social arrangement that has been resisted in various ways. The numbers of gay men and lesbian women are unknown and prob-ably unknowable because many never reveal their sexual preference, living lives that appear hetero-sexually oriented. There are also problems of definition, as Hess, Markson, and Stein note:

> Is homosexuality to be defined strictly in terms of behavior, or is self-definition the key? Many people who are attracted to persons of their own sex do not act on these feelings. Conversely, many people who have had homosexual relations continue to

define themselves as basically heterosexual (Hess, Markson, and Stein, 1988:306).

The common estimate by researchers is that about 10 percent of American adults (13 percent of males and 5 percent of females) are exclusively or substantially homosexual. Until the 1970s, gay men and lesbians were largely invisible. Before that time, almost all gay people sought to avoid the risks of disclosing their sexual preference.

For many, the homosexual individual is an outcast. Gays are seen as aberrations, perhaps even a dangerous deviations, from "normal" sexuality. People who believe that gays are immoral belittle their lifestyle; tell jokes about "queers;" deny their rights to housing, jobs, and memberships in organizations; and even engage in hostile acts (verbal and physical assaults) such as the "gay bashing" done by males. These homophobic attitudes and behaviors cause many homosexuals to have personal problems with self-concept and other adjustment problems. As Long and Sultan have argued, "We wish to suggest that many of the problems of adjustment that may be experienced by some homosexuals do not result directly from being homosexual, but are created by the way society views homosexuality" (Long and Sultan, 1987:227).

In fourteenth-century Europe, the common punishment for homosexuality was burning at the stake. The Puritans in the colonies continued the death penalty for this "crime." Around the time of the American Revolution, Thomas Jefferson and some "liberal" reformers of the day proposed changing Virginia law, replacing the death penalty for homosexuality with castration (Tivnan, 1987).

The legal status of homosexuals has progressed considerably since the days of death and castration, but they are still not treated equally because of their sexual orientation. For example, the marriage of homosexuals is not recognized by the state. In addition to losing the symbolic importance of having a union legitimated by the state, gays experience other negative consequences. Gould elaborates:

> While heterosexuals enjoy many rights and privileges by virtue of marriage, homosexuals in similar long-term relationships forfeit legal and

financial protections such as community property rights, inheritance, tax breaks, and insurance premium reductions (Gould, 1979:63).

The following discussion is adapted from Eitzen and Baca Zinn (1991:310—314). Society has defined what is appropriate sexual behavior end orientation. Consequently, those who differ from the approved orientation are objects of the derision and contempt of members of society and are discriminated against by individuals and by the normal way that the institutions of society operate. In short, their different sexual orientation makes homosexuals a minority group.

Gays confront three types of oppression: (1) ideological oppression, in which their behaviors are defined and stigmatized as immoral; (2) legal oppression, in which their activities are defined as illegal or they are treated unfairly by the courts and other agents of control; and (3) occupational oppression, in which jobs, advancement, and income are restricted or denied. This section examines each of these manifestations of institutional discrimination that homosexuals experience. There is a long tradition of fear and hatred of homosexuality in Western society, termed *homophobia*. Gays are considered by the majority as outsiders. They are targets of ridicule; they are restricted from social interaction and are stigmatized. Public opinion polls show that intolerance toward gays is common in society. For example, a 1989 Gallup poll revealed that only 47 percent of all adults believe that homosexual relations between consenting adults should be legal (Cited in Salholtz, 1990:21). Certain categories of persons are especially intolerant of gays: the poor, Protestants, those over 50, southerners, Blacks, and those who have not graduated from high school. Other polls show that the majority do not believe that homosexuals should be hired as doctors, ministers, or elementary school teachers.

Bias against gays is far more accepted among larger numbers of Americans than is bias against other groups. In surveys, about three-fourths of homosexuals say they have been harassed by people calling them names, and as many as one in four say they have been physically assaulted. According to a report by the National Gay and Lesbian Task Force, in 1989 over 7000 incidents of violence and harassment were reported against gay men and lesbians in the United States, including 62 bias murders (Goleman, 1990:9).

The exact amount of job discrimination against homosexuals is unknown, primarily because the government does not provide employment discrimination statistics for this group, as it does for women, Blacks, and other minorities. Two elements of discrimination confront homosexuals in the workplace: anticipated discrimination and actual discrimination.

Many homosexuals fear that they will lose their jobs if their sexual orientation is revealed. Or, if not fired, they may experience other forms of discrimination, such as being passed over for deserved promotions, being given relatively low salary raises, and being harassed. One study of 203 lesbians from New York City revealed that three-fifths of the women expected discrimination if their sexual orientation was discovered. Of this number, two-thirds expected to be fired, and 90 percent predicted that their co-workers would harass them with taunts, ostracism, and even violence (Levine and Leonard, 1984). These fears are likely based on reality. The New York State Health Code includes a section, for example, that states that employees can be fired for moral turpitude (which includes homosexuality). Similarly, if someone in the armed services is found to be a homosexual, they are dishonorably discharged. Since few legal protections are available to homosexuals, especially in the private sector, and homophobic attitudes are common, they have little choice in many cases but to hide their sexual orientation.

After employment, the hidden homosexual, knowing that retention and promotion depend on keeping the secret, must use a number of ploys to appear heterosexual. The strategies include bringing someone of the opposite sex to company social events, telling "appropriate" sexual jokes, and wearing "appropriate" clothing. But as Levine observes, "Needless to say, passing causes psychological problems, feelings of being on stage, anxiety over exposure and subsequent sanctions, strain from artificial behavior and talk" (Levine, 1979:156).

Actual discrimination against known homosexuals occurs frequently in the workplace. Many employers, personnel directors, school boards, and others involved in hiring do not hire homosexuals. They may refuse to hire gays and lesbians because they are bigoted or because they fear that the community or clients may object. Or they may feel that the exclusion of gays is justified because they believe that homosexuals are neurotic, morally degenerate, sexually dangerous to youth, a medical danger because of AIDS, or the like.

The very process of applying for a job is more problematic for homosexuals than it is for others. The application form may ask whether the applicant has ever been arrested, and if so, why. Since the laws criminalize homosexuality in many jurisdictions, homosexuals are more likely than heterosexuals to have a police record. Gays and lesbians are thus caught in a double bind. If, on the one hand, they disclose their arrest for homosexual behavior, they will be denied a job. If, on the other hand, they conceal this fact, they will be fired for lying, since most companies check information on application forms against official records. A similar situation occurs when the form asks about one's military service. Known homosexuals will have been dishonorably discharged, which is an obvious excuse for not hiring them. Finally, if applicants voluntarily disclosed their homosexuality on the application, they are not likely to be hired (Levine, 1979:154). For all of these reasons, a sexual orientation that deviates from the "normal" jeopardizes employment.

Homosexuals use two basic strategies for living in a society hostile to their sexual orientation. One is to conceal their sexual orientation from heterosexuals to avoid stigmatization, harassment, and discrimination. These secret gays segregate their lives into gay and "straight" activities. When in the straight world, they conceal their sexual orientation from family, friends, co-workers, and other associates. Those most likely to "stay in the closet" are from the working class. The structural and personal pressures against "coming out" are much greater for them than for those from the middle and upper classes.

Gay liberationists identify themselves openly as homosexuals. Rather than evade the efforts of straights to stigmatize them, they challenge society in an effort to transform it (Persell, 1987:544). There has been greater political activism by homosexual groups demanding an end to discriminatory practices. The result is that more and more individuals are choosing to avow openly their homosexual practices.

THE DOMESTIC PARTNER MOVEMENT

No state permits marriage between members of the same sex (indeed, no industrial nation, except for Denmark, which permits "registered partnerships," gives official recognition to homosexual marriages). Aside from the emotional benefits of marriage, homosexuals are also denied significant legal and economic benefits of marriage: coverage under their spouses' health and pension plans, rights of inheritance and community property, and potential savings from joint tax returns. Until recently, the courts have ruled consistently to deny these benefits to homosexuals in long-term relationships. Gays and lesbian partners face a "catch-22." They legally cannot wed and yet they face discrimination because they are not married.

"The family" has become the newest battleground for lesbians and gay rights. In the last ten years, two developments have made the economic and legal discrimination against gay and lesbian families hit home, mobilizing the community to take political and legal action. The first is AIDS. As partners and friends have died, homosexuals have grown more aware of their lack of family rights. They have not been able to have their partners included on the companies' health plans and have had no claims on their lovers' property. The second development is the growing number of gay and lesbian couples having and adopting children (Horn, 1990:9).

In 1988, the Census Bureau counted 1.6 million same-sex couples living together (Seligmann, 1990:38). Growing out of these realities, the domestic partner movement has entered the courts, legislatures, and workplaces to qualify for some of the legal benefits accorded married heterosexuals. Activists argue that "family" can no

longer be defined by marriage alone but by sharing lives in intimate and committed relationships of mutual caring.

Several landmark developments have greatly expanded the definition of what constitutes a family. Domestic partner benefit cases have been won in several municipalities, including Seattle, Santa Cruz (California), and Madison (Wisconsin). While many nonprofit groups offer domestic partner benefits, the private sector has been reluctant to redefine family. However, Lotus Development Corporation recently offered all family benefits to gay and lesbian employees and their partners. Cities and businesses that have established policies define domestic partners as two people who share the common necessities of life, take responsibility for each other's common welfare, and are each other's sole domestic partner. How does an employer or business determine who is a domestic partner? Courts have measured this by asking partners to prove that they are living together, that they are financially interdependent, and that they have had a relationship of a minimum length of time, demonstrating that the partners are not only seeking the rights of family but are also accepting its obligations (Horn, 1990, 1991). Cohabiting heterosexuals also benefit from the new legislation. Many are using domestic partner plans as well. Not only has the gay rights movement transformed our understanding of human sexuality; it is also expanding the definition of what constitutes a family.

GAY AND LESBIAN COUPLES

Studying gay and lesbian couples would greatly inform our understanding of the family; however, recent research on same-sex couples living together in family settings is sparse (Thompson and Walker, 1991:76). Social scientists have tended instead to study "homosexual lifestyles."

Pioneering research by Alfred Kinsey and his associates—first on men, in 1948, and then on women, in 1953—made it clear that homosexuality was much more common than anyone had suspected. Since then, several scientists have been interested in studying gay lifestyles (for example, Bell and Weinberg, 1978; Peplau, 1981; Harry,

1983). Their conclusions about sexual relationships point to a number of similarities and differences between homosexuals and heterosexuals and between gay men and lesbian women, some of which contradict the prevailing stereotypes. Alan Bell and Martin Weinberg (1978) studied 979 Black and White, male and female homosexuals. On the basis of interviews and questionnaires, they formulated five categories of homosexuals:

1. *Closed couples.* These homosexual couples were "closely bound together" and looked to each other rather than to outsiders for sexual and interpersonal satisfaction. They described themselves as "happily married."

2. *Open couples.* These couples were living with a special sexual partner but "not happy with their circumstances" and tended to seek satisfaction with people outside their partnership.

3. *Functionals.* These men and women tended to organize their lives around their sexual experiences. They engaged in a wide variety of sexual activity.

4. *Dysfunctionals.* This group conformed to the stereotype of the "tormented homosexual." They reported many problems due to their homosexual orientation.

5. *Asexuals.* These women and men were lonely, less overt about their sexual orientation, and had few friends.

The Bell and Weinberg study is also the best source on homosexuality among Blacks. In general, they found that Black male homosexuals were younger, had less education, and were employed at a lower occupational level than White homosexuals. Black homosexuals do not find a high degree of acceptance in the Black community (Staples, 1982:93). Black lesbians share the social stigma of their gay male counterparts. They are less visible and, according to Staples (1982), more likely to have stable and caring relationships than male homosexuals.

Gays are similar to heterosexuals in their desire to have an intimate relationship with one special person. Since homosexuals are denied marriage by law, homosexual couples must turn to cohabitation

relationships. Approximately three-fourths of lesbian couples live together, compared with somewhat more than half of all gay male couples (Harry, 1983:225). Blumstein and Schwartz (1983) found that lesbian couples and gay male couples faced many of the same issues confronting heterosexual couples who live together, married or not. They must work out issues related to the division of household labor, power and authority, and emotional obligations. But homosexual couples face additional problems. Because of the general antipathy toward homosexuality in American society, gay men and lesbian women are not encouraged to be open about their sexual preferences and their relationships. Hence, they may feel restricted in showing public affection toward their lovers. They are seldom extended such commonplace courtesies as having a partner invited to an office party or to a retirement banquet. Even heterosexuals who might like to welcome a gay friend's partner may not know how to go about doing so. Blumstein and Schwartz contend that the "couple" status of homosexuals is always in jeopardy:

> The problem with gay male culture is that much of it is organized around singlehood or maintaining one's sexual marketability. Meeting places like bars and baths promote casual sex rather than couple activities. The problem with the lesbian world is quite different. Women are often in tight-knit friendship groups where friends and acquaintances spend so much intimate time together that, it seems to us, opportunities arise for respect and companionship to turn into love and a meaningful affair (Blumstein and Schwartz, 1983:322-323).

GENDER

Gender is important in defining homosexual relationships. According to Letitia Peplau, the fact of being a man or a woman often exerts greater influence on relationships than does sexual orientation. Gay men in Peplau's study (1981) were much more likely than lesbians to have sex with someone other than their steady partners. This issue of sexual exclusivity is often a major source of tension in male homosexual relationships. Charles Silverstein has suggested that "at some point in the life of every gay couple, the monogamy battle will be fought" (Silverstein,

1981:140). The tendency for gay men to be less sexually exclusive than lesbian women parallels the difference in heterosexual males and females. And this difference is related to gender role socialization in society where "males are socialized to engage in sexual behaviors both with and without affection while women are expected to combine the two" (Harry, 1983:226).

In a major departure from the heterosexual pattern, homosexual couples tend to be egalitarian. Heterosexual couples, whether in cohabitation or marriage relationships, tend to accept the traditional gender roles for men and women. In contrast, homosexual couples are much more likely to share in the decision making and in all of the household duties. There are three likely reasons for this difference from the heterosexual pattern. One is the conscious effort by homosexuals to reject the dominant marriage model that prescribes specific and unequal roles. Another reason is that in same-sex relationships the partners have received the same gender role socialization. Another source of equality in gay relationships is that there tends to be little income difference between the partners, a condition rare in heterosexual relationships. Most homosexual couples are dual-income units. And since both partners in a homosexual relationship are of the same sex, they are subject to the same degree of sex discrimination in jobs and income (Harry, 1983:219).

An important implication of the equality found in homosexual relationships is that, contrary to the stereotype, the partners do not take the role of either "husband" or "wife." The prevailing assumption is that one takes the masculine role and is dominant in sexual activities and decision making, while the other does the "feminine', household tasks and is submissive to the first. Research consistently refutes this "butch/femme" notion, noting that only a small minority of couples reflect the stereotype. Those relatively few couples who conform to the stereotype generally are composed of individuals who are older, from lower socioeconomic levels, newcomers to the homosexual community, and male (Bell and Weinberg, 1978; Peplau, 1981).

A final stereotype about gays and lesbians is that being homosexual is such a powerful identity that it overrides every other aspect of a person. But according to Hess, Markson, and Stein,

> This is not necessarily the case. Just as heterosexuality does not obsess most men and women, coloring their every thought and act, the homosexual's choice of sex partner is only one part of a complex social person. The problems of daily life—work, leisure, comfort and safety, companionship, death, and taxes—beset the gay as well as the straight, and in many ways, they are harder for the homosexual to resolve because of discrimination and stigmatization (Hess, Markson, and Stein, 1988:308).

COMMUTER MARRIAGES

Commuter marriages have emerged from dual-career families in which marital partners are committed to both marriage and career. They differ in that husbands and wives in commuter marriages maintain separate households. The separation is the result of two demanding careers in different locations. They "commute" to one or the other household between periods of separation that are devoted to work. The patterns for this type of relationship vary. Some couples are together each weekend; others are together only once a month. Some couples are a day's drive away; others fly across the country. Some couples maintain commuter relationships for months, others for years (Rhodes and Rhodes, 1984:45).

Marital separation is not entirely new. In the past, there have always been circumstances under which husbands and wives lived in different locations. These have included war, immigration, economic need, and specific occupations such as those of pilots, truck drivers, politicians, entertainers, salespeople, and executives. These lifestyles have not usually required separate households. Furthermore, in these examples, it is typically the husband's work that separates the married couple. New commuter marriages are the result of women's participation in professions. Most often, it is the wife who opts to set up a temporary residence in a different geographical location. This contrasts sharply with the traditional pattern of the wife giving up her job to live with her husband.

It is estimated that there are 1 million commuter marriages in the United States (*Newsweek*, 1985:111). Most commuters are White, middle- to uppermiddle-class, well-educated professionals. Half of these couples have children.

Married couples who live apart view the careers of husband and wife as being equally important. Their lifestyle promotes women's equality by making it acceptable for women to be dedicated to their careers, to individual freedom, and to personal growth. However, this egalitarian marital form can be fraught with difficulties. Individuals' needs are pitted against family needs, and most commuters are ambivalent about their way of life. Yet most commuting couples express the belief that the strains in separate living are outweighed by the individual rewards they gain in their careers. Foremost among the advantages is the obvious freedom of each spouse to continue working at a chosen occupation. Closely connected with this benefit is the freedom to devote long and uninterrupted hours to work. This is a freedom that comes from not having to dovetail each other's schedules around meals, recreation, and sleep (Gross, 1984:468). The "other side" of this career—enhancing autonomy is a heightened comparison to the "togetherness" of more traditional couples, the energy required to maintain a separate residence, the personal loneliness, and the frequent social isolation that surrounds a lifestyle that is somewhere between marriage and singlehood.

Commuters tend to compartmentalize their lives into two areas: work and marriage. This may restrict interaction with people outside these realms and impose unique strains on the couple's relationship. Unlike the habituated togetherness of most married couples, commuters must work out the patterns of communication, sex, and domestic maintenance during their infrequent visits. Naomi Gerstel's study of commuter marriage found this to be a gain for couples as an interacting unit. "They invest themselves heavily in their marital relationship when they are together, and often regard this shared time as a special, important time to concentrate on the relationship. As a result, there is less trivial conflict" (Gerstel, 1977:364). The separation may provide a unique support for dual-career relationships, in that it offers a balance between separation and togetherness by easing the stress of unrelieved companionship (Douvan and Pleck, 1978:138). For many couples the strong emotional communication is intensified by the knowledge that time is limited, that separation is forthcoming (Kirschner and Walum, 1978:5 13).

In a study of 94 commuters, Gerstel identified certain conditions that make commuter marriages difficult. The length of the distance that had to be traveled was a primary limiting condition. Greater distances contributed to more stress and burden. Conditions of work, including income, the inflexibility of some work schedules, and the immobility of work-related materials, also produced difficulties. Finally, family conditions, especially the presence of children, produced stress. In addition, couples who had been married only a short time when they began to commute experienced severe problems. These conditions have led to Gerstel's conclusion that commuter marriages "work" best during particular stages of a family cycle and occupational sequence. They tend to work best at the stage when children are not yet born but when a level of trust and intimacy has been established, and when husbands and wives are establishing reputations in their careers. At this occupational stage, positions are harder to find than they will be later. And good first jobs often affect the possibility of good second jobs. Thus, it is useful as well as possible for an individual to optimize her or his career placement in this familial stage by commuting.

Commuter marriages also tend to work at a later stage, when children have moved out and more energy can be redirected to careers. This is the time when many women return to work. The reputations of those with steady careers are established. This is the final point at which one can choose to optimize his or her career involvement. Both spouses may not be able to find jobs in the same locale, especially those jobs they evaluate most positively. Thus, commuting may again be most appropriate (Gerstel, 1977:365).

The importance of "timing" in commuter marriages has also been suggested by Harriet Gross. She studied 43 spouses, representing 28 dual-career marriages, and found that older couples, those married longer, those in whom at least one spouse had an established career, and those who were freed from child-rearing responsibilities considered their life less stressful (Gross, 1984).

GENDER

Research on commuter marriages has been limited, but most studies have found varied sources of strain for husbands and wives (Gerstel, 1977; Kirschner and Walum, 1978; Gross, 1984). According to Gross, wives miss the emotional protection that they expected from the ideal husband, and they sense that this loss is the cost of their gain in independence. "More so than husbands in our culture, wives are programmed to think of marriage as an intimacy oasis—an emotionally close relationship that will be 'total'" (Gross, 1984:473). Though highly career-oriented, these women still give interpersonal relations, as compared to work-related rewards, a primacy in their lives that their husbands do not. Husbands, on the other hand, are less likely to express as much unhappiness about the loss of emotional closeness that living apart can produce. They do feel guilty about not providing the emotional closeness they sense their wives need. But in spite of women's expressed loss of intimacy, wives are more comfortable with the arrangement because it validates their equal rights in work and marriage.

SUMMARY

Families are changing as the world around them changes. Women have become less dependent on men. Many individuals have acquired affluence that allows for personal and sexual experimentation. These seemingly "private" matters reflect complex social issues. The lifestyles discussed in this chapter are adaptations to economic, demographic, and social changes in the larger society. Although the forms included here are diverse, they all expand the boundaries of women's and men's roles. Each of these alternatives represents a new definition of appropriate behaviors for women and men in public and private spheres. These lifestyle variations exist together with traditional family forms and in this way contribute to the diversity and flexibility of the family.

THE NEW WORKING CLASS

by Rebecca Piirto Heath

As recently as two years ago, leading newspapers were announcing the death of the working class. That obituary now seems premature. Although the structure of the working class is shifting, its spirit is thriving. What's changing is the working-class stereotype of a hard-hatted, blue-collared, middle-aged, white man. As the industrial age becomes more of a dim memory, the image of the group of people who drive the economy is changing, too. Indicators suggest that the working core of Americans is becoming younger, more ethnically diverse, more female, somewhat more educated, and more alienated from it's employers.

Trying to pinpoint the precise nature of this shift, however, is a prickly proposition. The difficulty comes from our uniquely American view of class. The common belief on these shores is that America, unlike Europe, is a classless society. We admit to racial, ethnic, gender, and cultural divisions. But to class? Most Americans think of class the same way they think of the British monarchy— something foreign.

Economic indicators show a steady polarization between incomes of the top-earning households and the lowest-income households. Only the richest Americans have seen any real income growth in the last decade. Incomes of the top 5 percent of Americans grew 37 percent between 1984 and 1994, compared with a meager 1 percent increase on the bottom.

Despite this evidence, many Americans find it most comfortable to believe that class divisions, if they exist at all, are minor obstacles. Even supposedly jaded baby-boomer parents still teach their children they can be anything they want to be. Despite growing rumbles of doubt, most of us still believe the old adage that an individual with enough gumption can pull himself up by his bootstraps, especially with a little hard work and a good education.

"No one wants to be working class in America," says Peter Rachleff, professor of history at Macalester College in St. Paul, Minnesota. For those who take issue with that statement, Rachleff asks another question: "When was the last time you saw a U.S. film about the working class?" British films, on the other hand, are full of working-class heroes. "We are bombarded by so much popular culture that tells us continually that this is a middle-class society," says Rachleff.

Michael Moore, author of *Downsize This* and a popular director and producer, has made a name for himself by poking fun at America's "classlessness." *Roger & Me* was a surprise hit documentary about Moore's attempts to track down General Motors CEO Roger Smith to ask him why the company's auto plant in Flint, Michigan, was closing and laying off thousands of loyal long-time workers. Moore says that getting a distributor for his films has always been an uphill battle. "There's something about working-class satire and irony that seems to be missing from our national language," he says.

This lack is ironic in itself, considering the relative novelty of a large middle class in this country. "The middle class didn't even exist until this century," says Moore. So what's behind all this American denial of its working-class roots? "It all started to change after World War II, when working-class people were able to own a home, buy a car or two, take extended summer vacations, and send their kids to college. Once they got some of the trappings of wealth, they got the illusion that they were like the man who lived in the house on the hill," says Moore.

CLASS IN A CLASSLESS SOCIETY

One reason why many surveys don't reveal the state of the working class is that they don't ask about it. Many definitions of the middle class are based on income. By one definition, the middle class includes households with incomes of $15,000 to $75,000. Such socioeconomic categories rarely include an explicit working-class group.

One survey that does is the General Social Survey (GSS), conducted by the National Opinion Re-search Center. Since 1972, it has asked Americans to classify themselves as lower, working, middle, or upper class. In 1994, 46 percent of American adults said they were working class, virtually equal to the 47 percent who claimed middle-class status. These proportions have varied little over the past 22 years.

In an effort to get at the characteristics underlying class affiliation, Mary Jackman, a professor of sociology at the University of California-Davis, and her husband, political scientist Robert Jackman, published *Class Awareness in the United States* in 1986. It was based on a landmark survey conducted by the University of Michigan's Survey Research Center in 1975. The study has been called "the most important study of class identification since Richard Center's 1949 *Psychology of Social Classes*." The Jackmans intentionally crafted the question to include five class divisions—poor, working, middle, upper-middle and upper. "This way middle was truly in the middle, which is more how people think of it," says Jackman. With this grouping, 8 percent identified with the poor, 37 percent with the working class, 43 percent with the middle class, 8 percent with upper-middle, and 1 percent with the upper class.

The Jackmans went on to analyze why people classified themselves the way they did. They asked them to rate the relative importance of attributes such as income, education, and occupation, as well as lifestyle and attitudes. Topping the list for most people was occupation, followed by education and people's beliefs and feelings. Up to 49 percent rated the kind of family a person came from as not important at all. "It seems that, for most people, social class is a combination of fairly hard-core economic attributes that you can identify pretty quickly and other cultural and expressive attributes that you can't identify quite so quickly—their lifestyles, values and altitudes," says Jackman.

Income turned out to be less valuable a predictor than occupation or education. "Education ends up being so important because it's a piece of social capital that reflects Americans' longterm focus," Jackman says. Occupations also played a role, although a less clear one. "The occupations that caused the most confusion about working- or middle-class status were the upperlevel blue-collar jobs or skilled tradesman," says Jackman. Lower-level clerical jobs also created confusion. But there was no debate over assembly-line workers and seven other solidly blue-collar occupations.

The occupational line is blurring even more today. With more companies downsizing, outsourcing, and turning to temporary workers, some highly qualified workers have been marginalized and are underemployed or working for lower pay and fewer benefits. At the same time, formerly semi-skilled blue-collar jobs demand higher-level skills. Even auto mechanics, a solidly working-class occupation in the 1970s, now require sophisticated knowledge of electronics. "For most functions, you just can't use a mechanic anymore. You really need technicians who can solve problems at a much higher level than in the past," says Myron Nadolski, dean of automotive and technical training at American River College in Sacramento, California.

TODAY'S WORKING CLASS

The work force isn't the same as it was 40 years ago. Neither is the working class. Since the Jackmans' study hasn't been updated and the General Social Survey doesn't ask respondents why they label themselves the way they do, differences between working-and middle-Americans must be inferred by their answers to other questions.

The average age of working- and lower-class Americans is declining, while the age of the middle and upper classes is increasing in line with national trends. On the other hand, the working class has become more average in its gender mix. The proportion of working-class Americans who are female increased from 48 percent in 1974 to 54 percent in 1994. The other classes have been predominantly female all along.

One of the most significant changes in the working class that is also in line with national trends is its increasing racial diversity. Back in the mid-1970s, Jackman found a clear delineation between the races in class attitudes. "You really have to deal

separately with blacks and whites because the distribution is so different," Jackman says. This is because, historically, blacks were left out of the economy altogether and have only recently begun to rise into the working and middle classes.

Racial diversity among the lower, working, and, to a lesser extent, middle class is increasing, while the upper class is becoming less racially diverse. Between 1974 and 1994, the proportion of whites who claimed working-class status decreased 9 percent, while the proportion of blacks grew 3 percent and those of other races rose 5 percent. The shift was even more pronounced for the lower class, and somewhat less so for the middle class. Meanwhile, the proportion of whites claiming upper-class status increased, while the proportion of blacks decreased.

The GSS supports the notion that income level plays an unclear role in class identification. In 1994, 74 percent of the working class and 63 percent of the middle class reported household incomes between $15,000 and $74,999. But 10 percent of the upper class also reported making less than $ 15,000, and 4 percent of the lower class reported making over $50,000 a year.

Educational level is a more reliable indicator that rises steadily with social class, although educational level for all groups has increased. The upper and middle classes still have the preponderance of bachelor's and graduate degrees, but higher degrees are becoming more common among the working class. The proportion of bachelor's degrees held by working-class adults more than doubled between 1974 and 1994, from 4 percent to 10 percent. The proportion of two- year degrees held by working-class respondents increased by 5 percentage points, to 6.5 percent. Two percent of the working class had graduate degrees in 1994.

Similarly, the occupations that make up the working class are less clear-cut. Between 1988 and 1996, the proportion of managers and professionals in the working class increased by 4 percent, to reach 17 percent in 1996. The proportion of technical, sales and administrative workers also rose slightly. Conversely, the proportions of service employees, farm workers, and craft and skilled workers have declined. (It is not possible to compare occupations before 1988 because the classification scheme changed.) In addition, the number of part-time workers has increased across the board, but part-timers remain most prevalent in the lower and working classes.

What does all this mean? Changes in the working class reflect changes in the work environment itself, says David Knoke, professor of sociology at the University of Minnesota, who is currently conducting a panel study of 1,000 work environments around the country to measure shifts in outsourcing, part-time and temporary employment, and cutbacks. "The number of people involved in non-full-time work has quadrupled in the past decade," says Knoke. Up to 30 percent of all U.S. workers are now "contingent" workers—temporaries, part timers, sub-contractors or independent consultants, according to Knoke.

Knoke and colleagues theorize that increased global competition has forced the elimination of companies' internal job markets. "It used to be that if you got a job with IBM out of college, you were set for life," Knoke says. "A series of job ladders was built into the organization that allowed people to count on a slow but steadily rising standard of living."

The likely effect of these shifts on workers is already being seen. "People involved in part-time work have a looser stake in the organization. There's more of a sense of having to fend for themselves," Knoke says. "People see themselves as more working class and having less of a stake in the middle class." Jackman agrees. "I believe there has been a hardening of awareness of class boundaries in the last 10 or 15 years because the situation for American workers has gotten grim, and it's happened so quietly."

The UPS strike last year crystallized these issues for American workers, which is one reason why the 180,000 striking teamsters had such overwhelming support from the public. "Workers across the country could identify with the striking UPS workers because they're all feeling the same pinch," says Deborah Dion, AFL-CIO spokesperson.

UNION RESURGENCE?

Not surprisingly, interest in organized labor is one of the attributes most common among the working class. "You can be working class without being a union member, but it's difficult to think of a union member who is not aware of working-class issues," says Rachleff of Macalester College. This relationship is borne out in GSS data. Union membership is one of the clearest delineators between the working and other classes. Although union membership among U.S. workers has fallen across the board, for the last 25 years it has remained highest among those who claim working-class status.

Unions understand the changing structure of the new working class and are targeting somewhat younger, more ethnic, better-educated workers, and different occupations than they did 25 years ago. Coincidentally, just around the time UPS capitulated to strikers' demands for more full-time jobs and a better pension arrangement, the AFL-CIO launched a five-city pilot ad campaign to help boost sagging union membership. More than one-third of all American workers belonged to unions in 1950. By 1997, less than 15 percent of workers (only 10 percent of nongovernment workers) were union members.

A recent AFL-CIO poll found that 44 percent of the general public employed in a non-supervisory job said they would vote to form a union at their workplace. Another 20 percent were less certain but still positive, saying it was better to join together at a work site to solve problems. "That 20 percent is made up of the same people we're trying to reach with our campaign—minority groups, young people, and women," says Dion.

The ads are four personal stories from real union members. Mike, a construction worker, represents the traditional white male, blue-collar core of the membership, but with a twist—he's young. A young black nurse named Arthereane talks about her love of helping children and her conviction that hospitals run best when they're run by doctors and nurses, not the profit motive. Erin, a working mother, balances family and her job as a chef with the help of her union. Michael, a worker at a Harley-Davidson plant, sings the union's praises for keeping the company from closing the plant, and making jobs more secure and the company more profitable. The tag line is: "You have a voice, make it heard; today's unions."

"These issues are the key because they are issues that workers everywhere are concerned about. Everything's going up except workers' fair share—the stock market's going up and executive salaries are skyrocketing," Dion says. She believes this is a pivotal time for unions to get this message out to people who may not realize the historic power of unions to raise wages and secure better benefits for workers.

Filmmaker Michael Moore also sees this as a pivotal period. "I think we're going to see a resurgence in interest in unions," he says. "In the last five years, it's dawned on a lot of people that unions have been asleep at the wheel. They really don't have that much in common with the man on the hill."

Moore features some of the newest members of the United Food and Commercial Worker Union in his latest film, *The Big One*. The 45 booksellers who start at $6 an hour at the Borders Books store in Des Moines, Iowa, voted in the union in December 1996. They are mostly young, with bachelor's or even graduate degrees. Many came to Borders from other professions—teaching, the arts, or independent bookstores driven out of business by the big chains. They say it's not about money so much as it is about respect.

"The way they pay us and treat us is a paradox,' says employee organizer Christian Gholson. "On one hand, they say the employees are the reason for Borders' success, then they say this is a transitional job and you aren't worth more than $6.50 an hour." So far only four of Borders' 200-plus stores have organized, but Gholson sees it as a worthwhile struggle. "In my perfect world, I'd like to make $8.00 an hour. That's not so much when you see the volume of business that goes through this store," he says.

The trend toward unionization is growing among health-care professionals as well as among upscale service businesses that depend on younger workers. Stores in the Starbucks Corporation and Einstein/Noah Bagel Corporation chains have also voted for union representation in the past year. As for Gholson, their issues are better wages, full-time hours, health benefits—and respect.

Social scientists see historic similarities between today's labor issues and those of the 1930s. "After the Depression, everybody's job became a lot more insecure," says labor historian Rachleff. "There were a lot of efforts by white-collar workers to unionize. The intervention of anti-communism stopped that and threw the labor movement back onto a much narrower social foundation." Knoke says that the contract between employers and workers has once more ended in the 1990s. "For a lot of people, it's turned into something like it was before World War II," he says. "There is great uncertainty. People are being forced out of jobs that are disappearing."

If globalization is creating a working class with a wider social base, what does a person like Gholson, who considers himself a writer and a poet, have in common with an auto-plant assembly-line worker? It seems like a clash of cultures. "It's very funny watching these enthusiastic young kids trying to get the old fogies of the union to take action and get involved," says Mike Moore.

The Jackmans' study found that beliefs and feelings were an important determinant of class in the 1970s. For today's working class, the commonality just might be age-old issues such as job security, autonomy on the job, occupational prestige, and the belief that hard work should be rewarded. The working class has always been the group most likely to rate job security as the most important reason for taking a job, according to GSS data. "There are differences between us and the old union people," admits Gholson. "But there's a middle ground where we all agree."

The mere fact that working-class identification has stayed so stable over the last 20 years, despite myriad macro economic and social changes, is significant in itself. "If we find people continuing to identify themselves as workers, there must really be something going on socially,' says Rachleff, "because there's so much stacked against their doing that."

Behind the Numbers

The General Social Survey (GSS) has interviewed a nationally representative sample of American adults aged 18 and older on an almost annual basis since 1972. Questions on social-class affiliation have been asked on a consistent basis throughout the survey's history, as have many other questions about demographic, social, and economic characteristics and attitudes. For more information about the GSS, contact the National Opinion Research Center, 1155 East 60th Street, Chicago, IL 60637; telephone (312) 753-7877. The cumulative database is in the public domain and is available from the Roper Center at the University of Connecticut in Storrs; telephone (203) 486-4882.

Aggression Against Women

by John Scanzoni

Previous chapters said a lot about the expansion of women's choices in postmodern societies. Those choices are both economic and sexual, and include the freedom to publicly maintain erotic friendships. However, there's a dark side to relationships between women and men that most of us would rather ignore. The dark side consists of the aggression that men inflict on women—sexual assault, sexual harassment, and physical force. Throughout history men have used their greater physical strength to limit women's choices. Male aggression continues to coerce and constrain women even today.

Many women and some men are trying to reinvent male violence by stopping it. The Liz Claiborne company sponsors big-city billboards urging, "STOP domestic violence: Don't die for love." The billboards also convey some chilling statistics: "Every 12 seconds a woman is beaten in the U.S.; 25% of the violent crime in America is wife assault; 4 women are killed every day by their husbands or partners; 60% of battered women are beaten while they are pregnant."

Sexual Exploitation

Early in 1992, heavyweight boxing superstar Mike Tyson was convicted of raping Desiree Washington, a contestant in the 1991 Miss Black America beauty pageant. In his defense he claimed she'd willingly gone with him to the hotel room, that they were having a good time, and that he didn't hurt her. He stated he was out to hurt boxers, not women. Washington claimed that Tyson had forced her to have sexual intercourse with him. She also alleged that leaders of a large African-American religious denomination (to whom Tyson had previously promised generous donations) had offered her lots of money to drop the charges.

According to novelist Joyce Carol Oates, Washington was a heroine in the stand against sexual abuse. Oates adds that press reports indicate some citizens (white and black) were sorry Tyson was convicted. A few black citizens remarked that they didn't care for the spectacle of a black woman accusing a black man of the crime that whites stereotypically attach to all black men. Other citizens wondered aloud where to place the blame for Tyson's action: A sex-saturated culture? Men's macho self-image and their view of women as sex objects? Oates cites an earlier biography of Tyson in which he himself vehemently rejected the labels of "poor guy" and "victim" that have trailed him all his professional life: "No one is to blame," concludes Oates, except Tyson.

A few months earlier, another rape trial drew as much if not more national attention. William Kennedy Smith (nephew of Senator Ted Kennedy) was acquitted of raping a white woman. They met at a chic Palm Beach, Florida, nightspot, danced and had a few drinks, and she returned with him to his family estate. She claimed that once there he forced her to have sexual intercourse against her will. His story was that she willingly consented. The jury took his word over hers. Once again press reports showed that citizens were divided: "Why did she go home with him if she didn't want It?" asked some. Other citizens believed he did it but the high-priced lawyer bought with Kennedy money "saved his neck."

These and similar media events have focused attention on a matter that until recently no one thought very much about—sexual assault in the form of *acquaintance rape*. During the early 1990s, popular TV series such as *Designing Women, L.A. Law, A Different World,* and *Civil Wars* devoted several episodes to it. In the late eighties and early nineties, "date rape" became a live issue on college campuses because for the first time officials were trying to cope with date-rape lawsuits. The women claimed that universities were not taking their charges of rape seriously and thus not punishing alleged offenders. One person who rejected the arguments of activist women was University of California Professor Neil Gilbert. On the major talk-show circuit and in the national media, Gilbert asserted that "rape" was an incorrect label for what some men did on dates. Men might be "insensitive," he acknowledged, "but you can't call that rape."

Alongside this mountain of attention from the media, numerous researchers have begun to focus on the topic of acquaintance rape. Does this newfound interest mean that acquaintance rape is a new thing? That it didn't happen before the 1980s? Laurie Bechhofer and Andrea Parrot cite an Old Testament Bible story showing that acquaintance rape has been around for at least 2,500 years. Amnon talked his unwilling half-sister Tamar into bed, and after he pleasured himself he threw her out of his house. When she reported the incident to her full brother Absalom, he responded, "Don't worry about it, it's no big deal." It was not until the 1950s that Kanin presented the first social science evidence for sexual aggression. Yet recall from Chapter 7 that Willard Waller figured a lot more sexual aggression went on among 1930s' daters than anyone realized. He based his suspicion on the essence of the Dating Game: Women were supposed to sexually titillate men enough to keep them interested, but not so much as to ruin their own reputation.

Although North Americans have been edging away from the Game since the 1960s, there's a lot of disagreement on what the new rules should be. Lillian Rubin points out that the sexual freedoms of recent decades may actually leave some women more vulnerable to sexual aggression than ever before. In the old Game, "nice girls" never said yes. In today's world, liberated women can't say no or so many men (and some women) seem to believe. Researchers will probably never know for sure if there's more or less acquaintance rape today than there was during the 1930s or 1950s, or the 1700s, or in ancient Israel. But for the first time in history it's become a live issue and will remain so for many years. The reason it's become a live issue is clear. Before the sixties, women's personal and economic choices were very narrow, so narrow indeed that they were wrapped up in the same man. Women had the freedom to marry the man they loved, but once married they were "taken." The married woman had given up the personal freedom to consider any other man. And the only economic choice she had was to hope that the man she loved could support her and their children.

ECONOMIC AUTONOMY

The Big Bang was about choices that today's women have more of than ever before. Chapter 15 shows that although women continue to face marketplace discrimination, increasing numbers of them are achieving economic autonomy, and many others want to. Economic autonomy simply means being able to support oneself, and any children, at a *reasonable* level ("reasonable" is defined by the person). Economic autonomy is what men have expected for themselves since the start of the Jacksonian era. To be sure, inflation, unemployment, a shrinking job market, and poor education make it difficult for any person to be autonomous. But according to Charles Jones and co-workers, the Big Change is that growing numbers of women prefer economic autonomy to having no option other than dependence on a man.

AVAILABILITY

Alongside, and indeed because of, economic choices, women (and men) also have greater personal choices than ever before. Chapter 5 said that availability means that every adult always retains the choice to select prospects and/or partners regardless of any relationship (including formal marriage) he or she may currently have. Today, not many persons need to be locked forever within the "quiet desperation" of the pre-sixties era. Nevertheless, to be available does not imply that one is *interested*. Neither Helga nor Kurt (Chapter 5) is interested in anyone else even though each retains that option. And after Karyn ends her relationship with Kurt she wants nothing to do with any man for a long time. Having a good job gives Karyn that choice.

Having that much control over their economic and personal lives is something new for women. It's a feature of postmodern societies. The difficulty comes in translating their newfound control into their relationships with men. Since ancient times, men have had far more economic and political resources, and thus greater control over their own lives, than women. One result has been that men

have thought of themselves as pursuers, or hunters, and women as their prize, or prey. It was quite common for men such as Amnon to get the sexual pleasures they wanted from women without giving women what they wanted. Taking something from someone without giving that person what he or she wants in exchange was how Waller defined *exploitation*.

It seems evident that men have sexually exploited women since time began. The rules of the Dating Game, as well as the rules of the Victorian courting era that preceded it, were designed to try to protect women from exploitation. What women needed and wanted was marriage; an honorable gentleman was supposed to promise it to his lady in exchange for sex. At the least (as in today's Japan) he should provide for the needs of his mistress and any children ("bastards") he might sire. Prostitutes have always been exceptions to the rules. And today's women now lack the protection of the rules as well. Many of today's women thus seem more vulnerable than before to sexual exploitation. The ancient exchange between sex and marriage has evaporated. Apart from religious conservatives, few people in modern societies view sex as something reserved for marriage. The rub is that many men still see themselves as hunters and women as their rightful prey. Another way to describe this is to say that some men hold "macho attitudes" toward women. Kanin used the term "sexually predatory." One result of how some men perceive women is acquaintance rape.

DEFINING RAPE AND SEXUAL ASSAULT

Although rape laws vary across the fifty states, Bechofer and Parrot have identified three conditions that are fundamental to a legal definition of rape. These three conditions provide the narrowest possible definition of rape. First, penile penetration of the vagina must occur, "be it ever so slight." Second, that penetration must be against the woman's will and without her consent. Third, there must be coercion, whether actual or threatened. A few states have dropped the narrower term *rape* and replaced it with a more general label, *sexual assault*. In these states sexual assault occurs when the man's penis penetrates the woman's vagina, anus, or mouth. Furthermore, since any unwanted penetration is a punishable crime, this definition includes men committing sexual assaults against other men both anally and orally. Most states, however, retain the narrower definition of rape. They prefer to place other kinds of nonconsensual sex under the *sodomy* and *sexual abuse* categories of crimes.

SEXUAL ASSAULT AMONG ACQUAINTANCES

The matter of acquaintance rape has become a public controversy both legally and socially. Citizen reaction to the Tyson and Kennedy trials shows that many people hold widely varying ideas and feelings about what rape is and is not. Feminists and other researchers carry on very active rape research programs. In addition, they vigorously advocate for changes in rape laws and in public attitudes towards it. Their objective is to broaden the definition of rape. The advocates wanted citizens and the courts to label certain behaviors as rape that in the past were not viewed as rape. And the advocates want those behaviors severely punished. The idea of a broad-based citizen movement against rape began in earnest with the publication of Susan Browmiller's book, *Against Our Will*. Bechhofer and Parrot consider themselves part of that movement. To help us understand what acquaintance rape is, they compare and contrast it with three other kinds of situations.

Stranger Rape   What do most people think of when they hear the work rape? A woman is walking along minding her own business. Suddenly a knife-wielding man she's never seen before jumps her and drags her into an alley while she tries to fight back. The stranger batters and bruises her into submission and then rapes her. Stunned and bewildered, she wanders to a hospital emergency room; she's treated for her wounds; the police are called; and a search is begun for her unknown assailant.

Ronald Homes divides stranger rape into two categories: attempted rapes and completed rapes. An attempted rape occurs typically during daylight hours on a street or playground or in a parking lot or garage. In an actual example, a 29-year-old man accosted a 65-year-old woman at 1:45 p.m. in a city's busy downtown area. He began to pull up her dress and wrestle her to the ground. Astonished onlookers rushed to the woman's assistance, chasing the man for several blocks before they trapped him in the lobby of the public library. A completed rape usually occurs in the victim's home from 6:00 p.m. to midnight. According to Holmes, fewer than 10 percent of all stranger rapes of either type are ever reported to police. In spite of the underreporting, Bechhofer and Parrot say that the vast majority of rapes are not done by strangers, but rather by men previously known to the women.

Anonymous Sex   Although the 1963 movie, Love with the Proper Stranger, doesn't convey exactly what Bechhofer and Parrot mean by "consensual sex with a stranger," it points in that general direction. The 1986 film describing the pre-AIDS singles' scene, About Last Night…is more on target. For Bechhofer and Parrot the term anonymous sex means that sometimes a man a woman (or two same-sex persons) who are total strangers meet and their erotic antennae tell them both, "Let's do it." The woman in particular defines this as something she wants and agrees to. Incidentally, the William Kennedy Smith trial was about two strangers meeting for the first time. Smith maintained that he had the woman's consent; she denied it. Before the AIDS epidemic, consensual sex with a stranger was a much more common occurrence among gay males than among either heterosexuals or lesbians.

Lovemaking   Consensual sex between acquaintances is what Bechhofer and Parrot call their third situation. For them, "acquaintance" means any man who is not a stranger. If he was not previously unknown to the woman, he is by definition an acquaintance. Being an acquaintance does not imply that the couple know each other on merely a casual basis. The man could be a neighbor, co-worker, friend, husband, cohabitor, sibling, cousin, or whatever. The woman may have known him for a few days, weeks, months, or years. How long she knew him doesn't matter at all. What does matter are two things: (1) She does not define him as a "stranger," as a person previously unknown to her. (2) She sleeps with him because she wants to. She perceives herself as willingly consenting to sexual intercourse with someone she knows.

HOW WIDESPREAD IS ACQUAINTANCE RAPE?

The National Crime Survey (NCS) carried out annually by the U.S. Justice Department reports that in 1982 some 52 percent of "completed rapes...were perpetrated by someone who was known to the victim." But Christine Gidycz and Mary Koss believe that the NCS figures are much too low. Their own national studies lead them to the conclusion that the majority of women who are assaulted by an acquaintance tend not to define their experience as rape, even though someone they knew coerced them into sex against their will. If a woman doesn't perceive her own experience as rape, she won't report it as such to the NCS interviewer. If all women who are actually coerced into unwanted sex could somehow be included in the NCS survey, the total percentage of completed rapes would be much higher than slightly over one-half.

THE ISSUE OF THE WOMAN'S CONSENT

In contrast to stranger rape,, acquaintance rape means two things: first, the woman knows who the man is, she does not define him as a stranger, and second, she does not willingly consent to intercourse. Bechhofer and parrot readily acknowledge that in real life distinctions among anonymous sex, lovemaking, and acquaintance rape are often blurred. Nonetheless, the central issue remains—the woman's own perception of her consent. Does she define herself as having coitus willingly or unwillingly? If it is unwilling, it violates her freedom of choice, and thus it is rape.

Chapters 2, 3 and 5 show that being in family or being in an erotic friendship rests ultimately on the person's own definitions of what's going on. His or her special relationship does not rely chiefly on something outward, or objective, such as a blood tie, or a marriage license. In similar fashion, whether a woman is giving her sexual consent is a matter of her own perception of what's going on. It does not depend on something outward, or

physically "real"—something that can be seen and judged by outsiders.

Date Rape   "Date rape" is merely one form of acquaintance rape. Date rape means that the rape occurred between persons who had known each other and were "out together." But we just learned that acquaintance rape is a much broader term that includes many other situations besides being out together at a party or bar.

Marital Rape   Until recently, the social and legal definitions of rape in fact rested on outward or physically real things. For example, one physical thing defining rape was the marriage license itself. A husband could never be accused of raping his wife. Indeed, say David Finkelhor and Kersti Yllo, a married man had a "license to rape." The license in and of itself transformed something that was previously wrong into something that after the wedding suddenly became right. Carol Bohmer reports that the "marriage exemption" made it legal for a man to demand sexual "services" from his wife anytime he pleased. His demands were justified on the basis of his economic support. As a result of major efforts by feminists and other reformers, most states have now removed the marital exemption. As a result, a wife in one of those states who feels she is not giving sexual consent can charge her husband with rape.

On the other hand, not only have some states retained the marriage exemption, they have even broadened it: They now apply the same exemption to cohabiting couples. In those states neither wives nor cohabiting women can charge their partners with rape. Marrying and/or moving in with a man is thought to be consent enough. Those outward facts give the man permission to demand and receive sex quite apart from the woman's consent.

When it comes to sentencing husbands convicted of wife rape, at least one state applies lesser penalties to them than it does to men convicted of raping "nonwives." The 1993 North Carolina legislature agreed to allow up to fifteen years in prison for husbands convicted of raping wives. By contrast, men raping "other" women could get up to life in prison. Chapter 5 described Helga as a victim of marital rape because, in her view, her husband was sexually forcing himself on her. Helga and Hans are an example of what Finkelhor and Yllo describe as force-only marital rape. In those situations, the husband uses only a minimal amount of coercion—no more than necessary—to get his wife to submit sexually. The coercion may include physical force such as pushing or shoving, but not necessarily so. These authors report that many husbands force their wives into having sex via constant verbal badgerings.

Finkelhor and Yllo contrast those situations with what they call *battering* rape. Here the husband beats his wife to a far greater degree than would be necessary simply to get her to submit sexually. The husband rapes her at the same time that he hits, punches, slaps, and in other ways hurts her. Perhaps the best-known example of battering rape is the John and Lorena Bobbitt case. She alleged that because her husband regularly beat her into having sex, she became "temporarily insane" and cut off his penis while he slept. A jury believed her and acquitted her of all criminal charges. Finally, Finkelhor and Yllo identify a third type of marital rape as *obsessive* rape. In this situation the husband adds "strange and perverse" activities to his rape and violence. Those activities include painful bondage and torture, such as burning the woman's breasts, buttocks, and genitals with cigarettes. He may also use foreign objects such as sticks or bottles to penetrate the woman sexually.

Consent and the Woman's Reputation and Demeanor   Besides the marriage license and or co-residence, a second set of outward, or physically real, things that some people look for to judge whether a rape has been committed is the woman's reputation and demeanor. If the woman's behaviors are judged to be "sexually provocative," then she "got what she deserved," and rape cannot be proven. In the 1991 film, *Thelma & Louise*, Louise was at a bar drinking heavily and dancing uninhibitively with a stranger that a waitress had warned her was of questionable repute. The pair then went outside where he roughed up Louise and attempted to rape her against her obvious resistance. After Thelma discovered them and shot the man to death, Louise wanted to go to the police. But Thelma refused saving, "A hundred people saw you

dancing 'that way' with him. Are they going to believe us? Wake up to the real world." Thelma was convinced that witnesses would testify that Louise had been "provocative"— that she had "asked for it." So how could you blame the man? Louise had "led him on."

Bohmer reports that very often, "provocative" behaviors or dress on the part of the woman are taken as proof, or as valid indicators, of her consent, no matter how strongly she protests to the man. A 1989 Florida case drew national attention when a man charged with rape was acquitted because the woman was wearing a tank top, a white lace miniskirt, and no underwear. The jury foreman stated, "We all feel she asked for it for the way she was dressed; her clothing was too enticing." The prevailing idea in North American culture has been that ordinary citizens can intuitively figure out whether it was rape because of something *outward*, no matter what the woman says. Outward evidence includes a woman's provocative clothing or lack of clothing and/or her overall demeanor. If she didn't behave like a "lady" (or if she was a wife or cohabitor), then there was no way to prove rape.

Additional outward circumstances making it very difficult for a woman to prove rape include her reputation. Someone known to be a "loose woman" is fair game for assault, say Bechhofer and Parrot. So is a woman who is either asleep or drunk. In one incident a woman and her boyfriend had been drinking together with his male friend. She fell asleep, but then woke up with the male friend cutting her face with a knife and trying to rape her.

Consent—Saying *Yes* and Not Saying *No*
Bechhofer and Parrot state that the cultural assumption—held over from the Dating Game, has been that unless a woman explicitly says no, then she's saying yes. The consent issue enters what Bechhofer and Parrot call the "gray zone" if the couple have in fact been "making out." At some point she may say enough, but he may feel she has tacitly given her consent to intercourse by participating in passionate foreplay. He thinks she has no right to tease him by stopping short of intercourse, and that she is now obliged to com-

plete the act. Nevertheless, Bechhofer and Parrot say that legally and morally, consent requires that she (or he) must first, say yes, and second, not say no. Making out cannot by itself be taken as evidence for consent if the woman does not define it that way.

Bechhofer and Parrot add yet another crucial point about consent. They believe that Tuesday's consent can never be assumed because of Sunday's agreement. Because a woman sleeps with a man today does not mean she's obliged to do so again the next day, next week, or whenever. That point is particularly relevant for couples in an ongoing erotic friendship. The woman (man) is free at any time to say no regardless of how often she (he) has said yes in the past. On a recent (April 29, 1992) national TV news special called *The New Rules of Love,* ABC devoted twenty minutes to the subject of a woman's sexual consent. In one of the scenes a group of college men were asserting their conviction that a woman's *no* actually means *keep on trying.* Furthermore, the men rejected the idea that a woman who sleeps with a man regularly has the right to say no whenever she wishes. One male quipped that on a "couple's golden wedding anniversary the man surely has a right to a 'piece.'"

RAPE MYTHS

According to Martha Burt, a *rape myth is* something many people use to distinguish a real rape from a nonrape. A *real* rape is limited to the stranger category described previously. Anything else cannot be rape. Burt says there are at least four types of cultural stereotypes, or rape myths, in North America. All of the myths apply to acquaintances. And they all boil down to this: If the woman knew the man, and if he didn't slap, punch, or hit her, or use a weapon—and thus by physical pain force her to comply—then it can't be rape. In addition, all four myths ignore the idea of consent and its legal and moral definition: She does say yes *and* she doesn't say no.

One myth is that nothing actually happened. In this stereotype, women are said to accuse men of sexual assault even though it isn't true. The woman wants to get revenge on the man because,

as the belief goes, he's no longer interested in her and wants to end their relationship. Or she makes up the accusations simply to convince herself she's sexually desirable. A second myth is that no harm was done. That was the gist of Absalom's remark to his sister Tamar—"no big deal." In this stereotype, unless a woman was a virgin or married to somebody else, what difference does it make? Burt adds that a corollary of the no harm myth is that only bad girls get raped. Since they're defined as loose women anyhow, what difference can it possibly make if some guy "has fun" with her? A third myth is that she wanted it. Underlying this stereotype is the idea that even when a woman says no she in fact means yes. Saying no is merely her way of being coy and playing hard to get. In the words of a 1950s' popular song, "Your lips tell me no-no, but there's yes-yes in your eyes." Burt says this myth applies particularly to a woman who's been doing consensual necking or petting with a man. If somehow she doesn't want it, she should walk away even if he gets violent. Burt adds that a dark corollary of this third myth is the belief that some women get turned on by being beaten up and raped. A final myth is that she deserved it. Examples of this would be Louise (in *Thelma and Louise),* and also the Florida woman with the white lace miniskirt *sans* underwear.

NEGOTIATION AND RAPE

Since consensual lovemaking requires that she say yes *and* not say no, how does a woman let a man know what she wants and doesn't want? Must she be verbal about her wishes? Is it possible to communicate her wishes nonverbally? Throughout North American society, persons tend not to be straightforward and explicit about sex. Most people rely chiefly on subtle, nonverbal cues and clues—the erotic antennae described in Chapter 5. By contrast, Bohmer reminds us that in some cultures persons are quite direct about sexual invitations, and do not hesitate at all to be explicit. She tells of a male friend attending a party in Iceland approached by a woman speaking Icelandic, which he did not understand. On translation, he learned that she'd asked, "Do you want to screw?" Being that forthright about sex, although very much a part of Icelandic society, is virtually unknown in North America.

Two Views of Sexuality   To a large degree, the matter of being verbally explicit about sex is connected to the two views of sexuality described in Chapter 4. The traditional view is that abstinence till marriage is morally superior. Since nonmarital sex is defined ahead of time as bad, illicit, and less than virtuous, non-married persons holding that view are understandably hesitant to openly discuss sex, contraception, and sexually transmitted diseases with a potential sexual partner. Furthermore, even persons who don't hold the traditional view are often uncomfortable about telling a potential sexual partner how they feel. They fear that the person will somehow view them as bad or immoral.

But Chapter 4 said that a second view of sexuality is called responsible indulgence. In this view, as the influential and widely respected columnist Ellen Goodman puts it, sex is defined as good *in and of itself* regardless of marital status. Although its pleasures are fully acknowledged, its inherent responsibilities are emphasized just as strongly. One of its chief responsibilities is that a person must never coerce his or her partner into having sex. It follows that avoiding coercion applies as much to married as to non-married persons— responsibility overrides the license. Furthermore, being responsible and avoiding coercion generally means being verbally explicit—it means talking about what one does and does not want.

Verbal Coercion   But merely talking about whether or not to have coitus does not guarantee that sexual coercion is avoided. We just learned that some men believe that even when a woman says no she means yes. Charlene Muehlenhard and Jennifer Schrag define verbal sexual coercion as times when the man uses any number of potent verbal and psychological strategies to get the woman into bed. These include making her feel guilty for leading him on, calling her frigid, or threatening to end their relationship. One national study of 6,000 college women reported that 44 percent of them had experienced unwanted sexual intercourse as a result of men's continual verbal badgering.

In her studies of communication between college women and men, Antonia Abbey found that two-thirds of the students reported that during the past year they'd experienced at least one sexual misperception. The average was five misperceptions. As expected, many more women than men reported being misperceived. "Misperceived" often means the woman thought she was merely being friendly but the man thought she was transmitting erotic signals, that she was interested. The students told Abbey that most of the misperceptions occurred at parties where alcohol was flowing freely.

Abbey also studied how misperceptions are resolved or negotiated. Communication is the sending and receiving of social signals. But Chapter 11 showed that negotiation is something quite different—it's what the persons do about the signals. Clarise senses that Bud perceives that she's signaling sexual interest, when in fact she has none. So what does she do as she becomes aware that he's misperceiving her? Clarise can let Bud know without talking that she wants nothing more to do with him— she can send out very strong nonverbal signals of *non*interest. Or she can try to get out of the situation by "playing dumb" (using evasive language aimed at making him think she's not getting his intended message). Or Clarise can do what 41 percent of Abbey's respondents did— not mince words and directly tell Bud no. Abbey reports that saying an explicit no was most troublesome for the woman when she and the man were just friends. On the one hand, having a platonic friendship made it easier to talk about his misperceptions of what was going on between them. On the other hand, it also often resulted in one or both of the friends becoming angry and upset.

One reason for getting upset is that in North American culture (unlike in Iceland), persons tend to be extremely fearful of sexual rejection. Thus, if the woman is subtle and tacit about not wanting sex, the man is less likely to feel humiliated and angry. If she's verbal, he can't escape the reality that she's turned him down. Although some men in Abbey's study were simply amused by being turned down, other men became quite angry. Because women are aware of the potential for men's anger (and possible violence), some in the study got upset and embarrassed over having to negotiate. They didn't like having to say no explicitly. Other women, however, felt relieved that their negotiations worked—the men had left them alone.

EFFECTIVE NEGOTIATION

Chapter 11 showed that the whole point of negotiation is to make something *work.* That means that negotiation is supposed to be effective, that things will turn out the way you want—you have some *control* over a situation. Although Clarise and Horace were friends, she wanted him to stop pestering her for sex. She negotiated by telling him, "No, I don't want to spoil our friendship." Since he too valued their friendship, he reluctantly said, "OK, I'll stop bugging you." Their negotiation was an example of what's called *win-win.* Clarise got what she wanted, but so did Horace (although not everything he had in mind). Because he valued her friendship and wanted to keep it, he gave up the idea of sleeping with her.

The many studies of acquaintance rape suggests a number of elements that might assist in effective negotiation. For the woman, "effective" means avoiding rape. Bechhofer and Parrot remark that some feminists refuse to discuss what women can do to avoid acquaintance rape; they claim that doing anything makes her responsible for what he does. Bechhofer and Parrot respond to that concern first by asserting that rape is "never the victim's fault." As Oates remarked about Mike Tyson, no one is to blame but him. Second, Bechhofer and Parrot believe that by making women (and men) aware of the risk factors, potential victims are empowered to get what they want, which is control over a situation before their acquaintance rapes them. The bottom line in this debate is this: Should women rely ultimately on men becoming moral and loving enough not to coerce them into sex? Or should women rely ultimately on themselves to control their own lives? Clearly, men need to become more moral in this regard. But a woman who trusts ultimately in male goodness takes the matter out of her own hands and places it with the man; she relinquishes control over a significant part of her life.

Equality	Traditionalism
←————————————————→	
Parity of educational options and employment opportunities	Scripted duties and opportunities
Interchangeability within home place and marketplace	Specialization within home place and marketplace
Decisions achieved via participatory problem-solving and negotiation	Decisions achieved via established norms and ultimate male authority
Explicit rejection of all forms of aggression within all expressions of primary relationships	Ambiguous stance toward aggression, especially regarding children

FIGURE 12.1   Continuum of Preferences for Gender Equality versus Gender Traditionalism

Gender Equality and Acquaintance Assault   One of the major elements known to influence any negotiations between women and men is what Chapter 10 called beliefs about gender equality. Recall from Chapter 10 that the more strongly women prefer gender equality, the more likely they are to want to keep their surname after marriage and to select nonpatriarchal wedding customs. Figure 12-1 shows that the polar opposite of gender equality is gender traditionalism. And gender traditionalism figures very much into the issue of acquaintance rape.

You will see immediately that Figure 12-1 is a continuum. The left side of Figure 12-1 covers citizens who strongly advocate gender equality, that is, interchangeability. Those persons endorse the idea that women and men should have the same opportunities and responsibilities for both paid work and home work. They believe, for example, that women should have access to any kind of training or education they want, from brain surgeon to bricklayer to bouncer. They also believe that women should have the same access as men to being hired, to wage increases, and to promotion. In addition, persons toward the left side of Figure 12-1 believe that men should participate fully with women in the routine chores of maintaining a household. And if the couple chooses parenting, men should participate fully in its burdens and joys. Advocates of gender equality believe that the more fully men participate in home work, the more fully women are able to participate in paid work.

Since the 1960s, there have been steady increases in the numbers of citizens who (regardless of their actual beliefs) will say they believe in gender equality. For example, if we compare 1960 with 1990, we find that during 1990 more persons were toward the middle and left of Figure 12-1 than were located there during 1960. Similarly, fewer persons were on the right side of Figure 12-1 than were located there during 1960. There has been a gradual but steady movement of citizens from right to center to left along the continuum of Figure 12-1. Regardless of their actual beliefs, fewer citizens today than ever before will admit that they believe in traditional behaviors for women and men.

Nevertheless, citizens located toward the right side of the figure do believe in traditional gender behaviors. They prefer that men specialize in paid work and women specialize in domestic work. In particular, they believe the woman should be the children's chief nurturer and caretaker. They hold that there are significant differences between the genders—biological, psychological, spiritual, and physical. Gender differences make it impractical and unworkable for women and men to be interchangeable. They don't agree that men can fit into the demands of parenting and do it as well as women. They are also doubtful that women can fit into the demands of certain kinds of paid work and do it as well as men. Earlier chapters showed that one of the most controversial examples of this belief in gender specialization is the belief that women can't do combat as effectively as men. During World War II, some 2,000 women pilots flew the identical fighter and bomber planes that men flew, but only in the United States. The women ferried the planes from factories to bases, where men then flew them overseas. The belief was that women were simply not interchangeable with men when it came to the rigors and dangers of actual combat.

It should come as no surprise that for decades almost every study of preferences about gender equality reveals that women believe more strongly in equality than do men. Men tend to be more gender-role traditional than women. And recent research reveals that the more traditional a man is, the more likely he is to believe that acquaintance rape is permissible. For example, 35 percent of college men admitted they would be likely to rape a woman if they believed they would not be caught. Robin Warshaw and Andrea Parrot report that men who feel that way tend to do so because of gender.

Some women too believe in highly specialized roles for men and women, based on cultural norms learned as children and reinforced as adults. And many women are in the middle of the continuum shown in Figure 12-1: They mix elements of traditionalism with elements of freedom, choice, and control.

Accepting the Old Script The fact that women vary among themselves regarding how gender traditional they are is connected specifically with acquaintance rape. First, for example, Warshaw and Parrot report that the more gender traditional a woman, the more likely she is to accept the "stereotypic sexual script." Chapter 7 called that script the rules of the old Dating Game. The whole point of the Game was that men should get as much as they can from women. Warshaw and Parrot add that this idea is built into the "macho sex role." Being macho also means that the man should ignore what the woman says—when she says no she's merely playing the Game. Everyone senses that she's supposed to say no even though she wants it as much as he does. His goal as a "real man" is to overcome her token resistance and give her what they both want.

The more gender-role traditional a man is, the more likely he is to accept the macho sex role. Several researchers such as Thomas Beneke argue that "rape is a man's problem...men solve it." He and other rape awareness advocates assert that if men regularly met in support groups for consciousness raising, they would eventually learn to accept the idea that it's *not* unmanly for a man to accept a woman's no as final. Very likely, the more strongly a man prefers gender equality, the easier it is for him to accept fresh views regarding a woman's protests and sexual intentions.

Abstinence versus Responsible Indulgence   Second, say Warshaw and Parrot, the more gender traditional a woman, the more torn she is between abstinence and responsible indulgence. Because she's not sure that sex is a good thing (nice girls can't do sex), she's nervous about talking openly, freely, and honestly about it. And because she's anxious about the morality of sex, she's also hesitant to negotiate explicitly with the man in a situation that has the potential for intercourse.

The Stroking Norm   Third, the more gender traditional a woman, the more likely she is to accept the "stroking norm." That's the old idea that women are supposed to put the needs of others, including men, ahead of their own. Chapter 7 said that in North American culture women are expected to nurture men and to take care of their emotional needs, but men are not equally responsible for women's emotional needs. Consequently, if the man persists in wanting sex, a woman who believes in stroking is more likely, even if reluctantly, to acquiesce, because "after all, he'll feel better if I give in."

Controlling the Sexually Charged Situation

Thus far we've learned that men who are more gender-role traditional are more likely to think it's no big deal to coerce (verbally and/or physically) a woman into having sex. In addition, women who are more gender-role traditional tend to be caught between the old Game and the new. Not being sure which Game is right, they're more vulnerable to sexual exploitation. They seem less willing and/ or able to negotiate for control over sexually charged situations. Researchers report that the sexually charged situation or setting is a critical element in understanding acquaintance rape. Jacquelyn White and John Humphrey say that the situation is built around, first, a location—a party, a car, or a dwelling with no one else around, and second, a situation that includes heavy use of alcohol and/or drugs. Finally, the situation may include previous intimacies (heavy petting, coitus), amount of money spent by the man, the

woman's type of dress, the man's and woman's reputations, and so on.

Clarise, for instance, dresses for a party (where alcohol is freely flowing) in a way that makes her extraordinarily sexually attractive. She defines the way she looks as a status symbol, not as a signal that she wants sex. She simply wants to have fun and enjoy herself. But some men at the party define her way of dressing as a signal of her sexual interest. According to White and Humphrey, Clarise finds herself in a sexually *charged* situation. A number of studies suggest that women who are less gender-role traditional tend to be more aware of and alert to the realities of that kind of situation. Clarise adheres strongly to gender equality She is determined to try to control the sexually charged situation. There is no guarantee she will be successful. It is quite possible that a man, because of his superior physical strength, will overwhelm her and force her into unwanted sex. Nevertheless, Clarise is wending her way through the minefields of a very different game than the one described in Chapter 7. By contrast, women who are more gender-role traditional appear less willing to face the intricacies of the contemporary sexually charged situation. They tend to be more sentimental about men and more trusting of them than someone like Clarise.

Controlling the War between the Genders

According to Warshaw and Parrot, a large part of facing reality is recognizing that women and men have been locked in the battle of the genders since time first began. Women are *less* gender-role traditional are *more* likely to accept that bottom-line reality. Instead of being sentimental abut the old Dating Game and its leftovers, those women readily acknowledge that the Game was but one example of that ancient battle. Women who prefer gender equality are also keenly aware of the ambiguities of today's fluid sexual scene. The old rules of battle are flaking away, and there are few new rules regarding what constitutes a fair fight between the genders.

Furthermore, women who are less gender-role traditional agree with Warshaw and Parrot that "in any battle, the outcome usually depends on which side has better fighting skills." Chapter 11 showed that "fighting skills" means, among several other things, the capability to negotiate effectively—to exercise control. Recall that while negotiating on previous occasions with her friend Horace, Clarise was able to achieve a win-win situation. Because each party got something of what they wanted, they each shared some degree of control. Clarise, however, is quite prepared to impose a win-lose situation on Russ, an acquaintance she runs into at the party, if that's what it takes for her to have control over her own body. When he gets too pushy and ignores her explicit no, Clarise warns him off using spicy profanity. When he continues to badger her, she threatens to scream, kick, run, or make a scene. According to Pauline Bart and P. H. O'Brien, those particular strategies are highly effective in thwarting acquaintance rape. Russ finally backs off—Clarise has won, Russ has lost.

SEXUAL HARASSMENT

For several days during October 1991, millions of Americans sat glued to their TV sets watching the Senate confirmation hearings of Clarence Thomas for the U.S. Supreme Court. What transfixed everyone was the testimony of Anita Hill. She charged that when she worked for Thomas some years earlier, he had *sexually harassed* her. Her testimony brought the issue of harassment onto the center stage of American consciousness. Before that media event, many Americans, men especially, had only a vague idea of what sexual harassment is all about. Hill described Thomas as "a boss who pestered her for dates and spoke graphically about pornography, bestiality, rape and his skills as a lover." Hill further alleged that Thomas "talked about pornographic materials depicting individuals with large penises or large breasts involved in various sex acts."

In commenting on the Hill/Thomas incident, A. Press and colleagues observe that harassment "may be as subtle as a leer and a series of off-color jokes, or as direct as grabbing a woman's breast. It can be found in typing pools and factories, Army barracks and legislative suites, city rooms and college lecture halls. It is…an exercise of power almost analogous to rape, for which women pay with their jobs…. Sexual harassment, the boss's

dirty little fringe benefit, has been dragged out of the closet."

Although those kinds of behaviors have been around probably as long as acquaintance rape, the label "sexual harassment" wasn't coined until 1975. As soon as it appeared, the popular women's magazine, *Redbook*, did a 1976 survey of 9,000 readers to find out how many of them had ever experienced harassment. Eighty-eight percent of the women reported they had indeed experienced it; 92 percent believed it was a serious problem on the job. Rosemarie Tong asserts that sexual harassment has several components: (1) It usually occurs in a formal setting, such as the workplace, school, religious meeting place, and so on. (2) Within this formal setting, a person or persons (usually but not always men) say or do things in a woman's presence that she perceives as having sexual overtones. (3) Because she defines the man's words and actions as annoying, unwelcome, and an imposition, she rejects his overtures, his unwanted behaviors.

HARASSMENT FROM SUPERIORS

The consequences of rejecting the man's unwanted overtures are significantly affected by the differing amount of authority that he has compared with what she has. If he is her superior, for example, her boss (as Clarence Thomas was to Anita Hill) or her teacher, then he's in a position to reward or penalize her in a number of ways. In situations where the man has an authority position over the woman, harassment includes the woman's perception that she'll be penalized if she rejects the unwanted behaviors but rewarded if she goes along with them. In the case of a woman employee, she perceives she'll be promoted or get a higher salary if she goes along with the harassment. If she doesn't put up with it she might get neither promotion nor money, and she might even lose her job. If she's a student, the rewards for going along might be better grades or financial assistance of some sort.

When Hill was asked why she didn't report Thomas at the time of the alleged harassment, she responded that she was afraid that she might lose her job and her entire career would be put in jeopardy. Before the Hill/Thomas case, women employees who felt they were being harassed were seldom encouraged to initiate grievance procedures or complain to management or personnel directors. If a woman did complain, she'd likely be perceived as a troublemaker and eventually be fired. And troublemakers have a tough time finding another job. Since the Hill/Thomas confrontation, however, *The Wall Street Journal* reports that American business has begun to shift in the direction of taking women's harassment complaints more seriously. Many businesses now encourage women to come forward with those kinds of complaints. And even before Hill/Thomas, *Business Week* asserted that companies were getting the message that they must seek to end sexual harassment.

The Wall Street Journal adds that a major reason businesses, as well as schools and universities, are scrambling to respond to women's complaints is recent court decisions awarding money to harassed women. "The Supreme Court ruled that students who claim they were sexually harassed and sue schools or school officials under federal law may seek money damages in addition to other damages." Before that ruling, businesses and schools were not required to pay money damages to women proving harassment. In the particular case on which the Supreme Court ruled, a high-school student claimed that a teacher "made unwelcome verbal advances [and] forcibly kissed her on the mouth." Months later his unwanted behaviors drifted beyond harassment into actual acquaintance rape: "On three occasions [he] pressured her into having sexual intercourse in a private office."

Harassment versus Acquaintance Rape   Legally, acquaintance rape differs from harassment because during harassment there is no actual rape, as defined previously. The harasser may, however, desire intercourse with the woman, and his harassing behaviors may be the prelude for coercing her into having nonconsensual sex. Under current U.S. law, a woman does not have to suffer actual assault to prove harassment and collect money damages. Interestingly enough, the same principle holds in Japan, a culture that is considered much more gender traditional than the

United States. A 34-year-old woman claimed that although her boss never touched her, he had sexually harassed her in a verbal manner. He had also spread unfounded rumors that she was a sexually promiscuous woman. She was forced to quit her job. The Japanese courts ruled that he had sexually harassed her and ordered the man's company to pay her monetary damages.

By no means, however, is it a simple matter for a woman to prove harassment in a court of law even if a man touches her but no actual sexual assault takes place: "Touching a woman's breast without permission isn't a crime in Arkansas if no force or threats are used," ruled a local judge in dismissing a suit by a 16-year-old girl against her teacher. She claimed that he'd invited her into his office to counsel her, and then began to ask questions about her sex life. Next, she says, he "touched her left breast, then moved his hand down toward her belt." At that point she got scared and left his office. The teacher denied her charges, but the school board suspended him with pay until they decided what to do next.

Harassment by Women   Although it is rare, the courts have occasionally ruled in favor of a man, charging that his female supervisor sexually harassed him. In a 1993 decision, a California jury awarded more than $1 million in damages to a man who claimed that his boss had sexually harassed him daily for six years. He said that she would enter his office and close the door, then embrace and kiss him. Sometimes, he added, she would "fondle my genitals."

Harassment from Peers

Thus far we've been looking at sexual harassment from superiors. Superiors can give rewards to women (or male) employees or students in exchange for going along with their harassment. And they can punish subordinates for not cooperating. We've also drawn a distinction between harassment and acquaintance rape. Not all men who harass women wish to have sexual intercourse with them. In the man's own perception, he believes that by his comments and behaviors he's "just having a little fun" with the woman. Because he doesn't intend to coerce her into sex, he doesn't see anything wrong with what he's doing. He doesn't perceive himself as intruding on the woman's privacy, eroding her dignity, or limiting her freedom.

Besides superiors, women are also subject to considerable sexual harassment from peers—men who have no formal authority over them, having neither rewards to give nor penalties to mete out. Since the women are with these male peers in an employment or school setting, it's difficult for the women to escape the harassment.

The Tailhook Scandal   In a much publicized example of peer harassment, the U.S. Navy investigated complaints by women officers and civilians who in 1991 had attended a convention of naval aviators in Las Vegas (the Tailhook Scandal). The women said that when they attempted to return to their hotel rooms, the male officers forced them to "run the gauntlet." The men blocked their way and not only made sexually degrading and insulting remarks about them, but also attempted to pull down their underwear. The men "groped and grabbed parts of their anatomy including breasts and buttocks." Moreover, this kind of harassment had been an annual event at those conventions for six years, and higher-ups knew about it.

The Navy Brass who investigated admitted that all the charges were true, but at first refused to discipline the men involved. Instead the Brass said that in the future they would " 'teach our people…the difference between acceptable and unacceptable behavior.' " The subsequent media outcry became so great, however, that Congress compelled the Pentagon to discipline the male officers involved in the harassment. Navy Secretary Lawrence Garrett was forced to resign in 1992 because of his failure to take the women's charges seriously in the first place, and to investigate them thoroughly. By 1993, the Pentagon reported that some 175 officers would face serious "disciplinary action" as a result of their involvement in *Tailhook*. In reality, not a single one of those officers was ever court martialed. Moreover, the admiral in charge of all naval operations was accused of undermining the entire *Tailhook* investigation; his

only "reprimand" was an agreement to take early retirement.

In a separate 1992 example of peer harassment, some girls in a Florida middle school complained about the boys' graphic sexual remarks aimed at them. They also complained to the principal about the boys' touching, patting, slapping, and grabbing them on their buttocks and breasts. Even though the remarks and grabbing occurred in school corridors as well as in class, the girls claimed that teachers ignored the boys' behaviors. When asked about it, the principal said, " 'There's a lot of what I call love taps. It's childish behavior, where they're showing their affection in some ways toward each other.'" The guidance counselor commented that although "consensual sex play among adolescents does occur, that is not the same as unwanted touching. If the girls tell me they feel uncomfortable and didn't want it to happen, I respect that. Unwanted touching can constitute criminal sexual abuse." One 14-year-old girl said that the boys "slap girls on the butt because they think it's funny and because they think that's how they're supposed to act. But now I won't take it from them. I told a boy who slapped me on the butt that if you ever do that again, I'm going to the guidance counselor and have you kicked out of school. They leave me alone now that they know I won't take it…I have my life…and I won't let anything get in the way." This same girl added that many other girls "don't know what to do. So they act like it's not really happening." She also added that most girls don't report harassment because they'll be marked as troublemakers: "Oh, you're the girl who got that boy in trouble."

These girls' experiences are borne out by a 1993 national study of 1,632 students in grades 8 through 11 conducted by pollster Lou Harris that was commissioned by the American Association of University Women (AAUW). The AAUW study describes "school hallways as a gauntlet of sexual taunts." Among other things, the researchers report more than 75 percent of girls and 56 percent of boys say they have been the "target of un-wanted sexual comments, jokes, gestures or looks, while two-thirds of girls and 42 percent of boys have been touched, grabbed or pinched." These and comparable findings lead AAUW officials to conclude that the climate of sexual harassment that pervades today's public schools undermines the learning process, especially for girls. For example, 70 percent of the girls said they were "very" or "somewhat upset" by the harassment, compared with only 24 percent of the boys.

Whether at work or school, many girls and women find themselves with male peers who sexually harass them by words and sometimes by actions. And since girls and women must share those social situations and physical spaces with those boys and men, they find themselves constrained. Women's freedoms are thus limited in ways that men's freedoms are not. Sexual harassment from peers places women in situations that are oppressive and painful, yet difficult to escape.

EXPLAINING HARASSMENT

Whether by superiors or peers, why is sexual harassment as widespread as many women and some men believe it to be? Nancy DiTomaso argues that harassment is an expression of gender discrimination. Simply by being in the workplace women become competitors with men for scarce economic rewards as well as for prestige. Attending the same schools also makes women competitors with men for grades, prestige, and sometimes financial aid. DiTomaso notes that harassment stems from the "fears that men have about losing their privileged place in the labor force." She adds that when women are competing with male peers for the same jobs, those peers tend to be more hostile than are the men who are the women's superiors. To give vent to their hostility and resentment toward their women competitors, many men behave in a sexually harassing manner. DiTomaso observes that most men themselves do not view their harassment as an expression of hostility. They view it just like the middle-school boys or male naval officers—"we're merely enjoying a bit of innocent fun."

DiTomaso concludes that whatever the complex explanations for male harassment, it is very real. And its reality has a profoundly negative effect on women's "access to good jobs, good training, and sufficient rewards." For example, the middle-school girl cited above sensed that the boys'

harassment was getting in the way of what she wanted to do with her life, and she simply wouldn't tolerate it. And the AAUW study agreed that sexual harassment is detrimental to girls' school performance and thus to their chances for future success in college and or the work force.

Harassment expresses gender discrimination because it's a problem that men face much less frequently than women. Every person (regardless of gender) confronts the stiff demands that are built into being a good student or a good employee in today's highly competitive world economy. However, women must in addition face the painful demands inherent in coping with harassment. Their options are to fight it head on or try to act as if nothing's happening. In either case the energies required to cope with something men rarely face means that women have fewer energies left over to compete in the marketplace. Disbursing energies in this fashion may be one reason that men continue to enjoy labor market advantages over women.

PHYSICAL FORCE

So far this chapter has considered constraints on women's choices in two realms—rape and sexual harassment. A third way of intruding on women's personhood and limiting their choices is use of physical force. As is the case with rape and harassment, it's difficult for researchers to know for sure whether there is more or less physical force against women today than there was years ago. Douglas Besharov concludes that it's growing. He asserts that, "Each year hundreds of thousands of wives are abused by their husbands."

Social researchers didn't pay much attention to violence within families until the late 1960s and early 1970s. Murray Straus was among the first to study it in a comprehensive manner. He said that although counselors had long been aware of wife beating, researchers had neglected it for several reasons. One reason was that everyone wanted to believe that the Modern (pre-sixties) Family was a place of sweetness and light, grace and harmony. It was socially defined as a *nonviolent* place. Since "everyone knows" that The Family is nonviolent, peaceful, and tranquil, researchers didn't bother to investigate whether what everyone knows was actually true or not.

Second, adds Straus, because most persons defined The Family as a nonviolent place, no one labeled acts of physical force in families as real violence. The 1960s had been marked by many incidents of horrific and unspeakable violence, including the assassinations of John Kennedy, Martin Luther King, Jr., and Robert Kennedy. In addition, for several years there had been numerous riots and unruly civil disturbances in cities and on college campuses throughout the nation. People could watch those happenings on TV and plainly see they were *real* violence. They also watched the first TV war—Vietnam—and daily saw acts of brutality on both sides.

But just as some people have difficulty imagining acquaintance rape as *real* rape, or grasping that sexual harassment is bitterly painful, many people—during the sixties and still today—have difficulty thinking of physical force in families as *real* violence. Straus says that many citizens impose a "perceptual blackout" on physical force in families, that is, whenever physical force is used, the persons who use the force and those on the receiving end don't generally define it as real violence. This tendency holds whether the force is used by husbands against wives or by wives on husbands, by parents on children or by siblings against one another. Rather, most people believe that real violence is what they see on TV news, not what happens at home, and surely not within their own four walls.

The Social Acceptability of Physical Force

In short, the use of physical force, like most things we've talked about in this book, is socially defined. Like a blood tie, or a marriage license, or sexual intercourse, the thing is not "real" in and of itself. The thing becomes meaningful and thus real based on how we perceive it—how we define it. Acquaintance rape, sexual harassment, and physical force have a great deal in common. One of the major elements they share is the variable of *social legitimacy*. That simply means the degree to which people conceive of those three kinds of behaviors as socially acceptable or not. In the past,

most people tended to think of all three as relatively acceptable social behaviors. To be sure, the behaviors were seen as unfortunate, but nonetheless inevitable. The rape myths discussed earlier showed that most people felt that if the woman knew the man, the act could not be defined as rape. Similarly, acts of "naughty fun" at women's expense were just that—fun, with no harm intended. Certainly few people defined the naughtiness as intrusive. And when it came to physical force between husbands and wives, many people accepted it as *simply there*—as an unfortunate part of life—like sometimes going hungry or getting evicted, or losing a limb, or becoming seriously ill. Not that anyone liked any of these things. "But," thought most people, "What can you do? That's life."

The degree of social acceptance, or legitimacy, of domestic force, was and is ratcheted upward many notches when it comes to children. Chapters 16 and 17 report that some citizens hold that God requires that they physically discipline their children. A few even believe that severe beatings are necessary to "drive the devil" out of the children and make them spiritual. On the other side, there is a minority of Christians who do not believe in physical force of any kind. Called *pacifists*, they are best known for the ways they perceive war They do not define war as an inevitable part of life. Nor do they believe that acts of military force are justified simply because the government says they're okay. Among other things, they refuse to serve in the military.

The matter of governments stating that certain physical force is okay while other force is not okay is much in the news these days regarding both capital punishment and abortion. Until the 1960s, most states believed they had the right to execute people. But during the 1970s and 1980s, a number of states said, "no, we don't have the right to execute people after all." More recently the U.S. pendulum has swung the other way, and state governments (along with the federal government) are once again saying that it's socially acceptable to execute. In contrast, most European countries continue to define capital punishment as unacceptable. Before the 1970s, most state governments said that abortion was an unacceptable act of physical force against the fetus. Then the U.S. Supreme Court decided it was okay. Some observers believe the Court may change its mind yet again and say that it's up to the states to figure out when abortion is or is not okay. Interestingly enough, it turns out that many people who believe that capital punishment is not okay feel that abortion is okay, and vice versa.

Physical Force within Primary Groups

Just as citizens and their governments can change their minds regarding whether or not physical acts of force such as capital punishment and abortion are legitimate, they can also shift their definitions regarding physical force among persons within primary groups. Recall from previous chapters that primary groups are special we-groups. They include platonic friendships, erotic friendships, blood families, and social families. Testifying before a U.S. congressional committee, Straus drew a sharp distinction between primary groups and what some sociologists call *secondary* situations. Secondary situations include people who work or share a class together, shop in the same store, ride the same elevator, share a hallway or sidewalk, sit together at a library or ball game, live in the same dorm or neighborhood, and so forth. One thing all these situations have in common is that it is never socially acceptable for co-workers, fellow students, neighbors, shoppers, and so on to punch, hit, kick, slap, pummel, stab, or strike one another with a blunt object. Nor is it ever acceptable to push, shove, or in any other ways beat up on one another

Sometimes violence happens in those kinds of situations anyhow. But if it does, no one would ever dream of saying, "Well, it's OK, the slapping was just work related." Or, "Since they're dorm mates or neighbors, it's no big deal if they beat up on each other." A person who uses physical force in any of those secondary situations is liable to be arrested and charged with criminal assault. Arrest is especially likely if the violence happens more than once, or if the attack leaves obvious marks such as bruises or abrasions, to say nothing of broken bones. By contrast, Straus reminded the congressional committee that in the United States a certain level of physical force is tolerated be-

tween erotic friends (spouses, cohabitors, girlfriends /boyfriends). He reported that if they slap, push, shove, or "mildly hit" one another, those types of physical force are culturally defined as *ordinary*—no big deal. People seem to expect it and don't get very excited about it. The other kinds of force listed above, such as striking with a blunt object or stabbing, are placed in a second and separate category and culturally perceived as extraordinary. In contrast to ordinary force, Straus says that most citizens seem shocked and surprised by extraordinary force within families and believe that something should be done about it.

Nevertheless, research carried out during the past twenty years concludes that many husbands and some wives use a certain degree of extraordinary force, and many more use a large amount of ordinary force, on one another. To demonstrate that physical force is far more common inside than outside of families, Straus reports that a man is twenty times more likely to experience violence of some kind at the hands of a family member than from an outsider. And a woman is 200 times more likely to experience violence of some kind from a family insider than from a stranger. Straus also reports that in the United States, 25 percent of all homicides are done by someone who was linked to the victim either by blood or marriage. In Canada, he says, the figure is 50 percent.

Measuring Force between Adult Partners   Straus and his colleagues surveyed national samples of U.S. households during 1975 and again in 1985. They measured violence between co-residing adults using what they called the Conflict Tactics Scale, or CTS. The CTS questionnaire is divided into two parts, the first of which is called "minor violence." Under minor (ordinary) violence they asked their respondents if during that year they had ever pushed, grabbed, shoved, threw something at, or slapped their partner.

Under the second part of their questionnaire ("severe," or extraordinary, violence that might cause injuries requiring medical attention) they asked their respondents if during that year they had ever kicked, bitten, punched, beaten up, choked, or burned their partner, or else threatened her or him with a knife or gun or actually used those weapons. In 1985, 161 of every 1,000 married or cohabiting couples reported either minor or severe violence. That translates into an estimated 8.7 million U.S. couples (16%) who experienced some kind of violence that year. The number of couples who said they experienced severe violence was 63 of 1,000, or 3.4 million couples.

Straus and his colleagues also compared the amounts of violence done by husbands and male cohabitors against their female partners with the amounts of violence done by women to their male partners. They found that 116 couples of 1,000 reported male violence that was either minor or severe. And 34 of 1,000 reported severe male violence. Straus reserves the label "wife beating" for this latter category.

At the same time, 124 couples of every 1,000 marrieds and cohabitors reported that the women did either minor or severe violence to their male partners. Finally, 48 of every 1,000 couples said that the woman did severe violence to her male partner. If we compare this 48 figure with the comparable 34 figure for men, and if we also compare the 124 figure for women with the comparable 116 figure for men, we come to a surprising and unexpected conclusion: Women seem to be more violent than their male partners! However, what seems to be is actually an illusion, as we shall see throughout the next few pages.

Straus acknowledges that a number of feminists, as well as other researchers, have been highly critical of the investigations of domestic violence that he and his colleagues have done. For one thing, he himself notes that all of the foregoing numbers are probably understated. That is, both spouses and cohabitors are almost certainly being less than truthful in telling the interviewer about the violent acts they do to their partners. They are also being less than candid about violent acts their partners do to them. Straus adds that instead of concluding that 16 percent of all couples experience some sort of violence in any given year, the figure is probably closer to a third.

Historic Roots of Male Force   But there's something far more fundamental at stake than the question of how much U.S. couples under report domestic violence. The more basic issue is an understanding of what's actually happening during partner violence. By way of illustration, hearing the final score of a baseball game gives us very little sense of the dynamics of that particular game. To figure out what went on we have to know the back-and-forth processes (hitting, pitching, running, fielding) that took place between the two teams throughout the nine innings. To learn about those dynamics, we must either watch the game or read a play-by-play account written by someone who did. Few if any researchers, however, have ever watched adult men and women slapping, hitting, pushing, biting, kicking, choking, or knifing or shooting one another.

To help us understand what's going on in situations of domestic violence, Russell and Emerson Dobash say we must first get a "vision of what our ancestors were like and what forgotten social baggage they left us." Their research reveals that throughout recorded history many women, wives in particular, have been the victims of male violence. Just as the Old Testament story of Amnon and Tamar reveals that acquaintance rape has been around for quite a while, Dobash and Dobash show that husband violence against wives has been with us just as long.

Let's say that a police officer orders a citizen to submit to arrest. If the citizen submits peacefully, the officer is prohibited from using physical force on the citizen. If the citizen resists, the officer is permitted to use "reasonable" force, including hitting him or her with a club or even using a gun if need be. The cultural rules surrounding the arrest scenario say that the person with legitimate *authority* (the officer) should avoid using force, if possible, but if the person decides force is necessary, he or she may use it in restrained measure. Everyone agrees it's much more desirable for police not to use force. But in U.S. society, force by police officers is defined as sometimes requisite to maintain law and order.

Dobash and Dobash say that during the early Roman period a similar logic applied to husbands' use of force on their wives. Cultural rules gave the husband the responsibility and authority to maintain *order* over his entire household. If husbands failed to maintain order within their four walls, the Romans believed society would collapse. If a wife submitted to whatever the husband asked her to do in the pursuit of order, the Romans believed he should not use physical force on her. If, however, she opposed him and he decided that the use of force was necessary, force was "condoned and even praised for its beneficial effects on domestic order. Violence was considered unfortunate and excesses were condemned; a few Romans even rejected the use of violence to control women. Nevertheless, in the interests of social order, the vast majority of Roman citizens (the men, anyhow) accepted husband violence as legitimate for male (patriarchal) control of women.

During the 1600s and 1700s, most Christian churches in the New World mixed beliefs inherited from the Romans, as well as from British common law, with religious views regarding the subordination of women to men. Christian theologians of the day taught not only that God had ordained Africans to be slaves to white men, but that God also expected wives to be obedient to their husbands. If wives were obedient, men had no right to use force on them. But if a husband, who after all had the responsibility to God to maintain family order, decided that violence against his wife was necessary for order's sake, then he had the authority, indeed the obligation, to use it.

The Notion of Family Privacy   By the 1800s, men were legally permitted to "chastise" their wives without any fear of charges of assault and battery. Wives were told to " 'kiss the rod that beat them' " because it rescued them from their waywardness. Additionally, during the Jacksonian and Progressive eras, the family household (husband, wife, dependent children) became more private than it had ever been before. Not only could a rapidly expanding and prosperous middle class afford the type of sturdy housing that effectively shut out nosy neighbors and relatives, it became part of North American culture for outsiders to keep away from the family's "own business." The implications of the powerful cultural norm of family privacy for husband violence are quite obvious. Before that era, if a husband used excessive force on his wife (or children) the neighbors were very likely to know about it and to try to stop it. But as families became enclosed within

solidly built walls and became ever more culturally private, community and neighborhood control over husband violence became virtually nonexistent.

In recent years, the idea of community control over police violence has gained widespread acceptance. By contrast, the concept of community control over male, as well as parental, violence within households remains foreign to most U.S. citizens. Moreover, conservative religious groups vigorously oppose that concept. A 1980 bill introduced in Congress would, for example, have provided federally funded local community shelters for women and children seeking "safe haven"— places where women could flee their physically abusive men. Successfully opposing those shelters, the conservatives argued they would become "antifamily indoctrination centers."

The conservatives' fear was and is that official places of this type would legitimate the idea that the government can interfere in the sacred, and thus private, interactions that occur between husbands and wives. They believe that government interference would undermine the divinely given authority of the husband over his wife. It is not that they necessarily condone a husband using force on his wife. But if, in their view, a husband is unfortunately driven to that extreme, the matter is between God, him, and his wife. Outsiders, particularly the secular authorities, have no role whatsoever in the matter. An even stronger reason for their political opposition is that the shelters would also house the mothers' children. Because they believe that God commands them to use physical force on their children, the idea of the State keeping children sheltered from their fathers simply cannot be tolerated.

GENDER AND PHYSICAL FORCE

This historical background opens the way for us to better understand violence among couples who are erotic friends—who claim they *love* each other. It also gives us a clue about explaining the numbers that imply women are more violent than men. First, according to Dobash and Dobash, this background tells us that the label "marital violence," along with labels such as "family violence" and "spouse abuse," miss the mark—they are inaccurate. These labels "neutralize, sanitize, and provide euphemisms for wife abuse." Dobash and Dobash claim that the reasons those labels are inaccurate is that they're "gender blind": They ignore the historical reality that although men have for centuries had official permission to use force on their wives, *women never have had nor do they now have permission to use force on their husbands.*

In addition, labels such as "marital violence" ignore the physiological reality that men are bigger and stronger than women. For instance, do the labels "spouse abuse" or "marital violence" create the same images in the mind when the average woman hits, slaps, kicks, or punches a man as when the average man does those same things to a woman? As we think about it, we're likely to conclude that the numbers describing U.S. women as being more violent than men are extraordinary misleading. They're misleading because women's hits don't mean the same thing as men's hits. Even if a woman punches a man ten times, it's not likely to hurt as much, or cause as many bruises, abrasions, or broken bones, as when he punches her even once. If she kicks him on five separate occasions, the pain and suffering are likely to be considerably less than if he kicks her just once.

WOMAN ABUSE

Given these historical and physiological realities, Dobash and Dobash assert that the only accurate label to describe what's going on in many contemporary households is the label *wife abuse,* not "marital" or "domestic" violence. They say that instead of being gender blind, the label "wife abuse" is *gender aware.*

However, even the label wife abuse is much too narrow to capture the complete picture of male violence against women. In recent years a number of studies have shown that some male cohabitors and boyfriends also use force on their woman partners. A few studies even suggest that violence may be somewhat more common among cohabitors than among marrieds or dating couples.

Consequently, a more accurate label to describe what's happening is *woman abuse.* This label is plain, simple, and direct. It means that because of our cultural history and male muscle mass, many men use force of various kinds to control women with whom they share an erotic friendship. Men do not commonly use violence on co-workers or store clerks or librarians. Furthermore, men rarely if ever use force on women with whom they are just friends.

The puzzle then is why many men use force on women they profess to love—women with whom they share a unique kind of primary relationship. Straus and others say that the marriage license is a license to *hit.* It gives the husband cultural permission to use force on his wife. But we just learned that men without licenses—male cohabitors and boyfriends—also use force on their female partners. Officially, there have been laws on the books for about a hundred years prohibiting woman abuse. The laws are hardly ever enforced, however.

Dobash and Dobash say that the laws are overriden because whenever a man and woman form what they call a permanent relationship (erotic friendship), two things happen. First, their social network (friends and families, i.e., outsiders) recognize them as having a unique bond—they belong to each other in a special way. Because they're enclosed within their own social boundary, outsiders tend to stay out of their business. Consequently, social network control of couple violence becomes minimal. Even if outsiders know that woman abuse is happening, they often try to ignore it.

The second and perhaps more crucial thing that happens is that men develop a sense of possession and rightful domination over "my woman." Underlying the idea that "she has become mine—my lover, my sexual property" is the notion that a man might sometimes need to use physical force of one kind or another on my woman. People seem to accept the idea that somehow, because of the exclusivity and monogamy inherent to erotic friendships, male violence, though unfortunate, "happens, and can't be avoided—after all, this ain't a perfect world."

Incidentally, the idea that sexual property helps to justify physical force within erotic friendships may in part explain partner violence among both lesbian and gay male couples. Many of the things, gender differences in particular, that account for violence among heterosexual couples would not apply. But notions of property and feelings of jealousy could apply equally among heterosexual and homosexual couples.

Control via Physical Force   In any case, to label force as severe or minor based on how much physical damage the force does is highly misleading. The basic question is rather, to what degree does the woman feel that her partner controls her life via whatever level of force he applies? Studies show that many wives live in constant foreboding of their husbands' greater physical strength. Whether he uses it or not, his strength is an ever-present potential resource for controlling her that she can never hope to equal. In contrast, few if any healthy men live in fear of their partners' physical strength even if their women hit, slap, kick, or punch them. Healthy men rarely if ever define their partner's violence as a means of potential or actual control over their own lives.

Intriguingly, Cathy Greenblatt reports that *if asked directly*, most of the respondents in her study did not perceive men's violence as a means of exercising control over women. Instead, most felt that men became violent because they "got out of control"—violence happens because men lose charge of their passions, arms, or legs. Her respondents felt that a man should *not* use physical force on women; they did not outrightly approve of it. Nevertheless they believed there might be valid reasons explaining why he lost control, for instance the woman's sexual behaviors such as flirting with another man or actually having an affair. Or the couple might be having an argument about something and he just "flew off and hit her even though he didn't mean to." Or he might be drunk or on drugs, and so forth. In short, Greenblatt's respondents felt the action is "deplorable, but the hitter cannot be held accountable for his behavior." What about when women use force on men? Once again, most respondents disapproved of violence, but they were also willing to tolerate a woman's use of force because, "after all they are not likely to create physical injury."

Greenblatt's findings are complemented by a national study showing that some 20 percent of Americans believe it's okay to slap one's spouse on "appropriate occasions." Although the authors didn't follow up by asking what occasions these might be, we can fill in the blanks from Greenblatt's study. Male slapping is tolerated if the woman "drives" him to it. Female slapping is tolerated since it's self-defense and she can't hurt him anyhow. Interestingly enough, 25 percent of college-educated persons approved of spousal slapping, compared with only 16 percent of those with eight years or less of schooling.

Gender Traditionalism and Woman Abuse
Greenblatt wondered why women and men alike tend to absolve men of responsibility for woman abuse by blaming the victim: Why is it okay to explain his behavior by saying he simply lost control? Why wouldn't that explanation be acceptable on the job? In a dorm or store? Greenblatt suggests that many citizens absolve men due to continuing beliefs in the gender traditionalism displayed by Figure 12-1. Many persons still believe that when partners disagree, men "have the right to the final say, and when they are thwarted…they have the right as well as the power to use physical force." Since their partners are physically weaker than they are, men have little to fear from them. Nor do men expect reprisals from the police, courts, neighbors, friends, or kin. Furthermore, because women are generally not as economically autonomous as men (it's more difficult for women to support themselves and children), most men have little fear their wives will leave them even when they use force.

Straus and Smith report that each of the many studies they have done over the past two decades reveals that "male-dominant' marriages have the highest level of violence." Hence they agree with Greenblatt that the more gender-role traditional men are the more likely they are to use force on their wives; and the more gender-role traditional women are the more likely they are to tolerate it. Believing the husband is the Head of The Family legitimates the man's physical force. If a man thinks of himself as the Head, then he's more likely to cave in to those primal urges to use force on his wife (or cohabitor or girlfriend) than if he views her as an equal partner. If a woman defines him also as the Head, she's more likely to live with force even though she doesn't like it. Furthermore, research shows that the more strongly a person holds to fundamentalist religious beliefs the more likely she or he is to believe that the husband is indeed the Head of the wife.

In short, the man has the privilege of flying off the handle and using force, even though his actions are judged as unfortunate. He remains the ultimate authority figure in families. The fact that he's excused for not controlling himself gives him effective control over his partner. Because she knows he might lash out at any time, she must mind her words and actions in ways that men simply never have to with women.

Men need only mind their words and actions with other men lest the men get violent with them. Even when men use life-threatening force on women, their partners still have a tendency to excuse them. One of the women in Greenblatt's study was choked several times by her husband. Nonetheless, she claimed, " 'it wasn't serious because he didn't really want to hurt me.' "

Defining Violence as a Means of Control Those choking incidents also suggest that Straus's definition of violence is misleading. Violence, he says, is "an act carried out with the intention or perceived intention of causing physical pain or injury to another person." In these reported choking incidents, neither the husband nor the wife believed that the husband intended to hurt her. As a result, Straus might not label the choking as violent. The more important point is that in choking her the man effectively controls his wife's behavior. Even if she thinks, "He loves me, he doesn't mean to hurt me," being choked is hardly a pleasant experience. In future she is likely to do all she can to avoid provoking an outburst. To keep the peace (and possibly her life), she will probably go along with his agenda.

Research evidence shows that few women are likely to initiate force against a healthy partner.

The great bulk of women's acts of force are undoubtedly in "retaliation or self-defense." Tiptoeing around her man doesn't always work. A little thing she does or says, something the kids do or say, something that happened at work, "ticks him off" and makes him violent. To protect herself, or the children if he's beating up on them, she might hit, slap, or kick him. Her aim is to resist his physical force and to gain some semblance of order within a highly volatile situation. Her attempted force might indeed shock him into ceasing his abuse. On the other hand, it might incite him to escalate the abuse. Some husbands go so far as to shoot their wives. National homicide statistics show that 76 percent of female homicide victims are murdered by their spouses, and 21 percent are murdered by strangers. In spite of media attention to crime in the streets, women have much more reason to fear being murdered by their erotic friends than by strangers.

At the same time, a number of women abused by husbands or partners resort to knives or guns as a means of protection during a violent episode, or as a means to forestall future abuse. The Bobbitt incident described previously is probably the best known example of women reacting violently to an ongoing pattern of extreme partner abuse. The actual degree to which women attempt to defend themselves can be surmised by comparing the numbers of murders women perpetrate inside their household with murders they perpetrate *outside*. For example, in considering murders of "strangers" in the United States, only 10 percent are done by women. The finding that 90 percent of strangers are murdered by men shows that they are exceedingly more violent with strangers than women are.

By contrast, in considering the murders of spouses in the United States, 48 percent are done by women, and 48 percent by men. Why is there such a wide gap (10 percent versus 48 percent) between murders by women inside and outside their households? Simply put, women have little reason to murder strangers, but do have reason to murder their partners. Among the 132 women in the Chicago jail during 1976, 40 percent were held on charges of killing their male partners after the men had consistently abused them.

Woman Abuse and the Law   Until recently, state laws treated wives much more harshly for murdering husbands than they treated husbands for murdering wives. The reason, says Tong, is rooted in English common law, which defined husband killing as a "crime against the state." Since God and the State had made the husband the wife's *lord*, killing him was a form of treason analogous to murdering the king. If on the other hand he killed her, that was an unfortunate by-product of his duty to curb her waywardness and thus almost certainly justified. In the United States, wives who murdered spouses were not allowed to plead self-defense, because in legal jargon self-defense means the murder was justified. On the other hand, if a woman pled insanity (temporary or otherwise), she might perhaps be acquitted of the charge. The reason, says Tong, is that insanity excuses her behavior but does not justify it.

As part of a broad-based effort to reform its domestic laws, Florida passed a 1992 statute aimed at granting women greater latitude in making complaints of abuse against their partners. The wording of the law, however, described the issue as *spouse* abuse rather than *woman* abuse, unintentionally implying that women are on a level playing field with men when it comes to physical force. As a result, when an officer responds to an abuse complaint (almost always made by the woman), the officer is now required to evaluate the man's statements as fully as hers. Ironically, the result of that well-intended legal effort to achieve equity has been a substantial increase in the numbers of *couples*—the woman as well as the man—being arrested. The man tells the officer that the woman has been just as violent as he and, "What's more she started it!" Unable to sort out who's telling the truth in the midst of a very stressful setting, the officer simply arrests them both. Hence a law designed to assist victims is turning out to place greater limitations on women than ever before. A number of advocates fear that as more abused women discover how liable they are to be arrested for complaining, they'll become even less likely to complain and will simply "take it."

African-Americans and Woman Abuse   Because of the severe economic discrimination faced by black men in the white-controlled marketplace, researchers have wondered whether black men are more abusive than white men toward their partners. How likely is it that black men will take out their frustration with white discrimination and prejudice by abusing women they love? On the one hand, on the basis of the national studies of the U.S. population described above done in 1975 and 1985, Robert Hampton and co-workers found that black women were indeed more likely than white women to report that their male partners had been violent towards them. However, the differences between black male violence and white male violence were less in 1985 than they had been during 1975. On the other hand, on the basis of a study done in 1982 in a major southeastern metropolitan city, Lettie Lockhart did not support the idea that black men are more abusive than white men toward their wives. She compared African-American with European-American couples and found no significant differences in the proportions of women reporting that their husbands were violent toward them.

Tong says that whatever the level of abuse they face, "black women are even more prone than white women to excuse their husbands' violent behavior." Because black women are keenly aware of the discrimination their men face, they are more likely to make greater allowances for them when they lose control. As one of the black women in Tong's study put it, "'If he can't have things his way out in Whitey's world, at least he can have them his way at home.'" Tong adds that black women are also less likely than white women to report their man's violence to the police. One reason for their hesitancy is that, although the police are slow to respond to *white* women's requests for help against male violence, officers are even slower in their responses to such requests from black women. Aware of how long it takes to get official help, black women see little advantage in calling for it. A second reason black women are less likely to report their partner's violence is black distrust in general of the police. African-Americans perceive the police to be on their side in few if any social encounters. Even white women are uncertain whether the police will take their side in situations of male violence. Hence it should not be surprising that black women are much less likely to expect that the police will support them against their partners.

WOMAN ABUSE AROUND THE WORLD

Anthropologist David Levinson observes that woman abuse and parental violence against children are "a reality of daily life for many people around the world." To illuminate his point, he cites a love poem from India:

> Your abuse is the ring in my ear,
> Your blows are my toe-rings,
> If you kick me, it is my pulse and rice,
> The more you beat me with your shoes,
> The more we are united.

Levinson wanted to find out whether some societies had more or less woman abuse than other societies. If they did, *why? To* satisfy his curiosity he compared ninety "small-scale and peasant" societies from North America, South America, Oceania, Africa, Asia, the Middle East, Europe, and the Soviet Union. He found that some of those societies had much less, and some much more, wife beating than other societies. Indeed, some societies had no wife beating at all, including a grouping of some 10 million people who live in Central Thailand. Levinson concluded that the more family life is "characterized by cooperation, commitment, sharing and equality," the less likely it is that wife abuse will occur." Hence, looking again at Figure 12-1, we can say that the more strongly women and men prefer gender equality, the less likely it is that men will use physical force on their female partners and that women will tolerate it. These conclusions appear to be valid not only in a postmodern society such as the United States but also among developing societies around the world.

In his study of the Central Thai people of Bang Chan, where wife abuse is nonexistent, H. P. Phillips reported that women and men do identical kinds of work inside and outside the household. Their lives are what Figure 12-1 describes as highly interchangeable. Both genders do plowing as well as paddling of river boats.

Both genders also own and operate farms on an equal basis, share equitably in the inheritances from their families, and divide property equally in the event of divorce.

Phillips adds that individualism is central to the Bang Chan people, alongside a commitment to the idea of controlling aggression within families. *Individualism* to those people means that the rights and interests of women are just as important as those of men. The notion that the husband/male possesses final authority or headship over the woman has never been, nor is it now part of their culture. At the same time, they are keenly aware of the potential for physically stronger males to use force on women, and they consciously seek to avoid it. Unlike many persons in the United States, they simply do not accept the notion that male violence, though regrettable, is inevitable and unavoidable.

CONCLUSION—THE IRRESPONSIBILITY OF AGGRESSION

The last several decades have witnessed an expanding array of both economic and sexual options for women. Nevertheless, women, throughout their life courses, continue to be more severely coerced and constrained than men. Chapter 12 examines three forms of aggression by which men exercise constraints over women. The first is known as rape. "Consent" requires that the woman say yes and not say no to a man's sexual overtures. Many men (including husbands) ignore one or both of those conditions and force women whom they know into intercourse against their will, which is sexual assault, or rape.

The second example of aggression and coercion is called sexual harassment. Although sometimes connected with acquaintance rape, a great deal of harassment occurs quite apart from an actual sexual assault. Harassment involves subjecting women (and sometimes men) against their will to sexually tinged words or actions that the women find demeaning and offensive. Generally occurring in formal settings such as work or school, harassment takes on added significance when the harasser is in a position of authority over the woman. In such instances, her willingness to tolerate the harassment may result in certain rewards, but her unwillingness to do so may lead to penalties.

The final example of coercion is called woman abuse. To one degree or another many men use physical aggression, or its threat, to control women. It is a curious fact that men use physical force most frequently on the woman they profess to love. Their shared sexual bond appears to create a feeling of possession that apparently legitimates the use of male force.

Around the world, as well as in North America, the more strongly men hold to ultimate male headship and authority, the more likely they are to use physical force on women. At the same time, the less women accept patriarchal ideas as a way to organize relations between the genders, the less likely they are to live with physical force. In other words, the *more* women strive for equality with men, the less willing they are to accept the one thing that perhaps more than any other signifies inequality and subordination—being subject to harassment and violence.

This book is about reinventing families in a responsible manner. As the Modern Family declines, how can persons create varieties of postmodern families that attend to the wellbeing of all their members as well as the largest society? One of the best kept secrets of the Modern Family is its pervasive physical and sexual aggression. Because it damages wellbeing, aggression within families is plainly irresponsible. Hence, constructing today's families requires figuring out ways to minimize aggression. It appears that one way to minimize it is to encourage the social and cultural conditions that promote equality between the genders.

Sisters

by John Allman
1971

Their brother, Eastwick, had promised them a surprise, and Amelia hoped it meant money. She and Elizabeth stood on the elevated Ditmars Boulevard last stop of the BMT in Astoria, from which trains clattered and squealed back to Manhattan, then to Coney Island. Elizabeth, puffy from weeks of confinement, was pleased her phobias weren't acting up, and she'd not once suggested they turn back, looking instead through the streaked windows of the station platform toward the Triboro Bridge behind them, admiring how lights strung on the cables made two beautiful loops over the East River. "Look!"

Amelia thought she meant the flow of traffic on the bridge, and said, "Aren't you glad we don't drive?"

Elizabeth stared at the bridge towers and turned and said yes she was. Amelia was adjusting her coat, tugging at it here and there, glancing at the hemline to see if her dress showed.

Elizabeth shook her by the arm. "Will you please stop that?"

The train pulled in, brushing them back, and Amelia held Elizabeth by the hand while the passengers disembarked. They took a corner seat opposite black graffiti on the engineer's compartment and settled in to wait for the conductor's squawks over the PA, the snapping doors. They were going to 59th Street, to change for the IRT. Elizabeth with her recent weight gain looked like the older sister. Amelia continued to fidget in her birdlike way, as if she was the one recently out of Creedmoor. But it was Elizabeth who would suddenly get dreamy, her speech thick from the three-cornered pill. "I hope he's not going to ask us to move in with him again, like the last time when he bought that awful house." Elizabeth shivered in her lightweight gray coat, the only one that fit her now.

Amelia patted her hand. "He probably got included in a new catalogue and wants to surprise us with how well he's doing."

"It's the only time he ever calls us." Elizabeth drifted, reading opposite her an ad for gin, with the man in it dressed like a Renaissance prince.

"Oh, he's very busy, that's all it is. It's the way he is, busy and forgetful." Amelia wondered if she would ever forgive Eastwick for spending their father's insurance money on the business that had failed and left her and Elizabeth with nothing but her job in Martin's Paints and Elizabeth's disability checks. And now President Nixon was freezing wages and prices, as if it wasn't enough last year to shoot students, to promise to end a war that never ended. She and Elizabeth might have had their own house by now. She might have married Martin Cordes the grocer and had children and lived over the store and rented Elizabeth a room like the one on Crescent Street that she herself had fled to when she tried to leave Elizabeth on her own.

"We brought them, didn't we?"

Amelia reached into her purse and rattled two amber vials of capsules and pills.

Elizabeth sighed. "I don't think I'll need them. I'm doing pretty well, aren't I?"

"Yes, dear," Amelia said. She began to fidget, plucking at her coat, pinching the material here and there, pulling off lint like nits. It was a complex choreography and would terminate only when Elizabeth said, as she did, that Amelia was making her nervous. A middle-aged man entered the train at 30th Avenue, his eyes bloodshot and wattles forming at his throat. Amelia smelled the whiskey and wondered why it was the fumes always carried such distances. And why did they always sit opposite her? The man, not much younger than herself, lowered his chin into his chest and fell asleep.

"Amelia, please stop that!"

Amelia took Elizabeth by the sleeve, and they slid down the long seat toward the door. The car was still nearly empty. She tried to fold her hands in her lap, as Elizabeth, enjoying the return of her ability to read that somehow always revived whenever she was in hospital, read aloud the advertisements for employment agencies and ointments and mouthwash. Amelia knew it would be only a matter of weeks before Elizabeth complained about the print swimming in the *National Geographic*. She herself would have to read the TV program aloud each night, and then Elizabeth would insert the audio plug in her ear, the color picture flickering for hours in silence like a muted life-support system, while Amelia read and drank tea and smoked cigarettes and later took out the dog.

The man shifted, muttered, suddenly popped open his eyes, hiccoughed, and went back to sleep. Amelia wondered if he would sleep past his stop. Here she was regretting Martin Cordes who might have turned out like this. With Elizabeth home now, there'd be new sweaters and blouses and skirts to buy, since Elizabeth couldn't fit into even the old large-sized ones hanging in the back of the closet, where Amelia put them, knowing Elizabeth's cycles would never change and that Elizabeth would never buy anything in the thrift store. "I know what kind of life they had. I can feel it when I put on their clothes. I hate it." Here Amelia herself was, a pinky knuckle swelling with arthritis, ligaments in her hand strained from lifting paint cans in the store, friends like little Adelaide shying away because how often can a person come with you into pinesol-urine halls and sit on a long wooden bench next to a woman who'd cut her hair in shreds and was weeping like a drunk? A goddamn nervous wreck. She began tapping her foot. Martin wasn't so great.

Elizabeth stopped reading aloud. "Did you take Sandy out? That's all I thought about, taking him for a walk. I felt so good. But the way he pulls on the leash. I don't know if I'm up to it." She turned to a new ad. "Do you think Eastwick will be happy to see me? I'm glad you didn't tell him."

So was Amelia. Besides, he had probably been out of town, at his flea markets, selling his little pewter people. "Yes, dear," she said. "Don't worry about Sandy. You can't expect to do everything at once." She patted her sister's hand, and Elizabeth nodded and said, yes, she'd be able to do everything soon. Amelia studied the graffiti on the engineer's door and next to it a man's name. What kind of need was it to have one's name read by thousands of strangers? What kind of need was it that flared and cooled in a woman, and she thought of a poem fire and ice by someone. You'd think doctors knew something by now. Maybe if Elizabeth wrote her name in the subway cars, she'd have no need to see it written in clinical reports.

"Look at that!" Elizabeth pointed to a column of black smoke rising through the elevated trestle. An old frame house was on fire below, on 31st Street, and a dark, acrid fog brushed past their windows. Amelia had just enough time to look out, straining her neck as she peered down, to see the color of the house, gray, and its upstairs windows breathing flame. They heard fire engines blatting and roaring beneath the noise of their train. A pity, she thought. Even though these houses were next to the El, even though the trains racketed past day and night, buzzing the windowpanes, forcing a person to adjust her heartbeat to the rhythm of arrivals and departures, still, many of them were nice houses, neat, clean, possibly even with a small apartment that provided an income. She began to pick at the lint and dog hairs on her coat. She glanced at Elizabeth who was pronouncing "hemorrhoids" from an ad. Two young black men got on at the stop before Queens Plaza. They scowled at the sleeping drunk and moved to the middle of the car, where the thin one began talking about ergonomics.

"Do you think I'll be afraid in the tunnel? Did you bring them?"

Amelia opened her bag again to display the vials.

Elizabeth leaned against her and whispered, "Doesn't he stink?" Then she straightened up, and pointed to the third floor of an office building, the lit windows, rows of desks, on the same level of the train as it curved away from 31st Street toward Queensboro Plaza and the tunnel into Manhattan. "I used to work there, Amelia. Remember? God."

It startled Amelia to remember there had been a time when her sister could hold a job. That tall, dark young woman with an English jaw from their father's side, and a talent in art from no one's side, who was quick-tempered, who laughed, who gossiped with Amelia about her dates with Donny Clendenon, the muscular young man who wanted to be an engineer, who thought Elizabeth was beautiful. Who disappeared years ago, even before Elizabeth's all-night binges, the hours of nonstop talk, the terrors, the pills. Before she had ripped the caps off her front teeth and thrown them in the trash can—looking like a vampire, her filed incisors pitiably tenuous in the gaping hole of her mouth. Before Amelia tried to move away; the room in the basement, the house owned by a Greek-American couple. A quiet, tree-lined street, within walking distance of Elizabeth, but far enough away. She could hear the father tell his children, "You don't bother the nice lady in the basement." That room with all its exits and entrances. A front door opening onto a small flight of stairs to the street and a broken chainlink gate. A back door leading into the furnace room. A staircase behind her studio couch leading upstairs to a door with no lock that led to the family hallway between the kitchen and their staircase which led to their bedrooms. All those doors and stairs. And then two boys pulling at her purse on the nice tree-lined street and calling her names and ripping the purse away while she cursed and felt her arm almost pulled out of its socket. And the policeman later asking if they were black when they weren't.

Elizabeth was leaning against the window, hands in her lap, and she turned to whisper in Amelia's ear, "What do you think the surprise is?" Amelia had tilted her head back and was gazing at the ads above without reading them, knitting and unknitting her fingers. Elizabeth, so much taller than Amelia, began to drone from a height. "Little Adelaide hasn't come to see us yet. If I was her I wouldn't come to see me either. I'm a tub. Look." She held up her long hand and wriggled her fingers. "They're so puffy with water I can hardly button my coat." Her tone, in someone else, would have been boredom condescension, the voice of doctors who Amelia had sat so often in front of. "Your daughter is a very . . ." one had said, outside the locked ward in Elmhurst General. She had yelled at him, "You mean my sister!" her little body gathered into a furious knot, exploding. She had held her hands almost comically over her head. "Wait a minute! Wait a minute!"

"Well, I don't know," Amelia said. "You can't tell with him."

"No. You can't." Elizabeth seemed to lose interest and began massaging her fingers, saying, "This little piggy went to market . . . "

Amelia looked at her watch. What did he want? His business was doing well. He'd been in three more gift catalogues under "E. D. Ferris Sculptures." There was his little statue of Shakespeare reading a book. There was the dog carrying a newspaper in her jaws. And the tree with a boy and girl somehow attached to it that Eastwick called "Eden." He had years ago changed his name from Henry and converted two rooms in his apartment into work and storage space. It was there he designed, manufactured, and assembled the pewter figures displayed in gift catalogues. She'd met him once at a flea market on Queens Boulevard, where he had brought his festively decorated pushcart, and wore his funny hat, and blew on the whistle he'd attached to an upright rod. He was singing ditties, tooting the whistle, and grinning so widely she thought he'd been overtaken by illness—short, grown plump, his hair quite thin, his eyelids wrinkled and loose so that they pushed upward in myriad folds, his blue eyes darting side to side, as he chuckled. It was like him to do this, to appear the fool. In his heart. In his heart, an emptiness, and in his eyes.

"I hope he's not going to ask us to move again. Do you have any gum or something? I'm so dry." Elizabeth made unpleasant smacking sounds opening and closing her mouth. "God." Amelia dug out a rectangle of sugarless bubble gum, unwrapped it, and placed it in her sister's extended hand. Elizabeth began chewing, saying, "Umph."

"We can't anyway," Amelia said, placing her purse between them. "We can't afford anything." She tried to emphasize the last word, without suggesting their funds were dangerously low. Or that it was Elizabeth's fault. Or that they couldn't afford

Sandy's dogfood, though she'd been reading about old people living on Alpo. She didn't want to imply that she couldn't get credit in the grocery run by that Indian man.

"You got anymore? I need another one." Elizabeth was sucking her cheeks together, and Amelia withdrew another stick of gum and placed it in her sister's hand. *You got a nickel?* Things tumbled together. Just as she again began thinking of Martin Cordes, Amelia remembered brick highrises separated by lawns and curved driveways, with only the fences and the gratings on windows to suggest an institution. Inside, the flaking green walls, the elevators with double doors and locks; the abandoned reception area on the first floor; odors of canned vegetables and Salisbury steak. People sat on benches along the path that led up to Building #31. They almost looked normal. The black man in dungarees, the middle-aged woman in the green coat (too heavy for September), the boy who looked up at the sky and who but for an odd wobble of the head appeared as capable as herself. Every time she went, the same woman, her age indeterminate, dark-blonde hair stringy, dirty, uncombed, as if she'd pushed through a briar patch, eyes bleared. "You got a nickel? I just need five cents more." Several patients lounged near the empty reception desk, observing her response. She knew what would happen if she gave in. They'd ask for cigarettes. A ride home. A pencil. She knew what giving the first nickel meant. "No dear, I have no money." The woman wandered to the front door, out into the path, looking for visitors. The other patients wandered off as well.

"Do you remember when I worked for the pickle company?" Elizabeth, chewing vigorously, turned away from reading the ad about pickles, where a stork resembling Groucho Marx held up a jar many times the volume of his body. The train had come to a halt at Queensboro Plaza, hissed open its doors, and was waiting for the arrival of the express. "I could have been a supervisor. Do you remember that?" She poked Amelia.

A four-room apartment with the old pull-chain toilet in the building on 28th Avenue. Windowpanes loose from dried-out putty. Their father's bedroom off the kitchen. The fire escape outside the bedroom she shared with Elizabeth since Eastwick was married and living in Bala Cynwyd and the downstairs cat came up the fire escape to their window bawling for the bits Elizabeth gave him. Father smelling of tires and motor oil from his job at Strauss Auto Parts and asleep over the detective novels he read by the score, the odor from his bedroom of something unwashed and sad ever since mother died, her breast cancer sudden, absolute, unexpected in a thin woman so active, her blue eyes and smallness like Amelia's and Eastwick's, and Elizabeth's olive skin and quick temper from father who was dark and handsome, though his father had had blue eyes, his mother, their Nana, still visiting them, though with the wine on her breath father would shout at her and later fall asleep over his book, the scent of Goodyears blending with his mother's port, and the girls holding their noses, giggling, until he awoke and said, "What's going on out there?" Nana already asleep on the couch in the small living room with the Admiral TV and combination Philco radio/phonograph, Mr. Stokowski the baker downstairs singing in his baritone and the planes thundering overhead going to LaGuardia Airport or her friend Bella's Uncle Frank the iceman roared with laughter that poured out of a first-floor window, into the alleyway, and Elizabeth said she didn't know how much she liked Donny. Amelia said it didn't matter and they put their hands over their mouths when Mrs. Webster next door was screaming and pulling the stove out of the wall because she had five children and a photographer husband home from the war with one leg, and his enlargement equipment filled up their bathroom. You didn't have room to sit and pee. Their mother's best friend, Elsie Webster, a big woman who said she'd be their mother now. Bitsy sitting on the couch, rocking forward to her knees, and back, banging her head into the small depression she'd made in the upholstery. Louise who spoke so low no one could hear her. Little Leon with the rock-like head other boys liked to beat on. Baby Eddie. And Sally, the oldest, her big breasts the talk of all the boys who hooted and guffawed.

"I just hated it!" Elizabeth said. "And the smell. God." She emerged briefly into clarity and anger

that Amelia hoped would last until they got to Manhattan. At least to 59th Street. The train sat, humming, doors open, a few more people drifting in. The woman wearing a hat like the one Amelia remembered on Nana—a kind of black beret fastened to her thin hair with a long hatpin—sat down away from them, a shopping bag tucked between her legs.

"I'm getting nervous." Elizabeth leaned against her sister. "Look." She extended her trembling hand for examination.

"It's just the waiting," Amelia said, taking the hand and bringing it down into Elizabeth's lap. "You're doing fine. Just think of something pleasant." She tried it herself. "Little Adelaide said she'd like to take a Circle Line cruise around Manhattan. I'll call her."

"Yeah, sure. We can all jump in the river." Elizabeth exhaled with force. "Why not." She leaned forward, as if to put her head between her knees. The woman with the beret tried to move further into the steel armrest she was already pressed into. "Jesus." Elizabeth seemed to address the floor. "I can feel the blood enter my head. My *brain*."

Amelia was thinking about money. Thirty thousand dollars. Gone. Like that. Eastwick's embarrassment, his upper eyelids wrinkled and pouched, his ear lobes pendulous. A grossness overtaking him. All that money in his ad agency that was going to return their money doubled in less than two years. In the beginning, his contacts from previous jobs, the one with UPS, a soft drink firm, an oil company. His ads appearing in *Good Housekeeping*. Then terrible things like the war and the arithmetic of dead bodies. His drinking worsened. Elizabeth's condition. Their incredulity as the admitting psychiatrist told them conventional therapy wouldn't work. Eastwick's horrified expression. More drinking. His promise to help and his protests he couldn't take this. Not this. The woman doctor leaning over her scarred desk, in her thick European accent telling them how important they were to Elizabeth. How much she loved her brother, the very man who sat trembling and nodding, while Amelia felt excluded even as she knew who would take Elizabeth back and forth, who would hold her hand after the electroshock treatments and tell her she seemed so much clearer (which she did), Eastwick spending his nights in terrible arguments with his wife, weeping, drinking, threatening to drive his car into a crowd of people.

Elizabeth sat up, the blood draining from her face. "God." Amelia noted the small pits in her sister's cheeks. She'd not thought about or noticed them for weeks. She remembered how they'd worked on Elizabeth's body. Vitamins. Tests for hormonal balance because her cycle was so irregular and she bled so much or not at all. No salt or sugar. Elizabeth improving, until one night as if from boredom she sat down and said, "It can't be that, it can't be that. I'm hearing voices. Voices!" And they both were frightened, Amelia now so anxious there were days she too was almost afraid to go out, and she thanked God she had to go to work. But they kept at it, as if somewhere they could find the rotted place where Elizabeth's mind had become unmoored. They surmised that if Elizabeth felt better about her appearance, she could go out more regularly. So they had her skin scraped, to eliminate the pits incurred by acne. For weeks, they watched the raw, red patches healing on her cheeks. And hoped she'd be able to walk down Steinway Street to look in shop windows or take a bus by herself. That was when she ripped the caps off her teeth—so recently paid for by Welfare (she still needed bridgework for two missing teeth). Amelia frightened for the first time because Elizabeth raved and threw the toaster against the wall, like Elsie Webster, while Amelia kept all the pills and structured each day around the probability of an episode; whether Elizabeth had enough cottage cheese on hand for her constant dieting (whether the new medication did not forbid the ingestion of cheese); whether that first analyst years ago who in addition to his treatment had become Elizabeth's lover for two weekends, whether that man should not be found and shot.

"Will you please stop that!" Amelia had been trying to turn down Elizabeth's collar but Elizabeth pushed her hand away. Amelia sighed. The train just stood here, and Eastwick would be polite but irritable. She imagined how he'd take their coats, swinging them over his arm, chuckling,

saying it didn't matter that they were late. When it did.

Hours later, in the bright light of the 59th Street station, Elizabeth, her coat open, was looking down at her stomach, touching it tentatively. "I think the chicken made me sick." Only a handful of people had changed from the IRT. A man with dark circles around his eyes was rubbing the arm of a large woman with orange-red hair who laughed loudly. Several teenage boys were shoving each other playfully down the other end of the platform. Elizabeth licked her lips, then brought her mouth down into an expression of sadness, like the mask, Amelia thought, on a high-school drama textbook. (Amelia was always the intelligent one, Elizabeth the talented one. "Born with a book under her arm," their mother said, "and this one drawing pictures of the doctor holding her upside down.") One for tragedy. One for comedy.

"Ugh." Elizabeth seemed to be tasting something sour. Amelia reached into her purse for the foil-wrapped antacid tablets, freed one, and said, "Here," lifting it to her sister's mouth. Elizabeth closed her eyes and took it. "If you chew it, it'll get into your system faster," Amelia said, snapping her purse shut.

"You know I can't stand the taste," Elizabeth said, opening her eyes and staring at the black "59" on the support post in front of her. She shivered and closed her coat. "What if I get sick in the tunnel?"

"You won't. Just don't think about it. Think about something pleasant." Amelia leaned gingerly over the platform, looking for the train. Elizabeth pulled her back, and Amelia struggled out of her grasp. "Don't do that!" Amelia scolded.

"Well, don't you do that!" Elizabeth put her hands over her face and sobbed. "What's wrong with me?"

Girls, come in! Eastwick had kissed each of them on the cheek and told them to have a seat in the small living room he'd brightened and enlarged with mirrors on white walls. Amelia hated having to see herself every time she stood in this room. And Elizabeth's furtive studies of her own image did nothing but darken her gloomy mood on seeing how deteriorated she looked, though with the extra weight, and in spite of periodic agitations, she seemed, Amelia thought, languid and removed. More bored than frightened. A bit spoiled. And as she tried to keep the attention off herself, watching Elizabeth smile wanly at the approaching white cat Eastwick had named Miranda, Amelia was startled to hear her brother conversing in low tones with someone in the kitchen.

It had been easy to conclude that Jessica was the surprise. A stiff-necked blonde woman with a round face like Eastwick's who often brought her hand to her mouth in mock dismay like the English actresses Elizabeth watched on Channel 13. Eastwick's broad, pinkish face lit by wine and excitement, his neatly trimmed mustache and designer peach shirt with thin stripes and French cuffs, almost out of fashion, reminding Amelia that this man wore party hats at flea markets. Jessica, a high-school guidance counselor, had met him at a handicrafts fair in Rockland County and thought him immensely amusing (the way she said it, like Joan Greenwood in *Kind Hearts and Coronets*). But she talked with her chin dropped to her chest, staring at Amelia over her glasses, smiling demurely, and sounding, too much for Amelia's taste, like one of the social workers she was always sitting with, while doctors' names were announced over the PA that was chiming *bong bong*. And Elizabeth saying, "You devil, you didn't say," prodding Eastwick and putting on her best goofy smile (it was always that, when she tried to conceal the missing eyetooth, curling her lip over the vacancy), Jessica laughing rigidly, her blue eyes as steady in their gaze as Amelia's.

"Here." Amelia opened her purse again, stepping further back from the edge of the platform. "I've been saving this." From the plastic vial, she dumped a blue three-cornered pill into her hand. Elizabeth scowled. "I thought I had to wait another hour." Amelia assured her it wouldn't matter. She had gotten so excited she'd used up the previous dose, her metabolism was up, it was the right time, biologically speaking.

Elizabeth threw her head back and exhaled violently. "How can I take it without water?"

"Just let the saliva collect in your mouth, then one, two, it's down."

"I can't, my mouth's too dry from that tablet." It was like the afternoons Amelia would call to remind her to take the two pills on top of the refrigerator. One for anxiety. One for depression. She never left more than one dose in the house. And Elizabeth would resist. Why didn't Amelia leave the pills in the house and she'd just use them when she needed them? Amelia reminded her the pills had to be in her system for days before they would work. They had to be taken regularly.

"I'm feeling better," Elizabeth said. "I am. I think I am."

Amelia returned the pill to its vial, and began to pluck lint from her coat, working up her left sleeve, then the right. She ought to call Adelaide, who usually came over for tea, talking with them in her jittery way, smoking, thin, her hair a synthetic black from the hair salon on Broadway she was always trying to get Amelia and Elizabeth into, arguing against grayness, sometimes talking about men as if her Hank might come back from whatever place he'd taken his good looks to. Sometimes she'd talk about their friend Lucille. Amelia remembered Lucille's flaccid arms around her when she went to see her that last time only a year ago, Lucille's abdomen swollen like a pregnant uterus, her husband Joe moving around the apartment as quiet as a deaf nurse, doing everything. Reminding Amelia of herself. Was cancer worse than being crazy? But if she'd been the way Lucille was years ago, outgoing, what would she have said when the doctor with his purplish mouth and creased dark face told her Elizabeth's illness was genetic, a form of schizophrenia, she'd seem normal for periods of time, but . . .? Lucille would have slapped his face. And that day Adelaide told her, after Amelia described how Elizabeth's cycle varied whereas her own was like clockwork, Adelaide said she, Amelia, could have had lots of children and probably would never have had veins showing in her legs.

Really younger! That's what Jessica had said, talking about her ex-husband and why she'd left him after he'd ruined his knees playing tennis with young women. As little-girlish as she seemed, tilting her head, pursing her lips, shrugging her shoulders, there was something more judgmental in her than Eastwick was aware of. Amelia would bet on it. "Oh, I can't," Elizabeth said, as Eastwick opened an expensive bottle of real French Burgundy. "Of course!" he said, and slapped his head. "Stupid!" He rushed into the kitchen for the small bottles of lemon-flavored seltzer. And Amelia reached over to brush back the coarse, gray wisp of hair that tended to fall over Elizabeth's right eyebrow, replying in the plural when Jessica asked her about herself, "Oh, we have this small apartment, and Elizabeth takes care of it, and the dog . . ." her portrait of their domestic economy skewed to Elizabeth's putative capabilities.

Elizabeth leaned now against the "59" on the steel pillar, her dyspeptic spasm replaced by a dreamy thoughtfulness, her body round and pressing outward in the thin coat. "I guess we'll be famous now, in that catalogue."

"I hope not!"

"Do you think he really likes Jessica?"

"I think he'll make a fat little statue sitting on a sofa with her legs crossed and call it, 'The Girlfriend.'" It certainly had been a surprise. Amelia flapping her hand at the cheeses Eastwick put out and telling him, "She can't have that with this medication." Elizabeth asking just a little? hovering dark and plump over the tray of Jarlsberg, Boucheron, and an oozy wedge of something unknown to either of them. "You know what might happen," Amelia warned, and Elizabeth annoyed asked for more seltzer then. But with the seltzer Eastwick came back pushing a table on wheels, just as Jessica was saying how once she almost died from eating shellfish, detailing her trip to the hospital in an ambulance, her husband in his tennis shorts limping, useless. Eastwick said, "Ta-daaa!" He snatched the white cloth away that covered the table—Amelia discerning beneath the cloth, before he had whipped it off, three peaks of something poking upward, as if the cloth were really a cerement. All happening again but slowly. Jessica gasping appreciatively. Eastwick saying, "I call it, 'The Sisters,'" smiling in his professional way, draping the cloth over his forearm like a waiter, while Amelia and Elizabeth stared. The

two pewter figures were holding hands. One had long hair, or a simulation of it scratched into a snoodlike tab that hung from a head rather small for a body made wide by a triangular dress. The other girl was kicking a leg outward and the dress seemed to billow. She too had a small head, her cartoon smile and pinhole eyes identical to the other's. The sisters were not pleased. "Which one is me?" Elizabeth asked. "I suppose I'm the one with the dress." She allowed herself to touch it, running her finger along the edge of the triangular garment that looked stiff as a frozen sail and was a geometrical variation on the shape of her hair. It gave the impression that the girl would be swept away in the first wind, were it not for the sister holding her hand. Eastwick protested that really it wasn't meant to be Amelia and Elizabeth exactly, and he was hoping for a big run next spring. On closer inspection, it was not clear why the other girl was kicking out her leg—whether she had lost her footing or was shooing something like a pigeon. It was difficult to imagine either girl in an actual physical universe. The figure with the nearly equilateral dress would never have been able to sit down or fit through a doorway. The other was doomed to pivot on one leg, like a geometer's compass, her tiny outstretched foot searching for contact. Amelia thought the girl in the billowing dress must be Elizabeth, while the more dowdy figure was herself, faithfully there, stolid, immovable. She said nothing at first, watching Elizabeth begin to worry her right cheek, searching out the small pits that had survived the skin scraping and smiling in a deadpan way that was startlingly similar to the expression on the pewter faces. "Are you going to put them in the catalogue?" Elizabeth asked. It was then Jessica said, "I wish I had a sister." "Do you?" Amelia responded.

"Do you think she liked us?"

"You were fine, just fine. Anyone would have thought so." Amelia stepped up and brushed the stray hair back off her sister's forehead and rubbed from a corner of her mouth the bit of white powder left from the antacid tablet. "Anyone." And she thought of Martin Cordes. The early days, when she shopped for just milk and bread in his store, embarrassed that other times she went to

Grand Union across the street for specials. He had such a nice smile, and his little accent, and she never had to ask for credit. Elizabeth was still holding a job, sharing the apartment, their father dead a few years. Eastwick using their money. Martin not much taller than she, his bushy eyebrows, an elfin twist in the corner of his mouth when she said something witty, his tidy hands at the slicing machine as he gathered a half-pound of ham off the whirling blade, the first dates in Italian restaurants where he rated the prosciutto and mozzarella and told her how much he respected her and about his late wife a Scotch woman whose legs Amelia remembered were terribly bowed. And he wasn't that much older than Amelia. But she couldn't remember if their few nights of sex had been exciting. He was so patient about Elizabeth who was getting worse and worse. He'd nod and make sympathetic sounds with his lips that she always thought tasted of cold cuts. "Well . . ." he'd say again and again. "Well . . ." All she could talk about was Elizabeth. Elizabeth's moods. Elizabeth's weight. And that time Elizabeth had come at her and she called the police who took them both to the hospital where she sat on a bench near some drunk who'd dropped his pants at a local bar, and Elizabeth was taken up in the elevator with a nurse and policemen who had handcuffed her. No harm to herself. Amelia swore never to call the police again. Never.

"Maybe I should take the pill now." Elizabeth tried to gather saliva in her mouth, working her jaws as if she were chewing something, but looking, Amelia thought, like a cow. "I can't, I just can't." Soon she would begin losing weight, buying slacks and blouses in sizes she already had in her closet. She couldn't wear the old clothes, and she couldn't give them away. "Someday I'll wear them. But not now." She'd talk about going on job interviews, if she could take the bus, if it didn't make her nervous. The TV flickering in the living room where she sat with Sandy the cocker spaniel, his long ears sour-smelling, a dried effluvium in the corners of eyes otherwise forever moist. The syringe-like audio plug inserted in her left ear— the hearing in her right ear damaged from a wrong medication. She *was* hearing voices.

They couldn't agree which of them was the pewter sister kicking her foot out. When Amelia said, "Oh, I suppose you're right," Elizabeth snapped, "Don't humor me. Just don't humor me!" She began to pace back and forth, rubbing her arms. "Listen," Amelia said, "it's coming." They heard a clink in the tracks. A soft rumble. They craned over the platform and peered into the tunnel.

that henry wouldnt & time lost l was taken by extraterrestrials little soft heads like starving children their underwater eyes & fuliginous man with darkness in his fingers the smell of burnt hair the daubed electro-jell did i cry out? tell me if i said anything melia you never talked back to daddy & henry & daddy saying dont run around the house like that in my panties dr esposito in out in out dr dorothy saying softness within you feel your finger a moistness donnys hand his thing in my hand his teeth scraping my nipples donny tongued and i wouldnt no the swelling they bent over me the light round & glaring like a dentists lamp they mumbled because they had no lips their mouths like gauze i heard them i was empty i wasn't no one mrs weber pulling the stove from the wall screaming & me & bitsy on the couch rocking back and forth the voice theres nothing here saying he wanted me eastriver dressballoon god wanted me floating between triboro bridge & hellsgate bridge the trains thumping between black hell lace the girders black lace hellsgate dr espositio said the tunnel the lid closing the dirt dumping thumping i did once i did the voice said open yr eyes the pink lining the satin pillow under yr daddyhead you died i ripped out my teeth before my lips rotted away they had no mouths they had my time they had white cotton fingers they were children spinning a rope jumping my name is alicia im from alabama my name is barbara im from barbados my name is cynthia im from cincinnati who i wa wa the trees green & floating astoria park like a country in a book like a fairytale dr expositio said its only a story dr expo said explaining i you sleep inside the bramblebush has sweet smelling little floribunda white stars & thorns donny you you the voice youll wake oh yes but youre there in the box i pulled my teeth away and sank in saltiness estuary that is the something pulling sucking the tide the tidal knot around the ankles tied he said you can do me then tied & i wanted him to dr exponential do mommy someday youll be a great artist you didnt say that & yr eyes looking away yr eyes underwater & daddy carrying a bunch of mommybones kissing them bones you wont breathe there the noise the noise of buses & trains the woman trying to bite her arm the smell im burning im cooking im lying on a metal table I cant swallow that im too dry melia too your finger down my throat like wouldnt you? gagging henry & our gray pewter legs kicking that woman & sandy home wagging eating my fingers only not hurting down my throat ten at a time in there closing my bowels opening because I couldnt nails & hair still growing drool coming out of my mouth their cotton fingers pressing my uterus my lungs nothing on the scale the top of my skull lifted like a lid so i could breathe & dr express changing among the girders the train taking me teeth gone one of henrys jokes mmma mmma w/o front teeth lips pulled over his gums their gauze mouths taking time my time that never was the voice you bad you bad

"It's coming."

Elizabeth braced herself.

AGING, THE FAMILY LIFE CYCLE, AND LIFE COURSES

by John Scanzoni

What does it mean to *age* responsibly? This has no simple answer. The idea that people age has always been intertwined with the idea that people live in families. Earlier chapters talked about the many ways people are making changes in families. Similarly, people are making changes in aging. Just as we've tried to figure out what responsibility means in terms of changing families, we'll now ponder what it means to *age* in a responsible manner.

"Hey," says Ned to Ted as they meet strolling their children in the park: "You have a good-looking kid! How old is he?" "He's 19 months old" replies Ted. *Old* at 19 months? How can a *child* be old? If Ted were wheeling his 98-year-old grandmother, we might agree that's old. But 19 months? The answer, of course, is that *old*, like *beauty*, lies in the eye of the beholder. Like all the labels used in this book, "old" can be perceived and defined in many ways. Ted is aware, for example, that although his child hasn't been around very long, the process of aging has already set in. In fact, aging began as soon as the child was born.

But that isn't what Ted's talking about, nor what Ned understands. What Ted actually means, and what Ned understands, is that his child is 19 months *grown*. For a child, aging is viewed as a process of growth and development. *Old* means movement toward becoming an independent and competent adult. For the toddler, many important and highly significant years lie ahead. The very core of our understanding of childhood is that nothing is ever standing still.

As children age, they grow physically stronger and mentally more alert. With each passing year they extend their degree of control over their lives. "What are you going to be when you grow up?" reminds them that childhood and adolescence are not permanent statuses. Nor do the youths want them to be. They want to grow up. They perceive adulthood as a time when they can finally take charge of their own lives instead of being controlled by adults. The curious thing is that, although every youth wants to age ("I want to be 16 so l can drive; 18 so I can vote; 21 so l can drink"), *no adult wants to keep on aging*. It's actually not so odd, because up to a point biological aging corresponds with an increase in the degree of control a person has over her or his life. The word "old" describes Ted's grandmother because, among other things, she has little control over her existence. She's at one polar extreme while her 24-year-old great-granddaughter, Monika, is at the other. Monika's just finished college and has taken a good job. She feels more m control of her life than she ever has before.

Already, however, Monika senses the paradox that with continued aging comes the threat of loss of control. She can't seem to do much, for instance, about the almost imperceptible decline she's recently noticed in her physical beauty. And although Monika's always managed to keep her weight under control, suddenly she finds herself 10 pounds above the charts and counting. Much grimmer is the news she's just received about her 30-year-old cousin, a professional dancer and dance instructor. He's been diagnosed with multiple sclerosis (MS). The incurable disease is gradually causing him to lose control of his legs. As that happens, he perceives his whole life becoming chaotic and pointless. Monika is shocked—it's bad enough to be 30, to say nothing of having one's life shattered by such an uncontrollable, and often fatal, illness.

Monika has a particular view of her past, present, and future life. Her view is probably shared by most persons of her age and education, especially if they've been fortunate enough to find a good job. She views her childhood and adolescence as having been a time of steadily increasing control of her life in every dimension—physical, mental, emotional, social, and financial. The present is seen as a kind of plateau during which her cousin's illness, along with many other things, impresses her with the fact that life can indeed spin out of control. Nevertheless, Monika views the future with guarded optimism. She expects to

be able to maintain full control of her life. To achieve that goal she intends to keep on growing mentally, emotionally, and socially, and she hopes to earn enough money to continue being economically autonomous. She intends to cope with her body's aging as best she can by staying fit via aerobic exercise and "eating right."

CONTROL AND RESPONSIBILITY

Arlene Skolnick describes Monika's view of her life as part of an emerging "life course revolution."' According to Skolnick, the *revolution* lies with the different ways today's persons are beginning to view the courses of their lives. Aging has always been an inevitable fact of being alive. The big question is, how do people respond to aging? Until the advent of modern medicine, sanitation, and nutrition, people passively accepted the idea that fate alone determined how long their lives would be. The science and technology of the twentieth century have brought about dramatic changes in how long people in industrial societies can expect to live. Now, instead of passively accepting fate, persons can actively take control to increase their longevity. The *quantity* of their years is expanded significantly through proper diet, sanitation, antibiotics and vaccines, laser surgery, and so on.

A growing number of researchers are saying that a similar kind of revolution is spreading in the social sciences such as sociology and psychology. Here the revolution focuses on the *quality* of the increased number of years available to many persons. These researchers believe that life quality is achieved in much the same way as life quantity: Persons actively seek to take greater control over their lives. Consequently, researchers are beginning to study "human control" (also known as *human agency)* in contemporary societies. Chapters 5 and 11 talked about the feelings of well-being that arise from perceiving that one is participating effectively in the control of one's erotic friendship. But a person's life consists of many realms. To feel good about herself in general, Monika needs to feel she has a reasonable amount of control not only over her erotic friendship but also over her health and her job.

That's where responsibility enters the picture. Control over one's life course goes with the moral obligation to love oneself. In part, the life course revolution means that a moral person is obliged to take charge of her or his life course as fully as possible. Loving oneself, and thus taking care of oneself implies that it's irresponsible to sit back passively and merely accept that "what will be will be." Taking over the management of one's life course is a topic to which sociologists have only recently turned their attention. Previously, sociologists were preoccupied with social control. The topic of social control is, "How does society get persons to do what they're supposed to do to achieve social order?" The answer? Socialization via The Family, church, and school. If people still don't conform, punish them via the legal system. Today, by contrast, sociologists are asking, "How can persons do what they must to achieve a sense of life-course control and thus experience the well-being that accompanies it?"

Premarital stage (expected to be childless)

Marriage (expected to be first marriage)

Pre-first child stage (expected to be brief)

First-child stage

Second-child stage

Third-child stage (and so on, if additional children)

Stage of youngest child in elementary school

Stage of youngest child in middle school

Stage of youngest child in high school

Youngest child leaves home

Parental empty-nest stage

Death of one spouse

Death of other spouse

FIGURE 14.1 Family Life-Cycle Stages

AGING AND THE FAMILY CYCLE

One of the most popular ideas that stemmed from the old views of socialization and social control was known as the family life cycle (FLC). It was popular because it blended important social behaviors with biological aging. The basic idea of FLC is simple indeed: As persons age biologically they behave in socially appropriate ways. The behaviors are "appropriate" because they promote the well-being of The Family and also of society. By way of illustration, biology courses often display diagrams describing the life cycle of a plant. A plant grows to maturity and then develops seeds. The seeds drop off or blow away and fall into the soil. Meanwhile, the parent plant dies. The seeds sprout a new plant, which follows precisely the same cycle of growth, reproduction, and death as the parent plant.

Figure 14-1 shows how in similar fashion the life-cycle idea was applied to the pre-sixties' family. A heterosexual couple—Lester and Amelia—married during their early 20s. Since neither had ever had children, they were placed in the *childless* stage of the family life cycle. Within a year they had their first child, and thus they shifted to the next stage, which was often called the infant stage. (The key to figuring out which stage a family is in is generally the age of the youngest child.) When the second child came along two years later, Lester and Amelia's family remained chiefly in the infant stage, even though they were also partially located in the *toddler* stage. Two years later their third child was born and they now found themselves partly in three stages: *preschool*, toddler, and infant. Since most of their energies and efforts were presumably devoted to their youngest child, they remained chiefly in the infant stage. Finally Nan, the fourth child, was born and they were now partly in four stages: *early grade school*, preschool, toddler, but most of all, infant.

Figure 14-1 displays the subsequent stages in the cycle. By the time Nan entered first grade, the family was chiefly in the early grade-school stage, even though the ages of Nan's older siblings placed the family partially in later stages. As Nan and her sibs matured biologically, family stages shifted accordingly, until finally Nan entered her junior year in high school. The family was now in the *later high-school* stage, and Nan's sibs were no longer living at home. When Nan went off to college, Lester and Amelia's family was finally in the *empty-nest* stage. Although parent birds in the wild seldom stay around the nest or each other once their offspring are mature enough to leave, few researchers have pushed the nest metaphor that far. Lester and Amelia remained in the empty-nest stage and enjoyed being grandparents. After a time, Lester retired from his lifelong job as an engineer, and they lived comfortably until his death. Although Amelia was physically healthy, she found herself unable to cope with the emotional trauma of life without Lester. Hence, within a year of losing him, she too died. Amelia's reaction to her husband's death was very different, however, from that of her neighbor Harriet. Harriet said: "For fifty years I lived my husband's life. Now it's time to live my own life." And she proceeded to do just that for a dozen more years.

Meanwhile, Nan and her siblings were attempting to repeat the life cycle of their parents. They fully expected to marry, have their own children, and watch them grow. They then expected their children to "leave the nest," just as they had left Lester and Amelia. Thus the family life cycle would be repeated generation after generation.

ROLE CONFORMITY AND THE LIFE-CYCLE APPROACH

Most sociologists once believed that a predictable family life cycle was the bedrock of social control and social order. Before the events of the 1960s and what's been going on ever since, it was the most common way to describe the aging of most persons. Today, however, the foundations of the FLC approach have been severely rocked by the life-course revolution, to say nothing of the sexual and employment revolutions. To their credit, FLC researchers were trying to show that aging is a lifelong process of change that begins in childhood. Nevertheless, in trying to describe aging, FLC researchers made an assumption that has since been undercut by the three revolutions. The assumption was that as people age, they conform to appropriate social roles. What FLC misses is that throughout their life courses, today's people are increasingly likely to keep on reinventing behaviors rather than merely conforming to existing roles.

Sociologists once described social roles as if they were something physically real, like a suit of clothes. Chapter 10 said that marriage is often

reified: People confuse it with a physical object that can be touched, smelled, heard, seen, or tasted. The same is true for a social role such as mother or husband. People often think of a role as if it's physically real and can be put on like jeans or a T-shirt. Instead, says Donald Hansen, we should think of a role merely as a *metaphor*—a figure of speech that helps us communicate important and often unique feelings, ideas, and behaviors. If a friend says, "I was walking on air," or, "I carried the weight of the world on my shoulders," we understand those words to be metaphors conveying joy or sadness. He wasn't really doing either thing. Similarly, when Nan says, "I've taken on the role of mother," we know it's not like putting on a dress, or a suit, or a robe. And it's certainly not like playing the role of Lady MacBeth in Shakespeare's play. While acting in a role like that, one generally follows the script telling one precisely what to say and do.

By way of contrast, Nan made changes in the script: She became a mother for several years and had two informal marriages before she ever got formally married. She did so even though the role of "mother" as scripted by the family life cycle simply doesn't allow for that kind of "deviant" behavior. Moreover, it was never part of Nan's own *anticipatory socialization* about the mother role: She never expected to behave that way. And she wasn't following any script because there are surely no cultural norms saying a woman should become a mother before a formal marriage.

Anticipatory Socialization   Meliza is a high-school senior. She's never been anywhere near a college in her life. Nevertheless, she thinks she has a pretty good idea of what her classes and social life will be like once she enrolls next year as a freshman. She got her ideas about college life from her parents and teachers, the media, and talking to college students, as well as from books, magazines, and catalogs. Meliza has been experiencing "anticipatory socialization" about college life. She's learning what to expect and she's picturing herself in the role of university student. She's anticipating what she will and won't do in that role. Once Meliza actually gets to college, however, she discovers that a lot of what she'd learned must be modified, and some of it doesn't work at all. As a result, she has to keep reinventing the role of university student in ways she never anticipated.

The same unexpected reinvention takes place when it comes to erotic friendships and parenting throughout people's lives. FLC researchers, however, ignored the idea of recreation. First, they assumed that as youth were growing up they would be socialized into traditional gender roles of husband and father and wife and mother, as in Figure 12-1. Second, they believed that having learned those roles, youth such as Nan would anticipate what the roles would be like. Third, they thought that the youth, on having taken on the roles, would fulfill them pretty much as they had anticipated they would. The assumption was that youth would in general behave in pretty much the same ways as their parents. Thus the family life cycle would repeat itself.

Family "Development"   Some researchers have tried to bring the FLC approach up to date by, among other things, changing its name to family "development."" But one of the most recent discussions of family development continues to concentrate on role conformity rather than role creation. For example, James White says there are "timing norms" about when a newly married couple should have children. The cultural norms state that a newly married couple can wait a couple of years to have children, but not ten or more years. Recall that Lester and Amelia conformed to that timing norm: two years after marriage they had a child. Consequently their family "developed" from the childless to the infant stage. Lester and Amelia believed the cultural norm that "being an only child is not a good thing," and so two years later they had a second child. Having that child caused their family to "develop" further. They also believed that "a woman's most important task in life is taking care of children," and so they had a third and a fourth child. As a result, their family developed still further. Their family kept on developing because of the connections between certain cultural norms prescribing what they were supposed to do, and the actual birth and growth of their children.

Conformity versus Construction   But according to White, Nan (or, from earlier chapters, Helga and Sondra) is labeled "deviant" because, among other things, she didn't conform to traditional norms saying that people are supposed to marry *before* having children. The label "deviant" doesn't do much to satisfy our curiosity about what today's erotic friendships and families are all about, however. Rather than say they're deviant, it makes more sense to say that Nan and the others are making certain kinds of choices. Those choices are part of their efforts to control their lives, even though the results may turn out to make them feel more out of control than they felt before.

Nevertheless, these women are constructing families with their choices. And at different times in their lives, they are likely to make quite different kinds of choices, resulting in different sorts of families. Thus, instead of our thinking of a role as something that is governed by a script, we can understand Nan's role as mother as a kind of metaphor. Her role describes particular behaviors and identifies unique feelings. Although in some ways her mother-role behaviors will be similar to those of her own mother, in many other ways they will be markedly different. The greatest contrasts are that Nan is unmarried, is not living with a man, and is employed full-time. Nor does she ever want a second child. Additionally, the way Nan constructs her role of mother can be very different from the roles constructed by other women in her same age bracket and similar economic circumstances.

By contrast, when Amelia was a young mother, just about every woman in her neighborhood played the role of mother in pretty much the same way. At that time, prevailing cultural images defining the Good-Mother role were captured by the traditional side of Figure 12-1. Today, Nan has the option of constructing gender roles that are less traditional and more flexible than ever before. Moreover, she can, if she wishes, change her gender-role behaviors throughout her life course. One result of that flexibility is that if Nan ever chooses to have a second child, she is free to construct the role of mother differently than she did the first time. Recall from Chapter 13 that

Sondra's mother role was very different the second time around than it had been with her first child. And when she joined her social family, her mother role shifted even more dramatically.

The issue of conformity versus construction is vividly illustrated by White's definition of the family. He says that the family development approach requires a parent-child bond of some sort; a social group that is not intergenerational cannot be a family. Hence, if an adult has no living relatives yet wishes to experience family, she or he has no choice except to have children either by natural or by social means, such as adoption or cohabiting with someone who has children (White mentions stepchildren as well). By White's reasoning, children are requisite to the idea of "family." The option of inventing social families quite apart from the presence of children doesn't exist.

Hence the FLC approach fails to take sufficient account of the 1960s and the years since. Recent decades have ushered in fresh kinds of social conditions, influencing women and men to respond very differently than before to the inevitability of lifelong aging. Rather than conforming to preexisting social roles that are supposedly appropriate for a particular chronological age, persons are instead recreating new roles—fresh ways of relating to one another and to children. Not only are people changing but broader political and economic conditions are continuing to shift as well. Consequently, persons such as Monika know that it's extremely difficult to anticipate the specifics of one's life course. Although Monika hopes for satisfying primary relationships (whether they be erotic friendships, social families, or just friends), she can't be certain about either their sequencing over time or their actual content.

Monika also looks forward to meaningful occupational experiences, but here too their sequence and content are unclear. She's aware, for instance, that economic experts are predicting that throughout their life courses people of her age and education may be forced to switch occupations several times. Furthermore, she's unable to anticipate exactly how her occupational trajectory will influence her primary relationships, and vice versa. Chapter 13

showed that before the 1960s, people like Lester and Amelia who graduated from high school and waited until their 20s to marry could, with considerable certainty, predict a lifelong marriage and a stable life overall. Today most persons simply hope for the best both in their occupations and their primary relationships. Throughout postmodern societies, we've moved from the image of aging marked by a predictable family *life cycle* to the notion of a very fluid and highly uncertain *life course*.

AGING AND LIFE COURSES

TRANSITIONS

The term *transition* has already appeared in this book several times. In Chapter 5, people shifting from one phase of their erotic friendship to another were said to be in transition. Persons moving out of an erotic friendship or perhaps moving into another were also in transition. Chapter 13 showed that "termination and transition" is a better way to describe the official ending of a formal marriage than terms such as "divorce" or "disorganization." Now we say that the idea of transition is central also to the life-course revolution identified a few pages ago. Why is the idea of transition so central?

Recently a number of researchers from sociology, psychology, and history have gotten excited about studying "life courses." Life-course students distill the best ideas from the family development approach while avoiding its pitfalls; they also add many new ideas. In contrast to the term "cycle," the term "course" carries the sound of flexibility as well as the image of choice. Carrie wants to drive to Chicago. She's not in a hurry and there are many roads, or courses, she can follow. She also works as a recreation specialist. Part of her job is to design trails throughout the city park for people who want to walk, run, or do calisthenics. She's free to create those trails, or courses, in the ways she thinks are best. The freedom to choose *what seems best* is the sort of freedom college instructors have in designing their courses.

This is part of what Arlene Skolnick means by applying the label "revolution."" She believes that today people have considerable freedom to do what they think is best. By comparison, what was best for Amelia and Lester was handed down to them as the *right* thing to do. The sole view of what was "right" and therefore "best" was pre-scribed by prevailing cultural norms. Today, the idea that there is only one prescription that works or works best is widely questioned. The freedom to keep on recreating new rules and roles through-out the course of one's life is, in Skolnick's view, a revolution. Nevertheless, let's not forget that people have always been creative in getting around established norms. Chapter 13 talked about desertion and extramarital sex as ways of coping with rules and laws against divorce. And Amelia and Lester were part of the Great Depres-sion generation that began to invent engagement sex. Even though the cultural rules said, "Premari-tal sex is neither right nor good," Amelia and Lester (along with other 1930s' couples) felt it was for them. Did they believe it was the right thing to do? Almost certainly not. They probably felt exceedingly guilty. Chapter 4 added that even though today some 80 percent of the population does It, when they're asked, relatively few persons will actually assert that premarital sex is right.

The Faces of Transition   Most people today make the transition from virgin to nonvirgin apart from marriage. Philip Cowan defines *transition* as a long-term process that reorganizes "Moth inner life and external behavior." As they started having sex, Lester and Amelia definitely passed through a transition, for two reasons. First, from that time forward each viewed himself or herself differently from before. Amelia had a particularly difficult struggle with what Cowan calls her "inner world," that is, her *identity*. She had trouble thinking of herself as the same "nice girl" she'd been before. She was terribly anxious because if her parents found out they'd call her a "fallen woman" unless she married Lester at once. Since the only means they used to prevent pregnancy was pulling out, she was deeply fearful that her parents would indeed discover the awful truth. Lester too felt guilty. Like Amelia, he felt he'd made a transition from one segment of his life to another. He became obsessed with the fear that if she got pregnant, he'd have to drop out of college and marry her

even though there were no jobs. For both of them, having sex strongly increased their commitment eventually to marry. Although they couldn't marry just yet, they each knew beyond any doubt that their partner was the person with whom they would spend the rest of their life.

The second reason we say Amelia and Lester experienced a transition was the fact of their new behavior patterns. Before doing It for the first time, they'd only had heavy petting sessions in the front seat of his father's car. Now they were doing it as often as they could in the back seat. In short, for outward behavioral reasons and because of their new identities, becoming sexual partners was for Amelia and Lester a crucial life-course transi-tion.

Life Markers   Cowan draws a distinction between what he calls a "life marker" and a genuine life-course transition. The classic illustra-tion of passing a marker but not making a transition is that of the married professional or executive man working seventy to eighty hours per week whose wife gives birth to a child. She passes through an indisputable transition into parenthood: Her behaviors change drastically, her view of herself changes, and so does her percep-tion of how others view her— she senses they view her much more positively than before. His behaviors change barely at all. If he's home on the weekends (and not out golfing), he tries to find time to play with the baby when it's awake. Second, his view of himself, his identity, doesn't alter in the slightest. He feels neither the need nor the responsibility to become connected with the child's life in any intrinsic sense. His wife sees herself as a different person, and thus she's experienced a life-course *transition*; he's merely passed a life *marker*.

Chapter 9 reported Larry Bumpass's reasoning that events such as marriage and divorce were losing their significance as life markers. What he meant to say was as that back in Lester and Amelia's time, most people experienced those two events as genuine transitions—marriage and divorce did indeed change people both inwardly and outwardly. But for growing numbers of persons today these events have lost that type of impact, and are often little more than markers. For instance, at the time of Nan's first formal marriage she'd already been living with her partner for two years. Legal marriage didn't change her outward behaviors in the slightest. Nor did she view herself much differently. Unlike her mother Amelia, she didn't have the transition to parenthood to look forward to— that was already long behind her! She had indeed experienced a vital transition a year earlier when she and her current partner entered the maintenance and change phase of their erotic friendship: Many of her behaviors changed, including setting aside casual sex in favor of monogamy. She decidedly saw herself differently than before, including, among other things, a strong desire to be a committed person: She hoped to stay with her partner indefinitely.

Markers, Transitions, and Stress   One reason it's important to be aware of the distinction between transitions and markers is that things have gotten much more complex than they appear on the surface. At one time marriage was a transition for just about everyone. Now it's not, except perhaps for religious evangelicals. For many people today marriage has become more of a life marker than a genuine transition.

A second reason the difference between transitions and markers is so important is because of their potential connection with stress symptoms. Chapter 11 described the things that can happen to people when they feel out of control, including stress symptoms such as sweaty palms, sleeplessness, extreme blushing, skin rashes, abdominal pains, anxiety and the blues, depression, and so forth.

According to Cowan, a life marker by itself is not likely to make a person feel out of control. Consequently, it's not likely to result in stress and its symptoms. If neither the executive becoming a parent nor Nan marrying her partner is changed either inwardly or outwardly, how could either feel out of control? Similarly, when Helga (Chapter 5) divorced Hans, she passed a marker, not experienced a transition, because the divorce changed nothing in her life. She felt neither out of control nor stressed. Helga had, however, experienced a transition several years earlier during her

separation from Hans. That painful process changed her outward behaviors as well as her own view of herself. It was painful in part because it was so stressful. Some of the stress sprang from her secret erotic friendship with Kurt.

Helga's history of stress had actually begun much earlier when she experienced the gradual transition from the maintenance and change phase she'd enjoyed with Hans into a dissolution phase. Throughout most of the downward spiral of that dissolution phase, she felt out of control and experienced numerous stress symptoms. Once she finally moved out of the house—after that transition was fully accomplished—she felt she was finally in control, and her symptoms began to disappear.

Does Helga's experience with dissolution and separation tell us that transitions are inevitably accompanied by stress? Do transitions always pose a threat to a person's sense of well-being? Not necessarily, says Cowan. He notes that some family life cycle and family development researchers did, and do, believe that getting married, having the first child, facing an empty nest, getting divorced, being a working mother, being a solo parent, changing jobs, going off to college, and so forth, are almost certainly going to be stressful events. But Cowan responds that it's not the event in and of itself that tells us whether it's stressful or not. We just learned, for instance, that if the person defines the event merely as a marker, it's much less likely to create stress.

Cowan adds that even if the person perceives the event as an actual transition, the amount of stress, if any, that she or he experiences depends on the level of *control* the person has during the process of transition. At the onset of her dissolution process, for instance, Helga felt only slightly out of control, and her stress symptoms were modest. The longer her dissolution phase wore on, however, the more out of control she felt, and the more intense the symptoms became. As it gradually dawned on her that leaving Hans was the only way to relieve her depression, gloom, and listlessness, she pondered plans to accomplish the separation. The mere fact of considering those plans meant that she was beginning to face choices and to exercise some control over her life. In fact, it was during that time that her feelings of well-being began to rise somewhat in anticipation of her actual separation.

For Hans the story was quite different. Cowan says that sometimes transitions simply *happen to* people. They neither want them nor have any control over them. Hans's experience of dissolution and separation was very painful and stressful on both counts: He didn't want either transition, and he felt absolutely out of control. The classic examples of *imposed* transitions stem from death or widowhood, natural disasters such as floods or hurricanes, terminal illness such as AIDS, physical or mental disabilities, war, and so on. Because persons rarely plan for such events and tend to feel utterly helpless during them, their sense of well-being drops dramatically.

CHILDHOOD, ADOLESCENCE, AND CONTROL

Cowan states that one major difference between the life courses of children and the adult life course is precisely that: Things always seem to be *happening* to children. Very little appears to be under the child's voluntary control. Transitions such as toilet training; entering day care or first grade, or middle or high school; the onset of puberty; and so forth, all seem to be processes imposed on the child by the towering adult world. Take, for example, adolescence (a social invention of the last hundred years or so). In premodern societies, after someone made the transition from childhood to puberty she or he was defined as an adult woman or man. Hence the person was soon married and compelled to behave as a responsible adult.

Contemporary societies create a gap between childhood and adulthood—adolescence. Adolescents are expected to make a gradual transition to adulthood. According to prevailing cultural norms, youth make the transition most successfully by learning and conforming to "proper" adult roles: "You'll be treated like an adult when you learn to behave like one," they're told. How does one behave like an adult? For one thing, since

prevailing cultural norms say that premarital sex is wrong, adolescents are told to say no to sex until they're married. Alongside the inherent "rightness" of chastity, adolescents are told that by being chaste they will avoid the hassles of birth control and the threats of disease, pregnancy, and abortion, to say nothing of the burden of parenthood. At the same time, adolescents are exposed to intense anticipatory socialization regarding adulthood. They're learning that they should expect to get married, to have children, and to be a good husband/father or wife/mother. For both genders, being good means conforming to the traditional norms described in Figure 12-1.

But instead of conformity, adolescence is often characterized by severe conflict between youth and adults. Youth make many choices to which adults object, especially when it comes to sex. There's no mystery why adolescents prefer choice over conformity. Choice supplies a sense of control and well-being. For the first time in their short lives, adolescents discover that they're able to take charge. Although lots of things continue to happen to them, they also can now *make* things happen. Jack Katz says that what most outsiders call deviance is perceived instead as a heady experience for the person actually making the choice. Sex, drugs, alcohol, fast cars, and so on are enormously exhilarating to many adolescents. The feelings of control and well-being come from violating the taboos against those things: The high comes from tasting the forbidden fruit.

Adolescence obviously qualifies as a major life-course transition: Not only do youth behave very differently from how they behaved as children; they also view themselves and one another very differently—their identities change. But earlier chapters revealed the perils of violating social control to exercise personal control. Choices inevitably have consequences. Exercising choice runs the risk that short-term exhilaration (immediate gratification) may be followed by longer term pain and depression because one's life has gotten more out of control than before. The most obvious example of that is spontaneous and unprotected sex resulting in infection with the HIV virus.

Gay and Lesbian Adolescents

That risks are often associated with transitions is clearly seen in a recent study of adolescent gays and lesbians living in a large metropolitan area. The authors claim that the United States has about 3 million homosexually inclined youth. Their research shows that there are some significant similarities as well as differences between heterosexual and homosexual adolescents. Heterosexuals justify their "deviant" premarital sexual activity in part by saying it represents natural biological drives: "This is the way I'm made." Adolescent gays / lesbians are following the lead of the adult same-sex community by making an identical argument. Just as heterosexual adolescents claim they have no choice regarding their sexual orientation, homosexuals say they don't either.

Both straight and gay adolescents do have a choice in the matter of sharing their transition from nonsexual to sexual being with their parents. Recall that Cowan claims that a transition is marked by two things: Changes in behavior and changes in identity (i.e., one's image of oneself). We can add a third element that was implicit in Cowan's discussion—a person's perception of how others view him or her. For instance, after Helga moved out from Hans, she sensed that her friends thought of her very differently than they had before. She knew that she'd finally proved to them that she was serious about terminating her relationship with Hans. She sensed they no longer felt uneasy that she'd been sleeping with Kurt while living with Hans. In short, the affirmation and approval of friends and / or families often adds a sense of completion and legitimacy to the transition. Marlis Buchmann calls it a validation of a person's social identity.

Andrew Boxer and co-workers report that gay adolescents are in a double bind when it comes to sharing their sexual identities and activities with parents and/or other significant adults. On one side, all children and youth are taught to be honest with their parents. On the other side, all youth are told they must be celibate. Most straight adolescents resolve that dilemma by being dishonest with parents and other adults. Although their transition to sexual being is affirmed by their friends, very few parents openly acknowledge it. At most, some adolescents sense their parents know, but a tacit agreement exists between the generations not to talk about it. One reason both sides tolerate that sort of duplicity is the comprehension that it's merely temporary. Later on the parents will fully accept their child's transition to sexual being, particularly in the context of marriage and parenthood.

By contrast, today's homosexual youth are keenly aware that their duplicity will not be resolved by subsequent conformity to parental expectations—by doing what their parents want. Adult same-sex persons report that in the past, many homosexual youth resigned themselves to the prospect of cross-sex marriage for a variety of reasons, not least of which was parental approval. But Boxer and colleagues found that the gay youth they studied were not choosing that course. Today's gay youth wished to add a sense of completion to their transition by gaining parental affirmation of their homosexuality. Although their biology was same-sex, they had after all been exposed to years of socialization aimed at making them cross-sex persons. Moreover, as part of their own quest to ascertain whether they could possibly go cross-sex, Boxer and colleagues report that over 70 percent of them had sexually experimented with heterosexuals. Most discovered that those cross-sex behaviors were much less satisfying than their same-sex experiences.

In short, their behaviors were homosexual, and so was their own view of themselves. They had experienced a transition from a culturally imposed heterosexuality to being gay/lesbian. They had also "come out" to many of their friends, but not yet to their parents. But they wanted to. The risks of their coming out to their parents pivoted around rejection, including parental attempts to restrict their same-sex friendships. Nevertheless, 63 percent of the girls and 54 percent of the boys in the study had shared their sexual identities with their mothers. And 37 percent of the girls had told their fathers, as had 28 percent of the boys. Interestingly enough, neither the girls nor the boys were consistently able to detect much negative reaction from their parents. Some reported that relationships with their parents actually improved somewhat because of their coming out.

It's likely that the youth who took the risks of coming out sensed ahead of time that their parents would not reject them and would at least be neutral toward them. Boys reported that neutrality was in fact the most common reaction they got from their fathers. Those who chose not to come out to their parents apparently felt that the goal of adding a sense of completion to their transition was not worth the risk of alienation from their parents, at least for now.

ECONOMIC SUPPORT AND PARENTAL CONTROL

Plainly, adolescence represents a major bridge between childhood and young adulthood. Adolescents are struggling to take control of their lives: They want the sense of well-being that springs from being able to make choices. Whether straight or gay, their transitions involve major changes in behaviors, shifts in identity, and a quest for the approval of significant others. But adolescence is by definition temporary; legal statutes prescribe its end somewhere between ages 18 and 21. Adolescents neither expect nor desire to be supported indefinitely by their parents—parental dollars strongly reinforce the control over their lives that they resent. Hence, to get their own dollars, growing numbers of U.S. high-school students are taking part-time jobs. A recent University of Michigan study reports that 74 percent of Minneapolis teenagers were employed compared with 21 percent in the comparable Japanese city of Sendai. The American youth worked almost sixteen hours per week, while the Japanese worked less than ten hours.

The outward reason growing numbers of adolescents hold jobs is to acquire the mass of consumer goods served up endlessly by the media. Nevertheless, the Minneapolis study reported that the most important thing adolescents buy with their money is greater independence from their parents. The study showed that because they had their own money they were treated, and actually felt, more like adults. The money was a means—a *resource*—for opening up choices, expanding their sense of control, and enlarging their feelings of well-being.

Earning money is a chief mechanism of anticipatory socialization: It provides adolescents with keen insights into the worlds of adulthood.

AGING INTO YOUNG ADULTHOOD

Education is touted as the best means both to earn a "good living" and to contribute to society. Adolescents are urged to graduate from high school and then attend vocational school or go to college. Throughout contemporary societies, economic independence (i.e., autonomy) is the hallmark—the bottom line—of what an adult is. The transition from youth to adult pivots around the behavioral shift of earning enough to support oneself. Part-time jobs while in high school or college rarely achieve that goal. Persons capable of supporting themselves right out of high school are for the first time behaving as full-fledged adults. Furthermore, they view themselves as adults, and so do friends and families: They have made the transition to adulthood. By contrast, college students depending partly or entirely on their parents for support have not made that transition. Parents and faculty often still refer to them as kids, a label rarely used to describe high-school graduates of the same age working in a local factory or office.

Buchmann, a German sociologist, studied what he calls the "passage" from youth to adulthood. He claims that youth in other Western societies are following the same types of passages as U.S. youth. He compared 1960 with 1980 high-school graduates from across the United States, collecting information about the first four years after their respective graduations. Buchmann was curious whether there were significant differences between the 1960 and 1980 graduates insofar as their "script of life" was concerned. We talked earlier about the script in connection with the family life cycle. The script consists of cultural rules telling youth what they should and shouldn't do to make their passage into adulthood as successful as possible. Buchmann's hunch was that 1960s' youth followed a much more standardized, or scripted, transition to young adulthood than did the 1980s' youth. His hunch was based in part on the Big Bang and Big Change described in Chapter 7. He reasoned that the many things occurring in the broader U.S. society during their childhood and adolescence would influence the 1980 graduates to choose a much more flexible life course—to interject it with considerable variety.

STRUCTURAL CHANGES

Among the many things "happening out there" are certain structural changes in the nature of modern societies. Politicians and business leaders of the nineties are debating how to respond to the shifting global economy in which the United States and all industrial (and emerging) nations find themselves intermeshed. One of the most worrisome concerns is that the payoff from educational investments is growing ever more uncertain. At the core of the American Dream is the belief that after a person (i.e., a male person) graduated from high school or college, he would be able to get and keep a good job all his life, and support his family in the bargain. Recently, however, many persons who finish school or college haven't been able to find and/or keep good jobs. A major reason they haven't, says Buchmann, is the steady decline in the sheer numbers of high-paying, highly skilled manufacturing jobs. Those blue-collar jobs (e.g., m the defense, steel, and auto industries), and many of the white-collar and management jobs connected with them, have simply vanished. A second reason is the microchip revolution. This "revolution" first generates a whole new range of computer-based technologies, and then makes them obsolete, all within the space of a few years. Most schools fail to prepare persons for those sorts of continually evolving technologies. For example, by the time a skilled tool-and-die maker replaced by last year's computer has finished learning fresh skills, those skills have in turn become outdated by still newer technologies.

Men's Life Courses   Buchmann describes the vast majority of the vanished manufacturing jobs, for example, tool-and-die maker, as male dominated. Since those kinds of occupations were made up almost entirely of males, they were defined as "men's work." One result of this enormous and far-reaching shift in the structure of male occupations is that today the course of many men's lives is much less stable and predictable than it once was. For example, two years after high-school graduation in 1970, Mal completed vocational college as a highly skilled machinist. Mal's father had worked as a master machinist all his life—fifteen years for one company, then thirty years for another. He was particularly proud of the fact that he'd earned such a good living that his wife never had to go to work. By the time he retired at age 65, Mal's father could look back on a comfortable life and ahead to an enjoyable retirement.

Mal wanted the identical thing for himself: He wanted to age within the context of the same sort of stable and predictable life course. Unfortunately for Mal, the 1970s, 1980s, and 1990s were marked by the structural changes just cited. After all the machinist jobs in his city were either automated or moved overseas, he was forced to attend evening classes to become a mainframe computer operator, earning much less than he did as a machinist. And after a couple of years, desktop computers replaced most mainframes and he was once again out of a job. He had to take an even lower paying job as a clerk in a local home-improvement store.

Women's Life Courses   Those same structural changes pressured hundreds of thousands of women such as Mal's wife Brenda. Unlike her mother-in-law, Brenda had to work to help pay the bills while Mal was experiencing his zigzag occupational course. Mal's continuing difficulties in holding a job, though not of his own making, resulted in conflicts Mal and Brenda were unable to resolve, and edged the couple into a dissolution phase. When Brenda refused to quit working even after Mal got his clerking job, they both sensed that separation and perhaps divorce were not far off. Comparing Mal and Brenda's life course with that of Mal's parents helps us understand why the label *revolution* makes a great deal of sense in describing today's life courses. Between the mid-1940s and the 1970s, both the economic and personal lives of adults proceeded in a relatively more-or-less predictable and stable fashion. Now, however, structural upheavals "out there" influence persons to make certain *choices*. Those choices in turn often result in significant *changes* for both their erotic friendships and their families. Consequently, predictable and stable life courses are being increasingly replaced by unpredictable and fluctuating life courses.

288

Life-course fluctuation is further stimulated by the cultural changes "out there" described in Chapter 10: Growing numbers of women are coming to accept the moral obligation to love themselves as much as (not more than) they love their neighbor. Her mother-in-law (Joy) perceived that Brenda was beginning to love herself in that manner. Because Joy defined that kind of love as Brenda's "problem," she blamed Brenda for her son's divorce.

Rebending the Tree   Buchmann says that women like Brenda, who come from blue-collar and lower- middle-class backgrounds, are the women most likely to be impacted by structural changes. They were socialized to love their husbands and children more than themselves. They learned to place their family's needs ahead of their own. The idea of becoming economically autonomous, and thus an equal partner, was never part of their anticipatory socialization. Nevertheless, structural changes pressured women such as Brenda to behave in economic and personal ways that they neither intended nor wanted: Brenda never wanted a job; and she surely never expected a divorce!

Judith Stacey's research shows that shifting economic conditions pressure even evangelical wives into behaviors that were never part of their youthful socialization. She studied lower-middle-class families—many of whom were devout religious evangelicals—living in Silicon Valley, California, during the early 1980s. The numerous computer industries of Silicon Valley are classic illustrations of the sorts of structural changes just described. Many of the thousands of jobs they offer are semiskilled; others are skilled or unskilled. Regardless of skill level, each new technological innovation renders many of the jobs obsolete. Men working at those jobs thus lose the economic means to support their family. After a period of unemployment, new technologies create new jobs for those men. No one knows, however, how long the new jobs will exist. The uncertainty of this economic seesaw makes it very difficult for the men to be their family's Head.

Wanting to be a good complement, the wife knows she should stoically accept their economic setback

and weather the storm until the next wave of technology gets her husband a new job. Nevertheless, Stacey reports that many evangelical wives ignore what they learned to be "right," that is, stay home to care for their children and submit to their husbands. Wives now feel sharp economic pressure to do what seems "best," that is, get a paying job. However, the wives' new behavior generates serious conflicts with the husbands, resulting frequently in separation and divorce. When some of the women and men later get remarried, they are taking another serious step away from their earlier religious socialization.

Perhaps the biggest question about childhood and adolescent socialization is how long it lasts: "As the twig is bent, so grows the tree," is a folk saying describing the widely held belief that how parents train children has enormous and lasting influence throughout their lives. The biblical promise that evangelicals learn is, "Train up a child in the way he should go, and when he is old he will not depart from it." Nonetheless, the question remains: How long does the bent twig influence the shape of the mature tree? The answer is that norms and beliefs learned as a child or adolescent last as long as they make sense for adults in the light of changing social conditions. In the case of women like Brenda, what they learned as youth failed to work during adulthood because of new structural conditions. The more Brenda changed her behaviors to fit the conditions, the more she forgot about the ideas she learned as a youth. Gradually, new ideas took their place because they made more sense for her adult life. The main reason she wouldn't quit her job after Mal went back to work was because she was learning to be economically autonomous: She was beginning to feel that being an equal partner with her man is for her a good idea. On the basis of her study of women like Brenda, Myra Dinnerstein concludes that *"adults continue to develop new values, beliefs, and aspirations as they encounter changing historical and social circumstances."*

Although Brenda didn't start absorbing those emerging cultural notions until she was thirty-something, Buchmann notes that growing numbers of today's females learn them much earlier, as children and youth. Many of those females, he says, come from upper-middle-class backgrounds where one or both parents are college educated. Recall from Chapter 10 that Kate's mother (Emma) was quite traditional, in part because she'd never been to college. But Kate's father had graduated from college and insisted that Kate do the same. Throughout the years she was growing up, he socialized her to anticipate becoming autonomous as well as an equal partner. And as she moved into adulthood and became aware of rapidly shifting economic conditions, Kate felt that her father's ideas made sense for her. Hence she put them into action for all the relationships she had with men, including her current long-term erotic friendship with Marshall. By contrast with Brenda, the norms she'd learned in her youth had greater lasting effects. The reason they did persist is that they made sense for her as an adult within the context of broader structural and cultural conditions.

In short, as Kate was making her transition to adulthood, the inner world of her own identity clear: "I am an economically autonomous person." Brenda's identity was just as sharp, but different: "I am a Good Wife and Good Mother." Although Kate experienced a number of other transitions during her 20s and 30s, her fundamental view of herself did not change. To be sure, it could have shifted in a more traditional direction. Kathleen Gerson, for example, reports that some women like Kate who begin adulthood wanting to be autonomous nonetheless experience a transition into accepting more traditional women's roles. Brenda headed in the opposite direction: She'd experienced a dramatic transition both in terms of her behaviors and her identity. For the first time in her life she viewed herself as an autonomous person. Furthermore, she reasoned that over the long haul autonomy was the best way for her to become an effective mother as well as a good erotic partner.

COMPARING 1960 WITH 1980—COMPLEXITY AND DIVERSITY

Buchmann's hunches regarding differences between 1960 and 1980 high-school graduates during their four-year transition to adulthood proved to be correct. Owing to the many changes occurring out there, today's youth are experiencing a much greater range and variety of life-course choices than youth of a generation ago. Buchmann agrees with John Modell that today's choices are captured by the terms "complexity and diversity." By contrast, 1960 graduates were more likely to follow the scripted family life cycle path than were 1980 graduates. Furthermore, because the 1960 path was simpler and more uniform, those earlier graduates, says Buchmann, were more likely to make a socially recognized transition to adulthood much earlier than were the 1980 graduates.

Buchmann used three tests to find out whether a person had made a socially recognized transition: "Are you still in school?" "Have you been married?" "Have you had a child?" The percentages of youth in each cluster of students answering yes to all three questions were much higher in 1964 than they were in 1984. All three of those behaviors conform to the cultural definition of what it means to be an adult. Persons who had done all three things thought of themselves as adults, as did their families and friends. Persons who had not, or who had done merely one or two of them, had not yet made the transition to full-fledged adulthood. It was not that the 1980s' cultural scripts had been "officially" altered; youth were simply paying less attention to the old scripts. Moreover, that trend of indifference to the standard life-cycle scripts seems to be continuing into the nineties.

Given that today's youth are increasingly indifferent to the scripts, how do they actually behave? Among other things, says Buchmann, growing numbers of high-school graduates appear to be delaying their entry into college for a year or two or perhaps longer. When they enroll, they may do so for a while as part-time, but later as full-time, students. If they do enroll in college immediately after high school, they may "stop out" of college for a year or two. Meanwhile, they may intersperse part-time with full-time employment. They may also intersperse periods of casual sex with periods of erotic friendships. If the latter, they may be girlfriends / boyfriends who each week spend several overnights together, or they may actually cohabit for a while. Two things that most high-school graduates do not appear to be doing during this initial four-year period is to marry formally and then soon afterward have a child. By comparison, the 1960 cluster of graduates moved along a much clearer, certain, and standard track: *As soon as possible*, they felt they had to do the three things that marked them as an adult: Finish school, marry, and have children. After all, the 1960 cohort was one of the last to graduate from high school before the upheavals of the mid- to late-sixties. Two major "revolutions" emerged from those upheavals, which in turn contributed heavily to today's life-course revolution. Chapter 5 identified one as the emergence of the erotic friendship; Chapter 15 describes the second as women's employment patterns, or what Chapter 7 called the Big Change. Buchmann claims that because both of those revolutions profoundly affected women, the life courses of most women have changed more dramatically during recent decades than they have for most men. That is not to say that the male life course has not changed. It has, as in Mal's case. But by comparison, Brenda's changes were greater and more significant.

Variations on Themes   John Gottman uses jazz to illustrate today's transitions from youth to adulthood. The art of jazz is that, while acknowledging a theme tune, musicians strive to create as many variations on that theme as they possibly can; *improvisation,* it's called. Most of today's youth follow a general theme that includes the goals of education, a good job, and meaningful primary relationships with adults as well as children. But the specifics of the general theme are open to a great deal of improvisation. Not only during the first four post-high-school years, but throughout their early adulthood, growing numbers of persons are interjecting unpredictable and often unexpected "notes" as they go along. For instance, people such as Brenda, Helga and Kurt, Sondra, and Kate and Marshall are making choices about school, work, sex, partners, informal and formal marriage, social families, children, and so on, that are clearly recognizable as belonging to the larger themes. But the sequence as well as the contents of their choices are no longer standard, scripted, or scored.

Instead, persons make choices that seem to make sense at the time. Recall that Helga's choices made sense to her, first because of the ways in which she

viewed her own complicated social situation, and second because of the ways in which she viewed her broader structural and cultural environment. Even after she'd made up her mind to leave Hans, she put it off for a while: She felt she had to wait until the "time was right." In short, instead of worrying a great deal about doing what they're supposed to be doing as defined by prevailing cultural scripts, today's young adults appear to have a somewhat different agenda. To be sure, they're following certain general themes regarding the importance of work, relationships, and families. And, they seem concerned to exercise as much control as possible over those and other parts of their lives and, as a result, achieve a sense of well-being. Finally, the fact that they're often frustrated while attempting to invent their own life courses does not diminish their determination to keep on trying.

AGING INTO THE MIDDLE YEARS

Earlier we said that life-course transitions occur when people change behaviors, when they think of themselves as being different, and also when they perceive that significant others affirm their new behaviors and identity. Persons begin to define themselves as young adults if they believe they're developing control over both the economic and personal dimensions of their lives. Hence, a young adult is someone who defines himself or herself as becoming weaned from parental controls.

SETTLING DOWN

What then is a midlife adult? How can we describe the transition to midlife? Ann Swidler, and later Arlene Skolnick, observe that *midlife* is something that has only recently been "discovered." Before the last couple of decades, persons were merely middle-aged. According to Swidler, the key phrase describing middle-aged persons was that they had settled down. Young adulthood was the time when men sowed their wild oats and played the old Dating Game; women merely played the Game. Men might also experiment with different occupations in search of their "life's work." But marriage and its aftermath symbolized settling down for both genders. Husbands and wives had committed themselves to a lifelong course of action centering around his occupation and her skills as wife and mother. Having put their hand to the plow, there was no turning back from either of those parallel rows. Thus, if a man's transition to adulthood was symbolized by a steady job, marriage, and children, his transition to middle-aged adult was symbolized by his own realization (acknowledged by others) that he had indeed *settled down*. He had given up the range of choices and options available to single young adults. Both he and his wife now had responsibilities; to fulfill them they had to conform to scripted roles.

Swidler notes that the contrasts between early and middle adulthood were once striking, indeed. Young adulthood was viewed as an escape from parental controls and a period of having considerable personal freedom regarding one's own life. By contrast, middleage adulthood meant relinquishing a great deal of that hard-won freedom. Choices, says Swidler, were replaced by conformity to culturally approved gender roles. Accordingly, for some persons "middle-age" may have begun when chronologically they were no more than age 25. If the husband kept on being a Good Provider, and if the couple was successful in having a stable marriage, then by the time they aged into their early to mid-30s they were culturally labeled as middle-aged. Their friends might tease the 30-year-olds by saying, "You're nothing but an old married couple." They were affectionately communicating that, "You've been together such a long time your lives aren't likely to change very much." The absence of change, the presence of predictability—those were the hallmarks of being middle-aged.

Interestingly enough, Skolnick notes that this sort of life-cycle certainty was a relatively new thing, having come on the scene around the 1920s. The certainty enjoyed by Mal's parents, for instance, was made possible, first, by medical advances reducing the risk of sudden or early death due to serious illness. As a result, Mal's parents were part of a generation that could expect to live many more years than their forebears. Second, until the 1970s there was a largely uninterrupted expansion of heavy manufacturing, male-dominated jobs.

Since neither of those factors was present to the same degree before the 1920s, the family life cycles of many couples back then were quite uncertain. Sudden death and/or male unemployment had devastating effects for many pre-1920s' families. Now, says Skolnick, after an interlude between the 1920s and the 1970s, the pendulum has once again swung in that same direction of life-course uncertainty. The luxury of looking forward to a predictable and stable middle-aged period of one's life is slowly evaporating.

REDISCOVERY OF CHOICE

But if today's *midlife* couples don't settle down, what then do they do? Women like Helga or Brenda, or the women in Dinnerstein's study (born between 1936 and 1944), *rediscover* the choices they previously relinquished when they got married, had children, and became full-fledged young adults. A best-selling 1976 book brought the term *middle-age crisis* into everyone's vocabulary. Gail Sheehy claimed that every middle-aged person goes through a radical transition in terms of both identity and behaviors. But Sheehy was writing about men and women both before recent structural and cultural changes in the larger society. Married under the old rules, midlife suddenly confronted them with new rules, or worse yet, no rules. Women and men who never expected to reenter school did so. Men who never expected to lose their jobs, and women who never intended to get serious about paid work, did. Persons who never expected to have "affairs," or be unwed parents, or cohabit, or get separated, divorced, and remarried, were surprised by their own behaviors—some pleasantly, others not. But the biggest shock of all for people like Mal and Brenda was that they were back where they were before they got married: Their lives were once again filled with choice and uncertainty. Their hopes for "settling down" had been rudely dashed. Unwittingly, they had stumbled into the *rediscovery* of choice.

THE REAFFIRMATION OF CHOICE

We began this chapter by saying that Monika, a college graduate in her mid-20s with a good job, already expects that her life course will be characterized by unpredictable twists and turns. She neither is married nor has children, and she doesn't intend either anytime soon. Nonetheless, she perceives herself as a young adult because she's economically autonomous, and she hopes that will continue. What makes her strikingly different from Brenda (when Brenda was her age) is that she does not intend ever to relinquish choice and control over her life. Since Monika hasn't given it up, her transition into midlife cannot be the rediscovery of choice. Instead, she expects her chronological aging will be accompanied by an ongoing lifelong *reaffirmation* of choice.

Permanent Availability   Monika knows several women like Kate and she takes them as role models. Chapter 10 showed that Kate, a professional woman, and Marshall maintained a richly satisfying informal marriage for over a decade. As she approached age 40, they formalized it because of their desire for a child. But at no point did either Kate or Marshall ever view themselves as settling down. Although they were strongly committed to each other and to developing a strong sense of we-ness, they were equally committed to the idea that each should nurture the other's sense of me-ness. Chapters 5, 11, and 13 said that *permanent availability is* the notion that a person is potentially a prospect for an erotic friendship regardless of whether she or he now has a partner. The fact that one may currently choose not to be a prospect in no way implies that one has given up that option in favor of settling down the way Mal and Brenda had done. Even if Kate or Marshall or Monika never expects to exercise that option, nonetheless each always retains it.

Permanent availability, along with commitment to the idea that each partner should be economically autonomous, means that the midlife courses of persons such as Monika, Kate and Marshall, and Kurt and Helga are likely to be quite unpredictable. But since their young adulthood was also unpredictable, that's nothing new. Furthermore, ongoing upheavals in the national and global economies increase the likelihood of midlife uncertainty. What does seem apparent is that the idea of a middle-age crisis will become increasingly irrelevant. Persons like Brenda, Mal, and

Hans had middle-age crises because they'd comfortably settled down. But as the goal of settling down becomes increasingly elusive for growing numbers of persons, it becomes replaced by the idea of learning to live with varying degrees of built-in uncertainty throughout one's life course.

In short, transitions into young adulthood are marked by an expanding range of choices and control over one's life. Slowly, a person begins to perceive of himself or herself as an adult. Throughout much of this century young adulthood merged into middle age as people made choices of marriage partners and (the men) employment and settled down. Other choices were severely limited by expected social roles. Today, by contrast, midlife choices and uncertainty have become expanded so that, apart from the ticking of the biological clock, young adulthood and midlife are becoming increasingly comparable.

AGING INTO THE LATER YEARS

"I must be getting old," was once a frequently heard folk saying. It contained a note of wry humor and also a sense of sad resignation to the inevitable. But that was before Jane Fonda, Paul McCartney, Barbara Streisand, Aretha Franklin, Bob Dylan, Frank Zappa, Paul Newman, Paul Simon, Art Garfunkel, Tom Hayden, Raquel Welch, and Robert Redford, along with other notables, turned 50 years of age. Now the predominant folk saying is, "You're as young as you feel." Fonda's trim and youthful body, clad in brightly colored tights, appears in video stores everywhere, convincing consumers that aerobic exercise is the new fountain of youth. The citizen's hope for continued youth is reinforced by reports from serious medical journals showing that exercise is a key element in controlling obesity and cholesterol levels, which in turn reduces the risk of heart disease. Additionally, the federal government has now imposed strict standards on food packaging, giving the consumer fuller information about fat content. Researchers say that fat contributes to heart disease and perhaps some forms of cancer. Citizens are told that reducing their fat intake should make them healthier.

Throughout the twentieth century, medical and related technologies helped prolong people's lives dramatically. As the century closes, growing numbers of middle- and later-year persons are hoping that being a nonsmoker, along with exercising and "eating right," will lengthen their lives still more. But it's not merely the quantity of years that interests them. Good health, they hope, should also enhance the *quality* of those years. Being able to exercise like, and be as trim as, Jane Fonda vividly symbolizes control over one's life even though the biological clock ticks away. Although they're aware that death is inevitable, many older persons hope to postpone it as long as possible and "have fun" doing so.

Many observers say that one way today's midlife and older persons try to have fun is to prolong indefinitely the enjoyment of sex. Before the 1960s, sexual pleasures were seen as perverse and decadent for older persons (i.e., those in their 40s and beyond). But Diana Harris and her colleagues claim that since the 1960s, the United States has experienced an "aging of sexual desire." They studied *Playboy* centerfolds between 1954 and 1989 and report that over time there has been an increase in the average age of the models. They attribute that increase to shifting cultural definitions about sexual pleasure. Growing numbers of midlife and older men (and women) identify pleasurable sex with persons of their own age, not just with younger persons. Viewing older models in the media reinforces the connection between sexual pleasure and maturity. Thus, say the researchers, "If we are to continue to have centerfolds, they should represent a broader array of womanhood than the adolescent angel of *Playboy's* youth."

SLIDING DOWNHILL VERSUS THE "NEW AGING"

Just as the transition to middle age was once marked by the perception that one had settled down, the transition to *old* age was once marked by the perception that one was "sliding downhill." Driving through steep mountainous areas, the motorist encounters signs warning of runaway vehicles. Due to faulty brakes or other causes, a vehicle may be unable to slow itself from disaster as it plunges downhill. "I must be getting old"

conveys the idea that a person views himself or herself on a seemingly uncontrollable downhill path plunging toward death. But one seriously doubts that Fonda, Simon, or Redford would ever use that folk saying. The reason they would not is that they, along with growing numbers of other persons, are redefining and reinventing their later years. Their transition to the later years is marked by keeping one eye on the biological clock while reaffirming the notions of choice and control that characterized their middle and early years. Skolnick labels their redefinition *"The New Aging."*

We learned, for example that Monika perceives that her middle years will be an extension of her younger years, a continued reaffirmation of choice and control. If asked, she perceives her later years in precisely the same mode. Skolnick contrasts Presidents George Bush and Franklin Roosevelt to illustrate the New Aging. Crippled by polio as a young man, Roosevelt had spent many years in a wheelchair unable to walk. He was also a heavy smoker and somewhat obese. In photos taken during 1945 at age 64 just before his death from coronary disease, he appeared to be sliding downhill as fast as he could—he looked very old. But when Bush became president at age 64, he didn't seem old at all. A nonsmoker, he was in excellent health and had a trim body caused in part, he claimed, by jogging and other forms of exercise. Furthermore, when he left office four years later Bush seemed hardly to have aged at all.

Bush was followed in office by the first baby boomer President, Bill Clinton, also an avid jogger. Matilda Riley is a leading expert on aging who at age 81 works full-time for the National Institute of Aging. She notes that the boomers (persons born during the dozen or so years after 1945), symbolized by public figures such as Clinton and Vice President Gore, represent the first generation to widely embrace the revised ideas known as the New Aging. The boomers are approaching their later years as "physically vigorous, intellectually strong adults who are in no mood for fading away and making room."

Enforced Retirement as Social Control   By contrast, the generation of Mal's parents perceived no options other than for the husband to retire from his job in order to make room for younger men. Indeed, Mal's father worked for a company that required its employees to retire at age 65. Enforced retirement is a striking example of what this chapter earlier called *social control*. Once a certain chronological age is reached, certain norms kick in: "By the time a married woman reaches age 30, she should have a child." "When a man reaches age 65, he should retire." By contrast, *personal control* represents the idea that behaviors such as childbearing and labor force activity ought to be matters of choice, not constraint. Furthermore, prevailing cultural expectations also strongly influenced the older couple's years after the man exited from his job. Retirement became a unique lifestyle quite distinct from that of the husband's work years. As the couple lived out their "declining years"—sometimes in a retirement community—their lifestyle became much less active and pressured, and much more leisurely.

But boomers such as Mal and Brenda have spent their middle years exercising choices (often painful), and attempting to control their lives (often ineffectively). Furthermore, young adults such as Monika will be spending their entire adult lives in a personal control rather than a social control mode. Consequently, argues Riley, it doesn't seem likely that persons who have spent many years learning both the pleasures and perils of choice will at age 65 suddenly, or easily, conform to conventional expectations regarding retirement. Instead, says Riley, they will favor "more choices and more varied roles for older people." As a result of their preferences for varied rather than prescribed lifestyles, Riley believes that "the potential for increased intergenerational strife will be tremendous "

CHOICE VERSUS COPING

Since the majority of persons currently in their late years were born before World War II, they're classified as preboomers. Recall that as Lester and Amelia entered retirement they could look back on a long and satisfying cycle of life safely governed by prevailing social customs. For them and for the majority of today's older persons, the view that their retirement years could be a continuation of an ongoing life course that they'd always been

inventing and reinventing seems quite foreign indeed.

First, they believe that throughout their lives they've been conforming to life-cycle demands. They do not view themselves as having created innovative life courses. Second, they perceive retirement as being a sharp disjuncture from the past: They define themselves as having moved through a significant transition from preretirement to retirement. Preretirement was a time of "doing what other people (especially the boss) want." Retirement "gives me the opportunity of doing what I want." Thus, for many of today's older persons, retirement is not a continuation of a lifelong pattern of choice and control. Rather, it is defined as the first time since youth for them to *rediscover* choice and control.

Rather than *choice*, however, the label that applies more accurately to the retirement period of many of today's older citizens is *coping*. More than anything else, Lester and Amelia spent their retirement worried about economics and health. As long as they had enough money, and as long as their health was good, they felt okay about themselves. But as Lester's health deteriorated due to Alzheimer's disease and the couple ran out of money, Amelia no longer felt able to cope with life and she got exceedingly depressed. Her daughter Nan stepped in and relieved Amelia of many of the burdens imposed by Lester's constant care. Nan's siblings helped out as well—not so much with Lester's physical care, but with needed financial aid. Emily Abel reports that in the United States the vast majority of needy and disabled older persons are cared for by their blood relatives. Most relatives provide this type of caregiving without any assistance from public or private agencies.

Furthermore, the caregiving tends to be gender linked: the caregivers usually are women. They either do the caregiving themselves, like Nan, or they orchestrate it for other family members. If no daughter is available, daughters-in-law are often expected to be the chief caregivers. A recent study, however, shows that a growing minority of men are also willing to behave as caregivers. Indeed,

295

the researchers report that some men are currently deeply involved as caregivers to elderly parents.

BOTTOM-LINE OBLIGATIONS

Why is Nan investing so much of her time and resources to help out her parents? For decades she's been quite distant from them not merely geographically, but emotionally as well. Lester and Amelia were extremely negative toward her because of her unconventional lifestyle; they never forgave her for it. All of Nan's sibs felt closer to their parents than she did. However, when their mother got to the end of her tether, each of those sibs came up with a good reason why he or she couldn't be the *chief* caregiver, although each agreed to contribute money. The sibs also agreed that Nan was the only one who couldn't legitimately refuse to be the chief caregiver. And even though Nan didn't particularly like her parents (much less love them), she concurred that she was the only one lacking a good reason not to be the chief caregiver. Hence she acknowledged her duty to take on that role.

Importantly, all of the sibs felt equally obliged to their parents, even though only one became the chief caregiver. And the sib who finally took on that demanding role had been more emotionally distant from her parents than any of the others had been. Chapters 2 and 3 showed that the *bottom line* of what families are all about is the shared obligation to help out whenever money, services, or goods are needed. These powerful "moral obligations" exist regardless of how little or how many emotional satisfactions family members do or do not share with one another. Two British researchers recently asked a sample of older persons if they "felt closer" to their relatives after those caregivers helped them out with their material or service needs. At the same time, the caregivers were asked if, after providing the needs of the older persons, they "felt closer" to them. "The most common response [from both caregivers and elderly alike] was to say that helping made no difference to their feelings towards each other." In other words, the sense of we-ness, or bonding, shared by family members didn't seem to depend very much on feelings of liking and/or loving. Instead, the idea that "we

are family" had emerged chiefly from the obligations to *give and receive* that had bound them together for many decades.

Elder Abuse   There is a dark side to the notion of family obligations to the elderly. Suzanne Steinmetz reports that sometimes caregivers such as Nan who are duty bound to help out their disabled elderly parents also get violent with them. All of us have been in stores or other public places where we've witnessed young adults slapping or hitting their kids out of sheer frustration—"They're misbehaving and embarrassing me." But the disabled elderly seldom appear in public. Hidden from view, someone as ill as Lester can be extremely annoying to Nan, or even to his wife Amelia. Nan feels very frustrated at having to take care of her father when she'd much rather be pursuing her own life. She's also angry at her sibs for failing to pitch in for his care as much as they'd promised. Hence when Lester "misbehaves," Nan sometimes loses control and slaps or punches him. Afterward Nan feels deep shame and guilt, but a week later it happens again. Amelia's the only one who sees it, but she doesn't say a word. Amelia's afraid that if she says anything, Nan wouldn't be able to continue as Lester's chief caretaker. If that happens, Amelia fears she'll once again have to play that role, and she simply doesn't have the energy to do it.

Apparently, there is sufficient hidden violence toward the elderly in the United States to worry the American Medical Association. For several years, the AMA has been urging pediatricians to be alert to signs of abuse among children, and to follow up on suspicions of child assault. The AMA recently issued a similar directive to physicians who treat elderly patients such as Lester.

CONCLUSION—THE OBLIGATION OF LIFELONG REINVENTION

The numbers of later life citizens like Amelia and Lester have been growing and will continue to grow rapidly in industrial societies. The National Institute of Aging (NIA) was organized during the late 1970s as part of the official U.S. response to their physical, mental, and emotional needs. A major mission of the NIA is to study the coping strategies of older persons. During the past several years a number of researchers have turned their attention and energies to that important question.

Some researchers have also begun to wonder about the aging of persons who are currently in their middle and early years. Nor have they forgotten later life people like George Bush and George Burns who are striking examples of the New Aging. Growing numbers of persons are now living into their later 80s and beyond, and many are leading healthy and active lives. Furthermore, millions of aging boomers expect to be considerably more vigorous and innovative during their later years. As researchers view the "lifecourse revolution" that's been occurring for almost all ages, some are thinking less about coping and more about choice and control.

"Coping" pivots around the idea of reacting effectively to unforeseen circumstances. The unexpected can include a dread disease such as AIDS, breast cancer, MS, or Alzheimer's. Or it might be the elimination of one's job, a pregnancy, or the sudden death of a parent, partner, or friend. There is no doubt that the more effectively persons learn to cope with the vagaries of life, the better off they are and the better they feel about themselves. By contrast, the notion of "control" takes us an important step beyond coping. Coping asks, "How do I / we deal with the changes that have happened to me/to us?" Control asks, "How do I/we *make* changes happen?"

Earlier chapters talked about the basic human need of people to belong—to be part of a primary group and thus experience a sense of we-ness. We also discussed something called me-ness, especially its growing significance for women. Chapter 11 said that a large part of me-ness is the desire to exercise control. Just as the need to belong is a basic human feature, control is equally a "basic feature of human behavior." Control of one's life course has many names: "Self-directedness, choice, decision freedom, agency, mastery, autonomy, self-efficacy, and self-determination." Control is important for many reasons, not least of which is that the more control people believe they have the *healthier* they are both physically and mentally.

Promoting the health of persons in their later years is NIA's all-encompassing objective. On the other hand there is no doubt that unexpected ill health (e.g., cancer, AIDS) causes anyone to feel out of control. But on the other hand researchers are also asking, "How can we assist later life people to develop a sense of mastery over their lives, thus helping them to generate good physical and mental health?" Those researchers are searching for ways to help today's older persons make the changes in their lives that they themselves desire. Increasingly, however, researchers are beginning to understand that achieving control, like producing physical fitness, is ideally a lifelong process. Monika, now in her 20s, intends to stay physically fit throughout her lifetime. She knows that waiting till age 45 to join a health club won't do it. The fitness she expects to have during her 60s, 70s, and 80s will simply be an extension of a lifelong pattern of keeping fit. She wants fitness to be as much a part of her lifestyle as "eating right," meaningful work, and satisfying primary relationships.

By the same token, the more Monika is able to make desired changes happen in her early and middle years, the more likely she is to keep on doing so during her later years. She takes very seriously the point made early in the chapter, that an important part of loving oneself is the obligation to take charge of one's life course as fully as possible. Monika hopes to develop a pattern—a lifestyle—of control and mastery over both her work and her relationships. She intends to experience lifelong life-course re-creation and reconstruction. As a result, she hopes to enjoy a high degree of physical and mental health throughout her years, including her later ones. She's keenly aware also that a sense of me-ness is difficult to separate from a sense of we-ness, and from responsibilities to the adults and children who are part of her primary groups. Hence she knows that as she and her post-boomer generation age into middle and later years, their life courses will inevitably be marked by the struggles inherent in forever trying to balance the obligations to oneself and to others.

GRADUATION DAY, 1965

by John Marzán

Fifteen years ago, when soldiers
Dragged your brother to that street
Crowded with others they had captured,
A burned-skin corporal named Vargas
Kicked him in the teeth,
And the long simple word of his blood,
Crawling to the shade of a jeep,
Dripped into the news of his arrest

So liquid and hot that it pierced
The skin your mother had hardened,
Who pushed the rush back in her heart
Long enough to sell the furniture,
Pack up your clothes and leave
The ground that came with a drinking husband,
The demon driving the fists that beat her,
And the famine that forever would be yours
Whom she bore to see prosperous, a man of peace

And often in the nightflights of nine years
You resumed to your childhood in that land,
Green without businessmen or politics,
To come before the image of your father,
Home from the canes with eyes bloodshot,
Angry for no reason,
Unbuckling his belt to hit you many times
Before you woke up to the screeching of the El,

The mice clinging to the blanket. It was
Enough to make you shut your eyes and leap
Back into the starless space inside
As if swimming underwater under a continent,
Looking for a glittering passage of light
Skin and scars and a name apart
From a cold metal bed in New York.

Millions of miles from a letter from prison,
Like the scream of a stump you had long forgotten,
Arrived to claim its continuity in you,
Repeating over the small town of a page
The democratic debate of the machine guns
As if today you understood his language
Or why the Yankees ever landed,
Why one day, while you wailed frightened,

Your pious mother, kneeled before her candle,
Cried out that she'd rather have him dead
As he stepped out to the meaning of his war,
Weeping unable to explain.

Here where the air corrodes his anguish,
Where his faded image
Translates into nonsense,
Seriously your life adjusts its tie and weighs
The advantages of accounting, of R.O.T.C.
Today a small state college on Long Island
Has offered you a scholarship
And the past is a stranger calling from a pier
Drowned out by the winds and a promise.

GRANDMA'S WAKE

by Emilio Díaz Valcárcel

We welcomed Uncle Segundo this morning. We sat waiting on one of the benches at the airport for four hours while mobs of people came and went. The people were looking at us and saying things and I was thinking how it would be to ride in an airplane and leave behind the *barrio*, my friends in school, Mamá moaning about the bad times and the cafes that don't let anybody sleep. And then to live talking other words, far from the river where we bathe every afternoon. That's what I was thinking about this morning, dead tired because we'd gotten up at five. A few planes arrived but Uncle Segundo wasn't to be seen anywhere. Mamá was saying that he hadn't changed a bit, that he was the same old Segundo, arriving late at places, and probably mixed up with the police. That he'd probably got in some kind of a jam up there in the North and they'd arrested him, that he hadn't paid the store and was in court. That's what Mamá was saying, looking all around her, asking people, cursing every time they stepped on her new slippers.

I'd never met Uncle Segundo. They said that he had my face and that if I had a moustache we'd be like made to order. That's what the big people argued about on Sunday afternoon when Aunt Altagracia came from San Juan with her bag full of smells and sweets, and told us to ask her for a blessing and then talked with Mamá about how drawn and skinny I was, and whether I attended Sunday school and whether I studied, after which they would almost come to blows because Aunt Altagracia would say that I was Segundo through and through. Mamá didn't like it at first, but later she would say yes, that I was really another Segundo in the flesh, except without the moustache. But one thing, my aunt would snap, let's hope he doesn't have his fiendish nature, for one time someone called him "one ear" and he slashed the man's back and he also castrated the dog that ripped up the pants he wore for calling on his

women. And Mamá would say no, I wouldn't have her brother's high-flown disposition, 'cause I was more like a sick little mouse if you were to judge by the way I sneaked around. Then Mamá would send me for a nickel's worth of cigarettes or to milk the goat, so that I wouldn't hear when she began to talk of Papá, and of the nights she couldn't sleep waiting for him while he played dominoes in Eufrasio's, and my aunt would turn all red and say she had it coming to her and that they'd warned her plenty and told her don't be crazy that man's a barfly don't be crazy watch what you're doing.

That was every Sunday, the only day that Aunt Altagracia could come from San Juan and visit this *barrio*, which she says she hates because the people don't have manners. But today is Tuesday and she came to see Grandma and to wait for her brother, because they wrote him that Grandma was on her last legs and he said all right if that's the way it is I'm coming but I've got to leave right away. And we were waiting four hours at the airport, dead tired, while all the people looked at us and said things.

Neither Mamá nor Aunt Altagracia recognized the man who came up dressed in white, looking plenty smooth and fat. He threw himself into their arms and nearly squeezed them both dry at the same time. As for me, he gave a tug at my sideburns and then stared at me awhile, then he picked me up and told me I was a real he-man and asked if I had a girlfriend. Mamá said that I'd been born a bit sickly and that from what I'd shown so far I'd turn out to be a sick little mouse. Aunt Altagracia said that they should take a good look, a real good look, for if I had a moustache I'd be the double in miniature of my uncle.

During the trip Uncle Segundo talked about his business in the North. My mother and my aunt both agreed that someday they would go up there, because here the sun makes one age ahead of time, and the work, the heat, the few opportunities to improve one's life.... We reached home without my being aware of it. Uncle Segundo woke me up tugging hard at my ear and asking if I could see God and saying straighten up 'cause nobody pays attention to people who hang their heads.

Uncle Segundo found Grandma a bit pale, but not as bad as they'd told him. He put his hand on her chest and told her to breathe, to come on and breathe, and he nearly turned the bed over and threw Grandma on the floor. He patted her on the face and then claimed she was all right, and that he'd come from so far away and that he'd left his business all alone and this was the only—listen, you—the *only* chance right now. Because after all he'd come to a funeral, and nothing else. My mother and my aunt opened their mouths to yell and they said it was true, he hadn't changed a bit. But my uncle said the old woman was fine, look at her, and what would people say if he couldn't come back from the North for the funeral next time? And he said it plenty clear: It had to happen in the three days he was going to spend in the *barrio* and if not they'd have to give him back the money he'd spent on the trip. My mama and my aunt had their hands to their heads yelling barbarian, you're nothing but a heretic barbarian. Uncle Segundo's neck swelled up, he started saying things I didn't understand and he took Grandma's measurements. He measured her with his hands from head to foot and side to side. Grandma was smiling and it looked like she wanted to talk to him. Uncle made a face and went looking for Santo, the carpenter, and told him to make a coffin of the best wood there was, that his family wasn't cheap. They spoke about the price for a while and then Uncle left to see the four women he's got in the *barrio.* He gave each one six bits and brought them over to our house. They lit a few candles and put Grandma in the coffin where she could've danced, she was so skinny. My uncle complained and said the coffin was too wide, that Santo had made it like that just to charge more, and that he wouldn't pay a cent over three fifty. Grandma kept on laughing there, inside the coffin, and moved her lips like she wanted to say something. Uncle's women hadn't begun to cry when two of their dogs started to fight beneath the coffin. Uncle Segundo was furious and he kicked them until they peed and came out from under and left, their tails between their legs, yelping. Then Uncle moved his hand up and down and the women began to cry and shout. Uncle pinched them so they'd make more noise. Mamá was stretched out on the floor, howling just like the dogs; Aunt

Altagracia was fanning her and sprinkling her with *alcoholado.* Papá was there, lying down at her side, saying that these things do happen and that it was all their fault, 'cause if they hadn't said anything to his brother-in-law nothing would have happened.

All that yelling began to draw people to the wake. Papá wasn't too happy about Eufrasio coming because he was always trying to collect debts with those hard looks of his. The twins, Serafin and Evaristo, arrived, and they tossed a coin heads or tails to see who would lead the rosary. Chalí came up with his eight children and sat them down on the floor and searched them for bugs while he mumbled his prayers. The Cane sisters came in through the kitchen looking at the cupboard, fanning themselves with a newspaper and saying things in each other's ears. The dogs were fighting outside. Canon came up to Mamá and said he congratulated her, 'cause these things, well, they have to happen and that God Almighty would fix things up so as to find a little corner on his throne for the poor old woman. Aunt Altagracia was saying that the wake would have been more proper in San Juan and not in this damned *barrio,* which she unfortunately had to visit. Uncle Segundo was telling Grandma to shut her damned mouth, not to laugh, for this was no joke but a wake where she, though it mightn't seem so, was the most important thing.

Mamá got up and took Grandma out of the coffin. She was carrying her toward the room when Uncle, drunk and saying bad words, grabbed Grandma by the head and began to pull her back toward the coffin. Mamá kept pulling her by the ankles and then the dogs came in and started to bark. Uncle Segundo threw them a kick. The dogs left, but my uncle went sideways and fell on the floor with Mamá and Grandma. Papá squatted down next to Mamá and told her that this was incredible, that they should please their brother after all the years he'd been away. But Mamá didn't give in and then Uncle began to stamp his feet and Aunt Altagracia said, see, this boy hasn't changed a bit.

But my uncle still got things his way. Cañón was stretched out in a corner crying. The Cane sisters came up to my grandma and said how pretty the old woman looks, still smiling as in life, how pretty, eh?

I felt sort of shrunk. My uncle was a big strong man. I, Mamá herself said it, will turn out to be just a sick little mouse, the way I'm going. I would like to be strong, like my uncle, and fight anyone who gets in my way. I felt tiny whenever my uncle looked at me and said that I wouldn't look like him even with a moustache, that they'd fooled him so many times, and what was this? He would end up telling me that I'd become the spitting image of my father, and that one couldn't expect much from someone with my looks.

Cañón began to talk with Rosita Cane and after a while they went into the kitchen, acting as if they weren't up to something. The other Cane was fanning herself with a paper and looking enviously toward the kitchen and also looking at Eufrasio who, they say, bought off Melina's parents with a refrigerator. Melina had left to give birth someplace else and since then Eufrasio just drinks and fights with the customers. But now Eufrasio was nice and calm and he was looking at the Cane girl and talking sign-language. He came up with a bottle and offered her a drink and she said heavens how dare you, but then she hid

behind the curtain and if Eufrasio hadn't taken the bottle away she wouldn't have left a drop.

The wake was now going full-steam ahead and the twins kept leading the rosary, looking toward the room where Aunt Altagracia was lying down. I was nearly asleep when the beating Uncle Segundo gave Cañón shook me up. My uncle was shouting and demanding to know what kind of things were going on and that they should all leave if each and every one of them didn't want to get their share. Rosita Cane was crying. My uncle grabbed his suitcase and said that all in all he was satisfied because he'd come to his mother's wake and that now he didn't have to go through it again. He went out saying that he didn't mind paying for the fare, or the box, or the mourners, and that in the whole *barrio* they wouldn't find such a sacrificing son. There's the coffin, he said, for whoever's turn it is. And he left, almost running.

When I went up to the coffin and looked at Grandma she wasn't laughing anymore. But I noticed a tiny bit of brightness flowing from her eyes and wetting her tightly closed lips.

1978
—Translated from the Spanish by Kal Wagenheim

CALLING HOME

by Dan Masterson

He dials his dead father's house,
where timers go off at noon, at dusk,
at nine, allowing the gooseneck lamp
to come on in the den, the radio
to sift through the kitchen walls
and awaken the neighbor's dog,
who no longer waits at the side door
for scraps.

Six rings—Mother
would have answered by now,
but she's kept in a vest that is tied
to a chair in the rest home he chose
from a list when he was in town.

Twenty rings, and counting:
the pilot light flickers in the stove,
a cobweb undulates
imperceptibly above the sink, the crystal
stemware chimes in its breakfront.

He closes his eyes and listens.
He would like to say something,
but there is nowhere
to begin.

Part Three

The United States: Democracy's Gorgeous Mosaic

In 1990 the passage of the Americans with Disabilities Act provided protections—for the first time—against systematic discrimination in employment, housing and public accommodations to the forty-three million U.S. citizens the Census Bureau identifies as having some physical or mental disability. It provided that the disabled must have access, the essential ability to enter a building or a bathroom unimpeded. Employers of 15 or more employees may not discriminate against them in hiring and must make "reasonable accommodation" to their disabilities. Millions of these mentally or physically challenged members of our society since have had greater opportunity to employ their abilities for their own benefit as well as for ours—in spite of attempts by some employers to use "undue hardship" as a loophole for providing particular accommodations. Who can deny that the leadership of someone such as the virtuoso violinist Itzak Perlman has changed significantly the way we see the physically challenged? And it is difficult to imagine that anyone who has worked with or watched the Special Olympics does not come away from them with a vivid sense of the personal qualities and particular abilities of the mentally and physically challenged who participate in them.

In coming to a new appreciation of the range of human abilities we find ourselves facing entrenched theories of intelligence that do not accommodate this range; indeed, the "one-and-only- one-true theory of intelligence" is too narrow to admit of the multiple intelligences we see at work readily in everyday life everywhere. **Chapter 7, Abilities,** begins with Howard Gardner's "The Theory of Multiple Intelligences." The most recent promotion of the "one-and-only-one-true theory of intelligence" is reviewed in Alfred E. Prettyman's "The Ring of the Bell Curve: Reverberations and Resonances. Daniel Goleman apprises us of the importance of "emotional intelligence" in "When Smart is Dumb."

Chapter 8, Values: Ethical and Religious, provides us with an historical summary of the sources, rituals and symbols of the civil religion—sometimes called "religious nationalism"—that is central to our constitutional democracy. Some observers, such as Stephen L. Carter in *The Culture of Disbelief* (1994), a work that is not included here, contend that there is today a pervasive tendency to denigrate both civil and personal religion. Lawrence M. Hinman in "The Ethics of Diversity: Gender, Ethnicity, and Individuality" examines how we might live morally in coming to grips with the challenges of cultural diversity. Moral dilemmas are at the heart of Randall Kenan's "Things of This World; or Angels Unawares"—a work of short fiction.

It was then New York Mayor David N. Dinkins who first described that city as "A gorgeous mosaic!" A microcosm of these United States. No one knew better than he—a coalition candidate—the importance of consensus and the difficulty of gaining or renewing it in the teeth of the conflicting claims of competing political and social groups. It takes far more than a steady focus. There is a ravenous irrationality abroad that must be acknowledged, as does Jayne Cortez in her poem "Madness Without Head," which begins **Chapter 9, Consensus and Conflict in Contemporary Society.**

Peter Edelman gives us a valuable analysis of the politics of passing legislation that might do harm to underrepresented segments of U.S. citizens and legal immigrants. Thing you may not consider a danger may be in daily use in your home, although they are toxic pollutants, according to "Scientific American." We are given new frames of reference for understanding Hispanic identity in Obler's essay. David Shipler helps us grapple with the complexities of decoding recism. Genny Lim's poem reminds us that "Children Are Color-Blind." Fanny Lou Hamer gives us a parable for living. Fixico's summary of federal Indian policy is sobering, yet hopeful.

IN A NUTSHELL

by Howard Gardner

Allow me to transport all of us to the Paris of 1900—La Belle Époque—when the city fathers of Paris approached a psychologist named Alfred Binet with an unusual request: Could he devise some kind of a measure that would predict which youngsters would succeed and which would fail in the primary grades of Paris schools? As everybody knows, Binet succeeded. In short order, his discovery came to be called the "intelligence test"; his measure, the "IQ." Like other Parisian fashions, the IQ soon made its way to the United States, where it enjoyed a modest success until World War 1. Then, it was used to test over one million American recruits, and it had truly arrived. From that day on, the IQ test has looked like psychology's biggest success—a genuinely useful scientific tool.

What is the vision that led to the excitement about IQ? At least in the West, people had always relied on intuitive assessments of how smart other people were. Now intelligence seemed to be quantifiable. You could measure someone's actual or potential height, and now, it seemed, you could also measure someone's actual or potential intelligence. We had one dimension of mental ability along which we could array everyone.

The search for the perfect measure of intelligence has proceeded apace. Here, for example, are some quotations from an ad for a widely used test:

> Need an individual test which quickly provides a stable and reliable estimate of intelligence in four or five minutes per form? Has three forms? Does not depend on verbal production or subjective scoring? Can be used with the severely physically handicapped (even paralyzed) if they can signal yes or no? Handles two-year-olds and superior adults with the same short series of items and the same format? Only $16.00 complete.

Now, that's quite a claim. The American psychologist Arthur Jensen suggests that we could look at reaction time to assess intelligence: A set of lights go on; how quickly can the subject react? The British psychologist Hans Eysenck suggests that investigators of intelligence should look directly at brain waves.

There are also, of course, more sophisticated versions of the IQ test. One of them is called the Scholastic Aptitude Test (SAT). It purports to be a similar kind of measure, and if you add up a person's verbal and math scores, as is often done, you can rate him or her along a single intellectual dimension. Programs for the gifted, for example, often use that kind of measure; if your IQ is in excess of 130, you're admitted to the program.

I want to suggest that along with this one-dimensional view of how to assess people's minds comes a corresponding view of school, which I will call the "uniform view." In the uniform school, there is a core curriculum, a set of facts that everybody should know, and very few electives. The better students, perhaps those with higher IQs, are allowed to take courses that call upon critical reading, calculation, and thinking skills. In the "uniform school," there are regular assessments, using paper and pencil instruments, of the IQ or SAT variety. They yield reliable rankings of people; the best and the brightest get into the better colleges, and perhaps—but only perhaps—they will also get better rankings in life. There is no question but that this approach works well for certain people—schools such as Harvard are eloquent testimony to that. Since this measurement and selection system is clearly meritocratic in certain respects, it has something to recommend it.

But there is an alternative vision that I would like to present—one based on a radically different view of the mind, and one that yields a very different view of school. It is a pluralistic view of mind, recognizing many different and discrete facets of cognition, acknowledging that people have different cognitive strengths and contrasting cognitive styles. I would also like to introduce the concept of an individual-centered school that takes this multifaceted view of intelligence seriously. This model for a school is based in part on findings from sciences that did not even exist in Binet's time; cognitive science (the study of the mind), and neuroscience (the study of the brain). One such approach I have called my "theory of multiple intelligences." Let me tell you something about its sources, its claims, and its educational implications for a possible school of the future.

Dissatisfaction with the concept of IQ and with unitary views of intelligence is fairly widespread—one thinks, for instance, of the work of L. L. Thurstone, J. P. Guilford, and other critics. From my point of view, however, these criticisms do not suffice. The whole concept has to be challenged; in fact, it has to be replaced.

I believe that we should get away altogether from tests and correlations among tests, and look instead at more naturalistic sources of information about how peoples around the world develop skills important to their way of life. Think, for example, of sailors in the South Seas, who find their way around hundreds, or even thousands, of islands by looking at the constellations of stars in the sky, feeling the way a boat passes over the water, and noticing a few scattered landmarks. A word for intelligence in a society of these sailors would probably refer to that kind of navigational ability. Think of surgeons and engineers, hunters and fishermen, dancers and choreographers, athletes and athletic coaches, tribal chiefs and sorcerers. All of these different roles need to be taken into account if we accept the way I define intelligence—that is, as the ability to solve problems, or to fashion products, that are valued in one or more cultural or community settings. For the moment I am saying nothing about whether there is one dimension, or more than one dimension, of intelligence; nothing about whether intelligence is inborn or developed. Instead I emphasize the ability to solve problems and to fashion products. In my work I seek the building blocks of the intelligences used by the aforementioned sailors and surgeons and sorcerers.

The science in this enterprise, to the extent that it exists, involves trying to discover the *right* description of the intelligences. What is an intelligence? To try to answer this question, I have, with my colleagues, surveyed a wide set of sources which, to my knowledge, have never been considered together before. One source is what we already know concerning the development of different kinds of skills in normal children. Another source, and a very important one, is information on the ways that these abilities break down under conditions of brain damage When one suffers a stroke or some other kind of brain damage, various abilities can be destroyed, or spared, in isolation from other abilities. This research with brain-damaged patients yields a very powerful kind cognitive profile. This vision stands in direct contrast to that of the uniform school that I described earlier.

The design of my ideal school of the future is based upon two assumptions. The first is that not all people have the same interests and abilities; not all of us learn in the same way. (And we now have the tools to begin to address these individual differences in school.) The second assumption is one that hurts: It is the assumption that nowadays no one person can learn everything there is to learn. We would all like, as Renaissance men and women, to know everything, or at least to believe in the potential of knowing everything, but that ideal clearly is not possible anymore. Choice is therefore inevitable, and one of the things that I want to argue is that the choices that we make for ourselves, and for the people who are under our charge, might as well be informed choices. An individual-centered school would be rich in assessment of individual abilities and proclivities. It would seek to match individuals not only to curricular areas, but also to particular ways of teaching those subjects. And after the first few grades, the school would also seek to match individuals with the various kinds of life and work options that are available in their culture.

I want to propose a new set of roles for educators that might make this vision a reality. First of all, we might have what I will call "assessment specialists." The job of these people would be to try to understand as sensitively and comprehensively as possible the abilities and interests of the students in a school. It would be very important, however, that the assessment specialists use "intelligence-fair" instruments. We want to be able to look specifically and directly at spatial abilities, at personal abilities, and the like, and not through the usual lenses of the linguistic and logical-mathematical intelligences. Up until now nearly all assessment has depended indirectly on measurement of those abilities; if students are not strong in those two areas, their abilities in other areas may be obscured. Once we begin to try to assess other kinds of intelligences directly, I am confident that particular students will reveal strengths in quite different areas, and the notion of general brightness will disappear or become greatly attenuated.

In addition to the assessment specialist, the school of the future might have the "student-curriculum broker." It would be his or her job to help match students' profiles, goals, and interests to particular curricula and to particular styles of learning. Incidentally, I think that the new interactive technologies offer considerable promise in this area: It will probably be much easier in the future for "brokers" to match individual students to ways of learning that prove comfortable for them.

There should also be, I think, a "school-community broker," who would match students to learning opportunities in the wider community. It would be this person's job to find situations in the community, particularly options not available in the school, for children who exhibit unusual cognitive profiles. I have in mind apprenticeships, mentorships, internships in organizations, "big brothers," "big sisters"—individuals and organizations with whom these students might work to secure a feeling for different kinds of vocational and avocational roles in the society. I am not worried about those occasional youngsters who are good in everything. They're going to do just fine. I'm concerned about those who don't shine in the standardized tests, and who, therefore, tend to be written off as not having gifts of any kind. It seems to me that the school-community broker could spot these youngsters and find placements in the community that provide chances for them to shine.

There is ample room in this vision for teachers, as well, and also for master teachers. In my view, teachers would be freed to do what they are supposed to do, which is to teach their subject matter, in their preferred style of teaching. The job of master teacher would be very demanding. It would involve, first of all, supervising the novice teachers and guiding them; but the master teacher would also seek to ensure that the complex student-assessment-curriculum-community equation is balanced appropriately. If the equation is seriously imbalanced, master teachers would intervene and suggest ways to make things better.

Clearly, what I am describing is a tall order; it might even be called utopian. And there is a major risk to this program, of which I am well aware. That is the risk of premature billeting—of saying, "Well, Johnny is four, he seems to be musical, so we are going to send him to Juilliard and drop everything else." There is, however, nothing inherent in the approach that I have described that demands this early overdetermination—quite the contrary. It seems to me that early identification of strengths can be very helpful in indicating what kinds of experiences children might profit from; but early identification of weaknesses can be equally important. If a weakness is identified early, there is a chance to attend to it before it is too late, and to come up with alternative ways of teaching or of covering an important skill area.

We now have the technological and the human resources to implement such an individual-centered school. Achieving it is a question of will, including the will to withstand the current enormous pressures toward uniformity and unidimensional assessments. There are strong pressures now, which you read about every day in the newspapers, to compare students, to compare teachers, states, even entire countries, using one dimension or criterion, a kind of a crypto-IQ assessment. Clearly, everything I have described today stands in direct opposition to that particular view of the world. Indeed that is my intent—to provide a ringing indictment of such one-track thinking.

I believe that in our society we suffer from three biases, which I have nicknamed "Westist," "Testist," and "Bestist." "Westist" involves putting certain Western cultural values, which date back to Socrates, on a pedestal. Logical thinking, for example, is important; rationality is important; but they are not the only virtues. "Testist" suggests a bias towards focusing upon those human abilities or approaches that are readily testable. If it can't be tested, it sometimes seems, it is not worth paying attention to. My feeling is that assessment can be much broader, much more humane than it is now, and that psychologists should spend less time ranking people and more time trying to help them.

"Bestist" is a not very veiled reference to a book by David Halberstam called *The Best and the Brightest.* Halberstam referred ironically to figures such as Harvard faculty members who were brought to Washington to help President John F. Kennedy and in the process launched the Vietnam War. I think that any belief that all the answers to a given problem lie in one certain approach, such as logical-mathematical thinking, can be very dangerous. Current views of intellect need to be leavened with other more comprehensive points of view.

It is of the utmost importance that we recognize and nurture all of the varied human intelligences, and all of the combinations of intelligences. We are all so different largely because we all have different combinations of intelligences. If we recognize this, I think we will have at least a better chance of dealing appropriately with the many problems that we face in the world. If we can mobilize the spectrum of human abilities, not only will people feel better about themselves and more competent; it is even possible that they will also feel more engaged and better able to join the rest of the world community in working for the broader good. Perhaps if we can mobilize the full range of human intelligences and ally them to an ethical sense, we can help to increase the likelihood of our survival on this planet, and perhaps even contribute to our thriving.

A Rounded Version

by Howard Gardner and Joseph Walters

Two eleven-year-old children are taking a test of "intelligence." They sit at their desks laboring over the meanings of different words, the interpretation of graphs, and the solutions to arithmetic problems. They record their answers by filling in small circles on a single piece of paper. Later these completed answer sheets are scored objectively: The number of right answers is converted into a standardized score that compares the individual child with a population of children of similar age.

The teachers of these children review the different scores. They notice that one of the children has performed at a superior level; on all sections of the test, she answered more questions correctly than did her peers. In fact, her score is similar to that of children three to four years older. The other child's performance is average—his scores reflect those of other children his age.

A subtle change in expectations surrounds the review of these test scores. Teachers begin to expect the first child to do quite well during her formal schooling, whereas the second should have only moderate ;success. Indeed these predictions come true. In other words, the test taken by the eleven-year-olds serves as a reliable predictor of their later performance in school.

How does this happen? One explanation involves our free use of the word "intelligence": The child with the greater "intelligence" has the ability to solve problems, to find the answers to specific questions, and to learn new material quickly and efficiently. These skills in turn play a central role in school success. In this view, "intelligence" is a singular faculty that is brought to bear in any problem-solving situation. Since schooling deals largely with solving problems of various sorts, predicting this capacity in young children predicts their future success in school.

"Intelligence," from this point of view, is a general ability that is found in varying degrees in all individuals. It is the key to success in solving problems. This ability can be measured reliably with standardized pencil-and-paper tests that, in turn, predict future success in school.

What happens after school is completed? Consider the two individuals in the example. Looking further down the road, we find that the "average" student has become a highly successful mechanical engineer who has risen to a position of prominence in both the professional community of engineers as well as in civic groups in his community. His success is no fluke—he is considered by all to be a talented individual. The "superior" student, on the other hand, has had little success in her chosen career as a writer; after repeated rejections by publishers, she has taken up a middle management position in a bank. While certainly not a "failure," she is considered by her peers to be quite "ordinary" in her adult accomplishments. So what happened?

This fabricated example is based on the facts of intelligence testing. IQ tests predict school performance with considerable accuracy, but they are only an indifferent predictor of performance in a profession after formal schooling (Jencks, 1972). Furthermore, even as IQ tests measure only logical or logical-linguistic capacities, in this society we are nearly "brain-washed" to restrict the notion of intelligence to the capacities used in solving logical and linguistic problems.

To introduce an alternative point of view, undertake the following "thought experiment." Suspend the usual judgment of what constitutes intelligence and let your thoughts run freely over the capabilities of humans—perhaps those that would be picked out by the proverbial Martian visitor. In this exercise, you are drawn to the brilliant chess player, the world-class violinist, and the champion athlete; such outstanding performers deserve special consideration. Under this experiment, a quite different view of *intelligence* emerges. Are the chess player, violinist, and athlete "intelligent" in these pursuits? If they are, then why do our tests of "intelligence" fail to identify them? If they are not "intelligent," what allows them to achieve

such astounding feats? In general, why does the contemporary construct "intelligence" fail to explain large areas of human endeavor?

In this chapter we approach these problems through the theory of multiple intelligences (MI). As the name indicates, we believe that human cognitive competence is better described in terms of a set of abilities, talents, or mental skills, which we call "intelligences." All normal individuals possess each of these skills to some extent; individuals differ in the degree of skill and in the nature of their combination. We believe this theory of intelligence may be more humane and more veridical than alternative views of intelligence and that it more adequately reflects the data of human "intelligent" behavior. Such a theory has important educational implications, including ones for curriculum development.

WHAT CONSTITUTES AN INTELLIGENCE?

The question of the optimal definition of intelligence looms large in our inquiry. Indeed, it is at the level of this definition that the theory of multiple intelligences diverges from traditional points of view. In a traditional view, intelligence is defined operationally as the ability to answer items on tests of intelligence. The inference from the test scores to some underlying ability is supported by statistical techniques that compare responses of subjects at different ages; the apparent correlation of these test scores across ages and across different tests corroborates the notion that the general faculty of intelligence, g, does not change much with age or with training or experience. It is an inborn attribute or faculty of the individual.

Multiple intelligences theory, on the other hand, pluralizes the traditional concept. An intelligence entails the ability to solve problems or fashion products that are of consequence in a particular cultural setting or community. The problem-solving skill allows one to approach a situation in which a goal is to be obtained and to locate the appropriate route to that goal. The creation of a *cultural* product is crucial to such functions as capturing and transmitting knowledge or expressing one's views or feelings. The problems to be solved range from creating an end for a story to anticipating a mating move in chess to repairing a quilt. Products range from scientific theories to musical compositions to successful political campaigns.

MI theory is framed in light of the biological origins of each problem-solving skill. Only those skills that are universal to the human species are treated. Even so, the biological proclivity to participate in a particular form of problem solving must also be coupled with the cultural nurturing of that domain. For example, language, a universal skill, may manifest itself particularly as writing in one culture, as oratory in another culture, and as the secret language of anagrams in a third.

Given the desire of selecting intelligences that are rooted in biology, and that are valued in one or more cultural settings, how does one actually identify an "intelligence"? In coming up with our list, we consulted evidence from several different sources; knowledge about normal development and development in gifted individuals; information about the breakdown of cognitive skills under conditions of brain damage; studies of exceptional populations, including prodigies, idiots savants, and autistic children; data about the evolution of cognition over the millennia; cross-cultural accounts of cognition; psychometric studies, including examinations of correlations among tests; and psychological training studies, particularly measures of transfer and generalization across tasks. Only those candidate intelligences that satisfied all or a majority of the criteria were selected as bona fide intelligences. A more complete discussion of each of these criteria for an "intelligence" and the seven intelligences that have been proposed so far, is found in *Frames of Mind (1983)*. This book also considers how the theory might be disproven and compares it to competing theories of intelligence.

In addition to satisfying the aforementioned criteria, each intelligence must have an identifiable core operation or set of operations. As a neurally based computational system, each intelligence is activated or "triggered" by certain kinds of internally or externally presented information. For example, one core of musical intelligence is the sensitivity to pitch relations, whereas one core of linguistic intelligence is the sensitivity to phonological features.

An intelligence must also be susceptible to encoding in a symbol system—a culturally contrived system of meaning, which captures and conveys important forms of information. Language, picturing, and mathematics are but three nearly worldwide symbol systems that are necessary for human survival and productivity. The relationship of a candidate intelligence to a human symbol system is no accident. In fact, the existence of a core computational capacity anticipates the existence of a symbol system that exploits that capacity. While it may be possible for an intelligence to proceed without an accompanying symbol system, a primary characteristic of human intelligence may well be its gravitation toward such an embodiment.

THE SEVEN INTELLIGENCES

Having sketched the characteristics and criteria of an intelligence, we turn now to a brief consideration of each of the seven intelligences. We begin each sketch with a thumbnail biography of a person who demonstrates an unusual facility with that intelligence. These biographies illustrate some of the abilities that are central to the fluent operation of a given intelligence. Although each biography illustrates a particular intelligence, we do not wish to imply that in adulthood intelligences operate in isolation. Indeed, except for abnormal individuals, intelligences always work in concert, and any sophisticated adult role will involve a melding of several of them. Following each biography we survey the various sources of data that support each candidate as an "intelligence."

MUSICAL INTELLIGENCE

> When he was three years old, Yehudi Menuhin was smuggled into the San Francisco Orchestra concerts by his parents. The sound of Louis Persinger's violin so entranced the youngster that he insisted on a violin for his birthday and Louis Persinger as his teacher. He got both. By the time he was ten years old, Menuhin was an international performer (Menuhin, 1977).

Violinist Yehudi Menuhin's musical intelligence manifested itself even before he had touched a violin or received any musical training. His powerful reaction to that particular sound and his rapid progress on the instrument suggest that he was biologically prepared in some way for that endeavor. In this way, evidence from child prodigies supports our claim that there is a biological link to a particular intelligence. Other special populations, such as autistic children who can play a musical instrument beautifully but who cannot speak, underscore the independence of musical intelligence.

A brief consideration of the evidence suggests that musical skill passes the other tests for an intelligence. For example, certain parts of the brain play important roles in perception and production of music. These areas are characteristically located in the right hemisphere, although musical skill is not as clearly "localized," or located in a specifiable area, as language. Although the particular susceptibility of musical ability to brain damage depends on the degree of training and other individual differences, there is clear evidence for "amusia" or loss of musical ability.

Music apparently played an important unifying role in Stone Age (Paleolithic) societies. Birdsong provides a link to other species. Evidence from various cultures supports the notion that music is a universal faculty. Studies of infant development suggest that there is a "raw" computational ability in early childhood. Finally, musical notation provides an accessible and lucid symbol system.

In short, evidence to support the interpretation of musical ability as an "intelligence" comes from many different sources. Even though musical skill is not typically considered an intellectual skill like mathematics, it qualifies under our criteria. By definition it deserves consideration; and in view of the data, its inclusion is empirically justified.

BODILY-KINESTHETIC INTELLIGENCE

Fifteen-year-old Babe Ruth played third base. During one game his team's pitcher was doing very poorly and Babe loudly criticized him from third base. Brother Mathias, the coach, called out, "Ruth, if you know so much about it, YOU pitch!" Babe

was surprised and embarrassed because he had never pitched before, but Brother Mathias insisted. Ruth said later that at the very moment he took the pitcher's mound, he KNEW he was supposed to be a pitcher and that it was "natural" for him to strike people out. Indeed, he went on to become a great major league pitcher (and, of course, attained legendary status as a hitter) (Connor, 1982).

Like Menuhin, Babe Ruth was a child prodigy who recognized his "instrument" immediately upon his first exposure to it. This recognition occurred in advance of formal training.

Control of bodily movement is, of course, localized in the motor cortex, with each hemisphere dominant or controlling bodily movements on the contra-lateral side. In right-handers, the dominance for such movement is ordinarily found in the left hemisphere. The ability to perform movements when directed to do so can be impaired even in individuals who can perform the same movements reflexively or on a nonvoluntary basis. The existence of specific *apraxia* constitutes one line of evidence for a bodily-kinesthetic intelligence.

The evolution of specialized body movements is of obvious advantage to the species, and in humans this adaptation is extended through the use of tools. Body movement undergoes a clearly defined developmental schedule in children. And there is little question of its universality across cultures. Thus it appears that bodily-kinesthetic "knowledge" satisfies many of the criteria for an intelligence.

The consideration of bodily-kinesthetic knowledge as "problem solving" may be less intuitive. Certainly carrying out a mime sequence or hitting a tennis ball is not solving a mathematical equation. And yet, the ability to use one's body to express an emotion (as in a dance), to play a game (as in a sport), or to create a new product (as in devising an invention) is evidence of the cognitive features of body usage. The specific computations required to solve a particular bodily-kinesthetic *problem*, hitting a tennis ball, are summarized by Tim Gallwey:

At the moment the ball leaves the server's racket, the brain calculates approximately where it will

311

land and where the racket will intercept it. This calculation includes the initial velocity of the ball, combined with an input for the progressive decrease in velocity and the effect of wind and after the bounce of the ball. Simultaneously, muscle orders are given not just once, but constantly with refined and updated information. The muscles must cooperate. A movement of the feet occurs, the racket is taken back, the face of the racket kept at a constant angle. Contact is made at a precise point that depends on whether the order was given to hit down the line or cross-court, an order not given until after a split-second analysis of the movement and balance of the opponent.

To return an average serve, you have about one second to do this. To hit the ball at all is remarkable and yet not uncommon. The truth is that everyone who inhabits a human body possesses a remarkable creation (Gallwey, 1976).

LOGICAL-MATHEMATICAL INTELLIGENCE

In 1983, Barbara McClintock won the Nobel Prize in medicine or physiology for her work in microbiology. Her intellectual powers of deduction and observation illustrate one form of logical-mathematical intelligence that is often labeled "scientific thinking." One incident is particularly illuminating. While a researcher at Cornell in the 1920s, McClintock was faced one day with a problem: while *theory* predicted 50 percent pollen sterility in corn, her research assistant (in the "field") was finding plants that were only 25 to 30 percent sterile. Disturbed by this discrepancy, McClintock left the cornfield and returned to her office where she sat for half an hour, thinking:

> Suddenly I jumped up and ran back to the (corn) field. At the top of the field (the others were still at the bottom) I shouted "Eureka, I have it! I know what the 30% sterility is!"...They asked me to prove it. I sat down with a paper bag and a pencil and I started from scratch, which I had not done at all in my laboratory. It had all been done so fast, the answer came and I ran. Now I worked it out step by step—it was an intricate series of steps—and I came out with [the same result]. [They] looked at the material and it was exactly as I'd said it was; it worked out exactly as I had diagrammed it. Now, why did I know, without having done it on paper? Why was I so sure? (Keller, 1988, p. 104).

This anecdote illustrates two essential facts of the logical-mathematical intelligence. First, in the gifted individual, the process of problem solving is often remarkably rapid—the successful scientist copes with many variables at once and creates numerous hypotheses that are each evaluated and then accepted or rejected in turn.

The anecdote also underscores the *nonverbal* nature of the intelligence. A solution to a problem can be constructed *before* it is articulated. In fact, the solution process may be totally invisible, even to the problem solver. This need not imply, however, that discoveries of this sort—the familiar "Aha!" phenomenon—are mysterious, intuitive, or unpredictable. The fact that it happens more frequently to some people (perhaps Nobel Prize winners) suggests the opposite. We interpret this as the work of the logical-mathematical intelligence.

Along with the companion skill of language, logical-mathematical reasoning provides the principal basis for IQ tests. This form of intelligence has been heavily investigated by traditional psychologists, and it is the archetype of "raw intelligence" or the problem-solving faculty that purportedly cuts across domains. It is perhaps ironic, then, that the actual mechanism by which one arrives at a solution to a logical-mathematical problem is not as yet properly understood.

This intelligence is supported by our empirical criteria as well. Certain areas of the brain are more prominent in mathematical calculation than others. There are idiots savants who perform great feats of calculation even though they remain tragically deficient in most other areas. Child prodigies in mathematics abound. The development of this intelligence in children has been carefully documented by Jean Piaget and other psychologists.

LINGUISTIC INTELLIGENCE

> At the age of ten, T. S. Eliot created a magazine called "Fireside" to which he was the sole contributor. In a three-day period during his winter vacation, he created eight complete issues. Each one included poems, adventure stories, a gossip column, and humor. Some of this material survives and it displays the talent of the poet (see Soldo, 1982).

As with the logical intelligence, calling linguistic skill an "intelligence" is consistent with the stance of traditional psychology. Linguistic intelligence also passes our empirical tests. For instance, a specific area of the brain, called "Broca's Area," is responsible for the production of grammatical sentences. A person with damage to this area can understand words and sentences quite well but has difficulty putting words together in anything other than the simplest of sentences. At the same time, other thought processes may be entirely unaffected.

The gift of language is universal, and its development in children is strikingly constant across cultures. Even in deaf populations where a manual sign language is not explicitly taught, children will often "invent" their own manual language and use it surreptitiously! We thus see how an intelligence may operate independently of a specific input modality or output channel.

SPATIAL INTELLIGENCE

> Navigation around the Caroline Islands in the South Seas is accomplished without instruments. The position of the stars, as viewed from various islands, the weather patterns, and water color are the only sign posts. Each journey is broken into a series of segments; and the navigator learns the position of the stars within each of these segments. During the actual trip the navigator must envision mentally a reference island as it passes under a particular star and from that he computes the number of segments completed, the proportion of the trip remaining, and any corrections in heading that are required. The navigator cannot see the islands as he sails along; instead he maps their locations in his mental "picture" of the journey (Gardner, 1983).

Spatial problem solving is required for navigation and in the use of the notational system of maps. Other kinds of spatial problem solving are brought to bear in visualizing an object seen from a different angle and in playing chess. The visual arts also employ this intelligence in the use of space.

Evidence from brain research is clear and persuasive. Just as the left hemisphere has, over the course of evolution, been selected as the site of linguistic processing in right-handed persons, the right hemisphere proves to be the site most crucial for spatial processing. Damage to the right posterior regions causes impairment of the ability to find one's way around a site, to recognize faces or scenes, or to notice fine details.

Patients with damage specific to regions of the right hemisphere will attempt to compensate for their spacial deficits with linguistic strategies. They will try to reason aloud, to challenge the task, or even make up answers. But such nonspatial strategies are rarely successful.

Blind populations provide an illustration of the distinction between the spatial intelligence and visual perception. A blind person can recognize shapes by an indirect method: running a hand along the object translates into length of time of movement which in turn is translated into the size of the object. For the blind person, the perceptual system of the tactile modality parallels the visual modality in the seeing person. The analogy between the spatial reasoning of the blind and the linguistic reasoning of the deaf is notable.

There are few child prodigies among visual artists, but there are idiots savants such as Nadia (Selfe, 1977). Despite a condition of severe autism this preschool child made drawings of the most remarkable representational accuracy and finesse.

INTERPERSONAL INTELLIGENCE

With little formal training in special education and nearly blind herself, Anne Sullivan began the intimidating task of instructing a blind and deaf seven-year-old Helen Keller. Sullivan's efforts at communication were complicated by the child's emotional struggle with the world around her. At their first meal together, this scene occurred:

> Annie did not allow Helen to put her hand into Annie's plate and take what she wanted, as she had been accustomed to do with her family. It became a test of wills—hand thrust into plate, hand firmly put aside. The family, much upset, left the dining room. Annie locked the door and proceeded to eat her breakfast while Helen lay on the floor kicking and screaming, pushing and pulling at Annie's chair. [After half an hour] Helen went around the table looking for her family. She discovered no one else was there and that bewildered her. Finally, she

sat down and began to eat her breakfast, but with her hands. Annie gave her a spoon. Down on the floor it clattered, and the contest of wills began anew (Lash, 1980, p. 52).

Anne Sullivan sensitively responded to the child's behavior. She wrote home: "The greatest problem I shall have to solve is how to discipline and control her without breaking her spirit. I shall go rather slowly at first and try to win her love."

In fact, the first "miracle" occurred two weeks later, well before the famous incident at the pumphouse. Annie had taken Helen to a small cottage near the family's house, where they could live alone. After seven days together, Helen's personality suddenly underwent a profound change—the therapy had worked:

> My heart is singing with joy this morning. A miracle has happened! The wild little creature of two weeks ago has been transformed into a gentle child (p. 54).

It was just two weeks after this that the first breakthrough in Helen's grasp of language occurred; and from that point on, she progressed with incredible speed. The key to the miracle of language was Anne Sullivan's insight into the person of Helen Keller.

Interpersonal intelligence builds on a core capacity to notice distinctions among others; in particular, contrasts in their moods, temperaments, motivations, and intentions. In more advanced forms, this intelligence permits a skilled adult to read the intentions and desires of others, even when these have been hidden. This skill appears in a highly sophisticated form in religious or political leaders, teachers, therapists, and parents. The Helen Keller-Anne Sullivan story suggests that this interpersonal intelligence does not depend on language.

All indices in brain research suggest that the frontal lobes play a prominent role in interpersonal knowledge. Damage in this area can cause profound personality changes while leaving other forms of problem solving unharmed—a person is often "not the same person" after such an injury.

Alzheimer's disease, a form of presenile dementia, appears to attack posterior brain zones with a special ferocity, leaving spatial, logical, and linguistic computations severely impaired. Yet, Alzheimer's patients will often remain well groomed, socially proper, and continually apologetic for their errors. In contrast, Pick's disease, another variety of presenile dementia that is more frontally oriented, entails a rapid loss of social graces.

Biological evidence for interpersonal intelligence encompasses two additional factors often cited as unique to humans. One factor is the prolonged childhood of primates, including the close attachment to the mother. In those cases where the mother is removed from early development, normal interpersonal development is in serious jeopardy. The second factor is the relative importance in humans of social interaction. Skills such as hunting, tracking, and killing in prehistoric societies required participation and cooperation of large numbers of people. The need for group cohesion, leadership, organization, and solidarity follows naturally from this.

INTRAPERSONAL INTELLIGENCE

In an essay called "A Sketch of the Past," written almost as a diary entry, Virginia Woolf discusses the "cotton wool of existence"—the various mundane events of life. She contrasts this "cotton wool" with three specific and poignant memories from her childhood: a fight with her brother, seeing a particular flower in the garden, and hearing of the suicide of a past visitor:

> These are three instances of exceptional moments. I often tell them over, or rather they come to the surface unexpectedly. But now for the first time I have written them down, and I realize something that I have never realized before. Two of these moments ended in a state of despair. The other ended, on the contrary, in a state of satisfaction.

> The sense of horror (in hearing of the suicide) held me powerless. But in the case of the flower, I found a reason; and was thus able to deal with the sensation. I was not powerless.

> Though I still have the peculiarity that I receive these sudden shocks, they are now always welcome; after the first surprise, I always feel instantly that they are particularly valuable. And so I go on to suppose that the shock-receiving capacity is

what makes me a writer. I hazard the explanation that a shock is at once in my case followed by the desire to explain it. I feel that I have had a blow; but it is not, as I thought as a child, simply a blow from an enemy hidden behind the cotton wool of daily life; it is or will become a revelation of some order; it is a token of some real thing behind appearances; and I make it real by putting it into words (Woolf, 1976, pp. 69—70).

This quotation vividly illustrates the intrapersonal intelligence— knowledge of the internal aspects of a person: access to one's own feeling life, one's range of emotions, the capacity to effect discriminations among these emotions and eventually to label them and to draw upon them as a means of understanding and guiding one's own behavior. A person with good intrapersonal intelligence has a viable and effective model of himself or herself. Since this intelligence is the most private, it requires evidence from language, music, or some other more expressive form of intelligence if the observer is to detect it at work. In the above quotation, for example, linguistic intelligence is drawn upon to convey intrapersonal knowledge; it embodies the interaction of intelligences, a common phenomenon to which we will return later.

We see the familiar criteria at work in the intrapersonal intelligence. As with the interpersonal intelligence, the frontal lobes play a central role in personality change. Injury to the lower area of the frontal lobes is likely to produce irritability or euphoria; while injury to the higher regions is more likely to produce indifference, listlessness, slowness, and apathy—a kind of depressive personality. In such "frontal-lobe" individuals, the other cognitive functions often remain preserved. In contrast, among aphasics who have recovered sufficiently to describe their experiences, we find consistent testimony: while there may have been a diminution of general alertness and considerable depression about the condition, the individual in no way felt himself to be a different person. He recognized his own needs, wants, and desires and tried as best he could to achieve them.

The autistic child is a prototypical example of an individual with impaired intrapersonal intelligence; indeed, the child may not even be able to refer to himself. At the same time, such children

often exhibit remarkable abilities in the musical, computational, spatial, or mechanical realms.

Evolutionary evidence for an intrapersonal faculty is more difficult to come by, but we might speculate that the capacity to transcend the satisfaction of instinctual drives is relevant. This becomes increasingly important in a species not perennially involved in the struggle for survival.

In sum, then, both interpersonal and intrapersonal faculties pass the tests of an intelligence. They both feature problem-solving endeavors with significance for the individual and the species. Interpersonal intelligence allows one to understand and work with others; intrapersonal intelligence allows one to understand and work with oneself. In the individual's sense of self, one encounters a melding of inter- and intrapersonal components. Indeed, the sense of self emerges as one of the most marvelous of human inventions— a symbol that represents all kinds of information about a person and that is at the same time an invention that all individuals construct for themselves.

SUMMARY: THE UNIQUE CONTRIBUTIONS OF THE THEORY

As human beings, we all have a repertoire of skills for solving different kinds of problems. Our investigation has begun, therefore, with a consideration of these problems, the contexts they are found in, and the culturally significant products that are the outcome. We have not approached "intelligence" as a reified human faculty that is brought to bear in literally any problem setting; rather, we have begun with the problems that humans *solve* and worked back to the "intelligences" that must be responsible.

Evidence from brain research, human development, evolution, and cross-cultural comparisons was brought to bear in our search for the relevant human intelligences: a candidate was included only if reasonable evidence to support its membership was found across these diverse fields. Again, this tack differs from the traditional one since no candidate faculty is *necessarily* an intelligence, we could choose on a motivated basis. In the traditional approach to "intelligence," there is no opportunity for this type of empirical decision.

We have also determined that these multiple human faculties, the intelligences, are to a significant extent *independent*. For example, research with brain-damaged adults repeatedly demonstrates that particular faculties can be lost while others are spared. This independence of intelligences implies that a particularly high level of ability in one intelligence, say mathematics, does not require a similarly high level in another intelligence, like language or music. This independence of intelligences contrasts sharply with traditional measures of IQ that find high correlations among test scores. We speculate that the usual correlations among subtests of IQ tests come about because all of these tasks in fact measure the ability to respond rapidly to items of a logical-mathematical or linguistic sort; we believe that these correlations would be substantially reduced if one were to survey in a contextually appropriate way the full range of human problem-solving skills.

Until now, we have supported the fiction that adult roles depend largely on the flowering of a single intelligence. In fact, however, nearly every cultural role of any degree of sophistication requires a combination of intelligences. Thus, even an apparently straightforward role, like playing the violin, transcends a reliance on simple musical intelligence. To become a successful violinist requires bodily-kinesthetic dexterity and the interpersonal skills of relating to an audience and, in a different way, choosing a manager; quite possibly it involves an intrapersonal intelligence as well. Dance requires skills in bodily-kinesthetic, musical, interpersonal, and spatial intelligences in varying degrees. Politics requires an interpersonal skill, a linguistic facility, and perhaps some logical aptitude. Inasmuch as nearly every cultural role requires several intelligences, it becomes important to consider individuals as a collection of aptitudes rather than as having a singular problem-solving faculty that can be measured directly through pencil-and-paper tests. Even given a relatively small number of such intelligences, the diversity of human ability is created through the differences in these profiles. In fact, it may well be that the "total is greater than the sum of the

parts." An individual may not be particularly gifted in any intelligence; and yet, because of a particular combination or blend of skills, he or she may be able to fill some niche uniquely well. Thus it is of paramount importance to assess the particular combination of skills that may earmark an individual for a certain vocational or avocational niche.

IMPLICATIONS FOR EDUCATION

The theory of multiple intelligences was developed as an account of human cognition that can be subjected to empirical tests. In addition, the theory seems to harbor a number of educational implications that are worth consideration. In the following discussion we will begin by outlining what appears to be the natural developmental trajectory of an intelligence. Turning then to aspects of education, we will comment on the role of nurturing and explicit instruction in this development. From this analysis we find that assessment of intelligences can play a crucial role in curriculum development.

THE NATURAL GROWTH OF AN INTELLIGENCE: A DEVELOPMENTAL TRAJECTORY

Since all intelligences are part of the human genetic heritage, at some basic level each intelligence is manifested universally, independent of education and cultural support. Exceptional populations aside for the moment, all humans possess certain core abilities in each of the intelligences.

The natural trajectory of development in each intelligence begins with *raw patterning ability*, for example, the ability to make tonal differentiations in musical intelligence or to appreciate three-dimensional arrangements in spatial intelligence. These abilities appear universally; they may also appear at a heightened level in that part of the population that is "at promise" in that domain. The "raw" intelligence predominates during the first year of life.

Intelligences are glimpsed through different lenses at subsequent points in development. In the subsequent stage, the intelligence is encountered through a *symbol system*; language is encountered through sentences and stories, music through songs, spatial understanding through drawings, bodily-kinesthetic through gesture or dance, and so on. At this point children demonstrate their abilities in the various intelligences through their grasp of various symbol systems. Yehudi Menuhin's response to the sound of the violin illustrates the musical intelligence of a gifted individual coming in contact with a particular aspect of the symbol system.

As development progresses, each intelligence together with its accompanying symbol system is represented in a *notational system.* Mathematics, mapping, reading, music notation, and so on, are second-order symbol systems in which the marks on paper come to stand for symbols. In our culture, these notational systems are typically mastered in a formal educational setting.

Finally, during adolescence and adulthood, the intelligences are expressed through the range of *vocational and avocational pursuits.* For example, the logical-mathematical intelligence, which began as sheer pattern ability in infancy and developed through symbolic mastery of early childhood and the notations of the school years, achieves mature expression in such roles as mathematician, accountant, scientist, cashier. Similarly, the spatial intelligence passes from the mental maps of the infant, to the symbolic operations required in drawings and the notational systems of maps, to the adult roles of navigator, chess player, and topologist.

Although all humans partake of each intelligence to some degree, certain individuals are said to be "at promise." They are highly endowed with the core abilities and skills of that intelligence. This fact becomes important for the culture as a whole, since, in general, these exceptionally gifted individuals will make notable advances in the cultural manifestations of that intelligence. It is not important that all members of the Puluwat tribe demonstrate precocious spatial abilities needed for navigation by the stars, nor is it necessary for all Westerners to master mathematics to the degree necessary to make a significant contribution to theoretical physics. So long as the individuals "at promise" in particular domains are located efficiently, the overall knowledge of the group will be advanced in all domains.

While some individuals are "at promise" in an intelligence, others are "at risk." In the absence of special aids, those at risk in an intelligence will be most likely to fail tasks involving that intelligence. Conversely, those at promise will be most likely to succeed. It may be that intensive intervention at an early age can bring a larger number of children to an "at promise" level.

The special developmental trajectory of an individual at promise varies with intelligence. Thus, mathematics and music are characterized by the early appearance of gifted children who perform relatively early at or near an adult level. In contrast, the personal intelligences appear to arise much more gradually; prodigies are rare. Moreover, mature performance in one area does not imply mature performance in another area, just as gifted achievement in one does not imply gifted achievement in another.

IMPLICATIONS OF THE DEVELOPMENTAL TRAJECTORY FOR EDUCATION

Because the intelligences are manifested in different ways at different developmental levels, both assessment and nurturing need to occur in apposite ways. What nurtures in infancy would be inappropriate at later stages, and vice versa. In the preschool and early elementary years, instruction should emphasize opportunity. It is during these years that children can discover something of their own peculiar interests and abilities.

In the case of very talented children, such discoveries often happen by themselves through spontaneous "crystallizing experiences" (Walters & Gardner, 1986). When such experiences occur, often in early childhood, an individual reacts overtly to some attractive quality or feature of a domain. Immediately, the individual undergoes a strong affective reaction; he or she feels a special affinity to that domain, as did Menuhin when he first heard the violin at an orchestral concert. Thereafter, in many cases, the individual persists working in the domain, and, by drawing on a powerful set of appropriate intelligences, goes on to achieve high skill in that domain in relatively quick compass.

In the case of the most powerful talents, such crystallizing experiences seem difficult to prevent; and they may be especially likely to emerge in the domains of music and mathematics. However, specifically designed encounters with materials, equipment, or other people can help a youngster discover his or her own métier.

During the school-age years, some mastery of notational systems is essential in our society. The self-discovery environment of early schooling cannot provide the structure needed for the mastery of specific notational systems like the sonata form or algebra. In fact, during this period some tutelage is needed by virtually all children. One problem is to find the right form, since group tutelage can be helpful in some instances and harmful in others. Another problem is to orchestrate the connection between practical knowledge and the knowledge embodied in symbolic systems and notational systems.

Finally, in adolescence, most students must be assisted in their choice of careers. This task is made more complex by the manner in which intelligences interact in many cultural roles. For instance, being a doctor certainly requires logical-mathematical intelligence but while the general practitioner should have strong interpersonal skills, the surgeon needs bodily-kinesthetic dexterity. Internships, apprenticeships, and involvement with the actual materials of the cultural role become critical at this point in development.

Several implications for explicit instruction can be drawn from this analysis. First, the role of instruction in relation to the manifestation of an intelligence changes across the developmental trajectory. The enriched environment appropriate for the younger years is less crucial for adolescents. Conversely, explicit instruction in the notational system, appropriate for older children, is largely inappropriate for younger ones.

Explicit instruction must be evaluated in light of the developmental trajectories of the intelligences. Students benefit from explicit instruction only if the information or training fits into their specific place on the developmental progression. A particular kind of instruction can be either too early at one point or too late at another. For example,

Suzuki training in music pays little attention to the notational system, while providing a great deal of support or scaffolding for learning the fine points of instrumental technique. While this emphasis may be very powerful for training preschool children, it can produce stunted musical development when imposed at a late point on the developmental trajectory. Such a highly structured instructional environment can accelerate progress and produce a larger number of children "at promise," but in the end it may ultimately limit choices and inhibit self-expression.

An exclusive focus on linguistic and logical skills in formal schooling can shortchange individuals with skills in other intelligences. It is evident from inspection of adult roles, even in language-dominated Western society, that spatial, interpersonal, or bodily-kinesthetic skills often play key roles. Yet linguistic and logical skills form the core of most diagnostic tests of "intelligence" and are placed on a pedagogical pedestal in our schools.

THE LARGE NEED: ASSESSMENT

The general pedagogical program described here presupposes accurate understanding of the profile of intelligences of the individual learner. Such a careful assessment procedure allows informed choices about careers and avocations. It also permits a more enlightened search for remedies for difficulties. Assessment of deficiencies can predict difficulties the learner will have; moreover, it can suggest alternative routes to an educational goal (learning mathematics via spatial relations; learning music through linguistic techniques).

Assessment, then, becomes a central feature of an educational system. We believe that it is essential to depart from standardized testing. We also believe that standard pencil-and-paper short-answer tests sample only a small proportion of intellectual abilities and often reward a certain kind of decontextualized facility. The means of assessment we favor should ultimately search for genuine problem-solving or product-fashioning skills in individuals across a range of materials.

An assessment of a particular intelligence (or set of intelligences) should highlight problems that can be solved in the *materials of that intelligence*. That is, mathematical assessment should present problems in mathematical settings. For younger children, these could consist of Piagetian-style problems in which talk is kept to a minimum. For older children, derivation of proofs in a novel numerical system might suffice. In music, on the other hand, the problems would be embedded in a musical system. Younger children could be asked to assemble tunes from individual musical segments. Older children could be shown how to compose a rondo or fugue from simple motifs.

An important aspect of assessing intelligences must include the individual's ability to solve problems or create products using the materials of the intellectual medium. Equally important, however, is the determination of which intelligence is favored when an individual has a choice. One technique for getting at this proclivity is to expose the individual to a sufficiently complex situation that can stimulate several intelligences; or to provide a set of materials drawn from different intelligences and determine toward which one an individual gravitates and how deeply he or she explores it.

As an example, consider what happens when a child sees a complex film in which several intelligences figure prominently; music, people interacting, a maze to be solved, or a particular bodily skill, may all compete for attention. Subsequent "debriefing" with the child should reveal the features to which the child paid attention; these will be related to the profile of intelligences in that child. Or consider a situation in which children are taken into a room with several different kinds of equipment and games. Simple measures of the regions in which children spend time and the kinds of activities they engage in should yield insights into the individual child's profile of intelligence.

Tests of this sort differ in two important ways from the traditional measures of "intelligence." First, they rely on materials, equipment, interviews, and so on to generate the problems to be solved. This contrasts with the traditional pencil-and-paper measures used in intelligence testing. Second, results are reported as part of an individual profile of intellectual propensities, rather than as a single index of intelligence or rank within the population. In contrasting strengths and weaknesses they can suggest options for future learning.

Scores are not enough. This assessment procedure should suggest to parents, teachers, and, eventually, to children themselves, the sorts of activities that are available at home, in school, or in the wider community. Drawing on this information, children can bolster their own particular sets of intellectual weaknesses or combine their intellectual strengths in a way that is satisfying vocationally and avocationally.

COPING WITH THE PLURALITY OF INTELLIGENCES

Under the multiple intelligences theory, an intelligence can serve both as the content of instruction and the means or medium for communicating that content. This state of affairs has important ramifications for instruction. For example, suppose that a child is learning some mathematical principle but is not skilled in logical-mathematical intelligence. That child will probably experience some difficulty during the learning process. The reason for the difficulty is straightforward: The mathematical principle to be learned (the content) exists only in the logical-mathematical world and it ought to be communicated through mathematics (the medium). That is, the mathematical principle cannot be translated *entirely* into words (a linguistic medium) or spatial models (a spatial medium). At some point in the learning process, the mathematics of the principle must "speak for itself." In our present case, it is at just this level that the learner experiences difficulty—the learner (who is not especially "mathematical") and the problem (which is very much "mathematical") are not in accord. Mathematics, as a *medium*, has failed.

Although this situation is a necessary conundrum in light of multiple intelligences theory, we can propose various solutions. In the present example, the teacher must attempt to find an alternative route to the mathematical content—a metaphor in another medium. Language is perhaps the most obvious alternative, but spatial modeling and even a bodily-kinesthetic metaphor may prove appropriate in some cases. In this way, the student is given a *secondary* route to the solution to the problem, perhaps through the medium of an intelligence that is relatively strong for that individual.

Two features of this hypothetical scenario must be stressed. First, in such cases, the secondary route—the language, spatial model, or whatever—is at best a metaphor or translation. It is not mathematics itself. And at some point, the learner must translate back into the domain of mathematics. Without this translation, what is learned tends to remain at a relatively superficial level; cookbook-style mathematical performance results from following instructions (linguistic translation) without understanding why (mathematics retranslation).

Second, the alternative route is not guaranteed. There is no *necessary* reason why a problem in one domain *must be translatable* into a metaphorical problem in another domain. Successful teachers find these translations with relative frequency; but as learning becomes more complex, the likelihood of a successful translation may diminish.

While multiple intelligences theory is consistent with much empirical evidence, it has not been subjected to strong experimental tests within psychology. Within the area of education, the applications of the theory are currently being examined in many projects. Our hunches will have to be revised many times in light of actual classroom experience. Still there are important reasons for considering the theory of multiple intelligences and its implications for education. First of all, it is clear that many talents, if not intelligences, are overlooked nowadays; individuals with these talents are the chief casualties of the single-minded, single-funneled approach to the mind. There are many unfilled or poorly filled niches in our society and it would be opportune to guide individuals with the right set of abilities to these billets. Finally, our world is beset with problems; to have any chance of solving them, we must make the very best use of the intelligences we possess. Perhaps recognizing the plurality of intelligences and the manifold ways in which human individuals may exhibit them is an important first step.

THE RING OF THE BELL CURVE

CRITICAL REVERBERATIONS AND RESONANCES*

by Alfred E. Prettyman

Since I first shared my thoughts about this singular book with some of you earlier this year, I have had the opportunity to reconsider them before addressing other audiences. I cannot say that my appraisal has grown less skeptical. But let me begin now as I began before. I examine *The Bell Curve*, Intelligence and Class Structure in American Life by Hernstein and Murray, from the two perspectives of my greater professional experience: those of book publisher and educator respectively.

The design of the book is masterful. Gold foil stamping is expensive and impressive on both a book's jacket and the book's spine. The black background accentuates the white print typeface of the sub-title, *Intelligence and Class Structure in American Life,* as well as the misleading color spectrum and shape of what appears to resemble a sound wave more than anything else, but is meant to characterize the "bell curve" of the book's hypothesis. The voluptuous, passion fruit apex of this mammary/phallic design element also may be reader-friendly for its subliminal evocation of the Laffer curve—which was an early rage of Reaganomics—or simply as a "rainbow" McDonald's arch.

The jacket and promotion flap copy are an ideal fulfillment of a trade sales force's need to have copy that is both informative and titillating. Writing such copy or having the authors write it (which is more difficult to get done) is a challenge I have faced in shepherding literally hundreds of text and trade books to publication. With text books you want promotion copy that implicitly co-opts competing texts so as to diminish their market share—and increase yours. Hyperbole in text book promotion copy will likely cause you to lose market share because every competing sales force quickly will point out the desperation of your exaggeration and arouse the likely indignation of faculty you seemingly have attempted to gull.

Hyperbole in promotional copy for trade books, especially fiction, is the norm. Here, too, the Hernstein-Murray book earns exceptional grades indeed. The jacket copy suggests a conspiracy to withhold from the American public vital information about the relationship of intellectual capacity and social stratification that could, if known, permit us to resolve crucial issues of public policy. Those of us with a knowledge of the literature claimed not to be aired in public, or with a knowledge of public relations, or a memory of World War II, would recognize this as a propaganda technique most aptly described as "the big lie." Mind you, the *big lie* is about the purported withholding of vital information from the American public. I will come soon enough to the quality of the arguments for the assured relationship between intellectual capacity and social structure and the implications of that relationship, if proven, for public policy.

There are few things a discerning public will react to as strongly as a claim that they have had information withheld from them by some elite of our society, to wit, "psychometricians and other scholars," as the flap copy claims; or that "decades of fashionable denial," somehow abetted by government policies, have some complicity in this deception. Such are among the promotional lures that sell books, the Devil catch the hindmost.

I find the quotation from Edmund Burke which frames the book, after the dedication page and before the Contents, a stunning disclaimer. The quotation is from Burke's *A Vindication of Natural Society*. He is quoted as saying, "There is a most absurd and audacious Method of reasoning avowed by some Bigots and Enthusiasts, and through Fear assented to by some wiser and better Men; and it is this. They argue against a fair Discussion of *popular Prejudices*, (italics mine) because, say they, tho' they would be found *without any reasonable Support*, (italics mine) yet the Discovery might be productive of the most dan-

gerous Consequences. Absurd and blasphemous Notion! As if all Happiness was not connected with the Practice of Virtue, which necessarily depends upon the Knowledge of Truth."

Is this really an acknowledgment that what follows is knowingly a discussion of popular prejudices for which, the authors wink, there is no reasonable support; but a discussion of which can do no harm as long as that discussion is conducted in the spirit of a search for **Truth?** If so, the text that follows is not merely supreme sophistry, but high-handed mischief indeed.

A skeptic might say that the book begins by pandering to the eager readers who have purchased it and to the book club members who feel they must have it on the coffee table even if they don't read beyond the first chapter. A book man or woman might say that the book wisely begins by engaging the interests of its core market. The title of the first chapter is, "The Emergency of a Cognitive Elite." Is one supposed to believe that never before has there been a sequestering of the sources or instruments for learning such that those considered unworthy might not have access to them—whether the perpetrators were the medieval church or the southern planters of the Chesapeake or Carolina plantations?

But every editor knows that qualifiers in titles are the bane of urging a reader on; so let the title stand and attend to the text.

The authors' thesis is that cognitive ability, more so than social class, has become "the decisive *dividing force*" (p. 25, italics mine) in our lives. This results in "the isolation of the brightest from the rest of society," a phenomenon they claim to be in extremes already. These extremely isolated bright people are to be called the "Cognitive Elite." These extremely isolated, bright people who are the "Cognitive Elite" are a unique product of our technological society, since, as the authors' postulate "A true cognitive elite requires a technological society." (p. 27) I ask myself, what is the difference between a Cognitive Elite, or CE, and the Alphas of Huxley's *Brave New World?* Well that's simple enough: an Alpha is genetically engineered; a CE is merely a spawn of technology.

Now as one who asks students to approach their readings by identifying the author's thesis (or claim) and the supporting warrants, data and illustrations that produce the conclusion or lead to a summary of the text, my next observation defies that classroom catechism. Not only do Hernstein and Murray have a thesis, they also have a **topic:** *"Our topic is the relationship of human abilities to public policy."* (p. 19, italics mine.)

So what we have here, quite clearly, is a thesis in the service of a topic. Or, to put it bluntly, a public policy agenda driving the entire discussion of a purported analysis of the impact of the emergence of a cognitive elite; about the significance of accepting certain average outcomes of IQ testing in the devising of social policy.

In the service of this agenda, we are asked to accept as "beyond significant technical dispute" (p. 22-23) the following six "conclusions:"

"1. There is such a thing as a general factor ('g', mine) of cognitive ability on which human beings differ.

2. All standardized tests of academic aptitude or achievement measure this general factor to some degree, but IQ tests expressly designed for that purpose measure it most accurately.

3. IQ scores match, to a first degree, whatever it is that people mean when they use the word *intelligent* or *smart* in ordinary language.

4. IQ scores are stable, although not perfectly so, over much of a person's life.

5. Properly administered IQ tests are not demonstrably biased against social, economic, ethnic or racial groups.

6. Cognitive ability is substantially heritable, apparently no less than 40 percent and no more than 80 percent."

None of these items has any logical connection to its successor or any other item in the list of six. And for me item six is a neo-Darwinian howler.

If, however, item one fails to be "beyond significant technical dispute" their project in this book becomes a house of cards.

We are asked to accept these six "conclusions"—as they are called by Hernstein and Murray—as they have been established by those the authors choose to classify as "the classicists" within "the professional intelligence testing community." They regard as "the archetypal classicist" none other than Arthur Jenson, an educational psychologist who has constructed his academic career, as has Hernstein, on arguing that there is a scientific basis for Aryan supremacy among the human beings. His work has been supported with grants in excess of one million dollars from The Pioneer Fund, a foundation whose endowment was established singularly for the support of research that would establish a scientific basis for white supremacy.

The claim that these six items are "beyond significant technical dispute" is a statement of the author's commitment, **not** a reliable report of how these items are regarded within the professional testing community. The authors make no attempt to prove the epistemological soundness of the argument upon which the entire book is founded, to wit, that there is an identifiable entity "g" such that it depicts intelligence and that the existence of such an entity is "beyond significant technical dispute." That claim is false. And the authors knew it was false to make such a claim, so better they postulate it with a reassuring flourish than waste time with a "proof" they know will fail scrutiny.

Of course if this claim is false it is also false to claim that intelligence is IQ and depictable as a single number, capable of ranking people in a linear order that is genetically based and immutable (Fraser/Gould: 12). Such a statement is a policy assumption, not an established principle of science. In pretending to establish it they offer, as Stephen Jay Gould points out, data based on *one* analysis, a multiple regression analysis of "social behaviors that agitate us, such as crime, unemployment, and births out of wedlock (known as dependent variables), against both IQ and parental sociometric status (known as independent variables). Gould's description of their procedure is telling: "The authors first hold IQ constant and consider the relationship of social behaviors to parental socioeconomic status. Then they hold socioeconomic status constant and consider the relationship of the same social behaviors to IQ. In general, they find a higher correlation with IQ than with socioeconomic status; for example, people with low IQ are more likely to drop out of high school than people whose parents have low socioeconomic status."

But in discussing the form and strength of that relationship they select only the item that seems to support their argument while effectively ignoring—or as Gould puts it "in one key passage almost willfully hiding" an item that does not support their argument. In fact, as Gould continues, "in violation of all statistical norms I've ever learned, they plot only the regression curve and do not show the scatter variation around the curve, so their graphs do not show anything about the strength of the relationships—that is, the amount of variation in social factors explained by IQ and socioeconomic status. Indeed, almost all of their relationships are weak: very little of the variation on social factors is explained by either independent variable...In short, their own data indicate that IQ is not a major factor in determining variation in nearly all the social behaviors they study." (Fraser/Gould: 18-19)

The authors knew this, so they constructed their house of cards in the following manner. They devote the four chapters of Part 1 to an exposition of what they call "The Emergence of a Cognitive Elite." Here they argue, in part, that "An IQ score is a better predator of job productivity than a job interview, reference checks, or college transcript." (p. 64)—which also is false. Knowing that, they grant that with this and every other general statistical relationship they claim in the book there are as many or more exceptions as there are data confirming the relationship. To me that sounds as if they grant that the statistical relationships which are the basis of all of their claims in arguing the thesis of this book are unreliable: that is, you cannot with certainty draw from them the conclusions the authors pronounce with such assurance. They say it again in the following manner, "For virtually every topic we will be discussing through the rest of the book, a plot of the raw data would reveal as many or more exceptions to the general statistical relationship, and this must always be

remembered in trying to translate the general rule to individuals." (p. 68)

If this is so one would have to assume implicit equivocations in their claims that "as America equalizes the circumstances of people's lives, the remaining differences in intelligence are increasingly determined by differences in genes," and that "success and failure in the American economy...are increasingly a matter of the genes that people inherit." (p. 91) Little wonder that they begin Part II by saying "you cannot predict what a given person will do from his (sic) IQ score." The exclusionary sexist pronoun is the authors', not mine. (p. 117)

Part III begins with Chapter 13 "Ethnic Differences in Cognitive Ability." The authors at once make the following categorical statements,"...ethnic differences in cognitive ability are neither surprising nor in doubt. Large human populations differ in many ways, both cultural and biological. It is not surprising that they might differ at least slightly in their cognitive characteristics. That they do is confirmed by the data on ethnic differences in cognitive ability from around the world." (p. 269) This last statement is not simply hyperbolic, it is demonstrably false. In *The History and Geography of Human Genes,* published by Princeton University Press in 1994, the authors Luca Cavalli-Sforza, Paolo Menozzi and Alberto Piazza provide us with the first genetic atlas of the world, based on a synthesis of research done over the past fifty years. The study, headed by Luca Cavalli-Sforza of Stanford University has the following to say about "The Scientific Failure of the Concept of Human Races."

"The classification into races has proved to be a futile exercise for reasons that were already clear to Darwin. Human races are extremely unstable entities in the hands of modern taxonomists... Although there is no doubt that there is only one human species, there are clearly no objective reasons for stopping at any particular level of taxonomic splitting...All populations of population clusters overlap when single genes are considered, and in almost all populations, all alleles are present but in different frequencies. No single gene is therefore sufficient for classifying human populations into systematic categories... From a scientific point of view, the concept of race has failed to obtain any consensus; nor is any likely, given the gradual variation in existence. It may be objected that the racial stereotypes have a consistency that allows even the layman to classify individuals. However, the major stereotypes, all based on skin color, hair color and form, and facial traits, reflect superficial differences that are not confirmed by deeper analysis with more reliable genetic traits and whose origin dates from recent evolution mostly under the effect of climate and perhaps sexual selection. By means of painstaking multivariate analysis, we can identify 'clusters' of populations and order them in a hierarchy that we believe represents the history of fissions in the expansion to the whole world of anatomically modern humans. At no level can clusters be identified with races, since every level of clusters would determine a different partition and there is no biological reason to prefer a particular one. The successive levels of clustering follow each other in a regular sequence, and there is no discontinuity that might tempt us to consider a certain level as a reasonable, though arbitrary, threshold for race distinction.

The word 'race' is coupled in many parts of the world and strata of society with considerable prejudice, misunderstanding, and social problems. Xenophobia, political convenience and a variety of motives totally unconnected with science are the basis of racism, the belief that some races are biologically superior to others that they therefore have an inherent right to dominate. Racism has existed from time immemorial but only in the nineteenth century were there attempts to justify it on the basis of scientific arguments. Among these, social Darwinism, mostly the brainchild of Herbert Spencer (1820-1903), was an unsuccessful attempt to justify unchecked social competition, class stratification, and even Anglo-Saxon imperialism. Not surprisingly, racism is often coupled with caste prejudice and has been invoked as motivation for condoning slavery, or even genocide. There is no scientific basis to the belief of genetically determined 'superiority' of one population over another... The claims of a genetic basis for general superiority of one population over another

are not supported by any of our findings. Superiority is a political and socioeconomic concept, tied to events of recent political, military, and economic history and to cultural traditions of countries or groups. This superiority is rapidly transient, as history shows, whereas the average genotype does not change rapidly. But racial prejudice has an old tradition and is not easy to eradicate." (Cavalli-Sforza et al: 19-20)

Since this is so, the Hernstein Murray hypothesis fails. But what we have then is, in reality, what the authors began with: a social policy agenda in search of a rationale other than bias. Not only do the author's political predispositions shape their view of policy, they also shape their view of intelligence.

It is possible to be generous and say that what Hernstein and Murray have labored over is more a panegyric for privilege than a scientific investigation of intelligence. I, as an editor or publisher would know of the existence of the Cavalli-Sforza study—as well as other studies, by neurologists and physiologists, ignored by the authors—so I will assume that Irwin Gilkes, the book's editor who, unfortunately, died, as did Hernstein, before the book's publication also knew. Perhaps that is why the authors' strategy in writing this book is to allow that everything they say is subject to contradiction.

Why, then, publish such a book? Because there is a market that will salivate for and purchase a book with such a ring. This market would not be unknown to Charles Murray. It is the potential market revealed by the 1990 General Social Survey (GSS) from the University of Chicago's National Opinion Research Center. This survey revealed that among white Americans 78 percent believe that black Americans prefer living on welfare, 74 percent believe Hispanic Americans prefer to live on welfare; 55 percent of whites believe black Americans more violence prone, while 50 percent believe Hispanic Americans violence prone; and, more to the point of this book, 53 percent consider black Americans less intelligent than they, and 55 percent considered Hispanic Americans less intelligent than they. Now that's a huge potential market! So much so that publishing a book such as this is a nobrainer. Even if discredited, as it has been in several ways by a variety of informed critics, it will sell. And it continues to do just that.

The book's last chapter, "A Place for Everyone," invites us to consider that what the nation's Founders meant by the self-evident truth that all men are created equal is that all men, and women, should have "human dignity" and a "valued place" in society. "You occupy a valued place if other people would miss you if you were gone." This is the nostalgia of feudalism, I say. What is important to Hernstein and Murray certainly is *Not* equality of opportunity or outcomes because "It is time for America once again to try living with inequality, as life is lived." (p. 551) This is familiar Murray doublespeak: there is great inequality in America, he is saying; let's codify it in social policy that keeps a tight leash on the Cognitive Elite (keeping in mind that Ashkenazi Jews have higher IQ scores than other ethnic groups) and keeps every one else in her/his lower place. Yes, reopen the plantations and the concentration camps.

Although I am aware that there may be some sympathy for the neo-Darwinian gamesmanship of Hernstein and Murray in odd places, even on this campus, I hope it will be unnecessary for me to respond to another student who comes to me for reassurance because his psychology professor has told him that the Murray-Hernstein thesis is science proven by scholarship and accepted by responsible scholars. Is this an irresponsible teacher, or just a careless teacher? Does IQ, as Howard Gardner asks, explain the embarrassing prevalence of white collar crime in business and politics or the recent sudden rise in crime in Russia? (Fraser/Gardner: 33) The theory of multiple intelligences pioneered by Gardner and others, accounts for multiple human faculties, properly identified as the *intelligences*. (Gardner: 26-27) Evidence from brain research, evolution, human development and cross-cultural compari-

son support such a theory of multiple human faculties.

Most of us who face the personal and compelling achievements of our students appreciate the significance of Rollo May's statement that it isn't the matter of who is more creative or ingenious that should concern us most; it is the matter of who, how many have the courage to use all of whatever they have that should concern us.

Cavalli-Sforza, Menozzi & Piazza: *The History and Geography of Human Genes*, 1995.

Fraser, Steven, Ed. *The Bell Curve Wars: Race, Intelligence and the Future of America*, 1995.

Gardner, Howard. *Multiple Intelligences, The Theory in Practice*, 1993.

Murray & Hernstein, *The Bell Curve, Intelligence and Class Structure in American Life*, 1994.

* Copyright © 1995 by A.E. Prettyman. ALL rights reserved. Delivered as one of the Inaugural Lectures upon the installation of Dr. Neal A. Raisman as President of Rockland Community College/State University of New York.

When Smart is Dumb

by Daniel Goleman

Exactly why David Pologruto, a high-school physics teacher, was stabbed with a kitchen knife by one of his star students is still debatable. But the facts as widely reported are these:

Jason H., a sophomore and straight-A student at a Coral Springs, Florida, high school, was fixated on getting into medical school. Not just any medical school—he dreamt of Harvard. But Pologruto, his physics teacher, had given Jason an 80 on a quiz. Believing the grade—a mere B—put his dream in jeopardy, Jason took a butcher knife to school and, in a confrontation with Pologruto in the physics lab, stabbed his teacher in the collarbone before being subdued in a struggle.

A judge found Jason innocent, temporarily insane during the incident—a panel of four psychologists and psychiatrists swore he was psychotic during the fight. Jason claimed he had been planning to commit suicide because of the test score, and had gone to Pologruto to tell him he was killing himself because of the bad grade. Pologruto told a different story: "I think he tried to completely do me in with the knife" because he was infuriated over the bad grade.

After transferring to a private school, Jason graduated two years later at the top of his class. A perfect grade in regular classes would have given him a straight-A, 4.0 average, but Jason had taken enough advanced courses to raise his grade-point average to 4.614—way beyond A+. Even as Jason graduated with highest honors, his old physics teacher, David Pologruto, complained that Jason had never apologized or even taken responsibility for the attack.

The question is, how could someone of such obvious intelligence do something so irrational—so downright dumb? The answer: Academic intelligence has little to do with emotional life. The brightest among us can founder on the shoals of unbridled passions and unruly impulses; people with high IQs can be stunningly poor pilots of their private lives.

One of psychology's open secrets is the relative inability of grades, IQ, or SAT scores, despite their popular mystique, to predict unerringly who will succeed in life. To be sure, there is a relationship between IQ and life circumstances for large groups as a whole: Many people with very low IQs end up in menial jobs, and those with high IQs tend to become well-paid— but by no means always.

There are widespread exceptions to the rule that IQ predicts success— many (or more) exceptions than cases that fit the rule. At best, IQ contributes about 20 percent to the factors that determine life success, which leaves 80 percent to other forces. As one observer notes, "The vast majority of one's ultimate niche in society is determined by non-IQ factors, ranging from social class to luck."

Even Richard Herrnstein and Charles Murray, whose book *The Bell Curve* imputes a primary importance to IQ, acknowledge this; as they point out, "Perhaps a freshman with an SAT math score of 500 had better not have his heart set on being a mathematician, but if instead he wants to run his own business, become a U.S. Senator or make a million dollars, he should not put aside his dreams.... The link between test scores and those achievements is dwarfed by the totality of other characteristics that he brings to life."

My concern is with a key set of these "other characteristics," *emotional intelligence:* Abilities such as being able to motivate oneself and persist in the face of frustrations; to control impulse and delay gratification; to regulate one's moods and keep distress from swamping the ability to think; to empathize and to hope. Unlike IQ, with its nearly one-hundred-year history of research with hundreds of thousands of people, emotional intelligence is a new concept. No one can yet say exactly how much of the variability from person to person in life's course it accounts for. But what data exist suggest it can be as powerful, and at times more powerful, than IQ. And while there are those who argue that IQ cannot be changed much by experience or education, I will show in Part Five that the crucial emotional competencies can indeed be learned and improved upon by children—if we bother to teach them.

EMOTIONAL INTELLIGENCE AND DESTINY

I remember the fellow in my own class at Amherst College who had attained five perfect 800 scores on the SAT and other achievement tests he took before entering. Despite his formidable intellectual abilities, he spent most of his time hanging out, staying up late, and missing classes by sleeping until noon. It took him almost ten years to finally get his degree.

IQ offers little to explain the different destinies of people with roughly equal promises, schooling, and opportunity. When ninety-five Harvard students from the classes of the 1940s—a time when people with a wider spread of IQ were at Ivy League schools than is presently the case—were followed into middle age, the men with the highest test scores in college were not particularly successful compared to their lower-scoring peers in terms of salary, productivity, or status in their field. Nor did they have the greatest life satisfaction, nor the most happiness with friendships, family, and romantic relationships.

A similar follow-up in middle age was done with 450 boys, most sons of immigrants, two thirds from families on welfare, who grew up in Somerville, Massachusetts, at the time a "blighted slum" a few blocks from Harvard. A third had IQs below 90. But again IQ had little relationship to how well they had done at work or in the rest of their lives; for instance, 7 percent of men with IQs under 80 were unemployed for ten or more years, but so were 7 percent of men with IQs over 100. To be sure, there was a general link (as there always is) between IQ and socioeconomic level at age forty-seven. But childhood abilities such as being able to handle frustrations, control emotions, and get on with other people made the greater difference.

Consider also data from an ongoing study of eighty-one valedictorians and salutatorians from the 1981 class in Illinois high schools. All, of course, had the highest grade-point averages in their schools. But while they continued to achieve well in college, getting excellent grades, by their late twenties they had climbed to only average levels of success. Ten years after graduating from high school, only one in four were at the highest level of young people of comparable age in their chosen profession, and many were doing much less well.

Karen Arnold, professor of education at Boston University, one of the researchers tracking the valedictorians, explains, "I think we've discovered the 'dutiful'—people who know how to achieve in the system. But valedictorians struggle as surely as we all do. To know that a person is a valedictorian is to know only that he or she is exceedingly good at achievement as measured by grades. It tells you nothing about how they react to the vicissitudes of life."

And that is the problem: Academic intelligence offers virtually no preparation for the turmoil—or opportunity—life's vicissitudes bring. Yet even though a high IQ is no guarantee of prosperity, prestige, or happiness in life, our schools and our culture fixate on academic abilities, ignoring *emotional* intelligence, a set of traits—some might call it character—that also matters immensely for our personal destiny. Emotional life is a domain that, as surely as math or reading, can be handled with greater or lesser skill, and requires its unique set of competencies. And how adept a person is at those is crucial to understanding why one person thrives in life while another, of equal intellect, dead-ends: Emotional aptitude is a *meta-ability*, determining how well we can use whatever other skills we have, including raw intellect.

Of course, there are many paths to success in life, and many domains in which other aptitudes are rewarded. In our increasingly knowledge-based society, technical skill is certainly one. There is a children's joke: "What do you call a nerd fifteen years from now?" The answer: "Boss." But even among "nerds" emotional intelligence offers an added edge in the workplace, as we shall see in Part Three. Much evidence testifies that people who are emotionally adept—who know and manage their own feelings well, and who read and deal effectively with other people's feelings—are at an advantage in any domain of life, whether romance and intimate relationships or picking up the unspoken rules that govern success in organizational politics. People with well-developed emotional skills are also more likely to be content and effective in their lives, mastering the habits of mind that foster their own productivity; people who cannot marshal some control over their emotional life fight inner battles that sabotage their ability for focused work and clear thought.

A DIFFERENT KIND OF INTELLIGENCE

To the casual observer, four year old Judy might seem a wallflower among her more gregarious playmates. She hangs back from the action at playtime, staying on the margins of games rather than plunging into the center. But Judy is actually a keen observer of the social politics of her preschool classroom, perhaps the most sophisticated of her playmates in her insights into the tides of feeling within the others.

Her sophistication is not apparent until Judy's teacher gathers the four-year-olds around to play what they call the Classroom Game. The Classroom Game—a dollhouse replica of Judy's own preschool classroom, with stick figures who have for heads small photos of the students and teachers—is a test of social perceptiveness. When Judy's teacher asks her to put each girl and boy in the part of the room they like to play in most—the art corner, the blocks corner, and so on—Judy does so with complete accuracy. And when asked to put each boy and girl with the children they like to play with most, Judy shows she can match best friends for the entire class.

Judy's accuracy reveals that she has a perfect social map of her class, a level of perceptiveness exceptional for a four-year-old. These are the skills that, in later life, might allow Judy to blossom into a star in any of the fields where "people skills" count, from sales and management to diplomacy.

That Judy's social brilliance was spotted at all, let alone this early, was due to her being a student at the Eliot-Pearson Preschool on the campus of Tufts University, where Project Spectrum, a curriculum that intentionally cultivates a variety of kinds of intelligence, was then being developed. Project Spectrum recognizes that the human repertoire of abilities goes far beyond the three R's, the narrow band of word-and-number skills that schools traditionally focus on. It acknowledges that capacities such as Judy's social perceptiveness are talents that an education can nurture rather than ignore or even frustrate. By encouraging children to develop a full range of the abilities that they will actually draw on to succeed, or use simply to be fulfilled in what they do, school becomes an education in life skills.

The guiding visionary behind Project Spectrum is Howard Gardner, a psychologist at the Harvard School of Education. "The time has come," Gardner told me, "to broaden our notion of the spectrum of talents. The single most important contribution education can make to a child's development is to help him toward a field where his talents best suit him, where he will be satisfied and competent. We've completely lost sight of that. Instead we subject everyone to an education where, if you succeed, you will be best suited to be a college professor. And we evaluate everyone along the way according to whether they meet that narrow standard of success. We should spend less time ranking children and more time helping them to identify their natural competencies and gifts, and cultivate those. There are hundreds and hundreds of ways to succeed, and many, many different abilities that will help you get there."

If anyone sees the limits of the old ways of thinking about intelligence, it is Gardner. He points out that the glory days of the IQ tests began during World War 1, when two million American men were sorted out through the first mass paper-and-pencil form of the IQ test, freshly developed by Lewis Terman, a psychologist at Stanford. This led to decades of what Gardner calls the "IQ way of thinking" that people are either smart or not, are born that way, that there's nothing much you can do about it, and that tests can tell you if you are one of the smart ones or not. The SAT test for college admissions is based on the same notion of a single kind of aptitude that determines your future. This way of thinking permeates society.

Gardner's influential 1983 book *Frames of Mind* was a manifesto refuting the IQ view; it proposed that there was not just one, monolithic kind of intelligence that was crucial for life success, but rather a wide spectrum of intelligences, with seven key varieties. His list includes the two standard academic kinds, verbal and mathematical-logical alacrity, but it goes on to include the spatial capacity seen in, say, an outstanding artist or architect; the kinesthetic genius displayed in the physical fluidity and grace of a Martha Graham or Magic Johnson; and the musical gifts of a Mozart or YoYo Ma. Rounding out the list are two faces of what Gardner calls "the personal intelligences": Interpersonal skills, like those of a great therapist such as Carl Rogers or a world-class leader such as Martin Luther King, Jr., and the "intrapsychic" capacity that could emerge, on the one hand, in the brilliant insights of Sigmund Freud, or, with less fanfare, in the inner contentment that arises from attuning one's life to be in keeping with one's true feelings.

The operative word in this view of intelligences is *multiple:* Gardner's model pushes way beyond the standard concept of IQ as a single, immutable factor. It recognizes that the tests that tyrannized us as we went through school—from the achievement tests that sorted us out into those who would be shunted toward technical schools and those destined for college, to the SATs that determined what, if any, college we would be allowed to attend—are based on a limited notion of intelligence, one out of touch with the true range of skills and abilities that matter for life over and beyond IQ.

Gardner acknowledges that seven is an arbitrary figure for the variety of intelligences; there is no magic number to the multiplicity of human talents. At one point Gardner and his research colleagues had stretched these seven to a list of twenty different varieties of intelligence. Interpersonal intelligence, for example, broke down into four distinct abilities; leadership, the ability to nurture relationships and keep friends, the ability to resolve conflicts, and skill at the kind of social analysis that four-year-old Judy excels at.

This multifaceted view of intelligence offers a richer picture of a child's ability and potential for success than the standard IQ. When Spectrum students were evaluated on the Stanford-Binet Intelligence Scale—once the gold standard of IQ tests—and again by a battery designed to measure Gardner's spectrum of intelligences, there was no significant relationship between children's scores on the two tests. The five children with the highest IQs (from 125 to 133) showed a variety of profiles on the ten strengths measured by the Spectrum test. For example, of the five "smartest" children according to the IQ tests, one was strong in three areas, three had strengths in two areas, and one "smart" child had just one Spectrum strength. Those strengths were scattered; four of these children's strengths were in music, two in the visual arts, one in social understanding, one in logic, two in language. None of the five high-IQ kids were strong in movement, numbers, or mechanics; movement and numbers were actually weak spots for two of these five.

Gardner's conclusion was that "the Stanford-Binet Intelligence Scale did not predict successful performance across or on a consistent subset of Spectrum activities." On the other hand, the Spectrum scores give parents and teachers clear guidance about the realms that these children will take a spontaneous interest in, and where they will do well enough to develop the passions that could one day lead beyond proficiency to mastery.

Gardner's thinking about the multiplicity of intelligence continues to evolve. Some ten years after he first published his theory, Gardner gave these nutshell summaries of the personal intelligences:

> *Inter*personal intelligence is the ability to understand other people; what motivates them, how they work, how to work cooperatively with them. Successful salespeople, politicians, teachers, clinicians, and religious leaders are all likely to be individuals with high degrees of interpersonal intelligence. *Intra*personal intelligence…is a correlative ability, turned inward. It is a capacity to form an accurate, veridical model of oneself and to be able to use that model to operate effectively in life.

In another rendering, Gardner noted that the core of interpersonal intelligence includes the "capacities to discern and respond appropriately to the moods, temperaments, motivations, and desires of other people." In intrapersonal intelligence, the key to self-knowledge, he included "access to one's own feelings and the ability to discriminate among them and draw upon them to guide behavior."

SPOCK VS. DATA: WHEN COGNITION IS NOT ENOUGH

There is one dimension of personal intelligence that is broadly pointed to, but little explored, in Gardner's elaborations; the role of emotions. Perhaps this is so because, as Gardner suggested to me, his work is so strongly informed by a cognitive-science model of mind. Thus his view of these intelligences emphasizes cognition—the *understanding* of oneself and of others in motives, in habits of working, and in putting that insight into use in conducting one's own life and getting along with others. But like the kinesthetic realm, where physical brilliance manifests itself nonverbally, the realm of the emotions extends, too, beyond the reach of language and cognition.

While there is ample room in Gardner's descriptions of the personal intelligences for insight into the play of emotions and mastery in managing them, Gardner and those who work with him have not pursued in great detail the role *of feeling*, in these intelligences, focusing more on cognitions *about* feeling. This focus, perhaps unintentionally, leaves unexplored the rich sea of emotions that makes the inner life and relationships so complex, so compelling, and so often puzzling. And it leaves yet to be plumbed both the sense in which there is intelligence in the emotions and the sense in which intelligence can be brought to emotions.

Gardner's emphasis on the cognitive elements in the personal intelligences reflects the zeitgeist of psychology that has shaped his views. Psychology's overemphasis on cognition even in the realm of emotion is, in part, due to a quirk in the history of that science. During the middle decades of this century, academic psychology was dominated by behaviorists in the mold of B. F. Skinner, who felt that only behavior that could be seen objectively, from the outside, could be studied with scientific accuracy. The behaviorists ruled all inner life, including emotions, out-of-bounds for science.

Then, with the coming in the late 1960s of the "cognitive revolution," the focus of psychological science turned to how the mind registers and stores information, and the nature of intelligence. But emotions were still off-limits. Conventional wisdom among cognitive scientists held that intelligence entails a cold, hard-nosed processing of fact. It is hyperrational, rather like *Star Trek's* Mr. Spock, the archetype of dry information bytes unmuddied by feeling, embodying the idea that emotions have no place in intelligence and only muddle our picture of mental life.

The cognitive scientists who embraced this view have been seduced by the computer as the operative model of mind, forgetting that, in reality, the brain's wetware is awash in a messy, pulsating puddle of neurochemicals, nothing like the sanitized, orderly silicon that has spawned the guiding metaphor for mind. The predominant models among cognitive scientists of how the mind processes information have lacked an acknowledgment that rationality is guided by—and can be swamped by—feeling. The cognitive model is, in this regard, an impoverished view of the mind, one that fails to explain the Sturm und Drang of feelings that brings flavor to the intellect. In order to persist in this view, cognitive scientists themselves have had to ignore the relevance for their models of mind of their personal hopes and fears, their marital squabbles and professional jealousies—the wash of feeling that gives life its flavor and its urgencies, and which in every moment biases exactly how (and how well or poorly) information is processed.

The lopsided scientific vision of an emotionally flat mental life—which has guided the last eighty years of research on intelligence—is gradually changing as psychology has begun to recognize the essential role of feeling in thinking. Rather like the Spockish character Data in *Star Trek: The Next Generation*, psychology is coming to appreciate the power and virtues of emotions in mental life, as well as their dangers. After all, as Data sees (to his own dismay, could he feel dismay), his cool logic fails to bring the right *human* solution. Our humanity is most evident in our feelings; Data seeks to feel, knowing that something essential is missing. He wants friendship, loyalty; like the Tin Man in The Wizard of oz. he lacks a heart. Lacking the lyrical sense that feeling brings, Data can play music or write poetry with technical virtuosity, but not feel its passion. The lesson of Data's yearning for yearning itself is that the higher values of the human heart—faith, hope, devotion, love—are missing entirely from the coldly cognitive view. Emotions enrich; a model of mind that leaves them out is impoverished.

When I asked Gardner about his emphasis on thoughts about feelings, or metacognition, more than on emotions themselves, he acknowledged that he tended to view intelligence in a cognitive way, but told me, "When I first wrote about the personal intelligences, I was talking about emotion, especially in my notion of intrapersonal intelligence—one component is emotionally tuning in to yourself. It's the visceral-feeling signals you get that are essential for interpersonal intelligence. But as it has developed in practice, the theory of multiple intelligence has evolved to focus more on metacognition"—that is, awareness of one's mental processes—"rather than on the full range of emotional abilities."

Even so, Gardner appreciates how crucial these emotional and relationship abilities are in the rough-and-tumble of life. He points out that "many people with IQs of 160 work for people with IQs of 100, if the former have poor intrapersonal intelligence and the latter have a high one. And in the day-to-day world no intelligence is more important than the interpersonal. If you don't have it, you'll make poor choices about who to marry, what job to take, and so on. We need to train children in the personal intelligences in school."

CAN EMOTIONS BE INTELLIGENT?

To get a fuller understanding of just what such training might be like, we must turn to other theorists who are following Gardner's intellectual lead—most notably a Yale psychologist, Peter Salovey, who has mapped in great detail the ways

in which we can bring intelligence to our emotions. This endeavor is not new; over the years even the most ardent theorists of IQ have occasionally tried to bring emotions within the domain of intelligence, rather than seeing "emotion" and 'intelligence' as an inherent contradiction in terms. Thus E. L. Thorndike, an eminent psychologist who was also influential in popularizing the notion of IQ in the 1920s and 1930s, proposed in a Harper's Magazine article that one aspect of emotional intelligence, "social" intelligence—the ability to understand others and "act wisely in human relations"—was itself an aspect of a person's IQ. Other psychologists of the time took a more cynical view of social intelligence, seeing it in terms of skills for manipulating other people—getting them to do what you want, whether they want to or not. But neither of these formulations of social intelligence held much sway with theorists of IQ, and by 1960 an influential textbook on intelligence tests pronounced social intelligence a "useless" concept.

But personal intelligence would not be ignored, mainly because it makes both intuitive and common sense. For example, when Robert Sternberg, another Yale psychologist, asked people to describe an "intelligent person," practical people skills were among the main traits listed. More systematic research by Sternberg led him back to Thorndike's conclusion: that social intelligence is both distinct from academic abilities and a key part of what makes people do well in the practicalities of life. Among the practical intelligences that are, for instance, so highly valued in the workplace is the kind of sensitivity that allows effective managers to pick up tacit messages.

In recent years, a growing group of psychologists has come to similar conclusions, agreeing with Gardner that the old concepts of IQ revolved around a narrow band of linguistic and math skills, and that doing well on IQ tests was most directly a predictor of success in the classroom or as a professor but less and less so as life's paths diverged from academe. These psychologists—Sternberg and Salovey among them—have taken a wider view of intelligence, trying to reinvent it in terms of what it takes to lead life successfully. And that line of enquiry leads back to an appreciation of just how crucial "personal" or emotional intelligence is.

Salovey subsumes Gardner's personal intelligences in his basic definition of emotional intelligence, expanding these abilities into five main domains:

1. *Knowing one's emotions.* Self-awareness—recognizing a feeling as it happens—is the keystone of emotional intelligence. As we will see in Chapter 4, the ability to monitor feelings from moment to moment is crucial to psychological insight and self-understanding. An inability to notice our true feelings leaves us at their mercy. People with greater certainty about their feelings are better pilots of their lives, having a surer sense of how they really feel about personal decisions from whom to marry to what job to take.

2. *Managing emotions.* Handling feelings so they are appropriate is an ability that builds on self-awareness. Chapter 5 will examine the capacity to soothe oneself, to shake off rampant anxiety, gloom, or irritability—and the consequences of failure at this basic emotional skill. People who are poor in this ability are constantly battling feelings of distress, while those who excel in it can bounce back far more quickly from life's setbacks and upsets.

3. *Motivating oneself.* Marshaling emotions in the service of a goal is essential for paying attention, for self-motivation and mastery, and for creativity. Emotional self-control—delaying gratification and stifling impulsiveness—underlies accomplishment of every sort. And being able to get into the "flow" state enables outstanding performance of all kinds. People who have this skill tend to be more highly productive and effective in whatever they undertake.

4. *Recognizing emotions in others.* Empathy, another ability that builds on emotional self-awareness, is the fundamental "people skill." Chapter 7 will investigate the roots of empathy, the social cost of being emotionally tone-deaf, and the reasons empathy kindles altruism. People who are empathic are more attuned to the subtle social signals that indicate what others need or want. This makes them better at callings such as the caring professions, teaching, sales, and management.

5. *Handling relationships.* The art of relationships is, in large part, skill in managing emotions in others. Chapter 8 looks at social competence and incompetence, and the specific skills involved. These are the abilities that undergird popularity, leadership, and interpersonal effectiveness. People who excel in these skills do well at anything that relies on interacting smoothly with others; they are social stars.

Of course, people differ in their abilities in each of these domains; some of us may be quite adept at handling, say, our own anxiety, but relatively inept at soothing someone else's upsets. The underlying basis for our level of ability is, no doubt, neural, but as we will see, the brain is remarkably plastic, constantly learning. Lapses in emotional skills can be remedied: to a great extent each of these domains represents a body of habit and response that, with the right effort, can be improved on.

IQ AND EMOTIONAL INTELLIGENCE: PURE TYPES

IQ and emotional intelligence are not opposing competencies, but rather separate ones. We all mix intellect and emotional acuity; people with a high IQ but low emotional intelligence (or low IQ and high emotional intelligence) are, despite the stereotypes, relatively rare. Indeed, there is a slight correlation between IQ and some aspects of emotional intelligence—though small enough to make clear these are largely independent entities.

Unlike the familiar tests for IQ, there is, as yet, no single paper-and-pencil test that yields an "emotional intelligence score" and there may never be one. Although there is ample research on each of its components, some of them, such as empathy, are best tested by sampling a person's actual ability at the task—for example, by having them read a person's feelings from a video of their facial expressions. Still, using a measure for what he calls "ego resilience" which is quite similar to emotional intelligence (it includes the main social and emotional competencies), Jack Block, a psychologist at the University of California at Berkeley, has made a comparison of two theoretical pure types; people high in IQ versus people high in emotional aptitudes. The differences are telling.

The high-IQ pure type (that is, setting aside emotional intelligence) is almost a caricature of the intellectual, adept in the realm of mind but inept in the personal world. The profiles differ slightly for men and women. The high-IQ male is typified—no surprise—by a wide range of intellectual interests and abilities. He is ambitious and productive, predictable and dogged, and untroubled by concerns about himself. He also tends to be critical and condescending, fastidious and inhibited, uneasy with sexuality and sensual experience, unexpressive and detached, and emotionally bland and cold.

By contrast, men who are high in emotional intelligence are socially poised, outgoing and cheerful, not prone to fearfulness or worried rumination. They have a notable capacity for commitment to people or causes, for taking responsibility, and for having an ethical outlook; they are sympathetic and caring in their relationships. Their emotional life is rich, but appropriate; they are comfortable with themselves, others, and the social universe they live in.

Purely high-IQ women have the expected intellectual confidence, are fluent in expressing their thoughts, value intellectual matters, and have a wide range of intellectual and aesthetic interests. They also tend to be introspective, prone to anxiety, rumination, and guilt, and hesitate to express their anger openly (though they do so indirectly).

Emotionally intelligent women, by contrast, tend to be assertive and express their feelings directly, and to feel positive about themselves; life holds meaning for them. Like the men, they are outgoing and gregarious, and express their feelings appropriately (rather than, say, in outbursts they later regret); they adapt well to stress. Their social poise lets them easily reach out to new people; they are comfortable enough with themselves to he playful, spontaneous, and open to sensual experience. Unlike the women purely high in IQ, they rarely feel anxious or guilty, or sink into rumination.

These portraits, of course, are extremes—all of us mix IQ and emotional intelligence in varying degrees. But they offer an instructive look at what each of these dimensions adds separately to a person's qualities. To the degree a person has both cognitive and emotional intelligence, these pictures merge. Still, of the two, emotional intelligence adds far more of the qualities that make us more fully human.

CIVIL RELIGION: MILLENNIAL POLITICS AND HISTORY

by Catherine L. Albanese

Many an American has visited the National Archives Building in Washington, D.C., to see the original copies of the Declaration of Independence and the Constitution. There the documents rest in a special case filled with helium and covered with protective glass to preserve them. Each night they descend into a steel vault where tons of metal prevent any accident or sabotage. Then the next day they rise to be viewed by tourists. Still more Americans have probably attended a ball game and stood in the bleachers with the crowd, singing "The Star-Spangled Banner" to the accompaniment of the local band. And nearly everybody remembers the ceremony that began the class day in primary and secondary school. Teacher and pupils rose and, facing the American flag—each person with hand on heart—recited a pledge of allegiance to the flag and "the Republic for which it stands." Nearly everybody remembers pledging, that is, except for the Jehovah's Witnesses.

Members of this large millennial religious body, which originated as a nineteenth-century new religion, refuse to salute the American flag. Arguing before the Supreme Court in 1940, the Witnesses claimed that the pledge of allegiance was an act of idolatry, homage to an earthly government by people who had made a covenant with God to do his will. In other words, the Witnesses were saying that the pledge of allegiance was a religious act and that, as such, it conflicted with the demands of their own faith. This argument by the Witnesses should prompt us to look again at the ceremonies just described. The solemn preservation and veneration of the Declaration and the Constitution, the singing of the national anthem, and the pledge of allegiance are acts that suggest, by their seriousness and deliber-

ateness, the rituals of organized religion. They are surely attached to ideas about the meaning of America, and they are encouragements to loyal and patriotic behavior. As rituals, they help people to center and orient themselves by reference to the nation.

For well over two decades the religion against which the Jehovah's Witnesses were protesting has been called by many scholars *civil religion*. While there are various definitions of it, civil religion generally refers to a religious system that has existed alongside the churches, with a theology (creed), an ethic (code), and a set of rituals and other identifiable symbols (cultus) related to the political state. As a shorthand definition, we might say that civil religion means religious nationalism. Historically, we know that the term *civil religion* was used by Jean-Jacques Rousseau (1712-1778) in Enlightenment France. And although the term did not come into repeated use in this country until 1967, the phenomenon to which it refers is as old as the beginnings of Western culture.

Thus, ancient Israel understood its government as a theocracy, literally a government by God—through his representatives. In its view of the state, religious and political institutions were united, and one person—a charismatic leader or, later, a king—was responsible for both. Even more, Israel's God was considered the true king, ruling by his law and under a covenant that he had made with the people. Before the idea of a divine covenant with Israel was affirmed, other covenants had been made between warring kings to establish relationships between them. So a covenant was a *political* agreement, and a king, of course, was a political figure, ruling by establishing control over territory. Hence, the empire of the biblical God was the Hebrew state, and as the Hebrew conception of God grew larger, his empire became the universe.

The roots of the majority religion in the United States are, like the roots of all Christianity, bound up with the history of Israel. But a second major source for Western European culture was Greco-Roman. By the time Rome was ruling the Mediterranean world in the first centuries of the Christian era, its empire was linked by a common ideal for living—the Roman Way of Life—and by a ritual centered around the emperor. The head of all the Romans and of the conquered nations, the emperor was thought to possess a spiritual double called his *genius*. Romans considered the genius of the emperor divine, so that throughout the empire people were required to take part in an annual ceremony rendering homage to the genius. In this way, the vast state composed of many ethnic and religious groups maintained a degree of unity. The Roman Way of Life, summed up in ritual homage to the emperor, acted as a social cement to bind the many into one.

With the Jews and, on the Mediterranean coast, some Muslims as clear dissenters, medieval Europe also held to a religiopolitical unity. Christianity united Europeans into Christendom, and religion was a political as well as pious act. Similarly, North America had its native civil religions in the traditional ways of the many Indian nations that populated the land. Here chiefs and holy persons were "civic" authorities in small, independent cultures, and they interpreted the meaning of their nations to other members. Later the European immigrants were not too different: The Puritans readily mixed religion and government. As early as 1749, Benjamin Franklin in Pennsylvania was speaking about the need for "public religion." A quarter-century afterward, the deliberations of the Continental Congress that gave birth to the United States were filled with attention to religious details.

With this double background, two models for civil faith in Western society had grown up. The first was the Hebrew model in which one nation, bound by ties of blood, history, and language, expressed these bonds in combined religious and political language and actions. The second was the Roman model in which different peoples, with different ethnic heritages, were brought together from the top down, so to speak, through formal ceremonies and ideals. In the United States, civil religion took something from each of these models. For this reason, its nature and its specific history have proved difficult to chart. Briefly, some of the major symbols of American civil religion rose out of Puritan experience, the expression of a people united by ethnic ties and traditions. But the

history of civil religion made it increasingly a bond designed to unite *many* peoples from *many* different nations into one state.

The distinction is important. A political state such as the United States means a civil government that contains within its jurisdiction distinct ethnic and religious groups. A nation, in the strict sense, means a group of people bound by language, past history, and real or alleged kinship, like each American Indian culture. A nation-state means a nation that has taken on a formal and political expression so that government is identified with one nation. Modern Japan is a nation-state.

Previous chapters have followed common usage in speaking loosely of the United States as a "nation." But here we need to be careful in our choice of words. Civil religion in this country was an attempt to create a nation and a nation-state, partially on the basis of the English Puritan national heritage, partially on the basis of more universal symbols derived from the Enlightenment, and partially through symbols that grew out of American political history. Yet as the years passed, more and more Americans did not share either the English Puritan national tradition or an ancestry in America during previous eras of its history. At the same time, the Enlightenment, as a cultural event, receded into the past. Thus, civil religion grew less meaningful. At best, civil religion was never more than the expression of many American people some of the time. Still, with its overtones of extraordinary religion, it is an important example of the religion of oneness in this country. It deserves scrutiny if we are to understand religious America.

THE FOUNDATIONS OF THE CIVIL RELIGION

Civil religion grew and changed throughout American history, and its presence was particularly visible in millennial fervor during wartime. Yet its essentials came from the seventeenth and the eighteenth centuries. By the time George Washington took his oath of office as first president of the United States, the fundamentals of the civil religion were in place. They had arisen out of New England Puritanism, but especially out of the fusion of Puritanism with the engagement of

Americans in the Revolutionary War. In this setting, the Puritan past was reinterpreted, linked more strongly to the Enlightenment (it had already been so linked), and joined finally to the historic tradition that Americans were creating by their own deeds in the war—deeds that were widely understood as the beginning of a millennial era. We will look first at Puritanism from the perspective of the civil religion and then at the era of the Revolutionary War. After that, we will be able to examine the civil faith as a religious system and to follow it in later American religious history.

PURITANISM AND CIVIL RELIGION

Centuries after the area we call New England was peopled by the Algonkians, it was colonized by English Puritan nationals, who brought with them a distinct culture and way of life. We encountered these New England Puritans in our study of Protestantism, but we need to look again at their relationship to the civil religion. They came to North America from an England experiencing visible religious dissent and millennial hopes. They grew up on tales of Protestant martyrs who had suffered and died for their convictions during the Catholic reign of Bloody Mary (1553-1558). They had read these tales as evidence of an unending war between God and Satan, and they thought of England as the particular place where that war was being waged.

When they immigrated from England to the colonies along the Atlantic coast of America, the Puritans came to see themselves as the true chosen people from an almost-chosen England. More and more they understood themselves and their projects in terms of a millennial vision inspired by the Protestant martyrs. Their covenant with God was a bond that expressed for them their elect status before him. They considered themselves predestined for paradise, and as "visible saints," they thought they should be busy in doing God's work on earth. The Puritans conceived of this work in two ways. First, they thought they should be an *example* for all the world to see—a society of God's elect in which righteousness had triumphed and sin would reign no more. Second, they believed they had a *mission* to spread the message and the meaning of their gospel to others. Since

Puritan society aimed to embody that gospel, the mission for them meant convincing others to live as they (the Puritans) were doing.

Puritan sermons expressed the sense of being an example for others by speaking of New England society as a light to the world and a city upon a hill. The sermons described the mission of Puritanism in the language of destiny and an errand into the wilderness. Being an example and performing a mission, both tasks that were conceived as Puritan obligations under their covenant with God, were also for the Puritans tasks that needed to be done with millennial fervor. By the third and fourth generation in America, the Puritans thought that the days of the world were numbered. In their view, their witness was perhaps the last chance for a sinful world to overcome the deceits of the Antichrist and to seize the truth of the gospel. In short, the Puritans were people who believed they did not have time to lose. For them God's business demanded total dedication in light of their conviction of a millennial future.

What made these themes especially important for American civil religion was that all of them were understood in political terms. Practically speaking, as we have seen, Puritan New England was a theocracy—a church-state aggregation in which government was in the hands of the "saints" (although not in the hands of the clergy). These saints, or fully converted members of the church, ruled the New England colonies in the name of those who were bound together in the civil or political covenant. While not all members of the political covenant were members of the covenant of "grace" (the church covenant), the ideal of the society was that the two should be one. More than that, the Puritans with their Calvinistic heritage formed the political covenant using the church covenant as a model. They came to interpret their government in terms of destined tasks and millennial visions. Government for them was the arm of God reaching into the world through the visible saints to create a society publicly committed to the Word. Although they believed that there might be—and were—sinners in New England, they insisted that the colonies—as public and political communities—should be holy. Indeed, when the Puritans were told they were to be as a city upon a hill, the civil character of religion in Puritan culture was being affirmed, for a city is a *political* unit. In the way the Puritans saw the world, the civil and the religious were fused, and—here at least—ordinary and extraordinary religion were united.

We can see from this description that there was much in Puritan society that resembled Old Testament understandings. The Puritans were aware of the similarities and, envisioned themselves as a New Israel. They linked their millennialism to an older religious model, so that they believed that the experience of the ancient Hebrews had parallels in the story they told about themselves. In other words, if all peoples have a sacred and traditional account about who they are and where they have come from, then the accounts of the ancient Hebrews and the seventeenth-century American Puritans were in some respects alike. When we studied the history of Jewish religion, we noted that the Jews early thought of themselves both as a chosen people and as a suffering people. Among the Puritans, there was the same double message. The Puritans thought of themselves as a chosen people, but they also thought of themselves as a suffering people. We have already glanced at their sense of chosenness, but now let us take a closer look at their conviction of suffering.

We need to remember at the start that suffering arises from subjective experience. We can finally only imagine the depths of other people's suffering, for none of us is able to experience what others feel. Moreover, language in some sense creates suffering. If people say that they are suffering and believe that they are, then they are. These warnings are necessary because it may be difficult for us to recapture the Puritan sense of their own suffering. From the point of view of outsiders, it may not seem nearly so intense, for example, as the suffering of the Jews.

Puritans saw themselves as suffering in two ways. First, they thought of themselves as suffering through outside forces. Like their ancestors during the reign of Bloody Mary, they were persecuted by the Church of England. In their view, the unkindness of the church and its corruption had forced

them to make the journey over an ocean. Here they thought of themselves as compelled to live— to use one of their phrases—in a "howling wilderness." They felt surrounded by "savages" (the Indians) in league with the devil. So both their fellow Christians in England and their environment in the New World became for them external sources of discomfort.

Second, the Puritans felt themselves to be suffering from conditions within their own souls. Especially after the first generation in New England, public sermons began to portray the Puritans as guilty sinners. They were not living up to their side of the covenant with God, preachers warned, and therefore all kinds of afflictions were coming to them. Ministers told that God was already forced to punish them through disease and harsh weather, through Indian wars and the failure of many of their children to be converted. We have encountered these sermons of affliction before, for they are the jeremiads that we noted in the last chapter. In fact, these jeremiads were rituals that probably relieved some of the guilt the Puritans experienced. By enumerating what they felt to be their sins and calling loudly for repentance, they were paying back the first penny on the debt they believed they owed to God. If the rest of the debt went unpaid, that was a matter for later concern. The present, at least, had been taken care of.

It is hard to put a finger on the reasons for the Puritan sense of guilt. It is possible that the Puritan break with people in England helped to bring it on. It is also possible that, after the first generation in New England, people looked back on the era of the pioneers with a certain awe. Nothing in the lives of settled farmers and tradespeople could quite match the tales of the heroism of those who had crossed the sea. But there was another reason for Puritan guilt—the sense of millennial chosenness itself. The Puritans had carved a lofty niche for themselves in a divine plan. They understood themselves as the elect nation who in the last ages of the world were giving an example and were possessed of a mission to all nations. As visible saints, they believed that they walked with their God and that they were emissaries of his Word. But the visible saints must have noticed that they and their friends were sometimes walking in unsaintly ways. Like all people, they had feet of clay; like all people, they blundered and made mistakes.

Hence, the gap between the Puritan vision of their role and their experience of themselves must have produced a sense of guilt. The theocratic ideology of the Puritans masked a tension in which being chosen and being sufferers were two aspects of the same story. The connection between these themes is important because, as we will see, much of the Puritan story became the public and official story of later American civil religion. When America became a chosen nation, there would be a good deal of anxiety attached. Americans would simultaneously proclaim their innocence and feel guilty.

THE CIVIL RELIGION OF THE AMERICAN REVOLUTION

By the late eighteenth century, the New England Puritans had thrown in their lot with other colonists in a growing rupture with Britain. In the era of the American Revolution, from the first acts leading up to the war to the final adoption of the Constitution in 1789, a civil religion was born. Much from that civil religion was a new version of the old Puritan story. Other parts of it had been gleaned from the Enlightenment, and still other aspects from the revolutionary experience of Americans. Let us look at each in turn.

The Puritans had been a melodramatic people. Some of the later Protestant search to simplify was already theirs, for their millennialism divided the world into a battlefield between two forces. On one side were God and his saints; on the other, the devil and his agents. In this dualistic world, reality was made up of sharp contrasts—good and evil, heaven and hell, truth and falsehood. Even more, the Puritans thought that there were especially significant divine and human actions, which contrasted sharply with the routine of everyday life. For the Puritan mentality, God acted through "remarkable providences" by which he saved the saints from Indian attack, brought them an exceptionally bountiful harvest, or softened the heart of a sinner for conversion. And humans acted in ways to be remembered when they, too, performed unusual or heroic deeds.

In the eighteenth century, the Puritan way of seeing things by means of dramatic contrasts was intensified by the Great Awakening. Jonathan Edwards, we recall, had worked to make his revival sermons "sensational." For Edwards, the more vivid and striking their language, the more the sinner might realize the terrors of hell and turn earnestly to God to seek salvation. Similarly, the behavior of congregations was also sensational. Accounts of the revivals were filled with references to the moans of anguish, the tears of repentance, the fits of fainting experienced by those who felt they were struck by the power of God. And as the revivals spread throughout the colonies, they brought interaction between people from different parts of the country and a growing sense of community that, some scholars believe, was essential for the occurrence of the American Revolution.

When the Revolution and the events preceding it did come, much of the rhetoric that stirred people, whether from church pulpits, political songs and rallies, or public newspapers, had a Puritan millennial and revivalist ring. As late as the close of the French and Indian War in 1763, Americans had regarded English soldiers with gratitude and had been proud to be part of the British overseas empire. Now, however, they saw the British as Satan's troops in a battle between the forces of good and evil. The Americans were "our Israel," and the British were the Egyptians at the time of the exodus.

THE STRUCTURE OF THE CIVIL RELIGION

By 1790 elements of creed, code, and cultus had come together to form a loose religious system. This system continued into the nineteenth and twentieth centuries, absorbing new elements and discarding old ones but keeping the same basic structure. Let us look briefly at this structure of the civil religion.

The creed of the civil religion rested on fundamental assumptions that the United States was a chosen and millennial nation. Both qualities could be understood either in Christian or in more general terms. Chosenness might come from God, from nature, or from historical events.

Millennialism could mean the coming of the kingdom of God or a golden age of peace and prosperity that Americans created for themselves without requiring God. In either case, chosenness was seen as separating Americans from members of other societies in the world. It was thought to burden them with the twin tasks of being an example of democratic equality and fulfilling a mission to bring that democracy to others. Millennialism split the world into simple alternatives of good and evil and at the same time encouraged both optimism and anxiety regarding America's future. Both chosenness and millennialism were attempts to create a nation out of a political state. They were religious concepts that, it was hoped, could forge one people out of many peoples, giving them a history and identity in the American Revolution, interpreted according to Puritan, Enlightenment, and new American themes.

The code of the civil religion was already contained in its creed. Being an example and fulfilling a mission meant that citizens in the chosen nation must engage in public activity. In this morality, loyalty and patriotism as inner qualities were not enough. Rather, as in the majority religion of Protestantism, citizens had to *work* for the collective good. Voting in elections became a symbolic action to sum up the duty of the citizen. But in the ideal formula of the code, civil religion required more. Citizens had to read and be informed so that they might vote intelligently. They had to be willing to enter public life themselves. And if they were male, the ultimate actions that might be required of them were service in their country's armed forces and even death in its defense. Here human sacrifice for religious reasons had not ended but instead was demanded in a new form. Meanwhile, on the domestic side, the code urged Americans to advance economically and technologically so that the millennium would come fully.

However, the code went beyond statements about how individuals should act in the United States. It was a statement about the political community and how it should behave toward the world. Being an example and having a mission were directives for foreign policy, and America would follow them in a series of encounters with other states. Al-

though the United States would not become a world power until the twentieth century, the rhetoric of the American Revolution already predicted as much. From this perspective, world leadership was a self-fulfilling prophecy. Similarly, the wars in which the United States engaged were always fought under the banner of moral crusade. As we will see later, nationalistic missionary labors did not disappear after the Constitution established separation of church and state.

At the same time, the code of the civil religion had its other side. Just as belief in the millennial mission of the Puritans had been linked to themes of guilt and repentance, in the United States the civil religion perpetuated the political jeremiad. In days of fast and thanksgiving and later in oratory and debate bewailing their country's failings, Americans continued to express the tensions of being chosen. Sometimes the guilt led to stronger statements about being chosen and stronger protests of innocence, as America refused to face its problems. This was the case, for example, in many conflicts created in the nineteenth and twentieth centuries by racism and nativism. Sometimes, too, the guilt became a great political upheaval in an attempt at moral purification. This was true in the crisis over slavery that led to the Civil War; and as we noted earlier, this was also the case in the Watergate scandal of the 1970s.

Finally, a cultus for the civil religion was already developed in 1790 and kept on growing in the next two centuries. First, the necessary conditions for ritual had been provided: There were sacred space and sacred time. Sacred space included shrines and significant places like George Washington's home, Mount Vernon, in Virginia, and Independence Hall in Philadelphia. In the planned development of the new capital in the District of Columbia, the city of Washington, with its classical buildings and memorials on a grand scale, furnished an ideal ritual setting. As time went on, historical sites—such as battlefields that had figured prominently in America's wars—offered other sacred places. In the revolutionary era, the Fourth of July and Washington's birthday were already coming to be sacred time. In later years, new commemorations joined them, such as

Memorial Day after the Civil War and Armistice Day after the First World War.

Second, there was a catalog of national "saints," individuals to be honored because they embodied the ideals of the civil religion. George Washington was only the first among a community of founders who came to be venerated in the public life of the country—men like Thomas Jefferson, Benjamin Franklin, and John Adams. The nineteenth century brought new heroes and saints, like Andrew Jackson and Abraham Lincoln, while the twentieth century contributed its own figures in men like Franklin Delano Roosevelt and John F. Kennedy.

Third, there were sacred objects as well as sacred figures. The original copies of the Declaration of Independence and the Constitution were the most remembered by the twentieth century, but from the beginning there were other relics of the Revolution. One Liberty Tree destroyed by the British in South Carolina, for example, had its stump preserved by being carved into cane heads.

Last, formal ritual practices were associated with the sacred space and time, commemorating the founders of the republic and venerating the objects that also helped Americans to remember. Fourth of July fireworks and more solemn sermons were early examples. Later, each special time was accompanied by its own ceremonial order of public addresses, processions, or other events. Important in all of these rituals was their use in attempts to unify people so that they would be a political community and a nation. Like all rituals, the rituals of the civil religion were endeavors to change the many into one.

THE MEANING OF THE CIVIL RELIGION

Creed, code, and cultus together formed the visible structure of the civil religion. But at a deeper level, its meaning was more than the sum of its parts. At the same time, that meaning was ambiguous. Civil religion pulled in different directions at once, and contradiction was basic to its makeup. Rooted in the Puritan and revolutionary past, it urged Americans toward a millennial future. At first glance, an ordinary religion based on life within the human political community of one country, it had extraordinary aspirations.

Because it was firmly based in the Judeo-Christian tradition and, indeed, in Protestantism, it saw America in a transcendent light. Civil religion, therefore, contained a good deal of the power of extraordinary religion.

Beyond that, the civil religion was a self-conscious and deliberate faith conceived by the leaders of the revolutionary era to meet their need for political ideology. Yet there was enthusiasm and spontaneity in the people's response to the new religion. Millennial excitement could not be produced at will: It had to exist first in the people. So the leaders who were trying to make a religion found it already made, the product of a Puritan past and a revolutionary present. All they did was to tap the power that was there and use it for their purposes.

In another contradiction, the civil religion perpetuated the problem that the conviction of chosenness had created for the Puritans. Such conviction led to guilt and anxiety. Belief in a millennium already begun brought fear of corruption and decline. Thus, a combined sense of millennial chosenness and accompanying guilt encouraged people to disguise serious problems that the country faced. To admit that too much was wrong could jeopardize America's belief in its status as a chosen and millennial nation. Acceptable lamentations were often, like Puritan jeremiads, somewhat hypocritical. In the later history of the republic, problems like racism, nativism, and inequities in the economic system tended to be kept hidden, confronted, if at all, only under carefully controlled conditions. These problems violated the basic identity that the civil religion gave to Americans. In that identity, as we have seen, chosen people, living in the millennium, had to be innocent and righteous. Americans could not admit the deepest sources of their guilt without destroying their sense of who they were.

Finally, people who believed that they were chosen and living in the millennium tended, by definition, to be an exclusive community. Yet the civil religion that expressed convictions about millennial chosenness was intended as a way to bind all Americans together. How, then, could a religion of exclusivity incorporate the increasingly diverse many ? As public consciousness changed and as racial, ethnic, and feminist sensitivities grew in the late twentieth century, how could a religion identified with a white, Anglo-Saxon, and male foundation accommodate those Americans who were self-consciously different? On the face of things, a tradition of exclusivity seemed a narrow basis on which to build for broad social consensus.

Despite these problems within the civil religion, it was an attempt to find some basis for public unity in the vulnerable federal republic. In the beginning, the vulnerability had more to do with the newness of the governmental apparatus than the character of the peoples it represented. But by the late twentieth century, government was vulnerable because of the diversity of peoples and interest groups it encompassed. Still, in a political state beset with boundary questions between social groups, civil religion proposed a common and, it argued, natural boundary based on its natural-rights philosophy. Civil religion was an attempt to merge the separate boundaries of the many into a single nation-state.

If there was a central meaning to the civil religion in the midst of these ambiguities, it was in millennialism in politics and history. Whether looking to past or to future, under God or under America, deliberate or spontaneous, hypocritical or sincere, the civil religion revolved around what were considered memorable deeds that Americans had performed to initiate an age unknown before in history. Here, actions had to be striking to be seen; events had to make history to be meaningful. For people who did not like to dwell in the past, Americans were very anxious to achieve a past on a grand scale. The sensationalist philosophy of Jonathan Edwards resounded in later American life, and all paths in the civil religion seemed to lead to millennial politics and history.

Civil Religion in the Nineteenth and Twentieth Centuries

So far we have examined the origins of civil religion in Puritanism and in the era of the American Revolution. We found that the New Israel of the Puritans continued into the revolutionary generation. We also found that the religion of the Enlightenment, as well as a new religion built around the deeds of patriotic Americans, merged with the New Israel. We noticed a distinct creed, code, and cultus in the civil religion that evolved, and despite its ambiguities, we discovered a core of meaning centering on values of millennial politics and history. In our study, we referred at times to the nineteenth and twentieth centuries. Now we give closer scrutiny to civil religion during these two centuries.

The Nineteenth Century

On the whole, nineteenth-century civil religion was rooted in the Puritan and revolutionary heritage. The legacy of the Enlightenment, in the nineteenth century and thereafter, became less clear. Its ethic of the golden mean was cast aside by Americans who were striving for ultimates. At least in the nineteenth century, its Freemasonic rituals came under challenge for their undemocratic secrecy, the clannish political tactics they fostered, and, said many ministers, their godlessness. Yet elements of the creed of the Enlightenment did continue. The proclamations of the Declaration of Independence—that all were equal in the sight of God and that all were endowed with natural rights—were, at least theoretically, sacred beliefs. Still further, Enlightenment ideas continued in new form by blending with a territorial version of millennialism in the age of manifest destiny.

Generally, themes of millennial chosenness, outstanding example as an innocent and righteous nation, and historic deeds and destiny shaped the civil religion. Especially in growing numbers of public schools, the civil religion was expressed in history books and readers that told of the Revolution and its heroes, aiming to inspire young Americans to patriotic behavior. And the civil faith was ritualized in regular annual observances as well as in a series of anniversary commemorations of revolutionary events. Since it is not possible to explore the nineteenth-century history of civil religion fully, we look first at the presence of (extraordinary) biblical millennial themes, especially in the Civil War, and then at a more ordinary millennialism that combined Puritan with Enlightenment ideas. Finally, we glance at how the memory of the Revolution relieved American anxieties and continued to shape the civil religion.

With the War of 1812 (1812-1814), the new conflict with Britain gave impetus to the civil religion. Congress had declared war because of the British impressment of American sailors into maritime service (in the context of a British struggle with France) and because of quarrels with Britain over land in the American West. While a considerable number of Americans opposed the war, once it had begun, many viewed it as a Christian crusade. Public fasts multiplied—some of them observed locally and others throughout the country. Because for political reasons the British had supported Pope Pius VII (1740-1823) against France, in American eyes this identified Britain with the Antichrist. Thus, the war was read as a millennial confrontation. American patriots believed that the last days were at hand, and when the fortunes of the pope sank, this was seen as a sign of fulfillment of the prophecies. For these Americans the War of 1812, like the Revolution, was a holy war.

If the War of 1812 was fought with strong millennial overtones, a half-century later it was the Civil War (1861-1865) that played out these themes as *the* millennial war of the century. The Civil War swept up legions of Americans in what they saw as the final battle between good and evil, as Northerners and white Southerners alike drew on the biblical heritage. In the South, the Confederacy was seen as the authentic New Israel facing the armies of Egypt. White Southerners believed that slavery was in the plan of God, for they considered blacks to be descended from the biblical Ham, the son of Noah who had shamed his father by viewing him naked and drunk (Gen. 9:20-25). According to the Bible, because of Ham's act Noah later cursed him and predicted for him a life of slavery. Hence, said southern whites, the enslavement of blacks was right and just. By contrast, southern whites argued, the northern abolitionists were atheists and unbelievers. War with such people was a defense of the cause of God and religion. For white Southerners, in a millennial vein, this war was the most important struggle through which the country had passed.

In the North, millennial dating convinced Americans that the end was at hand. According to one theory, the Antichrist had come to power in the year A.D. 606. A symbolic reading of the Book of Revelation (Rev. 11:3) indicated that his reign would extend 1, 260 years; and therefore, said convinced believers, the Antichrist must fall in the year 1866. Even in the liberal religious circles of Boston, distanced from the literal millennial belief of so much of Protestant America, the vision of Revelation marshaled people to the northern cause. There Julia Ward Howe (1819-1910), who did not believe in miracles or a special revelation in the Bible, wrote "The Battle Hymn of the Republic." She had visited an army camp, and after the experience the poem came to her, filled with images that must have arisen from long-forgotten childhood memories. Published in 1862, the hymn described the coming of Jesus for the biblical final battle. It was written in the dramatic language of the millennium, with echoes of Armageddon interwoven in its evocation of the march of the Union army. The point made by the circumstances of the hymn's composition was clear: Beneath the surface of liberal culture in America themes of Armageddon lived on, able to shape the interpretation of events and to give them powerful meaning.

So the war was fought in millennial terms. Then, five days after it ended, Abraham Lincoln was assassinated. He had just begun his second term of office, telling Americans that they should bear malice toward no one and have charity for all. As it happened, the president was shot on Good Friday, and that fact was not lost on others. He had been sacrificed, they said, as Jesus had been on the cross—one victim to redeem all the people. According to their thinking, while the sacrifice of Jesus pointed the way for men and women to enter heaven, the sacrifice of Lincoln brought them together in unity for a better earth. For them, blood had paid the price of liberty. Lincoln's blood, shed for his country, was seen as mingling with the blood of the nameless soldiers who had given their lives for their country. Popular oratory proclaimed these ideas, as a new divine man and event entered the civil religion.

While biblical interpretations—and especially biblical millennialism— dominated during times of greatest crisis for the country, at other moments themes of millennial chosenness became ordinary religion. The clearest example was during the era of "manifest destiny" in mid century (an era that we considered briefly in a Protestant missionary context in Chapter 5). Recall that the Enlightenment God of nature was thought to guarantee natural law and also natural rights. That guarantee had, in effect, allowed Americans to follow the dictates of their own self-interest, breaking the ties with Britain to achieve political and economic independence. The philosophy of natural rights took many turns in the nineteenth century, as it blended with a sense of national chosenness and a belief in the dawning of a new era. The result was the doctrine of manifest destiny that justified the expansionist ventures of Americans in the West.

Natural rights were viewed as rights given by nature to the political community. In the nineteenth-century understanding of these rights, nature grew less philosophical and more geographical. Americans began to think that the physical terrain, in its very contours, *contained* the law. In other words, there were natural boundaries to a country—rivers, oceans, sometimes mountains. According to the doctrine of manifest destiny, the existence of these boundaries was a law written into the landscape—a law that Americans should learn to obey, extending their state from one end of the continent to the other. By doing so, they said, they would be spreading the area of freedom and democracy at the same time that they improved the earth for farming, its predestined and highest use. In this view, true ownership of land came not from written documents but from the higher law of destiny that matched the land with the people most fit to cultivate it. These people, Americans said, were themselves. They argued that clear necessity demanded that they should have new territory, for like a biological organism, the United States ought to stretch to limits intended by nature. And they thought, besides, that the task of Americans was to regenerate conquered peoples by educating them in democracy. Indeed, for these Americans, Providence demanded that the United States absorb surrounding land to fulfill this mission.

The journalist John L. O'Sullivan used the term *manifest destiny* in 1845. In that year, an article in his *Democratic Review* argued regarding the question of Texas that it was America's manifest destiny to expand across the continent. After that, the phrase became a catchword to sum up a spirit and a time, but the ideas it expressed had been present in outline early in the century. Here we cannot trace the growth and changes in the country's commitment to the idea of manifest destiny throughout the century, but it is important to point out the continuance of the past in this new era and, later, into the period of the Spanish American War of 1898. Mainstream Americans still believed that they were a chosen people, whether they expressed that conception in the language of the Bible, of the Enlightenment, or of nineteenth-century ordinary culture. Likewise, they still believed that they must be an example to the nations and, even more, that they had a mission to perform. Whether they felt Providence, destiny, or the land commanded them, Americans believed that their mission was to establish a millennial age of empire. They were convinced that the natural right and providential plan for Americans was to hold more land.

It is clear from the hindsight of well over a century that Americans had manipulated language and ideals for their own self-interest. But as we noted earlier, this was a problem built into the very structure of the civil religion. Even without the use of the specific biblical language of the millennium, the problem would not disappear. Meanwhile, even as Americans ventured forward aggressively to make their future, they were deeply anxious, and they clung to would-be signs of divine favor tied to their heritage in the Revolution.

For example, when the Marquis de Lafayette (1757-1834) visited the United States as an old man in 1824, Americans staged what amounted to a revival in the civil religion. Lafayette had been the "adopted" son of George Washington. According to accounts at the time, the presence in the flesh of the son intensified the memory of the father, now dead for a quarter of a century. Thus, Lafayette made Washington live again for these Americans through the closeness of past ties with him. And with the presence of Washington came the presence of the Revolution—and the power of the Revolution newly made available. Heaven was surely speaking to them in the visit of Lafayette, Americans thought, for a rainbow hung over his ship both when it arrived and when it departed from port. Moreover, an eagle, the symbolic bird of America, was spotted flying over Washington's tomb as Lafayette walked into it to pay his respects. As Americans shared the news of Lafayette's descent into the tomb, it seemed to them as if they, too, followed him—not to death but to a rebirth in the spirit of the Revolution.

Then, some two years later, the deaths of both John Adams and Thomas Jefferson on the Fourth of July, 1826, awed and impressed Americans. The two had died hours apart on the fiftieth anniversary of the signing of the Declaration of Independence. Once more, Americans believed they had a sign from God as to the significance of their experiment in democracy. Again in the following decade, when the physical remains of Washington were placed in a new marble coffin, his body was declared physically nearly intact. No odor was reported to have offended those present; it was said that the broad temples and chest were still there; and one member of the party, it was told, quickly laid his hand on Washington's head. In these physical remains, Americans had a relic that for them had unusual power. The integrity of Washington's body seemed to them a sign of the integrity of America grounded on its past. Moreover, keeping in touch with the body of Washington was for them a way to keep in touch with the Revolution.

Less dramatically, keeping in touch came not through the deaths of the leaders of the Revolution but through the ceremonial recollection of the events through which they had lived. The fiftieth anniversary of the Declaration (1826), the hundredth anniversary of the birth of Washington (1832), the fiftieth jubilee of the Constitution (1839), the seventy-fifth anniversary of the Declaration (1851), the centennial of the Revolution (1876), and the centennial of the Constitution (1889) were all such occasions. Americans believed they could draw strength from their past as they faced the tensions that their millennial dreams of progress brought them. The ceremonies of the civil religion worked to reassure them of their cause and motives.

THE TWENTIETH CENTURY

With the twentieth century, civil religion continued to interpret for Americans the meaning of their existence as a political community. With the First and Second World Wars millennial themes were visible. In more peaceful times, the regular ceremonies of the Fourth of July, Memorial Day, the birthdays of Washington and Lincoln, and Thanksgiving recalled the heritage of the past. After the First World War, Armistice Day, later called Veterans Day (1954), joined them. But as time passed and the events of the Revolution became mostly chapters in history books, the power of the civil religion to inspire Americans began to fail. Even more, the second half of the century brought wars in Korea and Vietnam that did not lend themselves easily to familiar millennial interpretations. Moral ambiguity clouded the domestic scene as well, so that civil religion grew to be the faith of fewer Americans, less of the time.

The period preceding the American entry into the First World War (1914-1918) was a time of political isolation from foreign involvements—traditional during much of the country's history before the United States became a world power. Here the ideology of chosenness was expressed through the example Americans understood themselves to give to a "corrupt" world. According to the ideology, in its innocence and righteousness America was a new Eden, a garden of progress and peace. In fact, when Woodrow Wilson (1856-1924) was re-elected to the presidency in 1916, his campaign was built around the slogan "He kept us out of war." The First World War had begun over two years earlier, and Americans had tried to remain neutral. But by 1917 reaction to the loss of American lives through German submarine warfare made that impossible, and the country mobilized for war. Wilson, with a strict Presbyterian upbringing, brought moral earnestness to the effort. Under a committee on public information, the government began a propaganda effort to convince Americans of the righteousness of this new crusade.

Once again, the millennial account of the final battle between the forces of good and evil was recalled. The success of the campaign showed how deeply the millennial pattern was rooted in the American spirit. Motion pictures portrayed the Germans as wicked and barbarian Huns, promoting beliefs that Americans were fighting the agents of Satan. Some states passed laws to forbid teaching the German language in schools and colleges; citizens threw German books out of the libraries; German and Austrian artists and their music were banned from public performances. Speakers appeared at public meetings and at film theaters to deliver brief addresses in support of the war effort. Newspaper editorials and pamphlets repeatedly attacked the Germans as corrupt, and members of the Protestant clergy from their pulpits took up the cry of the New Israel engaged in a holy war against evil.

Billy Sunday—whom we have already met waving the American flag as he preached—declared that he thought that if hell were turned upside down, the phrase "made in Germany" would be seen stamped across the bottom. Meanwhile, Roman Catholic and Jewish leaders supported the Protestant interpretation of the war. Catholics were told that there was a parallel between the sufferings of Israel in the desert on the way to the promised land and the sufferings of America in the massive war effort. Jews in turn were told that they were once again fighting against the forces of oppression, as they had done so many times before in their history. From the side of ordinary American culture, the war whipped patriotism to new religious zeal. By 1918 at least one book—William Norman Guthrie's The Religion of Old Glory— was telling Americans of the greatness of their flag, suggesting a ritual for its worship.

According to the phrase that rallied millions of Americans, the war had been fought to "make the world safe for democracy." America had committed itself one more time in a mission to the world, combining extraordinary and ordinary versions of their belief in millennial chosenness to do so. As the "world's policeman," America had entered a new era in international affairs, but it read the new era through the pages of the old story of the civil religion. Then, after another period of isolation,

the Second World War (1939-1945) meant a return to the familiar themes, although less intensely than during the Wilson years.

Still, ideas of the dualism of good and evil rode the public airwaves. The totalitarian form of government in the Axis states (Germany, Italy, and Japan) lent itself easily to millennial interpretation. After Americans entered the war in 1941, convinced of the importance of bombing (some would say, despite evidence to the contrary), they used air power in dramatic displays of force. Making history became more destructive than at any time in previous wars, as the night skies were lit by missiles of death. When the United States finally dropped atomic bombs on Hiroshima and Nagasaki, Japan, in 1945, totalitarianism had been countered with a force as total. If the final battle of Armageddon had not come, Americans had done what they could to bring it.

In the midst of these years, Franklin Delano Roosevelt (1882-1945) presided over the country, publicly determined to make America an "arsenal of democracy." Elected to an unprecedented third term in office, he told Congress in January 1941 that America should support the countries that were fighting to defend the Four Freedoms— freedom of speech, freedom of religion, freedom from want, and freedom from fear. In the phrases of his oratory, he was calling all Americans to respond to their mission. For Roosevelt, it was not sufficient to be an example to the nations, as isolationist policy allowed. In so many words, he was urging the Puritans of the New Israel to march again, though they spoke in this worldly fashion and wore the uniforms of a government theoretically separate from religion.

Less spectacularly, civil religion continued through the annual calendar of public observances in which key moments or individuals from America's past were remembered. Like any ritual of remembrance, these observances were sacramental in nature. They were efforts to make the past present again, attempts to destroy the work of time in order to live in the power of moments remembered as the nation's greatest. Yet by the fifties, a long and gradual period of decline began to affect the observances and the spirit of the civil religion.

We cannot follow the whole story here, but as an example let us look at what happened to the annual Memorial Day commemorations.

Memorial Day began in the millennial aftermath of the Civil War, in an America mourning the death of Lincoln and deeply aware of all of the dead. In fact, there were both northern and southern theories of its origins. Northerners recounted that General John A. Logan, commander-in-chief of the Grand Army of the Republic, in 1868 established the observance by his orders. Southerners said the remembrance started in 1866 in Columbus, Mississippi, when women of the town paid homage to the war dead by decorating the graves of both Confederate and Union soldiers. The separate accounts suggest how deep the rupture had been between the two sides. They also suggest the intensity of feeling that marked these early Memorial Day commemorations. As time passed, the presence of veterans who had fought in the war continued to give intensity of feeling to the annual Memorial Day observances, but when the veterans began to die, a bond with the past was broken. Try as they might, later generations could not recapture the spirit that came with the presence of living witnesses to the war.

Then, in the fifties and afterward, time eroded the strength and significance of Memorial Day ceremonies even further. Remember that in both the North and the South, the day had paid tribute to countless soldiers who had given their lives in the cause of their country. By doing so, it had given expression to the sense of unity in the community that remained. By honoring those who died, people renewed their own belief in the need for sacrifice for the good of the entire American community. But the simple formula did not work when applied to the Korean War (1950-1953) and later the Vietnam War (1954-1973), with growing American involvement in the sixties. Many were less sure of the significance of sacrifices in foreign campaigns that were clouded with ambiguity. The community was no longer united in its support of war, and Memorial Day, therefore, could not express traditional themes convincingly.

In the fifties, newspaper editorials complained about the lack of enthusiasm for Memorial Day, while by the sixties, apathy was evident in accounts of poorly attended Memorial Day parades and gaudy souvenirs that cluttered and cheapened the observances. Journalists asked where the spirit of American patriotism had gone, and by the era of the Vietnam War, the answer was that it had become identified with right-wing causes. To be patriotic during the late sixties and early seventies was to make a cultural statement that identified a person with complaints against hippies, draft dodgers, and other long-haired individuals. To be patriotic meant to be a self-declared enemy of the Woodstock generation. Hence, far from being a solemn evocation of national unity, Memorial Day had become a reminder of division. The civil religion in some respects was failing, for the many were not being made into one.

If regular observances of the civil religion like Memorial Day reflected the decline of the tradition, so did the anniversary celebration of America's 200th year. January to December 1976 had been planned as a long remembrance of the events that established the United States. The Fourth of July was to be the high point of the yearlong observance, meant as a tribute to the deeds and values on which America was built. But coming on the heels of the nonvictorious end of the Vietnam War and the resignation of President Richard M. Nixon because of the Watergate scandal, the bicentennial caught many Americans not in the mood for celebration. The American Revolution Bicentennial Administration (ARBA), in charge of official government planning, was plagued with disagreements about how the bicentennial could best be commemorated. When early plans were floated to select one bicentennial city, prime candidates like Boston and Philadelphia thought approvingly of the financial gain for themselves from the influx of tourists. But when, for example in the case of Philadelphia, plans grew more concrete with a specific city neighborhood designated as the focus for the celebration, the city government responded to pressures from neighborhood residents. Local critics argued that the bicentennial would bring strange people, and especially black people, to their doorsteps. People in the Eastwick section of the city did not approve.

Finally, the ARBA settled on a decentralized plan for the bicentennial. No one city would be the center of solemnities. Throughout the country, small cities and towns began to erect signs that proclaimed each of them to be an authorized bicentennial city. In fact, the many proclamations mirrored the pluralism of the country at its 200th anniversary. The ARBA had stumbled into a version of America that fittingly summed up national life. In 1976 no one center could speak for all Americans, for there were too many languages to speak and too many stories to be told.

As if to emphasize the existence of different visions of America, the official ARBA had competition in its planning. The People's Bicentennial Commission (PBC), with its newsletter titled *Common Sense*, challenged the ARBA from a leftist perspective. For Americans of the PBC, the story of the American Revolution still had power to inspire, but a new enemy of America replaced King George III. In the late twentieth century, said the PBC, the real enemy of America was the giant corporation, and the power of the Revolution should be harnessed to fight the entrenched business establishment. So on the celebration of the 200th anniversary of the Boston Tea Party in 1973, 25,000 supporters of the PBC rallied for the enactment of their own interpretation of events. On the deck of their ship were oil drums prominently displaying the names of the largest oil companies in the United States. A group of the new Boston protesters threw the drums into the water, using the past to register dissent in the present.

Against this background of conflicting ideas of what America meant, the observances of the civil religion on the occasion of the bicentennial were sometimes lavish but mostly quiet and contained. There were gaudy mementos of every description, as commercial interests hurried to profit from events. But cities awaiting large numbers of tourists did not get nearly so many as they had expected. Police foreseeing fights and accidental deaths in the huge crowds at commemorations found that far less happened than they had anticipated. Generally, Americans observed the Fourth of July soberly more than enthusiastically. There were huge spectacles in big cities, such as a

procession of tall ships bearing masts that sailed through New York harbor. But in the atmosphere of the late twentieth century, the civil millennial dream had been interrupted. A new national consensus about the meaning of America had not been formed.

The slow decline did not go unheeded by thoughtful people. In fact, since at least the sixties, a number of scholars had begun to ponder the meaning of America as they examined the role of religion. It was one of these scholars, the sociologist Robert N. Bellah, who by 1967 employed the term *civil religion* to describe the religious system we have been examining throughout the chapter. For some sociologists, like Bellah, and for some historians, like Sidney E. Mead, scholarship about civil religion became an attempt to revitalize the tradition. Bellah's article "Civil Religion in America" spoke of the growing (at that time) conflict in Vietnam as America's third time of trial, a new crisis on the order of the American Revolution and the Civil War. Mead's many essays on the "religion of the Republic"—and later its theology—identified sectarianism as the cause of national disunity and praised the universal religion of the Enlightenment, born in the Revolution. This religion, he thought, offered Americans real hope of unity. In the year before the bicentennial, Bellah published a book length essay, *The Broken Covenant*. Subtitled *American Civil Religion in Time of Trial*, it began with historical assessment of the power of the traditional American account of origins and, in contrast, found the civil religion of the time empty and broken. Bellah called for a return to what he saw as the true and original meaning of an American covenant, to a millennium brought by God and not by human beings, and to the continuance of the old dreams and visions.

So in their awareness of the lessening hold of the civil religion, descriptive scholars had become theologians and preachers. Their reflection and writing were in fact an attempt to make the civil religion strong again. Although scholars have been less interested in civil religion in recent years and the so-called civil religion debate is largely over, we can learn much from the decade and more of scholarly exchange. In his article in 1967, Bellah identified the existence of civil religion by study-ing presidential inaugural addresses to find in them references to God. It is interesting that in the excerpts he included from the 1961 inaugural address of President John F. Kennedy (1917-1963), there were as many references to history or our "forebears" as to God. Later, at the height of the Watergate scandal, President Nixon continually referred to history as the judge of his deeds. He had wanted to make history, and so he had taped presidential conversations in the Oval Office to preserve them. His unwillingness to destroy the tapes—his bond with history—in the end helped bring him down.

In America from the beginning, making history had been closely identified with politics. The public space of government—and the conversa-tions and acts that took place there—gave many Americans a sense of clear direction in the ordi-nary world. In a key example, in 1823 as an old man Thomas Jefferson wrote to John Adams, including in his letter the wish that the two would meet again in heaven with their colleagues in the Congress. Happiness, for Jefferson, Adams, and many others, meant politics.

Indeed, in the late twentieth century the statement was still true. News accounts revolved around the (often crisis-ridden) doings of the president and Congress, while every four years, the country passed through a season of millennial revival as a presidential election campaign was waged. As Walter Cronkite ended his regular presentations of the evening news on CBS television in the seven-ties, he told millions of Americans, "That's the way it is." Meant to be a catchphrase to close the broadcast, the statement was philosophical—and religious. The real world, as proclaimed by Cronkite and CBS, was the world of public events and striking deeds. It was the world of political and, sometimes, military action, the account of goals achieved or woefully failed and of public acclaim captured or lost. Americans were still melodramatic people, and they were still sensa-tionalists. That is how they made sense of their world, lived their daily lives, and solemnized their actions in rituals.

Moreover, as the direct memory of Cronkite faded and the century waned, the civil religion still continued to define reality for Americans in extended moments of nationalistic feeling. The Iranian hostage crisis in 1980, the explosion of the space shuttle Challenger in 1986, and the invasions of Grenada in 1983 and of Panama in 1989 all evoked in different ways the patriotic cosmology at the center of the civil religion. When, in 1990, Iraq assumed control of tiny Kuwait and raised fears regarding the international oil supply, American public rhetoric turned more on Iraqi aggression against an "innocent" neighbor than on American defense of and desire for oil. Even with an ambiguous reference by President George H. Bush (b. 1924) to defending "our way of life," the rhetoric stood in the tradition of the "righteous" nation, taking its stand in time and history for the pursuit of transcendent values. The Persian Gulf War that followed (1991) was also fought on these rhetorical terms.

Yet as we have already seen, in such involvement in the historical moment, Americans showed little interest in the chronological account of the unfold-ing of the past. If they periodically looked to America's time of origins in the Revolution, they looked more to their problems and achievements in the present and to their plans for the future. Civil religion was the triumph of politics and history, but the history involved was, in reality, ahistorical. In an echo of Protestant restorationism, it was the history that Americans performed with an eye to the millennial new day that counted, not the weight of tradition. In effect, as we noticed earlier, the civil religion was caught in a double bind: it needed the past to be meaningful—to give the present a solid foundation. Yet the values it encouraged were values that rejected the past for the future.

As the past became older and the revolutionary events more distant, it was no wonder that many Americans had trouble relating to the founders and their foundation. At the same time, for Ameri-cans who were people of color and for immigrants who were newer and more diverse, the ties with the past that did remain in the civil religion proved not especially meaningful. Civil religion could give Americans a creed, a code, and a cultus, but it could not—save in exceptional wartime moments—transform them into one community. Ambiguous in its relationship to tradition, civil religion, with its belief in millennial chosenness, could not awake to the manyness of the present. It was caught between the past and the future. It had no formula for the community that needed to be created in the present from what all the people in the United States shared continuously in common.

Still, there was another side to the issue. From the first, civil religion was a religious system that had sprung up in addition to the churches. It had brought ordinary American history into touch with extraordinary religion. Yet unlike being Methodist or Jewish or Presbyterian, being a believer in the national faith did not mean belonging to an organization or breaking ties with a previous church to which a person belonged. Despite the contrary evidence of the Jehovah's Witnesses, a believer in the civil religion might also be a Baptist, a Catholic, or a Mormon. Indeed, a believer in the civil religion might conceivably be an atheist, since a good part of the symbolism of the civil religion could be used without reference to a God. Thus, despite its limitations, to some extent civil religion was an answer to the problem of manyness—an overarching religious system under which most of the denominations and sects might find their place. Whatever its problems, civil religion was a "one story" created to form the many into one.

In Overview

We have seen that civil religion is a recent name for religious nationalism as institutionalized in a loose religious system. Its foundations were laid by the New England Puritans and, later, by the patriots of the American Revolution, who linked Puritan millennial themes to Enlightenment religion and the experience and remembrance of their own deeds in the war. By the time of George Washington's first inauguration, the creed, code, and cultus of the civil religion were firmly in place, and through them the ordinary history of the country was linked to extraordinary religion.

The creed proclaimed the United States as a chosen and millennial nation, saddled with the twin charge of providing an example and fulfilling a mission to raise up others to democracy. The code emphasized patriotic behavior by citizens and government, with a view to setting example and accomplishing an American mission. But the code also institutionalized the jeremiad, the public lament about the guilt of America that substituted language for action to correct problems. Interlinked with creed and code, the cultus of the civil faith designated sacred space and time in national shrines and patriotic holy days. It offered national "saints," revered objects, and ritual practices to encourage Americans to keep touch with creed and code. Although there were many ambiguities in the meaning of creed, code, and cultus, the central affirmation was the millennial politics of making history by deeds of greatness.

In the nineteenth century, the War of 1812 and the Civil War carried forward the millennial theme, while the doctrine of manifest destiny applied the theme to the acquisition of land. Then in the twentieth century, the First and Second World Wars heightened millennial fervor, but beginning in the fifties a long period of decline occurred in the civil religion. Celebration of the cultus grew even less enthusiastic at, for example, Memorial Day observances and during the bicentennial. Against this background, a scholarly revitalization movement explored the meaning of the civil faith and tried to revivify and strengthen it. Beleaguered by its problems, civil religion could not create authentic community; it was the religion of, at best, many of the people some of the time. Yet it did offer a framework within which the many could come together as Americans and still pursue their separate religions. And it did provide a focus for national response during public crisis moments from 1980.

However, civil religion was only one piece of the religious territory, so to speak. Although they were many, Americans in their public space had created a dominant culture that, as one, told them who they were, advised them how to act, and provided them with rituals to express these meanings. George Washington was not the only divine man for Americans. Arguing politics and celebrating the Fourth of July were not the only American rituals. Beyond the civil religion there was general American culture. We need further examination of its religious dimensions, for we need to gain a clearer sense of what ordinary religion means in its American setting. As we will see, George Washington shared his power with Elvis Presley, and arguing politics yielded before the public spectacle of the American baseball game.

THE ETHICS OF DIVERSITY: GENDER, ETHNICITY, AND INDIVIDUALITY

by Lawrence M. Hinman

Introduction

We are puzzled, both as citizens and as philosophers, about diversity. The very motto of our country, *"e pluribus unum,"* speaks eloquently of a national hope: "out of many, one." Yet the pithiness of the Latin gives a misleading impression of clarity. What do we mean by *"unum"?* If we are seeking to be "one," does it mean that diversity should be eliminated? Surely uniformity is not our goal. Americans often have criticized societies such as that of contemporary China precisely because of their uniformity. Moreover, the American tradition of individualism would seem to value "the many" over "the one." Yet what should be the relationship between the one and the many, between unity and diversity? Often, our answers to this question are posed in terms of metaphors. For several decades, the metaphor of a melting pot captured our national ideal, if not our political realities. However, in the eyes of many, this metaphor threatened diversity and individuality, for in a melting pot everything gradually becomes the same. More recently, Jesse Jackson's metaphor of a patchwork quilt has challenged the melting pot metaphor, offering more hope of preserving uniqueness and difference within a context of unity. Yet we remain undecided, as a country and often as individuals, about exactly which metaphor most accurately captures the proper mix between the unity and diversity that we strive to achieve. Most of us reject the extremes of complete uniformity and complete diversity. We do not want everyone to be the same, but neither do we want such diversity that there is no meaningful sense in which we can call ourselves one people. Being part of a community means having things in common.

The issue of community and commonalties is not a purely political question. It is also an issue of lively disagreement among philosophers. For the last seventy years, philosophers have become increasingly discontented with, and mistrustful of, the philosophical 'canon' of essential writings and the Enlightenment belief in the universality of reason. Whereas initially this mistrust had a distinctively Marxist flavor, in the last thirty years post-structuralist thinkers such as Jacques Derrida, a contemporary French philosopher of the traditional structures of philosophy, have increasingly carried out a critique of the basic presuppositions of the modem age. Derrida, for example, has urged us to reread and rewrite the history of philosophy, paying attention precisely to those elements which usually are relegated to the margins of philosophy. The result has been a partial tearing down (or "deconstruction," to use a term introduced by Jacques Derrida), a radical reshuffling which brings to the fore previously neglected thinkers and ideas. With this reorientation, at least ideally, comes a greater receptivity to diversity.

Where Politics and Philosophy Meet: The General Education Requirements

One of the interesting ways in which this debate about cultural diversity touches the lives of college students is in the general education requirements of their particular college or university. At one time, general education was grounded firmly in a shared understanding of the classics of the Western tradition: Homer, Plato, Aristotle, Aeschylus, Euripides, Cicero, Augustine, Aquinas, Erasmus, Dante, Shakespeare, Montaigne, Descartes, Hume, Goethe, Cervantes, Kant, and Hegel. Now there is much less agreement among academics about (a) what constitutes the 'canon' of essential writings and (b) about whether we ought to expect students to study that canon. One of the obvious advantages of having and studying a canon is that there is a common ground of shared traditions and experiences that provide a basis for a more finely textured understanding among people. Yet one of the clear disadvantages has been that the canon, at least as traditionally understood, left out certain groups in society (such as racial and ethnic minorities, non-Europeans, and women) and neglected material vital both to their understanding of themselves and to our understanding of one another. The traditional core general education program in American universities, for example, contained nothing from or about Native Americans, even though they obviously are crucial to our understanding of ourselves as a country.

THE NEGLECT OF DIVERSITY

If we are to understand the proper role of diversity in the moral life, we must first have some understanding of why it seems to have little place in ethical theory. In recent years, there has been a growing emphasis on cultural diversity. This new emphasis raises intriguing issues for ethics. Some of these issues already have been dealt with in the chapter on ethical relativism, since the recognition of cultural diversity was a major motivating factor in the development of ethical relativism. There are other issues, however, which have not been as fully explored that relate directly to the way in which this issue is posed in contemporary discussions in America of cultural diversity.

THE IMPARTIALITY OF THE MORAL AGENT

Traditional ethical theories have ignored issues of ethnicity and cultural diversity for at least two reasons. The first of these centers around the notion of the moral agent which is at the heart of traditional ethical theories. Both Kantian and utilitarian theories are committed deeply to a notion of the moral agent radically stripped of almost all vestiges of individuality, and hence quite different from a unique moral decision-maker.

The Kantian Moral Agent

For Kant, moral agents are rational self-legislators, autonomous beings who give the moral law to themselves. Cultural background and ethnicity are excluded from relevance, for the question is how *any* rational agent would act. The very idea of universalizability implies that one acts in the same way as any rational agent would act in the same type of situation. Any considerations of individuality, gender, or culture would be set aside in order to act as a purely rational being.

The Utilitarian Calculator

Utilitarians exhibit a similar impartiality. The utilitarian moral agent is essentially an *impartial calculator,* a person who disinterestedly computes the utility of competing courses of action and chooses the one that maximizes utility. In calculating utility, the utilitarian may include factors relating to gender and ethnicity in the overall equations but the utilitarian moral agent as such exhibits no allegiance to a specific individual identity, gender, or ethnicity. Cultural diversity would seem to have no more place in utilitarianism than it does in calculus.

Thus we see one of the principal philosophical reasons for the neglect of diversity: The two major traditions in ethics both presuppose a notion of the moral agent that is so reified, so abstracted from the concrete situation, that no traces of individuality, gender or ethnicity remain.

GENDER, ETHNICITY, AND THE PHILOSOPHICAL CANON

There is a second reason why gender, ethnicity, and cultural background have played a relatively minor role in moral theory. Most of the work done in classical moral theory (and in many other areas as well) has been written by white males, about white males, and for white males. Historically, it has been difficult for women and members of minorities to acquire the university positions and research facilities that often are taken for granted in mainstream work. When they have done first-rate work, it often has been unrecognized, both during their lifetimes and afterward. Think of the major figures covered in standard histories of philosophy before the twentieth century: Plato, Aristotle, Aquinas, Montaigne, Descartes, Hume, Kant, Hegel, Marx, and Kierkegaard are but a few of the major figures. All of these figures in philosophy are men and all are part of our mainstream (largely Caucasian) European heritage.

This limitation had serious, although probably largely unintended, implications for the development of moral theory. Precisely because white males were the majority, there was virtually no need for them to be aware of their own ethnicity or gender, although it does not mean that they were unaffected by their own gender and ethnicity. On the contrary, their views often were profoundly affected by their gender and their cultural background on at least two levels. First, the problems they selected for study, the methods they employed, and the conclusions they reached were all often significantly influenced by their gender and cultural background. We shall call these *first-order influences*. There is also a *second-order influence*, one which helps to conceal the presence of the first-order influences. Because they were in the clear majority, these philosophers had no need to define themselves in opposition to some other group. Consequently, they did not have to acknowledge the presence of those first-order influences. Instead, they simply treated their own worldview as if it were the whole of reality itself.

This experience was not true for women and members of ethnic and cultural minorities, who by virtue of their situation in society had to define themselves in opposition to, or at least in contrast with, the dominant societal group. The awareness of difference is much closer to the heart of self-awareness for women and minorities than it is for white males. Consequently, women and minorities may be subject to just as many (although different) first-order influences as their white male counterparts, but they are much less likely to experience the second-order influences that encourage masking the first-order influences: They are much more likely to acknowledge their voices as women's voices, Native American voices, Chicano voices, African-American voices. White males, in contrast, are much less likely to acknowledge their own voices as white male voices; instead, white males are much more likely to think of their own voices simply as the voices of reason, of science, or of objectivity.

QUESTIONING THE CANON

Recently, the traditional canon (of the "classics") has come under increasing attack. The work of Carol Gilligan has profoundly influenced the way we understand the relevance of gender to morality. Much less work has been done by philosophers about the relevance of culture and ethnicity to ethics, so we shall have to mark out more of that conceptual terrain ourselves. Let us first consider the relationship between gender and ethics.

INTEGRATING DIVERSE VOICES

A deep ambiguity runs through Gilligan's work. Clearly, her work is *descriptive*. It articulates women's moral voices and the differences between their voices and men's without necessarily making any value judgments about which are better. However, at times her work also seems to have normative implications, suggesting that one voice may be as good as, perhaps even better than, another. Some of Gilligan's statements suggest that she thinks both men's voices and women's voices are of equal value in morality; other statements suggest that she sees women's voices as superior. In this context, we can set aside the question of what Gilligan herself says about this question and look at the various possible positions on this issue and consider them on their own merits.

The Separate but Equal Thesis

Assuming that, in general, men and women have different moral voices, one of the ways in which we could deal with the differences is to keep the two separate but equal. Men and women have different moral voices. Men's voices are right for men, women's voices for women. Neither is superior to the other; they are just different.

The problem with this thesis is fourfold. First, it is very difficult to retain the "but equal" part of such a position. Once the two voices have been separated, it is all too easy to dismiss the second voice as less important. Second, such a position tends to perpetuate gender-based stereotyping, since only males are given male voices and only females are given female voices. Third, it suggests that men and women have nothing to learn from one another, since each sex has its own moral voice. Fourth, males who have a "female voice" and females who have a "male voice" are looked down upon. The separate but equal approach is, as it were, a form of sex-based isolationism.

The Superiority Thesis

The second possible position is to maintain that one of these two voices is superior to the other. Historically, this belief has been the dominant position, most often with men maintaining (usually implicitly, occasionally explicitly) that men's voices are superior to women's voices in morality. In recent times, the roles have sometimes been reversed, with women claiming the superiority of women's voices.

There are two problems with this position. First, to say that one voice is completely true for everyone in all situations is interesting but obviously false. To say that one voice is partially true for some people in some situations is accurate, but it is so vague as to be unhelpful without further elaboration of the particular conditions under which one voice takes precedence over the other. Such additional elaboration then yields a position that is significantly different from the original thesis.

The second problem with this position is that it is exclusionary. It excludes whichever position is seen as not true—and that usually means that we cannot learn from that other excluded voice. If, on the other hand, we admit that we can learn from the other voice, then we find ourselves defending a version of one of the next two positions.

The Integrationist Thesis

The integrationist maintains that there is ultimately only one moral voice, a voice which may be the integration of many different voices. The integrationist need not claim to know precisely what this voice is, but must be committed to the claim that ultimately there is only one voice.

The principal difficulty with the integrationist thesis is that it is susceptible to losing the richness that comes from diversity. The integrationist position tends to be assimilationist, blurring the distinctive identities of the sources of its components. It celebrates a moral androgyny as a replacement for the sex-based voices.

The Diversity Thesis

The final thesis claims that we have diverse moral voices and that this diversity is a principal source of richness and growth in the moral life. We can learn from one another's differences as well as from similarities. The diversity thesis in the area of gender most closely embodies the pluralistic approach characteristic of this book.

The diversity thesis has two complementary sides. First, there is the external diversity thesis which suggests that different individuals have different (gender-based) moral voices, and that here is a fruitful difference from which we can learn. Men can learn from women, just as women can learn

354

from men. What makes this claim an external diversity thesis is that it sees diversity as something that exists among separate individuals.

The internal diversity thesis sees diversity as also existing within each individual. Each of us, in other words, has both masculine and feminine moral voices within us, and this diversity of internal voices is considered a positive thing. One of the attractions of this position is that it minimizes gender stereotyping, for it denies that men have an exclusive claim to masculinity or that only women can have a feminine dimension. Men can have both masculine and feminine dimensions to their moral voices, just as women can have both.

Nor is it necessary to think an increase in one type of voice necessarily leads to a decrease in another. Sandra Bem has suggested that masculine and feminine traits in general may be mapped along two different axes, such that an individual may be high in both (androgynous), low in both (undifferentiated), high in femininity but low in masculinity (traditional feminine), or high in masculinity but low in femininity (traditional masculine). This approach leads to the schema given above.

The principal strength of this scale is that it does not make masculinity and femininity mutually exclusive traits, which is in sharp contrast to models that plot masculinity and femininity on a single axis with "strongly feminine" and "strongly masculine" at the opposing ends of the scale. On Bem's scale, one can be high in both, or low in both, as well as high in just one or the other. More often than not, males identify with a masculine gender and females with a feminine gender. We are probably most familiar with figures who are high on only one of these scales, but we have occasional examples of individuals who are high on both scales.

One World, Two Genders

We all live in the same world. The moral challenge facing us is to decide how to do so in a way that promotes respect, understanding, and community. Separatist approaches to diversity offer the hope of preserving differences, but they offer little encouragement for learning from one another or for forging a genuine community. Those who espouse the superiority of one voice (usually their own) over others not only refuse to learn from the other gender, but also often fail to develop the understanding of the other gender necessary to genuine respect. The final voice offers the best hope of preserving uniqueness and simultaneously celebrating differences within the larger context of community.

Caring and Act Utilitarianism

Interestingly, there are some similarities between an ethics of caring and act utilitarianism. They are both, generally speaking, consequentialist theories, that is, both see morality primarily as a matter of consequences. Both are concerned with weighing the consequences of projected actions, and both see those consequences—broadly speaking—in terms of the pleasure or pain that they might cause.

But the differences are equally instructive. The act utilitarian usually employs some kind of calculus, some method of computing the total amount of pleasure and pain that would result from various courses of action. Gilligan's ethics of caring is consequentialist, but differs from act utilitarianism both in (a) what kinds of consequences count and (b) how they are measured. The care ethic focuses primarily on two kinds of consequences: (1) the extent to which people might be hurt by a particular decision and (2) the degree to which a particular decision might diminish the sense of connectedness among the participants in the situation. Connectedness itself becomes a moral value. Moreover, the method by which these consequences are determined has a strongly intersubjective component. Whereas utilitarian calculators might well attempt to weigh consequences in the isolation of their offices, the caring person attempts to weigh consequences by talking with the participants and allowing them to participate actively in the process. For those assuming the standpoint of an ethic of care, there is an essentially intersubjective moment to the decision-making process. Both what is valued and how it is valued have a strong intersubjective dimension.

Emotions play a much more significant role in the ethics of caring than they do in the utilitarian calculus. First, in an ethics of caring, emotions (especially compassion and empathy) are necessary in order to know how much pleasure or pain a particular action causes. How can you know how much pain a particular action may inflict on friends if you do not listen to what they say about their feelings and try to understand those feelings? This process of listening and understanding is not only an intellectual one, but also involves an emotional, or affective, component.

Second, there is another emotive dimension to the ethics of caring that is absent from act utilitarianism. Caring has an irremediably emotive component to it. To care about someone is not just to act in particular ways; it is also, and necessarily, to feel in particular ways. There would be something odd if a parent tried to add up impersonally all the hedons and dolors for a particular choice that will affect the family. Part of caring is to feel something for the other person. (There is also a double kind of evaluation going on; understanding how much the other person values a particular action of ours and how much we value them.)

This approach suggests a way of understanding the relationship between act utilitarianism and the ethics of caring. In an impersonal context where we are dealing with large numbers of people who are strangers to us, act utilitarian considerations may well be relevant. In personal contexts where we are dealing with people we know and care about, the ethics of caring may better capture the moral insights that utilitarianism captures in the other, larger scale contexts.

Ethics, Ethnicity, and Cultural Diversity

As we already have indicated, ethicists in the past typically have conceived of the moral agent in such abstract terms that the moral agent seemed to possess little personal identity. Although recent feminist scholarship has begun to explore ways in which women and men have different moral voices, virtually no comparable work has been done by philosophers in regard to ethnicity. Certainly, no one has done for the moral voices of ethnic diversity what Carol Gilligan has done for the moral voices of gender diversity. The following

remarks are offered in a tentative and exploratory vein as an attempt to begin to map out the conceptual territory within which a discussion of the relationship between ethics and ethnicity can take place.

Differences between Gender, Race, and Ethnicity

Both gender and ethnicity present issues of diversity, but the issues are not completely parallel. Consider some of the differences between gender and ethnicity.

- There are only two genders, whereas there are numerous ethnic identities.

- Gender commonly is regarded as an "either/or" matter (male or female); however, one can have more than one racial or ethnic identity.

- Although there is a biological imperative that demands men and women interact, there is no comparable imperative for people with different ethnic backgrounds. Nothing comparable to sexual attraction exists between different ethnic groups or cultures.

Despite these differences, it is clear that race and ethnicity have been used as a basis for discrimination at least as frequently as has gender. Indeed, precisely because different ethnic or racial groups can live without each other, the possibilities for discrimination—in its most extreme form, culminating in slavery and genocide—are even greater.

Race, Ethnicity, and Cultural Diversity

Race and ethnicity are distinct concepts, although they may overlap. **Race** is primarily a *biological* phenomenon that manifests itself in characteristics such as skin color, hair texture, body shape, and the like. Ethnologists generally distinguish among three main racial groups: Caucasoid, Negroid, and Mongoloid. Despite beliefs to the contrary, race is not a very precise concept, for there is a tremendous amount of variation within racial groups and a significant amount of overlap among them as well, as Steven Jay Gould has shown in *The Mismeasure of Man*. These variations are intensified by interracial reproduction. **Ethnicity,** on the other

356

hand, is primarily a *cultural* phenomenon. It refers principally to an individual's identification with a particular cultural group. There are many more cultural groups than there are races, and often differences in cultures are overlooked by outsiders. There are, for example, many southeast Asian cultures, but non-Asians often lump them all together as "Indochinese," which would be roughly equivalent to lumping the English, the Irish, the Portuguese, the Finns, the Spanish, the Italians, the Lithuanians, the French, and the Germans together as "Europeans." Although it is true that they all come from countries in Europe, they often perceive themselves primarily in terms of national and ethnic identities. But, they are only Europeans to outsiders. **Cultural background** refers directly to individuals' ethnicity and only indirectly and accidentally to their race. For example, a Caucasian American infant raised in Thailand by Thai parents may well be Caucasoid by race but ethnically and culturally Thai.

One can be high on several different cultural scales simultaneously. Think of an Italian who has married into a Jewish family. That person may become steeped in traditional Jewish customs without giving up an Italian heritage. Being at home in one culture does not necessarily preclude being at home in another, although there may be points of incompatibility between specific cultures. We can belong to two, or perhaps even more, cultures at the same time. This is not to say that there will not be some conflicts, but to be strongly identified with both traditions is to be committed to working out such conflicts in a way that respects both traditions as much as possible.

THE FACTS OF DIVERSITY

Do different cultures have distinctive moral voices? The obvious answer is "of course they do." In our consideration of descriptive moral relativism in Chapter Two, we saw that distinctive voices were clearly the case, at least in regard to (a) the particular actions which a given culture sanctions or condemns and (b) the peripheral values it accepts. Whether there is disagreement on central values is another question, and we have seen good evidence to suggest that there is widespread (but not total) agreement on certain values such as respect for innocent life.

To say that moral voices are distinctive is not to say that they are necessarily incompatible. We might find a much stronger emphasis on the concept of honor in Japanese society than we encounter in contemporary American society, but that does not necessarily make them incompatible, only different. Incompatibility, at least in the strict sense, occurs only when there are clearly opposing value judgments such as "honor is good" and "honor is bad." (For strict incompatibility, there must also be rough equivalence in the meaning of shared terms such as "honor." Cross-cultural comparisons of this type presuppose that understanding and judgment between cultures is possible; such comparisons also often demand a high degree of sensitivity to the nuances of another culture's worldview.) Differences alone do not constitute incompatibility. Often the relevant question is not whether different cultures have distinctive moral voices, but whether they can learn to sing together harmoniously when necessary.

Let us turn to a concrete example of the way in which a culture has distinctive voices so that we can understand more fully the nuances of the issues involved.

THE MORAL VOICES OF AFRICAN-AMERICANS

Consider the diversity of voices that are included in the African-American experience. Martin Luther King, Jr., Malcolm X, Alice Walker, and Maya Angelou are among the most powerful African-American moral voices of the second half of this century. These voices have many distinctive characteristics, but here I shall concentrate on just one element that is found in all four of these voices: *Affirmation of self-respect in the face of oppression.* Self-respect is a value found in virtually all cultures, as is opposition to oppression. In this respect, African-American culture is not unique. However, the affirmation of self-respect in the face of daunting oppression is a moral value which ranks higher on the scale in African-American culture than it does in, say, white American culture where the same on-going experience of oppression is not present. The speeches and writings of Dr. King and Malcolm X resonate with a deep affirmation of the self-respect of African-Americans, an opposition to any attempts to deny the worth of African-Americans, and a commitment to bringing about the social, political, and legal changes necessary to sustain and enhance that sense of self-worth among African-Americans. Martin Luther King's "Letter from Birmingham Jail" eloquently details the ways in which segregation "distorts the soul and degrades human personality" for all involved, those who perpetuate segregation as well as those toward whom segregation is directed. Malcolm X's *Autobiography* is a superb example of moral autobiography, a description of his journey toward an increasingly well-founded sense of self-respect.

The novels, poetry, and journals of Alice Walker and Maya Angelou demonstrate a similar commitment. They have given voice to those African-Americans whose suffering had previously been endured in silence. In *The Color Purple*, for example, Alice Walker traces the journey toward self-respect of an African-American woman whose life began in oppression and moved gradually toward autonomy. In a similar way, we find an account of the journey from oppression to increasingly full self-respect and self-determination in Maya Angelou's autobiography *I Know Why the Caged Bird Sings*.

Against this rich background of diverse African-American moral voices, we now can understand better the conceptual issues involved in linking ethnicity to ethics. There are two ways of forging this link, one considerably strong than the other.

Externalist and Internalist Accounts of Ethnicity and Ethics

The first way of linking ethnicity and ethics, the *externalist approach,* is through a shared set of social experiences and problems that are seen as largely independent of the identity of the persons in question. In the case of African-Americans, the heritage of slavery and the ongoing presence of racism in American society figure prominently among the shared experiences of African-Americans. The argument here would be that African-Americans have to deal with a set of

moral problems that are not usually encountered (at least in the same way) by the dominant white, male population of the United States. This way of understanding the link between ethnicity and ethics suggests that the connection is largely an external one. The analogy that suggests itself here is with professional groups that face particular moral problems not shared by the population as a whole. Physicians and psychologists, for example, must deal with questions of confidentiality and trust not shared in the same way by the population as a whole. African-Americans face a certain set of external problems not shared by the population as a whole; consequently, they develop distinctive moral voices to deal with those problems.

The drawback of this first approach is that it draws a comparatively sharp distinction between the group and the special moral problems it faces, and consequently, misses the ways in which specific moral problems partially constitute the identity of a particular group. The problems themselves are seen as largely external to the identity of the group itself. The distinctiveness of the voice derives primarily from the problems that it addresses, not from the members of the group themselves. The externalist account seems to miss the intimate connection between those problems and the very identity of the members of the group.

Ethics and ethnicity can be linked in a second, more intimate way through an *internalist account.* For example, the heritage of slavery and the experience of racism are powerful factors that are partially constitutive of the identity of African-Americans. Their voices are partially shaped by these forces, and it is misleading to think of their identity as something completely external to them. A particular sensitivity to the affirmation of self-respect in the face of oppression is one of the distinctive characteristics of African-American moral voices, and an internalist account of the link between ethics and ethnicity recognizes the extent to which this sensitivity is partially constitutive of the identity of African-Americans at this point in history.

"Thick" and "Thin" Conceptions of the Moral Self

These two approaches differ significantly in regard to the conception of the self that underlies each. The first approach is characterized by a "thin" conception of the self that sees the identity of the person as largely independent of empirical factors such as environment and ethnicity. Immanuel Kant strongly exemplifies this attitude. For Kant, the self was constituted primarily by reason and will; empirical conditions were generally excluded from the core identity of the moral agent. In our critique of Kant, we suggested a "thicker" conception of the self, one that included more empirical factors, as central to an individual's identity. In such thicker conceptions of the self, ethnicity may become an important part of identity. One's identity as a person, in other words, may in part be constituted by certain experiences largely unique to one's ethnic or racial group.

Ethnic identity is constituted by shared experiences. In the case of African-Americans, one of the most significant of these shared experiences is that of being subjected to racial discrimination. In other words, an important part of their ethnic identity is precisely the experience of having their ethnic identity devalued and degraded. It is, as African-American philosophers such as Laurence Thomas have pointed out, an experience that has a profound impact on self-respect and self-esteem. The affirmation of self-worth against a background that denies or diminishes that self-worth is a particular value for any group that has been the object of systematic and long-standing oppression. Among African-Americans, the experience of racism is certainly an experience that is partially constitutive of their identity, and this common experience partially shapes their distinctive moral voices. Their ethnic identity is part of who they are, part of their personal identity as moral agents, and ought to be affirmed in part because it was the object of discrimination in the past.

Thus we see why there is a special moral justification for Black pride or Latino pride in a way that there is not for Caucasian pride. It is not because Caucasians should not be proud, but rather because there is no special moral need for them to be proud specifically *of their ethnicity* in the way in which there is for Blacks, Latinos, and others who have been discriminated against precisely because of their ethnicity. Consequently, self-respect for them involves an affirmation of their ethnicity (against a background that has devalued their ethnicity) in a way that is not true for their Caucasian counterparts.

NORMATIVE OPTIONS

We have now seen one of the ways in which different cultures may have (partially) different values. The central normative question we face is how we should act in light of this fact. The range of possible responses is similar to those options regarding issues of gender.

Separatists

Again, we can begin our discussion by noting two extreme positions. On one hand, we have the voice of the *separatists*, who maintain that cultures ought to retain their own voices through isolating themselves from the cultures around them. The drive toward separatism is particularly strong when the gap between cultures is wide and the difference in power is great. Separatists often fear being swallowed up by the larger culture and losing their identity in the process. Indeed, they feel that there is much to be gained from having a community of people with shared values, experiences, interests, and history. Such a community not only provides security, but also eliminates the need to start over in every conversation. Persons of color do not need to prove that racism still exists or show that it still has pernicious effects when talking with those who have shared their experiences. For example, recent Vietnamese immigrants share understandings of cultural alienation in their new homeland. They can take such common ground for granted and move on to a discussion of further issues within this shared context.

Yet *strict separatism* is rarely a long-term viable option, because it usually will increase the power differential between the larger and smaller culture. Eventually this option leads to an even greater marginalization of the smaller, less powerful culture, in some instances leading even to its extinction. There are groups in America who still pursue this path, of course. Amish communities in Pennsylvania and other states are a highly visible example of a largely separatist tradition that has managed to survive and in certain respects flourish. Some Native American communities, such as the members of the Acoma Pueblo, also have pursued a largely separatist course, preserving traditional values in comparative isolation from white society. African-American leaders such as W. L. B. Du Bois advocated the value of separatism in part as a way of preserving the uniqueness of the African-American tradition. The long-term prospects for such communities remain unclear, especially in an increasingly technological and computerized society.

If the prospects for strict separatism appear cloudy, the same cannot necessarily be said for *limited separatism*. Many groups in our society have long pursued a course of limited separatism, interacting with the larger culture yet simultaneously retaining a distinctive sense of group identity. Religious groups, fraternal organizations, and ethnic clubs are but a few types of such communities. They often flourish in part by maintaining a place within the larger community, but at the same time retaining a limited sense of their own separate identity.

Supremacists

On the other hand, *supremacists* argue that (a) there is one culture that is morally superior to all others, and that (b) that superior culture is their own. In American society, we have seen this attitude in both white supremacist movements like the Aryan Nation and Posse Comitatus and Ku Klux Klan, and in some ethnic supremacist movements as well. The supremacist attitude is suspect on several counts. Historically, it often has been associated with hatred, intolerance, and cruelty. Philosophically, in those instances in which it rests on an *a priori* judgment that everything in one culture is superior to everything in another one, it is simply wrong. Indeed, supremacists depend on discrimination precisely in order to obtain a sense of their own self-worth.

Interestingly, we would rarely consider separatism to be an acceptable option for the dominant group in society, presumably in part because we recognize that such a course of action would cut off the smaller cultural groups from valued goods and resources. We recognize that there may be a value in having traditionally African-American colleges in America, or organizations for Latino students on campus, but we would be hesitant to endorse the same options for Caucasians alone. There are at least two reasons for this. The first is one that we have already discussed. There is a special moral justification for the affirmation of ethnicity among groups that have been discriminated against precisely because of their ethnicity. For such groups, the affirmation of self-respect necessarily involves the affirmation of their ethnicity in a way that is not true for groups that have not been discriminated against on the basis of ethnicity or who even have been the perpetuators of discrimination.

The second reason for this difference is historical. Dominant ethnic groups often have functioned unjustly to disenfranchise and to disempower minority groups. Historical examples of this phenomenon are all too common. The Turkish attempt to exterminate the Armenians, the German attempt to wipe out the Jews and the Gypsies and enslave other ethnic groups such as the Poles, and recent Bosnian calls for "ethnic cleansing"— these are but a few of the most prominent examples of this tendency in our own century. Presumably, separatist minority groups do not serve this same function. They do not attempt to disenfranchise or to disempower the majority group, since such minority groups do not control the distribution of power in the same way that the majority group does. If they were to function in this way, they too would be morally suspect, for they would turn into supremacist groups.

Integrationists and Assimilationists

The integrationist position in regard to ethnic and cultural diversity has a somewhat different shape than it does in regard to gender. Although we recognized that both males and females can have both masculine and feminine voices, there is still a strong and pervasive cultural pressure to identify people as either male or female. For example, English grammar forces us to classify individuals as male or female but not as Latino or French. The pressure in regard to ethnic and cultural identification is weaker. Moreover, individuals obviously could be from more than one ethnic tradition—for example, both Irish and Jewish. Such diversity in regard to being male or female is, at best, a much more subtle matter.

There are several possible models of integration, and these can be ranked according to the degree of sameness they seek to achieve. Some strive for assimilation and uniformity, while others emphasize cooperation within a context of at least minimally shared rules of interaction. At the far end of the spectrum, some models of integration shade into pluralism.

Pluralists

The middle ground between these extremes is essentially the same one described at the end of our chapter on relativism: A *cultural pluralism* that sees diversity as a source of strength, emphasizes the value of *dialogue,* and approaches such dialogues with a *fallibilistic* attitude. It is a pluralism that sees value in limited separatism, but also recognizes that we need to learn to live together while honoring our differences. We have much to learn from other cultures, just as they have much to learn from us. As pluralists, we can recognize that there are many ways of being right without giving up the possibility of taking a stand in those instances when we are convinced something is seriously wrong.

Consider the value of affirming self-respect in the face of oppression. As we have seen, given historical conditions, it is hardly surprising that this is an important value in African-American culture. Among groups who have not suffered such discrimination, the affirmation of self-respect may be a much less prominent value and may not involve an affirmation of ethnicity as part of self-respect. Thus, although white Americans also value self-respect, they may well not value it to the same extent or in the same way as their African-American counterparts. This is an excellent example of value pluralism, one in which different groups have partially different (but not necessarily incompatible) values. The advantage of a pluralistic approach to values is that it is able to

understand and appreciate such differences in values without resorting to an attitude of "anything goes." However, not all differences in values are as easily understood and appreciated as this one is. We shall consider how we live with diversity, and especially how we deal with moral conflicts in a pluralistic society, later in this chapter. Before turning to that issue, let us consider one last source of diversity.

VALUING INDIVIDUALITY

Individuals are the *loci*, the meeting points, of diversity. We already have seen some of the principal influences on an individual's identity: Gender, ethnicity, and culture. Each of these factors, often along with other influences such as our religious background and our socioeconomic class, help to shape who we are. What place does individuality play in the moral life?

Negative and Positive Morality

Morality sometimes is seen as having negative and positive elements. The negative elements are prohibitions that establish the *moral minimum* that is acceptable. To be concerned only with the moral minimum is like taking a course on a pass/fail basis: we are concerned primarily with what we need just to get by, to pass with a "C—." While being concerned with the moral minimum is preferable to not being concerned at all, it is still a long way from moral excellence. The positive element of morality focuses on *moral excellence.* Individuality finds its true place in the realm of the search for moral excellence, for there are often many different individual ways in which we can excel.

Moral Excellence

As we saw in Chapter Nine in our discussion of moral saints, genuine saints need not be cardboard figures. Consider the great moral figures of the twentieth century. Each is characterized by the quest for excellence in a certain area. Gandhi shows us the power of nonviolence in the twentieth century. He was, if anything, tenaciously, insistently nonviolent. Think of Mother Teresa. Her compassion and her spontaneous and joyful love set her apart from the rest of us and constitute her moral individuality. Yet it would be inaccurate to think of either of them as extensions of a theory or applications of some single principle. Their lives show a richness and vibrancy that is a sign of robust moral health.

Moral excellence is not restricted to public figures. We all know, or perhaps are, people with a special moral excellence. Think of the friend who truly can be depended upon, even under the toughest of circumstances. That is moral excellence, and it is one that we might choose to strive to embody. Or think of the friend who is able, even in the most difficult of circumstances, to put defensiveness aside and to listen genuinely to the concerns of the other person, which, too, is moral excellence. Or the person who is always fair, even in the face of great opposing pressures. Or the person who always can be counted on to respond in a caring and compassionate manner to the suffering of others. Moral excellences come in many different shapes and sizes.

Forging Our Moral Identity

We are all born as human beings into particular moral communities and traditions. We are not impartial, purely rational moral agents lacking in particularity. We are individual women and men, born at a particular time and place, having a particular ethnic and cultural background, specific likes and dislikes, individual hopes and dreams. The task for each of us as moral individuals is to forge our own moral identity.

Moral pluralism suggests that there is room for choice and creativity in the shaping of our individual moral identity and our moral values. In other words, although our moral values set some minimal limits within which we must act, we have a considerable degree of latitude within those limits to shape our own moral identity. Moral pluralism establishes the negative limits on behavior and points out possibilities for us, but it is our own individual choice to create our own identity. It is here that virtue ethics is of particular relevance, for it provides the most guidance to us in answering the question "What kind of person do I want to be?" The guiding concern here is not that our moral identity be unique in the sense that it be different from anyone else's; rather, the

crucial concern is that it be ours, that is, a freely chosen embodiment of the person we want to be.

The formation of our individuality involves more than just our moral values; it also involves striking a balance between our moral values and our nonmoral values. Many of our choices in life about career, family, friends, and leisure involve nonmoral values as well as moral ones. Finally, it is important for us to note that the development of individuality does not take place in a vacuum. We are always concrete individuals, situated in a particular time and place as members of various groups and communities. We can think of a community as a moral arena in which we have the opportunity to aspire to moral excellence.

LIVING WITH MORAL DIVERSITY

There is a richness in the diversity of theory as well as the diversity of experience which we (especially philosophers) have been too ready to ignore. One of the principal aims of this book has been to recognize and to value such diversity. Yet this goal is easier said than done, for moral conflicts—both real and imagined—present roadblocks on the path of the moral life. In order to complete our pluralistic account of moral values and to show the ways in which we can live with genuine diversity, we need an account of how to deal with moral conflicts. There are several ways in which we can respond to moral diversity and apparent moral conflict.

- We can live with diversity.

- We can seek imaginative ways of resolving conflicts.

- We can seek a compromise that all parties can live with.

- We can change our own behavior without demanding that others act differently.

- We can refuse to compromise and demand that others change.

Before turning to examine these options, a cautionary word is in order about the way in which internal conflicts come to be perceived as purely external ones.

INTERNAL AND EXTERNAL DIVERSITY

In discussing cases of moral conflict, it is easy to focus on *external* moral conflicts between two or more people with differing and conflicting values commitments. While these conflicts are the more visible type, we should be aware that there are also *internal* conflicts in which a single individual experiences the pull of conflicting values.

There is a danger, especially in situations of sharp conflict, that internal conflicts come to be seen as purely external in character. In situations such as the abortion debate in which external conflicts are starkly polarized, participants easily can lose sight of the degree to which they also experience the conflict as an internal one. Pro-choice advocates might lose sight of their own moral qualms about abortion, just as pro-life advocates might neglect their own feelings of empathy for some women with unwanted pregnancies. The danger is that people on both sides will ignore their own reservations because the other side already is advocating them so strongly. Psychologically, what happens in polarized situations such as these is that people allow their opponents to carry the burden of their own dissenting convictions. Most of us have had the experience of strongly defending a position, having our opponent capitulate, and then having doubts about our own position. These feelings are not merely the product of some perverse desire to take the opposite side in every issue. They may also be the result of letting the opposition carry the minority side of our own feelings. When we are able to acknowledge the full and sometimes conflicting range of our own values and feelings, we may well find that there is more common ground between ourselves and those "on the other side" than we thought.

LIVING WITH MORAL DIVERSITY

In Peter Weir's 1985 film *Witness*, we are presented with an interesting example of moral diversity. The movie skillfully plays off two ways of life, both moral within their own traditions and yet apparently mutually exclusive. Harrison Ford plays police detective John Book, who must live in disguise in an Amish community during his pursuit of a killer. The movie portrays Book

sympathetically as a detective genuinely committed to seeing justice done. If violence is necessary to accomplish this goal, Book does not shrink from it; but neither does he pursue violence for its own sake. The members of the Amish community, on the other hand, eschew violence; their commitment to pacifism lies at the core of their religious and moral identity. To betray that commitment would be to betray their deepest selves.

In one of the more striking scenes of the movie, a member of the Amish community named Daniel is confronted in town by several bullies who proceed to taunt him. Daniel does not fight back, but Book finally steps in and flattens the lead bully. Most non-pacifists would cheer, at least silently, when the bully gets what was coming to him. Yet I think that we can step back from a scene such as this one and draw several conclusions.

First, even if we are not pacifists, we might be glad that there are pacifists in our world. Even if we are happy to see Book punch the bully in the nose, we might still feel that our world is a better place because there are also people like Daniel in it. Daniel reminds us of another moral ideal, perhaps not our own, but one we can appreciate. Indeed, if there were more people like Daniel in the world, perhaps there would be both less violence and less need for violence. Daniel's presence in our own world may well prompt us to look harder for nonviolent alternatives before we resort to violence. We need not agree with Daniel in order to be happy that he is in our world.

Second, while there is an obvious moral conflict here about the moral value of violence, there is also a widespread area of agreement. If there is disagreement about whether justice can ever be brought about through violence, there is agreement that justice should be fostered. Indeed, there is also fairly widespread agreement about what counts as justice. Similarly, there is significant agreement about such issues as truthfulness, cooperation, and respect. Much moral diversity takes place within the larger context of moral agreement.

There is an added reason for valuing such diversity. It takes little reflection for us to realize that our values are not perfect. All we need to do is to look at virtually everyone else's values throughout history in order to see that none of them was without any moral blind spots at all. So, too, we can be assured that we are not immune to moral myopia, distortion, and blindness. We can be certain that some of our moral perceptions and judgments are off the mark— but the difficulty is that we cannot know *which* ones are. It is here that we depend on the values of others, for their blind spots may not be the same as ours. We count on others to help us see what we miss.

Thus we see the first way in which we can live with moral diversity: We can acknowledge it and encourage it, glad that there are others who see the world differently than we do. We might not agree with them, but *we may feel* our moral life as a whole could be more secure because they are part of our world.

MORAL IMAGINATION

The second way in which we can respond to moral diversity is imaginatively to seek new ways of acting that synthesize the diversity of apparently conflicting values. Some situations appear to be cases of moral conflict, but the conflict only exists because we lack the creative insight to devise a course of action that resolves the conflicting interests and values. Often a moral conflict has the following structure. One side says to do A because of value x; the other side says to do not-A because of value y. A morally imaginative solution would involve finding a course of action, B, that is compatible with both x and y.

Consider the following example, which may be a successful example of moral imagination. For the past several decades, our country has been experiencing a conflict that centers around the issue of poverty. On the one hand, some in our society— call them liberals for the convenience of the label—feel that the government must intervene to break the cycle of poverty. On the other hand, others in our society—we will stay with the standard labels and call them conservatives—feel that individuals are (or at least should be) responsible for their own lives and that government has no business intervening in the private sector and creating dependency on government by giving

people food and other necessities of life. Recently, there have been attempts to develop a third possibility (in addition to welfare or no support at all) that may synthesize these apparently conflicting values. Workfare, as it is currently known, would be a government program that provides the standard support usually associated with welfare but (in cases where appropriate) only for a limited time and under conditions that include job training and eventual employment. Undoubtedly many liberals and conservatives would perceive workfare as a compromise, that is, as temporarily setting aside some of their values for the sake of reaching a wider consensus on a course of action. Others, however, might experience it as a morally imaginative solution that does not involve giving up any of their values, a third possibility where previously they had seen only two alternatives. If such a possibility could be worked out properly (which is not a small "if"), it might provide for some individuals on both sides of the issue just the kind of morally imaginative synthesis we have been discussing here. The interests and values of liberals would be satisfied insofar as the program helped to break the cycle of poverty and provided a compassionate response to the economically less fortunate in our society. The interests and values of conservatives also would be honored insofar as the program reduced dependency, encouraged personal responsibility, and was directed toward minimizing the government's intervention in the private sphere. Much, of course, would depend on how well-developed the program was and how sensitively it could be administered. The success of the program also would depend on how well it dealt with recalcitrant cases, that is, those who apparently could develop work skills but in fact did not do so, despite apparent opportunities. Finally, it would depend upon how well the program responded to the issue of the suffering of children, none of whom had a choice about the economic or social conditions of the family into which they were born.

One of the results of moral imagination is that it allows us to forge a new course of action that incorporates the previously apparently conflicting values. When this solution occurs, the participants in the situation are not compromising, for they are not denying any of their values. Instead, they are revising their values and wholeheartedly committing themselves to a course of action that they now perceive as consistent with their values.

MORAL COMPROMISE

Sometimes, in the face of moral conflict, we are unable to find a morally imaginative solution that synthesizes the conflicting values of the various parties. Compromise becomes necessary. Although "compromise" sometimes carries the connotation of "betrayal" or "selling out," not all compromises are betrayals. A compromise is an agreement that partially preserves the interests of all parties in a consensus that is acceptable to everyone. There are times when moral compromise is appropriate and morally praiseworthy.

In his book *Splitting the Difference*, Martin Benjamin has elaborated a number of the reasons why it is often appropriate to reach a compromise. First, compromise fosters the continuation of a communal life. Disagreements, including disagreements in values, are inevitable. Unless we are able to compromise in at least some of the cases, our common life would grind to a halt. Second; we may be more willing to compromise because we are not absolutely certain about what the right course of action is. This uncertainty may stem from either of two sources. There may be factual uncertainties. For example, how we act—especially if we are utilitarians—often depends on what we anticipate the results of our action to be. Yet these results are notoriously difficult to predict. We could find that a given situation is so morally complex that we are not completely sure about how we should act. Benjamin compares these situations to judging an Olympic figure skating competition. There may be as many as seven different judges, with each judge evaluating a performance to the best of his or her ability. Generally we recognize that there is room for legitimate disagreement, and the final score is a compromise among the various scores. These are judgment calls in which compromise is eminently reasonable. Third, we may compromise because *some* decision has to be taken immediately and there simply is not time to find an alternative that does not involve compromise. Finally, we may find

ourselves in a situation of scarce resources that force compromises on us that in situations of more ample resources would not be necessary.

WHEN NOT TO COMPROMISE AND HOW

There are times when compromise is simply unacceptable. The moral price is too high, the suffering too great. There has been no shortage of such situations; the various genocidal programs of the twentieth century offer one set of examples, but they are not the only cases. Cases of child abuse offer another set of examples, ones that are often closer to home than is genocide. The moral theories we have examined help to articulate the moral minimum below which we should not allow ourselves or others to sink.

When discussing situations in which compromise is not acceptable, it is helpful to distinguish two types of cases. The first involves situations in which we will not compromise by acting, or agreeing to act, in ways which violate our moral values. Here the focus is on our own actions, on our refusal to cooperate with a possible compromise. In a second kind of situation we not only refuse to cooperate, but also actively try to stop other people from engaging in the objectionable activity. If we were to use abortion as an example, those in the first category would refuse to get abortions themselves if they were pregnant. Those in the second category would not only refuse to get abortions themselves if pregnant, but would also try to prevent others from getting abortions. Both are refusals to compromise, but the second involves an active intervention in a way that the first does not.

In both of these types of situations, it is important to reflect on *how* we refuse to compromise. Three points are noteworthy here. First, it is important to find ways of refusing to compromise that minimize polarization. We must look for ways of remaining connected with those with whom we disagree, which is often extremely difficult to do, but not always impossible. Often in such situations it is helpful to distinguish between people and their actions. We may refuse to cooperate with someone's actions, but we try to keep open other modes of communication and emotional connectedness with them.

Second, we can refuse to compromise, but do so *with respect*. Such respect was one of the striking characteristics of Gandhi's eventual refusal to cooperate with British rule of India. He refused to compromise on the large issue of Indian independence and he always agreed to compromise solutions on intermediate goals, but he never treated the British with disrespect. For a second example, recall the example of the villagers of Le Chambon given at the beginning of Chapter Ten. One of the startling aspects of their refusal to cooperate with the Nazis is that they were concerned with the welfare of the German soldiers as well as the Jews they sheltered. They wanted to be sure that *no one* was killed, including the German soldiers.

Third, we can refuse to compromise, but do so *imaginatively*, perhaps even *cleverly*. As the example of the villagers of Le Chambon shows, sometimes we can refuse to compromise without resorting to violence. When we resist, we hope to find ways of resisting that eventually will convert our adversaries to our viewpoint rather than beat them into submission.

LIVING MORALLY

Let me conclude with a different kind of metaphor in terms of which we can understand the issues of diversity—diversity in culture, in gender, and even in age. Think of ethics as architecture. Certainly there are occasionally matters of clear-cut right and wrong in architecture. From time to time, poorly constructed buildings do fall down, and people accidentally are killed or injured. Yet most of the time, other questions than those mathematical relations of size, weight, shape, and stress are much more interesting and relevant. Once we decide that a given group of buildings will not fall down, we can move on to more interesting questions about what life would be like in such a place. For example, what kind of balance is implied between communal living and individual privacy in the architecture? Buildings with few walls put a premium on communal life, perhaps at the expense of individual privacy. Buildings composed primarily of small, isolated rooms with no communal areas give relatively little value to a shared life, and emphasize the isolated individual as the primary unit. Our architecture reflects our values. For example, note the shift in American building away from large houses to small apartments and the implications for family life, both nuclear and extended.

We can learn about the moral life by studying different cultures in the same way that we learn about our everyday life from studying different architecture. Together, we might be able to build moral homes in which we can all live with dignity and mutual respect and in which each of us can flourish.

The Disparity Between Intellect and Character

by Robert Coles

Over 150 years ago, Ralph Waldo Emerson gave a lecture at Harvard University, which he ended with the terse assertion: "Character is higher than intellect." Even then, this prominent man of letters was worried (as many other writers and thinkers of succeeding generations would be) about the limits of-knowledge and the nature of a college's mission. The intellect can grow and grow, he knew, in a person who is smug, ungenerous, even cruel. Institutions originally founded to teach their students how to become good and decent, as well as broadly and deeply literate, may abandon the first mission to concentrate on a driven, narrow book learning—a course of study in no way intent on making a connection between ideas and theories on one hand and, on the other, our lives as we actually live them.

Students have their own way of realizing and trying to come to terms with the split that Emerson addressed. A few years ago, a sophomore student of mine came to see me in great anguish. She had arrived at Harvard from a Midwestern, working—class background. She was trying hard to work her way through college, and, in doing so, cleaned the rooms of some of her fellow students. Again and again, she encountered classmates who apparently had forgotten the meaning of *please*, of *thank you*—no matter how high their Scholastic Assessment Test scores—students who did not hesitate to be rude, even crude toward her.

One day she was not so subtly propositioned by a young man she knew to be a very bright, successful pre-med student and already an accomplished journalist. This was not the first time he had made such an overture, but now she had reached a breaking point. She had quit her job and was preparing to quit college in what she called "fancy, phony Cambridge."

The student had been part of a seminar I teach, which links Raymond Carver's fiction and poetry with Edward Hopper's paintings and drawings—the thematic convergence of literary and artistic sensibility in exploring American loneliness, both its social and its personal aspects. As she expressed her anxiety and anger to me, she soon was sobbing hard. After her sobs quieted, we began to remember the old days of that class. But she had some weightier matters on her mind and began to give me a detailed, sardonic account of college life, as viewed by someone vulnerable and hard-pressed by it. At one point, she observed of the student who had propositioned her: "That guy gets all A's. He tells people he's in Group I [the top academic category]. I've taken two moral-reasoning courses with him, and I'm sure he's gotten A's in both of them—and look at how he behaves with me, and I'm sure with others."

She stopped for a moment to let me take that in. I happened to know the young man and could only acknowledge the irony of his behavior, even as I wasn't totally surprised by what she'd experienced. But I was at a loss to know what to say to her. A philosophy major, with a strong interest in literature, she had taken a course on the Holocaust and described for me the ironies she also saw in that tragedy—mass murder of unparalleled historical proportion in a nation hitherto known as one of the most civilized in the world, with a citizenry as well educated as that of any country at the time.

Drawing on her education, the student put before me names such as Martin Heidegger, Carl Jung, Paul De Man, Ezra Pound—brilliant and accomplished men (a philosopher, a psychoanalyst, a literary critic, a poet) who nonetheless had linked themselves with the hate that was Nazism and Fascism during the 1930s. She reminded me of the willingness of the leaders of German and Italian universities to embrace Nazi and Fascist ideas, of the countless doctors and lawyers and judges and journalists and schoolteachers, and, yes, even members of the clergy—who were able to accommodate themselves to murderous thugs because the thugs had political power. She pointedly mentioned, too, the Soviet Gulag, that expanse of prisons to which millions of honorable people were sent by Stalin and his brutish accomplices— prisons commonly staffed by psychiatrists quite eager to label those victims of a vicious totalitarian state with an assortment of psychiatric names, then shoot them up with drugs meant to reduce them to zombies.

I tried hard, toward the end of a conversation that lasted almost two hours, to salvage something for her, for myself, and, not least, for a university that I much respect, even as I know its failings. I suggested that if she had learned what she had just shared with me at Harvard—why, that was itself a valuable education acquired. She smiled, gave me credit for a "nice try," but remained unconvinced. Then she put this tough, pointed, unnerving question to me: "I've been taking all these philosophy courses, and we talk about what's true, what's important, what's *good*. Well, how do you teach people to *be* good?" And she added: "What's the point of *knowing* good, if you don't keep trying to *become* a good person?"

I suddenly found myself on the defensive, although all along I had been sympathetic to her, to the indignation she had been directing toward some of her fellow students, and to her critical examination of the limits of abstract knowledge. Schools are schools, colleges are colleges, I averred, a complaisant and smug accommodation in my voice. Thereby I meant to say that our schools and colleges these days don't take major responsibility for the moral values of their students, but, rather, assume that their students acquire those values at home. I topped off my surrender to the *status quo* with a shrug of my shoulders, to which she responded with an unspoken but barely concealed anger. This she expressed through a knowing look that announced that she'd taken the full moral measure of me.

Suddenly, she was on her feet preparing to leave. I realized that I'd stumbled badly. I wanted to pursue the discussion, applaud her for taking on a large subject in a forthright, incisive manner, and tell her she was right in understanding that moral reasoning is not to be equated with moral conduct. I wanted, really, to explain my shrug—point out that there is only so much that any of us can do to affect others' behavior, that institutional life has its

own momentum. But she had no interest in that kind of self-justification she let me know in an unforgettable aside as she was departing my office: "I wonder whether Emerson was just being 'smart' in that lecture he gave here. I wonder if he ever had any ideas about what to *do* about what was worrying him—or did he think he'd done enough because he'd spelled the problem out to those Harvard professors?"

She was demonstrating that she understood two levels of irony: One was that the study of philosophy— even moral philosophy or moral reasoning—doesn't necessarily prompt in either the teacher or the student a determination to act in accordance with moral principles. And, further, a discussion of that very irony can prove equally sterile—again carrying no apparent consequences as far as one's everyday actions go.

When that student left my office (she would soon leave Harvard for good), I was exhausted and saddened—and brought up short. All too often those of us who read books or teach don't think to pose for ourselves the kind of ironic dilemma she had posed to me. How might we teachers encourage our students (encourage *ourselves)* to take that big step from thought to action, from moral analysis to fulfilled moral commitments? Rather obviously, community service offers us all a chance to put our money where our mouths are; and, of course, such service can enrich our understanding of the disciplines we study. A reading of *Invisible Man* (literature), *Tally's Corners* (sociology and anthropology), or *Childhood and Society* (psychology and psychoanalysis) takes on new meaning after some time spent in a ghetto school or a clinic. By the same token, such books can prompt us to think pragmatically about, say, how the wisdom that Ralph Ellison worked into his fiction might shape the way we get along with the children we're tutoring—affect our attitudes toward them, the things we say and do with them.

Yet I wonder whether classroom discussion, *per se,* can't also be of help, the skepticism of my student notwithstanding. She had pushed me hard, and I started referring again and again in my classes on moral introspection to what she had observed and learned, and my students more than got the message. Her moral righteousness, her shrewd eye and ear for hypocrisy hovered over us, made us uneasy, goaded us.

She challenged us to prove that what we think intellectually can be connected to our daily deeds. For some of us, the connection was established through community service. But that is not the only possible way. I asked students to write papers that told of particular efforts to honor through action the high thoughts we were discussing. Thus goaded to a certain self-consciousness, I suppose, students made various efforts. I felt that the best of them were small victories, brief epiphanies that might otherwise have been overlooked, but had great significance for the students in question.

"I thanked someone serving me food in the college cafeteria, and then we got to talking, the first time," one student wrote. For her, this was a decisive break with her former indifference to others she abstractly regarded as " the people who work on the serving line . " She felt that she had learned something about another's life and had tried to show respect for that life.

The student who challenged me with her angry, melancholy story had pushed me to teach differently. Now, I make an explicit issue of the more than occasional disparity between thinking and doing, and I ask my students to consider how we all might bridge that disparity. To be sure, the task of connecting intellect to character is daunting, as Emerson and others well knew. And any of us can lapse into cynicism, turn the moral challenge of a seminar into yet another moment of opportunism: I'll get an A this time, by writing a paper cannily extolling myself as a doer of this or that "good deed"!

Still, I know that college administrators and faculty members everywhere are struggling with the same issues that I was faced with, and I can testify that many students will respond seriously, in at least small ways, if we make clear that we really believe that the link between moral reasoning and action is important to us. My experience has given me at least a measure of hope that moral reasoning and reflection can somehow be integrated into students'—and teachers'—lives as they actually live them.

THINGS OF THIS WORLD, OR ANGELS UNAWARES

by Randall Kenan

On the sixth of June of that year a man of decidedly Asian aspect appeared in Mr. John Edgar Stokes's front yard, near the crepe myrtle bush he had planted in the southwest corner back in 1967, which now had ornery drooping limbs that Mr. John Edgar had to prune each year. The man lay face down and motionless in the grass, his legs in the gully, feet pointing toward the road. He wore dusty jeans and a bright red-and-blue flannel shirt. His shoes, brogans.

Not until the dog, Shep, continued to make such a ruckus after he had yelled at him for a score of minutes to hush up, figuring it was just somebody passing in the road, did Mr. John Edgar come out of his kitchen where he had just lingered over his eggs, bacon, and coffee, and then washed the dishes, to investigate what the matter could be.

When he first saw the man Mr. John Edgar gave a barely audible *Huh,* almost a sigh as if he had been pushed in the chest by some invisible hand. He stood there staring, contemplating whether or not he did indeed see a Chinaman, or what looked to him to be a Chinaman, from the back, face down in the southwest corner of his yard. Glory be, he thought, might be one of them migrant workers. Mexican. Dead drunk.

As he approached the prone figure it occurred to him—and he was annoyed that it hadn't occurred to him on the first go-round—that the man might well be dead.

He called to the corpse: "Hey. Hey there. What you doing?"

But the figure did not move.

"I say, you there. Feller. Is you quick or dead?"

Mr. John Edgar looked around and scratched his head, wanting to have a witness before proceeding. Not particularly eager to flip the thing over and say "Morning" to the Grim Reaper. He felt a creepy sort of sensation in the back of his neck.

But as he neared the man he heard what amounted to a groan and, sure enough, saw a slight twitching in the shoulder region of the body, and a kind of spasm in the leg.

Mr. John Edgar crouched down and nudged the man. "Scuse me, boy. You ain't sleep, is you?"

The body roused a bit more, now moaning louder, the sound making a little more sense, seemed he was saying: "Fall" or "Fell" or "Falling."

"Son? You all right?" Mr. John Edgar poked him again, and as if in reward the man, with some effort and a great sigh, raised his head.

"Jesus, son." Though the man's eyes were closed, Mr. John Edgar could tell the man was not Mexican. A Chinaman. Just like he had seen on TV. Look at them eyes, he thought. Just as slanted as a cat's. The man had a gash on his forehead and the fresh blood trickled down his face, over some already dried. Blood oozed from his mouth. "Jesus. "

Mr. John Edgar lifted the man before he even considered the act, reacting perhaps to the blood, his heart beating now a little faster. He didn't appear to have stumbled down drunk, Mr. John Edgar reasoned. Somebody must have beaten him. He felt a twinge of pity. Poor fool.

Mr. John Edgar lifted him and began toward the house. The man didn't seem to weigh more than a hundred pounds. If that. No more than two feed sacks. Still, carrying him wasn't too bad for an eighty-six-year-old man. Mr. John Edgar carried his groaning load into the kitchen and set him down on a cot he kept in the corner. He wet a rag and wiped the blood from the man's head and mouth. Didn't seem to be serious. But I ain't no doctor, he reminded himself. Might better call Doc Streeter.

At that very second the man's eyes blinked wide open with a start, but his voice was quite calm and soft: "No." His face held a look of such bewilderment and confusion and fear that Mr. John Edgar felt a tug in his belly.

"Boy, who messed you up like this?" Mr. John Edgar's voice came out firm and solid, tinged with a little anger, not at the Chinaman but at the fact that someone had perhaps taken advantage of him.

"Messed?...messed me?...mess?..."

"I say, did some of them white bastards jump you?"

"Jump? White? No. I...I fell..."

"You *fell?* What the hell you talking bout, boy? How you going to hurt yourself like that just falling down in my yard?"

The man looked around, taking in the kitchen, the oilcloth-covered table, the blue porcelain plates on the wall, the wrought-iron spider on the stove, the worn-through linoleum, the string of brilliant red peppers hanging over the door, Mr. John Edgar Stokes himself. He began to shiver.

"You all right, boy?"

Mr. John Edgar went to get him a blanket. As he put it over him, the man said, "Thank you," seeming less frightened but still confused. "Thank you. You are kind."

"How did you get into this condition, son?"

"I'm fine, really. I'm fine. I just need to...to...a little. Yes. A little..."

Mr. John Edgar watched him, expecting him to say more, but the man had closed his eyes. Now Mr. John Edgar felt confident he was just sleeping.

He sat down on the other side of the room, ran his hand over his face. What the *hell?* Should he call Doc Streeter? He'd wait. Figure out what the problem was.

He put on some soup. By the time the kitchen was smelling of chicken and tomato and parsley and salt, the man had roused himself. He seemed rested but still a bit weak.

Mr. John Edgar brought a cup of the soup to the man. "Bet you're hungry. It's going on eleven o'clock."

"Thank you. You're very kind."

370

He handed the man a cup of soup and a spoon, but the stranger began to tremble from the effort and the soup to slosh a bit.

"Here. Here." Mr. John Edgar took it and commenced to feed the man, spoonful by spoonful, carefully, grasping at this rare opportunity to nurture, and in some inexpressible way felt pleased each time the Chinaman swallowed and smiled. He finished the whole cup, burped, excused himself, and wiped his mouth with the back of his hand.

"That was good. I was hungry."

Mr. John Edgar walked to the sink. "So. You one of them migrant workers or something, is you? You don't look Mexican at all. How you come to be in Tims Creek? What's your…?" Mr. John Edgar turned around to see the man had dozed off again into—if his face told no lies—what had to be a healing sleep.

"Well, go on and sleep then," Mr. John Edgar muttered under his breath, and went outside to finish propping up his tomato bushes in the garden, heavy laden with plump green tomatoes promising many platefuls of eating, stewed and raw-sliced, in just a few weeks.

Shep sat at the edge of the garden, watchfully, his tongue out, panting in the midmorning sun. Shep, Mr. John Edgar reasoned, was getting old, though he still gallivanted about like a wet-behind-the-ears puppy. His sire, Yoke, had lived to be eighteen. And Yoke's dame, Sam, had lived to the grand old age of twenty, not faltering one step till the day she died. Maybe the same would be true for Shep.

Already the temperature had reached the high eighties and the humidity was thick as moss. Sweat beaded on the tonsure of Mr. John Edgar's head as he stooped and poked and tied, inhaling the sharp odor of the plants.

He had almost forgotten about the man when he heard the toilet flush. Mr. John Edgar figured he had better go and look in on him.

The man sat on the cot, his head in his hands.

"You ain't crying there, is you, feller?"

The man looked up, a smidgen stronger, with a hint smile. "No. Not at all. I'm just still a bit tired." The man had no accent as Mr. John Edgar could place, which puzzled him a bit. But then he had seen Chinamen on TV who spoke English better than the whiteman.

"You from round here?"

"No. Just passing through."

"Where you headed?"

"To see a friend."

"Round here?"

"Yes."

"Would I know—?"

"Oh, how rude of me. My name is—" The man stood as if to shake Mr. John Edgar's hand but crumpled over.

"Now now, why don't you just lay back now?" Mr. John Edgar helped him stretch out.

His head back on the pillow, cocked to one side, he said: "Chi. My name is Chi."

"Pleased to meet you, Mr. Chi. Now I should call Doc Streeter. He's the town doctor, you know. I spect you may need a look-see."

"No." The Chinaman said it with a firmness that took Mr. John Edgar by surprise.

"No? What you mean, 'No'?"

"No. I'll be fine. It's not serious. I just fell. I know. I've done it before. No need for a doctor. I just need to rest. Trust me."

"Trust you? I don't know a damn thing about you."

"Please. I won't stay long."

Mr. John Edgar furrowed his brow and frowned. He narrowed his eyes like an owl about to say "Who." "Ain't nobody chasing you, is they?"

"No. Nobody's chasing me."

"You wouldn't lie to me, would you?"

"No, Mr. Stokes. I do not lie."

"Well." Mr. John Edgar scratched his head. "All right. For a little while. But if you get worser, I'm calling Doc Streeter. Okay?"

"I won't get worse. I promise."

He walked out of the room and then it struck him: *"Mr. Stokes"?* But when he went back into the kitchen the man was deep in slumber. How did he know my name? But the man might have seen it on the mailbox or on something in the house when he went to the bathroom, Mr. John Edgar reasoned while walking to the porch.

That night Mr. John Edgar made them liver and onions, and cabbage and carrots, with some cornbread and bitter lemonade to drink. Chi seemed to enjoy the food though he didn't say much. Mr. John Edgar, after a while of silence, went off telling tales: About laying tracks for the railroads in his youth, about the biggest snake he had killed, about the price of corn and how he now leased all his land to the biggest landowner in town, Percy Terrell, the son of old evil Malcolm Terrell, against his better judgment. He talked long after they had finished eating. Chi said very little, and by and by Mr. John Edgar came round to the idea of what Chi was going to do.

"Well, you can stay on here tonight if you want. Ain't nobody but me." He said it without a second thought, for he trusted this strange Chinese man for some reason, though he couldn't quite put a finger on why he did.

Chi accepted with a gracious thank-you and Mr. John Edgar showed him the second bedroom and told him he could take a bath if he wanted, and laid out clean towels and some fresh clothes he thought might fit him.

In bed, his false teeth out, rubbing his bare gums together pleasurably, enjoying the wet friction, Mr. John Edgar considered the foolishness of what he had done by inviting a complete stranger into his house: He could sassinate me this very night, cut my head clean off in the middle of the night. But I've lived my life. What would it matter?

He turned on his side, oddly confident in his instinct, and glided off into sweet slumber.

The next morning he found Chi at the table looking somewhat better, a tad more dignified, upright, though he could tell the small Chinaman had not regained his full mettle. Mr. John Edgar scrambled up some eggs and fried up some bacon, and Chi munched with delight, saying Mr. John Edgar was a good cook.

Chi followed Mr. John Edgar around all that day: In the garden he helped him pick peas, chop collards and cabbage, and pull some of the last sweet corn; he rode with him into town in Mr. John Edgar's 1965 Ford pickup truck to buy some wire and nails and light bulbs; he helped him fix the roof of the pump house; all the while saying little, and Mr. John Edgar, perhaps induced by the Asian man's silence, talked on of his days of courting and sparking and of this gal Cindy and that gal Emma Jo and of that ole Callie Mae Harris's mama, Cleona, who was evil as a wet hen. Or he'd simply sit in silence enjoying the good company of his guest.

That night he roasted a hen, fried some mustard greens, and boiled some of the sweet corn they'd pulled that day and some rice. Again Chi complimented Mr. John Edgar's cooking, asking him where he'd learned to cook so well.

"A man living by himself'll pick up what he needs to, I reckon's all there is to it."

"You never married." Chi put it more as a statement than a question.

"No. Never got round to it."

They sat on the porch afterward, mostly in silence. Mr. John Edgar was now yarned out. After a spell of rocking he asked: "What it like in China?"

"I'm not from China."

"You ain't a Chinaman, then?"

"No. "

"Oh." Mr. John Edgar wanted to ask where the hell he *was* from then, but felt somewhat embarrassed, figuring he should know. So they rocked, saying nothing, listening to the twilight noises leavened by the sound of trucks and cars on the highway in the far distance.

372

The next morning Mr. John Edgar rose at about five and decided to clean his gun. As he moved to put it back in the closet off the parlor, outside the window something caught his eye. Mr. John Edgar stood perplexed: There in the backyard was Chi. Seemed at first to be doing some queer dance. No. No. Fighting some invisible somebody. No. Dancing. But no, the way he's a-moving ...

As he watched Chi, with his arms moving like a puppet's, Mr. John Edgar wanted to think him crazy, but something about the look on his face, the reverence with which he moved, with grace, yes, that's what it was, the grace of his movements, like a cat, made him think better of it. Looked like a ritual of some kind. Was he casting a spell? Praying? Maybe this was how they prayed where this feller was from. Clutching the gun, Mr. John Edgar stood at the window watching, and presently Chi sat down in the dew-misted grass. Motionless, his legs folded up before him, his head straight ahead toward the sun, his eyes closed.

Well, I'll be damned, Mr. John Edgar thought, half expecting the man to float; and at length, when he didn't, Mr. John Edgar Stokes took his gun back to the parlor.

By the time he got back to the kitchen, there sat Chi at the table, looking pert. He had regained all his dignity. The scar on his forehead was a mere red shadow, his black eyes glistened.

"Good morning, Mr. Stokes."

"Morning there, feller. Like some eggs and ham?" "Thank you. Please."

Mr. John Edgar went about preparing the meal as he had done for scores of years, humming. He truly wanted to ask what the man had been doing in his backyard facing the morning sun, but felt by turns embarrassed and guilty and prying, as if he had witnessed something private between this foreigner and his Lord. Best not to be nosy. Mind your own business.

They lingered over coffee, Mr. John Edgar ticking off those things he had to do for the day, waiting patiently to hear the man say it was time to go, thinking his hospitality had reached its limit and the polite thing would be for the man to move on,

seeing as he was hale and hearty. But at the same time he did enjoy the strange man's company. There was something comforting about it. So he got up to cut the grass, and as he stood at the shed door he heard a truck drive up.

Joe Allen Pearsall got out of his truck and Mr. John Edgar could tell he had bad news by the way he was slumped over in the shoulders, looking at the ground.

"Well, morning to you, Joe Allen. How you been?"

"All right, Mr. John Edgar. How you?"

Mr. John Edgar searched his own mind, trying to beat Joe Allen to the news. He hated surprises. Maybe something had happened to that crazy wife of his. Maybe somebody had died. Who? Zeke Cross? Carl Fletcher? Maggie Williams? Ada Mae...

"Mr. John Edgar. Something bad happened."

The old man wanted to say: "Well, I know that." But he said nothing, waiting for Joe Allen to complete his thought. Instead of letting more words drop out of his mouth—must be mighty bad or he woulda just said it—Joe Allen backed to the end of his truck, motioning for Mr. John Edgar to follow. He let the tailgate down.

They stood there for a good minute. Mr. John Edgar just stared, no saliva in his mouth. Not looking at Joe Allen, he asked: "Who done it?"

"Them Terrell boys. Say that he been shitting in their yard and that this morning he was in their cow pasture chasing a heifer. So...so...I was at the store when they done it."

By the time Chi had come around to the truck, Mr. John Edgar had the dog, Shep, already stiffening up in his arms, the tongue hanging pendulously; drool, and a mixture of blood and froth, leaving a gelatinous pool on the bed of the truck; the head a horrid confusion of tattered bone, flesh, white fluid, and what was left of a grey brain. Blood stained the tan coat.

As Mr. John Edgar carried Shep to the backyard, to where the yard met the garden, Joe Allen turned with questions in his eyes to the strange man at his side standing as perplexed and sad as he.

"Who... ?"

"I am Chi."

They stood, and it was obvious that Joe Allen wanted to ask Chi what he was doing there. But they were both distracted by the somber goings-on.

Mr. John Edgar laid Shep down and went into the shed to retrieve a shovel and an old quilt, faded yet still Joseph's coat-like in its patchwork colors.

"Let me do it, Mr. John Edgar." But he seemed neither to hear nor to see Joe Allen as he went about the task of digging a hole wide enough, long enough, deep enough. Chi and Joe Allen, useless pallbearers, watched Mr. John Edgar, who seemed neither to sweat a drop nor strain a muscle, as he went about the duty with a skill that would have made anybody who didn't know better think it his occupation.

Tenderly he swaddled the cooling pup in the quilt and lowered him to his forever bed. When the last shovelful of earth had been patted down, Mr. John Edgar picked up two large stones from a pile at the other end of the garden, stones swallowed by moss, and placed one at Shep's feet and one at his nose. He took a long pause, his breath miraculously even, a barely seen dew of sweat on his brown head, but he didn't seem to grieve or meditate or tremble in anger: He seemed only to wait, peering at the shallow grave, as if expecting the dog to claw out of the earth, brain intact, healed, panting, resurrected.

Presently he said under his breath: "Damn," turned and walked back to the shed, put the shovel down, and went into the house.

Chi and Joe Allen followed him with their eyes. Joe Allen shuffled awkwardly, clearly having no words or actions he felt would suffice. He regarded Chi with only slightly less suspicion than before.

"You from round here?"

"No. "

"I didn't think so. Never seen you before. Helping Mr. John Edgar out, is you?"

"Yes. I've been staying with him for a few days."

"Have? Wh—?"

The door slammed with a loud crack and they both pivoted to see Mr. John Edgar, gun in hand, marching toward his truck.

"Oh, Jesus. We got to stop him." Joe Allen ran toward the truck, Chi close behind.

"Mr. John Edgar. Mr. John Edgar! Now you can't just...You can't..."

But the old man paid Joe Allen no heed, cranking up the truck and backing out, running over a few marigolds to avoid hitting Joe Allen's truck. He shot down the road, pushing the old truck as fast as she would go.

Come on, Joe Allen motioned to Chi. They took off after him. Joe Allen, in his haste, ran over more marigolds.

The Terrell General Store was no more than five miles from Mr. John Edgar Stokes's house, barely within the town limits. He pulled up, the truck lurching to a stop. All three Terrell boys congregated on the front porch of the large warehouse of a store. One called out: "Well, if it ain't John Edgar Stokes. To what do we owe the pleasure." They all laughed.

Their jocular tone changed when Mr. John Edgar got out of his automobile and they could see he was carrying a Smith & Wesson. One Terrell boy whispered to another: "Better get Daddy," and the boy zipped off like a housefly.

Mr. John Edgar, his head held high, barely gave the boys a glance, but it was clear that the half-look equated them in his mind with hog slop. Choking his gun by the neck, he stomped along the side of the store.

By the time the boys ran up to Mr. John Edgar, Joe Allen and Chi had arrived and were among the boys who hollered at him.

The Terrell boys jumped in front of Mr. John Edgar but he did not stop; merely leveled his gun, cocked it, and kept walking. The boys got out of the way. "Crazy old nigger. What's he doing?"

Percy Terrell came bursting out the back door: "John Edgar Stokes. What you doing back here? What you aiming to do with that gun? Deer season is over. Now, John Edgar—"

Mr. John Edgar stopped in front of a hutch of hound dogs. Five dogs in all. Percy's prize coon dogs. Yapping in the confusion.

Joe Allen ran up to him from behind and whispered: "You oughtn't to do this, Mr. John Edgar."

"Nigger, I will kill you," one of the Terrell boys said, fist clenched, trembling, face all red. He took a step forward and Mr. John Edgar raised the gun to the level of the boy's heart.

"John Edgar!" Percy Terrell howled. The boy's eyes twitched with fear, given two seconds to contemplate his mortality. Another Terrell stepped forward and Mr. John Edgar, implacable, pointed the gun toward him; after the boy froze, toward the third; and finally toward Percy Terrell himself. They stood stock-still, less from the reality of the gun than from the look in Mr. John Edgar Stokes's eyes, a curse of loathing and damnation as if from God's own Counsel on Earth.

In a motion approaching nonchalance, Mr. John Edgar reeled to the hound dogs and aimed at the one on the end, the one Percy called Billy.

"Hell, no!"

The bullet went through the chicken wire, pretty and neat, not breaking a strand. The dog didn't make sound the first. He just fell over on his side like a spent toy. Mr. John Edgar got him square in the head. The blood came dripping down.

The youngest Terrell lunged toward him, but Mr. John Edgar just cocked his gun again, shot the ground, cocked it again, and pointed it at the boy. Mr. John Edgar began backing away, shaking his head no; but now the look on his face said that any more killing he had to do would be incidental and painless. Another Terrell boy babbled loudly and incoherently, his rage making him the color of raw beef, his arms flailing, yammering a high-pitched patois of hate: "Paw we gotta kill him nigger

sombitch killing cocksucker nigger Paw Paw do something."

Terrell shook his head gravely. "You done it now, you ole fart. John Edgar, you a dead man. You'll pay for this, you goddamn fool."

Mr. John Edgar got into his truck unaccosted and drove away, this time obeying the speed limit, followed by a shaken Joe Allen and Chi.

By the time Joe Allen and Chi got out of the truck, Mr. John Edgar had set himself down in his rocker on the front porch and was rocking.

"Now, Mr. John Edgar, you shouldn'ta done that, now. You reckon ole Terrell gone let you get away with that?"

Mr. John Edgar said not a word, answering Joe Allen with the creak of the chair on the floorboards, his gun in his lap.

Joe Allen tried to talk more but it became clear that Mr. John Edgar intended to keep silent. Flustered, Joe Allen went into the house and made a few phone calls. Chi sat with Mr. John Edgar in silence. Joe Allen came back, visibly worried, and just looked at the two of them. "Jesus H. Christ."

Dr. Streeter arrived first. The Reverend Barden came with Ed Phelps. Joe Allen recapped the entire incident, showing himself to be more than a little proud of what ole Mr. John Edgar had done, and smiled broadly at the end. The men all laughed and congratulated Mr. John Edgar in whoops and guffaws and slaps on the shoulder.

"Dog's dead, though." Mr. John Edgar continued to rock in the same rhythm, staring steelily into the front yard.

The men all became grave in countenance, heads bowed. It was Dr. Streeter who finally voiced everyone's unspoken curiosity. Turning to Chi, he scratched his white beard and fidgeted with his glasses in a lordly manner. "And who are you?"

Chi, who was standing now, looked as though he felt at home among this gathering. "My name is Chi. I am a friend."

"I see. You're not from around here, are you? Migrant worker or something?"

"No. Just passing through."

"We ought to hide him," Ed Phelps broke in. "Mr. John Edgar, you ought to hide. Ain't no telling what they'll do."

"Might not be a bad idea." Joe Allen looked worried.

Mr. John Edgar Stokes kept on rocking.

In the distance a siren came screaming. They could all see the sheriff's car zipping toward the house, followed by two other cars.

"Oh, Lord, my Lord." The Right Reverend Hezekiah Barden's face was wet with sweat. "What we gone do now? Terrell don't play, you know."

"You aren't afraid, are you, Reverend?" Dr. Streeter winked at Barden.

"Maybe we should pray?"

"Well,"—Dr. Streeter straightened his tie—"you better pray fast, Hez. Better pray fast."

Sheriff Roy Brinkley parked his car beside the road in front of the yard, the light still blinking on the top. Brinkley, a man of brood-sow girth and a small and jowly head, came rolling across the lawn with Percy Terrell at his right hand. The boys behind.

"Well, well, well." Dr. Streeter stood at the foot of the steps. "To what do we owe this visit from the county's finest?"

"Out of my way, Streeter. I ain't got time for your Yankee foolishness. You know why I'm here."

"Why?" Barden had composed himself, wiped away all the sweat with his Panama hankie. "Looks to me like the two things you're lacking is some white sheets and a cross."

"Now you know it ain't like that, Reverend." Brinkley himself was sweating now; the walk across the lawn had surely been an overexertion.

"Stop all this bullshit." Terrell pointed to Mr. John Edgar. "You all know good and well why we come here. To get him."

"To string him up?" Ed Phelps came down to ground level with Dr. Streeter.

"Yeah." Joe Allen stepped forward too. "Your boys killed his dog, you know. I don't see no sheriff coming for you."

"That was different and you know it." Brinkley wiped his red and sweating face with his bare hand.

"How come?" Ed Phelps shrugged.

"Cause John's dog was trespassing on Terrell's property. They was within their rights to shoot him. John was trespassing and maliciously destroyed property. He shoulda filed a complaint if he felt there was wrongdoing.

"Well, who do I file a complaint with now, you?"

"Shut up, Streeter." Terrell pointed. "This don't concern you."

"I'm not one of your employees, like the sheriff here. I can speak when and where I please."

"Well, talk all you want to. Roy, arrest that nigger and let's go so I don't have to listen to this fancy boy shoot off at the mouth. I got better things to do."

Rankled by what sounded like an order, Sheriff Brinkley advanced between Ed Phelps and Dr. Streeter and put his foot on the first step to the porch.

"Get the hell off my porch." Mr. John Edgar had stopped rocking.

"Now, John. You—" Brinkley took another step and Mr. John Edgar picked up his gun.

"I said get off my porch."

"You can't do this."

"I can and I am. I said get off my porch." He cocked the gun and took aim at Brinkley's belly.

Roy Brinkley trembled with anger, his belly quivering despite the tight brown uniform. "You broke the law, John Edgar Stokes. The law says you got to come with me."

"Well, the Bible say 'an eye for an eye,' don't it, Reverend? An Eye for an Eye and a Tooth for a Tooth. That's the onliest Law I'm studying about. Now get the hell off my porch or they'll have to scrape you off."

Sheriff Brinkley took one step back and almost fell into the Right Reverend Hezekiah Barden. He swung his great girth around and walked back to his squad car.

"Where the hell you going, Roy?" Terrell chased after him. "Arrest him. *Arrest* him, goddamn it. What do I pay...what were you elected to do? Goddamn it, arrest him, I say."

The men on the porch all laughed and slapped Mr. John Edgar's back. Mr. John Edgar again commenced to rocking, not smiling with the men.

Voices from the squad car carried to the porch.

"You fat fairy. You a goddamn coward is what you is. Scared of one old nigger with a buncha coons and a shotgun. He ain't gon—"

"Be quiet, Percy. Just hush."

"Scared is all you is. Scared. I gone take my boys and—"

"Hush, Percy." From the porch they heard static. "Luella? This is Sheriff Brinkley. I'm requesting assistance."

"Assistance, my left titty. You just scared. Afeared of a ole nigger."

"Hush, Percy, please! Yeah, at the residence of John Edgar Stokes in Tims Creek..."

On the porch the men became silent, looking to one another in puzzlement, looking to Chi in even greater puzzlement, each finding himself questioning the extent of his own courage on what had seemed earlier to have been a routine June day. The white men stood about the sheriff's car in the road; the black men on the porch, a strange Asian man in their midst. Chi said nothing, just looked from one group to another, seeming to drink it all into his Dead Sea-calm black eyes.

"Maybe." The Reverend Barden's face shone once again with sweat. "Maybe you ought to go on with them, John Edgar. Maybe..."

Two state patrol cars came down the road, one from each direction. Three tall troopers got out and conferred with Brinkley and Terrell. Two troopers were white, one black. They each had rifles in their hands. After a time they approached the house: The two white patrollers on either side, guns at the ready, the black one in the middle with Brinkley, Terrell, and his boys behind.

Before the steps Brinkley called out in a voice too loud: "In the name of the People of York County, the Governor of the Great State of North Carolina, and the Constitution of these United States of America, John Edgar Stokes, you are under arrest for willful and malicious destruction of property, resisting arrest, and threatening the life of an officer of the law. Now you come on down here and let me take you to the courthouse, why don't you?"

Mr. John Edgar just kept on rocking and rocking, as if the sights and sounds before him were no more than hoot owls and mist in the dark, unworthy of heed. All the men eyed one another tremulously, expecting everything, daring nothing.

"Go get him, son," Brinkley said to the black trooper.

As the black man, his eyes veiled behind smoky sunglasses, walked up the steps, Mr. John Edgar did nothing, outnumbered by two guns trained on his head and heart. The officer of the law took the gun from the old man without a struggle and pulled him forward, and Malcolm Streeter, M.D., was heard to say: "Pernicious infamy. O foul and black traitor of fate." But the man placed handcuffs on Mr. John Edgar Stokes just the same, and Brinkley, rocking on his heels in his newfound self-confidence and delight, commenced to recite: "You have the right to remain silent..."

"What difference does it make in Terrell County?"

"Now you stay out of this, Streeter. This is the law talking. "

"The law? Law? Jim Crow law if you ask me."

"Streeter, if you don't hush up I'll arrest you too."

"Go ahead, and you'll see more lawyers swarming over your precious courthouse than you're already going to see in about an hour. Come on, arrest me."

"Brinkley!" Terrell stepped forward. "Come on. We don't have to stand here and take this shit. Come on." They began to walk away.

"His master's voice, " Streeter said through clenched teeth.

Brinkley looked back but Terrell beckoned *come on* from the squad car's open door.

"If you harm one hair on that saintly man's head, I'll have your badge, your career, and your life. You pusillanimous hippopotamus!"

Dr. Streeter's words rang out to no avail as they stuffed Mr. John Edgar Stokes into the back of the sheriff's car. Terrell gloated and waved at the men as he got into the front seat, and began laughing as they drove off.

Word got out in the community in a hurry, and scores of people from all around Tims Creek followed the car containing Mr. John Edgar to Crosstown, and watched, yelling and screaming, as he was processed and spirited away behind steel doors. Though Brinkley's people were besieged by black and white telling them they had committed a heinous sin by putting an eighty-six-year-old man behind bars, the clerks and officers remained tight-mouthed as ordered and would not speak of release. Dr. Streeter and the Right Reverend Barden thundered about human rights and the travesty of justice, and placed phone calls to the state capitol and beyond well into the early morning. Early the next day Mr. John Edgar was released on five hundred dollars' bail, which Dr. Streeter promptly posted. Reporters from the York County *Cryer* and the Raleigh *News and Observer* and the Wilmington *Star* asked him questions; photographers snapped his picture; women hugged his neck and men shook his hand. He said little. Getting into the backseat of Dr. Streeter's car,

he looked up to see Chi. He asked him how he was doing.

"Fine, sir. I'm just fine. How are you holding up?"

"I do all right. For a old man."

Back home he sat in his parlor, contemplating the room, looking for pictures of family, knowing there were only a few: His mother, his father, both born slaves, dead for decades; his old sweetheart Lena Thompson, who he felt he would have married had he not waited so damn long; his nephew Joshua in Philadelphia; Joshua's two children. A daguerreotype, a large print, some snapshots, a few Polaroids, elementary-school pictures. Not much. Not enough to fill one of those good-size albums they sell at the department stores. All else was dull: Mementos of affectless happenings he could barely remember; gifts bearing little significance. Mr. John Edgar Stokes sat in his parlor on the day after his release from the county jail, troubled yet transformed, studying not just the present but the eighty-six years that had led him there. Amazed to now be awaiting a hearing, a trial. It had come up all of a sudden like a summer storm, but unlike a thundercloud this wouldn't leave things pretty much the way it found them.

Folk came by to talk, but he had very little to say to them. They left feeling a vague unease, not able to articulate their disquiet. Thinking, in the end, that that fine old gentleman, who had lived so long alone with his good dog, cooking, working in his garden, who had stopped farming some ten-odd years ago, had finally come upon the penultimate trouble of his life in the form of senility. Poor old gent.

He didn't have to cook, seeing as so many women-folk in the community had brought over pies, collard greens, spareribs, fried chicken, potato salad. He and Chi ate in unperturbed quiet, and afterward they returned to the dimly lit parlor and sat in quietude.

By and by Mr. John Edgar looked up to Chi and said: "You know, I hated to kill that dog. I surely did. But I had to. Just had to." He paused, looking out into the June-warm blackness of evening.

"Seems like up to now I been sitting right here in this chair waiting, waiting. But you know what?"

"No, sir."

"It sho was worth it. Worth it to see the look on that ole Terrell's face. I stood up to that cocksucker. Yes sir."

He smiled. Chi inclined his head thoughtfully and nodded with a strange look of understanding, complicity, and warmth.

"You know what else?"

"No. What, Mr. Stokes?"

"I wisht I could die. Die right now to spite his sorry ass. Yes sir. To show he ain't got no power over death. Yes sir. I could die right now—content."

"Could you?" Chi's black eyes seemed to shimmer in the lamp's faint light.

"Sho nuff could. With pleasure." He grinned.

When they found Mr. John Edgar Stokes he was sitting upright in a chair by his kitchen sink, his back straight as a swamp reed, not slouching one whit, clutching a large wooden spoon; his eyes stretched wide with astonishment, his mouth a gaping O—though his false teeth had held admirably to the gums—as if his last sight had been something more than truly remarkable, something wonderful and awesome to behold.

They found no sign of the man called Chi.

THE LAST CAMP

by Bernard Gotfryd

In August of 1944, after three weeks of hard labor at the Mauthausen stone quarry—three weeks of climbing one hundred and twelve steps six times daily with a heavy rock on my bare shoulders—I was shipped to the Messerschmitt plant at Gusen II, in Austria.

Gusen II was a fairly small camp set in a valley, surrounded by farmland. Outside the electric wire fence was a desolate perimeter bordered by another double wire fence; the concentric ring formed a corridor wide enough for the guards to patrol. The camp had eight watchtowers manned by SS guards with mounted machine guns. Far away, beyond the emptiness, one could see green fields with small clusters of trees silhouetted against the horizon.

Upon my arrival at the plant I became a planer operator. I'll never know what made the Nazis think I could do the job. In three months of trying to grasp the intricacies of the machine, as well as learning how to deal with the idiosyncrasies of my Nazi supervisors, I caused incalculable damage to the Third Reich by breaking a great many vanadium-steel-tipped knives. Vanadium, I was told, was the hardest steel in existence, and it was very expensive to manufacture.

The screeching of the planers, plus the adjacent lathe and drilling machines and several rows of sheet-metal workers who kept dropping aluminum and steel plates on top of a pile, created such a high-decibel noise that it was impossible to bear. I remember stuffing my ears with little balls of soft bread. The Nazis and the technical personnel plugged their ears with cotton or avoided the area whenever possible.

By autumn the Messerschmitt management had reason to be concerned about the diminishing labor force at the plant. Between recurrent epidemics of typhoid and dysentery and a chronic lack of nourishment, workers were disappearing faster than they could be replaced. Productivity was lagging far behind quota.

One day my supervisor, Herr Gruber, sorely tried by my performance with the planer but impressed by my proficiency in the German language, recommended me to head a food commando that the Messerschmitt management was about to set up. I suspected that this was his revenge for all the vanadium knives I'd managed to break.

In order to reverse the downward trend the Messerschmitt management offered food supplements to the most productive workers at the plant, or about ten percent of the work force. The food had to be brought in from the nearby Messerschmitt warehouse in St. Georgen. With the help of four Russian prisoners, a wagon with crates for the bread, two thermal tanks for the soup, and two SS guards to watch over it all, I was to do the job. Twice weekly we set off for the warehouse, brought back food to the plant, cut the bread, and distributed it according to lists drawn up by the plant supervisors. The final distribution of the food to the prisoners was done by a Russian POW, Andrei, and his assistants.

On my second trip to the warehouse I realized how easy it was to add more soup and loaves of bread to our wagon without incurring any great risks. So I added quantities of food and began passing on the extra portions to each listed department. In such a manner some prisoners who were not on the list were getting extra food. They wondered why, but they weren't complaining.

Early one morning, as we were walking over a frozen field of ice-covered furrows to the train that would take us to work my foot caught inside a rut, and I twisted my ankle. Almost immediately I started limping; I feared the injury would put me in sick bay, which could be the end of me.

In the pre-dawn darkness I heard someone ask in Russian, "What happened to your foot?" When I looked behind me I saw a broad-shouldered man of medium height dressed in a striped prisoner's uniform. In Gusen everybody wore the same uniforms. He moved closer as I tried to tell him in the little Russian I had picked up in Maidanek that my foot was hurting. It was still too dark for me to

be able to distinguish his features, but I could tell he was older than I. He asked the man next to him to help him lift me by my elbows; he asked me to fold and stiffen my arms and make myself as light as possible. In this way I was carried into the train and from the train to the plant.

I had no idea what made the Russian help me. Normally very few people went out of their way to help others unless they were of the same nationality. He and the other man carried me inside the plant through the long underground tunnel and deposited me at my station in front of the planer. As I was adjusting my machine another Russian prisoner whom I had never seen before came by and quickly handed me some chunks of ice wrapped inside a wet, torn sock. He told me to apply it to my ankle right away.

"Andrei said you must," he whispered in Russian, and he walked to his station.

My ankle was badly swollen, and I was in a good deal of pain; still I was intent on hiding my injury from the Nazis. The dour Herr Gruber kept casting glances at me as if he suspected something. I kept busy, pretending to focus my eyes on the moving knife and watching him at the same time. I didn't think Herr Gruber was a bad man, after all. Some weeks earlier I had found half a sausage and a slice of white bread inside a pocket of my French military tunic, which hung on the wall not far from his desk at the plant. Best of all, the sausage was wrapped in an undated German newspaper clipping announcing the Allied invasion of Normandy. I spent a long time trying to figure out how far it was from Normandy to Gusen; I hated to think how long it would take the Allies to travel more than a thousand kilometers. After secretly reading the newspaper clipping I hid it inside my shoe. Soon it disintegrated to a pulp, but I left it there, hoping the news would keep my foot warm.

Only Herr Gruber could have put the newspaper-wrapped sausage in my pocket. Herr Gruber rarely talked; he did so, in fact, only when he screamed at me for breaking a knife. I had trouble figuring him out. In particular I wondered if he had paid attention to his wrapping materials; did he want me to know about the Allied invasion?

Who was Andrei, and why did he care to help me? I wondered about that most of the day as I watched the tip of the knife whittling away at a row of steel brackets and tried to forget my ankle. In the afternoon, after the soup break, the Russian who had brought me the chunks of ice stuffed inside a sock returned with more. He left the sock on the door beside me and, without saying a word, walked away. Luckily, Herr Gruber was not at his desk.

Then came the shrill whistle, and it was time to go back to camp. I wondered how I would manage, but as soon as I stopped the machine I felt myself lifted off the floor by two Russians who appeared from nowhere. In the same manner as before they carried me outside, discreetly holding me under my elbows. Surrounded by hundreds of prisoners marching in ranks of five, we made it through the gate and into the train. It was a short ride back to camp, only fifteen to twenty minutes.

On the train I found myself standing between Andrei and his friend Dimitri and was at last able to get a good look at them. Andrei had a strong face with high cheekbones, a broad chin, and quiet gray eyes, unless the dim light inside the train was altering their color. There was something good and reassuring about him. It was difficult to determine his age, but he seemed to be in his mid-thirties. In camps people were aging fast and looked much older than they were in reality Dimitri, his friend, was taller, thinner, very blond, and very shy. I didn't know what to say to them and very apologetically in the best Russian I could muster, thanked them for being so kind to me. Turning my head from one to the other, I blurted out: "Thank you very much. It's very unusual what you are doing for me. I'm very grateful." Andrei looked at me, and his face lit up: "When the time comes we want you to be able to go home without a limp, because somebody will be there waiting for you. Don't worry about the ankle. All you have to do is keep applying the ice, and soon you'll be well again."

Dimitri was quiet. He offered me a drag of a thumbnail cigarette butt he had pulled out of his pocket and lit immediately my head began to spin. It must have been a camp cigarette made from some strange mixture of herbs. Andrei didn't smoke.

When we arrived in camp it was nearly dark. People were rushing in and out of the barracks, trading their bread rations for cigarettes or their clothing for bread or soup. Loud bargaining could be heard over some more complex transactions. Almost everybody had something to trade; of the babble of languages Russian could be heard most of all.

One Sunday, my day off, I was walking behind the barracks looking for a sunny spot to rest when I saw Andrei approaching me. "I would like to see you for a moment. It's such a beautiful day. Let's sit down in the sun and talk," he said in his clear, accentuated Russian. Some months had gone by, and I now had a better command of Russian.

"Young man," Andrei addressed me, "I'll get to the point. There isn't much time to talk. We like people like you who don't mind taking risks. And so I must tell you that we've watched you for a long time with your bread scheme, and we've come to the conclusion that you are one of us. That means that we trust you and would like you to join us. Many months ago, long before you arrived, we started organizing. You may call it a conspiracy, if you like. When the right time comes we must be ready to take over the camp in order to prevent a slaughter. You must understand that when we become useless the Nazis will destroy us. Did you know that more than thirty thousand Russian prisoners of war and many thousands of others died here building the Messerschmitt plant? We aren't willing to share their fate, not if we can help it, and we think we can help it. When we have rifles we will win. You see, we all have somebody back home. I have a wife and two little boys, parents and brothers and sisters—a big family, and I'm sure they're waiting for me. So I plan on going back. Did you understand everything I'm saying? If not, you can ask me questions."

I was flabbergasted. "Frankly," I answered, "I don't know what to say. I'm honored that you trust me. I really don't know what I can do for you—even if you want me to do anything at all— but I'll do whatever you ask. I also have a family that I would like to see again, but above all I would like to see the end of that monster. You know who I mean, don't you?"

Andrei nodded. "Yes, yes, I know. But I must go now," he said, and, lowering his voice, he continued: "Just keep supplying the bread so our people can stay alive. We have over two hundred people to worry about, and some aren't so healthy anymore. Every extra drop of soup or slice of bread is a big help. So far as I can tell, the Nazis don't know a thing about the bread scheme, and my people certainly won't tell, even if they're strung up. The only person that worries me is that new arrival who speaks Russian with a German accent. He claims to be a Czech. He just walks around and snoops. I never see him do any work. Very suspicious. Watch out for him. But above all, not a peep to anybody, not even God Himself. You understand, right?"

"Of course I understand," I answered as we shook hands Andrei had a strong grip; he hurt my knuckles.

"Oh, yes, one more thing. Now that you can walk again I suggest that when you ride the train you try to mix with different people all the time, so that we don't attract attention as a group. We think that there are informers among us. I'll talk to you only when I have something to tell you. Otherwise, act like a stranger and keep your ears tuned in." Andrei got up and walked toward the latrine.

I was overwhelmed. The whole thing seemed unreal. Suppose Andrei himself was an informer. Was it safe to continue oversupplying rations? Was it possible for a starved band of prisoners to organize a conspiracy inside a Nazi camp right under their noses? I had never heard of one, but then, if it was a conspiracy, how could anybody hear of it? I had doubts about some of the things Andrei had told me; still, I decided to go along with it. I knew that life in camps wasn't worth very much, but here in Gusen Andrei at least offered me a chance to fight back.

I had not even had a chance to thank Andrei for healing my ankle; every time I had started to open my mouth he had launched into a new sentence.

It felt good to sit outside in the warm sun. Spring was beginning, but the air was still cool. Some birds flew overhead, too far away for me to tell what they were. They never came close to the camp, as if they sensed what went on there.

I started daydreaming about Alexandra. I saw her knocking at the studio window during the snowstorm, and I saw her throwing me a kiss the last time we had met. I remembered her having brought me the sweater, and how she had cried. It was all just a little over a year before, and yet it felt as though a whole lifetime had gone by.

I wondered if Alexandra still thought of me, if she remembered me at all, and I hoped she hadn't been caught with any of the pictures I had passed on to her. Maybe it wasn't a good idea to think of her, but how could I not? Perhaps I should only concentrate on what was happening at Gusen and stop worrying about things I couldn't help. That made more sense. Hadn't Andrei said that one day when all this was over he intended to go home because his family would be waiting for him? I couldn't be sure if anybody would be waiting for me, and I dreaded even thinking about it. The deportation night was constantly on my mind, and nightmarish images from the ghetto kept flooding back.

Prisoners were moving about aimlessly all around me, dragging their feet, exposing their emaciated bodies to the sun. Others stretched out on the bare ground, too tired and starved to move. It made me shudder when I realized that m a matter of days I could be one of those lifeless ones. What could one do? Sit back and wait for the end? At that moment I was more than ever convinced by Andrei.

My friend Michael came by and joined me. I couldn't talk to him about Andrei, but I told him about the Allied invasion of Normandy, something I had mentioned to no one except Andrei. He didn't want to believe me. I swore to him that I had read it in a Nazi paper clipping that, unfortunately, had by now disintegrated inside my shoe.

"I don't want to sound like a cynic," he said, "but I think somebody is lying."

"Would a Nazi-controlled paper boast about an Allied invasion?" I asked Michael. "Usually they would underreport on Allied progress or not mention it at all. Can't you see?" I insisted.

I couldn't convince him, so I gave up. He didn't feel well, he told me. He was losing strength. I tried to instill some hope in him, even if the invasion was a newspaper lie. Michael and I had known each other since before the war. We were of the same age, had traveled together from one camp to another, and had sometimes even landed in the same barracks. I was sorry he didn't know how to dream.

In spite of the Messerschmitt food supplements people were still dying of malnutrition. Somehow, however, the core of the plant force kept functioning. Two Russian friends out of my food commando of five had died and were never replaced. Now the three of us were carrying a heavier load. In addition we had been assigned the chore of boiling fifty quarts of skimmed milk in a field kitchen twice a week for the prisoners who were spraying the airplane fuselages at the plant. It was ironic that the Nazis were so concerned with the lungs of a few paint sprayers while they let others die by the thousands Nothing they did made any sense.

April arrived, and with it came new hope. One day we were ordered to dig air-raid shelters outside the camp perimeter, and soon, sure enough, Allied planes arrived, bombing some locations in the vicinity. Although we were their targets we welcomed their bombs with open arms and no reservations. We didn't mind dying for freedom, and in order to end such evil. I prayed for the planes to return and bomb the Nazis again and again. I loved to watch the SS men with their automatic rifles run for their lives at the first sound of the camp siren. Suddenly they didn't look so tough at all. Andrei was right when he had said that we would win, because in our hearts we believed that we were free men. I knew what he meant. I could feel it when he said that our ideas would survive but the Nazi evil wouldn't. There was something magic in his words. Even though I didn't understand everything he said, I was willing to fight with him.

Around the middle of April, even as bombs were falling, an accident took place at the plant's loading ramp. As a freight train filled with Messerschmitt fuselages left the loading ramp a prisoner fell onto the tracks and was cut in half by the wheels. The man turned out to be the Czech about whom Andre' had warned me. I wondered who had contrived the accident. It had to be one of Andrei's men, I thought; I only hoped that the Nazis wouldn't take revenge.

An investigation followed, and the Gestapo were brought in. They brought dogs and led an interrogation, but nothing came of it. They questioned the German engineer of the train and everyone else who was in the vicinity when the accident occurred. The mere fact that they brought in the Gestapo was an indication that the Czech had been important to the Nazis. Andrei had been right. Normally they would hardly have noticed the death of a prisoner; this was what we were there for.

That same day one of Andrei's men was searched by the SS while returning from the plant to camp. They found on him a piece of metal resembling a trigger assembly component and took him in for questioning. They broke his ribs, knocked out his teeth, and shipped him half-dead to the crematorium in Mauthausen. He didn't talk, I found out later. If he had, almost certainly he would have lived.

The following morning I saw Andrei on the train. "Don't cut any extra bread," he said to me quietly, "until the excitement dies down. It's very easy to do something foolish, and this is what they're looking for."

Things were getting worse for the Nazis, as well as for us, day by day. There was a shortage of metals and tools at the plant; most of the machines were now idle. In lieu of our usual work we were ordered to sweep the plant or polish and oil the machines. Even grease was in short supply. Our bread rations were cut, the Messerschmitt food supplement was eliminated altogether, and no more German soup of bones, beans, and cabbage appeared.

Early one morning when we were on our way to the plant Allied planes flew over again, but they didn't drop any bombs. We were all sorry. We were ordered to abandon the train and lie on our backs in the field. Watching the sky, I thought I would have given my right arm to be up there so that I could bomb that miserable rat hole to dust. I could see little dark clouds exploding in the sky and kept praying for the Nazis to miss their targets. It was all over within a few minutes.

Soon artillery rumblings and bomb explosions became commonplace, and the whole camp trembled. We no longer went to the plant, but we also found food to be scarcer and scarcer. During the night of May third, 1945, the SS command disappeared from the camp, leaving behind a skeleton crew of lesser rank, and a Red Cross flag was hoisted on top of a tall mast in the center of the camp. Armed with vintage rifles, Austrian Home Guards, veterans of World War I, were brought in to guard us. They were in their fifties and wore vintage uniforms sizes too large for them. The watchtowers were still manned by SS men armed with machine guns, however.

The following day, May fourth, there was no bread. We were ordered to stay in the barracks and not to congregate outside. Dimitri came over to my bunk and sat down next to me. Almost in a whisper he said, "Tomorrow at midnight something will happen. Don't take off your shoes when you go to sleep. That's all," and he moved on.

The rest of the day was uneventful. Around midday two containers of watery soup were brought in to our barrack, not enough for three hundred people; that was all we ate that day. That morning I ate the bit of bread I had saved from my last breakfast and cleaned my pocket of every crumb; I was still hungry. My friend Ilya came over to tell me that the German kapos had received Red Cross parcels and were having a real party. He suspected that the parcels were meant for us, the prisoners, and not the kapos. Also, two prisoners were shot by an SS guard who caught them engaging in cannibalism. "Has it gotten this bad?" I asked. "Yes," Ilya said. "It could get even worse if this continues much longer." Ilya made a few comments about Andrei being a courageous man. I wasn't sure why he did so, but I carefully avoided getting involved in a discussion about

Andrei. Suppose Ilya wasn't a member of the conspiracy; even if he were, he wasn't supposed to talk about others who were. I pretended not to understand his references, though I had a funny feeling that Ilya was trying to tell me something. Confused, I decided to rest in my bunk. That way I would be ready when midnight arrived. Soon I was fast asleep, dreaming what the camp takeover would look like.

Suddenly I heard rifle shots and small explosions. Then a voice in Russian came over a bullhorn warning us to stay inside. There were more rifle shots and the sporadic rattling of a machine gun or two. Somebody yelled that Block #4 was on fire.

When the shooting stopped I ventured outside. All the watchtowers were burning, and some SS guards were on the ground, flat on their backs. Andrei appeared holding an automatic, still pointing it at a burning tower, with several hand grenades dangling from his belt. He wore a German helmet, which made him look very odd. There must have been more than a hundred armed Russian prisoners sweeping the camp grounds. They moved in small groups, crouching and surveying the ground.

The Austrian Home Guards were the first to be overpowered and disarmed; their rifles were used against the guards in the towers. The Home Guards had been taken prisoner inside one of the barracks. Nobody tried to harm them; they were for the most part old and harmless. The SS guards took off from their compound, leaving most of their heavy weapons and lots of canned food. There were about thirty of them, mostly Lithuanians and Ukrainians. At first they attempted to resist, but quickly they changed their minds.

The electricians of the conspiracy succeeded in cutting the power lines and telephone lines; later they secured an opening into the guardhouse. As I watched the camp gate being barricaded somebody called my name. I turned and saw Dimitri with a group of others rushing toward the main gate. "Come along," he yelled out, "we need help." I ran as fast as I could.

Andrei feared that the SS might decide to come back to take revenge; he thought it would be wise to fortify the gate. So we brought down a machine gun and several cases of ammunition and set up at the gate, lining up a long row of gasoline bombs against the fence. Other machine-gun nests were set up at various points; we filled potato sacks with earth and stacked them around the guns.

The place was beginning to look like an armed camp although not everybody had a gun. By now hundreds of Russians were engaged in fortifying the camp; whoever was still able to walk lent a hand. Captured food was brought to the camp kitchen where prisoner-cooks busily prepared our first soup in days. A group of armed prisoners left for the nearby farms and returned with a wagon loaded with foodstuffs. Everyone seemed to know what had to be done.

Andrei was the undisputed leader. He shouted commands to his lieutenants, who in turn passed them on down the ranks. So this was what he had been talking about.

I felt someone pulling at my sleeve; my next-bunk neighbor decided to wake me because I was yelling and making all kinds of sounds in my sleep. "Were you fighting a war?" he asked. "I guess I was dreaming. Don't mind me," I said apologetically.

The liberation scenes were still vivid in my mind when the morning lineup was called. The old Austrian guards were still everywhere, even in the towers. Was it possible that the SS guards had left? Was my dream real, or was I still dreaming?

It must have been early afternoon when suddenly we heard voices coming from the compound yelling "Amerykance, Amerykance." Three American reconnaissance tanks with white stars painted on them rumbled along a nearby road on their way to Linz. I ran outside with the hundreds of others who could still run. I was overwhelmed. I know I was screaming, but I don't know what it was I was saying. Two tanks stopped at the gate with their engines running, their steel bulks covered with dried mud. Helmeted soldiers with smiling faces appeared in the gun turrets, their eyes covered with goggles. I tried to remember the few words of English I knew, but I didn't think they

were appropriate. I addressed the soldiers in French. When one of them asked "Who are you?" I didn't know what to say, however; I wasn't sure who I really was. "Liberté," I yelled, not being able to think of anything else. The soldier just smiled and waved at me. Does this mean I'm free? I wondered as I ripped the cloth tag with my number—#88415, will I ever forget it?—off my jacket.

It would be impossible to describe the exhilaration that several thousand starved, sick, and exhausted people were able to generate when only two hours earlier they would not have dreamed that such an event was possible. Prisoners riddled with typhus and fever, prisoners who had not walked in days, rose from their bunks and crawled to see the tanks for themselves. Everyone was laughing and crying at once. We wanted to kiss the tanks, if we could only get close enough.

The Americans had not known that we—or the camp—existed. They had to move on, they told us, toward Linz; they assured us, however, that the war was almost over, would be in a day or two at most. Some hours later Red Cross ambulances arrived with Allied medical personnel, and the camp was turned into a field hospital.

Soon a strong odor of disinfectant permeated the place; everything seemed to be saturated with it. Inside the barracks long lines of sick prisoners, naked to the waist, their rib cages hollow-looking, stood patiently waiting to be examined by doctors. I walked away from the lineup; I wanted to get as far away from death as I possibly could. I couldn't stand being in Gusen another minute. Through the open window of the sick bay I saw piles of corpses, some with their eyes still open.

Before leaving I went to look for Andrei to say good-bye. I walked through the camp asking people if they had seen him, but no one could say for certain that they had, and some didn't even know what he looked like. With a heavy heart I walked alone through the gate. Outside I linked up with four friends; starved as we were, we set out on the road to Linz. Spring was in full swing; the warm air was invigorating, and the bright colors were nearly blinding. I was able to breathe at last. I couldn't believe I was free again.

MADNESS WITHOUT HEAD

by Jayne Cortez

They say it swoops down at midnight
  in a throat to throat search

They say it swaggers forward softens up the
system
and installs gratitude behind the eyes of a dreamer

They say it hides in the entertainment section
  of an electric cage
and enters through a voice of apologetic tremors
  and gyrating lips

They say it's a form of madness
the kind of madness disguising its mouth as a
  wagon wheel
a madness carving its tonsil into a machine gun
the madness painting itself black
and filling the balcony with darkness
the madness singing its heart out to the balcony
  through
the wagon wheel in machine gun moans
and when the moans become flames and the
  darkness dies
then this madness closes its mouth
  pulls back its heart
takes off the wagon wheel and puts on another
  pair
of lips and a rose
and then madness presses its lips to the rose and
starts a light show
and then madness fills the auditorium with
  lightness
and then madness becomes a soul lightener
  singing

through the lips of the rose in the light
of america the beautiful
and then madness pretending to need love
is infiltrated with applause
and then madness infiltrated with applause
and believing its own publicity
walks the waters in a fashion show to New
  Zealand
and then madness escalated with dreams
becomes too big for its lips
and then madness losing its lips becomes a security risk
and then madness sinking into grief without lips
becomes too little for its wigs
and then madness without wagon wheel without
  applause
without dreams without lips all alone now
sticks its head in the oven
and then madness losing its head becomes
madness without head
a madness that can't eat itself up
a madness that'll run in circles forever

the madness that swoops down a midnight
in a throat to throat search

They say it swaggers forward softens up the
  system
and installs gratitude behind the eyes of a dreamer
they say it interrogates the soul
and waits in the shade during the heat of initiation
  they say it hides

in the entertainment section of the electric cage
and enters through a voice of apologetic tremors
and gyrating lips

they say it's a form of impersonation
the kind of impersonation they call madness
the madness known as forever madness

THE WORST THING BILL CLINTON HAS DONE

by Peter Edelman

A Clinton appointee who resigned in protest over the new welfare law explains why it is so bad and suggests
how its worst effects could be mitigated

I hate welfare. To be more precise, I hate the welfare system we had until last August, when Bill Clinton signed a historic bill ending "welfare as we know it." It was a system that contributed to chronic dependency among large numbers of people who would be the first to say they would rather have a fob than collect a welfare check every month—and its benefits were never enough to lift people out of poverty. In April of 1967 I helped Robert Kennedy with a speech in which he called the welfare system bankrupt and said it was hated universally, by payers and recipients alike. Criticism of welfare for not helping people to become self-supporting is nothing new.

But the bill that President Clinton signed is not welfare reform. It does not promote work effectively and it will hurt millions of poor children by the time it is fully implemented. What's more, it bars hundreds of thousands of legal immigrants—including many who have worked in the United States for decades and paid a considerable amount in Social Security and income taxes—from receiving disability and old-age assistance and food stamps, and reduces food stamp assistance for millions of children in working families.

When the President was campaigning for re-election last fall, he promised that if reselected he would undertake to fix the flaws in the bill. We are now far enough into his second term to look at the validity of that promise, by assessing its initial credibility and examining what has happened since.

I resigned as the assistant secretary for planning and evaluation at the Department of Health and Human Services last September, because of my profound disagreement with the welfare bill. At the time, I confined my public statement to two sentences, saying only that I had worked as hard as I could over the past thirty-plus years to reduce poverty and that in my opinion this bill moved in the opposite direction. My judgment was that it was important to make clear the reasons for my resignation but not helpful to politicize the issue further during an election campaign. And I did want to see President Clinton reelected. Worse is not better, in my view, and Bob Dole would certainly have been worse on a wide range of issues, especially if coupled with a Republican Congress.

I feel free to speak out in more detail now, not to tell tales out of school but to clarify some of the history and especially to underscore the damage the bill will do and explain why the bill will be hard to fix in any fundamental way for a long time to come. It is also important to understand what is being done and could be done to minimize the damage in the short run, and what would be required for a real "fix": a strategy to prevent poverty and thus reduce the need for welfare in the first place.

Four questions are of interest now. Did the President have to sign the bill? How bad is it really, and how can the damage be minimized as the states move to implement it? Can it be fixed in this Congress? What would a real fix be, and what would it take to make that happen?

DID THE PRESIDENT HAVE TO SIGN THE BILL?

Was the President in a tight political box in late July, when he had to decide whether to sign or veto? At the time, there was polling data in front of him showing that very few people were likely to change their intended vote in either direction if he vetoed the bill. But even if he accurately foresaw a daily pounding from Bob Dole that would ultimately draw political blood, the real point is that the President's quandary was one of his own making. He had put himself there, quite deliberately and by a series of steps that he had taken over a long period of time.

Governor Clinton campaigned in 1992 on the promise to "end welfare as we know it" and the companion phrase "Two years and you're off." He knew very well that a major piece of welfare-reform legislation, the Family Support Act, had already been passed, in 1988. As governor of Arkansas he had been deeply involved in the enactment of that law, which was based on extensive state experimentation with new welfare-to-work initiatives in the 1980s, especially GAIN in California. The 1988 law represented a major bipartisan compromise. The Democrats had given in on work requirements in return for Republican concessions on significant federal funding for job training, placement activities, and transitional child care and health coverage.

The Family Support Act had not been fully implemented, partly because not enough time had passed and partly because in the recession of the Bush years the states had been unable to provide the matching funds necessary to draw down their full share of job-related federal money. Candidate Clinton ought responsibly to have said that the Family Support Act was a major piece of legislation that needed more time to be fully implemented before anyone could say whether it was a success or a failure.

Instead Clinton promised to end welfare as we know it and to institute what sounded like a two-year time limit. This was bumper-sticker politics—oversimplification to win votes. Polls during the campaign showed that it was very popular, and a salient item in garnering votes. Clinton's slogans were also cleverly ambiguous. On the one hand, as President, Clinton could take a relatively liberal path that was nonetheless consistent with his campaign rhetoric. In 1994 he proposed legislation that required everyone to be working by the time he or she had been on the rolls for two years. But it also said, more or less in the fine print, that people who played by the rules and couldn't find work could continue to get benefits within the same federal-state framework that had existed since 1935. The President didn't say so, but he was building—quite incrementally

and on the whole responsibly—on the framework of the Family Support Act. On the other hand, candidate Clinton had let his listeners infer that he intended radical reform with real fall-off-the-cliff time limits. He never said so explicitly, though, so his liberal flank had nothing definitive to criticize. President Clinton's actual 1994 proposal was based on a responsible interpretation of what candidate Clinton had said.

Candidate Clinton, however, had let a powerful genie out of the bottle. During his first two years it mattered only insofar as his rhetoric promised far more than his legislative proposal actually offered. When the Republicans gained control of Congress in 1994, the bumper-sticker rhetoric began to matter. So you want time limits? the Republicans said in 1995. Good idea. We'll give you some serious time limits. We now propose an absolute lifetime limit of five years, cumulatively, that a family can be on welfare. End welfare as we know it? You bet. From now on we will have block grants. And what does that mean? First, that there will be no federal definition of who is eligible and therefore no guarantee of assistance to anyone; each state can decide whom to exclude in any way it wants, as long as it doesn't violate the Constitution (not much of a limitation when one reads the Supreme Court decisions on this subject). And second, that each state will get a fixed sum of federal money each year, even if a recession or a local calamity causes a state to run out of federal funds before the end of the year.

This was a truly radical proposal. For sixty years Aid to Families with Dependent Children had been premised on the idea of entitlement. "Entitlement" has become a dirty word, but it is actually a term of art. It meant two things in the AFDC program: a federally defined guarantee of assistance to families with children who met the statutory definition of need and complied with the other conditions of the law; and a federal guarantee to the states of a matching share of the money needed to help everyone in the state who qualified for help. (AFDC was never a guarantor of income at any particular level. States chose their own benefit levels, and no state's AFDC benefits, even when coupled with food stamps, currently lift families out of poverty.) The block grants will end the entitlement in both respects, and in addition the time limits say that federally supported help will end even if a family has done everything that was asked of it and even if it is still needy.

In 1995 the President had a new decision to make. What should he say about the Republican proposal? The Republicans started considering the issue in the House in the heady post-election period, when it seemed not at all dissonant for them to talk of reviving orphanages and turning the school lunch program into block grants. The Administration concentrated its fire on these exponentially extreme measures and said nothing about time limits and the destruction of the entitlement. The President won the public argument about orphanages and school lunches, but his silence on the rest of the bill made it more difficult to oppose the time limits and the ending of the entitlement. For months, while the Republican bill was going through the House and the Senate, the President said nothing further. He might have said, "This isn't what I meant in my campaign rhetoric of 1992." He might have said, "This is totally inconsistent with the bill that I sent up to the Hill last year." He might have sent up a new bill that clearly outlined his position. He might have insisted that the waivers he was giving the states so that they could experiment with reform under the existing law were a strategy superior to the Republican proposals. He did none of these things, despite importuning from Hill Democrats, outside advocates, and people within the Administration.

The House Democrats had remained remarkably unified in opposition to the House Republicans' bill, which gave new meaning to the word "draconian." But when Democratic senators were deciding how to vote on the more moderate Senate bill, which nonetheless contained the entitlement-ending block grants and the absolute time limit, they looked to the President for a signal. Had he signaled that he remained firm in opposing block grants and the arbitrary time limit, there is every reason to believe that all but a handful of Democratic senators would have stayed with him. The opposite signal left them with no presidential cover for a vote against the Senate bill. It invited them to vote for the bill.

Prior to the Senate vote on September 19, 1995, the President sent the signal that he could sign the Senate bill (but warned that he would veto a bill that was too much like the House version). The Senate Democrats collapsed and the Senate passed its version of the bill by a vote of 87 to 12. To make matters worse, the President had been presented with an analysis showing that the Senate bill would push more than a million children into poverty. The analysis had been commissioned from the Urban Institute by Secretary of Health and Human Services Donna Shalala's staff (specifically Wendell Primus, the deputy assistant secretary for human-services policy), and Shalala had personally handed it to the President on September 15.

THE BOTTOM, REACHED

THIS was *the* major milestone in the political race to the bottom. The President had said he was willing to sign legislation that would end a sixty-year commitment to provide assistance to all needy families with children who met the federal eligibility requirements. In the floor debate Senator Edward Kennedy, who voted against the bill, described it as "legislative child abuse."

In late 1995 and early 1996 the Republicans saved the President from having to make good on his willingness to sign a welfare block-grant bill by sending him versions of the bill that contained horrible provisions concerning food stamps, disabled children, and foster care, which he vetoed. The Republican strategy at the time was to run against the President as a hypocrite who talked welfare reform but wouldn't deliver when he had the chance.

But President Clinton was not finished. Perhaps he saw some threat to himself in the Republican strategy. Perhaps he did not see the entitlement as being quite so meaningful as others did. It is important to remember that he is not only a former governor but the former governor of Arkansas. AFDC benefits in Arkansas were so low that he might not have seen the entitlement as meaning what it does in higher benefit states. He might have thought that as governor of Arkansas he would have been able to design a better program if he had received the federal money in the form of a block grant, without the restrictions, limited as they were, that were imposed by the federal AFDC program. And many people have remarked that he seems never to have met a governor he didn't like—an observation that appeared valid even after the 1994 elections reduced the number of Democrats in the gubernatorial ranks.

Whatever the reason, when the governors came to town for their winter meetings early last year, the President invited them to draft and submit new proposals on welfare and, for that matter, Medicaid. For a time it seemed to some observers that the President might even be willing to consider block grants for Medicaid, but it quickly became apparent that Medicaid block grants would have negative consequences for a much larger slice of the electorate than would welfare block grants. Large numbers of middle- income people had elderly parents in nursing homes whose bills were paid by Medicaid—to say nothing of the potential impact on hospitals, physicians, and the nursing homes themselves, all of which groups have substantial political clout. Welfare had no politically powerful constituency that would be hurt by conversion to block grants.

Hill Republicans, still pursuing the strategy of giving the President only bills that he could not sign, tied the governors' welfare and Medicaid proposals into a single bill. It was clear that the President would veto the combined bill, because by spring he had come out firmly block grants for Medicaid.

As of late spring it looked as if a stalemate had been reached, and that 1996 might pass without enactment of a welfare bill. Behind the scenes, however, White House political people—Rahm Emanuel and Bruce Reed, in particular—were telling Hill Republicans almost daily that if they separated the welfare and Medicaid bills, they could get a bill that the President would sign. In early summer a new dynamic arose on the Hill. House Republicans, especially freshmen, began to worry that they were vulnerable to defeat on the basis that they had accomplished so little of what they had come to Washington to do. Thinking that

Bob Dole was a sure loser anyway, they decided to save their own skins even though it would be to the detriment of the Dole candidacy. The Republicans decided to separate welfare and Medicaid, and began to move a freestanding welfare bill through Congress. The Senate and House bills were each roughly comparable to the respective Senate and House bills passed in 1995, but this time the conference outcome was very different: the conference produced a bill that was fairly close to what the Senate had passed. This time the Hill Republicans wanted the President to sign it.

The game was over. Now no one could ever say again with any credibility that this President is an old liberal.

How Bad is it, Really!

BEFORE I begin my critique, I need to say something about the motivations of those who genuinely support this new approach. Some of them, anyway, had in my estimation gotten impatient with the chronicity of a significant part of the welfare caseload and the apparent intractability of the problem. I believe they had essentially decided that handing everything over to the states was the only thing left to try that didn't cost a huge amount of money. They may well understand that there will be a certain amount of suffering, and may believe that the bucket of ice cold water being thrown on poor people now will result in a future generation that will take much more personal responsibility for itself and its children. I think they have made a terrible mistake, as I will try to show, but I respect the frustration that motivated at least some of them.

How bad, then, is it? Very bad. The story has never been fully told, because so many of those who would have shouted their opposition from the rooftops if a Republican President had done this were boxed in by their desire to see the President reelected and in some cases by their own votes for the bill (of which, many in the Senate had been foreordained by the President's squeeze play in September of 1995).

The same de facto conspiracy of silence has enveloped the issue of whether the bill can be easily fixed. The President got a free ride through the elections on that point because no one on his side, myself included, wanted to call him on it. He even made a campaign issue of it, saying that one reason he should be reelected was that only he could be trusted to fix the flaws in the legislation. David Broder wrote in *The Washington Post* in late August that reelecting the President in response to this plea would be like giving Jack the Ripper a scholarship to medical school.

Why is the new law so bad? To begin with, it turned out that after all the noise and heat over the past two years about balancing the budget, the only deep, multi-year budget cuts actually enacted were those in this bill, affecting low-income people.

The magnitude of the impact is stunning. Its dimensions were estimated by the Urban Institute, using the same model that produced the Department of Health and Human Services study a year earlier. To ensure credibility for the study, its authors made optimistic assumptions: two thirds of long-term recipients would find jobs, and states would maintain their current levels of financial support for the benefit structure. Nonetheless, the study showed, the bill would move 2.6 million people, including 1.1 million children, into poverty. It also predicted some powerful effects not contained in the previous year's analysis, which had been constrained in what it could cover because it had been sponsored by the Administration. The new study showed that a total of 11 million families—10 percent of all American families—would lose income under the bill. This included more than eight million families with children, many of them working families affected by the food-stamp cuts, which would lose an average of about $1,300 per family. Many working families with income a little above what we call the poverty line (right now $12,158 for a family of three) would lose income without being made officially poor, and many families already poor would be made poorer.

The view expressed by the White House and by Hill Democrats, who wanted to put their votes for the bill in the best light, was that the parts of the bill affecting immigrants and food stamps were awful (and would be re-addressed in the future) but that the welfare-reform part of the bill was basically all right. The immigrant and food-stamp parts of the bill are awful, but so is the welfare part.

The immigrant provisions are strong stuff. Most legal immigrants currently in the country and nearly all future legal immigrants are to be denied Supplemental Security Income and food stamps. States have the option of denying them Medicaid and welfare as well. New immigrants will be excluded from most federal means-tested programs, including Medicaid, for the first five years they are in the country. All of this will save about $22 billion over the next six years— about 40 percent of the savings in the bill. The SSI cuts are the worst. Almost 800,000 legal immigrants receive SSI, and most of these will be cut off. Many elderly and disabled noncitizens who have been in the United States for a long time and lack the mental capacity to do what is necessary to become citizens will be thrown out of their homes or out of nursing homes or other group residential settings that are no longer reimbursed for their care.

The food-stamp cuts are very troubling too. Exclusive of the food-stamp cuts for immigrants, they involve savings of about $24 billion. Almost half of that is in across-the-board cuts in the way benefits are calculated. About two thirds of the benefit reductions will be borne by families with children, many of them working families (thus reflecting a policy outcome wildly inconsistent with the stated purposes of the overall bill). Perhaps the most troubling cut is the one limiting food stamps to three months out of every three years for unemployed adults under age fifty who are not raising children. The Center on Budget and Policy Priorities describes this as "probably the single harshest provision written into a major safety net program in at least 30 years" —although it turns out that more states than the drafters anticipated can ask for an exception that was written to accommodate places with disproportionate unemployment. One of the great strengths of food stamps until now has been that it was the one major program for the poor in which help was based only on need, with no reference to family status or age. It was the safety net under the safety net. That principle of pure need- based eligibility has now been breached.

Neither the cuts for immigrants nor the food-stamp cuts have anything to do with welfare reform. Many of them are just mean, with no good policy justification. The bill also contains other budget and benefit reductions unrelated to welfare. The definition of SSI eligibility for disabled children has been narrowed, which will result in removal from the rolls of 100,000 to 200,000 of the 965,000 children who currently receive SSI. Although there was broad agreement that some tightening in eligibility was warranted, the changes actually made will result in the loss of coverage for some children who if they were adults would be considered disabled. Particularly affected are children with multiple impairments no one of which is severe enough to meet the new, more stringent criteria. Child-nutrition programs have also been cut, by nearly $3 billion over six years, affecting meals for children in family day care and in the summer food program. Federal funding for social services has been cut by a six-year total of $2.5 billion. This is a 15 percent cut in an important area, and will hamper the states in providing exactly the kind of counseling and support that families often need if a parent is going to succeed in the workplace.

So this is hardly just a welfare bill. In fact, most of its budget reductions come in programs for the poor other than welfare, and many of them affect working families. Many of them are just cuts, not reform. (The bill also contains an elaborate reform of federal child-support laws, which had broad bipartisan support and could easily have been enacted as separate legislation.)

This brings us to welfare itself. Basically, the block grants mean that the states can now do almost anything they want—even provide no cash benefits at all. There is no requirement in the new law that the assistance provided to needy families be in the form of cash. States may contract out any or all of what they do to charitable, religious, or private organizations, and provide certificates or vouchers to recipients of assistance which can be redeemed with a contract organization. So the whole system could be run by a corporation or a

religious organization if a state so chooses (although the latter could raise constitutional questions, depending on how the arrangement is configured). Or a state could delegate everything to the counties, since the law explicitly says that the program need not be run "in a uniform manner" throughout a state, and the counties could have varying benefit and program frameworks. For good or for ill, the states are in the process of working their way through an enormous—indeed, a bewildering— array of choices, which many of them are ill equipped to make, and which outside advocates are working hard to help them make well.

The change in the structure is total. Previously there was a national definition of eligibility. With some limitations regarding two-parent families, any needy family with children could get help. There were rules about participation in work and training, but anybody who played by the rules could continue to get assistance. If people were thrown off the rolls without justification, they could get a hearing to set things right, and could go to court if necessary. The system will no longer work that way.

The other major structural change is that federal money is now capped. The block grants total $16.4 billion annually for the country, with no new funding for jobs and training and placement efforts, which are in fact very expensive activities to carry out. For the first couple of years most of the states will get a little more money than they have been getting, because the formula gives them what they were spending a couple of years ago, and welfare rolls have actually decreased somewhat almost everywhere (a fact frequently touted by the President, although one might wonder why the new law was so urgently needed if the rolls had gone down by more than two million people without it).

Many governors currently crowing about this "windfall" of new federal money. But what they are not telling their voters is that the federal funding will stay the same for the next six years, with no adjustment for inflation or population growth, so by 2002 states will have considerably less federal money to spend than they would have had under AFDC. The states will soon have to choose between benefits and job-related activities, with the very real possibility that they will run out of federal money before the end of a given year. A small contingency fund exists for recessions, and an even smaller fund to compensate for disproportionate population increases, but it is easy to foresee a time when states will have to either tell applicants to wait for the next fiscal year or spend their own money to keep benefits flowing.

The bill closes its eyes to all the facts and complexities of the real world and essentially says to recipients, Find a job. That has a nice bumper-sticker ring to it. But as a one-size-fits-all recipe it is totally unrealistic.

Total cutoffs of help will be felt right away only by immigrants and disabled children—not insignificant exceptions. The big hit, which could be very big, will come when the time limits go into effect—in five years, or less if the state so chooses—or when a recession hits. State treasuries are relatively flush at the moment, with the nation in the midst of a modest boom period. When the time limits first take effect, a large group of people in each state will fall into the abyss all at once. Otherwise the effects will be fairly gradual. Calcutta will not break out instantly on American streets.

To the extent that there are any constraints on the states in the new law, they are negative. The two largest—and they are very large—are the time limit and the work-participation requirements.

There is a cumulative lifetime limit of five years on benefits paid for with federal money, and states are free to impose shorter time limits if they like. One exception is permitted, to be applied at the state's discretion: as much as 20 percent of the caseload at any particular time may be people who have already received assistance for five years. This sounds promising until one understands that about half the current caseload is composed of people who have been on the rolls longer than five years. A recent study sponsored by the Kaiser Foundation found that 30 percent of the caseload is composed of women who are caring for disabled children or are disabled themselves. The time limits will be especially tough in states that have large areas in chronic recession—for ex-

ample, the coal-mining areas of Appalachia. And they will be even tougher when the country as a whole sinks into recession. It will make no difference if a recipient has played by all the rules and sought work faithfully, as required. When the limit is reached and the state is unable or unwilling to grant an exception, welfare will be over for that family forever.

Under the work-participation requirements, 25 percent of the caseload must be working or in training this year, and 50 percent by 2002. For two-parent families 75 percent of the caseload must be working or in training, and the number goes up to 90 percent in two years. The Congressional Budget Office estimates that the bill falls $12 billion short of providing enough funding over the next six years for the states to meet the work requirements. Even the highly advertised increased child-care funding falls more than $1 billion short of providing enough funding for all who would have to work in order for the work requirements to be satisfied. States that fail to meet the work requirements lose increasing percentages of their block grants.

The states are given a rather Machiavellian out. The law in effect assumes that any reduction in the rolls reflects people who have gone to work. So states have a de facto incentive to get people off the rolls in any way they can, not necessarily by getting them into work activities.

The states can shift a big chunk of their own money out of the program if they want to. There is no matching requirement for the states, only a maintenance-of-effort requirement that each state keep spending at least 80 percent of what it was previously contributing. This will allow as much as $40 billion nationally to be withheld from paying benefits over the next six years, on top of the $55 billion cut by the bill itself. Moreover, the 80 percent requirement is a static number, so the funding base will immediately start being eroded by inflation.

Besides being able to transfer some of their own money out, the states are allowed to transfer up to 30 percent of their federal block grants to spending on child care or other social services. Among other things, this will encourage them to adopt time limits shorter than five years, because this would save federal money that could then be devoted to child care and other help that families need in order to be able to go to work. Hobson's choice will flourish.

The contingency fund to cushion against the impact of recessions or local economic crises is wholly inadequate—$2 billion over five years. Welfare costs rose by $6 billion in three years during the recession of the early nineties.

The federal AFDC law required the states to make decisions on applications within forty-five days and to pay, retroactively if necessary, from the thirtieth day after the application was put in. There is no such requirement in the new law. All we know from the new law is that the state has to tell the Secretary of Health and Human Services what its "objective criteria" will be for "the delivery of benefits," and how it will accord "fair and equitable treatment" to recipients, including how it will give "adversely affected" recipients an opportunity to be heard. This is weak, to say the least.

FIFTY WELFARE POLICIES

Given this framework, what can we predict will happen? No state will want to be a magnet for people from other states by virtue of a relatively generous benefit structure. This is common sense, unfortunately. As states seek to ensure that they are not more generous than their neighbors, they will try to make their benefit structures less, not more, attractive. If states delegate decisions about benefit levels to their counties, the race to the bottom will develop within states as well.

I do not wish to imply that all states, or even most states, are going to take the opportunity to engage in punitive policy behavior. There will be a political dynamic in the process whereby each state implements the law. Advocates can organize and express themselves to good effect, and legislatures can frustrate or soften governors' intentions. There is another important ameliorating factor many welfare administrators are concerned about the dangers that lie in the new law and will seek to implement it as constructively as they can, working to avoid some of the more radical negative possibilities.

Citizens can make a difference in what happens in their state. They can push to make sure that it doesn't adopt a time limit shorter than five years, doesn't reduce its own investment of funds, doesn't cut benefits, doesn't transfer money out of the block grant, doesn't dismantle procedural protections, and doesn't create bureaucratic hurdles that will discourage recipients. They can press for state and local funds to help legal immigrants who have been cut off from SSI or food stamps and children who have been victimized by the time limits. They can advocate an energetic and realistic jobs and training strategy, with maximum involvement by the private sector. And they can begin organizing and putting together the elements of a real fix, which I will lay out shortly.

THE JOBS GAP

Even given effective advocacy, relatively responsive legislatures and welfare administrators, and serious efforts to find private-sector jobs, the deck is stacked against success, especially in states that have high concentrations of poverty and large welfare caseloads. The basic issue is jobs. *There simply are not enough jobs now.* Four million adults are receiving Aid to Families with Dependent Children. Half of them are long-term recipients. In city after city around America the number of people who will have to find jobs will quickly dwarf the number of new jobs created in recent years. Many cities have actually lost jobs over the past five to ten years. New York City, for example, has lost 227,000 jobs since 1990, and the New York metropolitan area overall has lost 260,000 over the same period. New York City had more than 300,000 adults in the AFDC caseload in 1995, to say nothing of the adults without dependent children who are receiving general assistance. Statistics aside, all one has to do is go to Chicago, or to Youngstown, Ohio, or to Newark, or peruse William Julius Wilson's powerful new book, *When Work Disappears*, to get the point. The fact is that there are not enough appropriate private sector jobs in appropriate locations even now, when unemployed employment is about as low as it ever gets in this country.

For some people, staying on welfare was dictated by economics, because it involved a choice between the "poor support" of welfare, to use the Harvard professor David Ellwood's term, and the even worse situation of a low-way job, with its take-home pay reduced by the out-of-pocket costs of commuting and day care, and the potentially incalculable effects of losing health coverage. With time limits these people will no longer have that choice, unappetizing as it was, and will be forced to take a job that leaves them even deeper in poverty. How many people will be able to get and keep a job, even a lousy job, is impossible to say, but it is far from all of those who have been on welfare for an extended period of time.

The labor market, even in its current relatively heated state, is not friendly to people with little education and few marketable skills, poor work habits, and various personal and family problems that interfere with regular and punctual attendance. People spend long spells on welfare or are headed in that direction for reasons other than economic choice or, for that matter, laziness. If we are going to put long-term welfare recipients to work—and we should make every effort to do so—it will be difficult and it will cost money to train people, to place them, and to provide continuing support so that they can keep a job once they get it. If they are to have child care and health coverage, that will cost still more. Many of the jobs that people will get will not offer health coverage, so transitional Medicaid for a year or two will not suffice. People who have been on welfare for a long time will too often not make it in their first job and will need continuing help toward and into a second job. Both because the private sector may well not produce enough jobs right away and because not all welfare recipients will be ready for immediate placement in a private-sector job, it will be appropriate also to use public jobs or jobs with nonprofit organizations at least as a transition if not as permanent positions. All of this costs real money.

For a lot of people it will not work at all. Kansas City's experience is sadly instructive here. In the past two years, in a very well-designed and well-implemented effort, a local program was able to put 1,409 out of 15,562 welfare recipients to work. As of last December only 730 were still at work. The efforts of Toby Herr and Project Match

in Chicago's Cabrini-Green public-housing project are another case in point. Working individually and intensively with women and supporting them through successive jobs until they found one they were able to keep, Herr had managed to place 54 percent of her clients in year-round jobs at the end of five years. This is a remarkable (and unusual) success rate, but it also shows how unrealistic is a structure that offers only a 20 percent exception to the five-year time limit.

I want to be very clear: I am not questioning the willingness of long-term welfare recipients to work. Their unemployment is significantly related to their capacity to work, whether for personal or family reasons, far more than to their willingness to work. Many long-term welfare recipients are functionally disabled even if they are not disabled in a legal sense. News coverage of what the new law will mean has been replete with heartbreaking stories of women who desperately want to work but have severe trouble learning how to operate a cash register or can't remember basic things they need to master. A study in the state of Washington shows that 36 percent of the caseload have learning disabilities that have never been remedied. Many others have disabled children or parents for whom they are the primary caretakers. Large numbers are victims of domestic violence and risk physical retaliation if they enter the workplace. These personal and family problems make such people poor candidates for work in the best of circumstances. Arbitrary time limits on their benefits will not make them likelier to gain and hold employment. When unemployment goes back up to six or seven or eight percent nationally, as it will at some point, the idea that the private sector will employ and continue to employ those who are the hardest to employ will be even more fanciful than it is at the current, relatively propitious moment.

When the time limits take effect, the realities occasioned by the meeting of a bottom-line-based labor market with so many of our society's last hired and first fired will come into focus. Of course, a considerable number will not fall off the cliff. An increased number will have obtained jobs along the way. The time limits will help some people to discipline themselves and ration their years of available assistance. Some will move in with family or friends when their benefits are exhausted. The 20 percent exception will help as well.

But there will be suffering. Some of the damage will be obvious—more homelessness, for example, with more demand on already strapped shelters and soup kitchens. The ensuing problems will also appear as increases in the incidence of other problems, directly but perhaps not provably owing to the impact of the welfare bill. There will be more malnutrition and more crime, increased infant mortality, and increased drug and alcohol abuse. There will be increased family violence and abuse against children and women, and a consequent significant spillover of the problem into the already overloaded child-welfare system and battered women's shelters.

CAN THE WELFARE BILL BE FIXED THIS YEAR?

I am amazed by the number of people who have bought the line that the bill was some little set of adjustments that could easily be done away with. Congress and the President have dynamited a structure that was in place for six decades. A solid bipartisan majority of Congress and the President himself have a stake in what they have already done. Fundamental change in the bill is therefore not possible this year. So the answer to the question is no, not in any fundamental way.

One possible area for adjustment is in the immigrant and food-stamp provisions. These occasioned the most hand wringing from the President and some of the people who voted for the bill. They could be changed without redoing everything. The President has made some proposals for limited change on these items.

The bigger question is welfare. If there is going to be a short-term fix of the new law, it will be not in the fundamentals of the new structure but rather in some of the details. It might possibly include the following, although I hasten to say that even this list stretches credulity.

- *Jobs.* Congress could make extra funds available to the states for job creation, wage subsidies, training, placement, support and retention

services, and so on. The President has proposed a fund of $3 billion over three years for this kind of activity, saying it would result in a million new jobs. As campaign rhetoric, this was pure spin. It amounts to $3,000 per job. There is simply no way in which $3,000 per job will get a million jobs for people who have been on the welfare rolls for extended periods of time. The President has also proposed a modest additional tax credit for hiring welfare recipients. This, too, will have little practical effect.

- *Time limits.* The Democrats tried very hard to create a voucher covering basic necessities for children in families that had run up against the time limit. The idea failed by a narrow margin in the Senate, and is worth pursuing. Another item worth advocating would be raising the 20 percent exception to the time limit to 25 or even 30 percent.

- *Work requirements.* The states are chafing under the requirements about the percentage of the caseload that has to be participating in work or related activities. It would help a little if people were permitted to receive vocational training for longer than the twelve months the law allows.

- *Limits on state flexibility in the use of funds.* The law is excessively flexible on what the states can do with the blockgrant funds. A number of possible changes would be helpful: reducing the percentage that can be transferred out of the block; raising the requirement for states' contributions of their own funds; requiring states to comply with the plans they adopt; requiring states to process applications for assistance expeditiously; and clarifying the procedural protections for people denied or cut off from assistance.

- *Data.* It is vitally important that adequate data be gathered and reported on what happens under the new legislation. The new law contains some funding for research and some instructions about data to be gathered, but additional funds and specification would be helpful.

If reliable and affordable health care and child care were added to this list, and were available beyond a transitional period, it would help a lot. However, my crystal ball tells me that whatever is enacted in these areas will be modest at best, and the new structure will remain substantially in place. And of course not even these adjustments would solve the fundamental problems created when the previous structure was dynamited: the disappearance of the national definition of eligibility and of the guarantee that federal funds will be available for all eligible children.

WHAT WOULD A REAL FIX INVOLVE?

A real fix would involve, first, jobs, jobs, jobs—preferably and as a first priority in the private sector, but also in the public sector, where there is real work to be done. And then everything that enables people to be productive citizens. Schools that teach every child as well as they teach every other child. Safe neighborhoods. Healthy communities. Continuing health-care and day-care coverage, so that people can not only go to work but also keep on working. Ending the racial and ethnic discrimination that plagues too many young people who try to enter the job market for the first time.

When we discuss jobs, we need to be talking about opportunities for men and women both. That may seem obvious, but the welfare bill skews our focus. By allocating to long-term welfare recipients such a large share of the limited resources available for jobs and training, we may be draining funds and attention from others who deserve to be a higher priority. Inner-city young men come particularly to mind. We need to be promoting responsible fatherhood, marriage, and two-parent families. If young men cannot find work, they are far less likely to marry. They may have children, but economics and low self-esteem may defeat responsibility. Tough child-support enforcement is part of the solution, but genuine opportunity and clear pathways to opportunity are vital.

The outside world tends to believe that the inner city is hopeless. (I do not mean to neglect strategies to reduce rural poverty.) That is not the case. In the toughest neighborhoods, with all the dangers and pitfalls of street life, there are young people who beat the odds, stay in school and graduate, and go to college or get a job. These young people have exceptional strength and resiliency. But there are many more who could make it with a little extra support and attention. It is enormously important that we increase the number of young people who make it. We give a lot of lip service to prevention, whether of crime or drug abuse or teen pregnancy. But we will never prevent these negative outcomes as well as we could until we pursue a general strategy of creating opportunity and clear pathways to opportunity—a positive youth-development strategy.

Many of the jobs that welfare recipients and other low income people get do not pay enough to pull them out of poverty. Continuing attention to the minimum wage and the Earned Income Tax Credit will be necessary. States should insist, as the city of Baltimore has, that all their contractors pay all their workers a sufficient wage to keep them out of poverty (or at least approximately enough to keep a family of four out of poverty), and should fund their contracts accordingly. Current child-care and health-care policies are insufficient to allow low-wage workers to stay out of poverty even if transitional subsidies let them escape temporarily when they leave the welfare rolls. Federal and state childcare subsidies should help all workers who would otherwise be poor, not just those who have recently left the welfare rolls. And at the end of the day we still have 40 million Americans, including 10 million children, who do not have health coverage. We still have to deal with that as part of a real antipoverty strategy.

We have been reduced to the politics of the waitress mom. She says, all too legitimately, "I bust my tail. I don't have decent child care. I don't have health coverage. Why should 'these people' get what I don't have?" We started to bring greater equity to the working poor but, except for the recent minimum-wage increase, progress was halted by the 1994 congressional elections. A real fix would help the waitress mom as well as those a rung below her on the income ladder.

We are not just talking policy; we are talking values. We are talking people, especially young people growing up, who understand that they have to take responsibility for themselves, both as earners and as parents.

Personal responsibility and community responsibility need to intersect. The community has a responsibility to help instill and nurture values. The community has a responsibility to offer support, especially to children and youths, so that everyone has an opportunity to acquire the tools necessary to achieve the personal responsibility that is such a vital element in the equation. The community has a responsibility to help parents do their job. And community means something different from programs, something larger, although programs are part of the equation. Liberals have tended to think in terms of programs. The community's taking responsibility is a much larger idea. But communities cannot succeed in isolation. National leadership and policy are essential as well.

Welfare is what we do when everything else fails. It is what we do for people who can't make it after a genuine attempt has been mounted to help the maximum possible number of people to make it. In fact, much of what we do in the name of welfare is more appropriately a subject for disability policy. The debate over welfare misses the point when all it seeks to do is tinker with welfare eligibility, requirements, and sanctions. The 1996 welfare law misses the point.

To do what needs to be done is going to take a lot of work—organizing, engaging in public education, broadening the base of people who believe that real action to reduce poverty and promote self-sufficiency in America is important and possible. We need to watch very carefully, and we need to document and publicize, the impact of the 1996 welfare legislation on children and families across America. We need to do everything we can to influence the choices the states have to make under the new law. We *can* ultimately come out in a better place. We should not want to go back to what we had. It was not good social policy. We want people to be able to hold up their heads and raise their children in dignity. The best that can be said about this terrible legislation is that perhaps we will learn from it and eventually arrive at a better approach. I am afraid, though, that along the way we will do some serious injury to American children, who should not have had to suffer from our national backlash.

Everyday Exposure to Toxic Pollutants

Environmental regulations have improved the quality of outdoor air. But problems that persist indoors have received too little attention

by Wayne R. Ott *and* John W. Roberts

Imagine that a killer is on the loose, one who shoots his victims and flees. Police investigators would undoubtedly respond by visiting each crime scene and meticulously searching for clues. They would photograph the body, take fingerprints and question witnesses. An autopsy would recover the bullet for tests. The authorities could then use this information to establish exactly who was responsible.

But suppose the police took a different approach. What if they decided to start by examining all the guns that had recently been fired? Surely one of these weapons, they could argue, was involved. And they would be correct. They might even succeed in identifying the murderer—but not until after they had expended tremendous energy looking over a great number of firearms carried by law officers, soldiers and duck hunters. In a world of limited resources, they would probably run out of time and money before they came close to finding the culprit.

Surprisingly, officials charged with guarding the general population from toxic pollutants rely almost universally on the second strategy. Most environmental laws in the U.S. seek to control only the release of potentially dangerous wastes into the air and water, not the amount of contact people actually have with those pollutants. This focus on emissions rather than exposure essentially disregards the reality that toxic substances produce health problems only if they reach the body.

That oversight is, to some extent, understandable: for far too long, little information existed about the extent to which most citizens were exposed to the pollutants that the nation controls. Regulators seldom knew with any certainty the number of people affected by a given pollutant, the severity of exposure or the specific sources of the worrisome chemical. The result was that of officials focused on limiting pollution from the most apparent sources, such as automobiles and factories, while failing to address many other important but less obvious ones.

Fortunately, the science of assessing people's exposure to toxic substances has matured. In particular, scientists have developed highly sensitive analytical instruments and portable monitoring devices. Researchers have exploited this equipment in large-scale field studies, designed to gauge just where and how people are exposed to potentially dangerous chemicals.

Getting Personal

In 1980 one of us (Ott), along with Lance A. Wallace of the U.S. Environmental Protection Agency, launched the first serious efforts to assess everyday exposure of the general population to toxic substances. That program, carried out primarily by the Research Triangle Institute in North Carolina and other contract research organizations, later expanded to include some two dozen studies in 14 U.S. states. Using the same methods, researchers sponsored by private industry conducted similar studies in a 15th state (Alaska) and in one Canadian province. Most of these investigations employed monitoring instruments that were small and light enough for people to carry as they went about their normal activities. These devices showed which pollutants existed close by and in what concentration. In some cases, the researchers also made measurements of the food and water consumed. In certain instances, they determined the blood levels of various pollutants from breath samples.

So far these studies of "total human exposure" have examined the prevalence of volatile organic compounds, carbon monoxide, pesticides or dangerous particles in the daily lives of more than 3,000 subjects, a carefully chosen slice of the population meant to be representative of most

North Americans living in urban or suburban areas. Chemical analyses of the samples were detailed enough to identify the specific chemicals to which the participants were routinely exposed. For instance, the investigations of volatile organic compounds typically tested for some 30 different chemicals, including many known to cause cancer in people or animals.

It is difficult to know whether the contacts most people have with these substances pose an especially large health risk, because the capacity for low levels of each compound to cause sickness is exceedingly hard to estimate. Still, these studies produced results that were disturbing: most citizens were very likely to have the greatest contact with potentially toxic pollutants not outside but inside the places they usually consider to be essentially unpolluted, such as homes, offices and automobiles. The exposure arising from the sources normally targeted by environmental laws—Super-fund sites, factories, local industry—was negligible in comparison.

Even in the New Jersey cities of Bayonne and Elizabeth, both of which have an abundance of chemical processing plants, the levels of 11 volatile organic compounds proved much higher indoors than out. (Concentrations of the other volatile compounds tested were found to be insignificant in both settings.) The chief sources appeared to be ordinary consumer products, such as air fresheners and cleaning compounds, and various building materials.

Could everyday items with which people happily share their homes truly be more of a threat to their health than industrial pollution, even for people whose communities are surrounded by factories? In short, the answer is yes. For example, benzene—a chemical known to cause leukemia in workers continually exposed to high concentrations—is present in gasoline and in some household products. It is also one of about 4,000 chemicals found in tobacco smoke, so living with a smoker raises one's exposure to benzene enormously.

In 1985 Wallace combined all the existing information about how several hundred people located in five different states were exposed to this com-

pound. He found that the average concentration of benzene they inhaled was nearly three times higher than typical outdoor levels. He calculated that some 45 percent of the total exposure of the U.S. population to benzene comes from smoking (or breathing smoke exhaled by others), 36 percent from inhaling gasoline fumes or from using various common products (such as glues), and 16 percent from other home sources (such as paints and gasoline stored in basements or attached garages). He attributed only 3 percent of the average person's exposure to industrial pollution.

In contrast, government regulators usually consider only the gross amount of benzene released into the general environment, for which the largest share comes from automobiles (82 percent), followed by industry (14 percent) and domestic sources (3 percent). Cigarettes contribute only 0.1 percent of the total. Wallace's work aptly demonstrated that cutting all industrial releases of benzene would reduce health risks by only a tiny fraction. Yet even a modest reduction in cigarette smoking—the smallest source of benzene in the atmosphere—would significantly reduce the likelihood of benzene causing disease.

Many other volatile organic compounds that are quite toxic at high concentrations are also more prevalent indoors than out. For example, the chemical tetrachloroethylene (also known as perchloroethylene or "perc"), which has been shown to cause cancer in laboratory animals, is used to dry-clean clothes. Thus, the greatest exposure occurs when people live in a building with dry-cleaning facilities, wear recently dry-cleaned clothes or store such chemically laden garments in their closets. Moth-repellent cakes or crystals, toilet disinfectants, and deodorizers are the major source of exposure to paradichlorobenzene, which also causes cancer in animals. Studies have consistently indicated that almost all exposure to paradichlorobenzene comes from sources inside homes, from industrial emissions or hazardous waste sites.

Although assessments of the risks to health are somewhat uncertain, it is clear that less contact with toxic volatile organic compounds is better than more. Most people can limit potentially harmful exposure by avoiding products that contain such pollutants. But other worrisome vapors are difficult to avoid.

For example, the major sources of exposure to chloroform—a gas that provokes concern because it can cause cancer in animals subjected to high concentrations—are showers, boiling water and clothes washers. It forms from the chlorine used to treat water supplies. Because piped water is something that people simply cannot do without, the only way to minimize household exposure to chloroform is to drink bottled water (or tap water that is run through a good-quality charcoal filter) and to improve ventilation in the bathroom and laundry.

Better airflow can also help lower exposure to carbon monoxide, a product of incomplete combustion that robs the blood of oxygen and can be particularly harmful to people with heart ailments when inhaled at levels often found indoors. Although studies conducted in the early 1980s in Denver and Washington, D.C., confirmed that carbon monoxide levels rose precipitously when people were in or near motor vehicles, other research has demonstrated that indoor appliances, such as poorly operated gas stoves, grills and furnaces, can also cause extremely unhealthful conditions— even death. Fortunately, outdoor levels of carbon monoxide have steadily declined in the U.S. in concert with the reductions in automobile emissions, as required by federal regulations. Yet further progress will be more difficult because on the U.S. population now receives greater exposure to carbon monoxide than out.

Another environmental concern that appears more severe indoors is the danger from fine particles in the air. In one study, researchers used miniaturized monitors to collect minute particles in and around 178 homes in Riverside, Calif. Respondents carried devices that gathered particles 10 microns or less in diameter, ones small enough to penetrate into the lungs.

Curiously, exposures during the day were about 60 percent greater than expected from the particulate levels measured in samples of air concurrently taken indoors and outside. The higher exposures arose, at least in part, because people do not simply float through the air; rather they tend to stir up "personal clouds" of particle-laden dust from their surroundings as they move about. These investigators showed that most of these fine particles form through combustion—such as smoking, cooking, burning candles or firewood. Finding such pollutants indoors is troubling, because recent epidemiological studies have associated elevated concentrations of fine particles outdoors with premature death.

Even more disturbing were the results from two studies of indoor air contaminants conducted during the late 1980s Jacksonville, Fla., and Springfield, Mass. In those places, investigators found that indoor air contained at least five (but typically 10 or more) times higher concentrations of pesticides than outside air—and those residues included insecticides approved only for outdoor use. Evidently, potent chemicals targeted against termites in the foundations of these houses had found their way indoors. Such poisons can be tracked in on people's shoes, or they may seep through the soil as a gas into homes. Chlordane (which was taken out of products sold for home use in 1988) and some other pesticides contaminating the air indoors caused a greater share of exposure than the amounts found on food.

In addition, people sometimes apply inappropriate pesticides directly to indoor surfaces, unaware that they are causing their own high exposures. And even the most enlightened homeowners are often ignorant of past applications of dangerous chemicals. Pesticides that break down within days outdoors may last for years in carpets, where they are protected from the degradation caused by sunlight and bacteria. This persistence is well demonstrated by measurements of the pesticide DDT (dichlorodiphenyl-trichloroethane), which was outlawed U.S. in 1972 because of its toxicity. Despite that long- standing prohibition of Southern Jonathan D. Buckley of the University of Southern California and David E. Camann of the Southwest Research Institute found that 90 of the 362 Midwestern homes they examined in d 1993 had DDT in the carpets.

Indeed, that study showed that the ants lurking in people's carpets restricted to pesticides. In more than half of the households Buckley and Camann surveyed, the concentrations of seven toxic organic chemicals called polycyclic aromatic hydrocarbons (compounds produced by incomplete combustion which cause cancer in animals and are thought to induce cancer in humans) were above the levels that would trigger a formal risk assessment for residential soil at a Super-fund site.

SMALL PEOPLE, BIG PROBLEMS

The pesticides and volatile organic compounds found indoors cause 3,000 cases of cancer a year in making these substances just as threatening to nonsmokers as radon (a natural radioactive gas that enters many homes through the foundation) or secondhand tobacco smoke. And toxic house dust can be a particular menace to small children, who play on floors, crawl on carpets and regularly place their hands in their mouths. Infants are particularly susceptible: their rapidly developing organs are more prone to damage, they have a small fraction of the body weight of an adult and may ingest five times more dust—100 milligrams a day on the average.

Before 1990, when the EPA and U.S. Department of Housing and Urban Development established standard methods for sampling dust on carpets, upholstery and other surfaces, it was difficult to quantify the risk to children. Since then, however, improved techniques have allowed scientists to make more concrete statements about the degree of exposure. For example, we can now estimate that each day the average urban infant will ingest 110 nanograms of benzo(a)pyrene, the most toxic polycyclic aromatic hydrocarbon. Although it is hard to say definitively how much this intake might raise a child's chance of acquiring cancer at some point, the amount is sobering: it is equivalent to what the child would get from smoking three cigarettes.

The research also points out that, for small children, house dust is a major source of exposure to cadmium, lead and other heavy metals, as well as polychlorinated biphenyls and other persistent organic pollutants. Carpets are most troublesome because they act as deep reservoirs for these toxic compounds (as well as for dangerous bacteria and asthma-inducing allergens, such as animal dander, dust mites and mold) even if the rugs are vacuumed regularly in the normal manner. Plush and shag carpets are more of a problem than flat ones; floors covered with wood, tile or linoleum, being the easiest to clean, are best.

One of us (Roberts), along with several colleagues, has shown that people can prevent the accumulation of dangerous amounts of dust by using a vacuum equipped to sense when no more particles can be extracted. Other of our studies have indicated that simple preventive acts can help considerably. For example, wiping one's feet on a commercial-grade doormat appears to reduce the amount of lead in a typical carpet by a factor of six. Because lead exposure is thought to affect more than 900,000 children in the U.S., the use of good doormats would translate into a significant boost to public health.

Removing one's shoes before entering is even more effective than just wiping one's feet in lowering indoor levels of the toxic pollutants that contaminate the environs of most homes (such as lead from peeling paint and pesticides from soils around the foundation). By taking such precautions to avoid tracking in dust and using an effective vacuum cleaner—one equipped with a rotating brush and, preferably, a dust sensor—people can reduce the amount of lead and many other toxic substances in their carpets to about a tenth (or, in some cases, to a hundredth) of the level that would otherwise persist.

Unfortunately, most people are unaware of the ubiquity of indoor pollution or of how to reduce it. One innovative initiative by the American Lung Association in Seattle aims to remedy that problem by training volunteers (dubbed "master home environmentalists") to visit dwellings and help residents limit domestic environmental threats.

TROUBLE WITH THE LAW

The many findings now available from multiple studies of people's everyday exposure all point to a single conclusion—that the same air pollutants covered by environmental laws outdoors are usually found at much higher levels in the average American residence. This situation has come about, at least in part, because the U.S. has made remarkable progress in improving the quality of outdoor air over the past three decades by controlling automobile and industrial emissions. Of the hundreds of air pollutants covered under existing U.S. laws, only ozone and sulfur dioxide remain more prevalent outdoors.

So it is peculiar that more attention has not yet shifted toward indoor pollution, the main sources of which are not difficult to identify. In fact, they are right under people's noses—moth repellents, pesticides, solvents, deodorizers, cleansers, dry-cleaned clothes, dusty carpets, paint, particleboard, adhesives, and fumes from cooking and heating, to name a few.

Sadly, most people—including officials of the U.S. government—are rather complacent about such indoor pollutants. Yet if these same substances were found in outdoor air, the legal machinery of the Clean Air Act of 1990 would apply. If truckloads of dust with the same concentration of toxic chemicals as is found in most carpets were deposited outside, these locations would be considered hazardous-waste dumps. In view of the scientific results comparing indoor and outdoor exposure, it would seem that the time is now ripe for a major rethinking of the nation's environmental laws and priorities.

The initial version of the Clean Air Act, written in 1970, focused on outdoor pollution. Even in its 1990 revision, the law has not changed much. It does not address the fact that Americans spend 95 percent of their time inside: despite all the evidence available today, the act still relies exclusively on measurements taken at outdoor monitoring stations. Many other U.S. laws pertaining to air pollution, hazardous waste, toxic substances and pesticides are similarly flawed, because they do not require accurate information on the levels of exposure people receive.

Although the absolute level of health risk posed by many toxic pollutants may be elusive, scientists can now accurately measure the exposure caused by different sources. Hence, to protect public health best, the broad suite of environmental laws should be reexamined and judged by how effectively they reduce people's total exposure rather than by how they reduce total emissions. That effort would surely be substantial, both to recast a large body of legislation and to monitor how well the laws work to reduce exposure. But the payoff would be a dramatic reduction in health costs as well as an improvement in the economy and effectiveness of environmental regulation.

Americans concerned about toxic substances do not have to wait for their government to make these far-reaching changes. Reducing exposure normally demands only modest alterations in one's daily routine. Yet people cannot take the simple steps required without adequate knowledge. So increased education is needed. Laws requiring more detailed labeling would also help: If a product contains a dangerous pollutant, should not the manufacturer be required at least to list the chemical by name on the package? Armed with a better understanding of the toxic substances found in common products and in other sources at home, people could then make their own informed choices.

THE AUTHORS

WAYNE R. OTT and **JOHN W. ROBERTS** have long studied environmental threats to health. Ott served for 30 years in the Environmental Protection Agency, managing research on air pollution, toxic substances and human exposure. He now does research in the departments of statistics and environmental engineering at Stanford University. Roberts helped to develop the surface samplers used by the EPA to measure pollutants in carpet dust. In 1982 he founded Engineering Plus, a small firm in Seattle specializing in assessing and controlling exposure to dangerous pollutants in the home. He works frequently with the master home environmentalist program in Seattle *to* help reduce the exposure of families to indoor pollutants.

Further Reading

NON-OCCUPATIONAL EXPOSURE TO PESTI-CIDES FOR RESIDENTS OF Two U.S. CITIES. R. W. Whitmore, F. W. Immerman, D. E. Camann, A. E. Bond and R. G. Lewis in *Archives of Environmental Contamination and Toxicology,* Vol. 26, No. 1, pages 47-59; January 1994.

EXPOSURE OF CHILDREN TO POLLUTANTS IN HOUSE DUST AND INDOOR AIR. J. W. Roberts and P. Dickey in *Reviews of Environmental Contamination and Toxicology,* Vol. 143, pages 59-78; 1995.

HUMAN EXPOSURE TO ENVIRONMENTAL POLLUTANTS: A DECADE OF EXPERIENCE L A. Wallace in *Clinical and Experimental Allergy,* Vol. 25, No. 1, pages 4-9; 1995.

HUMAN EXPOSURE ASSESSMENT: THE BIRTH OF A NEW SCIENCE. W. R. Ott in *Journal of Exposure Analysis and Environmental Epidemiology* (available from Princeton Scientific Publishing), Vol. 5, No. 4, pages 449-472; 1995.

HISPANIC ETHNICITY, THE ETHNIC REVIVAL, AND ITS CRITIQUE

by Suzanne Oboler

The Mainstream Response: Creating a "Hispanic Ethnicity"

The experiences of Puerto Ricans and Mexican Americans in the United States were long excluded from popular historical knowledge, ensuring that until the mid-1960s, neither group received national attention and their respective histories in this country remained largely invisible and unknown to the public at large. In fact, despite their repeated efforts to make their demands for political inclusion heard, when the mainstream media of the late 1960s did cover their mobilizations, they were often portrayed as groups that were organizing for full citizenship rights for the first time:

> Tio Taco—or Uncle Taco, the stereotype Mexican-American sapped of energy and ambition, sulking in the shadow of an Anglo culture—is dead.... From the ghettos of Los Angeles, through the wastelands of New Mexico and Colorado, into the fertile reaches of the Rio Grande valley in Texas, a new Mexican-American militancy is emerging.... Given the plight of the Mexican—Americans, the only surprising thing about the *movimiento chicano* is that it took so long to get started.'

Thus proclaimed the June 29, 1970, issue of *Newsweek,* for example, noting the regional diversity of Mexican Americans' experiences in the western and southwestern states, even as it emphasized the historical and widely accepted stereotyped version of them as passive victims of their own lack of ambition. While the magazine's article recognized that the forms of their militancy of the 1960s did give credence to the assertion that the "death" was irreversible, *Newsweek's* description of the "new" Chicano militancy nevertheless ignored their long history of protest, revolt, and political organization throughout the Southwest and California. Thus, if one were to believe *Newsweek's* portrayal of the "newness" of the 1960s Chicano movement, the stereotypes of Mexican Americans' passivity and lack of ambition of the past could easily be reinterpreted as historical "facts."

In view of each group's specific forms of protest stemming from its particular demands and respective historical ties to the United States, it is not surprising that initially, when each group did receive national media attention, it was not as "Hispanics," but as Puerto Ricans and as Chicanos or Mexican Americans. But in the context of an emerging awareness of the two largest Spanish-speaking minorities on the national scene, one cannot help but remark on a curious, tiny article related to "Hispanics" published on September 13, 1969, in a major national newspaper. Almost hidden in the middle of column 5 on page 17 of section I of the *New York Times*, the title words—"Hispanic Heritage Week Set"—like the one-square-inch article itself, are almost lost in the midst of the pronounced headlines and photographs announcing the day's socialite "nuptials" and engagements. The article is so short that it is worth quoting in its entirety:

> Washington, Sept. 12 (UPI). President Nixon today designated next week as National Hispanic Heritage Week in tribute to the Spanish-speaking Americans and to promote ties with Latin American neighbors. In a proclamation, Mr. Nixon said that this particular week was set aside because it included the dates of September 15 and 16, when five Central American nations—Guatemala, Honduras, El Salvador, Nicaragua, Costa Rica and Mexico—celebrate independence days.

Although the Presidential Proclamation 3930 of September 12 explains that the recognition of Hispanic culture had been requested by Congress the year before, the question of why the very different historical and cultural legacies and experiences of the Mexican Americans and the Puerto Ricans were now to be homogenized precisely when their movements were emphasizing their indigenous Latin American roots, rather than Spanish European legacies, was never addressed. Why, one cannot help but ask, in this period of national emergence of Chicanos and

Puerto Ricans and in view of their specific divergent demands and cultural affirmation as two *distinct groups,* would the president of the United States designate a "Hispanic Heritage" week? Unfortunately, the article limits its explanation to noting that the choice of the week coincided with the independence days not only of Mexico but also of Central American nations whose populations at that time were numerically among the least represented in the United States.

In fact there were very few representatives of other Latin American nationalities in the United States at the time of the proclamation. Political refugees from the Cuban Revolution after 1960 constituted a recent and numerical exception. Like most of the South Americans and Central Americans in the United States at the time, the Cubans were racially and socially homogeneous representatives of the Latin American elite—white, middle- and upper-class bankers and professionals, often highly educated and literate in English. Many of them had previously visited the United States, owned real estate properties, had long established business and financial ties in Florida, and were familiar with American cultural values and norms. Still, compared with the Puerto Ricans and Mexican Americans, their numbers, like those of the Dominicans and of the Central and South Americans in the country at the time, were also not significant.

To a certain extent, the federal government's decision to proclaim a Hispanic Heritage Week must have been influenced by the new presence of Puerto Rican and Mexican-American leaders in Washington. Indeed, one plausible explanation for the proclamation is that recognition of a Spanish-speaking "ethnic group" was in keeping with the emergence of a new way of defining U.S. society, one based on the recognition of "ethnic groups" and the concomitant reevaluation of the theory of the melting pot. Moreover, as I suggested in chapter 2, people of Latin American descent—regardless of their country of origin, race, or class—had never been differentiated in terms of their individual nationalities; rather, following the rise of the ideological superiority of the "new breed" of American, they had been lumped together as "Mexicans" and non-Anglos as early as the period of the Conquest of the Southwest. In this respect, the use of a term such as "Hispanic" in the late 1960s and early 1970s to homogenize the experiences of people with ties to Latin America in the United States was not new. But it did serve to blur the distinctions between the newly affirmed national and cultural identities emphasizing indigenous and third world legacies and the concomitant and respective demands made by Mexican Americans/Chicanos and Puerto Ricans.

The proclamation made no mention of the largely mestizo, indigenous, and/or black populations that make up the majority of the Central American nations whose independence the proclamation celebrates, nor of the indigenous and mestizo cultural roots that both the Chicanos and the Puerto Ricans emphasized in their movements. Instead, it focused on the Spanish European legacy of "Hispanics" in the New World, excluding from its definition any consideration of indigenous and black populations. This emphasis cannot be underestimated, for a few years later in the mid-1970s, the federal government's guidelines for "racial and ethnic" categories were to emphasize that the designation "native American" was to be exclusively used for North American indigenous populations in the United States, drawing the line at the U.S.-Mexican border. As a result, as Jack Forbes has cogently argued, the ethnic and racial categories issued by federal agencies have meant that Native Americans from Latin America (regardless of their lack of Spanish language and culture) are considered, along with black Latin Americans, to be subgroups of the "Hispanic" category. One of the results of these categories, overtly adhering to political and bureaucratic criteria, has been in effect to obscure awareness of the indigenous and black roots of many Latin American immigrants in the United States, while simultaneously preventing indigenous refugee populations fleeing repression and discrimination by Latin American governments, or guerrilla actions on their villages, from seeking political asylum in the United States. Thus Nixon's proclamation, renewed every year and reinforced by later census definitions of Hispanics, paved the way for what Forbes called "a conscious effort . . .

to build a *historically European Spanish-based and Spanish dominated group rather than a regional 'Latin' group or a regional 'American' group*"—known today as Hispanics in the United States.

The struggle to raise the national community's awareness of the long historical and cultural legacies of Chicanos and Puerto Ricans during the specific period in which the term Hispanic began to be disseminated was thus largely dissipated by the fusion of the two groups into a newly created "ethnic group" with a new notion of its heritage and identity in the United States.

It is true that the post-1960s *public* awareness—*at the federal and national levels*—of the existence of populations of Latin American descent was unprecedented in the history of the United States. At the same time, it is important to note that the traditions, history, and experience of "the Hispanics" have since been in the process of being "invented" and affirmed by politicians, mainstream social scientists, the media, advertising sectors, and the public at large. Referring to the establishment of Hispanic Heritage Week, Edna Acosta-Belén has correctly noted that "this proclamation was a symbolic recognition of the major role played by Hispanic groups in the past and present of this nation, from the early days of exploration, conquest and colonization of the Americas to the modern technological world of today."

But while on one level the proclamation of Hispanic Heritage Week may indeed have acknowledged the presence of Spanish-speaking populations in the United States, it did so at the expense of publicly acknowledging the respective histories and demands of the two distinct national-origin groups, as well as the distinct political status of Puerto Rico. Thus, rather than signifying a new national and public recognition of these populations' "major role" in this country's history, the proclamation of Hispanic Heritage Week can instead be better understood, as the following pages suggest, as yet another sign of the significant shift in the mainstream perception of U.S. society as a "melting pot" and a consequent new approach to the way the "American community" would be imagined in the post-1960s period.

REIMAGINING THE AMERICAN COMMUNITY: THE DEBATE ON THE MELTING POT

Throughout much of the twentieth century, the image of the melting pot—whether in its "Anglo-conformity," "assimilation," or "cultural pluralism" versions—served to encapsulate the way the American community was imagined. Coined by the playwright Israel Zangwill in 1909, the term *melting pot* embodied the idea that the cultures of immigrants arriving in the United States would mix with one another to create a new "American" population. But by World War I, Zangwill's original vision had been "drastically" narrowed down to the belief that "to be 100 percent American . . . was to be Anglo-American." Even today, some scholars and sectors of the U.S. population still perceive the melting pot as "the dominant metaphor guiding our understanding of ethnic relations."

But in the early 1960s, a few scholars began to refute the image of the melting pot, focusing on the enduring impact of ethnicity to suggest instead that U.S. society should be perceived as a plurality of ethnic groups with competing interests. As racial minorities' diverse movements increasingly gained national attention, references to "new" culturally and politically homogeneous ethnic groups of "Hispanics," "Native Americans," "Blacks," and "Asians" began to appear in scholarly works and the national media of the post-1960s. The rejection of the melting pot definition of American culture was explained in terms of the emergence of a new notion of equality, an equality of difference, rather than of opportunities. Hence, Stephen Thernstrom's description of the 1960s celebration of ethnicity:

> In the 1960s and 1970s, the United States experienced a cultural earthquake. Or so it seemed from reading the press or watching the tube. The "unmeltable ethnics" were on the rise, and the WASPs—revealingly, the only remaining ethnic slur permissible in enlightened circles—were on the run.
>
> At congressional hearings on the bilingual education act, a congressman from New York announced that "we have discarded the philosophy of the melting pot. We have a new concept of the value of enhancing, fortifying, and protecting differences,

the very differences that make our country such a great country."

Thus, previously hierarchized at the symbolic level according to their origins and racial composition, ethnic groups, both old and "new," were now socially and culturally perceived horizontally by both scholars and public opinion makers.

Nevertheless, in spite of the 1960s celebration of ethnicity and the subsequent emphasis on ethnic studies and theories, the image of the melting pot continues to appear in some studies on ethnicity and race to this day, leading one study to note that the metaphor is "yet to be replaced." Some scholars continue to argue that the "melting pot really did happen," particularly in terms of past white European groups. At the same time, pointing to the "rapidity and thoroughness with which [old immigrant groups] assimilated," Thernstrom, for example, has argued that "channels of opportunity like those open to earlier immigrants have at long last opened to [blacks and various other American racial minorities]." The problems confronting the latter, he suggests, stem from the emphasis placed on securing *group* rights, which in his view are "likely to be ineffectual and probably counterproductive." As a result, the extent to which opportunities are actually open and made available to all persons within these groups is blurred. Arguing that "equality of persons and equality of groups… are two very different things" and recognizing the difficulty of coalition building between poor blacks and whites, Thernstrom suggests that rather than continuing to support affirmative action, which benefits more affluent and educated minorities, new measures should be devised aimed at achieving "greater equality of persons," measures that would "redistribute income toward the poor of all races."

Other scholars, however, have insisted that the lack of rights and recognition of nondominant ethnic *groups* in U.S. society has historically been determined by the dynamics of race and class. Non-white-European people and those of low-class status have long been citizens in this country and have experienced neither the assimilation nor the cultural pluralism predicted by either the melting pot hypothesis or later mainstream ethnic assimilation theories. Thus, rooting their analysis in the historical context of exclusion, as a result of which Chicanos and Puerto Ricans, like other minorities during the 1960s, mobilized for rights and group recognition, these analysts reject the concept of the melting pot as an explanation of various groups' experiences in the United States. They strongly suggest the need for a continued emphasis on group rights and affirmative action programs in the struggle to improve all minority persons' access to full citizenship, social justice, and rights.

Within the context of this debate, the case of the Hispanics is particularly interesting to explore, given that this "ethnic group" includes both Mexican Americans and Puerto Ricans—historically present as racialized national minority groups in the United States—as well as the large numbers of post-1960s Latin American immigrants who have now also been officially designated as Hispanics in the United States. As I argue in the following sections, the 1960s focus on ethnicity as an approach to understanding the current processes of incorporation of diverse groups with ties to Latin America obscures the class and racial dynamics of the interaction both within each group and between them and the society at large. In spite of the differences in their time of arrival, as well as their unique class and racial heterogeneity, the automatic incorporation of Latin American immigrants as "instant Hispanic ethnics," members of the "Hispanic" group *as it is defined in the U.S. context,* is at best reinforcing Latin American cultural traditions and language and at worst once again rewriting the respective histories of the Chicano and Puerto Rican populations. Indeed, as the issues raised by the bilingual education debate and the English Only movement exemplify, both the past invisibility of these groups as citizens of the United States and the concomitant historical stereotypes stemming from their foreignness to the style in which the "national community" is imagined continue to be solidified by the reemergence of these issues in increasingly nativist terms.

ETHNICITY AS AN EXPLANATION OF IMMIGRANT INTEGRATION

A series of scholarly reinterpretations of American history and contemporary society focusing on the political, social, cultural, and linguistic aspects of ethnicity in the United States appeared in the period from 1960 to the 1980s. Although these works continue to support the idea of the eventual assimilation of particular groups, their purpose was to document the ways in which each group's ethnic cultures and identities affected their assimilation trajectory and continued to persist in American society.

In 1963, for example, Nathan Glazer and Daniel Moynihan sought to explain the persistence of different ethnic groups in American society by arguing that they represented interest groups that established ties to the broader society in those terms. A year later, Milton Gordon developed a paradigmatic model that was to substantiate this approach to ethnic groups. Noting the extent of acculturation following the first generation, Gordon argued that the study of immigrants should distinguish between assimilation in terms of their cultural behavior, which had been "massive and decisive," and the effects of race and religion, which hindered their structural assimilation.

Others soon began to use Gordon's cultural/structural ethnic assimilation framework to present historical, cultural, linguistic, and sociological accounts of the experiences of past immigrant groups. Leonard Dinnerstein and David Reimers, for example, used it to present the history of U.S. immigration, providing a chronological account of the incorporation of the successive waves of immigrant "ethnics" into U.S. life. Joshua Fishman focused on specific aspects of cultural integration, studying the dynamics of language maintenance as indicative of the continued cultural "authenticity" of specific ethnic groups. While some have applied quantitative methods to the reconstruction of the experiences of Jews and Italians of the past, others have verified the process of assimilation of past Jewish immigrants using qualitative research among the second generation. Thus, as Silvia Pedraza-Bailey has pointed out, Gordon's study on various forms of assimilation has served as the basis for much of the research on ethnicity since the 1960s, whether to emphasize "ethnic identification" or to examine "tangible outcomes, such as occupation, education and income."

The framework has also been used in some studies about the populations who arrived in the post-1960s period from third world countries to analyze their progress in becoming "new ethnics." Joseph Fitzpatrick, for example, studied later waves of Puerto Ricans, focusing on the cultural differences underlying the assimilation process of this group, while Shih-Shan Henry Tsai explored the variations in the types of assimilation within the Chinese community. Both viewed the integration of these groups as continuing the patterns of previous waves of immigrant-ethnic groups. Speaking of the Chinese, for example, Tsai explains:

> The newcomers have demonstrated during the past two decades that they, like the eighteenth-century French Huguenots, nineteenth-century German forty-eighters, and the twentieth-century Russian Jews, have adapted to American culture and therefore have succeeded in their diaspore experience.

But since the 1980s, other studies on the more recent third world immigrant populations have increasingly criticized the ethnic assimilation paradigm, pointing to its inadequacy for understanding the experience of nonwhite immigrant groups arriving today in the United States. In his study of the Haitian population in New York, for example, Michel Laguerre concluded that it is "the racist structure of American society" rather than Haitians' own decision to adopt the U.S. ethnic categorizations "which compels them to use ethnicity in their adaptation process." As a result, he argues for "refining" the theory of ethnicity, to include generational, class, and racial dimensions in the process of studying the adaptation of nonwhite European immigrants to the United States—a point also raised by Clara Rodríguez in her study on Puerto Ricans.

Moreover, scholars have increasingly recognized the importance of accounting for the effects of transnationalism as new immigrant populations continuously interact across borders and between the home country and the host society, constructing in the process what one scholar has called a "transnational socio-cultural system." Shaping new identities, lives, and views on integration in the United States, the emphasis of this approach is on the effects of the restructured global economic context in shaping new immigrant flows, a context in which "the comforting modern imagery of nation-states and national languages, of coherent communities and consistent subjectivities, of dominant centers and distant margins no longer seems adequate."

Indeed, the transnational perspective has clarified that several factors contribute to the inadequacy of the 1960s ethnic assimilation paradigm for understanding the more recent experience of nonwhite immigrants—among them the historical elusiveness of the definition of ethnicity and ethnic identity, the lack of a clear theoretical framework that incorporates the shifting nature of the historical and economic conjunctures in which immigrants arrive in this country, and the neglect of the impact of the racial and class dimensions in assessing immigrants' experiences and life chances in U.S. society.

ETHNIC ASSIMILATION: A CRITIQUE

A review of the vast body of literature on ethnic groups of the period from 1960 to 1980 leaves little doubt as to the elusiveness of the definitions of ethnicity and ethnic identity. H. J. Abramson provided a brief history of the term *ethnicity* within the context of assimilation/pluralism versions of American society, noting that although the usage of the concept of ethnicity is recent, "the idea is old." Although Abramson suggests that this idea was conveyed in the past through terms like "immigrant group, foreign stock, language group, race and national background," other scholars have noted that the definition of ethnicity in the United States has always been historically contingent and cannot be separated from the class position of immigrants and minorities in this country. As Stephen Greer has noted, "ethnic" has been used to refer to poor white immigrants (at the turn of the century), then to black Americans (who were "yet to be included in the mainstream"), and finally, during the 1960s Great Society and civil rights era, no longer representing arriving newcomers but rather "a record of an alternative, a more truly American style."

Indeed, lacking in most studies on ethnicity is contextualization about the definition and uses of both the very notion of ethnicity itself and a recognition of the shifting meaning and historical nature of labels in society. If, as noted in chapter 3, naming oneself is, in Richard King's words, "an act of profound personal, social, and political significance," then of equal importance is recognizing the detrimental effects of focusing on identifying *which* particular fixed, subjective cultural traits underly "ethnic solidarity" for developing our understanding of both the historical contingency and continuous complex process of social life.

While not denying the importance of individual self-definitions or of group pride, some scholars have noted the recurrent lack of a contextual framework and of specific "objective" criteria in the study of ethnic groups leading to studies that emphasize instead the need to define ethnicity in terms of the society's economic processes. Criticizing "academic intellectuals" who suggest that ethnicity today is increasingly symbolic, David Muga, for example, discusses the relationship between ethnic attribution and economic opportunity. He points to the nativist backlash, racism, and discrimination and concludes that those who view ethnicity as symbolic only "speak for a middle strata and all those who have achieved material 'success' within a capitalist society while remaining blind to how ethnicity has been most authentically preserved among the economically and politically pressed."

Other authors have criticized ethnicity theorists for their neglect of class and racial considerations. Attributing this neglect to the tendency to conflate the 1960s racial and ethnic forms of organization, Joan Moore argues that "the idea of caste and the ethnic-assimilationist model continues to suit a large group of social scientists who find the

ferment of the 1960s repugnant. The ethnic-assimilationist model fits extremely well with the neoconservative emphasis on 'pure' market factors as an explanation of status mobility and on cultural factors as an explanation of failure."

Thus, precisely because the dynamics of race and class are rarely seen as significant in ethnicity theorists' perceptions of past immigrants' integration into American society, the focus on ethnic assimilation has meant that the *power differences* in ethnic and minority status attributions are often neglected in the analysis of a particular group's social mobility and usually obscure within-group variations.

Approaching this discussion from a different perspective, Michael Omi and Harold Winant focus on the shifting meaning of race in this country's history to construct a framework from which to conceptualize race. They underline the implications of the genocide of native Americans, the enslavement of African Americans, the invasion and colonization of Mexican Americans, and the exclusion of Asian Americans in the nation's history. The key to their analysis is the recognition of the significance of race and the need to specify the "racial formation" of a specific historical period—the political, economic, and social forces that shape both the content and significance of racial categories and meanings at each historical conjuncture.

These critics of "ethnicity" theorists argue against what they call the "immigrant analogy"—the idea that "blacks" and other "nonwhite minorities" could or should be analyzed in terms of their adherence to the patterns of assimilation of previous white immigrants. While they agree that in the 1960s "white-ethnics" returned to their roots and celebrated their advances from their *racially white* immigrant forebearers, they suggest that nonwhite, racial minority groups—long excluded from the immigrant advancement version of the melting pot by legally sanctioned discriminatory practices—organized not as "ethnic groups" but rather in racial terms. As the respective sixties movements of African Americans, Chicanos, Puerto Ricans, and other minority groups exemplify, this form of organization was a political device in their confrontation with the state and their struggle for social equality and full-citizenship rights before the law. Thus Omi and Winant suggest that rather than agree to "become" ethnics and accept the equal opportunity legislation that would allow African Americans, for example, to follow the "example" of previous white immigrant ethnics, "many blacks (and later, many Latinos, Indians and Asian Americans as well) rejected *ethnic* identity in favor of a more radical *racial* identity which demanded group rights and recognition." As I suggested in chapter 2, the historical acknowledgment of the presence of African Americans in the United States did not necessarily mean that they were perceived as equal members of the nation. As Ronald Takaki has argued, the citizenship and suffrage guaranteed by the 1790 naturalization laws to all men of white European ethnic origins arriving in the United States was historically denied to all men of color—establishing a "sharp distinction between ethnicity and race." Thus Omi and Winant argue that the important distinction between racial and ethnic forms of organization, long neglected in the literature on ethnicity, reemerged yet again during the 1960s and was at odds with the aims and goals of the various minority movements.

In fact, the strongest challenge to ethnicity approaches has come from analysts who critique the ways that the distinction made between race and ethnicity has shaped American history. Ideologically, the use of the term *melting pot* had contained an implicit idea of equality, at least at the level of the equality of rights and opportunities of all the citizens it embraced. Yet the very history of the United States bears witness to the existence of legally supported racial discrimination and widespread prejudice. As E. San Juan Jr. has argued, "From its inception, the United States has been structured as a racial order," and thus, as seen in chapter 2, race has historically been the basis for the construction of a social hierarchy according to which members of different ethnic groups were granted or denied citizenship rights and responsibilities.

The importance attributed to ethnicity in the political and social events of the 1960s to 1980s is indicative of the extent to which the social modes of clarifying the national identity of the United States cannot be separated from the historical forms that racism has taken. One has only to recall the black liberation movement's emphasis, during the years of the 1960s, on black pride, identity, and cultural heritage as an example of how social and political issues had to be raised and channeled within cultural referents in order to be heard in a now "ethnically awakened" multicultural society.

That sectors of the black liberation movement, like those of the Chicano and Puerto Rican movements, were to channel their demands within cultural referents is actually not surprising. For as seen above, the testimony to the power of cultural classifications is recorded most clearly in the history of race relations and their legislation in the United States. The 1896 *Plessy v. Ferguson* Supreme Court ruling in favor of segregation on the curious grounds that "legislation is powerless to eradicate racial instincts" is itself a telling example of the state's overt differentiation between prejudice and discrimination in terms of the power of these classifications. At the time of its enactment, this ruling contributed to the social recognition that blacks' lower socioeconomic position was in fact *illegitimate* in a social structure that "measured" status not only socioeconomically but also culturally and educationally. The use of segregation as a lived manifestation of status measurements contributed to the development of the "separate but equal" rationalization of a class society in which race has been the motive force underlying the social formation throughout most of U.S. history. Hence the distinction between race and ethnicity, as noted in chapter 2, stems at least in part from the historical distinctions made by the law itself between prejudice and discrimination. Not surprisingly, "minority" intellectuals and activists have increasingly played a significant role in exploring the implications of distinguishing race from ethnicity. Insofar as the minority movements and riots of the sixties showed the extent to which race had historically played a pivotal role in preserving and reproducing the social order, it is perhaps not surprising that many mainstream analyses of the 1960-80 "ethnic revival" period are being challenged specifically on racial grounds today.

The distinction between ethnicity theory and minority demands and practices during the 1960s is particularly interesting to explore in the light of the historically contingent definition of the term *ethnic* and the way its meaning has continuously been renegotiated in the context of the ongoing social and power *repositioning* of assimilated "acceptable Americans." While the latter are defined as those in a position to have the "benefit of social and political inclusion," their opposites, "unacceptable Americans," are perhaps not so easily defined. As seen in chapter 2, the very ideological definition of American national identity has historically been largely based on an "act of choice" by both the individual and the society.

Indeed, the struggle for "social and political inclusion" of minorities is exemplified through the battle to establish the (legal) right to bilingual education and its implementation in the schools. As Arnold Liebowitz has argued, "Official acceptance or rejection of bilingualism in American schools is dependent upon whether the group involved is considered politically and socially acceptable." This struggle in turn clarifies the role of the state in both protecting minorities and reinforcing through law the relationship between race, class, and language.

THE DYNAMICS OF ETHNICITY, LANGUAGE, RACE, AND CLASS: THE BILINGUAL EDUCATION DEBATE AND THE ENGLISH ONLY MOVEMENTS

Key to understanding the ongoing social and power *repositioning* of who might be considered an "acceptable American" is the fact that, unlike the present time, earlier immigrants did not "need advanced English language skills to get jobs and survive in the less complex economic order of the time. Whatever problems such groups had, they were not as critical to economic survival as such language skills are now."

Indeed, particularly since the 1960s, there has been what might be called a significant increase in linguistic discrimination through the gradual politicization of language (whether English or not). This is visible in the discussions on ethnicity and

the significance attributed to "de-ethnization" as the basis for assimilation and integration into U.S. society. Seen in these terms, language is an integral part of these ethnicity debates on what it means to be American, what it means for a new American national identity, an *American ethnic-nationalism* in a now-awakened "multiethnic" society.

According to Joshua Fishman, indifference to ethnicity among assimilated Americans matches their indifference to the English language: People speak English because it is the language used to communicate in this country, "rather than because it is beautiful, divine or indivisible from American tradition." Publications of the English Only movement, represented by such groups as U.S. English and English First, agree with this assessment of Americans' relationship to the English language, although they draw a different political conclusion. The aim of these interest groups is to achieve a constitutional amendment that would declare English the official language of the United States. In a 1983 justification of their support for the English Language Amendment, or ELA, U.S. English wrote, "We hold no special brief for English. If Dutch (or French, or Spanish, or German) had become our national language, we would now be enthusiastically defending Dutch."

The stated indifference of "assimilated Americans" to the language per se is particularly interesting to explore in view of the historical battles to ensure the prevalence of English among arriving immigrants today. The battle over language policy and usage has been most apparent in the educational system itself, long recognized as the principal site for immigrant socialization and Americanization processes. Yet, it is important to consider that historically, non-English and bilingual instruction were actually quite common in the United States. For this raises the question not of why bilingual education "emerged" in the 1960s but rather why it was not federally recognized by formal legislation before.

As Maria Matute-Bianchi noted, the recent history of language legislation and bilingual-bicultural education describing federal intervention in public schools was an "intervention that was unknown prior to the passage of the Elementary and Secondary Education Act of 1965." In this sense, history thus points to the increasing political relevance, for the state, of language policy and its effects on the socialization and Americanization of non-English-speaking minorities and immigrants alike.

The language-related policies and debates that have emerged since the passing of the Bilingual Education Act in 1968 are perhaps the clearest indication of this process. For when the sixty-five-year-old "separate-but-equal" justification for school segregation was challenged and revoked by the Supreme Court's 1954 *Brown* decision, a new period of legislative debates and court cases did begin. But, with them, the issue of the ability of legislative action to effectively "eradicate racial instincts" was once again the underlying motif of the legal battles that have since been waged. Like the 1896 *Plessy* case, the court decisions over the past thirty years have centered on the issue of racial discrimination in education. Today, however, the protagonists of these more recent cases are not only, or primarily, African Americans. Rather, they are sectors of the "Hispanic" population who, together with other minority and immigrant groups and their children, are formally challenging not only the racial prejudice of yesteryear but also the deeply embedded myth of the melting pot.

The trajectory of this challenge is most visible in the political impact that the court cases by minorities concerning the right to bilingual-bicultural education have had (or have failed to have) on the ideological belief of the melting pot image of the national community. Furthermore, the results of their challenge to the existing social hierarchy can be partially summed up in its "unanticipated historical consequences" on the power of legislation to deal with racial and ethnic tensions since the late 1960s.

The 1968 Bilingual Education Act is "often hailed as a masterpiece of ambiguity" for failing both to define "bilingual education" and to specify its goals. In this sense, it was a linguistic "side effect," so to speak, of the antidiscrimination provision stipulated by Title VI of the 1964 Civil Rights Act. Indeed, the passing of the Bilingual Education Act seems to have been more the result of the prevail-

ing liberal mood rhetorically proclaiming the "equality of difference" than of a well-thought-out project aimed at addressing the issues specifically related to providing equal educational opportunity to each child. The definition of what constituted an American education (that is, the question of nationality in a pluralistic society with an increasingly heard ethnic-minority voice) was more important than the recognition that even within minority groups, there were significant distinctions concerning their social and educational needs and cultural heritages.

It took five years, for example, for the Supreme Court decision in *Keynes v. School District no. 1* to begin specifying the existence of various and diverse ethnic groups within the category of "minority." This 1973 decision stated that Spanish-speaking students could not be sent to schools with primarily African American student populations as a means of circumventing the 1954 *Brown v. Topeka Board of Education* decision against segregation. Similarly, the practical implications of implementing "equality of opportunity" in the American educational setting were raised only after the *Lau v. Nichols* decision of 1974, which ruled that "access to educational facilities and resources alone cannot be the sole determinants of a child's educational rights." In spite of the *Lau* decision's recognition of the need for "affirmative action," the type of action and its practical application and punitive fines for noncompliance remained unspecified by the courts, and thus the decision was not pursued by most school districts until the *Lau* remedies were stipulated the following year. The issue of what would constitute an appropriate plan was theoretically resolved in the 1973 *Serna v. Portales Municipal School* in New Mexico. This court had "established bilingual education programs as viable solutions in language-related issues."

However, the lack of specification of both the quality of instruction and the means to determine need and eligibility for such programs led to further confusion. Court case decisions such as *Otero v. Mesa County Valley School District no. 51* (1975) were successful in dismissing bilingual programs on the grounds that "few students in the district experienced any real language difficulties.

Therefore, the lack of evidence to substantiate a violation of Title VI or the Fourteenth Amendment and the lack of numbers resulted in the dismissal of the claimed right to bilingual education."

But, while there were successful attempts against bilingual programs, some advances were made through other court cases, such as the *Rios v. Reed* case. This court ruling recognized not only the importance of bilingual education and the 1974 Bilingual Education Act, but also that

> it is not enough simply to provide a program for disadvantaged children or even to staff the program with bilingual teachers; rather the critical question is whether the program is designed to assure as much as is reasonably possible the language-deficient child's growth in the English language. An inadequate program is as harmful to a child who does not speak English as no program at all.

In spite of renewed federal support for bilingual education in 1978 and during the 1980s, the resistance of school districts to implementing adequate programs and their lack of concern as to their effectiveness— like the society's own growing antipathy, if not prejudice, against immigrants and minority children and adults alike—has continued unabated from the bill's enactment to the present day.

While many within the bilingual education community would hope that their efforts ensure English language proficiency as much as they guarantee that children do not forget their native language skills, there is no doubt as to the transitional nature of most language programs in the United States. Nevertheless, during the 1980s, numerous attempts were made to deny the validity of bilingual education. Cases such as the 1972 *Aspira of New York City Inc. v. Board of Education of the City of New York* had successfully argued for defining criteria to assess and evaluate language proficiency as a means for determining students' needs for bilingual programs. Yet faulty studies in the late 1970s and in the 1980s soon purported to measure their effectiveness. Together with support from individuals within the federal government, such as former U.S. secretary of education William J. Bennett, these studies bolstered groups such as the English Only movement

who used nationalist discourse to lobby against ethnolinguistic diversity and in favor of declaring English the official language of the United States. Their movement's agenda appears to be to move from "English-only in government to English-only in society." In so doing they consistently negate the founding principles, which included tolerance for language differences and in fact receive consistent support from the courts, which at various points have upheld the unrestricted right to use foreign languages in the United States.

The Bilingual Education Act of 1968 evolved from a bill sponsored by Senator Ralph Yarborough of Texas, which initially sought to address the psychological trauma resulting from linguistic discrimination and the consequent high dropout rates from schools among Mexican Americans and Puerto Ricans. Although later extended to include all students with limited English-speaking proficiency, "Hispanics" have remained a primary target of the anti-bilingual education groups as well as of the English Only movements. Yet for obvious reasons, such as social class and the time of arrival of different individuals and groups, there are mixed levels of language proficiency within the Hispanic community. For English is the first language of second and later generations of Chicanos and Puerto Ricans, as well as of the children of other Latin American immigrants, all of whom have been raised and socialized in the U.S. school system. More recent immigrants and their children, particularly if they have working-class origins, on the other hand, usually only encounter the English language for the first time when they arrive in the United States. Although this disparity in language proficiency within the Hispanic community seems self-evident, nevertheless the focus of both the detractors of bilingual education and the lobbyists of the English Only movements is primarily on the lack of English language abilities (and hence on the new immigrants) rather than on long-established English dominant groups within the Hispanic community, such as the Mexican Americans/Chicanos and Puerto Ricans. Similarly, these movements ignore the scientifically established fact that by the second or at most third generation, non-English-speaking immigrants (including "Hispanics") have become fluent English speakers.

Thus, the real issue for the detractors of bilingual education and the adherents of the English Only movement is not equal educational opportunity for each child but rather their persistent refusal to acknowledge or tolerate difference, or as Ana Celia Zentella has bluntly stated, "The root of the problem lies in an inability to accept an expanded definition of an American." Indeed, in the present context of the declining leverage and economic performance of the United States in the global context, as Fishman has suggested, recent nativist attacks on racial minorities and immigrants are increasingly fueled largely by the insecurity of the power classes—like that of those Anglos and non-Anglos alike who aspire to their ranks—about their leadership role and power in the United States. Movements to make English the official language of the United States "boil down to the 'who's in control here anyway; we who deserve to be or those riff-raff and upstarts?' " As a result, the politicization of the English language of the 1980s represented a "patriotic 'purification' campaign against 'foreign elements,' akin today to the anti-Catholic, anti-immigrant, anti-Black, and anti-hyphenated-American campaigns of past eras in American history."

HISPANICS: ETHNICS OR MINORITIES?

The above case study of the dynamics of ethnicity, race, and class in shaping the current national identity and image of the United States and the history of bilingual education legislation and the English Only movements points to the complexity of disentangling prejudices and discrimination against individuals within a group, in this case the Hispanic community. While it is difficult to disagree with Stephan Thernstrom that group rights and rights of persons are two very different things, language discrimination and the concomitant racial underpinnings are indiscriminately directed at now officially established ethnic groups such as Hispanics, with no regard for individuals' language skills, U.S. citizenship, or time of arrival in the United States. Besides going against the minimum principles of respect for individual rights, this in effect lays bare the extent to which

today, as in the past, persistent discrimination against *groups* based on long-held stereotypes about "foreign Others," rather than any serious consideration about the reality of the persons involved, continues to shape the "channels of opportunity" actually open to all individuals identified as its members. Thus, insofar as the political struggles against equality of opportunity are established in group terms, affirmative action policies aimed at improving the conditions of *groups* must be reinforced to ensure equality of opportunity and citizenship rights to all individuals.

At the same time, while the continued struggle for full citizenship, equal rights, and social and cultural inclusion in the "national community" requires that Latinos and other minorities affirm group rights and interests in political terms when confronted by nativist attacks, the complexity of the dynamics of "ethnic" and "minority" status in U.S. society stemming from the heterogeneity of race, class, and language within the Latino community in the United States cannot be overlooked in seeking to understand the meaning and social value of the label Hispanic in individual lives.

Arguing that it is important to distinguish between ethnic and minority group status, Joan Vincent identifies the differences between "ethnic groups" and "minority groups" as stemming from their differential positions of power and status in society:

> For individuals, ethnicity must consistently be placed in the context of alternative status articulation: the essence of minority status is that it cannot. Ethnicity may be seen to lose out in competition with economic status opportunities, whereas the maintenance of economic discrimination is the bedrock of majority-minority domination.

Thus, an ethnic group *chooses* to articulate its collective common cultural norms, values, identities, behaviors, and self-recognition in particular situations. But members of a "minority" group have to contend instead with the common experience of prejudice and discrimination "imposed from above."

Vincent's use of status and power as the basis for distinguishing between the social experiences of ethnic and minority groups is particularly important to bear in mind in analyzing the case of Latin American immigrants in the United States. For, unlike previous immigrant groups, the populations with ties to Latin America are characterized not only by national, linguistic, and religious differences but also, and perhaps more important in the U.S. context, by racial and class heterogeneity. Indeed, following Vincent, while white, middle- and upper-class Hispanics might be able to attribute an *ethnic* status to themselves, others would assign to many "non-white Hispanics" a *minority* status based on class and racial considerations. This distinction in turn raises questions about the effects of race and class in determining the types of insertion that different sectors within the Hispanic populations achieve in U.S. society.

Crucial for exploring the differentiated experiences in the United States of the populations with ties to Latin America is the fact that the understanding of the social hierarchy in Latin American countries has traditionally been based on a continuum rather than on division among the races. This does not necessarily mean that ethnicity, nationality, race, and language are not socially and culturally significant in Latin America, nor that class is secondary in establishing relationships and communications here in the United States. Yet it does point to two different ways of stratifying and classifying groups, which in effect differentially organize people's sense of self, feelings, and ways of belonging, participating, and positioning themselves in society, while simultaneously defining and legitimizing their political rights and social obligations—and hence their national and cultural identities both at home and abroad.

Indeed, the perceived prevalence of class over race in organizing the social hierarchies of Latin American societies is a Latin American cultural truism that can serve as a barrier against intragroup or ethnic solidarity for many Hispanics once in the United States. As the sociologist Martha Giménez poignantly stated: "Nationality is not as important in determining patterns of association and participation in the host society as social class.... *Middle and upper-middle class immigrants are more likely to share the values of the dominant classes including class, racial and ethnic prejudices.*"

The shift from a social hierarchy with representations based on class relations and differences to one in which race assumes a "legitimate" status in explanatory models of social and cultural differences thus raises the issue of how class distinctions are articulated with racial (as distinct from ethnic) practices within and among recently arrived groups from Latin America. The indiscriminate use of a homogenizing ethnic label such as Hispanic obscures both their respective experiences in this country and the power and status differences within the Hispanic population, while minimizing these distinctions in relation to the larger U.S. society. Given the unique heterogeneity of the population identified as Hispanic, it is important to address the neglect of the racial, class, and language dimensions that structure their daily lives and experiences as "ethnics" and "minorities" in U.S. society.

Decoding Racism

We're just as prone to see everything as racism as
whites are to see nothing as racism.
—David Greene,
an African-American employee
of the Defense Department

by David Shipler

Listening

Americans make choices constantly as they try to navigate through the racial landscape. They hear, or they do not hear. They speak, or they remain silent. They keep a racist thought to themselves, or they translate it into behavior—overtly or covertly. They select one or another mechanism by which to control the prejudices inside them. They confront or evade, question or teach, learn or regard themselves as above learning. They are not helpless in all of this, not mere prisoners of the past or pawns of the present. They are shaped by their surroundings, to be sure, but they also have free will. They act. They choose. And their first choice is how they listen.

Blacks and whites do not listen well to one another. They infer, assume, deduce, imagine, and otherwise miscommunicate. They give each other little grace and allow small room for benefit of the doubt. Dialogue is exceedingly difficult. Nor do blacks and whites listen well to themselves as they stigmatize, derogate, slur, slight, and otherwise offend. Quite innocently, whites make comments that trigger old stereotypes and then get defensive when blacks take umbrage. Blacks sometimes think their persecuted status cloaks them in permanent absolution for the sin of racial bigotry. And so they commit the sin without acknowledging it, infuriating whites and forestalling conversation.

It takes practice to learn to listen, and whites don't get much because most of them rarely think about race. If you are black in America, however, the chances are that you think about race every single

day. When this simple fact was mentioned by Richard Orange, the black consultant, to a workshop for Meridian Bancorp in Pennsylvania, the bank's chairman, Samuel A. McCullough, found it such a stunning revelation that he was still talking about it months later. It had opened a window onto a hidden universe. As a white man, he went through most days without race ever coming to mind.

That is the smooth luxury of the majority. Immersed in the harmony of sameness, bathed in familiar chords of culture, white people don't usually notice their whiteness, any more than someone speaking his native language notices his own accent. The senses are so soothed that they are dulled. This means that whites can be comfortably deaf to the racial overtones that blacks hear so vividly. And from across the line, blacks can imagine racial dissonance where none is intended. So it happens that blacks and whites tune in to different melodies.

If you are black in America, you stand somewhere along a spectrum of assumptions about what is really happening behind the code of white behavior. At one end are those African-Americans who tend to see racism in every adverse encounter with a white. At the other end are those who try mightily not to see it at all. Those extremes are the easiest positions; little thinking is required to apply ready formulas. But in the middle of the spectrum, where most blacks seem to be, deciphering whites' comments and actions is an exhausting effort. Was it because of your blackness that you were denied the promotion, excluded from the meeting, treated rudely by the salesclerk, ignored by the professor? Was the unpleasant remark, glance, or laughter an encrypted expression of racial prejudice?

Many African-Americans, reluctant to jump to automatic conclusions, find themselves expending enormous emotion trying to figure white people out. "It's very difficult," says Sharon Walter of the Houston Urban League. "I have had instances where I'm in a room with white people and there will be discussions going on, and I feel left out. . . . In waiting rooms or lobbies, you feel like you want to talk, 'cause you're sitting and waiting—the weather or sports or politics, whatever. And I've tried to initiate a conversation, and I could tell that they don't want to talk." But when a white person walks in, conversation begins. "I don't want to think it's racism," she says. "The better part of me wants to think otherwise."

"We all walk around with a little radar system," says Bruce King "Often it's confusing, because you're in conversations with people things happen and you don't know. You have to think about it, analyze it.... Those people who are oppressed have to put so much energy into rethinking, into going back over situations over and over and over and over again, always hoping that a comment maybe wasn't meant the way it sounded. Did they really mean that? What did they mean? Why am I angry right now if they didn't mean it?"

The label "racism" is such a fierce and categorical condemnation that its features are commonly disguised and submerged to create a benign mask of subtleties. Almost nobody wants to consider himself a racist. "My experience is that when many white people think of prejudice, they think of the institutions: Jim Crow, slavery; they think of the extremists, the hate groups," says Lauren Nile, the diversity consultant. Racism is not considered racism unless it wears a hood and burns a cross and explicitly keeps blacks down, agrees Jim Blacksher, the white civil rights lawyer in Alabama. But to "people of color," Nile believes, racism means something less dramatic: "the daily indignities, the look [of fear] on that woman's face when I was standing at the elevator, the fact that I can go downstairs to this pharmacy, and if I take too long looking at what I want, the pharmacist will start looking at me as if I'm going to shoplift something."

Racial aversion often takes the form of personal aversion, and someone who dislikes another individual personally rarely notices when the root of that distaste lies in racial stereotypes. Such failure of introspection can afflict both whites and blacks.

This can lead to stark black-white differences of interpretation, a Rorschach test in which contradictory perception becomes divergent reality. The late Mitchell Goodman, a white anti-war protester

from Vietnam days, once said that he thought black Americans possessed X-ray vision about this society, an ability to see through the platitudes and self-deceptions into the essentials. There is a valid point here, for whites could learn a great deal about themselves and their country if they would only listen to what blacks have to say. They might see how events are compiled into patterns. They might tune in to the racial vibrations in their own remarks. They might come to understand how insidiously their behavior is shaped by the shapeless caricatures that lurk in the unlit corners of the mind. Instead, whites usually just get indignant when they think blacks are imagining racism that isn't there. And those blacks who do fantasize about racism are often disgusted by whites' denials.

Some also manage a laugh at themselves, though. Wilbert Tatum, publisher of the *Amsterdam News* in Harlem, tells of a party on the yacht of the late media mogul Robert Maxwell. All the guests were asked to remove their shoes as they boarded. Tatum noticed that, unlike many of the white luminaries, he was not given any slippers to wear over his socks. He shambled around, looking at people's feet, and determined that none of the blacks had slippers. Feeling insulted, he confronted the attendant, who explained simply that slippers were being given to people who had holes in their socks.

An ambiguous episode occurred on a fine spring day when Trevor Woollery, a sophomore on Colgate's track team, came happily down to the track to stretch and warm up. "The weather is propitious for a good workout," he announced with delight.

A white teammate guffawed. "Did you say 'propitious'?"

Yeah, why?"

"Oh, I didn't know you knew such words!"

As an African-American stereotyped as mentally inferior, Woollery had no doubt about the meaning of the remark. He knew the white student, so he could fill in the character behind the comment. But wasn't it conceivable that the student would have teased a fellow white for using such a fancy word in such a mundane setting? "It is conceivable, yes. But they use the words all the time," Woollery said. And was he certain that it was because he was black? "Well, from my standpoint, yes."

Rarely is it possible to pass beyond speculation in such a matter. To know whether the white student was teasing innocuously or insulting racially would require a formidable capacity to read his mind. Only occasionally can the question be tested, and Senator John Danforth unwittingly provided such a case. In the lobby of a Senate office building, Danforth was approached by Roger Wilkins, the insightful black attorney, professor, and Pulitzer Prize-winning journalist. The two had never met. Wilkins stretched out his hand. "Hello, Senator. I'm Roger Wilkins."

Danforth shook hands. "Hello, Roger." And in that too-intimate use of a black man's first name alone, Wilkins heard the reverberating echo of white condescension across a long legacy. He told me the story to illustrate how thoroughly the practice was ingrained. But wait, I said, Washington is a town full of phony familiarity where even young secretaries give their elders the first-name treatment. Ah, Wilkins replied, but Danforth is different: well-bred, proper, an Episcopal priest. He knows better. But he's a politician, I countered. Wouldn't he have done it to a white man as well? Not a chance, Wilkins insisted. I wondered skeptically about this for a year or so, until I happened to attend a luncheon where Danforth spoke. Now I could check it out, for I had never met him either. I walked up to the senator, put out my hand, and told him my full name. "Hello, David," he said.

When I returned to Wilkins with the result of my experiment, he acknowledged that politicians use first names to diminish distance. Still, given the racial legacy, he argued, Danforth should have known better. "If you're a black person my age and were born in segregation, as I was, you are just steeped in the lore of segregation," Wilkins. "You had to understand it to negotiate it. One thing we all knew was that white people had to use first names with black people to establish the superior-inferior relationships. Black people started giving their kids names that required white people to address them with respect; they'd name their kids Major, General. You would expect that a man like Danforth would know that racial etiquette. On the other hand, Danforth thought he was doing a good racial thing by promoting Clarence Thomas for the Supreme Court, showing that he was tone-deaf on race."

Breaking the code is difficult because the motive is masked, the wellspring of the comment is concealed. Even a man with a good ear, with intuition finely honed, can be mistaken. Salim Muwakkil may be wrong, or he may be correct, in thinking that racism got him transferred out of Germany when he served in the air force. He dated an attractive German woman who picked him up almost daily in a nice Mercedes; he would see the faces of white officers peering enviously from the windows of their quarters as he rode away. Mark Vance, the high school history teacher in Oak Park, Illinois, may be right or wrong that racial prejudice induced a white mother to demand the transfer of her child out of his honors course in world history. The whites involved would surely deny—perhaps even to themselves—that bigotry played a role.

The accusation of racism flabbergasted Susan Jacox, a white official in a state university's development department. She fell into a misunderstanding that could have been choreographed in a comedy routine, except that nobody was laughing. Sitting in her office with her door open, she was concluding a meeting with three or four people who had been brainstorming over a problem. The session had gone well, and Susan was summarizing as she happened to notice the black assistant to the vice president for development walking by in the corridor. "I said hello to her, and she turned and nodded to me," Susan recalled, "and in the same breath I turned to the people in my office and said, 'I always believe in calling a spade a spade.'"

The daughter of a diplomat, Susan had grown up overseas, unexposed to most of the racist slang that young people learn in America. She had no idea that "spade" was a derogatory term for a black person; the black assistant evidently had no idea that "calling a spade a spade" meant telling a plain truth in plain language. "She came to later that afternoon and was furious with me for that insult to her," Susan said, "and I asked her what insult she was talking about, and she said, 'I'm not going to say it. Don't ask me to say what your insult was.'" For a time, they groped toward each other through obscurity until enough clues were given that "it dawned on me," Susan said, "that in the realm of card playing, spades are black." But that's not what she had in mind at all, she told the assistant. That's what the phrase means, the assistant said. "I didn't know that," Susan pleaded. "How could you not know that?" countered the assistant. "Well, I didn't. And I'm terribly sorry, and I will never, ever say that again."

Susan was stricken at the offense that she had caused. "So I called her that night from home, and I said, 'I am appalled at what I said and appalled that I used a phrase that has this connotation, and I apologize to you and I thank you for telling me discreetly, privately about it. And I will never, ever say that again, I promise you.'" The assistant thanked her, said she accepted the apology, and came to Susan the next day to say that she appreciated the call.

Several weeks later, Susan once again stepped into that battle zone of miscommunication that rages along the racial frontier. She had occasion to telephone the assistant one evening on some work-related matter and decided to compliment her. "She was a very beautifully tailored black person, a very elegant woman," Susan explained. "She was a refreshing, stunning-looking individual in the office. I complimented her frequently on what she was wearing.... As part of thanking her, and saying how super she was and how special her sparkle was to me, I said, 'You remind me of a sapphire.' And I was thinking on the phone about a magnificent blue and white silk pants-suit outfit she had worn, and she truly was as elegant as a star sapphire."

The comment brought a long silence. Then the assistant asked, "Do you remember *Amos 'n' Andy?*" Susan vaguely recalled seeing some of the shows when she was a young child, but she didn't get the connection. "Well," the assistant explained, "Sapphire was the woman on the show."

"So?" Susan asked.

"So! You've just called me 'Sapphire.'" And then came a torrent of invective about the program, about Susan as the worst racial bigot the assistant had ever known.

None of Susan's pleas of ignorance, her explanations about living overseas, were received as credible. "The next day, she studiously avoided looking at me," Susan said. "The tension was just horrible. As working hours ended, the assistant walked into Susan's office. "She said, 'I just don't know where to begin.' She would not look at me, she would not sit down. She was ramrod straight, absolutely furious, shaking with anger.... 'What crap do you hand me that you don't know those phrases? You claim to be so innocent of them, then you turn around and use the worst kind of slur possible. I detest you.... I will not accept this apology. You don't deserve to be treated civilly.' And she stormed out of my office, and I broke down. I was absolutely overwhelmed."

Susan pressed the university's vice president to institute diversity workshops, and the vice president hemmed and hawed, arguing that to do so would be to admit to a problem that did not exist. When the assistant heard that, she spoke privately to the vice president, and workshops were begun. Susan thanked the assistant for her intervention. In turn, the assistant circled around Susan, apparently looking for ways to have a conversation. One day, "she sat down next to my desk and sat forward and was really very eager, and didn't know what to say. I said, 'You don't have to say anything . . . this is a long process.'" Again she praised the assistant for standing up at the right time to get the diversity training started. "She said, 'Good,' and then left."

Two months later, Susan's husband was transferred out of state, and she left the job. The assistant did not attend her farewell reception.

At the other end of the spectrum, where blacks don't want to see racism, they can seem oblivious to what is obvious. It may have been just politics, but Clark Kent Ervin, an unsuccessful black Republican candidate for Congress, sat in his echoing storefront campaign office in Houston and proclaimed in sincere tones that George Bush's infamous Willie Horton ad contained not an ounce of racist appeal. Horton was a black murderer who raped a woman and assaulted her fiancé after escaping from a furlough program during the administration of Massachusetts Governor Michael Dukakis, Bush's opponent. By using Horton's African-American face to sinister advantage, the commercial pushed some powerful buttons of fear. But Ervin insisted that the ad was "about crime; it wasn't about a black person committing a crime. It would have been politically more correct, obviously, to have had a whole bunch of criminals of different races and religions and sexual orientations, and then we wouldn't have had that charge leveled against us. But it's essentially about crime."

African-Americans sometimes feel they have to educate one another. Renea Henry, a black Princeton student, took on the task with a fellow black Princetonian who had grown up affluent in a white community. He was driving with a white friend in a white neighborhood when a white cop pulled him over—and he had no idea why. "You think it's because you're black?" she asked rhetorically.

"Oh, no. It probably wasn't that."

When it happened again, and then again for no good reason, he began to accept her racial interpretation. Finally, he "got it" and had his white friend do the driving through white neighborhoods.

Sometimes whites are the ones who have to point out the racist dimension of an incident. Sitting around a table at Birmingham Southern University in Alabama, four white students and a black were telling of a black student recently charged— unjustly, they felt—with peering at a white woman in a shower. She had noticed a black man looking at her, she had screamed, he had run, and she had seen that he was wearing a yellow T-shirt. Campus police quickly found a black student doing his laundry in a nearby dorm and accused him, although his shirt was not yellow and he had checked in at the campus gate only two minutes before the incident—hardly time to park his car, go to the shower, then put in a load of laundry.

A couple of the whites believed that the authorities had been ready to grab the first black man who was handy. "I definitely saw it as racist," said Leigh Haynie, a white senior from Hartselle, Alabama.

But Carlton Chamblin, a black junior from Birmingham, thought otherwise. "More than an issue of race, it was an issue of justice," he said. "It wasn't like someone stole something and you don't know who stole it. I mean, she saw a black person. We can accept what she said.... That's why I don't make it an issue of race, because it was a black person," even though, he conceded, the wrong black person may have been accused.

It was an odd moment, with whites charging racism and a black dismissing the charge. Wesley Edwards, a white from Columbus, Georgia, tried to explain to Chamblin. "You know, if it had been a white person, they wouldn't have grabbed up the first white person on campus who happened to be near the place near the time, so easily. It made it very easy on the college to dispense with the problem." Chamblin thought for a moment, then nodded.

For some blacks, avoiding the racist interpretation is a protective doctrine that allows them to avoid a state of constant anger and to function with composure in a white environment. "I'm quite sure it's out there, and I've probably run into some situations where the intent was to let me know that they didn't like me because I was black," said Major Craig Adams, an air force navigator on C-130 cargo planes. "But I would say, generally speaking, I have never perceived things that way—or even if I thought it was, what I try to do is, I try to look at other alternatives. I say, 'Well, I think he's trying to tell me he doesn't like me because I'm black. What other reasons could there be for that?' I try to explore those before I look at it as a black-white issue."

Another black air force officer, Lieutenant Colonel Edward Rice, had something of a bizarre experience in this regard. He was sitting in the cockpit of a B-52, preparing for a flight evaluation, which is done periodically to keep pilots in top shape. The evaluator was white, and Rice's grave manner during the preflight checkoff seemed to be making the man nervous. "I'm normally very serious," Rice explained. "I don't joke around a lot during a flight." Finally, the evaluator couldn't take it anymore and said, "Come on, Rice, lighten up."

"I took no offense," Rice said. "I didn't think he meant anything other than relax a little bit. But the next day, he came up to me and said, 'Hey, I hope you didn't take offense to that remark. I didn't mean anything by it. I was just trying to say "lighten up," but I started to think about it.' " And the white evaluator went on to explain awkwardly that he was afraid that Rice might have interpreted it as a racial comment. That cracked Rice's seriousness, and he laughed deeply. "It obviously dawned on him that it could have been interpreted that way, even though it was clear to me in the circumstance that that's not what he meant."

In their interactions with blacks, white Americans fall along a broad spectrum themselves, from the self-questioning extreme of the flight evaluator to the dense, don't-get-it (or don't-care) mode of the majority. Unlike the black spectrum, which probably forms something of a bell curve with the bulk of blacks in the middle, the white spectrum seems to be skewed toward the less perceptive end, with a substantial tail that extends through the continuum into regions where whites get uptight, tiptoe around, walk on eggshells, choose their words, calibrate their statements, and otherwise display acute discomfort in dealing with blacks. As Wesley Edwards put it, "In any kind of interpersonal relationship between blacks and whites there's always that little impediment there of not being willing to be completely honest and open with each other.... It's always with us to some degree or another, whether we recognize it or not."

To avoid being accused of racism, these whites may use extreme restraint and careful calculation, which enforce the distance. That often seems the safest course, but it avoids intimacy—no teasing about a big word, no first names on first meetings. Hypersensitivity also brings paralysis, as it did to two white women at Princeton who felt so inhibited in a course on race relations, taught by a white woman and dominated by minority students, that they said practically nothing in class the entire semester. "Being white people, we don't feel qualified to speak," Anastasia explained simply. "I listen," added Loren. "I love hearing other people's stories, but I don't know what narrative I can tell to contribute." At the end of the course, some minority students expressed bitterness that the whites had said so little. But the two women had been intimidated by their whiteness and by their lack of suffering, which they thought deprived them of anything interesting to tell about themselves. Furthermore, they had accepted the admonition that as whites, they could never understand the black experience. This was all the more poignant for Loren, who was doing a concentration in Afro-American studies courses in which she routinely took a backseat. "I'm always second-guessing myself in those classes," she said. "I never felt the authority, and it's really hard for me. I don't know why I chose to concentrate on something that I'll never feel the authority in."

Other sensitive whites at this end of the spectrum have healthier reflexes. They listen to themselves and to the way their language comes across to blacks, and they deepen their understanding. Steve Suitts got an education when he reacted angrily to an anonymous memo that had been circulated about someone in his civil rights organization. "I think I referred to it as a pusillanimous and woolly-headed approach," he said. "I thought 'pusillanimous' might have been a little strong, but really what some of my black colleagues took offense to was my referring to it as 'woolly-headed.' Where I grew up in Winston County [Alabama], if somebody would bump into a door, we'd say, oh, he's just woolly-headed." In fact, the term "woolly-headed" may have racist origins, judging by its two definitions in *The American Heritage Dictionary:* "1. Having hair that looks or feels like wool. 2. Vague or muddled." The experience was a lesson to Suitts about how language naturally emerges from a warren of images and attitudes. "Sometimes you check yourself, sometimes you don't," he said, "and sometimes even with the best of intentions, what you say and what you do express a sentiment that others have heard as something quite different from what you heard it as."

But vocabulary is not always reliable as a guide to attitudes. "The operating theory in the civil rights movement was: If some southerner said 'Negro,' he was a liberal; if he said 'nigra,' he was a moderate; and if he said 'nigger,' he was a conservative," Suitts recalled. "I will always remember hearing a debate in Alabama by two old codgers who were sitting by a cedar tree on some red clay in a courthouse yard. I was interviewing them years ago.... And I'll never forget this fellow talking about the Negroes, and how the Negroes were taking over and how the Negroes were the closest thing to the ape that society had, and this other old white codger stopping him right in the middle and saying, 'Now, wait a minute. Niggers are people too.' "

Some whites who tune in to themselves discover their own prejudices, thereby taking a step toward controlling them. Jessica Prentice was unaware of her attitudes before she spent a year as the only white student at Tougaloo, the black college in Mississippi. She counted herself as liberal and open-minded but found herself seeing people's shortcomings through a racial prism. Some of her racist thoughts grew out Of "a certain snobbishness in general that I acquired over the years," she confessed. "In a racially charged situation, that can often play itself out in a racist kind of way. [At Tougaloo] I had a certain frustration, sometimes, finding intellectual peers." Instead of looking around and seeing specific individuals who didn't measure up, she added, "I would understand it racially, instinctively. And even though by the time I left, I -had found those people, it took a lot longer." She was jolted into self-examination when a black friend told her that no matter how nice and liberal a white person may be, "if you push them far enough the n-i-g-g-e-r word will come out of their mouths," as she remembered the comment. "That hit home, because in a certain sense I spent my whole time there dealing with my own racism. That was just a constant—my own prejudices," she confessed. "Some little thing would come up, and I'd just react in a way that five minutes later I'd be able to see was racist. I wouldn't react overtly, but just in my mind I would interpret it."

At another, less introspective part of the white spectrum, a dozen or so white middle-class parents are sitting in a church basement while their sons hold a Boy Scout meeting upstairs. We are there for an unhappy purpose, but you would never know it from the faces. We are discussing a flash of racism in the troop and the complicated fallout, which included the resignation of the black youngster who was the target. But no emotion is registering on the white faces, no pain, no hurt, no guilt, no concern, just bland complacency, as if this episode were nothing more than a shooting star that had skipped off the distant reaches of the atmosphere and never had a chance to penetrate the defensive layers of ignorance that surround the soul of morality.

The story is simple. Three boys—my son Michael, a white friend, and a black friend we'll call "Tommy"—had just joined the troop together from their Cub Scout pack and were wisely placed together in the same patrol. On one of their first camping trips, their white patrol leader, an older boy, ridiculed Tommy by calling him "blackie" and "black boy." Michael and the other white complained to the senior patrol leader, who notified the white scoutmaster. The scouts' version of a court-martial was convened, and the patrol leader was demoted. No counseling was done for him, and no support for Tommy was given by either the older scouts or the scoutmaster. Michael and his two friends, who were close pals, were worried that their patrol might be disbanded and they might be split up. Their parents—concerned that their alertness to racism would in effect result in punishment—asked the scoutmaster to be sure that didn't happen. The scoutmaster rudely ignored the appeal—at one point, he hung up on Tommy's father—and without warning, the boys were scattered into different patrols. Angry and upset, they discourteously demanded a meeting with the scoutmaster, who adopted an imperious air and made insulting declarations about the other white boy's mother. Michael and Tommy then resigned in protest; the other boy remained temporarily, later switched troops, and went on to become an Eagle Scout.

So, this evening, the white parents involved have decided to bring the matter before the other parents. We are sitting in a tight circle, all facing one another. I am expecting compassion, indignation, a resolve to mane amends with Tommy, to deal firmly with the scoutmaster. After all, a racist incident, plus the scoutmaster's abusive behavior, has led a black scout to conclude that he cannot be comfortable in this virtually all white troop. That should be a matter of grave concern.

Instead, the chairman of the parents' committee, an older white man, dismisses the entire episode, accepting the scoutmaster's denial that he insulted the mother or was nasty to the youngsters. We point out that two boys have resigned, that the racism has been handled mechanically, not sympathetically, that nobody has even called Tommy or his parents to apologize or inform them of the action taken. I mention that this may have been Tommy's first contact with racism, one that he will never forget. I look around the room. A chill has descended. The shields are up. The other parents are deflecting the discussion away from race; their faces are frozen, expressionless, almost lifeless. *They don't care*, I realize. *They don't care.*

Finally, we persuade them at least to talk to the boys. Two white fathers are appointed to the task. Weeks later, they write a report that, predictably, exonerates the scoutmaster. It makes no mention of the racial slurs or of the fact of Tommy's resignation. It is as bland and uncaring as the white faces in the church basement.

Most white people probably do not feel guilty race relations, and they certainly do not feel the guilt that black people think they should. They never owned slaves, they never discriminated. Many of their ancestors came to America after the Civil War and scrambled up the hard way. In fact, they are the new victims. If they are males, they are vilified, blamed, and pushed aside. Richard Orange finds that in corporations, most hostility comes from white men in their twenties and thirties who are trying to climb upward in an era of "downsizing" and affirmative action; they see undue, unfair competition from women, blacks, and other minorities.

Unsolicited comments by whites about race usually come to me in three forms. One is a category of complaints about blacks who get preference in hiring and then display either incompetence or dishonesty. Another is a lament about violence and disorder in the schools and neighborhoods of the inner city. The third is one story or another that casts the white as the target of black racism. Being the victim seems to have become the most fashionable American pastime.

To Larry and Rufus, twenty-one-year-old whites in Louisiana, the underdogs were white. "Blacks are killing whites, and it never hits the papers," said Rufus. "But one black gets killed and the whole place riots."

"It's so unequal," Larry added. "The cops will not pursue blacks for fear of being called racists.... A black can walk down my street, but a white can't walk into their neighborhood. If I went down there, I'd get stopped by a cop. They'd think I was down there buying drugs.... A black police officer let a black leave after he ran into my friend from the rear. My friend got a citation: failure to maintain control or something. My mother was in a wreck with a black person who was drunk with no license, no insurance. We had to pay for our car.... The blacks have an innate prejudism born inside against whites." And so on.

But white interpretations of black bigotry are subject to some of the same ambiguities that apply to black perceptions of white prejudice. That is to say, they are sometimes wrong. Laura, my daughter, laughed at herself for being so paranoid, when she arrived for a semester at Spelman, that when she went out walking to the supermarket with a few black women, she thought she heard one of them say, "Who's that white fool?" She was stunned, but only for an instant, because somebody asked, "What?" and the woman repeated her question: "Who's gonna buy the food?"

John Graham, the descendant of plantation owners, once went through something of the struggle that blacks experience in trying to delineate the racism within the coded behavior. "I worked as a waiter at one point down in New Orleans," he said, "and it was at a nice restaurant, and my captain for the room was black. I hadn't even said a word, and he immediately came down on me and was very negative the entire time we worked together. And there was nothing that I could do in terms of doing a good job or kind of being responsive to what he needed that ever made a difference. Now, it may very well have been that he just didn't like me not because I was white, but that he just didn't like me." But Graham leaned toward the racial explanation. I asked how the captain had dealt with black waiters. Graham paused in thought for a long time. "That's actually a very good point," he said finally. "There were some that he seemed not to be down on regularly, but there were also some that he was also a pain in the ass for." Graham hadn't thought about that before, and it seemed to diminish the weight of race.

Many blacks define racism as prejudice plus power, thereby labeling the practice so that it lies beyond the reach of powerless people like themselves. According to the formulation, if you're not in a position to translate your prejudices into discriminatory action, if you don't have the authority to make your attitudes felt in people's schooling, housing, jobs, and lives, then you cannot be racist.

Such a narrow rendering of the term will not be found in the dictionaries. But the issue is more than a semantic one. Many blacks have used it to confer a kind of immunity on themselves, a permission to be racist without admitting to it. As Gus Savage declared in defending an anti-Semitic campaign speech when he was a congressman from Chicago, "Racism is white. There ain't no black racism."

CONVERSING

Talking about race is one of the most difficult endeavors in America. Shouting is easy. Muttering and whining and posturing are done with facility. But conversing—black with white, white with black—is a rare and heavy accomplishment. The color line is a curtain of silence.

When Kathleen Sherrell, who is white, was seriously dating Bob Sherrell, the black man who became her husband, her brother and sister-in-law paid her an urgent visit with vitriolic appeal.

"They came in the door, and both of them started attacking me," Kathleen recalls more than two decades later. "Just a vicious attack: That I was trying to kill my father. I would kill my father. That I was rebelling, that that's all I was trying to do, was hurt my parents. On and on. 'You know those people are different. How are you going to handle your children?' The whole thing. And I kicked them out of my apartment. I called them names and told them to go back to church and pray...I didn't have much more to do with them until after we got married...My brother since then has come to me and said, 'That's one of the most shameful times of my life.' He has really talked about it as being something he's very ashamed of."

"But interestingly," Bob says, "he's never told *me* that." Bob is sitting beside Kathleen, and a wince of pain crosses his face. "I—I—I frequently—I think I've forgiven him. I think I have forgiven. I feel that I've forgiven. But I also feel that apiece of me really wants that out on the table. That needs to happen in order to have the closeness, because it is so phony to me to be received and to be hugged and welcomed when I know how they initially reacted to me in 1971. And it just still gnaws in way."

And has Bob raised it with the brother? His eyes flicker with surprise at the idea, and he shake his head: no.

If a black and a white in the same family who agree on the shamefulness of a racial episode cannot bring the subject into their conversation for more than twenty years, then a black and a white in a workplace who disagree cannot even think about talking the next day, the next week. In a newsroom, a white reporter wrote a summary of the story he was about to do on the civil war in Somalia. He commented on the country's "tribal politics," and a black reporter who saw the summary bristled. The black went to a white editor and objected to the word "tribal" as a racial allusion to primitive blacks. The white editor went to the white reporter and suggested it be changed. The white reporter, infuriated, defended the word. It had nothing to do with race, he said; Arabs and Jews in Israel, Muslims and Serbs in Bosnia, ethnic groups in confrontation around the world were properly described as "tribes"—a perfectly appropriate anthropological term. The white editor insisted, so the white reporter reluctantly changed it to "Byzantine politics." This so confused a second editor, who knew nothing of the black reporter's objections, that he called the white reporter and suggested that "Byzantine" be changed to "tribal." The white reporter had to be honest and mention the dispute. So, in the end, it came out in the paper as "murky."

The white reporter was still angry the following day, when he told me the story. He was mad not only that he had been misunderstood but that the black reporter had not gone to him directly and that the white editor had shown such cowardice. In that event, I suggested, why didn't he Sit down with the black reporter and talk it over? Perhaps they could learn something from each other. He thought for a moment. He hadn't considered such an approach, he said, but he might. Two weeks later, I checked. No, he had decided against a discussion; he was afraid that he would simply lose his temper. And so the incident will remain frozen in the memories of the two reporters just as they initially perceived it—as a piece of subtle racism, on the one side; as a case of false accusation and "politically correct" censorship, on the other.

It is always difficult to begin such a conversation. Anyone who has been present when a racist joke or racist slur is made knows how hard it is to be the first to speak up in protest, for much moral energy is required to overcome the inertia of silence. Usually, a vacuum of acquiescence prevails. If a black person is in the room, she notices what "good" whites fail to say. A doctor, the only African-American in a staff meeting at her hospital, was the only person to object when a white doctor complained about having too little help during a conference. "All I had to count on was this big, fat black woman who was sitting in the chair," he remarked

"I said, 'Excuse me? What's the relevance of that last statement to the issue?'" she recalled. "He blushed and tried to clean it up, but I never forgot it. Never forgot it." No whites seconded her disapproval. "They just kind of got real uncomfortable and shifted around in their chairs."

Blacks can be so hurt by white silence that the memory of the moment lasts for decades. The all-black Russian language class at Lincoln University was on edge, ready to pounce. Islanda Goode, Paul Robeson's niece, was fresh from Moscow, and she had just begun teaching here. She looked white, although she was biracial. She wrote on the board the Russian words for various colors: *byely* ("white"), *chyorny* ("black"), *krasny* ("red"), and *sinyi* ("blue"). From among the students, a woman's voice rang out: "Why did you put 'white' first? That's racist." Goode stopped short. She screwed up her face into deep thought and pretended to ponder the accusation. "Yes," she said finally, "it is deeply racist. So perhaps we should put 'yellow' first. But that would mean Asian, so non-Asians would find it racist. We could begin with 'blue,' except that's what we call gay people, so that would seem to favor them. How about beginning with 'green'?" By then, the class had started to laugh, and the complaining student had as well.

A little humor is a good antidote in a moment of racial tension, but it probably takes someone in Goode's unique position as an outsider-insider to defuse such a charge by laughing at it. Few white Americans would be bold enough to try, and it's a technique that can easily go wrong. Indeed, many techniques go wrong. Talking is not a panacea, and even when whites and blacks make an attempt, they often fumble around awkwardly with each other.

As a black man in a mostly white setting, and as a person who believed in clear communication, Bruce King traveled this terrain extensively. "When people say things that puzzle me and I don't understand it, I've learned to just ask them," he explained. a 'I don't understand what you're saying. Can you help me better understand it?' " That was enough to stimulate some useful discussion. But he also found that discussion could become burdensome, especially as a black alone at an all white dinner table, peppered with questions.

At the time, King was the director of minority affairs at Lake Forest College, north of Chicago.

He and his wife, Marcine, were the only blacks at a dinner meeting where I gave a speech about race and made the point that we don't talk to one another very well, don't listen to one another, and don't hear ourselves. Then we sat down to eat Unfortunately for King and his wife, my remarks prompted a barrage of inquiries from genuinely interested and concerned white people who had probably never had such an easy opening to vent their curiosity on African-Americans.

How does it feel to be black? What is it like to be black in Lake Forest? Why aren't you angry? "I was asked that question," King told me the next morning. "With all that's going on, how come you're not more angry? Shouldn't you be angry?'" He thought talking was healthy. "It gives people an opportunity to be honest and ask questions," he said. "But seldom are you in an atmosphere where they just come at you and they're constant. At our table, they were just constant. Before I could sit down, one of the women at the table said, 'I'm sorry he didn't tack more about solutions.' And she saw me coming to the table, and she says, 'Well, here's a guy who's going to give us the solutions to these problems.' At first, I thought she was joking, 'cause surely—even if you listen to your presentation last night, it's clear that there really are no clear-cut solutions. But I mean, every five minutes, it was like, 'So what is the solution? What is the solution to what happened in L.A.? What is the solution to black-on-black crime?' She wanted to know." He seemed bemused and weary. "It would have been nice to have a few more black people at the event, because I really seriously got tired of answering the questions," he said. "I mean, you would finish one, and somebody was coming with another one. And these were not just yes or no, and people wanted articulate answers."

Being on stage, even at casual parties, became so exhausting that King and his wife decided to avoid the subject of race if possible. "It's no longer fun to be someplace when you are speaking and having to think and articulate at a party," he complained. At a dinner the previous summer, he and his wife had been grabbed by a white woman on the staff who wanted to check his view on something a black student had told her: that she couldn't imagine how hard being black was in this environment. Was that true? King tried a short answer, explaining that most black students, including those who have gone to mostly white high schools, have never lived immersed in a predominantly white environment with no black family to go home to for support. Another white woman disagreed that the campus was such a hostile place. King replied by citing some of his unpleasant personal experiences. Soon he and his wife were encircled by a group of whites listening to the debate. "Then I was told that I was too sensitive," he said in annoyance, "that she didn't believe me or tried to write it off as me being sensitive. Then I was angry, I became frustrated, and we were ready to go home."

COPING

"Being a black person in a racist society is like being the moon going through meteor showers," Nell Painter, the history professor at Princeton, remarked laughingly. She admired undergraduates who expended enormous effort combating racism. But she had come to a different stage in life. "I am so hardened that it's almost impossible for me to see or feel things unless they're really gross," she said. "You could learn that there are some things that you just can't deal with and let them go, or you could spend all your time responding and being torn." She recalled a graduate student in his mid-thirties who was perpetually infuriated by the racism he saw around him. "My thought was, You're just going to have to let some of this go, because there are other things you have to do with your energy, and what's the use of getting an ulcer? I mean, you can get an ulcer and you can have an ulcer, or you can do your work and pick your fights." Techniques of survival are passed from generation to generation, both by example and by conscious decision, and no two parents are quite alike in teaching children how to cope with bigotry. In mixed marriages, the black partner tends to take the lead in setting the style and giving the advice, for the white mother or father rarely has a sense of what skills are needed by a youngster who is considered black.

Gina Wyatt was inclined to try to protect her three children, especially her two daughters. But Tony wanted all of them to learn to deal on their own, and he resisted the temptation to rush into school whenever a racial incident occurred. His thirteen-year-old son, Justin, began running into problems after he revealed in class that he was not merely white, as he appeared, but biracial. The teacher started grading him down, and other youngsters gave him trouble. A white boy told him that blacks shouldn't be allowed onto the golf course because they would tear it up and trash it. Justin exploded in anger and walked out of class.

He was coached through the crisis by both parents, primarily by Tony, who counseled firmness, hard work, and nonviolence. "I grew up violent," Tony said, "and I know that violence does not solve anything.... What I told him to do was to go back and just continue doing what he was doing and address the issue directly, because I want him to be able to confront these issues.... We really don't want to go out and rescue them every time. We do want to protect them, don't get me wrong. But they need to develop the skills to do it themselves."

The obligation to give a black child the tools he needs to function and survive amid racial bias adds a layer of duty to African-Americans' parenting that whites simply do not confront. So trying is the task that entire books of advice have been written to help point the way. In *Different and Wonderful: Raising Black Children in a Race-Conscious Society*, a married couple, Darlene Powell Hopson and Derek S. Hopson, who are black psychologists, lay out a series of steps designed to encourage open discussion and maintain a youngster's self-esteem amid pejorative portrayals of blacks. "Children should be taught about race at the earliest possible time," they state. "It is a parent's obligation to learn a child's innermost thoughts about race." If a child is afraid of white people, parents are advised, she should be helped to associate with whites "with whom you yourself feel comfortable."

Nancy Boyd-Franklin, a noted black psychologist, urges parents to assist children in developing a sense of "Blackness" and to give them "enough information about the realities of the world so that they are prepared without becoming immobilized or so bitter that they are unable to function." This

is a tricky balance to achieve, for children must be taught to believe in themselves and to embrace a "philosophy of hope" even where "an child succumbs to drugs, truancy, and/or other destructive activities," she writes.

Racial problems can be masked by their symptoms, and parents who don't talk openly with their children risk missing the core issues. Boyd Franklin cites the case of Melanie, a black girl who developed serious academic problems after moving from a public to a private school in New York City. During counseling, the mother was asked by the therapist to talk to her daughter about her experience in the new school. "Melanie burst into tears. She told her mother that she had never felt so alone. She was used to having lots of friends at her other school. Here she was the only black child in her class. None of the other kids ever invited her to do things with them." One child informed her that she was too black to be her friend.

The mother "was shocked," Boyd-Franklin writes. "She asked Melanie why she had not told her before. Melanie stated that she had tried but her mother was so angry at her for not doing well that she was afraid." The therapist then took several steps. First, she "normalized Melanie's struggle" by assuring her that the sense of aloneness was quite common for black youngsters in mostly white private schools. Second, she encouraged the mother to talk with her children about how she felt as one of the few blacks on her job, pointed out that Melanie and her mother shared the common trait of being "different," and asked the mother to explain how she handled it. Finally, the mother was urged to contact the teacher, call parents of schoolmates to arrange get togethers, and help Melanie maintain contact with her old friends in the neighborhood.

In large measure, parenting is autobiographical. Most of us raise our children approximately the way we were raised. And therefore, as African-American parents discuss race or avoid it, they often echo their own upbringing and reflect their own intimate sensations of comfort or awkwardness. For many blacks, race can be as difficult a subject of conversation as sex is to most parents. A riot of conflicting emotions storms through such dialogues. In an effort to help, Hopson and Hopson have drawn up a self-test for parents, who indicate the extent to which they feel exhausted, nervous, frustrated, irritated, disappointed, regretful, depressed, angry, embarrassed, guilty, desperate, calm, confident, patient, helpful, enthusiastic, friendly, happy, or concerned when they talk about race with their children. The authors note that many of those who have never had an open conversation on the subject "usually express regret. When racism surfaces the child is often devastated. ('Why didn't you tell me?' is a sad and frequent refrain.)"

Racial sensibilities are swaddled in ambiguity. That is something of the lesson that Sharon Walter of the Houston Urban League tries to impart to her children: Be tough-minded, but give some grace and don't automatically condemn others as racists. "I try to teach my children that racism is real, 'cause it is," she says. "But you can't let that stop you. I teach my children that you've got to be the best, not because you're black but just because you are.... If they come home and they tell me that something happened and they perceive it to be racist, I try to present two views.... One, so that they'll be able to recognize it, if it was, the next time it happens. Or the other side, so they'll be able to take a look and say, 'Well, maybe that wasn't racism. Maybe I did something.... Was I really up to par? Was I really all I should have been?' "

It is a great burden to place on children.

Children Are Color-Blind

by Genny Lim

I never painted myself yellow
the way I colored the sun when I was five.
The way I colored whitefolks with the "flesh" crayola.
Yellow pages adults thumbed through for restaurants,
taxis, airlines, plumbers...
The color of summer squash, corn, eggyolk,
innocence and tapioca.

My children knew before they were taught.
They envisioned rainbows emblazoned over alleyways;
Clouds floating over hilltops like a freedom shroud.
With hands clasped, time dragged them along and they followed.

Wind-flushed cheeks persimmon,
eyes dilated like dark pearls staring out the backseat windows,
they speed through childhood like greyhounds
into the knot of night, hills fanning out,
an ocean ending at an underpass,
a horizon blunted by lorries, skyscrapers,
vision blurring at the brink of poverty.

Dani, my three-year-old, recites the alphabet from
billboards flashing by like pages of a cartoon flipbook,
where above, carpetbaggers patrol the freeways like
Olympic gods hustling their hi-tech neon gospel,
looking down from the fast lane,
dropping Kool dreams, booze dreams, fancy car dreams,
fast foods dreams, sex dreams and no-tomorrow dreams
like eight balls into your easy psychic pocket.

"Only girls with black hair, black eyes can join!"

My eight-year-old was chided at school for
    excluding a blonde
from her circle. "Only girls with black hair, black
    eyes
can join!" taunted the little Asian girls, black hair,
black eyes flashing, mirroring, mimicking what
    they heard
as the message of the medium, the message of the
    world-at-large:
"Apartheid, segregation, self-determination!
Segregation, apartheid, revolution!"
Like a contrapuntal hymn, like a curse that re-
    frains in
a melody trapped.

Sometimes at night I touch the children when
    they're sleeping
and the coolness of my fingers sends shivers
    through them that
is a foreshadowing, a guilt imparted.
Dani doesn't paint herself yellow
the way I colored the sun.
The way she dances in its light as I watch from the
    shadow.
No, she says green is her favorite color.
"It's the color of life!"

It's In Your Hands

by Fannie Lou Hamer

Fannie Lou Hamer was born in Mississippi, one of twenty children of a sharecropper family. She began to pick cotton at the age of six and worked in the fields and as a plantation timekeeper until 1962, when she lost her job after registering to vote. Mrs. Hamer, who is the mother of two children and lives in Ruleville, Mississippi, was jailed in 1963 and severely beaten for attempting to integrate a restaurant. She has been under constant attack for her civil rights leadership and narrowly escaped being shot. Her home was bombed as recently as 1971.

As a field secretary for SNCC, Mrs. Hamer worked to organize the Mississippi Freedom Democratic Party and was one of its spokesmen at the 1964 Democratic Party convention in Atlantic City, where MFDP challenged the lily-white state delegation. The same year, Mrs. Hamer was one of three black candidates running for Congress from her state and garnered 33,009 votes. Since then she has thrown most of her energies into the organization of economic cooperatives in Sunflower County and into political leadership in her state. She is a dynamic public speaker and an outstanding grass-roots leader.

The special plight and the role of black women is not something that just happened three years ago. We've had a special plight for 350 years. My grandmother had it. My grandmother was a slave. She died in 1960. She was 136 years old. She died in Mount Bayou, Mississippi.

It's been a special plight for the black woman. I remember my uncles and some of my aunts—and that's why it really tickled me when you talked about integration. Because I'm very black, but I remember some of my uncles and some of my aunts was as white as anybody in here, and blue-eyed, and some kind of green-eyed—and my grandfather didn't do it, you know. So what the folks is fighting at this point is what they started. They started unloading the slave ships of Africa, that's when they started. And right now, sometimes, you know I work for the liberation of all people, because when I liberate myself, I'm liberating other people. But you know, sometimes I really feel more sorrier for the white woman than I feel for ourselves because she been caught up in this thing, caught up feeling very special, and folks, I'm going to put it on the line, because my job is not to make people feel comfortable— (drowned out by applause). You've been caught up in this thing because, you know, you worked my grandmother, and after that you worked my mother, and then finally you got hold of me. And you really thought, people—you might try and cool it now, but I been watching you, baby. You thought that you was *more* because you was a woman, and especially a white woman, you had this kind of angel feeling that you were untouchable. You know that? There's nothing under the sun that made you believe that you was just like me, that under this white pigment of skin is red blood, just like under this black skin of mine. So we was used as black women over and over and over. You know, I remember a time when I was working around white people's house, and one thing that would make me mad as hell, after I would be done slaved all day long, this white woman would get on the phone, calling some of her friends, and said, "You know, I'm tired, because *we* have been working," and I said, "That's a damn lie." You're not used to that kind of language, honey, but I'm gone tell you where it's *at*. So all of these things was happening because you *had* more. You had been put on a pedestal, and then not only put on a pedestal, but you had been put in something like a ivory castle. So what happened to you, we have busted the castle open and whacking like hell for the pedestal. And when you hit the ground, you're gone have to fight like hell, like we've been fighting all this time.

In the past, I don't care how poor this white woman was, in the South she still felt like she was more than us. In the North, I don't care how poor or how rich this white woman has been, she still felt like she was more than us. But coming to the realization of the thing, her freedom is shackled in chains to mine, and she realizes for the first time that she is not free until I am free. The point about

it, the male influence in this country—you know the white male, he didn't go and brainwash the black man and the black woman, he brainwashed his wife too.... He made her think that she was a angel. You know the reason I can say it, folks, I been watching. And there's a lot of people been watching. That's why it's such a shock wherever we go throughout this country, it's a great blow. White Americans today don't know what in the world to do because when they put us *behind them*, that's where they made their mistake. If they had put us in front, they wouldn't have *let us* look back. But they put us behind them, and we watched every move they made....

And this is the reason I tell the world, as I travel to and fro, I'm not fighting for equal rights. What do I want to be equal to [Senator] Eastland for? Just tell me that. But we are not only going to liberate ourselves. I think it's a responsibility. I think we're special people, God's children is going to help in the survival of this country if it's not too late. We're a lot sicker than people realize we are. And what we are doing now in the South, in politics, in gaining seats for black people and concerned whites in the state of Mississippi, is going to have an effect on what happens throughout this country. You know, I used to think that if I could go North and tell people about the plight of the black folk in the state of Mississippi, everything would be all right. But traveling around, I found one thing for sure: It's up-South and down-South, and it's no different. The man shoot me in the face in Mississippi, and you turn around he'll shoot you in the back here [in New York]. We have a problem, folks, and we want to try to deal with the problem in the only way that we can deal with the problem as far as black women. And you know, I'm not hung up on this about liberating myself from the black man, I'm not going to try that thing. I got a black husband, six feet three, two hundred and forty pounds, with a 14 shoe, that I don't want to be liberated from. But we are here to work side by side with this black man in trying to bring liberation to all people.

Sunflower County is one of the poorest counties, one of the poorest counties on earth, while Senator James O. Eastland—you know, people tells you, don't talk politics, but the air you breathe is polluted air, it's political polluted air. The air you breathe is politics. So you have to be involved. You have to be involved in trying to elect people that's going to help do something about the liberation of all people.

Sunflower County, the county where I'm from, is Senator Eastland's county that owns 5,800 acres of some of the richest black fertile soil in Mississippi, and where kids, there in Sunflower County, suffer from malnutrition. But I want to tell you one of the things that we're doing, right now in Sunflower County. In 1969 I founded the Freedom Farm Coop. We started off with 40 acres of land. Nineteen-seventy in Sunflower County, we fed 1500 people from this 40 acres of land. Nineteen-seventy I've become involved with Y.W.D.—Young World Developers. On the 14th of January 1971, we put $85,400 on 640 acres of land, giving us the total of 680 acres of land. We also have 68 houses. We hope sometime in '71 we will build another hundred houses on a hundred of the 640 acres.

This coming Saturday…young people will be walking throughout the world against hunger and poverty. It will be forty countries walking, millions of people throughout the world. In the United States it will be over 377 walks. These walkers are young people that really care about what's going on…And out of this walk—people will pay so much per mile for the kids that'll be walking—and out of this walk we hope to get a million dollars for Sunflower County…If we get the kind of economic support that we need in Sunflower County, in two more years…We'll have the tools to produce food ourselves.

A couple of weeks ago, we moved the first poor white family into Freedom Farm in the history of the state of Mississippi. A white man came to me and said, "I got five children and I don't have nowhere to live. I don't have food. I don't have anything. And my children, some of them, is sick." And we gave this man a house…

We have a job as black women, to support whatever is right, and to bring in justice where we've had so much injustice. Some people say, well, I work for $24 per week. That's not true in my case, I work sometimes for $15 per week. I remember my mother working for 25 and 30 cents per day.

But we are organizing ourselves now, because we don't have any other choice. Sunflower County is one of the few counties in the state of Mississippi where in that particular area we didn't lose one black teacher. Because . . . I went in and told the judge, I said, "Judge, we're not going to stand by and see you take a man with a master's degree and bring him down to janitor help. So if we don't have the principal…there ain't gonna *be* no school, private or public." These are the kinds of roles.

A few years ago throughout the country the middle-class black woman—I used to say not really black women, but the middle-class colored women, c-u-l-l-u-d, didn't even respect the kind of work that I was doing. But you see now, baby, whether you have a Ph.D., D.D., or no D, we're in this bag together. And whether you're from Morehouse or Nohouse, we're still in this bag together. Not to fight to try to liberate ourselves from the men—this is another trick to get us fighting among ourselves—but to work together with the black man, then we will have a better chance to just act as human beings, and to be treated as human beings in our sick society.

I would like to tell you in closing a story of an old man. This old man was very wise, and he could answer questions that was almost impossible for people to answer. So some people went to him one day, two young people, and said, "We're going to trick this guy today. We're going to catch a bird, and we're going to carry it to this old man. And we're going to ask him, 'This that we hold in our hands today, is it alive or is it dead?' If he says 'Dead,' we're going to turn it loose and let it fly. But if he says, 'Alive,' we're going to crush it." So they walked up to this old man, and they said, "This that we hold in our hands today, is it alive or is it dead?" He looked at the young people and he smiled. And he said, "It's in your hands."

"The Special Plight and the Role of Black Woman,"
Speech given at NAACP Legal
Defense Fund Institute,
New York City, May 7, 1971

TERMINATION AND RELOCATION IN RETROSPECT

by Donald L. Fixico

The years from 1945 to 1960 constituted one of the most crucial periods in the history of federal-Indian relations. Since 1960 Indians, bureaucrats, and the public have had ample time to digest the effects of termination and relocation policies on Native Americans and to formulate opinions about the intent of these policies. In everything that it represented, termination threatened the very core of American Indian existence—its culture. The federal government sought to de-Indianize Native Americans. The government hoped to ultimately negate Indian identity through assimilation into the mainstream society. First, however, government obligations to tribes had to be dissolved. Relocating Native Americans would help to achieve the goal of termination by removing them from the source of their cultural existence. Once Indians had given up their cultures for life in mainstream America, the government could abrogate special services to them. A former relocation officer recalled that "in the 50s Relocation was the instrument of termination," and "this was the policy of the Bureau."[1]

Between 1945 and 1960 the government processed 109 cases of termination affecting 1,369,000 acres of Indian land and an estimated 12,000 Indians. The end result of relocation is that over one-half of today's Indian population now resides in urban areas. So many changes within such a short time has had a tremendous effect on Native Americans; yet a high degree of tribal traditionalism has been retained.

Termination and relocation have often been mistakenly attributed to the nationalistic movement of the Eisenhower administration. Actually, the germs of both policies originated during the Truman administration. In fact, the results of two studies, the Hoover Task Force Commission Report and the Zimmerman Plan, laid the founda-

tions for termination and relocation. The Hoover Task Force Commission reported that Indians were ready to become "just" Americans and that they should begin to assume their roles as full citizens of the United States. The commission's report advised the dissolution of the federal government's involvement in Indian affairs and recommended that Native Americans utilize state services like other citizens. The Zimmerman Plan went farther by categorizing tribes into three groups based on criteria that supposedly measured readiness for withdrawal of federal trust.

It is unusual that the policy of termination and relocation began under Harry Truman, a president whose Democratic party traditionally advocated social justice for minorities and freedom of choice. However, Indian policy under the Truman administration disregarded Native American cultural integrity by reinstating the philosophy that Indians should be assimilated into the mainstream society. This irony is partially explained by the effects of World War II. Truman did not have the time to oversee Indian affairs, and the ensuing budget restrictions encouraged the move to reduce the costs of providing special services to Indians. Also, Truman's Fair Deal ideals, aimed at fitting everyone to a middle-class America, included Indians.

Today, many Indians and non-Indians alike remember well the negative repercussions of termination and relocation. They recall the fear and the threat that termination brought to Indian people. Relocation, also remembered for its negative impact, was overshadowed by the enormity of the fears surrounding the termination program. Termination was seen as an all-inclusive destroyer of Indian life-styles. George Pierre, former chief of the Colville Confederated Tribes of Washington, vividly described the fears that termination evoked in Native Americans:

> House Concurrent Resolution 108 adopted in 1953, sent the word termination spreading like a prairie fire of a pestilence through the Indian country. It stirred conflicting reactions among my people; to some it meant the severing of ties already loose and ineffective; others welcomed it as a promise of early sharing in tribal patrimony. Many outsiders realized that it provided a first step towards acquiring Indian resources. The great majority of

my people, however, feared the consequences. The action of Congress, accompanied by the phrase "as rapidly as possible," sounded to them like the stroke of doom.[2]

Many people remember termination as just another land grab for Indian properties. This seems to have been the case in many situations. In Nevada, Senator Pat McCarran repeatedly attempted to pass legislation to fee-patent certain lands for squatters living on the Paiute Reservation. In another case, one former relocation worker estimated that the Fort Peck tribes lost approximately a quarter of a million acres in land sales to non-Indians in Montana.[3] In the Klamath Basin, the lumber companies clearly became the actual beneficiaries of Klamath termination in 1961. Although federal officials expressed concern in preventing exploitation of the Klamaths, the lumber interests in southwestern Oregon dominated their actions. Lumber companies, banks, and numerous merchants depended on the Klamath timber cuttings. Although conservationists fought to prevent the lifting of restrictions on Klamath lands, they too were more concerned with the land. They argued that removal of trust restrictions would open up wilderness areas to lumber companies, and wildlife breeding and feeding grounds would be destroyed.[4]

Another dimension of Klamath termination concerns the monetary windfalls from timber sales that were distributed to members and the repercussions that followed. Each Klamath receiving the per capita payment of 43,000 dollars became game for local merchants, who aggressively sold them automobiles, televisions, and other goods at inflated prices. Many Klamath people were inexperienced in dealing with unscrupulous merchants and opportunists. There are numerous accounts of debauchery and schemes that tricked the Klamaths out of their properties. The same scene was repeated after the Menominee and other tribes received per capita payments. The government's plan for reducing the number of Indian people eligible for special services backfired when the suddenly rich Indians lost the monies and properties they had received after termination. They soon found themselves in need of assistance, and many tribes have since applied for

restoration of recognition. The Menominee have regained recognition and are again eligible to receive special services, and the Klamath now possess federal recognition.

The government was convinced that monetary settlements authorized by the Indian Claims Commission would improve tribal economies and benefit their livelihoods generally. By the end of the 1950s an estimated 42 million dollars was awarded to the tribes, while the total number of filed claims rose during the following years. In 1960 a claims attorney predicted that 25 million dollars would be spent on Indian claims, but by 1966 the figure had quintupled.[5] The Indian Claims Commission eventually awarded a total amount of 669 million dollars. In September 1978, Congress finally dissolved the Indian Claims Commission, and 133 unresolved dockets out of the original 617 were transferred to the U.S. Court of Claims.

Robert Bennett, formerly commissioner of Indian affairs, from 1966 to 1969, recalled that in the 1950s congressional reasoning for supporting the Indian Claims Commission was that a final dissolution of government obligations to Native Americans would result. Bennett stated that "the feeling grew up in Congress that if the people were to be paid for all their claims and unjustified acts on the part of the federal government, . . . this would mark the end of any kind of relationship with the federal government."[6] Finally, the government would pay its debts to the tribes once and for all. Such compensation would redeem the American government of its guilty history of mistreating American Indians.

Land has always been a common factor in federal-Indian relations. Since the early years of Indian-white contact, government officials have been convinced that division of tribal lands was the key to liberating Native Americans from impoverished communal life-styles and making them a part of mainstream America. In the 1950s, a deluge of legislation and federal actions poured forth efforts aimed at relocating Indians to urban areas. These efforts were motivated by the attempt to terminate costly government services to Indian people and to make lands available to interested whites.

Vast differences existed between the Indian policies of the 1950s and the early 1960s. Commissioner Dillon S. Myer and officials like H. Rex Lee, assistant commissioner during the early 1950s, took a direct approach in supporting termination legislation without regard to the possible harmful repercussions to Indian Americans. Although officials in the 1960s were also interested in eventually reducing government services to Indians, their actions were offered as reforms.

There were two types of individuals in government who were responsible for termination policy. Commissioner Dillon Myer, Senator Arthur Watkins of Utah, and Senator Pat McCarran typified the group identified as proassimilationists and Eisenhower men (although Myer was a Truman appointee). They were convinced that all Americans should conform to one society while participating in a personal struggle for achieving success. These men came from rural backgrounds that stressed hardwork ethics, and they admired individual accomplishments. Most had succeeded through their own efforts, and they believed strongly in laissez faire. Their approach to Indian affairs was often influenced by personal or political gains.

The second category included humanitarians like Senator Reva Beck Bosone of Utah, Senator Richard Neuberger of Oregon, and Senator James Murray of Montana. They worked in the best interests of the Indians and only introduced termination legislation when the tribal groups requested such bills. Some individuals, like Florida Senator George Smathers, originally favored assimilation, but after becoming familiar with the conditions of Native Americans and understanding their problems, they joined the ranks of the humanitarians to prevent the exploitation of Native American people. Certainly, numerous other federal officials played a part in the policies affecting Indians, but the ones mentioned above dominated federal-Indian affairs.

Without doubt, the Eisenhower administration encouraged the movement to abrogate government relations with Indians. Interestingly, Dwight D. Eisenhower symbolized the 1950s and the motives behind termination. His image as a World War II hero manifested another image that reflected a new Americanism. American citizens would have likely elected Ike as president of the United States in 1948 if he had chosen to be a candidate. Four years later, his popularity was still at its zenith, although no one really knew whether he was a Democrat or a Republican until he publicly declared the latter. The presidential election of 1952 held little doubt that Ike would win. His campaign platform called for a modernized middle-class society, encouraging citizens to redefine the American dream and to pursue it. At the time, most of the nation's citizenry were conservative, hard-working, and Republican. The mood of the country and the ideology and doctrines of the Eisenhower era amplified intense termination policy. The grand plan was for all Americans, including minorities, to conform to a middle-class society.

The architects of federal Indian policy failed to realize that assimilating Native Americans into middle-class America would take more time and effort than they wanted to provide. A large portion of the Indian population continually preferred to maintain distinct cultural communities within the larger urban communities. Furthermore, the existence of minority enclaves in large cities today is evidence that Indians and other ethnic groups were not ready to assimilate. Doubtlessly, urban Indians chose not to assimilate and white society did not encourage acceptance of Indians. One Apache suggested that whites maintained contradictory attitudes toward Indians. He asserted that white society deemed "everyone had a right to be himself, to be an individual. But on the other hand as soon as one person is different or tries to remain different, everybody asks, 'why can't he be like the rest of us?' "[7]

Several factors were at work in creating the appearance that the mainstream society was receptive to Indians. The Eisenhower administration attempted to unify all sectors of society into one culture. Ike envisioned a crusade to advance the American civilization into a position of world leadership, with the democratic principles of the United States serving as the cause. This ideology required all citizens to integrate into a middle-class society. If necessary, existing minority cultures would be forfeited in order to reach this grand ideal. As Americans enthusiastically embraced Eisenhower's grand plan, it appeared that assimilation of Indians into mainstream society would become a reality.

A grave error was made in assuming that Indians were ready for assimilation into urban life. Federal officials failed to comprehend the existing strength of Native American cultures and the tenacity with which Indians would try to preserve their heritage. The unfamiliarity of federal officials with the dynamics of traditional tribalism resulted in frustration for both them and the Indians. The officials became discouraged especially with apprehensive tribal governments that took lengthy periods of time to decide on termination questions. From the viewpoint of federal officials, the tribal leaders appeared unable or unwilling to deal with termination, and prodding was necessary to convince them to accept termination.

Traditionally, most tribes took whatever length of time was necessary to settle an issue by general consensus. Naturally, the more important the issue, the more time they required. In deciding on termination, or any significant issue, tribal officials continued to hold meetings for discussion until a nearly unanimous decision was reached. Sometimes this approach delayed action past the termination deadline set by Congress, as seen in the Klamaths' case; frequently, the magnitude of the issue caused strife within the tribal community.

Indians who successfully survived the withdrawal of trust status from their properties and assimilated readily into the mainstream were exceptions to the norm. Most Indians simply were not prepared socially, psychologically, or economically for the sudden removal of federal trust status. One individual said that recollections of the termination years of the 1950s brought back harsh memories, and she did not think Indians were ready for termination "because they couldn't take care of themselves even with help" from the government.[8] "We're not ready for termination right now," another elder Brule Sioux exclaimed. "I said at least twenty-five years is a short time.

But I think the next generation through education will stand to compete in this world with the non-Indians."[9]

The intense social and psychological adjustments that confronted Indians has been best described in novels like N. Scott Momaday's *House Made of Dawn* and Leslie Silko's *Ceremony*. Both books portray Indian veterans who are adjusting to a new way of life after World War II, while coming into contact with the American mainstream society. These two works are invaluably perceptive and vividly convey, from an Indian point of view, the intense human trauma of adjusting to a different culture.

In reality, relocation was difficult for Indians whose cultural integrity was challenged by urbanization. After finding the street life of the cities unbearable, many resorted to alcohol to escape the social and economic pressures of assimilation. Economic survival in the city forced many single Indian women into prostitution in order to provide for themselves and their children. "I have seen divorces, I have seen the kids, I have seen so many women that go to prostitute, you know they have to have money," lamented one Kiowa woman.[10]

From 1952, when the relocation program began, until the end of the 1967 fiscal year, 61,500 Indians received vocational training. Nonetheless, the unemployment rate for Native Americans during the 1960s averaged 40 percent. On reservations the unemployment rate was much higher. At Pine Ridge the rate was 75 percent for most of the year, and rose as high as 95 percent during the winter. Average Indian family incomes were horribly substandard in comparison with average American earnings. In 1964, for example, Native American family incomes averaged less than one-third of the national figure. In 1968 the net income for Indian families was about 1,500 dollars, while more than one-half of all white families earned at least 5,893 dollars. High unemployment and underemployment were partly attributable to the lack of education among young adults. The high school dropout rate for Indians averaged 60 percent in 1964.[11] Indian housing remained substandard both on reservations and in cities. On reservations 63,000 families lived in dilapidated houses without plumbing. Statistics indicated that Indians suffered far more health problems than other Americans. Whereas the average life span for white Americans was seventy years, an Indian could expect to live only forty-four years.[12]

Life in slum areas demoralized Native Americans, especially after relocation officers had led them to believe that their livelihoods would be vastly upgraded after moving to urban areas. For the small number who had received vocational training or attended college, improvement was possible. Many men worried about their families and their personal lives; and when they could no longer cope with their problems, they fumed to alcohol and/or abandoned their families to escape the tortuous reality of relocation.

The social and psychological problems of relocatees mounted as maladjustment to city life fostered an identity crisis that tormented many relocatees. After leaving their traditional social structures on reservations and in rural communities, which served as the basis for their psychological balance with kin and nature, they had nothing. Isolation and loneliness in the big cities confronted them. The city's alien environment was unlike anything they had experienced. Their perceptions of space, time, matter, energy, and causality differed vastly from that of the urban scene.[13] Their concepts of values, norms, and behavior, different in comparison with those of white society, bred cultural conflicts with other urban Americans. As members of a small minority attempting to adjust to the urban scene, Indian Americans felt inferior. Loss of morale and pride threatened their personal identity, causing many relocatees to wander and drift within the cities, searching for fundamental elements as they knew them traditionally in an attempt to reestablish some sense of their mental equilibrium. In seeking comfort through socialization, the relocatees tried to locate other Indians, especially those from their own tribe and reservation. Interactions with other Indians did not erase the loneliness or the coldness of an insensitive urban society. Some Indians contemplated self-destruction; the more depressed individuals committed suicide.

Difficulties with relocation to American cities were not unique to Indians. Other ethnic groups had migrated to metropolitan areas throughout the United States, and they shared many of the experiences that urban Indians encountered. But the dynamics involved in relocation from reservations to cities differed from that of migration from foreign countries. Groups from different nations have a better chance than Indians in adapting to urban areas for two major reasons. First, they elected to migrate to American cities and often desired to become quickly Americanized. Foreign immigrants left their motherlands for political, economic, and/or religious reasons, electing to come to America, where they could exercise their beliefs and strive to live their dreams. They shared a belief in many American ideals—individualism, attainment of wealth, and advancement. In contrast, many Indian relocatees did not leave their country but, rather, left the center of their culture and beliefs. In the cities, their beliefs in communal life-styles and their intolerance of close encounters with other people were misunderstood by the mainstream society.

Secondly, relocation and termination programs were aimed at destroying Indian cultures to speed up the process of assimilation. Immigrants, on the other hand, could move into cultural enclaves that already existed within the cities. No one expected them to give up the elements of their cultures since they shared the same basic ideas as other Americans.

Obviously, centuries-old Indian cultures could not be undone by the mere enactment of termination and relocation policies. Federal officials of the early Eisenhower years were interested in abolishing federal obligations and saw little importance in preserving Indian traditions. Stewart Udall, Secretary of the Interior during the Kennedy administration, recalled that the basic attitude of the Eisenhower administration was "a general demoralization and a feeling on everyone's part that there ought to be some simple solution" to the Indian problem. "Their so-called termination policy," he added, "is that what we ought to do is put them on their own and let them sink or swim."[14]

438

There were no "simple" solutions for reforming Indian conditions. Further reform measures actually compounded the problems for Indians who were attempting to assimilate into the American mainstream. Public Law 280 was enacted as an effort to convince Indian people to utilize state services, but provisions within the law also established state jurisdiction over reservations within certain states—a move which was received negatively by Native Americans. Former Indian Commissioner Robert Bennett recalled that "the Indian tribes have never been in favor of the extension of civil and criminal jurisdiction of states over Indian reservations, and they fought constantly since the enactment of this legislation to have it amended." The effort to alter the act focused on allowing Indian consent to its application, so that states unilaterally could not extend civil or criminal jurisdiction over Indians. Bennett recalled that "this policy placed great fear in the hearts and minds of Indian people because the Indian identity rests with the individual tribes and the tribal identity."[15] Nothing stopped state governments from extending their control over Indian communities until 1968, when the Indian Civil Rights Act amended the law to require referendums among the tribes affected.

Assimilation of Indians into the American mainstream at all costs was the objective of the early Eisenhower administration. Years later, in an interview, Senator Arthur Watkins of Utah described his efforts in Indian affairs to help Native Americans assimilate. "I was chairman of the Indian subcommittee of the Interior Committee of the Senate. For a number of years, at least while the Republicans were in power, I put over a lot of projects for the Indians, along with my western associates."[16] The Senator believed in immediate reform for Indians, and he dismissed the idea that Indians were *not* ready economically and socially for termination. Watkins and his associates pushed termination to its apex during the Eighty-third Congress, thus leading to a movement in Congress that continued through the early 1960s.

During the Kennedy years, some newspapers also supported the termination philosophy that Indians were ready for assimilation. Blind to the social and economic maladjustment that Indians encoun-

tered, an editorial in the Washington *Star,* on 27 August 1962, maintained that Indians should "join the rest of the Country and stop stagnating as museum pieces." The same piece stated its biased view that the "average Indian was not stupid" and did not require special treatment from the federal government."[17] Such commentary supported the belief that Indians could easily assimilate; and white conservatives could not understand why Native Americans did not easily adjust to the norms of the mainstream.

Congress continued to pass trust removal legislation through the mid- 1960s. The following statement of the Senate Committee on Interior and Insular Affairs in 1964 indicates the members' support for termination.

The Committee is deeply concerned about the failure of the Bureau of Indian Affairs to carry out the intent of House Concurrent Resolution 108, 83rd Congress, relating to termination programs for tribes, many of whom were reported by the Bureau itself as being ready for termination legislation more then ten years ago. As the Indian Claims Commission continues to make awards to tribes and substantial sums become available to the Indians, it becomes imperative that legislation be recommended to permit withdrawal of Federal Services where the Indians are able to conduct their affairs without supervision by the Bureau. At the beginning of the 88th Congress the committee plans to hold hearings on this subject, and the manner in which the Bureau has performed its responsibilities pursuant to the 1953 concurrent resolution.[18]

In April 1964, the House of Representatives passed H.R. 7883 to terminate federal control over one particular California Indian *rancheria,* but only with the permission of its residents. In 1958, Congress had authorized the eventual termination of trust for forty-one *rancherías.* Shortly thereafter, the government terminated fourteen more *rancherías,* and the other jurisdictions remained in various stages of trust withdrawals.[19] In 1966 the Department of the Interior announced the end of trust relations for four *rancherías:* Scotts Valley, Robinson, Guidiville, and Greenville; and in February of the following year, five more *rancherías*—North Fork, Picayune, Graton, Pinoville, and Quartz Valley—were also freed of trust restrictions.[20] In 1964 this number was amended to include more than one hundred *rancherías*.[21]

Since 1960 Native Americans from California *rancherías* and the Pacific Northwest have mingled with white neighbors in nearby communities and appear adjusted to white American norms. One Colville tribesperson wrote to President Johnson to report: "Our tribe is ready for Termination and Liquidation. Of the 45 Indians in our tribe only a few live on the reservation." Her tribe was one of many Colville tribes; she estimated that most of her people were fairly well educated, and she asserted that they had been fighting several years for their equal rights as citizens.[22] A majority of California Indians expressed similar sentiments about termination and claimed that they were ready to supervise their own affairs.[23]

Although many Indians of California and the Pacific Northwest requested termination of federal supervision, they frequently experienced social and psychological problems while adjusting to their new status. Relocation to urban areas was eased by socialization with other urban Indians. Father Wilfred Schoenberg, a Jesuit priest at the Pacific Northwest Indian Center, wrote to President Lyndon Johnson about urban Indian adjustment and the need for assistance in the cities. Schoenberg stressed that Indian centers were essential to the survival of Indian people in metropolitan areas because they provided a tangible cohesiveness for relocatees, something to cling to during the painful period of urban adjustment. He maintained that federal officials had neglected Indian problems, and he hoped a new era in federal-Indian affairs would bring relief to the Indian people.[24]

President Johnson depended on his Secretary of the Interior, Stewart Udall, to fulfill federal obligations to Native Americans and to oversee Indian affairs. He reported to the president when inquiries were made, but the Interior Secretary actually drew his information from the commissioner of Indian affairs, whose office was in daily contact with the tribes. Thus, it was important for the secretary and the commissioner to be in close communication.

Secretary Udall asserted that the Bureau of Indian Affairs could do more to help Indians in the relocation process. He suggested a change in its leadership, proposing that the BIA needed a dynamic commissioner to replace Philleo Nash and to formalize a new policy to help Indians.[25] Increased dissatisfaction with Nash paved the way for the appointment of Robert Bennett, a Wisconsin Oneida, as the new commissioner of Indian affairs in 1966.

The reforms of the Johnson Administration in its "War on Poverty" caused problems for Commissioner Bennett. Dissatisfied Indians who suffered economically sharply criticized the federal government.[26] Years later, in an interview Bennett recalled that the whole political climate in Washington had changed dramatically since the 1950s. He particularly believed that Congress would not consider approving a piece of legislation like the infamous termination measure H.C.R. 108 during the mid-1960s. In fact, President Johnson expressed opposition to unilateral termination in a message before a national meeting in Kansas City in February 1967. Afterward, federal Indian policy moved in a different direction, dedicated to the development of human and natural resources on reservations with federal assistance.[27]

Even during the 1970s, Native Americans remained angry about termination during the 1950s. A Northern Cheyenne stated during an interview in 1971: "I'm . . . 100 percent against this termination, [in] any shape or form, and I've been this way for as far back as I [*sic*] can remember."[28] Even when tribespeople did not fully understand the termination policy, they denounced it as part of a protest against past injustices. Their complaints consisted of objections against numerous legislative measures, trust status removal by the Interior Department, BIA control, and the failure of the government to achieve liberation for Indians from second-class citizenship. Naturally, the BIA was the target for some very harsh criticism. One Indian spokesman stated on television in 1970: "The only thing to do with the B.I.A. is to abolish it. I want to make something right now certain, that I am not for termination, I am for the abolishment of the Bureau of Indian Affairs."[29]

On Indian-white relations, John Dressler, a wise and elderly Washo, clearly expressed the differences between the two peoples:

> Today, what plays an important part within our Indian nation communities—our Indian people and their culture—is the introduction of the white man's culture, and we became bicultural. And it's difficult at times to define the white man's culture and use it as our culture also because of the educational processes that exist. There is no other means. We cannot accept it any other way because I feel its necessary that we adopt some areas of the white culture with ours, we being the minority in this case. This is what makes it difficult for a lot of our people to understand. At times, with some of the people, it gets to the point where they become frustrated because they see no sense in participating in the white man's culture and entirely forgetting their own.[30]

Fortunately for Indian Americans, the termination and relocation policies during the 1960s and 1970s were not as harmful as those applied in the 1950s. Today, Indians are better adjusted to the norms of the dominant society, whereas previously termination and relocation had thrust Native Americans into an alien culture without regard to the possible social and economic upheavals facing them. Federal officials in the Bureau of Indian Affairs and Congress were at fault for professing that the time had arrived for the red man to live as a white man in the city. To some extent, the Indians' voluntary attitude in leaving their homelands after World War II enhanced the government's conviction that they were ready for termination and relocation. The conditions on reservations also convinced federal officials that they were right in assuming that Native Americans were ready to assimilate into urban society. In effect, termination was thought to be the answer to the Indian problem. For the most part, termination frightened American Indians, while bureaucrats envisioned it as the panacea for all of their own problems in working with Indians.

As an attempt to Americanize Indians, the federal Indian policy of termination and relocation failed. Ironically, the federal government did not learn from its history of relations with Native American peoples that no single policy can be devised that will successfully serve all Indians, who represent many different tribes, languages, and cultures. Even within the tribes, there are differences represented by various kinship systems, social roles, and political status; and yet, the federal government's attempt to design a termination program to suit individual tribes drew criticism for not establishing one definite policy. Such a paradox has continually plagued the federal government, and Indians have suffered the consequences.

Footnotes:

1. Stanley D. Lyman, interview by Floyd O'Neil and Gregory Thompson, n.d., Pine Ridge Agency, South Dakota, interview no. 1031, box 54, acc. no. 24, Doris Duke Indian Oral History Collection, Special Collections, Marriott Library, University of Utah.

2. George Pierre, *American Indian Crisis* (San Antonio: The Naylor Company, 1971), p. 39.

3. See n.1.

4. Psychosocial problems of Indian residents in Klamath County after termination are discussed in Charles C. Brown, "Identification of Selected Problems of Indians Residing in Klamath County, Oregon—An Examination of Data Generated since Termination of the Klamath Reservation" (Ph.D. dies., University of Oregon, 1973).

5. Haney D. Rosenthal, "Their Day in Court: A History of the Indian Claims Commission" (Ph.D. dies., Kent State University, 1973).

   An early study of the Indian Claims Commission Act is Thomas Le Duc, "The Work of the Indian Claims Commission under the Act of 1946," *Pacific Historical Review* 26 (February 1957),pp. 1-16. A discussion of the end of the commission, and information on Arthur Watkins as the chief commissioner, is in the "Post-Senate, Claims Commission" folder, Arthur V. Watkins Papers, Special Collections, Archives and Manuscripts, Harold B. Lee Library, Brigham Young University, Provo, Utah.

6. Robert Bennett, interview by Joe B. Frantz, 13 November 1968, Washington, D.C., Oral History Collection, Lyndon B. Johnson Presidential Library, Austin, Texas; a similar interview with Bennett, no. 836, is in the Doris Duke Indian Oral History Collection, Special Collections, William Zimmerman Library, University of New Mexico, Albuquerque.

7. Philip Cassadore, interview by J. Bell, 14 October 1970, Arizona, folder A—Doris Duke Indian Oral History Collection, Arizona State Museum, University of Arizona, Tucson.

8. Lenora DeWitt, interview by Gerald Wolf, 25 August 1971, Lower Brule, South Dakota, interview no. 39, pt. 1, tape 786s, microfiche, American Indian Research Project-Doris Duke Indian Oral History Collection, University of South Dakota, Vermillion.

9. Moses Big Crow, interview by Herbert Hoover, 31 August 1971, Vermillion, South Dakota, interview no. 50, pt. 2, tape 745, ibid.

10. Lena Haberman, interview by Georgia Brown, 12 June 1971, La Mirada, California, interview no. O.H. 639, Doris Duke Indian Oral History Collection, Oral History Collection, California State University, Fullerton.

11. Memorandum, Stewart Udall to Lyndon B. Johnson, 20 January 1964, executive file FG, box 203, Lyndon B. Johnson Presidential Library.

12. The Indian Health Program, U.S. Public Health Service Report (August 1972), DHEW Publication no. (ASM) 73-12,003, pp. 1-36.

13. For a discussion of Indian-white differences in perceptions of space, time, matter, energy, and causality, see Vine Deloria, Jr., *The Metaphysics of Modern Existence* (New York: Harper and Row, 1979). Differences of perceptions are also explained in Jamake Highwater, *The Primal Mind: Vision and Reality in Indian America* (New York: Harper and Row, 1980).

14. Stewart Udall, interview (no. 3) by Joe B. Frantz, 19 July 1969, Washington, D.C., tape 1, Oral History Collection, Lyndon B. Johnson Presidential Library.

15. See n. 6. Robert Bennett commented on the Indian reluctance to accept P.L. 180 because of the limitations and restrictions of the law, which are covered in the following articles: Linda Cree, "Extension of County Jurisdiction over Indian Reservations in California, Public Law 180 and the Ninth Circuit," *Hastings Law Journal 25*, no. 3 (May 1974, pp. 535-94; Joel E. Gurthals, "State Civil Jurisdiction over Tribal Indians-A Re-Examination," *Montan Law Review* 35, no. 2 (Summer 1974), pp. 340-47; and Louis D. Persons II, "Jurisdication: Public Law 280-Local Regulation of Protected Indian Lands," *American Indian Law Review* 6, no. 2 (Winter 1978), pp. 403-15.

16. Arthur V. Watkins, interview by Ed Edwin, 14 January 1968, Washington, D.C., Oral History Collection, Dwight D. Eisenhower Presidential Library.

17. Jenkins L. Jones, "Time for Indians to Join U.S.," Washington *Star*, 27 August 1962.

18. Joseph J. S. Feahers to Alan Bible, 9 December 1964, box 245, Alan Bible Papers, Special Collections, University of Nevada Library, Reno.

19. Harold T. Johnson to Clair Engle, 23 April 1964, "Indian Affairs-General folder," Clair Engle Papers, Tehama County Library, Red Bluff, California.

20. "Three California Rancherias Terminated by the Bureau of Indian Affairs," 1 September 1965, news release by the Department of the Interior, and "Four More California Rancherias Terminated," 25 February 1966, news release by the Department of the Interior, box 34, Records of the Department of the Interior, Lyndon B. Johnson Presidential Library.

21. "Federal supervision Terminated at Greenville Rancheria, California," 15 December 1966, news release by the Department of Interior; and "Federal Supervision Terminated at Quartz Valley Rancheria, California," 27 January 1967, news release by the Department of Interior, ibid.

22. Adeline Crosswell to Lyndon B. Johnson, 26 August 1964, box 74, Gen LE-IN, White House Central Files, Lyndon B. Johnson Presidential Library. A study that disagrees with the suggestion that the Colvilles were ready for termination is Susanna A. Hayes, "The Resistance to Eduction for Assimilation by the Colville Indians, 1872-1972" (Ph.D. dies., University of Michigan, 1973). Hayes contends that the Colvilles retained many socialcultural traditions despite the effects of government policy, including termination, over a hundred year period.

23. U.S. Congress, Senate, H.R. 10911, "to provide for preparation of a roll of persons of California Indian descent and the distribution of certain judgement funds," 90th Cong., 2d sess., 4 June 1968; a copy of this bill; which was urged by many California Indians, is in box 76, Wayne Morse Papers, Special Collections, University of Oregon Library.

24. Wilfred P. Schoenberg to Lyndon B. Johnson, 8 May 1966, Gen-IN 2, White House Central Files, Lyndon B. Johnson, Presidential Library.

25. See n. 14, John Carver, Jr., interview (no. 5) by William Moss, 7 October 1969, Washington, D.C., Oral History Collection, John F. Kennedy Presidential Library, Waltham, Massachusetts; this interview substantiates the poor relationship between Udal and Hash. Udall's views on Indian affairs are clarified in Stewart L. Udall, "The State of the Indian Nation-An introduction," Arizona Law Review 10 (Winter 1968), pp. 554-57.

26. See n. 6.

27. Ibid.

28. Allen Rowland, interview by Al Spang, 5 March 1971, Lame Deer, Montana, interview no. 864, Doris Duke indian Oral History Collection, Special Collections, William Zimmerman Library.

29. Panel Discussion on "Termination" for the television show, "The Advocates," 24 January 1970, taped by Michael B. Husband, interview no. 450, ibid.

30. John Dressler, "Recollections of a Washo Statesman," p. 134, Oral History Project, Special Collections, University of Nevada Library..

Review Questions and Glossary

To The Student: Here are some steps that will help you to review the readings in a time-saving manner while also increasing your ability to think critically about them.

Essays: Always ask yourself, before you begin reading, "What is this essay about?" That is a way of asking, What is the *thesis* of this essay? Just as in every English composition course you have to state clearly what your thesis is when you write an essay, the authors of the essays in this text must do that as well. The *title* and introductory paragraphs of the essay usually give you the first general statement of the author's thesis. The *sub-titles* within the essay highlight how the author is going about explaining that thesis in detail. In this process the author may use anecdotes (brief stories that illustrate the point that is being made), numerical data (including graphs, tables or other specific statistical information) and supporting arguments based on these data, stories and graphic illustrations, in order to present the strongest support that she/he can give the thesis. The last paragraphs of an essay usually summarize what the author has said in explaining his/her thesis.

A few of the essays are simply extended anecdotes (longer stories illustrating a theme). An essay such as "Mastering the Arts of Democracy" (16) is a nuts and bolts "how-to" essay.

Stories: If you can answer the questions, "Who are these characters? How are they interacting?" You will be able to follow the development of each story readily. The development of the short story excerpt from James' *The Bostonians* (13) is driven by the dialogue through which the man and two women interact. James' narrative description of the details of their appearance and the psychological attributes of their personalities helps us to follow this *interior* tale of *manners*. Chestnutt's *The Sheriff's Children*, (14) which takes place in a different post-Civil War milieu than James' tale, is very much driven by a series of external actions. But here too we learn much about the characters (one of which is a lynch mob) in this tale from the author's description of how the characters look and think.

Poems: The most effective way to enter the poet's vision is to **sound** the poem: read the poem aloud so that you can begin to appreciate how the poet is using rhythm and imagery (sound and sight) in the creation of the poem. Pay attention to the images evoked and what they mean of themselves as well as in association with one another. Try this with two decidedly different poems, "Ivory Bracelets" (26) and "Madness Without Head" (44) and you will see how effective an approach it can be.

To The Instructor: You will find that the review questions which follow for each Chapter can be used for in-class discussion or assigned to be handed in at a following class, with the student simply writing the answer in the space provided and tearing the page from the book. These questions also can be used, with or without modification, as test items.

NATIONAL IDENTITY AND THE DEMOCRATIC PROCESS

Introduction RECOGNITIONS: HOW DO WE SEE EACH OTHER

1. What is *civicism?*

2. Why is it necessary that each citizen have *staying power* in learning to *recognize* others as we would recognize ourselves?

3. What exactly is our national culture?

4. Why are the metaphors "melting pot" and "tossed salad" inadequate in describing our diversity?

5. Why is "whiteness" not a norm which assigns everyone else value, and not a race?

6. What does it mean to say that whiteness, as a norm or race, is an insistence on privilege?

7. How does the author explain that multi-culturalism, properly understood, is not enthnocentrism?

8. In what ways are *nonrecognition* and *misrecognition* forms of oppression?

9. What does Judith Shklar mean by saying that *each* of us as citizens must have "standing"?

Part I—National Identity and the Democratic Process

Chapter One — Grafting a New Society

1. (a.) What other creation myths do you know?

   _____

   _____

   _____

   _____

   _____

   (b.) How would you compare them to this Aztec myth of Quetzacoatl?

   _____

   _____

   _____

   _____

   _____

2. (a.) What were the differing world views of the Native Americans, Europeans and Africans who met in this "new world"?

   _____

   _____

   _____

   _____

   _____

   (b.) What does it mean to say that European religious beliefs were basically *celestial* while the religious beliefs of Native Americans and Africans were basically *terrestrial*?

   _____

   _____

   _____

   _____

   _____

   Documented Essay Question: Who were the first (pre-Columbian) Americans? Where did they live? What were their societies like? (*Please use space at top of following page for your outline.*)

447

_____
_____
_____
_____
_____
_____
_____
_____
_____
_____

3. (a.) How, according to Takaki, was savagery *racialized* by the colonists of New England?

_____
_____
_____
_____
_____

(b.) How was the savagery attributed to the Irish by the British in the Old World different?

_____
_____
_____
_____
_____

4. Lebsock tells us that of the Indian, West African and English women in Virginia in the 17th century, "not one of the three groups has what we think of as 'traditional' sex roles." Describe a woman of each of these different cultures whose role was non-traditional.

_____
_____
_____
_____

5. What aspects of Puritanism are being condemned by Hawthorne in *Alice Doan's Appeal*?

_____
_____
_____
_____

CHAPTER TWO — CONSTITUTIONAL GOVERNMENT AND THE COMMONWEAL

6.   What other governments in the world can you identify which consider that the citizens of their nation have "unalienable Rights" including "Life, Liberty and the pursuit of Happiness"?

_____

_____

_____

_____

_____

7.   How is the operation of each of the three branches of our constitutional government (Legislative, Executive and Judicial) evident in the events of this week's or this month's news?

_____

_____

_____

_____

_____

8.   What, according to Hamilton, were the motives of "many *inconsiderable* men" who would have been pleased to see the Constitution voted down?

_____

_____

_____

_____

_____

9.   Identify and explain the Articles and Sections of the Constitution that might reflect the Indian models Weatherford cites— particularly those he claims Benjamin Franklin (1706-1790) may have influenced.

_____

_____

_____

_____

_____

CHAPTER THREE — IMMIGRANT LIVES

10.   How are the Shimerdas *quintessential* immigrants of their time?

_____

_____

_____

_____

_____

11. (a.) What were the personal characteristics and social conditions that distinguished the immigrants of the First Immigration from those of the Second Immigration?

_____

_____

_____

_____

_____

(b.) What does Higham regard as the "paradox" of immigration in American History?

_____

_____

_____

_____

_____

12.   Given John Hope Franklin's historical analysis, how might the expectations African Americans have of our social and political culture differ from those of other immigrant groups?

_____

_____

_____

_____

_____

451

CHAPTER FOUR — POLITICS AND SOCIAL PRACTICE

13.   What brings the characters in James' *The Bostonians* together; and how pleased is each of them with this meeting?

_____

_____

_____

_____

_____

14. (a.) In what ways is the post-Civil War community of *The Sheriff's Children* different from that of the post-Civil War community of *The Bostonians*?

_____

_____

_____

_____

_____

(b.) What kind of father is the Sheriff?

_____

_____

_____

_____

_____

15.   What are the ten *arts of democracy*?

_____

_____

_____

_____

_____

(a.) Why are these democratic practices regarded as *arts*?

(b.) What are the hallmarks, benefits and 'how-to's' for each of these arts?

(c.) Give specific illustrations of how you realistically could practice each of these arts.

16. (a.) How are the six eighteenth century values that contributed to the U.S. democratic tradition evident in today's society?

(b.) How are both "conservatism" and "liberalism" in U.S. politics outgrowths of our liberal democratic tradition?

ACTIVITIES (PART 1)

A. Make an informal survey of the historical ethnic or national cultures of three of your friends. How many of those friends or their family members speak a language other than English?.

B. What information (in books, films, journals...) does your local library or college library have on the history of Indian habitation in your state? Volunteer to make an oral presentation on one of these sources to your classmates.

C. What information on the history of immigration in your state can you find through your state's historical society?

D. If you have access to a computer, you may want to search for the information in B. and C. above by going to the Web site **www.loc.gov**—which is the Library of Congress archives.

E. In the 90 or more years of Oppechancanough's life (late 1550s to 1646 —Nash:*"Three Worlds Meet"*) he saw great changes in his life and the differing lives of those who were not American Indian. As a group project, report on similar major changes in the lives and eras of Benjamin Franklin (1706-1790) Tecumseh (1768-1813) and Frederick Douglass (1818-1895).

PART II— CONTENDING CLAIMS AND INTERCULTURAL COMMUNICATION

CHAPTER FIVE — OURSELVES AND OTHERS

17. How great is the range of humanity celebrated by Whitman in *Faces*? Give specific examples.

_____

_____

_____

_____

_____

_____

18. Some aspects of our shared national identity are not assets when interacting with non-US citizens. What are they, according to Stewart and Bennett and how might we change them?

_____

_____

_____

_____

_____

19. What is the scientific failure of the concept of human races, based on this excerpt from the thirty year study of **The History and Geography of Human Genes**, by Cavalli-Sforza, Menozzi, and Piazza.

_____

_____

_____

_____

_____

20. (a.) What is ethnic stratification?

_____

_____

_____

_____

_____

(b.) How is it related to prejudice and discrimination?

_____

_____

_____

_____

_____

21. (a.) What are the three criteria upon which Yinger bases his topology of ethnicity?

_____

_____

_____

_____

_____

(b.) Based on these three criteria, where would you locate yourself on Table 1.1 "Varieties of Ethnic Identity"?

_____

_____

_____

_____

_____

22. What is the myth of a white America? Explain in detail, based on Eoyang's reflections on diversity.

_____

_____

_____

_____

23. How does Sean's confusion about racial and sexual characteristics mirror social confusion about race and gender?

_____

_____

_____

_____

_____

24. Write a brief paragraph summarizing facets f your personal cultural identity. Now adopt an additional culture at random (Finnish, Nigerian, Mexican, Chinese, etc.) and write a brief paragraph on how this might change your self-image and the ways in which you interact with your current friends. Then consult a current encyclopedia, world almanac or similar reference to see to what degree you might have stereotyped your *additional* cultural identity. If you know someone of that identity, as them to read your second paragraph to see what misrecognitions you may have included.

_____

_____

_____

_____

_____

25. Why does Primo Levi say that "To refuse to communicate is a failing"?

_____

_____

_____

_____

_____

CHAPTER SIX — CLASS AND POWER

26.   What are the stories hidden by the surfaces of *Ivory Bracelets*?

_____

_____

_____

_____

_____

27. (a.) How do you distinguish between social differentiation, social inequality and social stratification?

_____

_____

_____

_____

_____

(b.) According to Kerbo, what are the causes of increasing income inequality in the United States?

_____

_____

_____

_____

_____

(c.) How do you distinguish between social differentiation, social inequality and social stratification?

_____

_____

_____

_____

_____

(d.) According to Kerbo, what are the causes of increasing income inequality in the United States?

_____
_____
_____
_____
_____

28. Zinn and Eitzen's *Moving Away from the Nuclear Mold* substantially assays the structural transformation of U.S. families. What are the varieties of our families?

_____
_____
_____
_____
_____

29. What evidences do you find of the new working class in your neighborhood, community, village or city? Be specific; check your local newspaper, for example.

_____
_____
_____
_____
_____

30. What are the varieties of aggression against women historically and in your time?

_____
_____
_____
_____

31. How would you describe the relationship between the brother and sisters in Allman's *Sisters*?

_____
_____
_____
_____
_____

32.   What are the distinctions between the following:

(a.) life cycle / life course

_____

_____

_____

_____

_____

(b.) role conformity / role creation

_____

_____

_____

_____

_____

(c.) life transition / life marker?

_____

_____

_____

_____

_____

(d.) Give concrete examples, based on your personal experience, of (a.), (b.) and (c.)

_____

_____

_____

_____

_____

33/34. In what ways is the son of the poem *Graduation Day* different from the son in the short story *Grandma'a Wake*?

_____

_____

_____

_____

_____

_____

_____

_____

_____

_____

_____

_____

_____

_____

_____

_____

_____

_____

_____

_____

_____

_____

_____

35. What feelings does Masterson convey in the meditative *Calling Home*?

_____

_____

_____

_____

_____

_____

_____

_____

_____

ACTIVITIES (PART 2)

A. *Documented Essay Question:* In the proposed or approved national budget for this year (a summary of which usually is published in **Business Week** or similar financial magazines; or is attainable from your local Senator or Representative as well as from the Congressional website) what do you find that fits Kerbo's description of "wealthfare" costs to the taxpayer? How does it compare to welfare costs? Is the burden of paying these and other costs, given current tax laws, carried equitably by persons in all income brackets? How and why might you want to change allocations in this budget? How and why might you want to revise current tax laws? For internet search, go to **www.loc.gov,** when the homepage for the Library of Congress appears, click on "text only," (upper right) find listing for Congress or *Thomas* (middle left) click on that and access current budget information.

_____

_____

_____

_____

_____

_____

_____

_____

_____

_____

_____

_____

_____

B. Do an informal survey of the different forms of aggression against women that you observe over the period of a week, including illustrations from television features and movies, local television and radio news, and among your acquaintances and friends, at work or social events. Summarize your findings and comment on your reactions to them.

C. As a group project, do a class presentation on the lives of the following three women, emphasizing the qualities they exhibited in making their unique contributions to our society:

Elizabeth Cady Stanton (1815-1902)
Mary McLeod Bethune (1875-1955)
Ada Dee (1935-   )

D. **1)** What is the demographic composition of your city (town or village), county and state in terms of the number and variety of ethnic and national cultural groups comprising the total population? Keep in mind Yinger's discussion on *"Drawing the Boundaries of Ethnicity."* **2)** What persons whose cultural identity is different than yours do you count among your acquaintances or friends – distinguish between the two? **3)** Would you describe your communication with them as *cross-cultural or intercultural?* Why? Give concrete examples to support your description.

E. Select a destination for a trip out of the United States. Keeping in mind Stewart and Bennett's analysis, write a detailed action plan for how to best prepare for that trip.

Part III—The United States: Democracy's Gorgeous Mosaic

Chapter Seven — Abilities

36. (a.) What is IQ theory?

_____

_____

_____

_____

_____

   (b.) Why is IQ theory one-dimensional, according to Gardner?

_____

_____

_____

_____

_____

   (c.) What are the multiple intelligences and how do they function?

_____

_____

_____

_____

_____

37. What are the serious flaws in the recent defense of IQ theory presented in the book *The Bell Curve*?

_____

_____

_____

_____

38. (a.) What is emotional intelligence, according to Goleman

_____

_____

_____

_____

_____

(b.) From your own experience, give examples of when "smart" was really dumb.

_____

_____

_____

_____

_____

CHAPTER EIGHT — VALUES: ETHICAL AND RELIGIOUS

39.   What, in specific detail, are the three components of civil religion? Give examples from both history and contemporary life.

_____

_____

_____

_____

_____

(a.)   What does Albanese mean when she says" civil religion was the triumph of politics and history, but the history involved was, in reality, ahistorical;... it was the history that Americans performed with an eye to the millennial new day that counted, not the weight of tradition."

_____

_____

_____

_____

_____

(b.)   What evidence do you find, in today's life and the news about it, that there is a preoccupation with millennialism?

_____

_____

_____

_____

_____

40.   What is the relationship between *caring* and *act utilitarianism*?

_____

_____

_____

_____

_____

(a.) Give examples, from your own experience, when you have made a choice, or had to consider a choice, between a decision that was caring and one that was an instance of act utilitarianism. Be specific as to **why** you chose one over the other.

_____

_____

_____

_____

_____

_____

41.   How is *intellect* different from *character*?

_____

_____

_____

_____

_____

(a.) What scenario of events might have been created to prevent this young woman from leaving Harvard?

_____

_____

_____

_____

_____

(b.) What particular conclusions might one draw about the young man's lack of character in the light of Goleman's exposition? (38)

_____

_____

_____

_____

_____

42.   What values are explored in Kenan's *Things of This World*?

_____

_____

_____

_____

_____

_____

43.   What is the significance to you of *"The Last Camp?"*

_____

_____

_____

_____

_____

_____

471

CHAPTER NINE — CONSENSUS AND CONFLICT IN CONTEMPORARY SOCIETY

44.   Cortez' poem vividly presents a vortex of madness in all its forces and disguises. Can you identify situations in contemporary life that are examples of such *Madness Without Head*?

_____

_____

_____

_____

_____

45.   What new legislation has been passed to amend or modify this "bargain with the devil" legislation that President Clinton signed?

_____

_____

_____

_____

_____

46.   Make an inventory of the toxic pollutants you face daily. How can you reduce your exposure?

_____

_____

_____

_____

_____

47.   What is the essence of Oboler's critique of Hispanic identity and (re) presentation in these United States? What is your response to it?

_____

_____

_____

_____

_____

473

48.   Identify three situations in which you decoded racism or failed to decode racism effectively. Explain in specific detail.

_____

_____

_____

_____

_____

_____

49/50.   There are fundamental insights about the human condition in the parable of Fannie Lou Hamer (49) and poem by Genny Lim (50); what are they and what do they mean to you?

_____

_____

_____

_____

_____

_____

51.   What failures of intercultural communication are evident in the federal policies of termination and relocation? Be specific.

_____

_____

_____

_____

_____

_____

_____

_____

ACTIVITIES (PART 3)

Documented Essay:

A. The Indians of America continue generally to be misrecognized and unrecognized by those of us who are not "Native Americans." Recent historical glamorizations in the films *Pocahontas* and *Dances with Wolves* are no exceptions. A real American Indian movie such as *Pow-Wow Highway* is nearly impossible to view because of its lack of availability through regular theater and video distribution channels. And stereotypes continue to abound about Indians in the U.S.. In some regions of the country it is reported that there is a dogged belief that at the age of 18 years, every American Indian gets a car and a $1500 per month "per cap" from the federal government. This is completely untrue. Perhaps such stories are fueled by the impression that American Indians are now flush with money from gambling income on their reservations. The facts are that only 20 tribes, of a total of 554 federally recognized tribes in the country, are doing well; and seventy-five percent of all Indians do not live on reservations.

Write an essay on the historical or contemporary life of American Indians that recognizes *their* identity. You may consider selecting a tribe from your region of the country, see the list that follows. Among other references you may want to consult *Native Roots* by Jack Weatherford and *Indian Givers*, also by Jack Weatherford—each of which is available in affordable paperback editions.

_____

_____

_____

_____

_____

_____

_____

_____

_____

_____

B. **1)** As a group project explore the arguments for and against passing laws mandating English as the "national language." **2)** Contrast these arguments with the historical arguments for forcing Indians to speak English. Consider how many Indian languages there were 200 years ago and how many there are now. What has been the impact on the cultures of Indians in the United States.

C. In addition to the major changes we see in our economy, there is a similar growing change in our values, life styles and views of the world. It is said that we live in three different worlds of meaning and value: Traditionalists, those 29 percent of the populace who believe in, among other things, a "nostalgic image of small towns and strong churches that defines the Good Old American Ways;" Modernists, those 49 percent of the populace who "place high value on personal success, consumerism, materialism, and technological rationality;" and Cultural Creatives, those 24 percent of the populace who do not like sound bite news but prefer to explore things in depth, are opposed to hedonism, materialism and cynicism, have strong social consciousness, are committed to service to others and maintaining personal physical and spiritual (not necessarily religious) health. (American Demographics 2:97).

1) What challenges to our ability to communicate effectively with each other does this change in our national culture present? Be specific.

2) What modes of intercultural communication would you propose to meet these challenges? Give concrete examples.

D. What new insights of American Indian life are evident in Sherman Alexic and Chris Eyre's recent film "Smoke Signals?" A paperback edition of this screen play is available: **Smoke Signals (1998) ISBN 0-7868-8392-8.**

Major Native Nations

United States

Northeast

Abenaki
Brotherton
Cayuga
Chickahominy
Chippewa (Ojibway)
Fox
Huron
Maliseet
Mattaponi
Menominee
Miami
Mohawk
Mohegan
Montauk
Nanticoke
Narragansett
Nipmuc-Hassanamisco
Oneida
Onondaga
Ottawa
Pamunkey
Passamaquoddy
Paugusset
Penobscot
Pequot
Piscataway
Poosepatuck
Potawatomi
Rappahanock
Sauk
Schaghticoke
Seneca
Shawnee
Shinnecock
Sioux
Stockbridge-Munsee
Tuscarora
Wampanoag
Winnebago

Southeast

Alabama
Biloxi
Catawba
Cherokee (Eastern)
Chitimacha
Choctaw (Mississippi)
Coharie
Coushatta
Creek
Edisto
Haliwa
Hourna
Lumbee
Miccosukee
Santee
Saponi
Seminole

Texas Kickapoo
Tunica
Waccamaw

Oklahoma

Apache
Caddo
Cherokee
Cheyenne-Arapaho
Chickasaw
Choctaw
Comanche
Creek
Delaware
Iowa
Kaw
Kickapoo
Kiowa
Miami
Modoc
Osage
Otoe-Missouri
Ottawa
Pawnee
Peoria
Ponca
Potawatomi
Quapaw
Sac and Fox
Seminole
Senecca-Cayuga
Shawnee
Tonkawa
Wichita
Wyandotte

Plains

Arikara
Assiniboine
Blackfeet
Cheyenne
Chippewa
Crow
Delaware
Gros Ventre
Hidatsa
Iowa
Kickapoo
Mandan
Omaha
Plains Ojibwa
Potawatomi
Sac and Fox
Sioux
Winnebago
Wyandotte

Rocky Mountain Area

Arapaho
Bannock
Cayuse
Coeur d'Alene

Confederated Tribes of Coiville
Flathead
Gosiute
Kalispel
Klamath
Kootenai
Nespelem
Nez Percé
Palute (Northern)
Sanpoll
Shoshoni (Northern)
Spokane
Umatilla
Ute
Walla Walla
Warm Springs
Wasco
Washo
Yakima

Southwest

Apache
Chemehuevi
Havasupai
Hopi
Hualapai
Mohave
Maricopa
Navajo
Paiute
Pima
Pueblo
Tohono O'Odham (Papago)
Yaqui
Yavapai
Yuma
Zuni

California

Achumawi
Atsugewi
Cahulla
Cupeño
Diegueño
Gabrieliño
Hupa
Karok
Luiseño
Maidu
Miwok
Mohave
Mono
Ohlone
Paiute
Patwin
Pomo
Serrano
Shasta
Shoshoni (Western)
Tolowa
Washo
Wintu

Wiyot
Yana
Yokuts
Yuki
Yurok

Northwest Coast

Bella Bella
Bella Coola
Chehalis
Chinook
Clallam
Coos
Coquille
Gitksan
Haida
Heiltsuk
Hoh
Kalapuya
Kwakiutl
Lillooet
Lummi
Makah
Molala
Muckleshoot
Nisgha
Nisqually
Nooksack
Nootka
Puyallup
Quileute
Quinault
Rogue River
Sauk-Suiattle
Shasta
Siletz
Siuslaw
Skagit
Skokomish
Snohomish
Squaxin Island
Stillaguamish
Suquamish
Swinomish
Tillamook
Tlingit
Tsimshian
Tulalip
Twana
Umpqua
Wishram

Alaska

Ahtena
Aleut
Athapascan
Eyak
Haida
Inuit
Tlingit
Tsimshian
Yupik

GLOSSARY

Vocabularies vary from person to person. It is important that you take note of words you need to look up and learn if you are to understand clearly the content of your readings. Some of the words unfamiliar to you are defined explicitly within the particular text in which the unfamiliar words appear; some can be understood implicitly from their context. For all college level reading a good, affordable paperback dictionary is an essential study aid. This glossary lists only those words essential to understanding the unifying theme of this text. When you see the note *(See 63)* after an entry, it means that the word glossed has a clear contextual use and fuller exposition in the reading of that number; the number of each reading is found in the Table of Contents.

acculturation—The process of *adapting to* a different culture while maintaining the shared beliefs and activities of a person's ancestral culture. *(See 20 and 21)*

assimilation—The process of *adopting* a new culture through identification with its shared beliefs and customs while leaving behind a person's ancestral culture. *(See 20 and 21)*

bigot—A person who is blindly intolerant, narrow-minded, prejudiced. *(See 3 and 12)*

caste—An exclusive social class based on a person's lineage (race).

civicism—The principle that a person shares both the *rights and duties* of citizenship in a society. *(See Part I, Intro)*

civil religion—A religious system with a theology (creed), an ethic (code) and a set of rituals and other identifiable symbols (cultus) related to the political state and existing alongside that of the churches; religious nationalism. *(See 39)*

class—The layering or stratification of persons into groups based on such social inequalities as power, prestige, influence and income. *(See 27 and 29)*

constitutional democracy—Government based on a written, democratic constitution. *(See 15)*

commonweal—The common good; for the good of everyone in a society.

consensus—Mutual agreement or consent.

conservatism—In the United States it is belief in the strength of free enterprise in the marketplace with minimal government interference, belief in individual (not government) responsibility in fulfilling social and economic needs, and belief in government action in matters of personal morality. Some conservatives explain these beliefs on the basis of their point of view that there is a "natural hierarchy" (Darwinian) among human beings. *(See 16 and 18)* European conservatism is different in that it favors paternalistic government willing to use the power of the state to protect or assist individuals. *(See 15)*

cross-cultural communication—a comparison of interactions among people from the same culture to those from another culture. (Lustig & Koester, 1993) *(See 18)*

culture—Learned customs and traditions that govern human behavior. *(See 15, 18 and 39)*

custom—A traditional practice based on one's culture.

demonise(-ize)—To convert into an evil spirit or demon. *(See 3)*

dialect—A particular form or variety of a language; a manner of speaking a language based on one's class or geographical location.

emigrant—A person who leaves a country. *(See 11)*

ethics—A system of morals or rules of behavior concerned with human character and conduct. *(See 40)*

ethnicity—As a segment of a larger society, an ethnic group is comprised of members who are thought, by themselves or others, to have a common origin and to share important elements of a common culture around which they participate in shared activities. *(See 20 and 21)*

ethnic encapsulation—Ethnocentricity that is manifested by members of an ethnic group spending most of their time with one another, in the course of which they develop strong negative feelings toward people not like them.

ethnocentric—A belief in the superiority of one's own cultural group. *(See 18)*

fascism—An extreme form of nationalism through a totalitarian control by the state of all aspects of social and individual life in order to achieve the goals of a state as articulated by an authoritative central leader.

high context cultures—communication in high context cultures is more indirect, even spiral rather than linear, less speaker or verbal centered; more a matter of contextual understanding of the cues of subjective culture—as is Japanese culture. *(See 18)*

homophobia—To have an aversion to or strong dislike of homosexuals, whether male or female. *(See 28)*

immigrant—A person who *enters* a country not of their origin. *(See 11)*

indigenous—To originate naturally in a country; native born. *(See 2, 3 and 11)*

intercultural communication—a symbolic, interpretive, transactional contextual communication process to discover shared meanings between those of different cultures who have dissimilar interpretations and expectations of what competent behaviors are. (Adapted from Bennett & Bennett, 1996) *(See 18)*

jingoism—A boastful patriotism that favors aggressive, even warlike, foreign policy toward other nations; national chauvinism. *(See 39)*

liberal democratic tradition—The beliefs in individualism, liberty, equality, an open society, the rule of law, and limits on government that are fundamental values of the democratic tradition in the United States. *(See 16)*

liberalism—A political value system characterized by a belief in government based on the consent of the governed as well as the belief that certain rights are guaranteed to all persons simply because they are human beings. In U.S. politics, it is an activist view of government, committed to the improvement of the average person's condition of life, including the elimination of poverty and other forms of deprivation; personal morals are matters of personal choice, not government prescription. *(See 15)*

libertarianism—Extreme forms of left-wing or right-wing belief in least government. *(See 15)*

life marker—An event in a person's life that does not change that person's behavior or identity. *(See 32)*

life transition—An event in a person's life that changes that person's view of her/himself as well as her/his behavior. *(See 32)*

low-context cultures—direct, verbal, speaker-centered, generally non-allusive, pragmatic communication —as, for the most part in American (United States) culture. *(See 18)*

morality—A doctrine of actions as either right or wrong. *(See 40 and 41)*

melting pot—A vessel in which things are melted; a metaphor for assimilating in a new society.

mosaic—A design of small pieces of colored glass or marble fitted together.

misrecognition—To deflect the identity of a person or group in a manner that is confining, demeaning or contemptible. *(See 2–5, 22, 28, 32 and 36-38)*

multicultural—For the United States a society comprised, for the most part, of acculturated ethnic and national immigrants as well as historically subjugated Indians (Native Americans), African Americans; people who maintain their own traditions, more or less, and are receptive to—if not really knowledgeable about—the distinctive traditions of others. *(See Part I, 22 and 40)*

national identity (shared)—See civil religion

nationalism—The favoring of the interests, independence, unity or domination of a nation.

nativism—A disposition to favor the natives of a country in preference to immigrants. *(See 11)*

nonrecognition—A form of misrecognition that disregards a person, imprisoning them in a reduced mode of being. *(See Part I and 47)*

objective culture—the institutions and artifacts of a culture, such as economic system, social customs, political structures and processes, arts, crafts and literature. (Stewart & Bennett, 1991) *(See 18)*

paradox—Something that is apparently absurd but is or may be true. A self-contradictory statement.

patriarchal—The dominance of male choice and direction; the favoring of male privilege. Governing by paternal right. *(See 27 and 28)*

political culture—the collection of beliefs, institutions, and artifacts that have to do with our shared life as Americans. *(See 15 and 39)*

racism—A belief in the inherent superiority of people of a particular lineage (ancestry) over those of another lineage or other lineages; discriminative treatment based on such beliefs. *(See 12, 20 and 47)*

role conformity—Individual behavior that follows prescribed stages of development in life-cycle analyses of society. *(See 32)*

role creation—The individual construction of a life course based on one's experiences. *(See 32)*

scapegoat—An object of false blame for the distasteful or inconvenient things that happen to a person. *(See 2, 3 and 5)*

sexism—Discrimination against, patronizing of or stereotyping of another sex. *(See 28)*

social differentiation—The non-hierarchical individual qualities and distinct social roles that people have. For example, the social role of an infant is not *ranked* relative to that of an adolescent or adult; the roles are simply different, as are those of farmer, red head, secretary, actor, chauffeur, brunette, nurse-practitioner, plumber, tall woman, poet, full-time mother, single male lawyer, fat shortstop, double-dutch jumper, bald male cyclist, cellist, make-up artist, greying female pediatrician, dance therapist, hoarse teacher, one-legged barber, acoustic engineer. *(See 27)*

social inequality—The social condition where people have unequal access to valued resources, services and positions in society. This unequal access may be based on the *social evaluation* of a person's difference within a group or society. It may be based also on a social role placing that person in a position to have greater access to acquire a greater share of valued goods and services within the society. *(See 27)*

social stratification—Human beings are stratified, as are layers of rock, from high to low, based on their unequal access to valued resources, services and positions. This social inequality has become *hardened* or *institutionalized* in a system of social relationships that determines who gets what and why they get what they get. *(See 27)*

socialism—The theory of social organization which places the means of production and distribution in the hands of the community, rather than private individuals; all members of the community or society share in the work, the products and their value.

standing—The expectation that in a republic committed to political equality, each citizen must have the same rights, the same recognition. *(See Part I, Intro)*

stereotype—In the print industry a fixed, conventionalized representation, made possible in a solid, metallic plate for printing an unchangeable letterpress image appearing in books, magazines and newspapers; to describe a person or group simplistically, without dimension, change or complexity.

subjective culture—the physiological features of culture, including assumptions, values and patterns of thinking. (Stewart & Bennett, 1991) *(See 18)*

welfare—The assumption of responsibility by government (whether national or state and local) for the general social welfare of the population through the direct provision of goods and services. Such public welfare seeks to enforce work norms among its recipients as well as to maintain low wage labor. It can be instrumental in keeping down social disorder. *(See 27)*

wealthfare—Federal government subsidies for agriculture, research and development for major corporations, tariff protections for selected industries, other direct federal government services that corporations otherwise would have to pay for out of their own profits, such as the Federal Aviation Administration's total funding of the air guidance systems and airport landing systems—as well as research and development costs for new airline technology; other industries, such as tobacco and certain food corporations, have their international promotion and sales subsidized by federal tax write-offs. In short, most of what government does, it does for the nonpoor. *(See 27)*

white privilege—The assumption of a standpoint from which to look upon the world as a chosen people; a perspective of dominance, normativity and privilege as opposed to one of subordination, marginality and disadvantage. *(See Part I and 22)*

xenophobia—The fear or hatred of things foreign.

481